# Public Health for the 21st Century

## 2nd edition

# Public Health for the 21st Century

## NEW PERSPECTIVES ON POLICY, PARTICIPATION AND PRACTICE

## 2nd edition

*Editors: Judy Orme, Jane Powell, Pat Taylor and Melanie Grey*

 Open University Press

Open University Press
McGraw-Hill Education
McGraw-Hill House
Shoppenhangers Road
Maidenhead
Berkshire
England
SL6 2QL

email: enquiries@openup.co.uk
world wide web: www.openup.co.uk

and
Two Penn Plaza
New York, NY 10121–2289, USA

First edition published 2003
Second edition published 2007

A catalogue record of this book is available from the British Library

ISBN-10: 0 335 22207 2 (pb)
ISBN-13: 978 0 335 22207 0 (pb)

Library of Congress Cataloging-in-Publication Data
CIP data has been applied for

Typeset by RefineCatch Limited, Bungay, Suffolk
Printed in Poland EU by OZGraf S. A. www.polskabook.pl

The **McGraw·Hill** Companies

# Contents

*List of figures and tables*                                                      xi
*Notes on contributors*                                                          xiii
*Foreword*                                                                      xviii
*Acknowledgements*                                                                xxi
*Introduction*                                                                      1


## PART 1

## Policy for 21st century public health                                            5

*Editors' overview*                                                                  5

1  JUDY ORME, JANE POWELL, PAT TAYLOR AND MELANIE GREY                               7
   Mapping public health

    *What is public health?*                                     7
    *A public health for the 21st century*                        9
    *An evidence base for public health*                          9
    *Historical perspectives on public health*                   10
    *Who contributes to public health?*                          14
    *Building capacity in public health*                          15
    *Where does public health take place?*                        19
    *The international context*                                   19
    *Devolution*                                                  19
    *The regional context and 'powers of well-being'*            21
    *Conclusion*                                                  23

2  DAVID J. HUNTER                                                                  24
   Public health policy

    *Introduction*                                               25
    *The state of public health policy*                           25
    *Conclusion*                                                  40

3 **CHRIS MILLER**     42
Public health in the local authority context: more opportunities
not to be missed?

    *Introduction*     43
    *The policy context*     45
    *Cross-cutting themes for public health*     46
    *Public health in alliance with a restructured local government?*     48
    *Local Strategic Partnerships*     51
    *Local Area Agreements*     53
    *Public Service Agreements*     55
    *'Double' devolution*     56
    *Conclusion*     57

## PART 2
## Participation and partnerships in 21st century public health     61
*Editors' overview*     61

4 **STEPHEN PECKHAM**     63
Partnership working for public health

    *Introduction*     64
    *What are partnerships?*     64
    *Why partnerships for public health?*     65
    *The nature of public health*     66
    *Joined-up governance*     68
    *The collaborative dimension*     71
    *Types of partnership*     73
    *Who are the partners in public health?*     75
    *Partnerships with communities*     79
    *Conclusion*     81

5 **GILLIAN BARRETT, JENNIE NAIDOO AND JUDY ORME**     83
Capacity and capability in public health

    *Introduction*     84
    *The public health workforce*     84
    *Public health skills and competencies*     86
    *The public health professional project.*     88
    *Conclusion*     91
    *Case study: asylum seekers*     92

6 **PAT TAYLOR**     98
The lay contribution to public health

    *Introduction*     99
    *Structure of this chapter*     99
    *What is lay involvement and why is it important to public health?*     99
    *The changing nature of public involvement in the NHS*     100

*Lay perspectives in the history of public health*                    103
*Understanding lay perspectives*                                      107
*Medical perspectives on lay involvement*                             109
*Promoting an effective lay contribution to public health*           112
*Conclusion – challenges and opportunities*                          115

7   SELENA GRAY                                                        118
The contribution of health services to public health

  *The contribution of health care to population health*              118
  *The three domains of public health practice*                       121
  *Quality improvement*                                               124
  *Health improvement*                                                130
  *Organizational structures for delivery of the three domains of public*
  *health practice*                                                   132
  *Sustainability*                                                    133
  *Conclusion*                                                        134

8   ALISON GILCHRIST                                                   135
Community development and networking for health

  *Introduction*                                                      136
  *Community development for health*                                  138
  *Promoting health 'in the community'*                               138
  *The 'community' dimension to health and well-being*                141
  *Informal networks and health*                                      142
  *The concept of social capital*                                     143
  *Networks and community participation*                              144
  *Building relationships, sharing power*                             145
  *Indirect outcomes of social networks*                              148
  *Networking in practice*                                            149
  *Conclusions*                                                       151
  *Acknowledgements*                                                  152


PART 3
Major contemporary themes in public health                            153
*Editors' overview*                                                   153

9   DAVID EVANS                                                        155
New directions in tackling inequalities in health

  *Introduction*                                                      156
  *The evidence for socio-economic inequalities in health*            157
  *The UK policy response*                                            159
  *UK policy effectiveness*                                           161
  *Potential policies for reducing inequalities in health*            163
  *Conclusion*                                                         168

10 MURRAY STEWART                                                           170
   Neighbourhood renewal and regeneration

   *Urban policy and neighbourhood renewal: historical context*             171
   *The development of the neighbourhood focus*                             172
   *Neighbourhood policies and health inequalities*                        176
   *Public health and the neighbourhood*                                    180

11 COLIN FUDGE                                                              185
   Implementing sustainable futures in cities

   *Introduction*                                                           186
   *Urbanization, urban change, development and policy*                     186
   *Ecological modernization*                                               195
   *Strategic issues for the future of sustainability*                      199
   *Acknowledgements*                                                       202

12 STUART McCLEAN                                                           204
   Globalization and health

   *Introduction*                                                           205
   *The globalization debate*                                               205
   *Globalization – a contested term*                                       206
   *Key features of globalization in relation to public health*            207
   *The Janus faces: positive and negative impacts on public health*       209
   *The promoters of economic globalization and other key
   players*                                                                 211
   *Global trade policy and the UK health care context*                    213
   *Global inequalities in health: the local impact of global
   divisions*                                                               215
   *Globalization and emerging public health risks*                        217
   *Health care organizations*                                             220
   *Conclusion: the challenges for public health in a global era*           221

13 MELANIE GREY, MIKE STUDDEN AND JOYSHRI SARANGI                           223
   Protecting the public's health

   *Health threats and emerging health protection policy*                   224
   *The organizational framework for protecting health*                     231
   *Health protection: principles and practice*                             234
   *Overview: the challenges*                                               246

PART 4
Evaluation evidence and guidance in 21st century public
health                                                                      249
*Editors' overview*                                                        249

14 TONY HARRISON                                                            251
   Evidence-based multidisciplinary public health

*Introduction* 252
*Defining evidence-based multidisciplinary public health* 253
*The development of evidence-based public policy and*
*public health* 255
*Main problems of evidence-based systems for multidisciplinary*
*public health* 260
*The role of theory in evidence-based public health* 266
*Conclusion* 268

15 **JON POLLOCK** 269
Epidemiology for 21st century public health

*Defining the scope* 270
*Identifying appropriate epidemiological approaches for contemporary*
*public health* 271
*Epidemiology: changes to support 21st century public health* 273
*Future developments in public health epidemiology: concepts*
*and methods* 278
*Conclusion* 285

16 **JANE POWELL** 287
Health economics and public health

*Key concepts in health economics for public health*
*professionals* 287
*Incorporating health economics in public health guidance* 289
*Economic evaluation methods* 289
*A case study example: the economic evaluation of family and child*
*alcohol services* 290
*Strengths of economic evaluation* 298
*The ethical stance of public health professionals* 298
*The ethical stance of economists* 299
*Efficiency and equity – the trade-off and ethical dilemma* 299
*Conclusion* 300

17 **STUART HASHAGEN AND SUSAN PAXTON** 302
Frameworks for evaluation of community health and
well-being work

*Introduction* 302
*Powers of well-being in Scotland* 304
*The Scottish Community Development Centre: Learning*
*Evaluation and Planning framework* 307
*Case study – Building Healthy Communities in Dumfries and*
*Galloway* 316
*Conclusion* 320

18 **GABRIEL SCALLY** 322
Sustainable development and public health: arm in arm

*Introduction* 323

*Recapturing the common ground*    324
*Conclusion*    328

*Glossary*    330
*Bibliography*    346
*Index*    391

# List of figures and tables

**Figures**

| | | |
|---|---|---|
| I.1 | Overview of book structure and the major themes of the chapters | 3 |
| 1.1 | The determinants of health and well-being in our neighbourhoods | 8 |
| 1.2 | Public health for the 21st century | 10 |
| 1.3 | Overview of the organizational structure for public health (England) | 20 |
| 4.1 | Strategies for partnership | 68 |
| 4.2 | Individuals, communities, the public and health | 70 |
| 4.3 | The collaborative dimension – a framework | 72 |
| 4.4 | Types of partnership | 74 |
| 5.1 | The role of public health specialists, practitioners and the wider public health workforce in meeting the needs of asylum seekers | 95 |
| 6.1 | Levels of public involvement | 114 |
| 7.1 | Potential improvements in total cancer mortality due to specific intervention in persons under age 75 | 120 |
| 7.2 | Domains of public health practice | 121 |
| 8.1 | Social networks | 137 |
| 8.2 | Different approaches to health promotion | 140 |
| 8.3 | Actions that facilitate and maintain networks | 150 |
| 9.1 | Themes and principles of the *Programme for Action* | 161 |
| 9.2 | Life expectancy at birth in years, by social class and gender | 162 |
| 11.1 | Percentage of world population 1950–2150 in three age categories and medium fertility scenario | 188 |
| 11.2 | Percentage of population living in urban areas in 1996 and 2030 | 189 |
| 11.3 | World's urban agglomerations with populations of 10 million or more inhabitants in selected years | 190 |
| 11.4 | Number of urban agglomerations from 1950 to 2015 with one million or more inhabitants | 190 |
| 12.1 | Outline conceptual framework for globalization and health | 208 |
| 13.1 | Overview of organizations contributing to the protection of the public's health (England) | 232 |

13.2   The barriers to understanding of risk between the expert and the
        public                                                                237
14.1   Simplified model of evidence-based policy and practice                 259
14.2   Locating different research traditions in public health                264
17.1   Risk factors in Labonte's model                                        304
17.2   A model of community well-being                                        309
17.3   LEAP action planning and evaluation framework                          312

**Tables**

1.1    The key public health challenges                                       9
1.2    National standards for specialist public health                       15
1.3    Healthy communities and examples of the roles which support them      16
1.4    Healthy communities: work activities                                  18
2.1    Key policies, reports and initiatives in public health 1997–2006      26
7.1    Quality and outcomes framework for UK general medical services
        2006/07                                                              128
7.2    United States and Australian research into adverse events in hospitals 129
7.3    Potential for NHS and other health care organizations to contribute
        to sustainability                                                    133
11.1   Chronological policy history                                          192
13.1   Infectious and environmental hazards – the disease burden in the UK   226
13.2   Organizations and their functions in protecting health               228
13.3   Risk and uncertainty – levels of proof, descriptors and examples
        in regulation and control mechanisms                                 235
13.4   Examples of surveillance systems in the UK                            239
15.1   Activity areas in classical and public health epidemiology            272
17.1   Quality of life                                                       311

# Notes on contributors

## The editors

The editors are all members of academic staff at the University of the West of England, Bristol. The original idea for this book sprang from discussion and delivery of modules on our well established postgraduate programme in public health (MSc in Public Health).

**Judy Orme** is Reader in Public Health and Director of the Research Centre in Public Health in the Faculty of Health and Social Care at the University of the West of England, Bristol. Her research interests include vulnerable young people and risk, particularly relating to drug prevention and alcohol use and the sociology of public health.

**Jane Powell** is an economist and social scientist with experience in the economic evaluation of public health programmes and interventions. She is the programme lead for the MSc Public Health programme in the Faculty of Health and Social Care. Her research interests extend across the field of public health and include alcohol research and the economic evaluation of service provision and delivery in vulnerable groups including the prison population.

**Pat Taylor** is a Senior Lecturer in Health and Social Care in the Faculty of Health and Social Care at the University of the West of England, Bristol. She has a social work qualification but has worked primarily in community development and the voluntary sector and has extensive experience of working with community-based and service user led groups and in helping them establish their role in partnership working. She has worked within the NHS and social care to promote public and service user/carer involvement and to develop its potential to influence mainstream practice. She continues this interest in her current research. She is currently leading the patient/service user and carer initiative in the new social work degree and within the faculty as a whole, and retains strong links with practice in the field to enable her to fulfil this role.

**Melanie Grey** is Principal Lecturer in Environmental Health and Head of the School of Environmental and Interdisciplinary Sciences in the Faculty of Applied Sciences at the University of the West of England, Bristol. Her research interests include assessment of environment and health risks and evaluation of interventions. Other interests are education and training development for environmental health and health protection practitioners.

## Other contributors

**Gill Barrett** is Senior Lecturer in Health Promotion at the University of the West of England, Bristol. She has a background in nursing and health promotion. Gill's research interests include health promotion, interprofessional education and health communication.

**David Evans** is Reader in Applied Health Policy Research in the Faculty of Health and Social Care at the University of the West of England, Bristol. Previously he was Director of Community Development and Public Health for Bristol North Primary Care Trust and was one of the first NHS directors of public health from a background other than medicine. His research interests include user and community involvement in health, the evaluation of initiatives to tackle inequalities in health and the development of multidisciplinary public health.

**Colin Fudge** is Professor of Urban Environment and Pro Vice-Chancellor at the University of the West of England, Bristol. He has held senior positions in government and academia in the UK, Sweden, Australia and the EU, was awarded an Honorary Fellowship of the Royal Institute of British Architects for his work on urban sustainability, and the title of Royal Professor by the Swedish Academy of Sciences. He is Chair of the EU Expert Group on the Urban Environment, Founding Director of the WHO Collaborative Research Centre on Healthy Cities and Urban Policy, Visiting Professor, Italy and Sweden and a Board Member, Chalmers University. He has written more than 80 articles and reports, 10 books, numerous book chapters and presented more than 100 conference papers.

**Alison Gilchrist** worked for many years as a community development worker in inner-city neighbourhoods in Bristol and was active in various local and national networks. For 11 years she taught community and youth work at the University of the West of England, Bristol and during this period undertook doctoral research into the value of networking for community development. This was published as *The Well-connected Community: a Networking Approach to Community Development*, by The Policy Press in 2004. In 1999 she joined the Community Development Foundation (CDF) as their Regional Links Manager, responsible for CDF's work with regional levels of government. In October 2003 she was appointed to the post of Director, Practice Development and is now based in Leeds. She has lead responsibility for CDF's cohesion and diversity work, and brings an equalities perspective to this. The Community Development Foundation is a non-departmental public body, sponsored by the Department for Communities and Local Government. It is a leading authority on community development, with a specific remit to advise government at national, regional and local levels of decision making.

**Selena Gray** is Professor of Public Health and Director of the Centre for Clinical and Health Services Research, Faculty of Health and Social Care, University of the West of England, Bristol. She was a founding Director of the South West Public Health Observatory and has extensive experience of health services research with over 30 peer reviewed publications on a wide variety of public health topics. She is currently Registrar of the Faculty of Public Health, and a past Council Member of the UK Public Health Association.

**Tony Harrison** was, until recently Principal Lecturer in Housing and Urban Studies in the Faculty of the Built Environment at the University of the West of England, Bristol. He is a social scientist whose main research interests include evidence-based policy and practice, planning and healthy cities. He now lectures part-time at the University of the West of England, Bristol, and combines this with consultancy work.

**Stuart Hashagen** is Director, Scotland with the Community Development Foundation and Co-director of the Scottish Community Development Centre. He works in most of the Scottish Community Development Centre programmes, to help develop good practice in community development. As well as working with community health projects and programmes, he is also involved in regeneration, community planning and environmental issues. Scottish Community Development Centre programmes include training and support on skills in planning and evaluation, community engagement, developing effective partnerships and promoting participation. He is a past convenor of the Poverty Alliance and currently a management committee member of a community-based housing association in Glasgow.

**David Hunter** is Professor of Health Policy and Management in the School for Health, Wolfson Research Institute, Durham University. His research interests are in public health policy and practice, and health policy and management; he has published extensively in these areas. His recent books include *Public Health Policy* (2003) and (co-edited with Sian Griffiths) a second edition of *New Perspectives in Public Health* (2006). His latest book, *Managing for Health*, is to be published by Routledge in early 2007. He is Chair of the UK Public Health Association and is an Honorary Member of the Faculty of Public Health and Fellow of the Royal Society of Physicians (Edinburgh).

**Stuart McClean** is Senior Lecturer in Health Science (sociology and social anthropology) at the University of the West of England, Bristol. Stuart received his PhD from the Department of Sociology and Social Anthropology at the University of Hull. His research interests include the resurgence of alternative medicine and healing practices in Western societies, the role of creative arts in health, and the global dimensions surrounding health. His book, *An Ethnographic Study of Crystal and Spiritual Healers in Northern England: Marginal Medicine, Mainstream Concerns*, is published by Edwin Mellen.

**Chris Miller** is Reader in Health, Community and Policy Studies and Director for the Research Centre for Local Democracy at the University of the West of England, Bristol. He is Editor of the international *Community Development Journal*.

His research interests include participation, non-governmental action, governance, and public service organizational development.

**Jennie Naidoo** is Principal Lecturer in Public Health in the Faculty of Health and Social Care at the University of the West of England, Bristol. She has a background in sociology, health promotion and education. Jennie worked in health promotion and research prior to taking up her post at the University of the West of England, Bristol. Her research interests include gender and health, health promotion in primary care, and health and ethnic minority groups. She has written extensively on health promotion, theory and practice.

**Susan Paxton** is currently the Senior Development Officer with the LEAP Support Unit, based at the Scottish Community Development Centre. She is jointly responsibility for delivering the Healthy Living Centre Support Programme and provides training and consultancy support to HLCs using or intending to use LEAP for Health to plan and evaluate their work. Susan is also Chair of the Scottish Community Development Network, a members-led organization for both paid and unpaid community development practitioners.

**Stephen Peckham** is Senior Lecturer in Health Services Delivery and Organizational Research at the London School of Hygiene and Tropical Medicine, and works as an academic lead within the NHS Service Delivery and Organization Research and Development Programme. Stephen has published widely on primary care and health policy. His main research interests are in health policy analysis, inter-agency collaboration, primary care, public health and public involvement. Recent research includes a three-year project examining the links between community organizations and primary care on public health issues, primary care support for carers and decentralization in health care services. He is currently jointly leading a project examining autonomy and decentralization in the NHS, is involved in an NCCSDO-funded project on out of hours work force issues and is also working on a project on public health ethics.

**Jon Pollock** is Principal Lecturer in Epidemiology. His interests are in health services research and the contribution of epidemiology to studies of child health, care of the elderly, service provision and the evaluation of health and social care interventions.

**Joyshri Sarangi** is a consultant public health physician who works as Consultant in Communicable Disease Control and Regional Epidemiologist in the South-west region. She has extensive practical experience in the management of health protection incidents and in policy issues, and is a visiting lecturer at the University of the West of England, Bristol.

**Gabriel Scally** is Regional Director of Public Health for the South-west region of England. Gabriel has undertaken a number of assignments abroad for British and Irish governmental agencies including projects in Nigeria, Zambia, Zimbabwe and Seychelles. He was a member of the General Medical Council for the UK from 1989 to 1999 and has served on the Professional Conduct, Education, Health and Standards Committees. He is also a former member of the Northern Ireland Board for Nursing, Midwifery and Health Visiting. He has published papers on poorly performing doctors and most recently on clinical governance. He has edited a book on public health and is currently Joint Editor of *Clinical Governance Bulletin*, a journal published by The Royal Society of Medicine.

**Murray Stewart** is Visiting Professor of Urban and Regional Governance at the University of the West of England, Bristol. He has undertaken extensive research on urban regeneration, partnership working, mainstreaming and community involvement and was a member of the national evaluation teams on New Deals for Communities, Local Strategic Partnerships, Local Area Agreements and Single Local Management Centres. He has led two major cross-national European Union projects. His broader community interests include board member of Quartet Foundation, Chairman of the Bridge Foundation for Psychotherapy and the Arts, and Chair of the North Somerset Fair Share panel. He was Deputy Chairman of the Lloyds TSB Foundation for England and Wales 1997–2005.

**Mike Studden** is the Regional Head of the Environmental Hazards Unit, for the Health Protection Agency in the South-west Region. He qualified as an environmental health practitioner in 1969 and spent nearly 30 years in local government latterly as Head of Environmental Services for the largest city on the south coast of England. After completing an MSc in Environmental Risk Management he moved into the private sector on consultancy projects in waste management, sustainable development and strategic environmental appraisal. He returned to the public health field as head of the newly established Environmental Hazards Unit at the South-west regional office of the Health Protection Agency in 2004.

His interests include comparative risk assessment as a tool for resource allocation in environmental public health, environmental public health policy and sustainable transport.

# Foreword

The term public health may conjure up a variety of ideas. For some it means drains and sewage. To others it might mean visions of people queuing up for mass X-rays, immunization and screening. For still others it might summon up thoughts about housing conditions, slum clearance and school dinners. And in the contemporary world for some, public health embraces a vision of creating a healthy environment and an environmentally sustainable planet.

All these visions are valid and are grounded in the historical facts of the gradual and eventually systematic improvement in the health of the public that we have witnessed since the early part of the 19th century in Britain. The conquest of killer infections, the improvement in housing conditions and nutritional standards, the regulations introduced to control dangerous occupational hazards like asbestos and other carcinogenic agents and in recent times the decreasing acceptability of cigarette smoking have, among other things, made us as a population much healthier than we once were. Indeed some would argue that the health benefits which we enjoy are really a human right. We have attained them and all that is required is that we somehow maintain the status quo.

This is a deceptive if appealing conclusion. It is deceptive on a number of grounds and it is those grounds which make public health so challenging and which in their different ways the chapters in this book deal with. The right to health and the improved health status we now enjoy were actually very hard won. Protecting our environment in the future will require even harder effort. At every stage in the history of public health there have been vested interests that opposed measures that improved or protected public health. It may seem blindingly obvious in 21st century Britain that it is bad for children to go to work at the age of 6 in a coal mine or a factory, or that to provide the means to remove human excrement from houses is good for the health of the people that live in them, or that protecting populations from the ravages of measles and whooping cough, rickets and diphtheria prevents suffering and death. But it was not always so. When these and virtually every other public health measure were originally proposed, there were those who opposed what we now take for granted.

The conclusion is also deceptive because there is still a long way to go. The clean water, sanitation and decent housing now enjoyed by the great majority of Britons are not universal; large parts of the world do not have even these basics. In many places children still do go to work in factories and sweatshops at very young ages. Here in Britain the population is healthier at aggregate level than any time in the past and people are living longer. The combined benefits of improved medical technologies and better social conditions have produced benefits which earlier generations could only dream of. However, at the same time as the overall health of the population has improved, the inequalities in the health of the population have got worse. Differences between the best and the worst off in economic terms is mirrored in their health and sickness and in rates of death. The differential rates of death are theoretically preventable because they are apparently linked to human behaviour and lifestyle. Notwithstanding this simple relationship, health inequalities have remained stubbornly resistant to efforts to eliminate or reduce them.

The conclusion is deceptive for a third reason. While one might argue that protecting people from unnecessary and preventable pain, suffering and death is a matter of social justice, it is perfectly possible to construct the alternative argument. This is that social justice is irrelevant and that restrictions and regulations like wearing seatbelts, driving within speed limits, or regulating the sale of alcohol to children are fundamental infringements of our liberty; another and different right! All the measures listed in the previous paragraphs, while resulting in benefits for many, have seriously curtailed the activities of some others. This may have taken the form of reducing profits, managing the free rein of the market or of restricting liberties in various ways. Public health occupies the very uncomfortable territory where the rights of some clash with rights of others. To give one person a right to health is to restrict or even eliminate the utility of some other person or group. In Britain in recent years controversies about MMR immunization, banning smoking in public places, speed cameras, and the debate about the so-called nanny state all eloquently attest to the fact that the struggle for the health of the public continues over different interpretations of rights and justice.

This of course makes public health very exciting and as this volume demonstrates in a very exciting position at the beginning of the 21st century. The problems it addresses are scientifically challenging, are practically difficult to deal with and are about some of the most hotly contested political and philosophical issues of the day. Public health, as this book demonstrates, deals with the big issues. It operates in the territory in which the biology of the human body connects with the world of work, the home, and the family and the wider determinants of health. So public health operates at the point where human psychology, sociology, economics, politics, geography and medicine intersect and overlap.

But public health is much more than an interesting scientific challenge. The health of the public affects us all. We are the public, and it is our health. Population patterns of health influence us directly. Factors like the general level of affluence in the population, the levels of immunity, the effectiveness of screening programmes will affect us. As taxpayers too, the burden placed on health services by gross inequalities in health will affect us directly. And of course there are issues of justice and fairness, or injustice and unfairness which are of fundamental interest to public health. Why a male child born in the North-west region of England should have a life expectancy years less than his counterpart born in Surrey, speaks volumes about the need to generate a decisive role for public health.

The second edition of this text is a very welcome addition to the public health library. The sweep of its interests and the vision it encapsulates marks it out as a true standard bearer for public health into the 21st century. Its approach is comprehensive and its subject matter compelling. In spite of the challenges ahead for public health, the book reminds us of the quality of those practising and writing about the subject in the UK today.

Professor Mike Kelly
*Director of the Centre for Public Health Excellence*
*The National Institute for Health and Clinical Excellence (NICE)*

# Acknowledgements

Thanks go to all the contributors for their co-operation, inspiration and enthusiasm for this project and also to their various sources of support. Our thanks also go to our colleagues at the University of the West of England, Bristol, who have given encouragement and practical support at key times in the development of this book and who have contributed to creating a stimulating collegiate environment in public health for us at work.

Finally, thanks go to our families for putting up with our absences, both mental and physical.

# INTRODUCTION
## What is this book about?

In our second edition we aim to contribute to strengthening public health practice in the 21st century.

> Strengthening public health means that we need to inspire, we need to explain, and we need to communicate. We need to create a commitment to change and spelling out the health challenges powerfully and imaginatively helps to create that impetus. Some of the great public health leadership of the past which connected directly with the public and which could influence policy makers is not there in great plenty in today's world, yet it is needed just as badly.
>
> (Donaldson 1999)

The Chief Medical Officer, Sir Liam Donaldson said this at the London School of Hygiene and Tropical Medicine in 1999. This is the challenge laid down for all those who contribute to improving public health and well-being.

One of the big ideas in public health today is to turn our National Sickness Service into a National Health Service. Derek Wanless identified the importance of encouraging people into good health lifestyles. This should prevent costly treatment as a result of chronic ill health into the future (Wanless 2004). Well-being has become more important. The connections between healthy communities and the environment are clear. Our future good health depends upon looking after the planet and taking as many steps back from disturbing its natural rhythms as possible (Lovelock 2006). Many professions, volunteers, citizens and community activists have different contributions to make in helping the population to be 'fully engaged' in improving health and building sustainable communities.

Throughout this book, we analyse and reflect upon the influence of history, theories, research and practice on contemporary public health practice. We explore the meaning of public health for the 21st century within the current debates and policy changes that are reshaping its context. We examine the vital connections between public health knowledge and professional writing and the rationale for the current commitment to public health. We demonstrate how different disciplines, epidemiology and health economics, make important contributions to public health.

We hope that readers will find this book thought provoking, informative and above all helpful in taking public health forward to meet the challenges of the 21st century.

## Organization of the book

### Structure

This book has been edited as a resource to inspire the development of future public health with contributory chapters by authors in public health academia and practice.

It is structured into four parts. In order to give overall coherence to this wide ranging book, each of the four parts has its own editors' overview. Reading this introduction to the whole book in conjunction with the overview of each part is, in itself, a useful exercise for getting to grips with the scope of 21st century public health. Each chapter has an editors' introduction that introduces each chapter's subject matter.

## Who is this book for?

Some of you will be interested in reading this book as a whole. There will also be readers who are interested in particular parts and chapters. Each chapter can stand alone for those wishing to dip into a specific issue, for example, to find guidance in and to learn more about networking, lay perspectives and the contemporary role of epidemiology for 21st century public health.

This book is intended first, for those people for whom developing and implementing policies for health improvement, health protection and the reduction of inequalities in health is the central focus of their practice. Our intended readership also includes a wider audience of professionals, lay people and students who would not immediately label their work as 'public health', but who would see that they contribute to the wider health and well-being of their communities.

## Contents

The aim of Part 1 is to present an overview of the field of public health and its policy context (see Figure I.1). First, the editors map the field of public health and consider what it is, the importance of its history, who does it and where they do it. Aspects of the public health policy context that underpins effective multidisciplinary action are then discussed. Public health policy including modernization and its implementation is evaluated critically as are the roles of local authorities in health improvement.

In Part 2 the authors identify the partners in public health and assess the capacity and capability of the public health workforce, including lay people and communities, to meet new objectives of multidisciplinary public health.

Public health resources and action have to address some all pervasive public health problems. For example, regeneration, improving health in the cities of the world, looking at the wider picture of global influences on health and health inequalities and the increasing importance of the health protection agenda all underpin

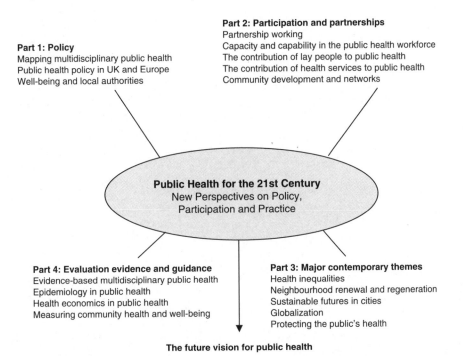

**Part 1: Policy**
Mapping multidisciplinary public health
Public health policy in UK and Europe
Well-being and local authorities

**Part 2: Participation and partnerships**
Partnership working
Capacity and capability in the public health workforce
The contribution of lay people to public health
The contribution of health services to public health
Community development and networks

**Public Health for the 21st Century**
New Perspectives on Policy,
Participation and Practice

**Part 4: Evaluation evidence and guidance**
Evidence-based multidisciplinary public health
Epidemiology in public health
Health economics in public health
Measuring community health and well-being

**Part 3: Major contemporary themes**
Health inequalities
Neighbourhood renewal and regeneration
Sustainable futures in cities
Globalization
Protecting the public's health

**The future vision for public health**

**Figure I.1** Overview of book structure and the major themes of the chapters

recent change in public health policy, participation and practice. Each of these themes is considered in Part 3.

In Part 4, the authors outline ways in which disciplines such as epidemiology, community development and economics can work together and move forward. A difficult challenge for 21st century public health action with its focus on health communities, sustainability and well-being is providing good underpinning research evidence. The authors outline three separate approaches to evaluation from epidemiology: economics; community health and well-being.

The book is concluded with Chapter 18 in which Gabriel Scally presents a vision for the future of public health in the 21st century. He focuses on several core themes which include learning from historical public health, the need to function in a shared power world, the impact of excessive consumption on the health profile of populations and the impact on the well-being of the planet. Focus moves to the global issues of AIDS, transportation, obesity and tobacco as complex public health issues which impact considerably on sustainable development. This concluding discussion will help to create the impetus to strengthen public health referred to by Liam Donaldson earlier by inspiring everyone with an interest in public health to consider these health challenges and commit to change.

# PART 1

## Policy for 21st century public health

### Editors' overview

What is the broad policy framework for public health at the start of the 21st century? How has it evolved, and what may happen in the future?

These are the fundamental questions addressed in Part 1. It provides readers with an overview of the development and context of public health and public health policy and its potential scope in contemporary society. It explores current debates in relation to the influences of social, political and cultural factors. It takes a critical look at how public health fits into current government policy.

Understanding the context of policy development in public health is an essential precursor to effective multidisciplinary public health activity. Overall this part of the book engages readers in an interdisciplinary context through the analysis of, and reflection upon, public health theories, research and practice. It includes reference to wider international developments in public health.

The chapters focus on three aspects of the public health context: mapping public health; current public health policy and its implementation; public health, well-being and local authorities.

In Chapter 1 the editors map the field of public health and consider what it is, the importance of its history, who does it and where they do it. This provides an accessible introduction to the whole field of public health practice.

In Chapter 2 David Hunter takes a critical look at current public health policy and its implementation. Hunter questions whether the current and developing administrative and policy framework is appropriate for the problems which need to be tackled in the development of multidisciplinary public health. His chapter briefly considers the policy context in Wales, Scotland and Northern Ireland. First, he reviews the present state of public health policy and its recent history since 1997, then he examines the constraints on implementing public health policies, before considering the future of public health policy. He provides public health professionals with suggestions about what needs to happen if there is to be a sustained shift in policy towards health as distinct from health care.

In Chapter 3 Chris Miller reflects on the government's modernization agenda and the contribution of local authorities to the well-being of the population. The implications of the modernization agenda are then examined focusing on generic threads that affect public health work. These include partnership working, user involvement, community focus, leadership and quality of service provision. Miller provides unique insight into political processes and their impact on the health of the public.

# 1

## JUDY ORME, JANE POWELL, PAT TAYLOR AND MELANIE GREY
## Mapping public health

In this chapter, we seek to define multidisciplinary public health in terms of its scope. Our core aim is to map the people, professionals, disciplines, settings and actions that contribute to multidisciplinary public health in the 21st century.

### What is public health?

The start of the 21st century is an exciting era for public health theory and practice. Improving the public's health and well-being is a high profile feature of government policy. Public health action has expanded into a far wider arena as it recognizes that factors in people's social, economic and physical environment have a profound impact on their health and can create deep inequalities. It involves a wider range of people than ever before from many different disciplines and professions working in partnership with the lay public and across agency and organizational boundaries. There is a growing need for a diverse public health workforce with an expanded range of expertise and skills.

Under the banner of public health, work is being undertaken in major areas such as addressing inequalities in health, tackling challenges of renewal and sustainability in our communities, and taking on board the impact of globalization on health. The definition of health was set out by the World Health Organization (WHO) as '. . . a state of complete physical, mental and social well-being and not merely the absence of disease or infirmity' (WHO 1948). It is a utopian 'goal' perhaps, but it sets a focus that has significance for the population as a whole, or subgroups within it through collective action (HM Government 2005).

The term public health is generally understood as a broad concept. Attempts have been made at more focused descriptions in a continuum of definitions between science and art which are far from compatible. However one agreed characteristic is that the basis of public health is *population* focused – in contrast to the *individual* patient focus of most health professionals. The term public health traditionally describes work done by health professionals while local authority and environmental professionals use the term 'well-being' often to describe the same phenomenon.

Public health can be conceptualized in two ways: public health as *actions* and public health as *resources*. Public health actions refer to activities to improve health by professionals and lay people, and by individuals, groups and communities. It is within this idea of public health action that the rationale for partnership and multidisciplinary practice is established. Public health resources refer to the sources of information and expertise that contribute to public health action. There is clearly a strong interdependent relationship between public health activity and public health resources; in this book we deal with both aspects.

Increasingly sustainability and the agenda for public health are being integrated. The Government's strategy on sustainable development, *Securing the Future*, is acknowledged as an excellent public health document, both for health protection and health improvement (HM Government 2005). Figure 1.1 presents the determinants of health and well-being that form this view. The links between healthy communities and sustainable development and change are numerous and encompass the social and economic determinants of health, quality of life and an ecological model of health where health is a resource for life (Barton and Grant 2006).

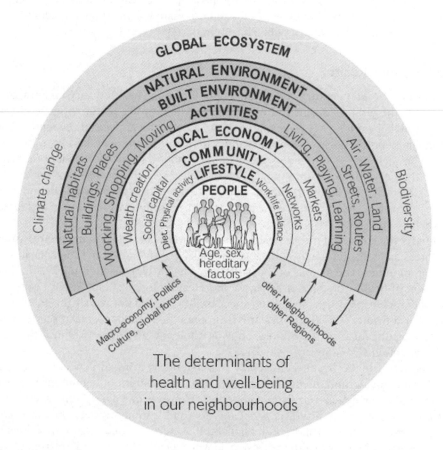

**Figure 1.1** The determinants of health and well-being in our neighbourhoods
*Source:* Barton and Grant 2006

There are key public health issues such as nutrition, pollution and community safety that draw together different groups of organizations, professionals, interest groups and community activists. At European, UK and devolved government levels there is general recognition of the main threats to sustainable communities which fall neatly into two public health clusters, that is, health protection and health improvement-related threats (Palmer 2006) (see Table 1.1).

The Sustainable Communities Plan is to:

> meet the diverse needs of existing and future residents, their children and other users, contribute to a high quality of life and provide opportunity and choice. [We] achieve this in ways that make effective use of natural resources, enhance the environment, promote social cohesion and inclusion and strengthen economic prosperity.
>
> (ODPM 2003: 7)

These recent documents and reviews demonstrate that the interconnectedness and interdependency between individual health, community and population health and the wider determinants of health and the resources in an ecological model of health is recognized at the heart of policy making.

## A public health for the 21st century

It is important to scope public health in an innovative way, building on our previous scoping and mapping (Orme *et al.* 2003) and reflecting the breadth of health and well-being and the importance of sustainable change. This new mapping demonstrates the convergence of the public health and sustainable change agendas. It recognizes that public health work involves a wide range of professionals and people. It also reflects the contribution of professionals working within the natural and built environments to public health action or work. Some of these people would not immediately label their work as 'public health' (see Figure 1.2).

## An evidence base for public health

The challenge of developing evidence-based public health is considerable. (See Part 4 for fuller discussion.) It involves, among other things, complex theoretical and

**Table 1.1** The key public health challenges

| Health protection-related threats | Health improvement-related threats |
|---|---|
| • Climate change and global warming | • Poverty and social exclusion |
| • Persistent toxic substances, resistance to antibiotics and food safety | • An ageing population |
| | • Transport and regional imbalances |
| • Loss of biodiversity | • Sedentary lifestyles |

*Source*: adapted from Palmer (2006)

**Figure 1.2** Public health for the 21st century

methodological debates across disciplines, realignments of power and influence within the public health profession and community, a synthesis of various types of evidence into guidance for people working in public health practice (NICE 2005). This is not to say that an evidence-based approach should dominate all aspects of public health. Public health is a complex activity, involving long-term goals and fundamental shifts in both policy and practice. This means that it is 'both an art and a science, but it should not be an act of faith' (Gowman and Coote 2000). It should make risks of failure clearer, encourage monitoring of outcomes and add to the evidence base which will inform future decisions.

## Historical perspectives on public health

Contemporary public health practice has however not been written on a blank slate, but has evolved and developed through centuries. History informs practice, so it is useful to consider briefly the roots and development of today's public health theory and practice (Scally and Womack 2004). This historical context is also important in understanding the rationale for many of the contributions to public health in this book. In this section we draw out the key lessons of the past.

### The 19th and early 20th century origins of public health practice

The history of public health illustrates the interrelationship between public health information and public health action. The early public health movement was built on a social and environmental approach based on political and social action focused on getting the state at mainly local levels to regulate such things as clean water, sanitation, better standards of housing and improving the environment.

Eminent doctors such as Snow (see Box 1.1) and Chadwick are credited with early public health action, but other commentators such as Szreter (1988), emphasize that these campaigners worked with trade unions, charitable organizations and philanthropists to persuade politicians and municipal authorities to make

---

**Box 1.1**  The history of public health

---

In the mid-1800s, outbreaks of disease were thought to be spread through odours in the air (the miasma theory) until one physician, John Snow, treating an outbreak of cholera in Broadgate, a poor area of London, observed that the disease also affected a single patient in a more affluent area some distance away. Snow discovered from the patient's maid that while the patient herself did not visit the Broadgate area she preferred to drink the water from the Broadgate pump which she thought was sweeter.

Snow hypothesized that cholera was transmitted through water rather than by 'bad smells'. He linked the data on sources of disease with mortality data in London, established an association and then a causal link between the events, taking action to close the water pump which was 6 feet from a cesspit contaminated with cholera.

So began the basis of evidence-based public health, with a physician observing events and taking time to engage with ordinary people to find out about their habits and practices.

---

environmental improvements. Such action required political motivation and public support.

The public health movement did not move towards a more medical focus until the last decade of the 19th century, when the emphasis changed from environmental issues to bacteriology and germ theory and more individual approaches to improving health based on preventing disease and carrying out immunization programmes. Following on from this, individual health education and hygiene became a major focus for public health interventions.

Contemporary observers have argued that the early public health reforms led to greater improvements in population health than anything subsequently achieved by the NHS (Baggott 2000). The realization that disease was no respecter of social class or wealth, and that the health of the most deprived members of society had to be of concern to the population as a whole, was a strong factor in encouraging the population to be concerned about the living conditions of the poor. These 19th century reforms created the basis for the system of public health located at the level of municipal or local authorities. Large cities across Europe can trace some of their historical amenities such as open spaces, parks, swimming and Turkish baths and health centres to the particular public and local political action in the 19th century.

Public concern about the state of the population's health has reappeared throughout the 20th century.

- The poor state of army recruits revived concerns about the conditions influencing the health of the working classes.
- The creation of the National Health Service (NHS) in 1948 was a direct result of pressure from trade unions to provide better conditions for workers who had contributed to the war effort as soldiers and civilians. Debates at that time showed a clear expectation that providing a free and accessible illness service for the

whole population would result in a reduction of the need for such services in the long term.

- Preventive health activities remained with the local authority with the medical officer of health heading up a team of public health workers including environmental health officers, health visitors and welfare officers dealing with population health issues. But in 1974, a reorganization moved the medical officer of health along with health visitors into the NHS. Public health medicine became recognized within the medical profession with the establishment of its professional body, the Faculty of Public Health in 1972 (Warren 2000).

- The improvements in living conditions and the impact of immunization on infectious diseases meant that public health, located within the NHS, began to focus more on 'preventable' medical and psychiatric disorders, such as diseases of the circulatory system, cancers and depression.

- As public health in the UK became more medically focused the World Health Organization (WHO) has been influential in broadening out the concept of health and establishing an appreciation of the range of determinants of health and disease. The original and classic definition of health (see page 7) with its holistic emphasis on health and well-being, underpinned the later Health for All movement and the declaration of Alma Ata (WHO 1978). This clearly acknowledged the gross inequalities between advantaged and disadvantaged peoples as politically, socially and economically unacceptable (Tones 2001). However in the developed world confidence in advanced medical care meant that the WHO perspective was initially understood only in relation to health in the developing world.

- A significant shift in public health thinking in the UK occurred during the 1980s, with the publication of the Black report (Townsend 1988) demonstrating the continuing presence of health inequalities in the UK.

- A broader ecological perspective on health, emerged as the 'new public health' (Ashton and Seymour 1988). Significant developments in this period included the Healthy Cities movement (Ashton 1992; Davies and Kelly 1992) and the 1985 Targets for Health for Europe (WHO 1985). This was followed by the Ottawa Charter in 1986 (WHO 1986) with its five main strategies for health improvement. The developing environmental movement at this time resulted in the agreement of Agenda 21 which sets out how developed and developing countries could work towards sustainable development (United Nations 1992; Allen 2001).

- Another significant event in the 1980s was the publication of a report on public health in England (Acheson 1988) which is summarized in Box 1.2.

- The Acheson Report recommended that a director of public health should be appointed in each health authority. The director would act as a chief medical adviser and 'would advise on priorities, planning and evaluation, co-ordinate the control of communicable disease and develop policy on prevention and health promotion' (Baggott 2000: 47).

- In 1992 the government published the first document 'Health of the Nation'

---

**Box 1.2** The new public health

---

Donald Acheson, the Chief Medical Officer for England, defined public health in a much wider context than before as:

> the science and art of preventing disease, prolonging life and promoting health through the organised efforts of society. These efforts will address policy issues at the level of the population's health and will tackle the role of health and disease, as well as considering the provision of effective health care services. Public health works through partnerships that cut across disciplinary, professional and organisational boundaries, and exploits this diversity in collaboration, to bring evidence and research based policies to *all areas* which impact on the health and well being of populations.
>
> (Acheson 1988)

Acheson's definition reveals key ideas embedded in much contemporary public health, identifying partnership and multidisciplinary working, collaboration, an evidence-based approach and the width of action from population health gain through to the provision of health care services. It also illustrates the complex and contested nature of public health.

---

which recognized the importance of maintaining good health. This document, which was criticized because it over-focused on the responsibility of individuals for their own health, but was nevertheless a significant development in the growing recognition of public health as a key aspect of national policy.

- The 'green movement', saw a re-emerged concern for the environment as quite a separate development through the 1980s. The Rio Earth Summit held in 1992 included no reference to health. It has taken until the 21st century for a strong connection between sustainable development, our ecological footprint and the consequences for our health to emerge.

- Following the change of government in 1997 there was growing governmental concern with health inequalities and the first minister for public health was appointed.

- The 'new Labour' government commissioned Sir Donald Acheson to report on inequalities in health and this marked a significant resurgence of interest in addressing the 'health gap' between richer and poorer people and tackling the root causes of poor health and health inequality such as poverty, homelessness, lack of life chances and unemployment (Acheson 1998) (see Chapter 9).

- Saving Lives: Our Healthier Nation (Secretary of State for Health 1999) built on the targets of the *Health of the Nation* (Secretary of State for Health 1992) but significantly gave more recognition to the health inequalities and the role played by social and economic factors in creating them. It identified key priority areas for health improvement – cancer, accidents, heart disease, stroke and mental health.

- The publication of *Shifting the Balance of Power: Next Steps* (Department of Health 2002b) indicated the government's intention to make primary care trusts (PCTs) the local focus for health development within the NHS including public health. The intention was to make PCTs carry the main responsibility for leading the development of local health improvement and modernization plans. They were expected to achieve specific targets for health gain and partnership, and to work at a local and community level with a range of regeneration and neighbourhood renewal initiatives. This move to put primary care at the centre of public health development was ambitious and with a few exceptions has not been particularly successful because of other pressures. PCTs had to reduce the use of expensive hospital services and develop alternatives in the community, as well as balance budgets. This has taken precedence over the development of public health (see Chapter 7).

- The same tensions are mirrored in the difficulties of developing public health activities in GP practices. There have been some significant successes in developing opportunistic health promotion within GP practices and there is potential to develop a greater focus within Practice Based Commissioning. However, there is some scepticism about whether this will be realistic.

- *Tackling Health Inequalities: Summary of the 2002 Cross-Cutting Review* (HM Treasury and Department of Health 2002) – aimed to establish the evidence for health inequalities and identify a strategy for delivery. A single target was introduced 'by 2010 reduce inequalities in health outcomes by 10%, as measured by infant mortality and life expectancy at birth'. Interventions thought to have the most impact were reducing smoking, Sure Start programmes, preventing teenage pregnancy, improved housing, immunization, breastfeeding and targeting the health of the over 50s.

- *Securing our Future* (Wanless 2002) and *Securing Good Health for the Whole Population* (Wanless 2004) were reports by Derek Wanless commissioned by HM Treasury to assess the resources needed in the future for the NHS. These reports demonstrated the impossibility of continuing with the traditional approaches in the NHS of curing illness and made the case for the 'fully engaged scenario' of achieving good health for the whole population. It made a powerful case for a strong national public health strategy as the driver for future spending on health.

## Who contributes to public health?

This section presents a scoping exercise for the contributors to public health. It provides an insight into the range of perspectives from different disciplines that contribute to public health.

Box 1.3 shows how the public health workforce was defined by the Chief Medical Officer of England (Department of Health 2001b).

---

**Box 1.3**  The public health workforce

- Those who have a role in health improvement and inequalities reduction, e.g. teachers, local business leaders, social workers, transport engineers, housing officers, other local government staff across the public, private and voluntary sectors, as well as doctors, nurses and other health care professionals.

- Professionals who spend a major part, or all of their time, in public health practice. These include those working with individuals within a group and/or communities, for example health visitors, environmental health officers and planners as well as those who use research, information, public health science or health promotion knowledge and skills in the public health field.

- Public health consultants and specialists who work at a strategic or senior manage-ment level or at a senior level of scientific expertise, for example public health epi-demiology and statistics. These people have the ability to manage change, formulate strategy, to lead public health programmes and to work across organizational boundaries.

---

## Building capacity in public health

The national standards for specialists in public health have recently been updated to reflect the challenges of moving public health forward and are presented in Table 1.2. It has been acknowledged at the highest levels of government that building capacity in public health is essential to avoid potentially spiralling costs that might arise from a larger national sickness service in the future (Wanless 2004).

In Table 1.3 some of the roles that contribute to sustainable public health in healthy communities are identified and briefly described by drawing on some previ-ous work (Grant *et al.* 2006 unpublished). Table 1.4 outlines the main work activities of public health. It includes people involved in leisure, building and architecture,

**Table 1.2** National standards for specialist public health

| | |
|---|---|
| A | Surveillance and assessment of the population's health and well-being |
| B | Promoting and protecting the population's health and well-being |
| C | Developing quality and risk management within an evaluative culture |
| D | Collaborative working for health and well-being |
| E | Developing health programmes and services and reducing inequalities |
| F | Policy, strategy development, implementation to improve health and well-being |
| G | Working with and for communities to improve health and well-being |
| H | Strategic leadership for health and well-being |
| I | Research and development to improve health and well-being |
| J | Ethically managing self, people and resources to improve health and well-being |

*Source*: Skills for Health (2002a)

**Table 1.3** Healthy communities and examples of the roles which support them

| Professions | |
| --- | --- |
| Public health specialists | Are trained in core public health skills. Disciplines include: epidemiology, health information, statistics, preventive medicine, health promotion, communicable disease, environmental health, health surveillance and evaluation of health services. |
| Community development practitioners | Develop working relationships with communities and organizations and encourage people to work with and learn from each other. They work with communities to plan change and collective action. |
| Architects | Design buildings that create a built environment that meets certain objectives and supervise construction. |
| Architectural technologists | Experts in the materials for built environment design and construction. |
| Town planners | The planners and controllers of construction, growth and development in a town or other urban area. |
| Housing professionals | Professionals with the skills and experience to match people to types of housing at the right time and in the right place. This might be in the private, public and voluntary sectors. |
| Transport planners | The planners and controllers of construction and use in terms of travel and journeys of the road, rail, air and sea systems. |
| Urban regeneration managers | Professionals that create the redevelopment of deprived areas in a large city. |
| Civil engineers | Engineers who design roads, bridges and dams etc. |
| Environmental scientists | People with knowledge to predict the impact of events on the environment and to gather evidence to support hypotheses about environment impacts and change. |
| Urban designers | These people design the layout of cities and towns. |
| District nurses | Provide high quality, culturally sensitive nursing care for people in their own homes or community setting and promote and maintain independent living through co-ordination of support services. |
| Teachers and lecturers | These people are responsible for the knowledge and skills of the whole population. They educate all children up to the age of 16 years and have a role in widening participation in education and training and creating life opportunities. |
| Health activists | People who use vigorous campaigning through a variety of means to bring about political and/or social change. |

| | |
|---|---|
| Fire and rescue services | Support community fire safety initiatives and work as advocates to prevent fatalities from fire in deprived communities. |
| Flood planners | These people are responsible for the surveillance of the rivers and seas and for the response to, and control of, environmental events that affect them. |
| Police | Support community safety initiatives and neighbourhood renewal. Also enforce the law with regard to new public health laws, for example, a ban on smoking in public places serving food. |
| Social workers | Social work is about working with people to achieve change. The social work profession promotes social change, problem solving in human relationships, and the empowerment and liberation of people to enhance well-being. |
| Primary care professionals | Primary Care Trusts carry the main responsibility for health improvement plans. They are expected to achieve targets for health gain and are required to work in partnership with a range of organizations across sectors. |
| School nurses | Help young people to make choices for a healthy lifestyle, to reduce risk-taking behaviour and to focus on issues such as teenage pregnancy. They contribute to personal health and social education and to citizenship training. |
| Health visitors | The overall purpose of health visiting is to improve health and well-being; enabling people to improve their own health. This is achieved through holistic assessment, which takes account of the needs of individuals, families and groups. |
| Health trainers | It is sometimes hard to change the habits of a lifetime without some support. NHS-accredited health trainers will be giving support to people in the areas with highest health need. |
| Community hygiene workers | Refuse collection from houses and within the community. |
| Pest controllers | The identification and solution of pest infestation in premises including homes and businesses. |

**Table 1.4** Healthy communities: work activities

| Work activities | |
| --- | --- |
| Health protection and emergency planning and response | Plays a critical role in protecting people from infectious disease and prevention of harm from hazards. They also prepare for new and emerging threats, such as a bio-terrorist attack or virulent new strain of disease. |
| Health promotion | Work includes community development, strategy development, partnership development and appropriate production and targeting of health information for different audiences. |
| Occupational health | Contribute to public health action through assessment of change within society and its translation into healthy workplace development. They take a lead in assessing and responding to health needs in the workforce. |
| Community development | A process which entails the mobilization, participation and involvement of local people on common issues important to them. |
| Environmental health | Use surveillance of local public health needs to target resources to public health work within an area. As service providers, they have a central role to play in linking environment with health and quality of life. |
| Neighbourhood renewal and Regeneration | Aims to improve standards of health, education, housing and the environment, and reduce crime and to close the gap between deprived neighbourhoods and the rest of the community. |

education, employment, housing, planning, transport, emergency response and community safety. One of the overall aims of this text is to explore the similarities and overlap in the core public health agenda and the wider agenda of contributing to well-being, as well as to identify challenges to and opportunities for working together. Implicit within our mapping is the belief that successful public health endeavour requires that professionals and disciplines commit to collaborative working to create sustainable change in health and well-being within a joined-up policy environment. The move towards establishing regional Teaching Public Health Networks (Rao 2006) supports the *Choosing Health* requirements of educating the whole workforce about the determinants of health. This initiative recognizes that it should involve not only the traditional public health workforce but also those for whom an appreciation of the public health approach and public health principles is vital if behaviour and practice are to lead to changes in the population. This is considered to be a massive undertaking and one that has never been attempted before.

Contributors to public health require appropriate organizational structures to facilitate public health action and resource development. The next section provides an overview of the organizations involved in the delivery of and settings for public health.

## Where does public health take place?

Leadership, advocacy and the collective working of the contributors to public health, require organizational structures and policies to drive forward and steer the direction of resources for public health action. The concept of 'settings' in public health practice is particularly useful for multidisciplinary working. Settings can be described as the domains of the living environment, the working environment and the leisure/ cultural environment (see Figure 1.1). Healthy Cities, health services, prisons, workplaces, neighbourhoods, communities and schools are just some of the settings where public health professionals work collaboratively.

Consideration of settings allows connections between people, environments and behaviours to be explored. It enables interrelationships between different groups of people within a setting to be addressed. It looks outward as well as inward to encourage participation and partnership and raises awareness of the wider impacts on health, sustainability and inequalities at a local, national and global level (Dooris 2006).

Public health action should be understood within the context of international, national, regional and local domains and reflect the way political and administrative, economic and social systems are organized. Figure 1.3 provides an overview of the main organizational structures that influence public health in the UK.

## The international context

International organizations, agreements and regulations can drive public health action. An example of this is international disease surveillance and rapid alert and response systems which coupled with international regulations control the spread of disease. International agreements on climate change started with the Montréal Protocol of 1986 banning ChloroFlouroCarbons (CFCs) from use in refrigerator coolants. (See Chapters 11 and 12 for more about international environmental agreements and sustainability.)

The importance of the level of decentralization in driving public health action is illustrated in Box 1.4.

## Devolution

An important factor in how public health strategies are implemented is the degree to which devolved government develops in Scotland, Wales, Ireland and England. The resulting diversity provides something of a natural experiment where we may learn from difference about what works in practice in tackling the key public health challenges.

'The advent of devolution will lead to differences in the way that the health systems of the four countries develop in the early years of the next century. All the indications are that this diversity will be healthy with opportunities to tailor services more closely to within-country needs and similarly building on local ideas and innovations. The importance of retaining and developing the traditional bonds and networks between the four UK countries will also be important

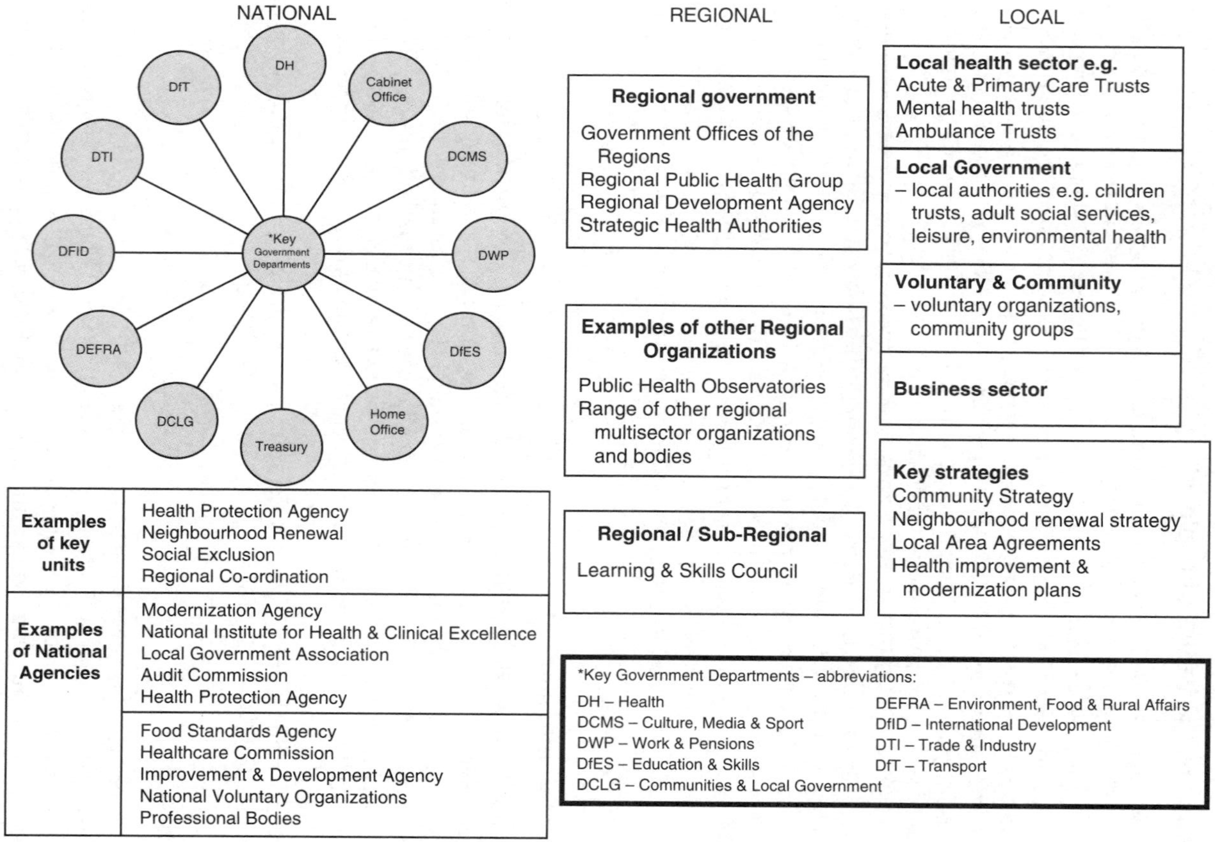
NATIONAL
REGIONAL
LOCAL
DH
Cabinet Office
DCMS
DWP
DfES
Home Office
Treasury
DCLG
DEFRA
DFID
DTI
DfT
*Key Government Departments
Examples of key units
Health Protection Agency
Neighbourhood Renewal
Social Exclusion
Regional Co-ordination
Examples of National Agencies
Modernization Agency
National Institute for Health & Clinical Excellence
Local Government Association
Audit Commission
Health Protection Agency
Food Standards Agency
Healthcare Commission
Improvement & Development Agency
National Voluntary Organizations
Professional Bodies
Regional government
Government Offices of the Regions
Regional Public Health Group
Regional Development Agency
Strategic Health Authorities
Examples of other Regional Organizations
Public Health Observatories
Range of other regional multisector organizations and bodies
Regional / Sub-Regional
Learning & Skills Council
Local health sector e.g.
Acute & Primary Care Trusts
Mental health trusts
Ambulance Trusts
Local Government
– local authorities e.g. children trusts, adult social services, leisure, environmental health
Voluntary & Community
– voluntary organizations, community groups
Business sector
Key strategies
Community Strategy
Neighbourhood renewal strategy
Local Area Agreements
Health improvement & modernization plans
*Key Government Departments – abbreviations:
DH – Health
DCMS – Culture, Media & Sport
DWP – Work & Pensions
DfES – Education & Skills
DCLG – Communities & Local Government
DEFRA – Environment, Food & Rural Affairs
DfID – International Development
DTI – Trade & Industry
DfT – Transport

**Figure 1.3** Overview of the organizational structure for public health (England)

---

**Box 1.4**   European action: smoking bans

---

The European Union represents its member states and is a geographic and political region originally established as a common market for free trade and now with a wide and substantial influence over social environmental and economic policy and regulation in the UK.

The 'Europe against Cancer' programme which ran until 2002 is an example of a public health measure that took a long time to come into effect. The EU resolution banning smoking in public places occurred as early as 1989, but even with the introduction in the late 1990s of the tobacco advertising directives there were too few regulatory teeth to enforce an impact on member states' governments. Finally, the main public health action occurred between 2005 and 2007. The implementation of a ban on smoking in public places at national and regional level came first in Ireland and then in devolved administrations of the UK.

This is a good example of how EU powers were too decentralized. The EU helped to delay for some 15 years a smoking ban in public places. It was the level of devolved power to administrative structures in national governments that eventually brought in the smoking bans.

---

in ensuring that learning and expertise are shared and that the UK-wide matters (e.g. training and professional self-regulation) are held firmly and consistently together.

(Donaldson 2000: 39–42)

The publication of four public health strategies across the UK highlights the centrality of public health improvement in government policy. In England *Choosing Health: Making Healthy Choices Easier;* in Wales *Health Challenge Wales* and *Designed for Life;* in Scotland: *Improving Health in Scotland: The Challenge;* and in Northern Ireland *Investing for Health.*

The UKPHA (2006) have identified the key organizational challenges or issues that result from the publication of four public health strategies across the UK (see Box 1.5).

## The regional context and 'powers of well-being'

At regional and local level, statutory organizations such as local authorities, the police, the health services and non-governmental department agencies, for example the Health Protection Agency and the Environment Agency have powers given to them by parliament. Local authorities have a wide 'well-being' agenda driven by statutory powers enabling them to promote the social, environmental and economic well-being of a community and the individuals within it (The Stationery Office 2000). (See Chapter 17 for more on community development and the powers of well-being.) A new English White Paper on local government reform entitled 'Strong and prosperous communities' was published in October 2006. It aims to 'enable local partners to

---

**Box 1.5**   Organizational challenges for public health

- Where does public health sit in the structure of government at central, regional and local level? Is it identifiable at all the levels?
- How does the structure from central to local organizational level influence co-ordination and coherence of public health strategies?
- How well are local government services integrated with primary health care services?
- How well does the structure of an organization engage voluntary and community groups and ordinary people?
- How dominant is the inequalities focus in the public health agenda?
- How do structures for devolved administrations influence the approach to public health action?
- How do organizational structures reflect the need for different levels of approach for different public health challenges? For example a structure which enables a focus on local community engagement for health inequalities and health improvement and a structure which enables a focus on central and regional organization to support local public health action for health threats, health protection and civil contingency in the event of a major health threat.
- Is there an articulated 'well-being and sustainable communities' agenda which connects local government, health services and community partners?

*Source*: adapted from UKPHA (2006)

---

**Box 1.6**   Sustrans for well-being and sustainable communities

Sustrans was set up to influence sustainable transport systems through a cycle route network. Its public health action is to implement projects like 'Active Travel'. Cycling as opposed to car use reduces pollution and improves health and well-being through exercise.

Sustrans was set up as a charity in 1977 as Cyclebag, in response to an energy crisis that was encouraging the whole world to look at different ways of travelling. Sustainable transport was the wider framework within which cycling and walking would become increasingly relevant. Sustrans works at national and devolved government level as a pressure group influencing policies and funding for sustainable transport and at local level with local people, local authorities, partners and other landowners to identify potential new cycling and walking routes. The National Cycle Network currently runs within 2 miles of 75 per cent of the UK population and the aim is to bring the Network to as many people as possible (walkers, wheelchair users, cyclists and horse riders). This will mean running through every city, bringing communities together and providing links to shops, schools and farther afield to other towns and cities.

respond more flexibly to local needs; to reduce the amount of top down control from central government; and to enable citizens and communities to play their part (DCLG 2006). This is discussed in detail in Chapter 3.

The integration of the wider 'well-being and sustainable communities' agenda of local government with public health is important in tackling inequalities. There is evidence of voluntary and community engagement developing in all countries of the UK (UKPHA 2006). This is essential in tackling inequalities and social exclusion and for engagement in the wider sustainable community agenda. The work of Sustrans is an example of a Non-Governmental Organization (NGO) contributing to public health at a national, regional and local level (see Box 1.6).

## Conclusion

This chapter has set out a map of 21st century public health. We have summarized the history of public health in the past 200 years so that readers can understand how current practice has developed from the pioneering work of public health thinkers and practitioners in the past. The challenges then for public health in the 21st century, which this book explores, are in making sense of complexity and differences, based on sound evidence, so that actions and interventions taken by all contributors will impact on health outcomes and that this is sustainable into the future.

# 2

# DAVID J. HUNTER
## Public health policy

**Editors' introduction**

Government policy on public health, along with related policy on issues which affect health such as education, employment, food and transport, provide the broad framework for action to improve the health of the population; policies can facilitate new opportunities for health improvement but they may also hinder progress.

It is therefore crucial that public health workers develop a critical understanding of current public health policy and programmes at both national and local level. In this chapter, the author provides a refreshing insight and critique into the important area of public health policy development and implementation, which should prove useful for everyone working in the field of public health, in whatever capacity.

The government's commitment to public health is evidenced by a range of policy initiatives since 1997. The author takes a critical look at current policy developments and examines how they have been put into action. He questions whether the current and developing policy and administrative framework are 'fit for purpose' and appropriate for the problems and challenges posed by the development of multidisciplinary public health in the 21st century. He identifies and discusses barriers and difficulties posed by the breadth of policy development.

The chapter is in three sections. The first section reviews the present state of public health policy and its recent history since 1997. In particular, it assesses two tensions in health policy. The first is between a 'downstream' agenda fixated on acute health care on the one hand and an 'upstream' agenda centred on public health interventions designed to maintain and improve health, and avoid or delay contact with the NHS on the other. The second tension is between those who support a strong role for government in tackling health improvement and those who see government's role as largely one of encouraging individuals to make healthier lifestyle decisions. Charges of acting as the 'nanny state' sit uneasily with the government.

The second section examines the constraints on implementing public health policies and the bias in public health towards the NHS and health care. It questions how far this can be influenced and changed.

The final section and conclusion consider the future of public health policy and make suggestions for what needs to happen if there is to be a sustained shift in policy towards health as distinct from health care.

## Introduction

This chapter takes a critical look at current public health policy and its implementation. It questions whether the current and developing policy and administrative framework are 'fit for purpose' and appropriate for the problems and challenges posed by the development of multidisciplinary public health and concludes that they pose major barriers and other difficulties which, if not addressed, will seriously impede implementation. Though centred on the position in England, the chapter briefly considers the differing policy contexts elsewhere in the UK post-devolution. The impact of devolution affords opportunities for policy learning with growing evidence of increasing policy divergence in health across the four countries.

The chapter is in three sections. The first section reviews the present state of public health policy and its recent history since 1997. In particular, it assesses the deep rooted tension in health policy between an 'upstream' agenda centred on public health interventions, and a 'downstream' agenda fixated on acute health care. It also charts the recent shift from government exercising a strong leadership role to one where it sees its role as an enabling one, helping people to help themselves without interference from the nanny state. The second section examines the constraints on implementing public health policies and the bias in public health towards the NHS and health care; it questions whether this is inevitable. The third section considers the future of public health policy and makes suggestions for what needs to happen if there is to be a sustained shift in policy towards health as distinct from health care.

## The state of public health policy

### The new Labour government May 1997: public health renaissance

Public health underwent something of a renaissance following the election of the Labour government in May 1997. The new government acted quickly to appoint the first ever minister for public health as a member of the ministerial team in the Department of Health. Her remit only extended to England as plans for devolution to Scotland, Wales and Northern Ireland were already well advanced. The new minister was anxious to map out a new approach to health policy to demonstrate the government's commitment to a more socially equitable and cohesive society.

There was a recognition that improving health and narrowing the widening 'health gap' between social groups were policy challenges that transcended any single department's responsibilities. They were cross-cutting issues and therefore key features of the government's concern that there should be 'joined-up' solutions to 'joined-up' social problems. The minister for public health immediately set in progress three initiatives:

- the development of a new health strategy to replace *The Health of the Nation*, the first ever health strategy for England which existed from 1992 to 1997 (Secretary of State for Health 1992);
- an evaluation of the impact of *The Health of the Nation* at local level, the findings from which would inform the new strategy (Department of Health 1998c); and
- an inquiry into inequalities chaired by a former chief medical officer, Sir Donald Acheson, to demonstrate where the scientific evidence showed interventions to be effective in tackling inequalities (Acheson 1998).

The Acheson inquiry made 39 recommendations only three of which directly concerned the NHS. This only confirmed the government in its view that improving the public's health and tackling inequalities had to be part of concerted action across government. (See Chapter 9 for a detailed discussion of tackling inequalities in health.)

Table 2.1 lists key policies, reports and initiatives in public health since the Labour government came to power in 1997.

**Table 2.1** Key policies, reports and initiatives in public health 1997–2006

| | |
|---|---|
| 1997 | Election of new Labour government; commitment to public health action to reduce health inequalities. |
| 1998 | Acheson *Independent Inquiry into Inequalities in Health* published. |
| 1999 | New national strategy for health in England published: *Saving Lives: Our Healthier Nation.*<br>Initiatives such as health action zones, healthy living centres and Sure Start started to be launched to improve health and reduce inequalities in health. |
| 2000 | Health Development Agency set up; remit included strengthening the evidence base of public health.<br>*The NHS Plan* published; signalled organizational change and attracted criticism about the lack of emphasis on public health. |
| 2001 | National targets on health inequalities published.<br>*Shifting the Balance of Power* published – devolving NHS responsibility to the 'front line'.<br>House of Commons Select Committee reports on public health published, which criticized the lack of government emphasis on public health.<br>*The Report of the Chief Medical Officer's Project to Strengthen the Public Health Function* also published.<br>Two reports: *Tackling Health Inequalities* (consultation document) and *Vision to Reality* (progress report on tackling health inequalities) published. |
| 2002 | Wanless Report published on future health trends and resources required; it supported public health action to bring health and economic benefits.<br>*Tackling Health Inequalities* report published on action needed. |

HM Treasury and Department of Health *Tackling Health Inequalities: Summary of the 2002 Cross-Cutting Review* published, which committed the government to placing tackling health inequalities at the heart of public service delivery. Public Service Agreement (PSA) target on health inequalities: *by 2010 to reduce inequalities in health outcomes by 10 per cent as measured by infant mortality and life expectancy at birth.*

2004     Wanless's second report published on the state of public health; it was critical of lack of progress in rebalancing the NHS from a sickness to a health service and called for a workforce development plan to consider the needs of those contributing to the wider public health; it also wanted to see more investment in evidence-based public health interventions to demonstrate cost-effectiveness.
New health strategy for England published, *Choosing Health: Making Healthier Choices Easier*, in response to Wanless report; it heralded a shift in the role of government away from the 'nanny state' to one of enabling people to make informed lifestyle choices; it called for closer partnership working between the NHS and local government.
New PSA targets announced, the majority of which are concerned with improving health and tackling inequalities; targets can only be achieved through joined-up action and shared priorities across government.

2005     *Choosing Health* Delivery Plan published setting out 171 targets.
The Health Development Agency is wound up and its activities transferred to the renamed National Institute for Health and Clinical Excellence (NICE) and within NICE to the Centre for Public Health Excellence.
*Commissioning a Patient-Led NHS* published which was met by a storm of opposition from NHS staff; it set in motion the third major NHS reorganization since 1997 and one which sought to reintroduce market-style competition that the government had promised to end.
*Tackling Health Inequalities: Status Report on the Programme for Action* published by the Scientific Reference Group on Health Inequalities chaired by Sir Michael Marmot; the report shows 'a continuing widening of inequalities as measured by infant mortality and life expectancy at birth'.

2006     New health strategy published, *Our Health, Our Care, Our Say* which emphasized the need to shift the focus of care away from acute care hospitals to primary and community care settings; this would mean giving more attention to long-term conditions and public health.
Operating framework for the NHS in England for 2006/07 published by Department of Health with health inequalities and sexual health listed as two of the six priorities for action.

## New policies and other initiatives

Richard Sennett has argued that governments are consumers of policy, 'abandoning them as though they have no value once they exist' (Sennett 2006: 176). It does not matter if these policies fail to get implemented – what matters is that policy makers are seen to be at the cutting edge of what is fashionable and in vogue. Certainly, in public health as in other policy domains the government has shown great restlessness with an endless stream of bewildering strategies and reports (see Table 2.1). Whereas most of those engaged in public health thought that the 1999 health strategy, *Saving Lives: Our Healthier Nation* (Secretary of State for Health 1999), would remain the government's touchstone for its efforts to improve health, this did not prove to be the case. Not that the strategy was without flaws. Although widely welcomed, some commentators felt it remained rather too firmly wedded to a health care model which was less about supporting communities to remain healthy than about keeping individuals alive (Fulop and Hunter 1999). The strategy focused mainly on disease-based areas which demonstrated clear limits on how far it represented a move 'upstream'. A key finding from the evaluation of the first health strategy for England, *The Health of the Nation* (1992–97) was that the dominance of the medical model underlying the strategy 'was a major barrier to its ownership by agencies outside the health sector, notably local government and voluntary agencies' (Department of Health 1998c). Commenting on the 1999 health strategy, the Local Government Association and the UK Public Health Association in a joint report concluded that 'the traditional concerns of public health medicine focused primarily on alleviating sickness and preventing premature death' remained a 'dominant and overly narrow perspective' (Local Government Association and UK Public Health Association 2000: 2).

Almost simultaneously with these policy developments, the government launched a further raft of new programmes and initiatives most of which have long since disappeared. These included Health Action Zones (HAZs), Health Improvement Programmes (HIMPs), Healthy Living Centres (HLCs), Sure Start (with its pledge to end child poverty within a generation), and New Deal for Communities. Judging by the sheer number of announcements and their scope and range there could be no doubting the government's resolve and drive in respect of raising the priority attached to improving the public's health and narrowing the gap between rich and poor.

At the same time, the Health Education Authority was replaced by a new body, the Health Development Agency (HDA), charged with strengthening the evidence base for public health in line with similar developments that were already underway in respect of evidence-based medicine. The new Agency's remit included a commitment to disseminate the evidence about what interventions worked and those that did not work, as well as to provide developmental support to those organizations struggling to apply the evidence in practice. The HDA proved short-lived and was integrated with the National Institute for Clinical Excellence (NICE) in 2005 to form the National Institute for Health and Clinical Excellence (NICE) when the government decided to reduce the number of arm's-length agencies it had set up.

While welcoming the government's commitment to public health evident in the outpouring of policy statements, ministerial speeches and so on, critics accuse the government of suffering from 'initiativitis'. This actually makes the job of 'joining up' policy and management more difficult because each initiative tends to operate in isolation and receives its own dedicated funding and its success is judged according to criteria specific to that particular initiative (Hunter 2003).

The appearance of *The NHS Plan* in July 2000 gave a clear signal that the government's attention and energy were being progressively directed towards the NHS and its problems, the extent of which the government had underestimated during its initial years in office (Secretary of State for Health 2000). Aware that the NHS was a key electoral issue, especially after the prime minister's personal pledge to end waiting lists, ministers could not afford to ignore what was happening in 'down-stream' acute care services while being distracted by 'upstream' health concerns. Initially opposed to 'big bang' structural reform of the type from which the NHS had become weary over decades of successive structural changes, the government embarked on the most comprehensive and complex organizational changes the NHS had witnessed (Department of Health 2001a). It proved to be the first round in a series of successive restructurings which continue to dominate the NHS. Inevitably such major changes give rise to disruption and planning blight and have certainly put at risk the government's early focus on public health.

## Reviews and reports strengthening public health

As if sensing the change of mood about its commitment to public health, the government published a number of other policy documents and reports testifying to its determination to fulfil its public health objectives and perhaps seeking to reassure its critics that its eye had not been taken off the health ball altogether (Department of Health 2001b–d). None of them, however, made much of an impact or served to restore the government's weakened public health credentials.

It took two influential reports produced by the former banker turned government adviser, Derek Wanless, to put public health back at the centre of policy. The first report, commissioned by the Chancellor of the Exchequer, was intended to assess future health trends and the resources required over 20 years up to 2020. Rather unexpectedly, Wanless gave an important boost to public health.

The review team argued that 'better public health measures could significantly affect the demand for health care' (Wanless 2002: paragraph 1.27). On top of any health benefits, a focus on public health was also seen to bring wider benefits by increasing productivity and reducing inactivity in the working age population. There was optimism too, about the potential for public health interventions. 'Despite methodological difficulties and the length of time needed for research, there is evidence suggesting that some health promotion interventions are not only effective, but also cost-effective over both short and longer time periods' (Wanless 2002). See Chapter 16 for more on the Wanless reports.

Most important, especially coming from a hard nosed banker, was a conviction that good health is good economics and that far from being a cost, investment in health is a benefit to individuals, employers and the government. Healthy communities attract investment, while unhealthy ones do not. What was required, according to Wanless, was a better balance between curing sickness on the one hand and preventing disease on the other. The review team expressed concern that perhaps too much effort and emphasis was being placed on 'downstream' acute care services in preference to 'upstream' interventions designed to maintain and improve health, and avoid or delay contact with the NHS. The Wanless review therefore gave an important and timely boost to those advocating a more assertive approach to public health interventions both inside and outside government.

The message was reinforced in a second report published in 2004 which looked specifically at the state of public health and whether the government was on course with its policies (Wanless 2004). Wanless was critical of the government's failure to implement its own policy and of the workforce's weak capacity and poor capability and general lack of 'fitness for purpose'. In particular, it lacked many of the essential skills to change individual behaviour (for example social marketing) and was spread too thinly across multiple organizations thereby failing to make a sustained impact. He was particularly exercised at the absence of a workforce development plan or of any systematic attempt to harness the wider public health workforce and its contribution to health improvement. He repeated his criticism of the government's fixation on acute care and hospitals and called for a rebalancing of the NHS so that it became less of a sickness service and more of a health one. Wanless's prescription lay principally in getting 'a realignment of incentives in the system to focus on reducing the burden of disease and tackling the key lifestyle and environmental risks'.

The government's response to Wanless's second report was muted which in part reflected tensions between the Treasury and Department of Health over who was driving health policy. The Department's defence was to argue that the government's priority had been to sort out the NHS and now that the task had been largely done, it was appropriate to turn attention to wider health issues. The Wanless report coincided with mounting evidence over the sharp rise in obesity, especially among young children who were presenting with Type 2 diabetes in alarming numbers, growing alcohol misuse, a rise in sexually transmitted infections and so on. Wanless's critique of slow progress was further defused by the announcement of a major public consultation to ascertain people's views on how public health challenges could best be tackled. The fact that a perfectly serviceable health strategy which had been lying more or less dormant since 1999 remained to be implemented did not seem to register with ministers. The thinking among special advisers and some ministers was that public health needed to be modernized in keeping with other public services. What they understood by this became clear with the publication of a new public health White Paper in late 2004 with the telling title, *Choosing Health: Making Healthier Choices Easier* (Secretary of State for Health 2004). It focused on six main priority areas identified in Box 2.1. The new strategy received a mixed response. The fact that public health policy was once again centre stage was widely welcomed by the public health community but this was coupled with misgivings about some aspects of the proposals. It was apparent that the 'quiet revolution' which had begun to sweep through the NHS was now to be extended to public health. The NHS was being subjected to the language of business and customers and to market-style incentives that went far beyond anything that had been contemplated in 1997 when the government had been elected. Indeed, at that time the government was committed to abandoning its predecessor's NHS internal market reforms. The political rhetoric changed after 2002 and was no longer about 'big' government or 'top down' change. Instead, though few believed it, the emphasis was on devolution, putting power back to the front line, reducing central control, and giving patients and public more choice. It was also about increasing capacity to meet the tough targets and on driving up quality and efficiency, making use of the private sector to do so and to provide competition for NHS monopoly providers. Indeed, the government's new mantra was one of choice and competition although

---

**Box 2.1**   Choosing health priorities

The *Choosing Health* strategy set out six priorities:

- tackling health inequalities
- reducing the number of people who smoke
- tackling obesity
- improving sexual health
- improving mental health
- encouraging sensible drinking

---

few in the public health world were persuaded that such notions would make their task easier.

There is nothing exceptional about these priorities but a comparison between the 1999 and 2004 health strategies is revealing in terms of the shift in emphasis away from what government could and should do about improving health, and what individuals should do for themselves (Hunter 2005). Whereas the stress in 1999 was on government to provide leadership where only government action could achieve the objective, by 2004 the emphasis was on government being less interventionist with its role largely confined to enabling and facilitating people to make better informed choices about their lifestyles. Hence there was no plan at this time to legislate for a ban on smoking in public places in England despite developments in Scotland and elsewhere to introduce such a ban (see below).

With the marketization of public policy well underway, the government's redefinition of the public realm to give a greater place for personal choice and for diversity in service provision has made many working in public health uneasy about their role and where they fit. The government seemed to add to their unease by recommending that health trainers, drawn from local communities, be recruited to work with people to help them change their behaviour and lifestyles. There was also an emphasis on social marketing in order to find new ways of encouraging people to change their behaviour. Since then a major initiative is underway to introduce social marketing tools and techniques into the NHS (National Social Marketing Centre 2006). In short, it seemed as if health was to be defined and marketed in terms of personal fitness, body imagery and individual achievement – a far cry from traditional public health values and concerns based upon enlightened government action (at global, national, regional and local levels) in developing and enacting healthy public policy coupled with action at local level to help people change their behaviour.

No sooner did the new health strategy appear with its promise of additional resources and a renewed commitment to improve health than the NHS became caught up once again in a further major and distracting restructuring. Indeed, it is possibly the most far-reaching and destabilizing in its history and its effects are likely to be felt for some time to come. However, the government could not entirely forget about public health. First, its own public service agreements agreed between spending departments and the Treasury (see Table 2.1) placed significant emphasis on public health and tackling health inequalities. Second, on the smoking ban issue the government was forced to retreat from the widely criticized position set out in *Choosing Health* and, following a free vote in Parliament, there was a majority for an outright ban. It will take effect from summer 2007, well over a year after similar measures were introduced in Scotland which followed the earlier example of Ireland.

Third, and perhaps most significant of all, the government came under strong attack for not doing enough about public health from its Chief Medical Officer in his 2005 annual report (Department of Health 2006a). In a hard-hitting chapter, Sir Liam Donaldson was critical of NHS organizations for raiding public health budgets to reduce deficits and make the books balance. Acknowledging the government's 'major and unprecedented commitment to public health over the last eight years', he laments the vulnerable state in which public health services now find themselves. The causes, he claims, are lack of growth, the weakening effects of repeated management reorganizations, and the 'compelling and emotive' competition for resources from clinical services. The situation is a result of systemic failings rather than the fault of any person or group of people. But 'at its heart is a set of attitudes that emphasizes short-term thinking, holds too dear the idea of the hospital bed and regards the prevention of premature death, disease and disability as an option not a duty' (p. 44).

This thinly veiled attack on government policy coincided with a major, if in places slightly confused, speech delivered by the Prime Minister, Tony Blair, in which he reiterated the government's commitment to public health but pointed out that 'we are now in a new era, the time of conditions of affluence, of degenerative and man-made diseases' (Blair 2006). Amidst the endorsement of a concept of the State as enabling, of the importance of personal lifestyle change, and of the need for commercial companies to get more directly involved in sending health messages to employees and the public, the prime minister acknowledged that perhaps paternalism and the nanny state had their uses. He conceded that in formulating policy he had undergone his 'own personal journey of change'. Whereas a few years back he 'would have hesitated long and hard over issues like the smoking ban', now 'I have come to the conclusion we need to be tougher, more active in setting standards and enforcing them' (Blair 2006). He cited legislation in a number of public health areas – food, air, water quality, drinking and driving, speed restrictions, school meals – to make the point that the government did not shirk from legislative action where needed.

It is also possible to detect another shift in the government's stance on public health. Following a review of the mortality target to reduce life expectancy between social groups and reduce health inequalities carried out by the Prime Minister's Delivery Unit in late 2005/early 2006, the government's focus is now firmly on ensuring that the NHS and acute health care services pay sufficient attention to public health. The view taken, reasonably enough, is that major gains can be achieved in public health if the NHS would only give these priority. Such a development opens up a long-running sore in the public health community with those wedded to the wider public health concerned that a medical model of public health is once again in the ascendant at precisely the time when it seemed as if the prospects for a different approach looked encouraging partly as a result of many non-clinicians being appointed to senior public health posts in primary care organizations (PCOs). It is unclear if many will survive the halving of the number of primary care trusts.

This section has reviewed some of the highlights emerging from the steady stream of documentation establishing the case for rebalancing policy so that it gives proper attention and weight to health as distinct from health care. But, if there has been a common and persistent complaint running through the various policy pronouncements that have appeared since 1997, and reaffirmed by the CMO's critique, it has been that there remains an unhelpful bias in favour of the NHS and of avoiding ill health and disease rather than maintaining good health. The contribution other sectors and agencies can clearly make to the public health effort is too often overlooked or treated as an add on. The NHS continues to have the lead role regardless of whether it actually chooses to exercise it or not. It is a familiar story told over many years and one that has been repeated ad nauseam in countless reports from numerous quarters. Hardly surprising, therefore, to find that other key stakeholders have not been engaged in ways that are essential if the wider public health agenda is to be seriously addressed (Elson 2004). The section below – Public health: constraints on implementation – probes a little further the implementation gap in respect of public health.

## Devolution and public health policy

It is important to acknowledge that none of the policy documents reported above apply to Wales, Scotland and Northern Ireland. Nor is there a separate public health minister in these countries. Some documents, notably the health strategy, *Saving Lives: Our Healthier Nation*, and *The NHS Plan* have their equivalents in the other three countries. But growing divergence is evident and this is notable in all kinds of ways and not simply in producing separate inventories of policy documents. The language of political discourse is different and the NHS in Wales and Scotland (Northern Ireland remains a special case and has been omitted from this discussion) is not being subjected to constant organizational change. Nor is the language of choice or markets in evidence (Blackman *et al.* 2006).

In contrast to England, the Welsh and Scottish Plans both open with a strong commitment to putting health first. But there is scepticism in some quarters over whether this really signals a break with the past. Greer (2001: 21), for instance, who has studied the progress of public health across the UK asserts that the English Plan is 'primarily focused on health care services organisations'; Scotland is 'speaking of public health but still focusing on health care services'; and Wales is 'focusing on integrated public health activities and promotion'. Both Wales and Scotland appear to be addressing the public health infrastructure deficit more directly having established new bodies dedicated to the strengthening of the public health function. Nothing comparable has emerged in England despite a failed attempt in 2005 to establish an elected regional assembly in the North-east. However, as Greer also points out, it makes little sense to take England as a baseline for intra-UK comparative purposes, tempting though this may be. It is not a case of England doing better or Scotland or Wales doing worse – each jurisdiction has chosen different priorities and means of achieving them coming to a different view of their respective costs and benefits (Greer 2006; UKPHA 2006). Greer has given labels to the distinct approaches evident within the UK (Greer 2004). English policy is characterized by markets and management, Scottish by a new professionalism, focusing on integrated services (there is not purchaser–provider split) and managed clinical networks. Welsh policy is described as primarily 'localist'. Further discussion on devolution can be found in Chapters 1 and 3.

## Public health: constraints on implementation

Reasons advanced for the lack of effective implementation of policies favouring public health are many and include:

- lack of clarity of the public health function especially as performed by public health medicine specialists;
- a policy stance that seems to be more symbolic and concerned with gesture politics rather than with real change;
- lack of leadership and poor management;
- weak incentives to ensure sustainable change and a shift in priorities;
- the absence of clear boundaries – improving health is everybody's business (the risk being that it becomes nobody's responsibility);
- the results of interventions to improve health often take many years to take effect and these are sidelined in favour of short-term considerations that bring immediate and visible results;
- giving the lead role for public health to the NHS which, many would claim, is preoccupied with ill health rather than health; health care services have an insatiable appetite for growth and expansion and they are where the powerful vested interests in health policy are located; and
- poor evidence not only about the cost-effectiveness of public health interventions but also about what makes them successful.

In their study of what incentives exist for NHS managers to focus on wider health issues, Hunter and Marks (2005) report that those interviewed were critical of current targets, the impact of restructuring the public health workforce, the patchiness of the evidence base, and the quality of public health information. They also criticized the 'jigsaw' approach to policy making where policies were developed in isolation from each other and without reference to their impact on health improvement. Interviewees believed progress would only be possible with the emergence of public health organizations which would have public health at their centre. Such organizations would require cultural change as well as change in the mind set of practitioners together with system change (Marks and Hunter 2005).

## Public health: patchy implementation?

It is possible to contest some of these explanations for patchy implementation, like the issue of the evidence base, where comparisons with evidence-based medicine are not sensible or valid. But a key factor in public health's failure to deliver, it is suggested, may have its roots in confusion about its core purpose and the multiple roles it is expected to perform. These are:

- health promotion, including the wider public health;
- improving the quality of clinical standards; and
- protection of public health and management of risk: communicable disease control and so on. (See Chapter 13 for more about health protection.)

Although these three domains, articulated by the Faculty of Public Health, are interrelated up to a point, they are also discrete and demand different skills as well as presenting particular challenges (Griffiths *et al.* 2005). Without an appropriately skilled workforce functioning within a clearly understood policy setting, it seems unlikely that significant progress will be made.

The weakening of public health's leading role in health improvement is not confined to England. Julio Frenk, Mexico's Minister for Health and a former senior official in WHO, claimed well over a decade ago that 'public health is experiencing a severe identity crisis, *as well as a crisis of organisation and accomplishment*' (Frenk 1992: 68, my italics). The US Institute of Medicine in 1988 claimed that 'public health, as a profession, as a governmental activity, and as a commitment of society is neither clearly defined, adequately supported nor fully understood' (Institute of Medicine 1988). In a more recent report, the IOM insisted that the public's health can be supported only through collective action, not through individual endeavour (IOM 2003). The situation is little different throughout most of Europe particularly when the idea of what constitutes the public realm is under challenge from the growing penetration of public services by market forces and the effects of globalization.

Periodically, public health has found itself at a crossroads in terms of the opportunities and challenges facing it. Yet, on each occasion, despite repeated attempts to refocus public health on its core business, the specialty has continued since the early 1970s to be buffeted by successive NHS reorganizations and has found itself more and more at the mercy of general managers who have strengthened their grip on the NHS and on its priorities. Few managers have been advocates for public health and have sought instead to use expensive clinically trained public health professionals to pursue their own agendas around evidence-based medicine, contracting, commissioning and clinical governance. For the most part, public health specialists appear to have been willing accomplices. Or, for whatever reason, they have felt unable to speak out.

Of course, all these essentially health care tasks are included in the mix of roles listed above and ascribed to public health practitioners but it is arguable whether such a complex and varied set of tasks can easily be vested in a single specialty or individual. Little wonder, then, that the practice of public health has 'shifted uneasily between the analysis of health problems and the administration of health services' (Berridge 1999: 45). While the commitment to tackling poor health and health inequalities may be genuine, the energy and resources appear to be directed to other more immediate and pressing concerns thereby dashing hopes of implementing national policy locally (Exworthy *et al.* 2002).

## Little emphasis on practice

But there are other aspects of the public health function which have hampered implementation. There has always been a tension between public health *science* and public health *practice*. Both are essential to improving health but public health practice remains a much neglected area of the public health function. A similar conclusion is reached by Nutbeam and Wise (2002) when they assert that public health medicine has been more concerned with knowledge acquisition than with its application to change practice. At issue here is the training available to public health trainees and the balance between competencies and skills designed to equip them with an ability to acquire and handle evidence on the one hand and manage change on the other. Too little emphasis is placed on change management skills and there is a notable absence of appropriate management and leadership development opportunities (Hunter 2007). The final section of this chapter, on the future of public health, returns to this theme.

## Insufficient joining up

Another impediment to implementation is the compartmentalization of policies and structures mentioned earlier. The government has rightly argued that complex problems demand complex solutions and that there is a premium on ensuring that policy and management is joined up both horizontally across departments and agencies, and vertically between levels of government.

The rhetoric has been impeccable, while the reality has been disappointing. In practice, the government has approached policy and its implementation from exactly the opposite, 'reductionist', point of view – breaking a problem down into its component parts and then attempting to solve them in a linear fashion. The accompanying preoccupation with endless targets, performance management systems and all the other paraphernalia of modern managerialism has prevented the very 'joined upness' that the government says it seeks. There is a curious mismatch between ends and means with the chosen means almost certainly making the desired ends less, rather than more, likely to be achieved.

Moreover, despite the mantra of 'joined-up' policy emanating from the prime minister's office, the persistence of departmentalism is evident all around. Nor is it denied within the Cabinet Office where reports from the Performance and Innovation Unit pull few punches in their critique of the government's approach to implementation (Cabinet Office 2001a, b). They note that 'too many new policies and initiatives can wreck delivery by diverting management time – carrying out instructions gets in the way of better outcomes' (Cabinet Office 2001a: 6). In another report on leadership the Unit comments on the need for 'horizontal' leadership within and across sectors and for leaders 'who are able to see the whole picture, and create a common vision with other agencies' (Cabinet Office 2001b: 11). The emphasis on targets was criticized too, since it could 'stifle innovation and initiative with leaders concentrating on centrally-set targets' to the exclusion of more important issues affecting their organizations.

## Politics and power

Finally, if there is genuine concern about implementation failure and its causes then attention has to be given to the politics of change and the power plays that exist. It is both incorrect and naive to allege that if only the evidence existed in regard to which interventions worked then implementation would follow. Impediments to change often owe more to political than technical factors. 'Unless and until we are willing to come to terms with organisational power and influence, and admit that the skills of getting things done are as important as the skills of figuring out what to do, our organisations will fall further and further behind' (Pfeffer 1992: 12).

## Regionalism

It was hoped that the creation of elected regional assemblies in England would give a new focus to public health (Hunter *et al.* 2005). There is limited evidence to suggest that regional bodies have finally discovered public health and its importance to economic regeneration. *The NHS Plan* began the process of strengthening the wider regional role and the move was widely welcomed, especially by those concerned with the wider public health and keen to remove its sole locus from within the NHS. However, as was reported earlier, the NHS fell victim to continuous reorganization and the regional role has not been developed. Nevertheless, there remains some optimism because the new top tier of the NHS below the central department is in most parts of the country based on the existing regional government offices. The newly combined posts of regional directors of public health and regional medical directors could become more influential than their predecessors but only if they are adequately supported to enable them to operate effectively and in a balanced fashion across the three domains described earlier. The risk otherwise is that public health will once again be distracted by the constant pressure emanating from the NHS as described by the CMO in his 2005 annual report (Department of Health 2006a). Indeed, it might have been better to break down the regional role into its component parts, retaining the more medical health service elements within the NHS while confining the new regional public health function, involving the work of the regional offices of government, to a dedicated senior post. The risk then, of course, would be that the NHS would pay even less attention to its public health responsibilities than currently. So there is no perfect or easy answer to the question of where best to locate the lead public health function. Perhaps the lead role should vary according to where public health (or which of its three domains) can make the most impact.

Finally, the future of regional government remains uncertain with no significant pressure to revive elected assemblies. Rather the focus has shifted to local government and the desire to move to single tier authorities and devolve more powers to local level – the so-called concept of 'double devolution'. However, even here there are major traps which the government is anxious to avoid especially after its bruising over NHS reform. It may be, therefore, that a revival of regionalism can be expected as a way of devolving government from the centre. (See Chapter 3 for further discussion on regionalism.)

## Local government

It has been a long-standing complaint that local government's significant contribution to public health – certainly greater overall than the NHS's – has been ignored or marginalized. Despite all the talk of 'joined-up' government local government has always played second fiddle to the NHS, which has retained its lead role on public health matters. Part of the blame lies with local government itself and its failure to seize the initiative over a breakdown in the effective governance of health (Elson 2004). The President of the Society of Local Authority Chief Executives admitted that 'local government is not very good at talking about health and the role it plays in achieving good health for its citizens' (Duggan 2001: 4). The new policy context, especially the development of local strategic partnerships and local area agreements (LAAs), provides 'opportunities for local authorities to reclaim their original role as champions of the health of local communities' (Duggan 2001: 7). In a significant development, the cross-cutting spending review on health inequalities led by the Treasury and completed in July 2002 gave local authorities a lead role in achieving new targets designed to improve health and tackle inequalities (HM Treasury and Department of Health 2002). Moreover, as noted in Table 2.1, over half of the public service agreements drawn up between spending departments and the Treasury in 2004 have a public health focus.

There are also numerous examples of new joint arrangements in place where local authorities have taken the lead in exercising greater influence over public health. There are growing numbers of joint appointments between the NHS and local government and the government is actively encouraging these. In Manchester, a joint health unit has been established within the City Council by the Council and Greater Manchester Health Authority in a move to pass the lead role for public health to the local authority. The new English White Paper 'Strong and prosperous communities' (DCLG 2006) identifies local authorities as the local strategic leaders. Partnership working is to be strengthened by a new duty to consult with others in the preparation of LAAs, and a duty to co-operate with named others including PCTs, NHS Health Trusts and NHS Foundation Hospitals, on agreeing on targets and their achievement.

Finally, local authority overview and scrutiny committees (OSCs) offer a significant opportunity for local government to assess the extent to which the NHS has achieved a balance between both improving the health of local populations and treating ill health. The ultimate goals of health scrutiny are to improve health and reduce inequalities. However, although for the most part, OSCs have been slow to develop their public health function a recent study provides evidence to suggest that the focus of health scrutiny reviews is changing to broader public-health related issues (Coleman and Harrison 2006). Short of resources and support, like training, OSCs have tended to be reactive and to focus on NHS issues like hospital mergers, change of use or bed closures. OSCs seem destined to have a more influential role in future in respect of commissioning health and social care services. Under government proposals they will also develop a relationship with the new local involvement networks (LINks) which will replace the Commission for Patient and Public Involvement in Health and patient forums (Department of Health 2006c). But beyond OSCs, and more broadly, as Elson urges, local government needs 'to create sufficient leverage to make the promotion of the public's health a mainstream part of public policy once more' (Elson 2004).

## Europe

The concern in this chapter has principally been with developments in England. However, there is a European dimension which ought not to be overlooked, even though it has not so far assumed the importance some observers at one time predicted, possibly because the European project as a whole has lost direction and momentum over the past few years. The European Union was principally conceived to develop a single economic market. Social policy, including health, issues have therefore tended to receive little attention and have remained the strict preserve of member states. But recent public concern over food safety and other issues like the environment, obesity, and the state of mental health has raised the importance of public health on the EU agenda. For many years, the UK has been 'in a state of active denial about the influence of Europe' (Mossialos and McKee 2002: 991). This is no longer a tenable position to adopt although agreeing what the EU's role in health policy should be is unclear.

Public health issues have never been accorded much prominence in the EU but the situation has slowly begun to change for the reasons noted above and a new public health programme has been adopted (Commission of the European Communities 2001: 2). It focuses on three strands of action:

- improving information and knowledge for the development of public health;
- responding rapidly to health threats such as those arising from communicable diseases; and
- addressing health determinants and tackling the underlying causes of ill health.

The new public health policy represents a significant departure from the EU's approach to public health hitherto. No longer is public health seen as a series of separate action programmes, largely disease orientated. In its place, a more structured approach linked to clearer policy objectives has been introduced (Merkel and Hubel 1999). The focus is on health determinants, health status and health systems rather than specific diseases or conditions. During its presidency of the EU in the second half of 2005, the UK singled out health inequalities as one of its two health themes and hosted a major conference showcasing developments in Europe.

It remains to be seen how far the EU is really prepared to pursue a vigorous public health policy since to do so may conflict with the overriding aim of the EU which is the creation of a single market. Anything which could interfere with its smooth running has not been accorded priority. Yet, a change of climate about the importance of health in a well run economy does appear to have occurred. Only time will tell whether this is more than a rhetorical flourish.

## The management of change

Before concluding this section, there is a more general issue in regard to the success of public health which concerns the change management model the government has adopted. Its essentially mechanistic, reductionist nature is proving dysfunctional. As was suggested earlier, the transmission of policy into practice is complex although perhaps the government understands this which is why it is restlessly searching for new ways of connecting with the public and influencing health choices and behaviour. There are serious, and often neglected, issues about whether, and how, national policy can be effectively implemented locally and what needs to be in place for this to occur.

In his report on system failure, Chapman (2004) argues that a major impediment to 'joined-up' management and organization (in other words, implementation of 'whole systems' policy making) is the adherence to a linear rational model of policy making that is no longer a guide to the policy maker. He asserts that 'a new intellectual underpinning for policy is required' (Chapman 2004: 23). The complexity and breadth of the public health agenda is not in any doubt. It may therefore be more fruitful to start from this point and to view the various moves to tackle health, as distinct from ill health, as resembling a complex adaptive system. Such a system has been described as 'a collection of individual agents with freedom to act in ways that are not always totally predictable, and whose actions are interconnected so that one agent's actions changes the context for other agents' (Plsek and Greenhalgh 2001: 625). Complexity-based organizational thinking is concerned with the whole system rather than with artificially viewing the system as comprising discrete parts or sectors. There is growing awareness that if sustainable progress is to be made in securing an 'upstream' change agenda, then moving away from current models of implementation is an essential prerequisite. However, the precise nature and shape of whatever might replace these models remains unclear.

## Conclusion

The problem in public health seems to lie in constant policy and organizational churn which prevents sustained focus on implementation and on the cross-agency partnerships needed for such a task. Contributing to the problem is a tendency in all health care systems for resources and effort to be concentrated on health care services even in those cases where those resources have been allocated for public health purposes. However, there is also a case to be made for government adopting a different model of policy and implementation if real progress is to be made. Treating public health as a complex adaptive system would herald such a new approach and it might then be possible to devise new management systems and health improvement tools and techniques with which the public health workforce could then be equipped. There might also be a more prominent leadership role for local government and regional bodies in respect of the wider public health, leaving the NHS to focus on what it is best placed to do to promote public health.

### Suggested further reading

Chapman, J. (2004) *System Failure: Why Governments Must Learn to Think Differently*, 2nd edn. London: DEMOS.

Department of Health (2006) *On the State of the Public Health: Annual Report of the Chief Medical Officer 2005*. London: Department of Health.

Department of Health (2006) *A Stronger Local Voice: A Framework for Creating a Stronger Local Voice in the Development of Health and Social Care Services*. London: Department of Health.

Hunter, D.J. (2003) *Public Health Policy*. Oxford: Polity Press.

Hunter, D.J. (ed.) (2007) *Managing for Health*. London: Routledge.

Marks, L. and Hunter, D.J. (2005) Moving upstream or muddying the waters? Incentives for managing for health, *Public Health*, 119: 974–80.

Sennett, R. (2006) *The Culture of the New Capitalism*. New Haven and London: Yale University Press.

# 3

## CHRIS MILLER
# Public health in the local authority context: more opportunities not to be missed?

**Editors' introduction**

For many years change and reorganization have been permanent features of the working lives of people working in all parts of the public sector, including public health workers. New government policies and directives, and new plans and programmes, have been introduced frequently and rapidly as part of the government's agenda of 'modernization'. What has this meant? And more specifically, what does it mean for people who work in the field of public health?

In this chapter, the author takes a critical look at the government's 'modernization agenda' and explains the part of public health within it. He argues that the government's commitment to reform and to the modernization of health and social care services provides a real opportunity to give visibility to the breadth of public health. He provides a concise history of the roles that different political parties have played in the modernization of health and social welfare, examining the complex relationship between public health and politics.

The author discusses new Labour's journey through its commitment to reform of public institutions, relationships between citizens, the promotion of community relations and the reform of social policy. He examines the precursors to modernization, how it has happened, why it has happened and the dilemmas it has created for public health. The discussion helps readers to understand what is expected of modernized services and how modernization affects professions and agencies upon whom the success of public strategies depend.

The author moves on to consider the impact on public health of three new arenas outside of the health sector: regional government offices, regional assemblies, local strategic partnerships (LSP), arguing that these developments provide new opportunities for public health.

The author then examines the implications of the modernization agenda for public health, focusing on the common threads of partnership working, user involvement, community focus, leadership and quality of service provision. He concludes by considering the very practical implications of current modernization activity for front-line public health professionals. He recognizes the potential for public health to emerge as a powerful lever for change within the modernization agenda.

## Introduction

In the original chapter for the first edition (Miller 2003) I suggested that despite some major concerns over modernization, there were some real opportunities for public health professionals to make closer links with those working from within a local authority context and to develop a broad-based public health strategy. Modernization is concerned with the reform of public institutions, the relationship between them and the citizen, the promotion of particular instruments and social relationships in the delivery of social welfare, and the reform of specific policy areas. Public services needed modernizing 'to create better government to make life better for people . . . brings services to the people, is more accountable and brings more power to local communities' (Cabinet Office 1999).

This chapter argues that although the picture remains uneven and is still in the process of maturing, public health in England, and especially those public health professionals with a specific responsibility for such matters, have yet to take full advantage of a relatively favourable policy environment. They may have in fact, missed the opportunity to do so (Department of Health 2003).

The Local Government Act 2000 (The Stationery Office 2000) opened up new opportunities by creating new governance structures, new forms of local authority political leadership, and opportunities for executive devolution while authorizing local authorities to act in pursuit of local well-being. Similarly, the two Wanless Reports (2002 and 2004) despite the over-riding focus on individual 'responsibilization' give emphasis to the fully engaged citizen in health care and tackling the wider determinants of ill health. Thus within the new consumerist and well-being discourses lurk opportunities for public health professionals to promote a broader strategy for better health care outcomes (Newman and Vidler 2006; Cameron et al. 2006). Opportunities have also been provided, but not always taken, to work in partnership with local authority and non-governmental partners on both local strategic matters and the implementation of national initiatives. Yet as Newman et al. (2004: 205) note, 'The policy reforms for the health service, local government and other sectors are oriented towards fostering active citizenship, overcoming social exclusion and promoting public participation in decision making'. Recent announcements, ahead of the forthcoming White Paper on local government reform, announcing proposals for 'double devolution' are yet another reminder that these could be powerful vehicles to promote a broad-based public health agenda.

However, one could argue that at least within England, there has been a retreat away from a broad social model back to one that gives emphasis to personal responsibility and lifestyle choices and that Primary Care Trusts (PCTs), acting perhaps in response to other competing centrally-driven government targets on individual hospital admissions and discharges, have focused their energies on both commissioning and developing better relationships with hospital-based Trusts and community-based providers rather than the new local authority governance arrangements (McDonald 2006). Further they have often opted for a minimal level of engagement to meet their statutory duty of public consultation and involvement.

The fate of the additional monies allocated to each PCT to carry out the work identified by Wanless and specified in the *Choosing Health* White Paper (Department of Health 2004a) highlights the problem facing the public health profession. These were not ring-fenced for such purposes and consequently have been used as contributions to solve existing problems in those PCTs facing a financial deficit. The example in Box 3.1 provides an example of such an initiative.

Such examples of funding for new major initiatives being swallowed up by existing budget deficiencies and badly thought-out implementation strategies suggest both a lack of national political leadership in relation to public health and a profession lacking in coherence, sense of mission and authority. Where a social model of public health is being pursued it is just as likely to be driven by other non-public health specific professionals, such as those involved in regeneration and community sustainability or work with young people (Department of Health 2002d). This may also reflect greater public knowledge and awareness of public health matters thereby pushing it up the agenda of a range of professionals. A failure to build working partnerships with local authorities will ensure that public health will remain locked within a world dominated by medicine, missing the opportunity to ground public health debates and policy within a local democratic discourse in which institutional as well as personal responsibilities for public health can be developed.

---

**Box 3.1**   Health trainers

There is emergent evidence that in such PCTs the planned public health initiatives have again stalled with projects put on hold for at least a year. In those PCTs where new projects have got underway, including the appointment of health trainers, identified in the White Paper, pressure on local finances and government insistence that break-even budgets be achieved within a year, has meant that these too have been placed in jeopardy.

Similarly, there is evidence that those appointed as health trainers often from black and ethnic minority communities have been well if not over-qualified for the role and yet recruited on relatively low salaries. The appointment of these workers, for whom the posts represented an opportunity often denied to get a foot on a career ladder and now faced an uncertain employment future, also reflects a much criticized practice in relation to the recruitment of black and ethnic minority staff within the NHS. It stands accused of repeatedly appointing over-qualified black and ethnic minority staff on low salaries to short-term and insecure posts for what is considered work that is marginal to the organization's primary task. An uncertain employment future also reflects a much criticized practice in relation to the recruitment of black and ethnic minority staff within the NHS.

## The policy context

'New' Labour was first elected to government in 1997 with 43.2 per cent of the vote share and an overwhelming majority of 179 seats and then re-elected in 2001 and won again in 2005, a historic third term for a Labour government, albeit with 35.3 per cent of the vote share and a much reduced but still healthy majority of 66. Now in its tenth year of office the 'new' Labour government has been through a number of iterations of the policy-making cycle involving the identification of new social issues, reviewing progress in relation to previous social interventions, the introduction of specific policy responses, some of which have been mainstreamed immediately while others have been constructed as time-limited experimental projects, to evaluating, revising and sometimes abandoning some of its own initiatives in the light of experience.

During those ten years, government departments have been reorganized and senior and junior ministers have departed or been re-shuffled and new ones appointed, sometimes heralding a new policy initiative or approach or bringing their 'personal stamp' to the task. Over the period some, such as John Reid, have been called upon to take responsibility for a number of major and apparently diverse portfolios, such as health, defence and the Home Office, among others. During sometime prolonged periods the government's radical welfare reform agenda has been overshadowed or blown off course by other events, especially in foreign policy, back-bench revolts, the occasional but destructive ministerial misdemeanour, the tension between the prime minister and the Chancellor of the Exchequer and more recently following Tony Blair's announcement that he is to stand down as party leader before the next election, the leadership transition process. All of this is the normal stuff of government but is a reminder of the gap that can come to exist between strategic policy goals, planning and implementation.

During its lifetime 'new' Labour, as part of its 'modernization' agenda had developed a raft of strategic and specific policies both in relation to discrete areas, such as public health, education or housing. A number of core themes or issues, such as social inclusion, life-long learning or workforce up-skilling and the 'respect' agenda, have been designed to underpin all policy initiatives. In its drive to 'modernize', it has paid particular attention to the values, organization and delivery of public policy with attention focused on user choice, greater professional accountability and the creation of a more entrepreneurial organizational approach, as set out for example in the White Paper, *Creating a patient-led NHS* (Department of Health 2005b). Its commitment has been to revitalize public policy following 18 years of neo-liberal government and create a health and welfare system in tune with contemporary times. What it identified were the many serious failings of public policy, but in rejecting the traditional social democratic or 'old' Labour strategies, which were perceived by the party leadership as inappropriate to current circumstances, 'new' Labour embarked upon a period of intensive 'third-way' policy-making activity.

This extensive reform programme has led in some quarters to accusations of 'policy initiative-itis', or fatigue, and professional and organizational exhaustion after a lengthy period of continuous change. Despite strong indications that it will allow greater devolved autonomy for the best achieving providers, the government continues to be accused of over-centralization, micro-management, over-regulation and a fundamental lack of trust in welfare professionals (Hood *et al.* 2000; Miller *et al.* 2007). This point was recently acknowledged by Ruth Kelly, the new Minister for Communities and Local Government in a speech to the Local Government Association in which she talked about the government as having 'got into the habit of responding to too many new challenges with what some would call a centralizing measure'. However, after 10 years of very proactive government 'new' Labour is beginning to look somewhat weary and careworn, increasingly fragmented, incoherent and in danger of having lost sight of its overall agenda amidst the detail of policy implementation and shifts of emphasis consequent upon unforeseen events. If the government appears weary and lacking in inspiration it is also not surprising to find front-line professionals also feeling weary but in this case from too much change. It is possible that the government will be revived and will rediscover its ambitious reform programme either through new policy initiatives, such as the new local government White Paper (DCLG 2006) or, more fundamentally, a change in leadership or it may continue to lose its sense of direction and fail in its attempt to secure a fourth general election victory thereby failing to achieve its goal of the party of the centre and automatic choice of government.

## Cross-cutting themes for public health

Since its 1997 election victory the Labour government has displayed a determination to pursue a number of cross-cutting themes. A number of these have been central to public health policy including: a commitment to 'joined-up' thinking and practice, the introduction of greater accountability and improved governance, service user and community involvement, sustainable policy, and the transformation from a dependency to a more 'positive' or enterprising welfare approach. The latter was first articulated in the Green Paper, *From Welfare to Work* (Department of Social Security 1998) as well as in a desired shift from an emphasis on 'rights' to 'responsibilities', and more recently as 'active citizens' able to make choices and as the second Wanless Report (2004) clearly states, take more responsibility for their own well-being, or self-care, and that of the community (Department of Health 2005b; Newman *et al.* 2004; Cameron *et al.* 2006).

An exploration of the persistence and imperviousness of a number of challenging so-called 'wicked' social issues despite various government interventions over some 50 years led among other things to the recognition that no single body or profession could solve such complex and intractable problems. This reflects an acknowledgement of the inter-connectedness of social issues and public solutions, and the need to tackle these through systematic initiatives involving all relevant organizations and professionals. This broadly collaborative and co-ordinated approach contrasted with the existing deeply rooted professional and organizational 'silo' mentalities, in which strictly demarcated areas of responsibility had been fiercely guarded and little communication or joint-action had taken place between professions or organizations. This was characteristic of UK policy and practice since the creation of the post-war welfare state. This was a bold but risky strategy not because it was ill-conceived but because the government was vulnerable to accusations of policy failure each time the many absences of professional and organizational collaboration were revealed. Further the effective pursuit of policy to tackle 'wicked issues' required not only a shift in practice and orientation at a local level but also the wholesale re-organization of central government departments and ministries, something that 'new' Labour has so far avoided. Instead it has introduced 'think tanks' or special co-ordinating cross-departmental units to influence departmental behaviour and given individual ministers, including the deputy prime minister, the task of ensuring cross-departmental working. Such measures have proved inadequate and departments have continued to compete for the more immediate and tangible benefits of additional resources, status and power.

In adopting a more holistic approach to social issues 'new' Labour has had to wrestle with three persistent and inter-linked problems.

- The first is to identify solutions that do indeed seek to address all core aspects of any major social concern, such as social inclusion or public health.

- The second is how to ensure that those responsible for policy implementation, professionals, managers, elected members or appointed board members, feel able to think 'outside the box', embrace the spirit of the collaborative impulse and comply with policy expectations.

- The third is how, in the face of both passive and active resistance to policy change, to find the balance between setting targets for implementation and demanding accountability for actions taken while allowing for some local discretion in policy direction based upon local requirements. In addition, it has to ensure that the requirements of potentially competing policies do not overwhelm or submerge such new ways of working.

On first gaining office, 'new' Labour was impatient for change but anticipated resistance from both politically hostile local authorities and reluctant professionals, and was already working with a view to further electoral success. Consequently, its response to such challenges, common to some degree in all policy implementation processes, was to drive change through by presenting sometimes exceptionally well-researched accounts (Scottish Executive 1998; Scottish Executive Health Department 2001) as to the weaknesses of previous efforts and the scale of the current problem, identifying and being enthusiastic about the planned future direction linked to a wider vision, and fixing specific achievement targets that where possible were conditional upon future central government funding. In other words, it used a combination of rational argument, persuasion, blue sky visioning and appeals to popular concerns, backed up by managerial direction, detailed regulation, auditing and financial control.

The common complaint is that it too quickly abandoned persuasion, was itself confrontational rather than collaborative in relation to local authority and health care professionals and elected or non-elected members. It over-emphasized enforcement through mechanisms of accountability and regulation, and failed to sufficiently listen to the concerns expressed by front-line professionals choosing instead to interpret these as the expressions of self-interested professionals seeking to defend past practice, status and reward. As a consequence it would seem to have made even those professionals and managers who are most sympathetic to its overall strategy risk averse and calculative in which policy imperatives they choose to pursue.

There is also some evidence as areas of discretionary activity decline of a growing emotional distancing from professional practice, thereby seriously undermining the likelihood of success (Miller *et al.* 2007). In such a context, the more difficult and challenging policy changes in relation to measuring outcomes, such as partnership working and broad-based public health strategies are likely to be neglected. Such a shift can be detected in the growing emphasis on both the individual lifestyle, through the development of the 'health trainer' role, medical model of public health and the lack of attention given to the more challenging wider socio-economic determinants of health.

## Public health in alliance with a restructured local government?

The Labour government has been concerned, only partly out of self-interest, with what has become known as the 'democratic deficit'. This is characterized by falling membership levels in political parties, a low turn-out in elections, especially local ones, the poor credibility of politicians, the perceived distance between those responsible for decision making and those affected by the decisions taken, and disenchantment with the political process. Labour's response has been threefold. First, it has introduced specific reforms and practices to particular institutions. Second, it has attempted to recast the focus of attention at a local level towards issues of governance. This has included, for example, the creation of over-arching local stakeholder bodies, such as Local Strategic Partnerships (LSPs), concerned with strategic issues in relation to the area's well-being and development. New duties have been imposed upon local authorities, which take them beyond their traditional concerns for the delivery of specific services, to develop strategies to further the area's economic, social and environmental well-being. Similarly, the Public Health Green Paper (Secretary of State for Health 1998) described the role of the NHS as part of a network of public bodies concerned with enhancing individual and collective well-being. Third, it has emphasized the need to create a socially inclusive society by investing in the processes of engaging service users and citizens. Labour has given considerable weight to the concept of the active citizen who is fully engaged in the labour market, in their communities, and in the democratic processes.

The reform of political institutions has included with various degrees of success reforming the House of Lords, devolution in Scotland, Wales and Northern Ireland, the creation of a Greater London Authority, and regional devolution within England. Devolution in England has been confined to strengthening the role of the regional Government Offices (GOs). These are responsible for the sponsorship and monitoring of Regional Development Agencies (RDAs), 'the economic powerhouse for the region', acting as champion for the Department of Trade and Industry's strategy on innovation and small businesses, and significantly for regional governance. The White Paper (Department of Transport, Local Government and the Regions 2002) brought together under the GO all existing government regional offices, including the Department of Health's regional public health team, and provided it with an enhanced role in such areas as crime reduction and the community cohesion agenda.

The White Paper set out the possibility of an elected regional assembly (ERA), to be preceded by a referendum to establish the level of local support. Such plans have now been shelved following their rejection in a referendum in the North-east, the region predicted as most likely to favour an expansion of regionalism. The lack of progress in this area has implications for public health as ERAs had the potential to become a key body in relation to GOs and public spending reviews. With responsibilities devolved from central government it was anticipated that ERAs would work to an overall vision for the region, setting priorities for and delivering regional strategies. With one-third of the seats allocated as 'top-up' seats to non-governmental organizations and the business community there were opportunities for regionally based public health bodies to have a stronger voice. The collapse of elected regional assemblies has led, however, to new initiatives, to devolve responsibilities to local level. (For further discussion of these issues see Chapter 2.)

The attempt to subject the health sector to greater direct democratic account-ability, as evidenced in a limited way by the inclusion of public health within the ill-fated regional structures, has been expanded considerably within Labour's local government reforms. A number of measures have been introduced including locally elected mayors, a new internal system of cabinet and scrutiny committees designed to give back-bench elected councillors greater authority and an enhanced role while making for a more effective and accountable decision-making process. Critically, as part of their remit in health improvement and reducing health inequalities, the Overview and Scrutiny Committees (OSCs) have since 2003 been given powers to examine local NHS provision, including public health. Such powers should be strengthened further by the proposed introduction of Local Involvement Networks (see below) to be established by local authorities and with specific links to OSCs.

Of even greater significance for public health is the duty imposed on local author-ities under the Local Government Act 2000, to take a lead role in the drawing up of a 'sustainable community strategy' revised in a speech by the prime minister in 2005. This is to be devised in relation to social, economic and environmental well-being and thus closely linked to an inclusive public health agenda. The strategy sets out the vision and priorities for the area and must be produced with the involvement of all key actors. It will further develop and ensure the effective delivery of the Local Area Agreements (LAAs) (see below). The Act also provided local authorities with the power, and is therefore permissive and not mandatory, 'to do anything which they consider is likely to achieve' the objective of local well-being. Although local author-ities have a lead role, the community strategy is to be generated within the framework of a broad 'Community Partnership' providing an over-arching framework within which other local initiatives can operate (Department of the Environment, Transport and the Regions 2000a). This is linked to both the sustainable development strategy, based on work undertaken through Agenda 21, and the local authority's 'duty of Best Value'. Local neighbourhood strategies are also expected to form part of the broader community strategy. The Act states clearly that central to its purpose is the aim of allowing 'local communities to articulate their needs and priorities' (p. 38). Further, 'community strategies must give local people a powerful voice in planning local approaches to economic, social and environmental well-being and in holding core public services and politicians to account' (p. 16). The Local Government Act 2000 gave local authorities the power to promote social, economic and environmental well-being in their areas which are described in Box 3.2.

---

**Box 3.2**   Local authority powers of well-being

The **Local Government Act 2000** gave local authorities the power to promote social, economic and environmental well-being in their areas.

The framework below (New Economics Foundation 2006) for understanding well-being proposes that local authorities need to consider how economic, social and environmental well-being links with, and is influenced by, people's personal well-being. Indeed it proposes that these areas are important precisely because of their effect on people's personal well-being. By placing people's well-being at the core of policy formation, councils can be more innovative and potentially more efficient and effective too.

The New Economics Foundation worked with Nottingham City Council to measure the well-being of young people in the city (Marks 2005). The use of the well-being indicators provided valuable new information to policy makers in a range of areas including education, crime and sport.

Overall, the pilot study shows that measuring well-being is a powerful way in which local government can use its 'well-being powers' to join up different local services and gain important insights into the ultimate impacts of policy. The New Economics Foundation recommends that government puts together a larger pilot which uses well-being measurement over five regions for several years and further explores the implications of well-being for a range of policy agendas including education and preventive health measures (New Economics Foundation 2006).

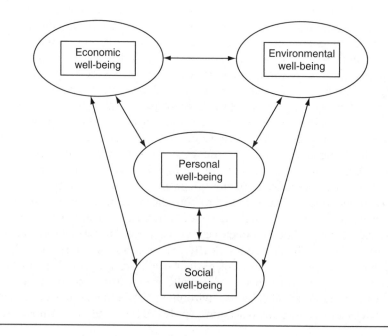

## Local Strategic Partnerships

A Local Strategic Partnership (LSP) is a non-statutory and non-executive body, as outlined in the Act, and responsible for strategic co-ordination and linking with other plans and bodies at regional, sub-regional and local level. LSPs are to be established in every local authority and accredited by regional GOs but initially were a requirement only in the 88 priority, or designated, areas eligible for support under the Neighbourhood Renewal Fund. However, it was clear from the outset that all English authorities would move in this direction since there was little difference between the expectations as laid down for partnership development between the designated priority areas and the rest. The local authority has the critical lead role in initiating and maintaining momentum for the LSP, ensuring appropriate representation within it and scrutinizing its work. Partnership strategies focused on specific policy areas, such as public health or children's services, are thus subjected to scrutiny by the LSP. (For further discussion of Local Strategic Partnerships see Chapter 10.)

LSPs are identified as the key mechanism to bring together under one umbrella, local authorities, residents, private, voluntary and community sector organizations. They are expected to act as the partnership overseeing all other partnerships, a 'partnership of partnerships', exercising a powerful influence over their constituent elements and beyond. The former office of the deputy prime minister recently recommended the creation within each LSP of a 'core body' able to take decisions on behalf of the larger partnership and underpinned by the various local thematic partnerships that sit within it. The core body is expected to include key actors including the local health partnership. This core body, along with the local authority Overview and Scrutiny Committee is to be responsible for the implementation of the cross-cutting themes within Local Area Agreements (LAAs) – explained later in this chapter. The extent to which an LSP will be able to require detailed changes to service-specific strategies still remains unclear, as the expertise will ultimately lie within the more specialized partnerships. Nevertheless, service-specific strategies are increasingly devised with reference to the broader strategy identified by the LSP. As LSPs grow in confidence and build up a knowledge base they will also be able to identify potential connections and gaps between the more service-specific strategies.

The primary task of the LSP is to produce a Sustainable Community Strategy for the area along with local neighbourhood renewal strategies that aim to bring improvements to health as well as securing greater employment, reducing crime, improving housing, better education, and reducing the gap between disadvantaged neighbourhoods and the rest. LSPs are expected to contain all local partnerships and other initiatives so as to facilitate greater effectiveness among service providers. The emphasis is on being strategic, inclusive, action-focused, efficient, establishing clear links between the aims and objectives of the LSP with performance management systems of its individual organizational members, and building on best practice (Department of the Environment, Transport and the Regions 2001b). LSPs are seen as essential 'for developing new ways of involving local people in how public services work' (Neighbourhood Renewal Unit 2001: 5) and 'providing the strategic co-ordination within the area and linking with other plans and bodies established at regional, sub-regional and local level' (Department for Communities and Local

Government 2006). The link between the LSP and the GOs is potentially important as the latter feeds directly into central government.

The White Paper, *Shifting the Balance of Power* (Department of Health 2001a) made much of the importance of regional accountability for public health to the Department of Health. For example, regional directors of public health have been appointed in each region and working with a small team have been co-located within the GOs. The importance of an integrated multi-sectoral approach in addressing the 'wider determinants of health' at this level has also been given emphasis in the role of the regional director in bringing a health perspective to other policy areas and raising the public health profile within LSPs.

Three community participation funds, accessible only to the 88 designated areas in receipt of regeneration funds, the Community Empowerment Fund, Community Learning Chests and the Community Chests, were introduced in 2001 to support local organizations' engagement in public participation. These were subsequently merged in 2005 into the Single Community Programme, which is managed by the Neighbourhood Renewal Unit via the government offices to the local Community Empowerment Network created in each of the areas. These have been followed, after the 2002 Treasury Cross-Cutting review of the Voluntary and Community Sectors in Service Delivery, by the introduction of the 'Change Up' and 'Futurebuilders' initiatives (see Box 3.3).

Such initiatives at the regional and local levels but beyond the health sector reflect efforts to establish a broad strategic overview, in which public health is given specific mention, through collaborative working. Such links widen the scope and range of those with a responsibility for or interest in public health. They provide opportunities for those organizations with a public health remit to raise the public health profile, direct attention to the public health implications of the work of other organizations, and ensure that public health secures a higher level of priority in neighbourhood, community and regional strategies. Indeed some would argue that such links should be extended further to the point where the responsibility for public health is the responsibility of local government. In its recent document, '*A Stronger Local Voice*' (Department of Health 2006c), following the decision in 2004 to abolish the Commission for Patient and Public Involvement, which has survived a mere 12 months, and a subsequent review during 2005/06 of patient and public involvement, the

---

**Box 3.3**   Change Up and Futurebuilders initiatives

- 'Change Up' was a £80m fund for the period 2003–06 to support sub-regional and local initiatives to ensure that by 2014 the needs of front-line VCS organizations would be met by a nationwide support structure.

- Futurebuilders is a £125m fund to invest in exemplar schemes that demonstrate the distinctive approach and added value that the sector can contribute to public service delivery and are managed by the Active Communities Unit, which following the May 2006 Government reshuffle is based in the Third Sector Unit of the Cabinet Office and reporting to Ed Miliband, Minister for the Third Sector.

government has announced plans to establish Local Involvement Networks (LINks) in every local authority with responsibility for social service provision to 'promote public and community influence in health and social care'. Critically, LINks will be established by local authorities, including the identification of the membership, and will receive additional funding for this purpose. LINks, which replace Patient Forums, will be expected to establish a specific and strong relationship with Local Authority Overview and Scrutiny Committees, including the power to refer matters to them. They will also have formal links to the Strategic Health Authority (SHA).

Further at the very local level public health professionals should not encounter much resistance as health matters have long been a concern to community and voluntary organizations, and especially within women's organizations (Health Education Unit and Open University 1991). The emphasis given to joined-up policies and seamless services can also work in favour of those with a public health interest now that it has been specifically identified as a critical aspect of social, economic and environmental development. However, the extent to which health sector professionals or organizations will be represented within LSPs is not proscribed. In such fluid circumstances it is important that professionals and civic organizations act both assertively and in collaboration to ensure a strong presence. Another concern is the extent to which the learning that takes place within such deliberative fora and the strategic priorities that emerge penetrate those agencies concerned with health provision so as to impact upon front-line provision. The earlier example of the appointment of health trainers suggests there is some way to go. There will continue be some resistance from within the medical profession to what might be seen as inappropriate 'interference' in health issues by external bodies lacking in professional expertise.

## Local Area Agreements

Local Strategic Partnerships are to be responsible for the development and delivery of Local Area Agreements (LAAs) which is itself based upon the local Sustainable Community Strategy. These are seen as central to further devolved decision making, in what is described as a 'more mature' relationship between central and local government, in part by providing a vehicle for the rationalization of funding streams. The expectation, however, is that LAAs will be a critical mechanism by which, 'crucial shared business gets done between partners in a locality and between that locality and Government' (Office of the Deputy Prime Minister 2006a). LAAs are three-year agreements with six-monthly performance reviews, matched against templates developed by government, and agreed between central government, represented by the government office, and a local area represented by a local authority and its key partners through the LSPs. Capacity-building support for the LSP is available, in addition to that provided to those in receipt of Neighbourhood Renewal Funding, through a variety of initiatives including, web-based toolkits, advisers and through the Improvement and Development Agency for local government (IDeA) and Department of Health support for health partnerships. The creation of LAAs began in 2005 with 21 pilot authorities and two further rounds have followed with all top tier local authorities required to have one in place by 2007. LAAs are seen as mechanisms to deliver co-ordinated programmes to ensure sustainable communities, improve central and local government relations, enhance efficiency by strengthening partnership working and provide a framework in which the local authority can further exercise its community leadership role. According to the government they will be a key mechanism by which 'crucial shared business gets done between partners in a locality and between that locality and government' (Office of the Deputy Prime Minister 2006a).

The agreements are structured around four areas or blocks of policy: children and young people, safer and stronger communities, healthier communities and older people, and economic development and enterprise. The field of healthier communities and older people is essentially a broad cross-cutting public health agenda but key elements of public health, such as improvements to the quality of public spaces, liveability and improved quality in deprived areas, economic well-being and the health and well-being of children and young people, are also to be found prominently in the other three blocks. A central government designed template sets out in some detail what items must be included, signposting both a number of outcomes and indicators of how they might be measured, within the LAA document which is to be 'signed off' by ministers. For those local areas with a record of good performance across a range of policy areas there is the opportunity to be designated 'Single Pot' status. Such areas will have the freedom to spend any pooled funding on any of the agreed outcomes rather than grouping funding and outcomes under each of the four blocks. All areas will have the ability to pool funds within each block. In addition they will have the freedom to combine some mainstream funding between organizations to meet shared LAA outcomes. Further, the government promises streamlined payment mechanisms and the possibility of investing any efficiency savings in delivering LAA outcomes.

LAAs will also further strengthen the role of regional government, as it is the government office in the regions that represents central government in making the agreement and has the responsibility to ensure that regional priorities and strategies are reflected in LAAs (see Box 3.4). Each LAA is required to demonstrate how a number of critical factors are to be addressed, such as how local people and the voluntary and community sectors are to be involved in the design and delivery of the LAA, the roles and responsibilities of, and within, the partnership, including specifying the lead body for each agreed outcome, and the ways in which funding streams are to be pooled.

Each upper tier of local authority will be the accountable body for the financial management of the LAA and will be responsible for the performance management arrangements and the identification of the designated lead body for each agreed outcome. The latter represents a major challenge in how to ensure that individual partners within the Local Strategic Partnership are responsible and accountable to government for the delivery of agreed outcomes. This provides the local authority with a critical leadership role in relation to public health bodies, including PCTs. The government expects the local NHS to be actively involved in the agreement and delivery of LAAs with PCTs as key partners in the identification, design and delivery of provision and in contributing, with the agreement of the Strategic Health Authority (SHA), mainstream funding to the LAA. SHAs will be responsible for ensuring that Local Delivery Plans for health care are aligned with the LAA and are expected to share responsibility with the GO for the six-monthly performance review. Such

---

**Box 3.4**   What's in an agreement? Making local area agreements work for the third sector

---

LAAs are central to the government's modernization and devolution agendas and mark a change in relations between local and central government. LAAs will simplify funding streams flowing from central government, focus local strategic partnerships on agreeing a core set of outcomes for an area, and allow local areas more freedom to spend on locally agreed priorities. LAAs signify a shift away from the 'Whitehall knows best' model of governance; they will allow for a greater flexibility for local solutions.

*Source*: BVSC The Centre for Voluntary Action (2006) www.bvsc.org/files/images/layout/laa.gif

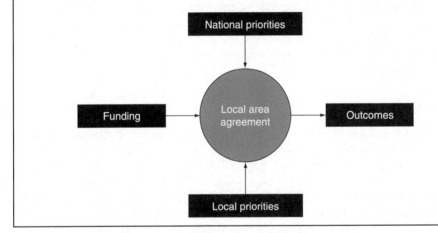

measures should provide the means for improved co-ordination and 'joined-up' working, making LAAs a key mechanism for joint planning and delivery. This is further strengthened by the introduction of an outcome-based performance framework jointly shared by PCTs and local authorities.

## Public Service Agreements

Another example of new mechanisms designed to secure clear outcome-related agreements between both government departments and between government and local authorities is the introduction of Public Service Agreements as a mechanism for identifying key outcomes. These were first introduced in 2000 as Local Public Service Agreements (LPSA) on a pilot basis in 20 authorities and representing voluntary agreements negotiated between government and the local authority that now cover virtually all upper tier authorities. A second generation of LPSAs are promised. At national level, PSAs are negotiated between the Treasury and all major spending departments. As an illustration, the 2004 PSA with the Department of Health gave emphasis to improving the health of the poor by reducing mortality rates, health inequalities and the underlying determinants of health inequalities. It was in this context that it is already taking action to tackle the causes of ill health and reduce health inequalities that the government launched the White Paper, *Choosing Health: Making Healthy Choices* (Department of Health 2004a), with its focus on individual responsibilities and good health. The White Paper argues that it is based on research indicating that the overwhelming majority (88 per cent) of those taking part in a survey agreed that health was an individual responsibility and that the role of the state was both minimal and should be oriented towards enabling individual citizens make health-related choices. This lead to the Commission on Sustainable Government to produce a 'Corporate Citizenship Assessment Model', in addition to a series of web-based resources including practical guides on how to create and maintain sustainable partnerships, examples of 'good practice' and links to other sites. Sir Nigel Crisp, NHS Chief Executive described the Model as one of his 'five new priorities for the next 10 years'. The Commission is an independent government body, whose Chief Executive is Jonathon Porrit, and was founded in 2000 but whose role was further expanded in 2006 to include a 'watchdog' function, monitoring cross-government department progress towards sustainable development.

## 'Double' devolution

A new White Paper on local government reform was published in October 2006 (DCLG 2006), the product of a two-year consultation process and a change in Ministerial Office. It had been anticipated that at the heart of the reforms would be a strategy for greater devolution, or 'double' devolution as it was being termed, meaning both devolution from central to local government and subsequent devolution from local authorities to neighbourhoods, other organizations and individual citizens (ODPM 2006b). In previewing the White Paper, *Deal for Devolution*, the then Minister for local government, David Miliband, argued that it would be based on the subsidiarity principle, that is, that the starting point should be to devolve as far as possible and that proposals would be clearly visible in the LAAs with an enhanced means by which citizens can challenge performance. Miliband highlighted the role of the Ward Councillor who could again speak and act on behalf of their communities, hold authorities to account, be accessible to and advocates for local residents, and foster improved relationships between service providers and local communities. Such an enhanced role could, he argued, be possible only if citizens were more engaged, and highlighted the Expert Patients Programme as an example of existing good practice. Miliband referred to this as the 'process of empowerment' in a speech to New Local Government Network Conference in January 2006 in which citizens are 'at the heart of our conception of vibrant local government', a shift that would impact on top-down accountability as bottom-up accountability was strengthened.

Ruth Kelly, Miliband's successor, began in a similar vein when she spoke of a 'bonfire' of top-down targets and regulatory mechanisms and having reached a 'tipping point' in our democracy. However, the published White Paper, which somewhat oddly appeared ahead of the Lyon's review of local government funding due to be published at the end of 2006, is more tempered in approach without losing all of the devolutionary thrust. The White Paper does make provision for central regulation to be reduced, strengthened partnership arrangements via LSPs and LAAs, an enhanced role for local councillors, a strong emphasis on building local leadership, an extended role for voluntary sector organizations, new mechanisms for citizens to make their concerns known, a new duty for local authorities and others to consult and opportunities for citizens to take over the management and ownership of local assets. Overall, however, the emphasis is on a strengthened and co-ordinated political leadership, including the local elected councillor, described as 'democratic champions' and the 'bedrock of local democracy', that is firmly located in the local authority. The White Paper continues the trend of devolving service provision through extended commissioning of services to the voluntary and community sectors but, despite some strengthening of citizen participation and voice, seeks to ensure that local political leadership remains in local authorities.

Specifically, in relation to public health, the White Paper continues to knit more closely together local health care provision with local authority structures and to bring greater local political control and co-ordination into the health services. Thus, legislation will create a new thematic partnership for 'health and well-being' to sit alongside the existing Crime and Disorder Reduction Partnership and children's trusts to underpin the LSP. This will be backed by a new duty to 'co-operate' for PCTs and local authorities to 'enable local partners to achieve a truly integrated approach to delivering local government and NHS priorities' (Annex B, p.17). A new duty will be introduced for local authorities to establish Local Involvement Networks (LINks) as a mechanism through which citizens can influence both service delivery and local priorities of health and social care bodies and can refer concerns to the local authority overview and scrutiny committee. The White Paper anticipates a much strengthened citizen voice when LINks are combined with the proposed 'Community Call for Action' mechanism by which local people can request the locally elected councillor to trigger a response from the local authority on any matter of concern. Similarly powers are to be offered to overview and scrutiny committees enabling them to require local service providers to provide an account in relation of failing services which strengthens their existing power to require PCTs to provide similar information. The Committee will also be able to scrutinize the response of the local authority and local PCTs to reports of Directors of Public Health on health improvement.

In line with the White Paper's central thrust that the local authority is to be the local strategic leader and 'place-shaper', partnership working is to be strengthened by a new duty to consult with others in the preparation of Local Area Agreements, and a duty to co-operate with named others, including PCTs, NHS Health Trusts and NHS Foundation Hospitals, on agreeing on targets and their achievement. Directors of Public Health will be both jointly appointed and accountable to both local authority and PCT chief executives and the practice of joint appointments is to be encouraged in relation to other senior management positions. This raft of new duties suggests a continuation of leading from the centre yet in key respects, such as strengthening local leadership, the White Paper is reluctant to dictate preferring to offer a range of options even though some options, such as a directly elected mayor, may be more likely to generate creative and innovative ways of moving forward.

## Conclusion

This chapter has illustrated a variety of existing and emergent opportunities for public health professionals to work collaboratively within a local democratic framework both with other local authority professionals as well as the community and voluntary sector to develop broad-based strategies and interventions to tackle the wider socio-economic determinants of ill heath and health inequalities. As the government moves ahead with its strategy for 'strong and prosperous communities' contained within the 2006 White Paper, the ability and commitment of PCTs to work with local authorities will become even more important. Yet there is only limited evidence that public health has so far made sufficient use of such opportunities. The 1990s emphasis on the health inequalities agenda, that galvanized a wide range of professionals from epidemiologists to community development practitioners and voluntary and community organizations, seems to have lost some of its bite. Although a range of health interests continues to try to persuade PCTs that greater collaboration is a worthwhile endeavour, on a practical level such as the question of organizational coterminosity, movement has been slow. Indeed in some notable cases such as Birmingham, PCTs appear to have rejected coterminosity despite extensive local authority devolution and a major reorganization of the PCTs across the city.

A number of explanations can be offered as to why the public health profession has been slow to react. Perhaps the fundamental reason lies in the government's apparent retreat from its own broad-based public health agenda. In its place has been a growing almost exclusive emphasis on the not unimportant lifestyle issues, such as smoking, alcohol abuse, teenage pregnancy and obesity. In addition, the government appears to have retreated from an explicitly interventionist position and suggested that by popular demand it will assume that individuals are sufficiently capable and responsible enough to make their own health-related decisions, with at most some friendly guidance and advise when this is sought. However, it cannot ignore the risk associated with the social and economic costs should individuals make the wrong decisions. Similarly, a withdrawal from a somewhat hectoring posture does not mean a refusal to work towards an environment better designed to contribute positively to public health. While government messages in the field of public health remain at best ambiguous and lacking identifiable political leadership then it is unlikely that public health professionals will feel sufficiently authorized to seize any local opportunities.

A second explanation that is closer to the front line is that PCTs appear to be more concerned about reducing financial deficits and by targets for hospital admissions and discharges and to that extent see hospital trusts as their primary partners, rather than the local authority, and have chosen to invest resources in commissioning services. This is again not an unreasonable response given the pressures on NHS funding but it is also an easy option and allows health care professionals to remain safely within the familiar field dominated by medicine. Further, a minimalist approach to local authority partnerships helps to prevent local authority Overview and Scrutiny Committees of back-bench councillors having too much influence on what are still defined as health matters which have previously not been part of a locally elected councillor's brief. Moreover, the sometimes complex, confused and sometime difficult nature of local authority partnership boards have not made them an attractive option, although the creation of an inner 'core body' may change this. Ironically, it may also make LSPs less democratic and more managerial and therefore less attractive to other partners especially those from the voluntary and community sectors. Further, local authorities have not played a major role in identifying public health concerns and mobilizing around such matters. Conversely, as PCTs focus more on matters of patient assessment it is less likely that a political leadership in relation to public health can develop or be sustained. However, a combination of the proposed development of LINks, the further strengthening of OSCs, and the prominence given to LAAs and stronger links to SHA and regional government offices make this minimalist approach increasingly unsustainable.

Similarly, there is some evidence that from a public health perspective the contribution of other non-governmental actors from the voluntary and community sector, who are increasingly involved in local governance arrangements, is perceived as marginal to public health outcomes and, therefore, not worth the necessary investment in developing a working relationship. There are a number of issues here. The first is that many local voluntary and community sector organizations are both small in size, often targeted at what appear to be narrowly defined communities of interest, reluctant to become engaged with those who lie outside their boundaries and are often in competition with other voluntary and community organizations. To that extent they are not ideal vehicles for those seeking a universal approach to public health. The second is that the majority of voluntary and community sector organizations are more concerned with the well-being agenda and do not focus necessarily on those government targeted priority groups, currently very narrowly defined, for public health interventions. Rather those concerned with specific health conditions such as obesity, cancer, smoking cessation or sickle-cell anaemia tend to be supported by self-help groups. Such groups, however, tend to be less involved in local governance arrangements and would require a different strategy to access them.

The third challenge is that community-based organizations are often seen as 'unrepresentative' even of those they claim to be and often of the wider community. Consequently, for PCTs who are unused to engaging with the voluntary and community sector, other than those large professional NGOs providing health care, the territory appears uncertain and hazardous and they are naturally wary of being drawn into local politics. It is not that PCTs are unaware of the need to engage with ethnic minority communities but ironically in the context of their concerns about the representativeness of local organizations tend to believe that this can be done, as in the case of health trainers, by the appointment of individuals who are subsequently used as though they were 'representative'. The fourth area of difficulty is the lack of systematic evidence, as recognized by health care professionals and medics in particular, that the interventions of voluntary and community-based organizations has any discernible impact on public health outcomes. In an 'evidence' driven health environment the 'soft' contribution of voluntary and community organizations can appear very marginal. What such arguments ignore is that such organizations, however small and narrowly focused, can provide health care professionals access to social groups who would otherwise be difficult to reach, especially for example in relation to ethnically diverse communities or young people, and who would usually be prepared to take public health messages to those communities with whom they have contact. Further they can often do so in innovative and creative ways that would be beyond the scope of health care professionals. Community sector organizations also can provide invaluable insights into local public health concerns supported by a wealth of 'street knowledge' and experience about what works locally that would otherwise take a considerable time to accumulate when done by outsiders and only if first they could gain the trust of the local communities to provide it. In fact, health care professionals are often insufficiently aware of the importance of such data and only come to recognize it after they have engaged with the sector over a period of time. Thus without such engagement it is unlikely that they themselves would initiate research to uncover local knowledge and practices. Again the introduction of LINks with the requirement to work with the voluntary and community sectors will require public health professionals and PCTs to engage more energetically and seriously than hitherto.

Finally, the government has struggled at a national level to deliver its ambitious commitment to collaborative and joined-up working. It has shown a reluctance to engage in any major overhaul of government departments but choosing instead to create cross-departmental mechanisms to drive through the agenda. However, these have not challenged the fundamental power of individual departments that continue to protect and whenever possible expand the sphere of influence. To expect, therefore, that this can be achieved at a local level without being mirrored centrally is perhaps over-ambitious especially when this involves, as it does in relation to public health, bringing together two quite different cultures: one that is dominated by professional expertise, and the other that still retains a system of democratic accountability. When combined with the absence of strong internal pressure within the health sector from public health professionals it is unlikely that the potential within the new governance arrangements will be fully realized.

---

**Suggested further reading**

Department of Health (2006) *A Stronger Local Voice: A Framework for Creating a Stronger Local Voice in the Development of Health and Social Care Services*. London: Department of Health.

Department for Communities and Local Government (2006) *Strong and prosperous communities: The Local Government White Paper*. London: DCLG. CM6939–1. Volumes 1 and 2.

Cameron, E., Mathers, J. and Parry, J. (2006) Being well and well being: The value of community and professional concepts in understanding positive health, in L. Baud, K. Clarke and T. Maltby (eds) *On Behalf of the Social Policy Association, Social Policy Review 18: Analysis and Debate in Social Policy, 2006*. Bristol: The Policy Press.

Newman, J. and Vidler, E. (2006) More than a matter of choice? Consumerism and the modernisation of health care, in L. Bauld, K. Clarke and T. Maltby (eds) *On Behalf of the Social Policy Association, Social Policy Review 18: Analysis and Debate in Social Policy, 2006*. Bristol: The Policy Press.

Office of the Deputy Prime Minister (ODPM) (2006) *The Challenges of Local Governance in 2015*. The Tavistock Institute, SOLON Consultants and the Local Government Information Unit, local: vision. London: The Stationery Office.

# PART 2

## Participation and partnerships in 21st century public health

### Editors' overview

Who plays a part in making public health action happen? Is there a large enough workforce with the necessary skills? How do people and organizations work together to take public health action forward? How are the public involved?

These are some of the questions addressed in Part 2. Participating in public health action, and working in partnership to achieve better health for the population, are central themes in multidisciplinary public health. This part of the book examines different conceptual frameworks, dimensions and processes involved in participation and partnership, setting them in their policy context and in the real world of practical experience.

User involvement and collaborative working are now major themes in all government policy. Policy makers recognize that joint working does not just happen by goodwill and common sense. It needs attention to the structures and processes that underpin collaborative working – issues which are explored in these chapters.

Multidisciplinary public health involves a wider range of professional groups than ever before, both within and outside the NHS; this wide range is explored in these chapters. There are challenges for health professionals to move out of their discrete professional specialisms and to work with other health professionals. Public health action also requires the public to be accepted as important contributors in working for better health. The need to engage with non-health workers and lay people pushes health professionals' thinking towards even greater shifts.

In Chapter 4 Stephen Peckham asks the question 'Who needs to work together and how can they do it?' This chapter examines the way that concepts for collaboration and partnership are embedded within public health policy and goes on to examine the nature of these partnerships. It considers the development of partnerships in the UK context and the different forms they take.

Recent government policy emphasizes strengthening the public health function by expanding capacity and capability. In Chapter 5 this issue is examined by Gillian Barrett, Jennie Naidoo and Judy Orme. They question government notions of 'capacity and capability' in public health, their application in practice and discuss issues about professional identity in public health. They examine which professional groups are involved in the current expansion of public health and why. They critically examine recent interrelated initiatives to support policy implementation. They discuss what is meant by 'public health professionals' and whether they always see themselves as contributing to public health.

In Chapter 6 Pat Taylor examines the lay contribution to public health. The 'public' is seen as a key partner in contemporary public health, and lay involvement is expected at all levels of public health activity. Taylor outlines the policy context for lay involvement before discussing some of the inherent problems, contradictions and conceptual and practical barriers. She discusses the reality as well as the potential for lay involvement in public health. Key questions are posed about expectations for lay involvement by different partners in current public health practice.

In Chapter 7 Selena Gray explores some of the evidence that demonstrates that equitable access to health services does have an impact on health at the population level. She describes a model of public health practice that includes three domains; namely, health improvement, health protection and health service delivery and quality, and demonstrates how engagement with health service provision is an integral part of public health practice.

In Chapter 8 Alison Gilchrist examines the role of networking for health gain. She demonstrates the importance of social relationships in promoting general health and interagency working, arguing that robust and diverse networks provide useful mechanisms for emotional support, critical advice, communal learning and collective organizing. She links this with the concept of social capital, and discusses three aspects of networking: partnership approaches, personal networks and networking practice. The skills and strategies of effective and inclusive networking are identified as a vital dimension of public health.

# 4

# STEPHEN PECKHAM
## Partnership working for public health

**Editors' introduction**

An overarching theme in contemporary public health is the need for people to work together. The notion of collaboration and partnerships between agencies, professionals, communities and individuals is fundamental to policy for multidisciplinary public health.

Who needs to work together and how can they do it? This chapter examines the way that concepts for collaboration and partnership are embedded within public health policy and goes on to examine the nature of these partnerships. It considers the development of partnerships in the UK context and the different forms they take.

All public health workers – who by the very nature of their work are likely to find themselves working in partnerships with other people, organizations and the public – will find this chapter useful. It will help them to think critically about what 'partnership' and 'collaboration' actually mean in theory and practice, and why and how partnerships are successful. It also helps readers to find their way around the plethora of local, national and international partnerships.

The author starts by discussing definitions of partnership in current practice. A broad understanding of partnerships is identified and discussed, with a continuum of degrees of collaboration from isolation to integration. The discussion goes on to link the degrees of collaboration to the purpose of collaborations, the nature of the organizations involved and the influence of the wider context on them.

The next section discusses why partnership working is relevant and important for public health to achieve its objectives, with different contributions coming together to maximize resources for health improvement and addressing health inequalities. It acknowledges potential pitfalls and identifies opportunities for partnership working.

In the final section, the author takes an in-depth look at who are the partners in public health, basing discussion on national and international activity. He particularly concentrates on local relationships, where recent development has mostly focused. He concludes by summarizing key benefits and problems within current partnership developments in public health.

## Introduction

This book has stressed that 21st century public health is viewed as a collaborative endeavour – a shared responsibility. However, it has also been described as everyone's business, but no one's specific responsibility. Recent government policy on public health has, more than before, explicitly recognized the need for a more multidisciplinary and multisectoral approach to public health with an emphasis on collaboration between agencies and individuals. (See Chapters 2 and 3 for an overview of recent and current public health policy.)

This chapter examines how concepts of collaboration and partnership (as a mode of organization) are embedded within current public health policy. It explores what form such collaborations take, how public health collaborations have developed in the UK and identifies partnership as a pragmatic endeavour – an incremental response to getting things done. The aim of the chapter is to provide frameworks for thinking about public health partnerships and to explore the interrelationship between policy and practice. Thus this chapter will explore the patterns of intra- and interorganizational relationships as they relate to public health policy and action.

The chapter starts, however, by defining partnerships and why partnership is of relevance to public health. Four broad approaches are discussed relating to the nature of public health, government policy, organizational approaches and working with the public and local communities. The chapter then discusses the nature of partnerships, examining the concept of partnership and ways of thinking about partnerships, using examples throughout.

## What are partnerships?

The terms partnership and collaboration are often used interchangeably to explain ways of co-ordinating activity – whether between individuals or organizations. Warren *et al.* (1974) define 'co-ordination' as: 'A structure or process of concerted decision making wherein the decisions or action of two or more organizations [or individuals] are made simultaneously in part or in whole with some deliberate degree of adjustment to each other' (p. 16). In common usage, partnership conjures a picture of some formal or informal relationship – such as a GP or solicitor partnership, marriage or perhaps 'partners in crime'. However, the notion of partnership is not without problems.

The Audit Commission (1998) has suggested that partnership is a slippery concept and difficult to define precisely. Writing in the 1980s, before new Labour's attachment to the concept, Challis *et al.* (1988) argued that partnership is a word in search of a way of giving it effective meaning in practice. Partnerships are formal structures of relationships among individuals or groups, all of which are banded together for a common purpose. It is the commitment to a common cause – frequently purposive change – that characterizes these partnerships, whether the partners are organizations or individuals, voluntary confederations of independent agencies or community assemblies developing multipurpose and long-term alliances (El Ansari *et al.* 2001). Embedded in such a definition is, however, the notion that partners are equal. This is rarely the case in reality and different professions and organizations come to partnerships with different values, levels of power, levels of commitment and resources. It is also true that partnerships do not have to be formal structures and many local partnerships, particularly between professionals or lay and professional people are informal but characterized by common purpose. For some commentators it is precisely this lack of a specific definition of 'partnership' which is seen as an advantage providing 'a form of organizational governance whose flexibility, responsiveness and adaptability is ideally suited to the demands of contemporary society [thus] collaborative activities can reflect local circumstances, needs and agreed joint objectives and remain appropriate to the expertise and levels of trust of local partners' (Glendinning 2002: 117).

Partnership is an umbrella term and is often used interchangeably with words such as interagency, joint working or interprofessional all of which can have more specific meanings. While accepting the problems surrounding the definition of 'partnership' it is this term which will be used for the remainder of the chapter to denote collaborative arrangements developed in relation to public health.

## Why partnerships for public health?

This section explores why partnerships are relevant to public health. Since 1997 there has been an increasing concern to develop joined-up processes at national, regional and local levels, as well as increasing vertical partnerships between levels. The Labour government has pursued a 'collaborative discourse' (Clarence and Painter 1998) that has included 'joined-up government at the centre and joined-up governance at local levels' (Powell and Exworthy 2001: 21). Many attempts to promote greater collaboration (possibly including the current policy drive) have been 'largely rhetorical invocations of a vague ideal' but collaboration has become the *zeitgeist* of the Labour government (Hudson 1999) as a result of its 'third way' philosophy (Powell 1998). Partnership approaches are the government's response to tackling cross-cutting problems (Newman 2001; Sullivan and Skelcher 2002). In public health as elsewhere in government policy, various mechanisms have been introduced which cannot be considered simply rhetorical. Box 4.1 highlights a range of strategies which are employed in developing partnerships.

The need for national collaboration for public health was clearly recognized in *The Health of the Nation* White Paper (Secretary of State for Health 1992). In fact government policy on public health partnerships has traditionally operated at both national and local levels addressing (to some degree at least) partnership on public health policy, organizational partnerships and joint working between professionals.

The relative emphasis on these aspects of partnership have been changing over the past 10 years reflecting the general shift in public health policy from the Conservative government of the 1980s and 1990s to the new Labour government elected in 1997. The next sections explore the context of these developments outlining five broad themes for partnership relating to the nature of public health, organizational issues, government policy working with the public and the need to address health inequalities.

---

**Box 4.1** Strategies employed in developing partnerships

---

Three broad strategies have been employed in developing partnerships:

- co-operation based on agreement between different organizations/individuals;
- incentives such as funding; more flexibility over resource allocation such as that given to areas with health action zones who were able to use health and local authority resources more flexibly than authorities outside these zones (Matka *et al.* 2002); and
- authoritarian approaches setting out specific organizational forms or other 'must do' requirements; these include local strategic partnerships, Local Area Agreements.

These strategies have been applied at both national and local levels and have been variously called joint working, partnership and collaboration.

---

## The nature of public health

The need for partnership can be seen to arise from the widely recognized fact that most advances in health are the result of improvements in people's economic and social status – better housing, higher incomes, better education and so on (McKeown 1976). These improvements are not just the consequences of government intervention but derive from the actions of individuals, communities, organizations and international circumstances. Collaboration is one of the key pillars of primary health care (the others being participation and equity, see Macdonald 1992). Collaboration was also a key element of the Health for All approach promoted by the World Health Organization during the 1980s (WHO 1991). Moreover, as suggested in Chapter 8, social and community ties have been identified as important protective elements which promote health. Recognition of the importance of healthy communities has been reflected in government health policy since 1997 with, for example, the early creation of health action zones, healthy living centres, health improvement programmes and the development of primary care organizations (Peckham 2004; Peckham and Exworthy 2003). All these organizations have had a broad and ambitious brief to employ both individual and community approaches for addressing local health problems.

Clearly this encompasses a range of activities undertaken by a wide range of actors and hence gives rise to the notion that public health is everyone's business (Secretary of State for Health 1999, 2004). Current policy and practice are framed by government policies on public health in England that aim to develop a three-way partnership between individuals, communities (and local agencies) and government to achieve better public health. Similar emphasis can be found in government proposals in Scotland, Northern Ireland and Wales (Scottish Executive 1998; Secretary of State for Northern Ireland 1998; Secretary of State for Wales 1998).

While the need for involving a range of agencies, and individuals, in public health has long been acknowledged (in both policy and practice) the current government has perhaps more fully embraced action which sits more firmly in the wider social model of health with its emphasis on intersectoral action and participation as advocated by WHO. An example is in Scotland where local authorities are required to develop community planning to provide a strategic framework for joint planning, partnership working, and to address fragmented public policy and service provision (Fernie and McCarthy 2001). As Barnes and Sullivan argue 'Partnership was understood to be the key vehicle that would enable the resources of government to be brought to bear on improving health, reducing inequalities and improving services in a coordinated and cohesive manner' (Barnes and Sullivan 2002: 81).

Policies to tackle health inequalities can be identified across government (Department of Health 2001c) including tax and benefit reform, welfare to work, interventions in the early years of life and across the life course, diet and nutrition programmes, among many others. The government's approach to health inequalities also emphasizes the need to tackle these by building partnerships at and between national, regional and local levels (Secretary of State for Health 1999, 2004; Bull and Hamer 2002). These policies have been pursued at a local level using primary care and partnership working as the main local vehicles for policy implementation. At a regional level there is greater strategic co-ordination bringing regional public health directors into the existing government regional offices.

The need for partnership also arises in part from the acknowledged limits of organizational individualism where agencies work in isolation from each other. Huxham and Macdonald (1999), for example, identify four 'pitfalls of individualism' which all have direct relevance to public health:

- *repetition:* where two or more organizations carry out an action or task which need only be done by one;

- *omission:* where activities which are important to the objectives of more than one organization are not carried out because they have not been identified as important, because they come into no organization's remit, or because each organization assumes the other is performing the activity;

- *divergence:* the actions of the various organizations may become diluted across a range of activities rather than being used towards common goals;

- *counterproduction:* organizations working in isolation may take actions which conflict with those taken by others.

All of these clearly relate to approaches to public health where action needs to co-ordinate the work of health, local government and other voluntary and private agencies (see Box 4.2).

Pratt *et al.* (1998) have also argued that the decision to use a partnership approach should be related to goals to be achieved. This can be shown diagrammatically as in Figure 4.1. Public health goals are collective, although health is also an individual goal.

Public health strategy needs to balance these approaches but if the goals are to maximize population health then co-evolution or co-ordination are the best strategies for partnerships.

---

**Box 4.2**  School meals – a partnership approach

---

The responsibility for the health of young people falls on both local health agencies who provide child and adolescent health services and local education authorities (LEAs) who are responsible for schools. However, until the recent government prioritizing of childhood obesity and improved nutrition for school meals, LEAs had not taken any lead role in school meals as they were not responsible for health issues. Conversely local health authorities saw school meals as being outside their remit. Individually health and education authorities may have taken divergent approaches to tackling the issue and in addition schools themselves, families and private school meal providers may have all followed very different approaches to tackling obesity and nutritional problems. Importantly, isolated action by individual schools or by the education authority to address school meal problems may have been focused more on process issues of delivering meals that children eat rather than on the relative nutritional and health benefits of school meals.

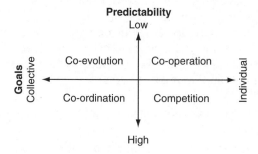

- Collective public health goals – where the gains are uncertain then separate agencies should develop responses towards a collective goal.
- Collective public health goals – where the gains are high, e.g. accident prevention then co-ordination is best achieved through partnership working.
- Individual goals – gains are generally uncertain because individuals cannot control the determinants of their health so a strategy of co-operation would be best to achieve individual outcomes.
- Where individual gains are high but the context uncertain, agencies may compete in achieving the best individual outcomes.

**Figure 4.1**  Strategies for partnership

## Joined-up governance

The drive towards 'joined-up' thinking, generating 'joined-up' solutions are a response to the need to address what have been described as 'wicked issues' (Audit Commission 1998; Clarence and Painter 1998; Powell and Exworthy 2001; Glendinning *et al.* 2002). In other words, the issues facing local communities – such as tackling health inequalities, promoting health, tackling social exclusion and so on – are multifaceted and require multiagency and multidisciplinary attention. No previous government has tried so systematically to create 'joined-up government' (Bogdanor 2005) in order to address complex issues which cross departmental boundaries. Early examples were the Social Exclusion Unit and the Rough Sleepers Unit; these were followed by 'tsars', for example to counter drug trafficking and use, and a similar approach has been used in co-ordinating services, for example the National Service Frameworks (NSFs) for older people and for children. This new approach has also been embodied in government policy documents such as *Saving Lives: Our Healthier Nation* which emphasized the important role of integration and partnership 'working across Government to attack the breeding ground of poor health – poverty and social exclusion – and we believe in creating partnerships with local authorities, health authorities and other agencies to tackle the root causes of ill-health in places where people live' (Secretary of State for Health 1999: 3) and the more recent *Choosing Health* public health White Paper (Department of Health 2004a). The emphasis was also embodied in *The NHS Plan* identifying the NHS's role in helping to 'develop Local Strategic Partnerships, into which, in the medium term, health actions zones and other local action zones could be integrated to strengthen links between health, education, employment and other causes of social exclusion' (Secretary of State for Health 2000: 111) and the requirement to develop Local Area Agreements (Boyne and Law 2005).

The increasing emphasis on community and public involvement is of particular relevance to public health. Research on health inequalities has identified the important connection between individual, relative inequality within any given geographical community, as well as inequality between communities (Wilkinson 2005). It is widely recognized that there are inequalities in health status, morbidity and mortality between deprived and affluent communities shaped by a range of individual, geographical and social factors. The relative effect of these will vary according to specific circumstances. At the same time early life factors and/or the cumulative effects on social cohesion of life events caused by deprivation play a significant role (Wilkinson 1996, 1997, 2005). Thus developing approaches to reduce health inequalities will require tailoring towards individual circumstances and addressing specific characteristics of local areas and communities. There has tended to be little recognition of the role of the community in promoting its own health through community-based action and community health initiatives (Petersen and Lupton 1996; Taylor *et al.* 1998). Yet, individuals, families and communities provide significant amounts of self care and ill health prevention as illustrated in Figure 4.2 and this is increasingly being recognized by governments who are keen to support prevention and self care (Zakus and Lysack 1998; Department of Health 2004a, 2005d, 2006d). (See Chapter 6 for discussion of the lay contribution to public health.)

Despite the domination of a medical approach to public health most advances in health are the result of improvements in people's economic and social status – better housing, higher incomes, better education and so on. These improvements are not just the consequences of government intervention but derive from the actions of individuals, communities, organizations and international circumstances. Recognition of the importance of healthy communities would appear to be reflected in current health policy. For example, the creation of health action zones, healthy living centres, health improvement programmes and the development of primary care organizations

| Who | | Act as | How | Who with | Comments |
|---|---|---|---|---|---|
| **Individuals** | | Patients, health providers, health educators | Self care, user care, user involvement, complaints, preventive care | Themselves, health professionals, other users | Individuals undertake a range of self-directed and motivated preventive health measures and have contact with professionals on an individual basis |
| **Families** | | Patients, health providers, carers/parents, supporters, advocates | Direct care, shared care, user involvement, complaints, preventive care | Themselves, health professionals | Contact with individual health care practitioners and professionals providing support and information (e.g. health visitors) |
| **Communities of Interest** | **Informal networks** | Supporters, health providers, information providers | Friend and kinship networks, self-help groups | Themselves, health professionals | May work collaboratively with specific health professionals but main emphasis is on mutual support (e.g. self-help groups) |
| | **Formal networks** | Health providers, supporters, advocates, information providers | Community associations, patient groups | Members | May provide a range of information and support services to members. This may involve specialist and professional health providers (e.g. patient participation group, food co-operative) |
| | **Community/ voluntary organizations** | Providers of services, supporters, advocates | Campaigning, delivering services, participating in working groups | Members, users, health professionals, health agencies | More formalized than networks and may have specific aims to provide services as well as support users (e.g. MIND, SCOPE, Royal National Institute for the Deaf) |
| **Geographical communities** | | Polity, electors, providers, advocates | Voting, campaigning, developing networks between other groups | Health agencies, local authorities, government | E.g. neighbourhood health action group, environmental groups |

**Figure 4.2** Individuals, communities, the public and health

all have a broad and ambitious brief to employ both individual and community approaches for addressing local health problems.

Self-evidently, in adopting a more enlightened public health perspective, individuals and communities need to be seen as equal partners in promoting and producing health alongside many others. The medical and health professions are just one part of a range of individuals and organizations which have an impact on health including local authorities, voluntary organizations, and private companies and those that work within them.

So, partnership or collaboration is an essential ingredient of public health in four key ways:

- tackling the key determinants of health (as conceptualized in the social model of health) requires action by a range of international, national and local agencies;
- seeing public health as a shared responsibility;
- needing to avoid overlap and duplication; and
- recognizing the important role individuals and communities play in promoting their own health.

But this still raises the question of what a partnership is and what sort of partnerships are needed to deliver public health. While accepting the need to address international aspects and the important role of cross-national partnership arrangements this chapter will focus on the UK context.

## The collaborative dimension

However, it would be simplistic to view partnerships as either existing or not existing, as in reality we would expect to find different degrees of partnership. This collaborative dimension (Hudson *et al.* 1997, 1999) can be analysed using a framework which distinguishes between isolation, encounter, communication, collaboration and integration (see Figure 4.3). Each of these represents points on a collaborative continuum ranging from weak to strong. In fact the first and last points are not strictly collaborative measures, since isolation involves *no* interagency activity, while integration is strictly an *alternative* to collaboration.

In those interorganizational or professional relationships characterized by *isolation* and *encounter* we would expect to find loose knit and lowly connected networks with infrequent and ad hoc interaction. Different members of the partnership may have very different organizational goals and interests and there may be interprofessional rivalry and stereotyping. Where communities are involved there may be levels of distrust and conflicting values and priorities. An example here would be the historically low level of interaction between general practice and public health in the UK, where they have been organizationally isolated but also premised upon different values, with general practice focusing on individual, reactive patient care and public health on population-based proactive preventive care (Taylor *et al.* 1998).

Where relationships are characterized by *communication* we would expect to find more frequent interactions and a willingness to share information about mutual roles,

| Isolation | No partnership exists and agencies or individuals work in isolation from each other. |
| Encounter | Some interagency and interprofessional contact, but this is informal, ad hoc and marginal to the goals of the separate organizations. |
| Communication | Separate organizations or professionals do engage in joint working of a formal and structured nature, but this still tends to be marginal to separate organizational goals or individual roles, and needs to be able to demonstrate how such activity will help achieve these respective goals or fulfil individual work roles. |
| Collaboration | Separate agencies recognize that joint working is central to their mainstream activities; this implies a trusting relationship in which organizations are seen to be reliable partners. |
| Integration | A situation where the degree of collaboration is so high that the separate organizations no longer see their separate identity as significant and may be willing to contemplate the creation of a unitary organization. |

**Figure 4.3** The collaborative dimension – a framework

responsibilities and availability. Communication is an important first step in providing the foundations for partnership and collaboration, however the partnership may remain relatively loose knit. For example, there may be a limited acceptance of the notion of membership of a team with workers' prime loyalty being to the employing organization. Joint working often gives rise to a high degree of expectation of reciprocation. This may be particularly true in cases where communities are involved in developing public health action and there may be justifiable expectations on statutory agencies to deliver services or address the concerns identified by the local community. However, communication provides an approach which allows agencies or workers to achieve their own goals better than if they worked in isolation (see Box 4.3).

---

**Box 4.3**  Communication to meet organizational goals

*Example 1*

Public health professionals can achieve their own objectives better by working with others e.g. a health promotion worker making contact with youth workers to achieve greater access to young people to promote sexual health. In such circumstances both the health promotion worker and the youth worker work together but are guided by their own goals.

*Example 2*

Public health networks draw together professionals in local areas based upon the premise that individual primary care trusts do not have the capacity to fulfill all public health tasks on their own. In particular, these networks have focused on sharing expertise, information, knowledge and skills and have been a force for continuity in provision of public health (Faculty of Public Health Medicine and Health Development Agency 2001; Fahey *et al.* 2003; Abbott *et al.* 2006).

Where *collaboration* develops we would expect to find a willingness to participate in some formal and structured pattern of joint working and an acknowledgement of the value and existence of a team and agreement on the membership. Collaboration will be characterized by relatively close knit and highly connected networks enjoying a high degree of mutual trust and respect. Participants would not be looking for immediate reciprocation and there would be a high degree of recognition of common interests, goals and interdependency. In such arrangements you might find mutual secondments and other forms of cross-boundary deployment, clustering or co-location of personnel joint planning joint service delivery; and joint commissioning.

Such characteristics are often demonstrated in joint projects. These are generally local and small scale but also include more ambitious projects such as healthy living centres (see Box 4.4).

Finally, with *integration* we should see very close knit and highly connected networks, little regard for reciprocation in relationships, a mutual and diffuse sense of long-term obligation, very high degrees of trust and respect, joint arrangements which are mainstream rather than marginal, joint arrangements which encompass both strategic and operational issues, some shared or single management arrangements and the establishment of separate, unified organizations. To some extent the joint appointment of directors of public health starts to build a more integrated approach although responsibilities remain split across local authorities and primary care trusts.

It would also be wrong to characterize the relationship between different agencies as being unidimensional – simply a linear continuum between isolation of one agency to integration with other agencies.

## Types of partnership

Additionally, Hudson and Hardy (2001) identify six key types of partnerships: governing partnerships; accountability partnerships; purchaser–provider partnerships; NHS–local authority partnerships; partnerships with patients/publics; and

---

**Box 4.4**   Healthy Living Centres

The Healthy Living Centre initiative was a government programme managed by the New Opportunities Fund launched in January 1999. Healthy Living Centres were expected to seek to influence the wider determinants of health, such as social exclusion, poor access to services, and social and economic aspects of deprivation which can contribute to inequalities in health.

There was no blueprint for projects. The initiative was designed to be flexible enough to allow for innovative proposals based on local needs, supporting national and local health strategies. Local communities and users were expected to be involved in all aspects of design and delivery of a project. Projects covered a range of activities including, for example, smoking cessation, dietary advice, physical activity, health screening programmes, training and skills schemes, arts programmes and complementary therapy.

central–local partnerships. Yet these perhaps simplify the multiplex nature of inter-professional partnerships and partnerships between professionals and patients and the public. Importantly Powell and Exworthy (2002) have argued that partnerships do not just exist horizontally within these levels but that they can also be vertical, between levels.

Stewart (2002) has suggested that partnerships can be categorized as being strategic (or co-ordinating), facilitative or implementing partnerships. However, like most frameworks for partnership this categorization suffers problems from the fact that some formalized partnerships have more than one of these roles and often the members are not clear what their role is. However, Stewart's categorization is useful as it highlights different functions of partnership. Examples of all these types of partnership can be found in public health (see Figure 4.4).

This framework demonstrates that there are necessary stages of development in partnerships. Collaborative working in public health at any level may require the development of strategic partnerships where initial discussion takes place about values and principles before facilitative and implementation partnerships can be developed.

In order to assist in discussion and analysis Ling (2000) has suggested that partnerships can be described by four key dimensions:

- their membership;
- the links between members;
- the scale and boundaries of the partnership; and
- the wider context within which the partnership operates.

In practice the dimensions described by Ling are defined by, for example, the context and purpose of the partnership such as stopping smoking initiative, a healthy schools project or in child protection committees. Similarly the membership of a partnership will be directly related to the availability of partners so that two healthy living centres in different areas focusing on say young people are likely to have different

| Type of partnership | Example | Characteristics |
|---|---|---|
| Strategic | Local Strategic Partnership | Brings together key statutory and other agencies to set context and agreements for collaboration. |
|  | Local area committee | Brings together local agencies and community representatives to establish the principles for collaborative working. |
| Facilitative | Public health network | Provides a repository of skills to pursue public health activities. |
| Implementation | Sure Start | Focus on improving health and providing the services to support health improvement. |

**Figure 4.4** Types of partnership

members depending on local agency structure, local community profile and range of community and voluntary organizations and so on.

In practice partnership occurs at a number of levels (Hudson 1987; Rummery and Glendinning 1997; Exworthy and Powell 2000). These include:

- internationally between governments and international agencies, as in UNESCO or the World Health Organization;
- at a national level, regionally or, for example, in the UK between devolved areas/ regions within national government;
- between key local agencies (such as local government, health, voluntary agencies) – as in neighbourhood action areas, Sure Start, and local strategic partnerships;
- locality or area based such as community partnerships, Sure Start, healthy living centres, Neighbourhood Renewal; and
- between individuals – joint working.

In understanding partnership it is important to identify what a successful partnership will require. A review of partnerships undertaken in 2003 suggests that successful partnerships have two dimensions – process success and outcome success. Successful processes require the commitment and engagement of partners; agreement about purpose; involve high levels of trust, reciprocity and respect; favourable political and social conditions (finance, institutional arrangements, legal structures); satisfactory accountability arrangements and adequate leadership and management. Partnerships are more likely to achieve successful outcomes if they include improved service delivery to users and the public; achieving greater equity; improvements in efficiency and effectiveness; improved experiences for staff and informal workers and overall improvements in health status (Dowling *et al.* 2004). Measurement of partnership success requires, therefore, some attention to identifying relevant criteria along these two dimensions.

## Who are the partners in public health?

Partnership can be contextualized in both formal and informal ways. Formal partnerships include organizational arrangements such as cross-representation and joint budgets; informal arrangements are those such as professionals working alongside each other, and local networking. There are important and ongoing relationships between NHS public health specialists, environmental health officers, nurses, doctors, community workers and so on, that operate within, but independently of, organizational and institutional arrangements.

Generally, formalization occurs at all levels with policy gradually increasing institutional and organizational structures to support this. Informal approaches have tended to be seen as less important but have also occurred predominantly at senior management levels and between professionals working in the community. In recent years there has been an increase in joint educational approaches through multidisciplinary public health training (for example, at the University of the West of England, Bristol). However, professional networks still tend to be uniprofessional although the Faculty of Public Health has broadened itself into a more multidisciplinary professional body in line with government policy.

## International partnerships

International collaboration is an expanding feature of public health. Increasingly it is recognized that public health issues transcend national boundaries and action between countries (such as in the European Union or WHO) is becoming important. Mobility between countries, international trade (particularly in foodstuffs) and common health problems mean that countries can no longer be isolated in their approaches to public health. The need for global responses to diseases like HIV/AIDS (and, increasingly, the transfer of other diseases through global travel) means dealing with poverty and health issues in many developing countries and requires co-operation at an international level (McKee *et al.* 2001). (Chapter 12 discusses globalization and its impact on health.)

## National partnerships – joined-up government

At the national level, joined-up government has been promoted in policy making and service delivery through cross-departmental programmes and initiatives such as Sure Start, the Teenage Pregnancy Unit and the Rough Sleepers Initiative. These seek to overcome the long recognized problem of departmentalism, that is, the strong tradition and culture that civil servants and ministers seek to defend and, if possible, augment their own sphere of responsibility; ministers thus become 'barons'. Issues that cut across more than one department (such as health inequalities) might suffer from a lack of departmental ownership or sufficient accountability. This has led Kavanagh and Richards to conclude that 'It is questionable to what extent joined-up government can be properly established when departments remain crucial holders of resources and continue to dominate policy-making and policy delivery' (Kavanagh and Richards 2001: 17).

Since 1997 there has been an increasing attempt to link up government departments. In England, for example, single regeneration bids, now explicitly including joint health and social care targets, have been set for the NHS and local government, and the Neighbourhood Renewal Unit has a presence in both the Department of Health and the Office of the Deputy Prime Minister. The Cabinet Office has also provided a focus for co-ordinated approaches such as the Social Exclusion Unit and more recently the Treasury has undertaken a number of cross-cutting spending reviews including one into tackling the causes of health inequalities (HM Treasury and Department of Health 2002). The next Government Spending Review will report in 2007. These approaches are a clear attempt to join up policy and government action and have more recently been reflected in changes to regional structures bringing the NHS more closely aligned with regional government offices and regional public health forums bringing together local authorities, the NHS and regional agencies. But joined-up government remains a complex task and while the Labour government since 1997 has attempted to develop more joined-up policy this is not always without problems (see Box 4.5).

---

**Box 4.5**   Joined-up policy

---

Examples of how government policies either complement or contradict each other.

1.  The Department of the Environment, Transport and the Regions has a key role in transport policy, which as the Acheson Report (1998) states, will in turn affect road safety (road accidents are a major cause of death for disadvantaged children) and air pollution from traffic.

2.  The Department of Health and the Home Office both have key roles in determining drug policy. Both also have a role in prison health, and the responsibility for over-seeing prison health services has recently passed to primary care trusts. At an individual level, goals may conflict; usually a health care provider will have a detailed history of their patient, but in high security prisons, security requirements prevail and even the name of the patient may not be known.

3.  Children's health is a further example where two government departments need to co-ordinate their interests; historically, this prevented the full development of school nursing, which is provided by primary care trusts in settings (schools) in which the Department for Education and Skills has the policy lead, but it is now recognized that school nursing is a key element of public health. The range of services needed to improve equality for children is well illustrated by the Green Paper, *Every Child Matters* (Department for Education and Skills 2003); these include extended schools, child and adolescent mental health services, speech and language therapy, reforms to the youth justice system, and ending bed and breakfast accommodation for homeless families.

4.  An example of policy conflict and conflict of interest is provided by MAFF, the Ministry of Agriculture, Food and Fisheries. The Phillips Report (2000) on the BSE crisis in the mid-1990s considered that the ministry did not adequately protect the inter-ests of consumers, since it also existed to promote the interests of farmers. Lang (2000) also considers that the Department of Health was very weak in the 1980s, and was over-ridden by MAFF, so that risky practices in feeding livestock persisted. The Food Standards Agency was set up in 2000, reporting to the Department of Health rather than MAFF, which was superseded in 2001 by DEFRA, the Department for Environment, Food and Rural Affairs.

---

With devolution, cross-national relationships are developing between England, Wales, Scotland and Northern Ireland. As Powell and Exworthy (2002) have demon-strated in their study on health inequalities policy, national and cross-national approaches to partnership are becoming more common and important, and are likely to continue to provide both an attempt at joined-up policy and to join up the mechanisms of central government. However, they and others (Davies *et al.* 2000) argue that this is not yet by any means perfect. UKPHA (2006) argue that although the major public health challenges facing each of the four countries of the UK and Ireland are identical, one feature of most of the countries is that their health and public health systems are in the process of transition of varying degrees of radicalness. (Perspectives on 'joined-up' government are also discussed in Chapters 2 and 3.)

## Local partnerships

For most public health workers and activists it is at the local level that partnerships are more likely to be developed or experienced. Local partnerships now constitute a wide range of activity encouraged by central government policy initiatives but also developed through local action (see Box 4.6).

Since 1997 the government has tried to develop a new framework for addressing public health at local level. Examples include a statutory duty of partnership upon health agencies and local authorities with provisions for local strategic partnerships, the development of joint investment plans, healthy living centres and Sure Start projects which have sought to widen partnerships beyond health and local authorities with a wider public health remit.

Drawing on Stewart's (2002) framework of strategic (or co-ordinating), facilitative and implementing partnerships it is useful to examine local partnerships in more detail. Historically, strategic or co-ordinating partnerships would include health action zones (HAZs) and currently would include local strategic partnerships. HAZs were established from 1998 onwards to develop partnership approaches to tackling health inequalities. They were given additional funding and developed a core staff with partnership, both horizontally across major local agencies, but also vertically with other local agencies. The evaluation of health action zones has suggested that collaboration is an important ingredient in success but that having a long history of partnership is helpful and that a commitment to partnership does not address imbalances in power between different members. These are well recognized problems (Gillies 1998a; Department of Transport, Local Government and the Regions 2002; Stewart 2002).

However, the evidence from the HAZ evaluation is that there have been successes partly due to the changing national context, with new policies supporting a partnership approach, providing local freedoms, for example, flexibilities through new approaches to funding (Secretary of State for Health 2000; Barnes and Sullivan 2002). Local strategic partnerships (LSPs) across the country bring together the public, private, voluntary and community sectors to action the local community strategy. LSPs are a key element of intersectoral partnerships in England (DETR 2000d,

---

**Box 4.6** Local partnerships

- A wide range of formal and informal groupings at local level may constitute partnerships, such as action on stopping smoking, healthy schools initiatives, child protection committees, community safety groups, drug action teams and so on.
- Tackling teenage pregnancy is predicated on local partnerships.
- The nature and range of such groups will vary from area to area, and some have a long history, some have developed for one specific reason and others are highly informal, based on ad hoc groupings of individual workers.

2001b) and have key roles in engaging communities in partnership arrangements and provide rationalization of other strategic planning processes. Tackling health inequalities is central to the process 'ensuring committed NHS participation in local strategic partnerships by bringing knowledge, expertise and resources to the partnership' (Department of Health 2001c).

In 2000 the Secretary of State for Health, Alan Milburn, highlighted Sure Start as making one of the most important contributions to health improvement in the UK (Milburn 2000). Sure Start is one of many community partnership approaches which seeks to address individual problems through community-based responses but by working with the local communities involved. Sure Start is based on a similar approach pioneered in the USA and has a strong neighbourhood focus, with each programme serving the local community 'within pram pushing distance'. The programme is targeted on children and families in deprived circumstances. It is being delivered through local partnerships with the aim of providing a range of support services, including childcare, early learning and play opportunities, and support with parenting skills, as well as improved access to primary health care (see Box 4.7). The future of Sure Start is, however, under discussion. Initially the government wanted to roll out Sure Start approaches across the whole of the country. The first findings from the national evaluation suggest that while there are strengths to the programme there are also some concerns about whether the programmes are delivering value for money (Department for Education and Skills 2004).

## Partnerships with communities

Increasingly, community-based approaches to health have been incorporated into a range of government policy objectives at a local level emphasizing partnerships between local communities and statutory agencies within programmes such as

---

**Box 4.7**   Rose Hill – Littlemore Sure Start

The Sure Start project started in 1999 in an area of Oxford with the second largest 0–16-year-old population. The area also had the highest number of people reporting a limited long-term illness and high levels of unemployment. Rose Hill had a high proportion (25 per cent) on the school roll of children from Asian families and a high number of children on the special education needs register. There were no locally based health services in the area and few resources for under-4s and their families.

The project has worked with local parents to establish a centre based at the First School for 0–3-year-olds providing a community café, health clinics, crèche, playroom and so on. The project has also worked with the local early education project. The project is a partnership between statutory and voluntary services and local families. There are parent representatives on the project group, and a research group is conducting a local evaluation of the project.

The focus of work is on prevention rather than crisis intervention and thus should be seen as playing an important role in addressing local health and welfare issues from a public health perspective.

Standard Regeneration Budget, New Deal for Communities and the Neighbourhood Renewal programme. The emphasis is on the need for local regeneration activity which engages local communities as citizens, service users and neighbours (Audit Commission 2002). The focus is on deprived neighbourhoods and the Neighbourhood Renewal programme aims to build on the experiences of previous programmes to improve local neighbourhoods so that 'within 10–20 years no one should be seriously disadvantaged by where they live' and to 'narrow the gap on [worklessness, crime, health, skills, housing and physical environment] measures between the most deprived neighbourhoods and the rest of the country' (Social Exclusion Unit 2001a: 8). More importantly neighbourhood renewal is a cross-departmental approach and there is an attempt to join up policy initiatives across government – especially between local government and health. Such partnerships can be seen as both facilitation and implementation partnerships but they face many difficulties in relation to community engagement, imbalances in power, problems of governance as new ways of working challenge traditional local authority and health service models of bureaucracy, management and budgetary control.

Finally, at a more individual level joint working has traditionally developed health promotion (both in local authorities and the NHS) and public health departments around specific issues to meet individual patient/client needs (for example, diet and smoking) or targeted at specific population groups (such as young people and pregnant women). However, some general practices have also developed joint working arrangements for public health. While these have involved inter-professional working the emphasis has been predominantly intra-organizational within the NHS.

More rarely wider collaborative approaches have been pioneered such as the Arts for Health Movement and Local Exchange Schemes or time banks (Cowe 2000) (see Box 4.8).

Local partnerships can, therefore, be seen to have a range of agencies involved, an organizational context, an individual context and a range of purposes. What all the local partnerships share is an attempt to draw together local agencies and professionals to avoid overlap, improve co-ordination and bring a range of approaches, professionalisms, perspectives and resources to bear on local problems. In some cases this approach is defined and set by central government or is at least reliant on a context which has been set centrally. However, it is also true that many initiatives derive from local circumstances, personal agendas and endeavours despite continuing

---

**Box 4.8**   Rushey Green time bank

The time bank is closely related to the local exchange trading schemes where community members trade skills. In the time bank people trade hours of activity.

There are a dozen or more time banks in the UK. One of these pioneering schemes was led by a GP who saw the potential for time banks to have a health impact. He instigated a scheme in Rushey Green in 1999 which encourages local people to offer time to other local residents. Tasks on offer include story telling, fishing, odd jobs, baby sitting and visiting elderly and house bound people.

problems of traditional management approaches and poor interagency co-ordination (see Box 4.9).

## Conclusion

The discussion in this chapter has demonstrated that partnership is a fundamental concept which underpins public health policy and action. This is both a strength and a weakness. Clearly the nature of public health and the need to address inequalities in

---

**Box 4.9**    Obesity as a public health problem – joined-up responses

Obesity in England has grown almost 400 per cent in 25 years, and three-quarters of the adult population is now overweight. Childhood obesity has tripled in 20 years. The economic cost in England arising from its consequences, such as heart disease, could be £7.4 billion a year, and the Wanless Report (2003) predicted that our health care system could only remain affordable if we become fully engaged in maintaining our own health and therefore tackle issues such as obesity.

All governments need to consider the extent to which they are prepared to intervene to alter the individual behaviour of their citizens. In the UK, governments that do so are often accused of being a 'nanny state'. However, such are the concerns about the 'obesity epidemic' that this type of intervention is now being attempted, and there have been several reports on obesity, such as the House of Commons health select committee report (2004) and the global plan from the World Health Organization (2004). The Food Standards Agency has recommended curbing the aggressive marketing of food to young children.

There are also many debates on the extent to which we have real choices in the food we eat. Many poor people live in 'food deserts' where they have access only to a limited range of shops, with little fresh food, and parents with little money will not risk buying unfamiliar foods which their children may not eat. Poor people buy calories which are cheap, not vitamins and other micro-nutrients (Philip *et al.* 1997).

Blythman (2004) analyses the power of the large supermarkets, which sell more than 80 per cent of the food we eat. Five giant companies control three-quarters of the world's banana trade; two provide two-thirds of the bread in the UK. The food industry lobbies government intensively, for example in delaying EU regulations for food labelling. It also seeks to improve its image; Cadbury produced a Get Active Campaign of tokens for sports equipment endorsed by Richard Caborn the sports minister, which required the consumption of large amounts of chocolate to get the tokens.

Inactivity is also a factor; in the UK only 40 per cent of men and 26 per cent of women take enough exercise (30 minutes of moderate activity on five or more days a week). The Department of Culture, Media and Sport therefore also has an important role, as has the Department for Education and Skills in promoting sport in schools.

To effectively tackle such a multifactorial public health problem as obesity, joined-up responses are essential. The continued need for innovative forms of partnership and collaboration between the agencies and organizations identified above is clear (Department of Health 2004a).

health requires multisectoral action which, if it is be effective, requires some level of co-ordination. The multisectoral approach requiring action by all those agencies and individuals which have an impact on health, strengthens approaches to address health problems and inequalities. However, it is their co-ordination which creates problems both in terms of 'joining up' policy and action and ensuring accountability. Thus public health may be everyone's responsibility but how do we ensure that responsibility is taken up and also held to account?

Partnerships are also generally based on ideas of voluntarism and current policy; emphasizing the development of formal partnerships raises questions about whether such enforcement of collaborative working is possible. Public health policy continually emphasizes and requires new forms of partnership working by PCTs, in regeneration schemes and in local strategic partnerships. However, research on partnership has identified the need for partnerships to develop through the establishment of relationships between different agencies and individuals. Such partnerships are more likely to be successful and be sustained.

Yet, in the very policy push towards establishing partnerships many traditional partnerships are being reorganized, dismantling the very relationships which support sustained collaboration. Having recently dismantled health action zone structures (devolving aspects of their work to PCTs, local strategic partnerships and other local agencies), PCT reorganization in 2006 is a further disruption to public health. The public health role was already spread very thinly when it was devolved to primary care trusts and new partnerships have been slow to develop. In formalizing partnerships the government has also attempted to establish who partners should be, and there is a danger that insufficient co-ordination will be achieved between different partnerships such as public health networks and other local health partnerships in the community.

Despite this there is still a strong sense of support for partnership and many policy makers, workers and representatives from community and voluntary agencies are committed to developing partnership approaches. Recent policy changes do provide a context and some new frameworks which make partnerships easier through changes in funding regulations, structures and the ability to experiment with new organizational forms. Ultimately the success of public health partnerships is likely to rest upon the flexibility for actors at all levels to develop real and appropriate partnerships within a policy framework that recognizes variation and flexibility, but which provides clarity on purpose and accountability.

Suggested further reading

Laverack, G. (2005) *Public Health. Power, Empowerment and Professional Practice.* Basingstoke: Palgrave Macmillan.
Sullivan, H. and Skelcher, C. (2002) *Working across Boundaries: Collaboration in Public Services.* Basingstoke: Palgrave Macmillan.

# 5

## GILLIAN BARRETT, JENNIE NAIDOO AND JUDY ORME

Capacity and capability in public health

### Editors' introduction

Public health work in the 21st century needs people with a wide range of knowledge and skills. What are the competencies – the combination of knowledge, attitudes and skills – which we need to develop in the public health workforce? Are there enough people being trained? Do we have the right range of expertise?

In this chapter, the authors address the question of capacity and capability in the public health workforce. The chapter aims to help public health workers and trainers from all disciplines and professional backgrounds to see themselves as part of a wider workforce, with responsibilities continuously to develop their skills and knowledge, and to apply them in new situations, often in multidisciplinary teams.

The authors first review the scope of the public health workforce, identifying different levels of skills and expertise, and some barriers to collaborative working within and across these levels. They discuss the range of public health skills and competencies and highlight the issue of multidisciplinary practice. They argue that a mapping exercise, matching the National Standards skills and competencies with existing professional skills and expertise, would provide a useful baseline from which to assess the existing public health workforce and future training needs.

The chapter moves on to review the concept of the 'professional project' in public health. Particular challenges are identified and discussed, including issues of multidisciplinary working, challenging the dominance of health professions, using the evidence base for public health, and issues about integrating and financing training in public health.

The authors argue that the important progression to make is to a true multidisciplinary public health where contributions from the range of professional groups are recognized and valued.

The chapter concludes with a case study focused on asylum seekers to illustrate the range of professional groups who can potentially contribute to the health and well-being of this marginalized group of people with complex needs.

## Introduction

Public health concerns the development of the full potential for health and welfare of the whole population. Public health priorities will obviously differ depending on the state of development of the society. For example, developing countries may prioritize infectious disease surveillance and control, whereas developed countries may prioritize the prevention and treatment of chronic conditions. Public health depends on the capacity and capability of a large workforce, employed in a variety of roles and organizations, to protect and promote the population's health in a range of contexts and environments and throughout the life cycle. The potential workforce for public health is huge, spanning not just health but also education, social care, environmental health, housing, transport and voluntary sector staff. This leads to many complexities when trying to develop capacity and capability in public health.

This chapter first reviews the scope of this public health workforce, identifying different levels of skills and expertise, and some of the barriers to collaborative working within and across these levels. The range of public health skills and competencies is then discussed, and the issue of multidisciplinary practice is highlighted. The concept of the professional project is then reviewed and related to developments in public health practice. Particular challenges are identified and discussed, and the potential for developing capacity and capability in different ways is illustrated using examples of good practice.

## The public health workforce

The following discussion refers to the UK. While some features are specific to the UK, many more are representative of developed countries in general. The British government clearly recognizes that people from a range of backgrounds and at all levels of seniority contribute to the public health workforce (Department of Health 2001b). The Chief Medical Officer's *Project to Strengthen the Public Health Function* (Department of Health 2001b) identifies three different levels of involvement in public health.

- Specialists from a variety of professional backgrounds, with the ability to manage strategic change and lead public health initiatives. These include consultants in public health medicine, directors of public health, leads in public health and health promotion and environmental health officers.

- Practitioners who spend a substantial part of their working time furthering health by working with communities and groups. These include public health nurses, community nurses, community and youth workers, and health promotion specialists.

- Professionals whose work includes elements of public health and who would benefit from a better understanding of public health. These include social workers, teachers, police officers and voluntary sector workers.

This framework is important because it acknowledges theoretical views of the broad determinants of public health, for example the importance of social capital for public health (Popay 2001; Duggan 2002), and hence the potential of a wide variety of professionals to promote public health. It is helpful to consider public health in three domains, such as health improvement, health protection, and health and social care quality (Griffiths *et al.* 2003) to ensure that the breadth of public health skills are both recognized and valued, and that their development is supported.

## Challenges

However, this 'three levels' framework also presents many practical challenges. Not all these players necessarily see themselves as having a public health function, and the range of professional and disciplinary backgrounds is immense. Whether the multidisciplinary public health banner is sufficient to weld a commonality of purpose among these diverse groups is questionable. Adequate funding for public health training and accreditation, and a supportive policy context which recognizes the multidisciplinary roots of public health, are key prerequisites if a unifying public health purpose and function is to evolve. An increased understanding of the different contributions that different disciplines and areas of work contribute to the public health function will support its integration and enhancement. The delivery of *Choosing Health* (Department of Health 2004a) and the fully engaged scenario envisaged by Wanless (Wanless 2002) requires the whole workforce to have an understanding of, and an involvement in, key public health issues. This ambitious undertaking is being attempted through the establishment of regional Public Health Teaching Networks which are discussed later.

A separate challenge is the historical dominance of public health medicine in the field of public health and the problems this poses for true multidisciplinary practice (McPherson and Fox 1997). The picture is complicated due to the relative weakness of public health medicine within medical specialties, which leads to a defensiveness and policing of the boundaries of public health medicine in an effort to assert identity and retain autonomy (Lewis 1991). Sociologists term this process 'professional closure' – an attempt to close ranks, limit the number of people admitted to the profession, and thus retain a protected monopoly provider position which is more likely to be well rewarded both financially and in terms of power and kudos (Freidson 1986; Annandale 1998). One could argue that the introduction of the voluntary register for public health practitioners, which follows closely the traditional curriculum of medical public health specialists (Faculty of Public Health Medicine 2002), also demonstrates an attempt at professional closure, as predicted by sociologists. However in practice the range of professionals and the commitment to supporting the process within the field may highlight the benefits for more comprehensive professional development of a portfolio approach to public health education and training. The movement towards sustainability does also provide a real opportunity to gain maximum benefit from, and enhance a multidisciplinary approach to, public health. This is mainly due to the broadening of the term sustainability from the early concepts derived from the 1987 Brundtland Report (World Commission on Environment and Development, 1987), where sustainable development is defined as development that meets 'the needs of the present generation without compromising the ability of future generations to meet their needs' and focused on three pillars of environmental protection, economic growth and social equity, which were subsequently built on at the World Summit on Sustainable Development (WSSD), which took place in Johannesburg on 26 August to 4 September 2002.

Public health and a range of other professions are associated with a specific and broad-ranging skills mix which includes considerable areas of overlap. For example, teachers have educational skills; community workers have community development skills; public health nurses have needs assessment skills; environmental health officers have risk assessment and management skills, and so on. Rather than re-inventing these skills anew, public health should draw upon existing expertise, including professional training and accreditation schemes as well as accredited specialists, for instance in health promotion or environmental health. This is not only desirable, but essential given the lack of specialist public health capacity and capability on the ground (Singleton and Aird 2002).

Commentators have also identified the crucial need for developing a more flexible skills mix among existing NHS staff in order to deliver quality care and the targets for staffing (Buchan 2002). Buchan comments that the introduction of new roles and skill mix will pose the most challenging test for the human resources agenda, and the priority should be on developing the skills of existing staff rather than introducing new types of workers. However, *Choosing Health* (Department of Health 2004a) focused on the role of working with individuals to help them adopt healthier lifestyles and identified health trainers as a new type of public health practitioner, with skills and experience in helping to change behaviours. All spearhead PCTs recruited health trainers by April 2006 and the programme will be extended to all PCTs in April 2007. The challenge for health trainers will be the level of support they receive, how well they integrate into and complement a multidisciplinary public health workforce, and how effective they are in providing a sustainable long-term benefit to their local communities.

## Public health skills and competencies

There is a growing consensus as to what constitutes public health skills and competencies, and how they should be assessed. The ten key areas for specialist public health practice are:

- surveillance and assessment of the population's health and well-being;
- promoting and protecting the population's health and well-being;
- developing quality and risk management within an evaluative culture;
- collaborative working for health and well-being;
- developing health programmes and services and reducing inequalities;
- policy and strategy development and implementation to improve health and well-being;
- working with and for communities to improve health and well-being;
- strategic leadership for health and well-being;

- research and development to improve health and well-being; and
- ethically managing self, people and resources to improve health and well-being.

## Voluntary Register information – acting as a catalyst for public health specialist training

The UK Voluntary Register for Public Health Specialists (UKVRPHS) was established in 2003 with the aim of promoting confidence in specialist public health practice in the UK through independent regulation (McEwen 2006). Evidence needs to be presented against each sub-area for all of the ten key areas and demonstrated in two ways: acquisition of and knowing how to apply knowledge ('knows and knows how'), and practical application of knowledge ('shows how').

The three routes to full registration are: (1) the standard route, (2) dual registration and (3) retrospective portfolio assessment. From June 2003 the Register accepted applications for the Specialist Register for those working across the ten key areas of public health, these people being recognized as 'generalists'. From 2006 the register also accepts retrospective portfolios for assessment for 'defined specialists'. Defined specialists are competent in all ten key areas and have expertise in some specific areas. The two arms of the register (generalist and defined specialists) are of equivalent status (www.publichealthregister.org.uk).

The public health workforce also needs to be sustainable and build on expertise in different and complementary areas. In this way, the workforce as a whole will have the required expertise in diverse areas without swamping any one profession with too many demands for excellence in disparate spheres.

## Public health training needs

A mapping exercise, matching the National Standards skills and competencies with existing professional skills and expertise, would provide a useful baseline from which to assess the existing public health workforce and future training needs. Training needs may be 'top–up' programmes reinforcing potential public health roles and expertise of existing professionals as well as initial training programmes for new staff. For example, this process of targeted educational enhancement may be particularly important for those professionals who have applied unsuccessfully for director of public health posts in primary care trusts. The important progression to make is to a true multidisciplinary public health, where contributions from the range of professional groups are recognized and valued. If this does not happen in a proactive and productive way, it is unlikely that we will come near developing the capacity and capability in public health that the Chief Medical Officer drew attention to in his report (Department of Health 2001b).

The emphasis on and commitment to 'joined-up working' is analysed in other parts of this book (see Chapter 4). The assumption, however, that groups can and will work across professional and organizational boundaries is not necessarily borne out in practice. Interprofessional education and training can help to instigate and facilitate partnership working (Centre for the Advancement of Interprofessional Education

1997). Skilful management and expertise in multidisciplinary education in public health is needed to ensure that the needs of professionals who are anxious to forge their own identity and not keen to be assimilated in one agenda are addressed appropriately. It could be argued that there are certain areas of focus within public health which act as real vehicles to enable professions to work together and to cross boundaries, for example social capital, neighbourhood renewal, sustainable development and building healthy communities. There are also cross-cutting themes that have not been appropriated by any one profession, for example sustainability and health inequalities, which could be used to facilitate multidisciplinary work in public health.

## The public health professional project

Larson (1977) discusses the concept of the 'professional project', which is useful when thinking about public health practice. Key aspects of the professional project are about acquiring a monopoly in valued areas of expertise. This monopoly is supported by specific training that restricts the number of practitioners and certifies a certain level of competence; this, in turn, is recognized and supported by the state. Foucault (1979) uses the concept of 'governmentality' to encompass all those procedures, techniques, mechanisms, institutions and areas of knowledge – including professions – that empower political programmes. Foucault therefore emphasizes the fluidity of the professional project, which is constantly being renegotiated within a political and technological context.

The professional project is a fairly accurate description of public health specialists. For capacity and capability in public health to develop in an effective multidisciplinary manner, some aspects of the professional project, such as state recognition and support and certified training and education, need to also apply to practitioners and the wider workforce. The public health professional project is widening, ensuring that public health will not remain a beleaguered medical specialty. Its potential as a multidisciplinary resource and activity enhancing the public health in its broadest sense is increasingly being fulfilled. A key question for practitioners and the wider workforce is whether the identity of being a public health professional, or engaging in the public health professional project, will complement or challenge existing professional identities and what changes it would bring in terms of status and income. This in turn will impact on the ability to generate genuine multidisciplinary working in the interests of the public health.

## Issues of multidisciplinary working

The Department of Health (2001f) in *Research and Development Strategy for Public Health* recognizes the central importance of partnership, participation of all stakeholders and the plurality of approach in public health. While the policy context appears to be supportive, practical difficulties abound. These include developing effective communication, establishing genuine teams and teamwork, escaping the dominance of public health medicine, practising evidence-based public health, and the provision of appropriate training and education.

Communication across professional groups and different sectors can be problematic. There is a range of different jargon with no unifying means of communication. There is a need for communication which understands and respects contributors' unique positions and strengths and builds on these. To facilitate this process, interprofessional education and training in public health is essential, as well as multidisciplinary forums on public health where practitioners can learn together and develop a common means of communicating. Innovative approaches to multidisciplinary training could include the use of 'real world' scenarios as exemplified by the case study focused on asylum seekers later in this chapter.

Genuine teamwork seeks to develop and utilize partners' specific skills and expertise, recognizing the value of practitioners at different levels, in different organizations and agencies, with different remits and priorities, as well as the collaborative advantage that can be gained through working together. This requires practitioners to be confident in their identity and expertise, and to feel supported by their own employing organization. One practical way of demonstrating confidence and commitment is for employers to support staff training in public health.

Teamwork is essential because public health skills and competencies cover such a broad area that it is unrealistic to expect any one person to be expert in all fields – indeed, it would be quite a challenge to have a team which encompassed all these skills within its membership. Arguably, the key public health skills are those of facilitation, leadership and partnership – skills that serve to combine expertise and resources for public health goals. Innovative ways of spreading expertise and resources are needed. One example of this is the development in England of public health networks spanning several primary care trusts which 'By pooling resource, particularly specialist skills, . . . could help to provide the capacity needed for effective public health, which a single Primary Care Trust could not' (Shaw and Abbot 2002: 29).

A key theme in the English White Paper *Our Health, Our Care, Our Say: A New Direction for Community Services* (Department of Health 2006d) is that there must be much better integration between the workforces in health and in social care and that to encourage integration 'we will bring skill development frameworks together and create career pathways across health and social care' (Department of Health 2006d: 5). One initiative which may help this development is the establishment of regional Public Health Teaching Networks across England which will link educational institutions and service departments more closely. The aim will be to maximize the skills and resources available to teach public health and to ensure that all relevant workforce groups are exposed to public health learning as part of their pre- and post-qualification training and continuing professional development (Dunkley and Rao 2006).

There is now an extensive database of research and evidence about effective public health interventions (National Institute for Health and Clinical Excellence 2006). This evidence base can effectively guide the work of a wide range of practitioners, not only those whose work directly impacts on health, such as doctors, nurses, health visitors and environmental health officers, but also those who make an indirect impact, such as housing officers, architects, environmental engineers, teachers, and police, probation, fire and prison officers (Department of Health 2001b). However, in the UK the ability to use this evidence in practice to improve health is much less well developed than the ability to collect good quality evidence (Nutbeam 2002). While research and evaluation skills are important to determine whether evidence exists and how sound it is, the priority now is to take effective action to protect and promote the public health.

Effective action depends on an understanding of the socio-economic and political context of policy, and an overt and transparent ethical and value base. It is important to recognize the catalytic work of the National Institute for Health and Clinical Excellence (NICE) in England, both at a national policy level and at a regional and local level. NICE produces guidance in three areas of health (NICE 2005):

- public health – guidance on the promotion of good health and the prevention of ill health for those working in the NHS, local authorities and the wider public and voluntary sector;
- health technologies – guidance on the use of new and existing medicines, treatments and procedures within the NHS; and
- clinical practice – guidance on the appropriate treatment and care of people with specific diseases and conditions within the NHS.

The provision of appropriate training and education requires not just relevant curricula and programmes, but also financing and resourcing so that relevant personnel are able to undertake opportunities for further training and education in public health.

On the point of training provision, public health does not currently fit into the existing curricula of most professions. There is an urgent need for training needs analysis to be undertaken for all professionals who contribute to public health. The potential for integration of some aspects of their training can then be explored so that common ground can be secured in relevant areas of their work. This could involve environmental health officers, health promotion specialists, community nurses, community development workers and general practitioners. The provision of recently developed postgraduate programmes in public health that are underpinned by inter-professional educational approaches means that these students are more likely to establish important common ground.

With regard to financing and resourcing, there are gaps in all areas nationally, although there are also examples of good practice demonstrating the way forward. Funding streams for public health education and training are not clearly identified at present. The role of Managed Public Health Networks could be to undertake a skills audit and subsequently work with Workforce Development Confederations to co-ordinate appropriate access to training opportunities and to ensure these opportunities meet identified needs. This would need to be supported by a funded development programme, agreed with Workforce Development Confederations and linked with academic institutions, to fill gaps in capability and capacity in public health (Faculty of Public Health Medicine 2002). As already mentioned, regional Public Health Teaching Networks in England may enhance capacity and capability through their scoping and co-ordination function. The government's commitment to building capacity and capability in the field is welcomed; funding this does, however, need to be supported.

Primary care trusts are starting to respond to the need for continuing professional development in public health by linking with relevant education providers. Funding streams for local authority professionals such as environmental health officers are not clearly identified, and continuing professional development is often supported on an individual basis with no co-ordination in the field.

It is necessary to look at the ability of providers to deliver the range of education and training to facilitate necessary capacity and capability. It is also necessary to decide at what level – local, regional or national – to assess training needs in order to skill up the workforce. The process needs to operate at all levels in a synergistic way without duplication.

## Conclusion

If the full potential of public health is to be achieved, capacity and capability in public health needs to extend beyond its current narrow medical and health boundaries to embrace a wide range of different professionals and activities. This broadening-out process depends on several different, mutually supportive factors, including a diverse workforce which recognizes and embraces its public health role, appropriate training and education opportunities, and a supportive political and policy context which encourages a broad perspective on public health.

The central task is to recognize existing competencies and expertise as public health skills, not to attempt to build up capacity and capability from nothing. Abundant public health skills and competencies exist already, ranging from community development workers and social workers to public health and community nurses to voluntary sector workers and beyond. What is needed is a vision and purpose which binds such diverse workers together in a common public health agenda.

To some extent this is being provided by the policy context, which recognizes varying levels of public health skills and competencies, a broad public health workforce, and the need to go beyond public health medicine. However, this public recognition needs to be backed up by practical support for multidisciplinary training and education in order to deliver a broad public health identity and commitment, and mechanisms to encourage collaborative working for public health.

The concept of the professional project enables identification of key aspects of this process – effective communication to facilitate collaboration and teamwork, evidence-based practice to inspire trust and confidence in the public health enterprise, and appropriate recognized training and education opportunities for public health staff at all levels and in different roles. It is possible to chart progress in all these areas, although scope for further development still exists.

People and action skills are high on different professional agendas, and health promoters in particular are skilled at bringing people and agencies together to work collaboratively. This range of contributory skills and specialisms are vital to the furtherance of public health and this needs to be acknowledged instead of being ignored. Thus it is only by recognizing the vision and skills encompassed by this range of different contributory professions that public health can become an effective force for change and positive health.

## Case study: asylum seekers

## The needs of asylum seekers

The following case study, focused on asylum seekers seeking refuge in the UK, has been developed to illustrate the range of professional groups who can potentially contribute to the health and well-being of this marginalized group of people with complex needs.

Although asylum seekers are not a homogeneous group, they are likely to share a range of public health needs associated with their experiences of migration. Being a marginalized group they may be exposed to a range of health problems associated with social deprivation and social exclusion. However, they may also experience the following problems specific to their asylum seeker status. They may suffer a number of physical health problems associated with their exposure to atrocities in their country of origin and during their journey to the UK. This may include physical injury from the effects of war or trauma associated with torture and rape. In addition, asylum seekers experience high levels of stress and depression associated with the experience of uncertainty, separation from family members and cultural bereavement. For some, these mental health problems will be compounded by psychological trauma associated with witnessing the destruction of their own homes, the ill-treatment of family members or the psychological after-effects of torture and rape.

Asylum seekers include families, single adults (predominantly young single males) and unaccompanied children; their health needs are likely to be affected by their age, gender and family composition. Some of the complex range of public health needs likely to be experienced by asylum seekers are identified below.

### The need for security, shelter and safety

Asylum seekers who depend on state support are required to accept the accommodation offered to them or lose their benefits. Housing arranged through the National Asylum Support Service (NASS) is allocated on a 'no choice' basis to disperse asylum seekers away from London and the South-east. In order that this process does not impact upon council taxpayers or social housing waiting lists, the properties used tend to be located in deprived areas (Anie *et al.* 2005) and classified as 'difficult to let' (Wellard 2003). Many asylum seekers are housed in substandard or unsuitable accommodation. In a recent report on the living conditions of asylum seekers in London, many cited examples of vermin infestation, poor furnishing, inadequate heating and damp (Ramadan 2006). Some accommodation was described as dangerous with, for example, water from a leaking roof flooding a room and seeping dangerously close to electricity cables. Disabled asylum seekers report being dispersed to unsuitable accommodation resulting in social isolation because of access difficulties (Roberts and Harris 2002) and problems with personal care needs because of inadequate bathroom facilities (Ramadan 2006). A further problem relates to inappropriate attitudes of some housing staff with incidents of rudeness, disrespect and intrusion of privacy being reported by Ramadan (2006).

Asylum seekers report feeling unsafe (Ramadan 2006) with many experiencing hostility and abuse from some members of the public and racially motivated attacks have been reported in a number of areas within the UK (Wong and Butler 2000; Anie *et al.* 2005). Asylum seekers need information on areas and situations that may expose them to increased risk, in addition to advice on how to optimize their personal safety.

Mechanisms to enable asylum seekers to report the experience of crime are also required because of language barriers, lack of familiarity with UK procedures and 'concern that their involvement with police may affect their claim for asylum' (Wong and Butler 2000).

Current legislation restricts asylum seekers from accessing employment within the UK (Refugee Council 2006a). Asylum seekers who were granted a work permit under previous legislation or those whose claim remains outstanding after 12 months can work but difficulties arise through lack of recognition of professional qualifications (Lynch and Cuninghame 2000) or barriers to obtaining verification from an asylum seeker's home country (D'Cruze 2000). Employment restrictions mean that many asylum seekers are dependent upon the state for financial support. Although children are eligible for benefits at the full income support rate, adults receive only 70 per cent of income support benefit.

An increasing number of asylum seekers face destitution because of administrative errors made during the asylum application process, legal aid restrictions and delays or gaps in the provision of support services (Marsden *et al.* 2005; Morrell and Wainwright 2006). Such problems can threaten the security, shelter and safety of asylum seekers who may be rendered homeless and vulnerable to abuse. They are also likely to experience extreme poverty resulting in hunger, deterioration in physical and mental health and potential exploitation from unscrupulous employers.

### The need for community and social support

The practice of dispersal means that asylum seekers may not have access to the support of friends and family members resident in the UK or community groups who share a similar culture. Although the original intentions of NASS was to disperse asylum seekers according to their cultural and social needs, the process is now predominantly driven by the availability of housing (Refugee Council 2006b).

### The need for access to a range of services

Asylum seekers need access to a range of primary and secondary health care services because of their complex physical and mental health needs. They need an empathetic response with services provided by staff who have received adequate training to enable them to understand the perspective of the asylum seeker and the traumatic experiences that they may have encountered.

Although asylum seekers are entitled to the full range of NHS services in the same way as any other UK resident, in reality they experience a number of barriers to access. Within the UK general practitioners are gatekeepers to most NHS services and therefore entitlement is dependent upon registration with a GP practice. General practitioners are free to decide which patients they will accept onto their lists and, according to Vernon and Feldman (2006), many asylum seekers experience difficulty registering with a general practitioner.

Possible reasons for this are identified as language difficulties resulting in lengthy consultations (Jones and Gill 1998); a reputation for high mobility (Jones and Gill

1998); and the potential for asylum seekers to affect practice payments if they refuse vaccinations or cervical cytology screening (Department of Health 2000b). Many asylum seekers have no option but to accept temporary registration which limits their access to routine preventive health services and means that the general practitioner has no access to NHS past records.

Once registered with a general practitioner, asylum seekers are entitled to access NHS services although they are not automatically entitled to free NHS prescriptions, dental or eye care. In order to receive these services they need an HC2 certificate and, whereas asylum seekers supported by NASS receive this certificate automatically, those not in receipt of NASS support are required to complete an HC1 form which is 16 pages long and only available in English.

An additional barrier relates to lack of information on the part of asylum seekers and professionals regarding entitlement to NHS and other services. Many asylum seekers are not familiar with the UK model of health service provision (Vernon and Feldman 2006). Martell and Murray (2001) and Hampshire (2001) highlight the problem that asylum seekers may have no concept of a general practitioner or practice nurse because for many, primary care does not exist in their country of origin.

Language barriers mean that asylum seekers need access to quality interpreting services. This may be provided through 'hands free' technology or through face-to-face interpreters. Family or community members are sometimes used as interpreters but this may be inappropriate and can create problems in respect of confidentiality.

All children, whether unaccompanied or part of an asylum-seeking family, have the right to access education (Refugee Council 2006c) but evidence suggests that not all children receive an immediate school place (Lynch and Cuninghame 2000). In addition, schools may not have adequate resources to meet the language needs of children for whom English is a second language (Lynch and Cuninghame 2000). An additional difficulty that may be experienced by asylum-seeking children is that of integration within UK schools. Difficulty can arise as a result of language barriers, racial hostility, bullying (Hampshire 2001; Free 2005), and unresolved stress associated with the experience of trauma, loss and grief (Wong and Butler 2000).

## Strategies to meet the needs of asylum seekers

The needs of asylum seekers are diverse and broad ranging, and a comprehensive range of strategies is required to address these needs. The role of public health specialists, practitioners and the wider public health workforce in meeting asylum seekers' needs is set out in Figure 5.1.

Next, the applicability of the national standards for specialist public health in helping to develop an integrated strategy is considered. The ten key areas identified in the national standards for specialist public health practice (discussed earlier in this chapter) are all applicable to meeting the needs of asylum seekers. An example is presented for each of the ten standards to illustrate their relevance in practice.

It is also possible to map the ten standards across the three levels of involvement in public health; this may be a helpful exercise in assessing public health educational and training needs.

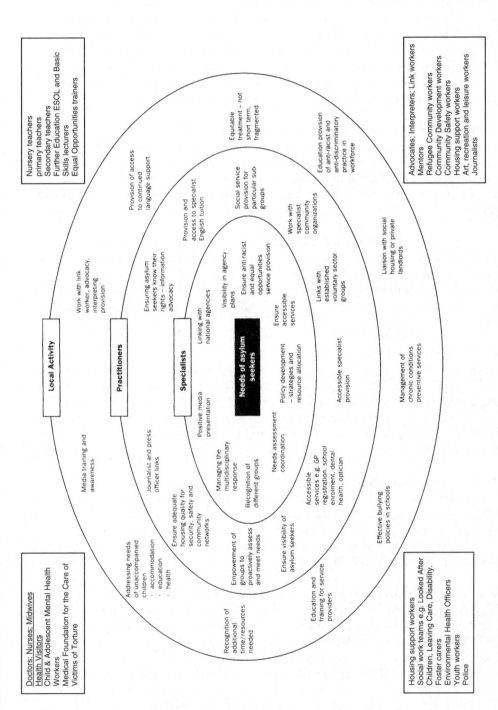

**Figure 5.1** The role of public health specialists, practitioners and the wider public health workforce in meeting the needs of asylum seekers

Doctors: Nurses; Midwives
Health Visitors
Child & Adolescent Mental Health Workers
Medical Foundation for the Care of Victims of Torture

Nursery teachers
primary teachers
Secondary teachers
Further Education ESOL and Basic Skills lecturers
Equal Opportunities trainers

Advocates; Interpreters; Link workers
Mentors
Refugee Community workers
Community Development workers
Community Safety workers
Housing support workers
Art, recreation and leisure workers
Journalists

Housing support workers
Social work teams e.g. Looked After Children, Leaving Care, Disability.
Foster carers
Environmental Health Officers
Youth workers
Police

**Local Activity**

**Practitioners**

**Specialists**

**Needs of asylum seekers**

Media training and awareness

Work with link worker, advocacy, interpreting provision

Provision of access to continued language support

Equitable treatment – not short term, fragmented

Journalist and press officer links

Ensuring asylum seekers know their rights – information advocacy

Provision and access to specialist English tuition

Social service provision for particular sub-groups

Education provision of anti-racist and anti-discriminatory practice in workforce

Addressing needs of unaccompanied children
· accommodation
· education
· health

Ensure adequate housing quality for security, safety and community networks

Positive media presentation

Managing the multidisciplinary response

Linking with national agencies

Visibility in agency plans

Ensure anti-racist and equal opportunities service provision

Work with specialist community organizations

Ensure accessible services

Links with established voluntary sector groups

Liaison with social housing or private landlords

Empowerment of groups to proactively assess and meet needs

Recognition of different groups

Needs assessment coordination

Policy development – strategies and resource allocation

Accessible specialist provision

Ensure visibility of asylum seekers

Accessible services e.g. GP registration, school enrolment, dental health, optician

Management of chronic conditions preventive services

Recognition of additional time/resources needed

Education and training for service providers

Effective bullying policies in schools

### Surveillance and assessment of the population's health and well-being
In addition to visible and easily recognized health needs such as respiratory or gastro-intestinal illnesses, asylum seekers may have hidden health problems. For example, they may have experienced torture leading to enduring mental health problems and/or ongoing depression due to loss of family, home, work and community. Health needs assessment in these cases would need to be sensitive and may well require specialist input, a longer time-scale and additional resources.

### Promoting and protecting the public health and well-being
Asylum seekers, especially children, may not be up-to-date with UK immunization programmes. The fact that they are often registered as temporary residents with general practices may result in fragmented service provision, and lack of continuity in record keeping may mean future immunizations and preventive programmes are missed.

### Developing quality and risk management within an evaluative culture
Research documenting health needs of asylum seekers exists in a variety of formats including academic journals and anecdotal accounts. National agencies such as the Audit Commission, and voluntary organizations such as The Refugee Council or Asylum Aid, provide literature reviews and policy recommendations based on these.

### Collaborative working
Statutory services are often inaccessible to asylum seekers, and one of the main barriers is language. Working collaboratively with link worker, advocacy and interpreting providers is an essential component in ensuring that asylum seekers have access to the full range of health, education, housing and social services to which they are entitled. High quality face-to-face interpreting and advocacy services should be prioritized.

### Developing services and programmes and reducing inequalities
Asylum seekers are likely to be a small group within the local population, but one with a high level of health needs. In developing public health programmes and services for this marginalized group, care needs to be taken to ensure the process is transparent and equitable. National guidelines and resources may provide useful additional support for developing specific services.

### Policy and strategy development and implementation
To date, asylum seekers are entitled to reduced levels of income support which will inevitably result in high levels of poverty. Increasing numbers face destitution. The links between poverty and ill health are well established. One proven avenue to improving health is to reduce poverty, which can be tackled at local and national levels. In addition to lobbying for adequate income levels, supportive strategies such as benefits advisers, interpreters and legal representatives are needed to ensure asylum seekers receive all the benefits to which they are entitled.

### Working with and for communities
Asylum seekers bring a wealth of skills and expertise to their newly established communities. Facilitating and empowering these communities to work in partnership with statutory agencies to address community needs brings benefits to everyone. User involvement in agencies helps to ensure appropriate service provision and maximum uptake.

### Strategic leadership
Strategic leadership includes working towards positive media representation of asylum seekers and their contribution to the community. Asylum seekers should not be represented as a specific isolated group who make demands on services but rather as a marginalized group who share features with other excluded groups. By meeting their needs, services are improved for everyone. Proactive press releases and fostering a good working relationship with the local media are important strategies.

### Research and development
Asylum seekers are subject to many social factors which will impact negatively on their health, for example poor housing, discrimination, low income and poor access to services. Research can help to identify which strategies are most effective in tackling these factors and promoting health. Research needs to be sensitive, ethical and take into account the possible risk of over-researching this vulnerable group.

### Ethically managing self, people and resources (including education and continuing professional development)
Good communication is central to effective management. This is particularly important within a multidisciplinary team where different agencies and professions use different terminologies within their areas of expertise. It is therefore vital to ensure that all forms of written and verbal communication have minimum jargon and are understood by all. Good communication with user representatives is also essential. This is especially relevant for asylum seekers who may not speak English, for whom interpreting and translation services need to be provided and costed.

An understanding of the diverse needs of asylum seekers, including an appreciation of the cultural and political contexts which influence their beliefs and regulate their lives is required in order to respond empathetically and provide appropriate services. Those involved in public health provision have a responsibility to take advantage of educational and continuous professional development initiatives in order to ensure that they have relevant knowledge, skills and attitudes to provide culturally sensitive and equitable services.

---

Suggested further reading

Evans, D. (2005) Shifting the balance of power? UK public health policy and capacity building, *Critical Public Health*, 14: 51–63.

Barrett, G., Sellman, D. and Thomas, J. (2005) *Interprofessional Working in Health and Social Care. Professional Perspectives.* Basingstoke: Palgrave Macmillan.

# 6

## PAT TAYLOR
## The lay contribution to public health

**Editors' introduction**

The public are no longer seen as passive recipients of paternalistic professional efforts to improve their health. Rather, they are active participants in plans and programmes which aim to improve their health and well-being, drawing on the resources of their own perspectives, experience and knowledge. The 'public' – lay people – are key partners in contemporary public health and lay involvement is expected at all levels of current public health activity.

This chapter will be useful for all public health workers as it examines the contribution of lay perspectives to public health, addressing questions of why and how lay people can and should be involved in public health practice.

The author starts by considering current policy for public involvement in the overall historical context of lay involvement in the NHS. She identifies that most of the policy for public involvement concentrates on patient involvement in health *services* rather than on the wider arena of public health. She then considers why lay perspectives are important to public health and shows the place of lay perspectives and lay action in the development of health services and public health action in the UK.

The chapter outlines the nature of lay perspectives on health and demonstrates that they are a different and unique contribution to multidisciplinary public health. But there are significant difficulties in accessing and articulating lay views in the face of the dominance of the biomedical model in any public discussion on health. Medical perspectives on lay involvement are examined and key obstacles in health professional approaches to public involvement are discussed.

The author concludes by looking at ways of promoting an effective lay contribution to public health. She identifies four approaches and four levels to lay involvement and shows that the connections between them need to be understood by those responsible for developing lay involvement. Public health particularly requires strong links to local and informal networks within communities and local populations, in order to establish the full contribution of lay involvement.

## Introduction

Today we need a new outlook. An approach that accepts that there are wide determinants of ill health – and a wide ranging programme of action is necessary and indeed is underway to deal with them . . . an approach which also understands that the NHS can make a specific contribution to improving health prospects by working with the communities it serves: making the task of tackling health inequality something done with local people not just done to them.

(Milburn 2002)

The quote above highlights a significant change in the way the public are being perceived in government policy – no longer as passive receivers of expert health care but as active participants in the processes of health improvement. How realistic is this aspiration in practice? How has the rhetoric of policy actually opened up opportunities for lay people to articulate and influence the agendas for health improvement and health service development?

## Structure of this chapter

The chapter starts by considering why lay involvement is important to public health and the changing nature of public involvement in public services. In the brief resume of public health history in Chapter 1 there is clear evidence that lay people have played many different roles in health improvements as community activists, politicians and members of trade unions. This chapter gives a brief resume of the history of lay involvement in the NHS from the inception of the NHS in 1948. It then outlines lay perspectives in health and demonstrates that there is a different and unique contribution that lay perspectives bring to a multidisciplinary public health. A discussion of medical perspectives on lay involvement follows.

The chapter concludes with a section on promoting an effective lay contribution to public health. It identifies four approaches and four levels of public involvement and further shows that there are key practical, attitudinal and conceptual obstacles to promoting an effective lay contribution to multidisciplinary public health. It considers some of the conceptual leaps needed for public health to ensure that it accesses a vibrant and rich vein of lay input to inform its future development.

## What is lay involvement and why is it important to public health?

The term 'lay' needs to be defined in relation to something else, for example, lay people as opposed to professionals. Other terms such as the public, service user, patient can often be used to mean lay involvement in relation to a specific service or organization. Frankel *et al.* (1991) define lay or popular understanding of health as 'the process by which a person interprets health risk through routine observation and discussion of illness and death in personal networks and in the public arena as well as from formal and informal sources such as television and magazines' (Frankel *et al.* 1991).

The lay perspective is a crucial area of knowledge for public health. Listening to, and understanding, lay people's experience of their health, ill health and how it is affected by their daily lives can:

- give insight into patterns of behaviour and lifestyles which can identify new areas for investigation in relation to mortality and disease;
- help us to understand factors which underpin and create health inequalities;
- suggest new factors which influence people's health and their ability to use existing resources;
- help us to understand how people live and manage their lives in different circumstances, which is crucial to understanding how information and support can be most effectively offered;
- encourage people's interest and achieve their active involvement in maintaining their health; and
- create continuing mechanisms for dialogue and debate and for successfully implementing and monitoring programmes of health improvement with the ownership of the people they aim to help.

This can only be done by in-depth engagement and ongoing dialogue with people within the context of their everyday lives.

## Lay involvement and public health action

In Chapter 1 we distinguish between public health action and public health resources. Public health action refers to the wider activities in society that can promote health and well-being and can include the activities of organizations, groups, communities and individuals who may not necessarily perceive themselves as being primarily involved in health. It is this concept of public health action that underpins the drive for partnership working and is the starting point for understanding the lay contribution to public health. The development of public health action may influence and alter the nature of public health resources. Lay perspectives may eventually be seen as a form of public health expertise; this has happened within health services where patients with long-term chronic illness have now better established their right to have their experience of managing their illness equally valued. The Expert Patient Programme has been set up by the government to give patients and carers an opportunity to understand more about their medical condition and the services and resources available to support them, as well as recognizing their own skills in managing their own health (Department of Health 2001e).

## The changing nature of public involvement in the NHS

### Four eras of public involvement

Public or lay involvement in the NHS can be understood within two models.

- *The democratic model* which sees involvement in relation to people as citizens with rights to receive public services and responsibilities to be involved in their development and accountability.

- *The consumerist model* in which the relationship is between the lay person and a particular service or organization.

As lay involvement has developed in the NHS there has been a merging of aspects of both models.

Milewa *et al.* (2002) have reviewed the changing nature of public involvement in the NHS since the inception of the health service in 1948. They identify four distinct periods: pre-1974, 1974–90, 1990–97 and post-1997.

### Prior to 1974: democratic accountability in local authorities

The NHS had public representatives throughout its structures. Some were the elected members from the municipal authorities in which local NHS services were provided and others were appointed as lay members on hospital boards and committees.

The medical officer of health and other public health specialists such as environmental health officers, health visitors and social workers were outside the NHS structure, working with local politicians and the local democratic processes within the local authority to address the wider health needs of local populations.

### 1974–90: Community Health Councils in health authorities

In 1974 medical officers of health and community nurses left their local authority colleagues to enter the NHS. The role of the medical officer of health as an influential, but independent figure within the local authority able to identify key local health concerns was lost. The new directors of public health within health authorities did not have the same sphere of influence or independence.

After 1974 the roles of lay representatives on health committees were reduced. Community health councils (CHCs) were set up within the NHS in 1974 to represent the 'interests of the public', but this was essentially a token gesture to lay representation. The community health councils had a statutory responsibility for aspects of public consultation in relation to health service changes and worked behind the scenes to promote patient interests. The CHCs struggled to gain recognition for their work despite the resurgence of interest in patient and public involvement (Buckland *et al.* 1994) and were eventually abolished in 2002.

In the 1980s the increasing interest in managing the NHS and in using market approaches within public services brought the 'needs' of individual patients back into focus with an emphasis on responsiveness, accessibility and quality. The model of lay involvement in this period was 'patient as consumer', but there was little interest in any other public representation within the wider processes of health care planning and service delivery. One exception to this was the variable development in England of joint planning structures between health and social care. This included health and social care organizations and voluntary organizations. In some areas these structures included service user-led organizations (Challis *et al.* 1988). Milewa *et al.* (2002) assert that this did signal a change in policy from seeing patients as 'passive recipients' to seeing them as more active 'consumers' of health care. It also created an opportunity for groups of health service users to express their views within the different mechanisms created for 'consumer' feedback (McIver 1991; Barnes 1999).

### 1990–97: the Patient's Charter and *Local Voices*

In 1990 the Patient's Charter gave patients some procedural rights in their use of services and in 1992 *Local Voices* (National Health Services Management Executive 1992) was issued as an advisory document to encourage health authorities, who were purchasers of health care on behalf of their local communities, to consult their communities about their health needs. This stimulated a variety of initiatives in local areas, from local community activities, user and self-help groups to more market research methods such as surveys, focus groups and patient panels.

Research undertaken at that time (Lupton and Taylor 1994) indicated significant differences in public involvement activity depending on which part of the health authority took responsibility for it. Managers developing quality assurance tended to favour market-based methods, public relations tended to prioritize information giving, and public health specialists were more inclined to work with local democratic networks and community-based groups. Some commentators (Harrison and Mort 1998) viewed public involvement activity as primarily concerned with legitimizing managerial decisions or curbing professional autonomy. Others also indicated that there had been an increasing degree of service user involvement and influence in service delivery (Pickard 1998; Barnes *et al.* 1999).

### 1997: new Labour

Public and service user involvement remained firmly on the policy agenda with the change of government in 1997 and continues to remain central within all the subsequent health service reforms. This Labour government has built on the foundations developed over the past 12 years by giving central recognition to public and patient involvement in all major policy and modernization initiatives in the NHS.

Changes in primary care were major planks of the modernization agenda from 1998. Primary care groups (PCGs) gave an equal place for a lay representation on management boards alongside clinicians and health service managers. PCGs operating at a local level, meant that in some areas local community activists were able to become involved in a formal NHS structure with local health professionals and able to bring a lay perspective into health service decisions (Taylor *et al.* 2001). PCGs were short-lived and were replaced by Primary Care Trusts (Department of Health 2001e) covering much larger geographical areas in which the separation between clinicians and lay members returned in the creation of a professional executive and board. However, it could be argued that the experience of PCGs, as well as policy requirements, had helped public involvement become better established within trust structures.

In 2002 new structures for patient involvement were created through patient advice and liaison services (PALs) in each PCT and NHS Trust. Patient forums were attached to, but independent of each trust (Department of Health 2001e). At this time local authorities re-established a formal relationship between health and the NHS by being given responsibility to include health within its statutory powers of overview and scrutiny (OSC). The patient forums were intended to act as a co-ordinating mechanism for patient and public involvement activities in each local trust area, including those relating to wider initiatives on health within other agencies and in the community. However, they have not generally lived up to these expectations with many experiencing difficulties in achieving full membership. The forums were originally affiliated to the National Commission for Patient and Public Involvement (Department of Health 2001e). It was intended to act as a national body for their concerns, but was abolished in 2004 in a review of 'arms length' (from the Department of Health) bodies. A recent government consultation document (Department of Health 2006c) is proposing that patient forums are replaced with local involvement networks (LINks) based on local authority areas and have a specific relationship with the overview and scrutiny bodies. It might be argued that the emphasis on public involvement and consultation with the NHS and PCTs has weakened the role of the independent forums, but the variable quality and level of support available to them has also been identified as underpinning their difficulties.

This section has shown that most experience of public involvement in health is related to patients and health services rather than public health. But in the early 21st century, as well as policy relating specifically to health services, there are parallel policy initiatives relevant to the development of lay perspectives in public health. They include the Sure Start programme, Neighbourhood Renewal Strategy and the regeneration programmes. These all include very clear intentions to involve local communities in their programmes and are likely to offer opportunities for lay people to contribute to the health of their communities.

The next section looks specifically at the involvement of lay people in public health, as distinct from the development of health services.

## Lay perspectives in the history of public health

A consideration of the place of lay perspectives within the history of public health may help to develop an understanding of the part they have played in establishing the modern public health knowledge base.

The history of public health identifies different historical periods in which public health consciousness was higher in society in general and viewed as a wider social responsibility. It is in these periods when there have been clear alliances forged between health professionals and lay people. Then there were other periods when public health activity has been confined to specific public health services such as disease surveillance and protection, and the responsibility of experts.

There are two clear traditions which have underpinned lay input into public health action. One is the voluntary and charitable tradition. The other tradition stems from the activities of the organized Labour movement.

### Voluntary and charitable tradition and the Labour movement

The 19th century was characterized by a high level of public health activity with social concerns generated by the growth of cities and the fear of the spread of disease and social unrest. The charitable activities of the rich were not wholly altruistic, but were underpinned by self-interest and moral superiority. Ashton and Seymour (1988) identify the Sanatarians, led by Chadwick, a doctor who worked to persuade municipal authorities and politicians and campaigned for widespread legislation to establish modern standards of clean water and sanitation. The Personal Preventors such as Eleanor Rathbone and Josephine Butler, the founders of modern health visiting, began from a starting point of being voluntary visitors to the poor, and went on to found the tradition of working with families to improve their own life circumstances as well as campaigning for better housing and social conditions. Immunization and child surveillance followed on from these actions. The Rowntree surveys on poverty supported these changes (Owen 1965). Social philanthropists such as Peabody and the Cadbury and Fry families established 'model' housing schemes to demonstrate the importance of decent housing to people's health and well-being.

The Labour movement, with its concern for the working and living conditions of workers, also contributed to public health activity. Working class people had an enduring dislike of charitable activity because of its potential for being patronizing and judgemental and these attitudes still endure within many communities experiencing discrimination and disadvantage. Unions provided their own organizations for holidays, sports and convalescent homes. Organizations such as the Co-operative Societies, the Ramblers and Workers Educational Association were established by the trade unions. The Labour movement also supported mutual aid societies, forerunners of modern building societies, enabling working people to contribute to insurance for essential health care, sickness benefit, funeral costs and early unemployment support (Gladstone 1979; Richardson and Goodman 1983; Brenton 1985). For many older people, growing up before 1945, their first experiences of social and health support might have came from trade unions and mutual aid organizations.

## The welfare state and the NHS

The two world wars were also times of wide social concern for health and social needs. In the First World War there was widespread concern for the health status of recruits to the armed services prompting debates about adequate diet, housing and health services. This provided an opportunity for the trade union movement to be successful in their demands for better social provision for improvements in social conditions and welfare benefits. The social upheavals of the 1930s mass unemployment and the Second World War consolidated these demands and led to the Beveridge Report (Beveridge 1942) and a political commitment to the establishment of the welfare state to tackle the 'five giants' of poverty, disease, ignorance, squalor and idleness.

The establishment of the NHS and other welfare services in 1948 was accompanied by a widespread expectation that many social problems would be solved. This and the success of earlier public health activists and the success of immunizations led to a general complacency about the wider threats to the population's health. Confidence in the power of drugs grew in the public mind as the key solution to all aspects of health.

## Lay action in the 1970s

It was not until the 1960s that it became clear that these expectations were not being fulfilled and a growing body of evidence demonstrated enduring poverty and disadvantage among different groups in the population and in particular geographical areas. During the 1970s there was a resurgence of lay action which took a variety of forms. The voluntary sector resumed its role in highlighting the problems for different groups of people suffering disadvantage and campaigning for improvements and recognition from the public services. New kinds of voluntary and community action grew alongside the traditional voluntary groups founded within the charitable tradition of 'noblesse oblige'. These groups drew their forms of organization more from the traditions of self-help and the Labour movement and were helped by state investment in community development projects (Brenton 1985; Smithies and Webster 1998).

This renewal of voluntary and community action in the 1970s contained within it the beginnings of social movements that would be sustained throughout the following two decades. New social movements such as Women's Rights, Disability Action, Action against Racism, provide some pertinent examples (Barnes and Sullivan 2002). These new forms of lay action had wide ranging influences. They often worked at the level of local authorities and health services, working to improve services and set up new forms of social support. They were influential in taking part in the early interest in service user consultations in the setting up of community care services in the early 1990s (Lindow 1993). They also worked to influence the larger and more well established voluntary organizations to become more responsive to the people they purported to represent and so built up a greater awareness of the need for interest groups to be in touch with their constituencies. Barnes and Sullivan (2002) note that these new lay movements wanted to go further than gaining improved services and support, they wanted to achieve a transformation in social attitudes and understanding towards their members and their experiences emphasizing the importance of service taking a holistic view of people and their lives (the social model of disability) rather than concentrating solely on a particular illness or disability (medical model of disability).

## The early community health movement

The 1970s also saw the beginning of a community health movement with the first community health project being set up in 1977 in London (Smithies and Webster 1998). These projects were often connected to other community activities and developed health-related activities in local communities using community development methods to help local people articulate and take action on health concerns (see examples in Box 6.1).

Individual health professionals did get involved in these projects, but were not often given organizational backing. Overall, community health work remained outside mainstream NHS consciousness. The community projects related instead to other community activities and to local authorities, joining and being supported by the Health for All and Healthy Cities movements.

While the NHS and mainstream health services remained relatively isolated from

---

**Box 6.1** Community perspectives on health

---

**Mental health support groups** – often when local people meet there are shared discussions about people's health problems. This can result in people realizing how many share the same problems of low-level depression and feelings of low self esteem and lack of confidence. From this kind of informal contact people can move to set up self-help groups to provide regular time for sharing concerns and support for people to try to get involved in new activities. These groups may also address the issue of the effects of drugs and help people understand what alternatives are available to them.

**Community swimming sessions** – parents on an inner city estate meet at a parents' evening in the local primary school and raise the issue of activities for their children in the school holidays. Many options are discussed, one being to organize a regular outing to the local swimming baths which is within walking distance, but across a busy road and too far for younger children to go alone. Many mothers say it is difficult to organize all their family in order to walk back and forward to the baths, but are prepared to go on a rota and take a larger number of children once a week. The community worker negotiates with the pool to have one of the lifeguards available to help the two mothers who undertake the rota. The pool also gives a discount for a group swim making it a cheaper option for each family. Through the enthusiasm of a small group of local mothers this initiative runs for four mornings a week all through the summer holidays and is deemed a great success with at least six regular attenders learning to swim. They then work with the community project to set up a regular Saturday swimming club for both adults and children which has now been in existence for five years. The original mothers have now gone on to join many of the other sports activities available at the sports complex and have set up a slimming club which meets after each Saturday swimming session.

**Environmental clean up campaigns** – a student health visitor undertakes a health needs assessment as part of her placement in a health centre of an inner city area. In the course of contacting people to find out their views she becomes aware of local peoples dislike of 'professionals coming in to judge us'. She decides to present her findings to a local meeting and to ask local people what they think should be done to improve health in the local area. The meeting is well attended and many issues discussed, but one that gets unanimous support is the need to clean up the area of litter and dog dirt. A small local action group is formed and they negotiate with the council to provide rubbish skips over one weekend and to put dog litter bins in strategic parts of the area. They also enlist the support of local businesses to donate refreshments. Over the appointed weekend local residents turn out to clear up the area and something of a carnival atmosphere prevails with a local busker and several budding rock bands sharing their talent. Once the clean up is complete people see the potential of turning a piece of waste land into a small park and play area and go on to raise funds to develop this.

much of the efforts of these social and community movements, they did raise important issues in relation to health services and had some significant success in changing services to reflect their concerns. Lay action from within the women's movement changed practices within the maternity services and lay concerns about the welfare of children in hospital were expressed through a campaign to allow parents to stay with their children in hospital – these days regarded as good practice (Williamson 1992).

This section has attempted to demonstrate that lay action has played a significant part in contributing to the development of health improvement and health services, but that this contribution has not always been explicitly recognized. Since the creation of the NHS in 1948 it seems that lay perspectives and lay action on health have been overshadowed by a belief held by professionals and the public alike that health is the exclusive domain of the NHS. The new policy framework for public involvement and its place in the modernization agenda for public services (see Chapter 3) requires a renewed understanding of lay perspectives on health.

## Understanding lay perspectives

What is the lay perspective on health and illness? There is a large and respectable body of sociological literature which deals with the lay understanding of health. This may be influenced by professional perspectives, but it is very different to health professionals' understanding of health. Sociological studies of lay perspectives on health focus on people's experience of health and illness in the context of their overall life experience. They are therefore more diverse and more complex than those of professionals whose focus is on their specific expertise.

For many people, health is integral to the way they live, something they appear to take for granted until they experience ill health. However, when time is taken to explore their perceptions of health, people demonstrate knowledge derived from a range of sources about what it means to be healthy and what kind of actions they should take to maintain good health. Such information is gained from their upbringing and family culture, peer groups and friendship networks, from the media as well as from health professionals. People also identify complex ways in which they manage their concerns about health and illness within their own personal understandings of the world and what is necessary to carry out their 'normal' daily routines.

Such decisions are influenced by their gender, their family responsibilities, age and cultural background. Blaxter (1990) identified differences in people's attitudes to their health at different times of their lives, with young men viewing health as physical fitness and middle aged people emphasizing the importance of mental and physical well-being. Older people stress the importance of retaining physical functioning as well as seeing peace of mind and contentment regardless of levels of ill health. She found differences in social status in relation to people's ability to express their ideas about health in multidimensional ways.

Pill and Stott (1982) studied people's attitudes to ill health in a case study of working class women in Wales. They developed two broad categories:

- people who had a passive or 'fatalist' attitude towards their health status as something outside their direct control and who were content to accept the intervention of medical professionals when necessary. Religious and other belief systems are often invoked to explain unexpected events including ill health and cure and they link to people's attitudes to their health status and to their attitudes to medical intervention; and

- people who viewed their health as something under their personal control and who were more likely to take actions to keep healthy as well as having a questioning attitude towards the interventions of health professionals.

Turner (1985) identifies distinct behaviour attached to when people decide to seek help and who they choose to seek help from. He describes the 'lay referral system', a process people may go through prior to seeking medical intervention. This included seeking advice from family and peers and others within their cultural systems. (See Chapter 8 for a fuller discussion of networks.)

Graham (1993) describes the reasons given for smoking among young mothers well aware of the negative health consequences of the activity. For them the short-term benefits of smoking as a stress reliever when coping with the care of young children in poor physical circumstances outweighed the longer-term effects. Studies of carers (Finch and Groves 1983) have repeatedly shown that they ignore their own symptoms of ill health in order to maintain their caring roles.

Studies of whole communities and their attitudes to health and well-being are also part of the sociological tradition. Cornwall (1984) carried one significant study of community attitudes to health and illness in East London which illustrated the impact of historical perspectives and networks of support in influencing people's health behaviour.

## Lay knowledge vs. medical knowledge

Williams and Popay (2002) identify the epistemological and political challenges of lay perspectives in understanding their relationship with health professionals. They show that lay knowledge about health is a completely different kind of knowledge to that of medical knowledge.

Lay knowledge cannot be understood by using the positivistic tradition of research underpinning medicine, including public health medicine. The positivistic tradition is based on the ability to control conditions to isolate a variable to be understood and measured. It is essentially a reductive approach to knowledge and creates an 'objectification' of the patient as the object to be 'done to'. Traditionally the role of the 'patient' was one of acceptance of this role in exchange for the interventions of medical expertise (Stacey 1976). While this role of acceptance is still common, particularly for short-term patient experience, it has been challenged by people with long-term contact with medical experts as alienating and denying the totality of their experience (Morris 1991; Oliver 1996). The impartiality of scientific knowledge has been increasingly challenged, concealing specific professional interests and not always serving the interests they purport to serve. In the new modernity (Beck 1992) there are many 'competing truths' which need to be continually negotiated and public health partnerships are no exception.

The key characteristic of lay perspectives is the variety and combination of factors they identify as influencing their decisions on health. The sociological studies highlighted above can suggest and illuminate some of the characteristics of lay perspectives, but can only suggest possible connections between social characteristics and individuals and are unable to give definitive predictions of how any one individual will understand their own health status. Lay perspectives must be researched using methods such as ethnography and narrative analysis, methods very different from those traditionally used within the positivistic tradition.

## Medical perspectives on lay involvement

Why does the history of lay action on health show that it has remained outside mainstream thinking within the NHS? This section looks at medical perspectives, and identifies some of the obstacles to lay involvement in public health.

### Medical epidemiology vs. lay epidemiology

Epidemiology is the main basis for public health knowledge and is defined in the Oxford English Dictionary as the science of understanding epidemics and diseases as they affect a given population. Lay perspectives on disease are acknowledged to be an important part of epidemiological research (Ben-Shlomo et al. 1996; Bartley et al. 1997), but there are acknowledged problems in accessing these views. Other issues such as how lay perspectives inform the agenda for research and, more importantly, their contribution to how the results of research are acted upon are crucial aspects of public health. Don Nutbeam (2002) commented that the UK had a world class reputation in describing public health concerns, but had demonstrated a very limited capacity to do much about them. Clearly involving lay perspectives in the search for effective measures of improving health is valuable.

Frankel et al. (1991) define lay epidemiology as: 'The process by which a person interprets health risk through routine observation and discussion of illness and death in personal networks and in the public arena as well as from formal and informal evidence arising from other sources such as television and magazines'. One might also add 'and through their contacts with health and other welfare professionals'.

Fundamentally, epidemiology is based on experimental research methods which seek to establish direct relations of causality between factors and in doing so explain the patterns of disease and ill health in any given population (see Chapter 15). The lay person's perspectives on health are complex and influenced by a host of other circumstances. They are difficult to evidence and research and so have remained marginalized and unrecognized within mainstream public health discourse. 'Lay epidemiology remains marginalised information scarcely recognised beyond sociology as legitimate knowledge. Despite most health professionals recognising that lay people have ideas about the causes of ill health, these ideas tend to be viewed as interesting, but irrational' (Moon et al. 2000: 151).

The above quotes indicate the dominance of the biomedical model in controlling and limiting the discourse in public health. Lay views are not judged as significant within this discourse or, more significantly, their very diversity makes them difficult to identify using the traditions of positivism at the heart of epidemiology. Even when lay people are included in partnerships they will experience difficulties in getting their perspectives recognized and taken seriously. The tradition of the passive patient in receipt of expertise still influences the discourses of public health where the public are viewed as recipients of advice and expertise in relation to their health and lifestyles. Discourse within health care is littered with references to 'patient information', 'patient education' and 'patient compliance', implying that the only issue in relation to lay people using the NHS is to tackle their lack of understanding about health and health-related issues as defined by biomedical discourse. The underlying assumption that people are 'empty vessels to be filled' in relation to their health is slowly beginning to change through the evolving agenda for patient and public involvement.

## The dominance of the biomedical model

The underlying tensions of professionalism and the quest for exclusive expertise is a powerful factor in understanding the difficulties faced by lay people in public health partnerships. The biomedical model is concerned to reduce the encounter with the lay person, to isolate the problem to specific and achievable intervention within the sphere of specific medical expertise, so retaining the power and status in the encounter.

Even if the patient wants to work with a holistic view, wanting to understand the specific medical issue within the wider context of their lives, they find this blocked within the medical consultation. The result of these encounters, often taking place at a time of individual vulnerability, ensures that the public acquiesce to the dominant medical interpretation, they remain passive in relation to their own health and any views they have about their health remain within private and informal discourse.

GPs and primary care professionals, as the agencies of universal open access, are often at the 'sharp end' of this relationship, overloaded with people seeking expert advice for all kinds of health concerns, only some of which can be dealt with by medical intervention. Many have responded by prescribing medicines when they know that another type of support or service might be more appropriate. Or in referring on to other agencies they retain the separation between the medical intervention and other support which could influence health. The result of these encounters is to attain the goal of professionalism – for the public to see health as entirely defined by health professionals and to which they have little to contribute.

There is evidence to show that people will not feel able to express their real views in normal one-off encounters with health professionals or in one-off interviews, but need time and trust to open up (Hogg 1999). Attempts to stimulate discussion about health with lay people will often first focus on their concerns about current NHS services rather than ways in which they manage their own health (Taylor *et al.* 1998). Interviews with individuals about their health will tend to reproduce medical discourse or reflect medical definitions of their conditions even when this is not explicitly requested (Mykhalovskiy and McCoy 2002).

Another concern of the new policy agenda is to open up the public health arena to a wider range of professional groups outside the medical profession. If this is successful it may help youth workers, teachers, social workers and community development workers to bring a wider understanding of what constitutes public health action and to widen access to groupings of the population outside their role as patients. It could, however, lead instead to an increase in the army of public health specialists or experts who continue 'doing public health' to people who continue to be unrecognized as actors in the debate. However, research has shown that this kind of interprofessional and interagency working often leads to a greater awareness and willingness to include lay people and local communities as active and equal participants in the public health debate (Taylor *et al.* 1998).

User movements have clearly identified barriers which can result in lay people being marginalized by professionals in partnership working (Beresford and Croft 1993; Barnes 1997). Box 6.2 identifies some examples of this marginalization.

Williamson (1992) gives an excellent account of the way lay people seeking change within certain aspects of the NHS had to build up complex and co-ordinated campaigns to deal with these barriers, support people involved and build up strategic alliances with key people within the system who would act as advocates and create the right opportunities for the lay representatives to make their contribution most

---

**Box 6.2**   Ways of marginalizing the lay perspective

- *Defining the agenda* – lay people tend to respond to questions about health in terms defined by health professionals. They tend to be able to participate more easily in areas which are not already in a professional domain – hence the often heard comment from a professional involved in public consultation 'all they wanted to talk about was dog dirt'.

- *Education* – emphasis can be put on the need for the public to be educated in order to participate. While the public may need relevant information and support to participate, the 'finding out' process should be two way. This two way process can begin by attending to the use of professional jargon which can block all forms of partnership working.

- *Involvement as a therapeutic process* – seeing involvement as a way of letting people 'have their say' as an end in itself and a way of ticking monitoring sheets without any intention of taking lay views seriously.

- *Incorporation* – putting lay representatives onto committees and projects within the organization and absorbing them into the organizational culture and taking no interest in how these lay representatives can connect to the communities or interests they came from.

- *Exploiting* – expecting lay representatives to give their time and effort voluntarily without engaging with their need to be resourced in ways appropriate to their situations.

- *Dismissing and discounting* – lay people who are prepared to take part in consultations and long-term involvement being taken as unrepresentative and too articulate to represent the 'average' member of the public, without showing much interest in the experiences of lay people who have taken this route.

effectively. Increasingly some of these barriers have been recognized within the NHS in the new policy for public involvement and are now being recognized in good practice guidelines and in monitoring processes.

## Promoting an effective lay contribution to public health

How can an effective lay contribution to public health be developed? First, it is helpful to consider the range of approaches to lay participation in public health, and the levels at which people are prepared to be involved.

### Four approaches to public involvement

It is possible to identify four approaches to public involvement.

### The consumerist approach

The first is a consumerist approach in which people are asked for their views on specific issues or services by those responsible for those services. This is focused on their specific relationship with the issue and service, and is often time limited with the boundaries decided by the service providers. It does not encourage any wider dialogue on health issues, but nevertheless may encourage an interest in greater participation if other opportunities exist to capture this (Winkler 1987; Lupton *et al.* 1998). Consumerist initiatives may take many forms from surveys and focus groups to patient panels and councils. They often attempt to address the issue of bias in their choice of participants.

### The representatives' approach

A second approach is the quasidemocratic approach of appointing public 'representatives' to sit on NHS trust boards and on different structures within health organizations. This supersedes the earlier inclusion of locally elected councillors on health authorities and in the past 20 years has been seen as a form of public accountability (Day and Klein 1987). The emphasis for these roles is to contribute to the development of their organization, by ensuring that public interests and perspectives are considered. The key issue for this kind of involvement is to ask how far these appointed 'representatives' are viewed as legitimate representatives by local communities and communities of interest and how well they can keep in touch with their communities.

These first two approaches lend themselves to an organizational agenda requiring specific evidence of public involvement. It allows the organization to define the terms of the encounter and be able to control the level of feedback.

### The interest group approach

A third approach is through the activities of organized interest groups who have an independent status, though this may be greatly influenced by the availability of funding. Such groups develop their own agendas which they then attempt to promote using whatever means available to them. They can be small self-help groups or part of a much larger network of groups within a national network or voluntary organization.

Participants in these groups are likely to have developed skills over time in taking part in consultations and organized involvement events and may have developed their own research to underpin their perspectives.

As discussed in the earlier section, interest groups who challenge accepted professional opinions are often viewed by health professionals as unrepresentative and are seen as isolated and unconnected to wider 'public opinion'. However, another perspective may be that such groups represent the articulated tips of icebergs of public opinion which is hidden and undeveloped. Interest groups who may now seem well organized and articulate probably started as small groups of like minded people (often as informal discussion and self-help groups) which over time have developed into networks and larger organizations able to raise funding and lead campaigns for social change. They are interested in not only improving resources and services but often aim to change or transform society's attitudes to the issues they raise. They can be viewed as genuine tips of large icebergs of lay opinion. They are the public expression of much larger bodies of lay opinion which may still be difficult for individuals to fully articulate in their individual encounters with professionals. However, it remains a perfectly valid concern to check how far such groups are representative of more general public opinion. This can be done by surveys and other consumerist methods or it can be developed through the network approach identified below.

**The network approach**
A final approach to public involvement is to access the informal networks and activities within communities to find out the way people understand and live their lives and to find ways to help them articulate their perspectives and influence the development and delivery of services. Chapter 8 discusses the realities and spread of networks in greater detail and the ways in which they can be fostered and worked with. The need for public health to address inequalities as a priority implies that it needs to have good sources of information into all parts of local communities using as many information sources as possible.

Figure 6.1 provides a way of thinking about levels of public involvement. People come in and out of this kind of action as their personal circumstances allow. One individual has limited capacity to be active in all aspects of life so while they might be active in one issue they may be a non-participator in others, happy for others to speak on their behalf. However, the experience and skills built up in campaigning in one arena will broaden an individual's experience and knowledge of how 'things are done' and may lead to broader participation in other areas. Individual circumstances, wider opportunities, timing, attitudes and social support all influence an individual's decision to participate, as illustrated in the case study in Box 6.3. This level of activity within communities has been identified as 'social capital' and has recently been identified as important in promoting health and addressing inequalities (Gillies 1998c; Campbell *et al.* 1999). (Chapter 8 looks at social capital in more detail.)

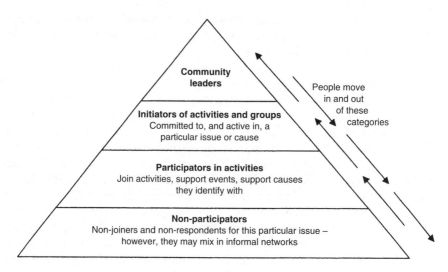

**Figure 6.1** Levels of public involvement

---

**Box 6.3**  Case study example of lay involvement in public health

A young mothers' group on a housing estate has been meeting weekly at a local community centre for the past three years. The group was started by a local health visitor as a postnatal support group but has run independently for two years. There is a core group of eight women who maintain activities through an informal committee structure; about 25 other women attend the group with fluctuating levels of commitment. The group receive funding for their crèche worker from the local community association and are able to use the premises free of charge. The group raise funds for their activities by charging members, running a stall at the local community festival each year and doing occasional car boot sales. Over the past two years the group have organized children's activities and outings during the summer and Easter holidays, and run a successful babysitting network. Their meetings alternate between organized sessions with speakers and informal coffee get togethers.

  Individual members take part in other activities in the area and report back to the group. Several members attended an information session on the 'five a day' initiative (to encourage people to eat five portions of fruit and vegetables a day) at their children's school, run by the school nurse. When this was reported back to the group it stimulated a lot of discussion about the difficulties of buying affordable fresh food in their area. One of the mothers discussed this concern with the school nurse who put them in touch with a fruit and vegetable co-operative in a neighbouring town. After a group visit to this co-op several members of the group became enthusiastic about starting a similar one on their estate. Five women from the group are now working with other people from the community association, two local farmers and the local allotment group to set up this initiative and have recently run a one-off 'farmers' market' to publicize their project.

This work on healthy food has stimulated a more general interest in health. A small sub-group have begun to support each other to lose weight and take regular exercise, committing themselves to a 'weigh in' (known in the group as the 'naming and shaming session') each month; this has been a great success, with the sub-group gaining more members as weight goals were reached. At one of the meetings two of the slimming group commented that now they are exercising regularly they are feeling the effects of their smoking. This stimulated a heated debate about smoking and whether people should believe all the publicity about smoking and health.

The group decided to approach the local health centre to ask a GP to come and speak at their meeting. The GPs passed on the request to their health visitors, one of whom offered to go along to the group. But her colleagues were concerned that in the current climate of staff shortages they should not take on new work. Instead, they decided to send information to the group about the smoking cessation clinic which runs at the health centre every Tuesday evening and where new clients would be welcome.

The group received this response with comments like, 'I told you those doctors aren't interested in our estate', 'You wouldn't catch me going to the health centre when it isn't necessary', 'How can I get out on Tuesday evening with two small children to look after' and 'I'm not keen on going out after dark'. The subject of smoking was dropped and the group moved on to planning their summer outings. The original slimmer who raised the topic decided to use the babysitting network and to go to the clinic, but not to tell the others of her decision at this stage.

**This case study illustrates**

- the way in which health awareness was built up incrementally in this group of lay people;
- the group as a mechanism for informal discussion and information processing as well as a focus for organizing activities;
- the importance of building up skills based on what people feel they can do and are interested in within a 'safe' environment of trust and with people in the same situation;
- the acceptance of different levels of involvement for different issues; and
- the impact of contact with health professionals.

## Conclusion – challenges and opportunities

This chapter has attempted to demonstrate that lay perspectives have always been integral to public health and historically have had greater recognition than at present. As discussed in the sections on lay and medical perspectives on involvement, there are many and often conflicting opinions on what influences health improvement. The power of biomedical discourse in defining the terms of engagement for health and illness is a significant barrier for lay participation in health improvement. It both limits the boundaries of discourse in health and further seeks to control and limit any efforts made to link lay perspectives into the public debates about health and illness.

This chapter has offered a framework of four approaches to public involvement and has tried to identify and explain the connections between them. In using any one approach it is important to understand what the other approaches might offer. Anyone seeking to understand the contribution of lay perspectives in public health may need to realize that they are likely to be hidden and outside the public domain except where there has been concerted attempts to bring the lay perspective into the public arena. This would be through campaigning and the action of self-help, voluntary and community organizations. Inevitably lay perspectives will be partial and sporadic as they are often incompletely articulated. Sometimes, lay opinion is just like unconnected pieces of driftwood and expressed by individuals without clear public support. Rather than dismiss lay opinions as unrepresentative and 'quirky' it is important for more public health professionals to know how to check the links back into local communities. Public health needs to have clear strategies to link into networks and informal activities of local communities.

There are, of course, resource issues which need addressing. A constant concern for all lay activists is finding the resources, support and time to sustain their activities. They struggle to find people to become involved and willing to stay involved. Lay activity is sustained by an ever changing group of people who come in and out of involvement as their circumstances allow. Varied and diverse opportunities need to exist to maximize lay activity so that people can engage in particular areas of interest like the state of the pavements or the lack of fresh vegetables. Grassroots professionals in their day-to-day dealings with local people are an obvious resource for public health to access lay views. However, public health professionals have to be prepared to be open, non-judgemental and to listen. We have also outlined in this chapter that the inhibitions that local people may feel towards service providers, especially when they are particularly vulnerable or dependent, require consideration for professionals wanting to develop access to lay views.

Developing an effective lay contribution poses challenges for people engaged in public health. Health professionals must be able to understand, value and respect the way lay perspectives interact with professional interventions for individuals and communities in relation to health and illness. This must first involve medical professionals in accepting the contribution of lay perspectives in defining and determining health knowledge and information. They must be prepared to work with lay perspectives and those of other professionals to ensure that health interventions and health improvement can be made effective. It remains to be seen if the emphasis in policy on public involvement discussed at the beginning of this chapter will translate into realistic opportunities for a better engagement of lay people in the public health agenda.

**Suggested further reading**

Barnes, M. (1999) Users as citizens: collective action and the local governance of welfare, *Social Policy and Administration*, 33(1): 73–90.

Beresford, P. and Croft, S. (1993) *Citizen Involvement: a Practical Guide for Change*. Basingstoke: Macmillan.

Birchall, J. and Simmons, R. (2004) *User Power: the Participation of Users in Public Services*. London: National Consumer Council.

Department of Health (2006) *A Stronger Local Voice: a Framework for Creating a Stronger Local Voice in the Development of Health and Social Care Services*. 275857 DH publications www.dh.gov.uk/publications

Hogg, C. (1999) *Patients, Power and Politics: From Patients to Citizens*. London: Sage.

Taylor, M. (2003) *Public Policy in the Community*. Basingstoke: Palgrave Macmillan.

Taylor, P., Vegoda, M. and Leech, S. (2001) Exploring the experience of a group of lay members on primary care groups, *Local Governance*, 27(4): 231–8.

# 7

## SELENA GRAY
## The contribution of health services to public health

**Editors' introduction**

There has long been debate about the extent to which health care, as opposed to wider social and environmental determinants, contributes to population health. This chapter will explore some of the evidence that demonstrates that equitable access to high quality health care does have an impact on health at the population level.

It will describe a model of public health practice that includes three domains; namely, health improvement, health protection and health service delivery and quality, and demonstrate how engagement with health service provision is an integral part of public health practice. For some practitioners this will mean a very direct involvement with the planning, commissioning, quality assurance or delivery of equitable high quality appropriate services to ensure that maximum gain is secured for a local population from a safe, comprehensive and equitable health care. For others it may be to work with health professionals to ensure the active provision of information and support to individuals and communities of appropriately tailored health promotion messages, delivered in an appropriate, culturally sensitive and sustainable fashion. Still others will wish to have an active engagement and partnership with health care professionals in order to advocate and build the case for regulatory or fiscal changes that will improve health.

Finally, the potential role of hospitals and other health care facilities as key players in sustainability will be explored.

## The contribution of health care to population health

### The contribution from medicine

In the 1970s the contribution that medicine made to improvements in public health were widely considered to be marginal. Writers such as McKeown (1976) argued cogently for example that the dramatic improvements in mortality rates from tuberculosis and other infectious diseases preceded the introduction of effective immunizations and treatments. Illich (1976) was an ardent proponent of the view that medical care had a marginal impact at a population level, and in many cases actually damaged health. However, in more recent years this account has been challenged. The changing demography of the population, with an ageing population with a higher burden of chronic disease, and the development of effective interventions for conditions such as coronary heart disease, hypertension and cancer have led to a re-balancing of this view.

## Evidence of impact

Bunker (1995) estimated the amount of life expectancy that could be attributed to health care. He concluded that clinical services, including preventive services and therapeutic interventions accounted for five of the 30 years increase in life expectancy in the USA since 1990, half of the seven years increase since 1950, and an estimated five years of pain or disability free life. Mackenbach (1996) and Mackenbach et al. (1988) using a different methodological approach, calculated that in the Netherlands between 1950 and 1984 that male life expectancy would have fallen by a year without the improvements in medical care, in contrast to the actual rise of two years, and that approximately four of the six years of life expectancy gained in women was attributable to medical care. Other evidence of the effectiveness of health care interventions at population level has been well summarized by Nolte and McKee (2004).

## Avoidable deaths

In the late 1970s and early 1980s, the concept of avoidable deaths was developed (Rutstein et al. 1976, 1980; Charlton et al. 1983). These were deaths that might in theory be avoidable, based on both preventive and curative interventions. An example would be deaths resulting from treatable conditions, such as appendicitis, or cancers such as Hodgkin's disease for which effective treatments are available. Analysis of these death rates in different populations demonstrated enormous variation, showing significant differences in the provision of effective health care. These indicators have subsequently been applied in many different contexts to identify both the potential contribution of health care to mortality improvement, between communities and over time, and also to identify variations in outcomes which might be due to variations in access or quality of health care, for example work by Treurniet et al. (2004).

Further evidence of the effectiveness of health care interventions at a population level has also come from observational research following the re-unification of Germany. Reviewing life expectancy and avoidable deaths, Nolte et al. (2002) concluded that of the observed increase in life expectancy of 1.4 years in men and 0.9 years in women in East Germany over the time period 1992 to 1997, 14–23 per cent was accounted for by declining deaths from conditions amenable to medical intervention (Nolte et al. 2002) such as hypertension, cerebro-vascular disease, and breast and cervical cancer.

## Modelling scenarios

Another approach has been based on using modelling exercises where specific conditions have been examined to try to estimate the potential gain for population health of different strategies.

### Cancer

To underpin the development of a national cancer strategy for England (Department of Health 2000c), modelling was undertaken to identify what interventions would be most likely to achieve the proposed target reduction in cancer mortality rates of 20 per cent. It was concluded that about one-fifth of this targeted reduction could come from improvements in treatment, one-fifth from improvements in screening programmes, and the remaining three-fifths coming from changes to diet, alcohol and tobacco use (see Figure 7.1). This suggests that the improvement of treatment and screening services is a key part of any population strategy to improve cancer death rates alongside primary prevention efforts.

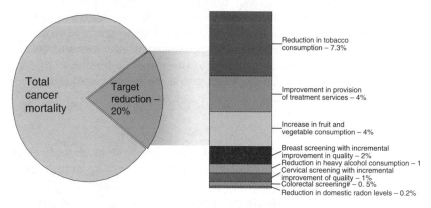

* estimates produced for the under 65 age group and assumed to apply to under 75 age group
# phased introduction of new modalities

**Figure 7.1** Potential improvements in total cancer mortality due to specific intervention in persons under age 75*
*Source*: Department of Health (2000c: 16)

### Coronary heart disease

There has been a dramatic decline in both the number and rate of deaths from coronary heart disease in the UK and many other countries over the last 25 years. Modelling the potential effects of both health interventions and population risk factor changes, Ünal *et al.* (2004) concluded that health service interventions and treatments accounted for 20 per cent of the reduction, and population risk factor changes for 80 per cent, of the life years gained between 1981 and 2000 in England and Wales.

Although the extent to which the reduction in heart disease deaths are a result of improvements in population risk factors such as diet and tobacco use, or the development of much better ways of treating heart disease continue to be debated (Kelly and Capewell 2004), it seems clear that both have played a part and that tackling heart disease requires both the provision of effective services and primary prevention.

## The three domains of public health practice

### The domains of public health practitioners in the field of health care

A useful framework for considering public health activity is outlined by Griffiths *et al.* (2005) and has been adopted by the UK Faculty of Public Health. This considers that there are three main domains for public health practice, namely health improvement, health protection and health service delivery and quality (see Figure 7.2). Examples of activities that take place in the field of health services delivery and quality and contribute to population health include: needs assessment; service planning and commissioning; delivery; quality improvement and patient safety programmes. This spans both secondary (hospital) and primary and community care, and requires engagement and partnership with doctors and other health care professionals such as dentists, nurses and pharmacists.

Public health practitioners whose work is more focused in the health improvement domain may also need to engage with health care professionals to ensure the active provision of information and support to individuals and communities of appropriately tailored health promotion messages, and also to build effective coalitions to advocate and build the case for regulatory or fiscal changes that will improve health.

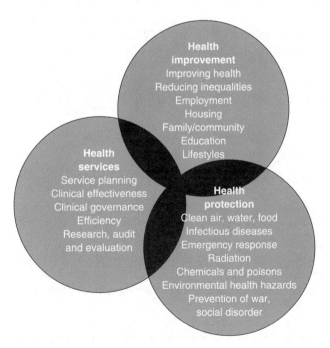

**Figure 7.2** Domains of public health practice
*Source*: adapted from Griffiths *et al.* (2005)

The extent to which public health practitioners are directly involved in commissioning and quality assurance of health care systems may vary depending on both where they are located within health and social care systems, and on the professional skills and background of practitioners. In the UK, the move of the public health function from local authorities to the NHS in 1974, and the location of public health in health care commissioning and purchasing organizations following the NHS structural changes in the 1980s, meant this was an active area of work for many in public health at that time. This was facilitated by the fact that at that time senior public health posts in the NHS were open only to those with a medical background, which gave them a natural interest and aptitude to work in this area. With the opening up of senior posts in public health to those from any background with the appropriate skills and training in England in 2003, and the closer working with local authorities, there has been a welcome move to an increased emphasis on both health improvement and health protection. However, in order to retain a balanced public health function, it is necessary that work is undertaken in each of these three domains, and integrated at the population level by the director of public health or equivalent.

These areas will be explored further in the following sections.

## Health needs assessment

A key area of practice for public health professionals is the identification of the health needs of their local population and the assessment of whether these needs are currently being met by existing services. This requires the application of epidemiological tools to identify need (Stevens and Raftery 1997), an assessment of current services and an assessment of the effectiveness of available interventions and the potential for benefit. These need to be complemented by approaches that include the views of local populations. Systematic health needs assessment can inform the planning and commissioning of appropriate levels of the right sort of health care for different populations (see below).

## Service planning and commissioning

Arrangements for planning and/or commissioning health services vary between different countries and health care systems. In some, the identification of population needs and commissioning services to meet them is separated from the delivery of care, whereas in others the processes of planning and delivery are integrated. Irrespective of the details of local arrangements, those planning and commissioning services need to be able to undertake an assessment of the health needs of their local populations, to commission appropriate services and importantly, to put in place arrangements to monitor the quality of those services. Further discussion about quality is considered below.

Within the UK at present, different models are emerging, with a move in England to encourage 'practice-based commissioning' (Department of Health 2006e). This initiative is intended to engage general and other primary care professionals at local level in the commissioning of services through providing both information about current service usage and the ability to influence where and what services are purchased on behalf of the local population. It is intended that this initiative will lead to better responsive services.

### Delivery of services

While public health practitioners are more often involved in planning, commissioning and quality assuring health (and in some cases integrated social care) programmes, they have traditionally been the advocate and often the lead for a key range of community-based programmes aimed at improving public health. This includes particularly immunization, screening, family planning and antenatal care, family visiting programmes, school health, and health education programmes, although this is no means a complete list. Because of their importance both screening and immunization programmes are discussed further below.

As health needs change within populations, these basic core public health services may need to adapt and change. For example in recent years the UK has pioneered the development of a universal smoking cessation service, as a key element of a wider tobacco control policy. There is currently debate to the extent to which universal parenting programmes might be useful and many school health services are re-introducing weighing of children again as malnutrition takes a back role and childhood obesity emerges as a public health problem.

## Screening

Public health practitioners may be involved at several levels in screening programmes. First, in reviewing the evidence systematically to support the introduction or otherwise of a new screening programme is a skilled task requiring rigorous assessment against established standards. One example of a set of such criteria is that developed by the UK National Screening Committee (www.nsc.nhs.uk) which reviews new programmes by considering the condition, the test, the treatment options and effectiveness and acceptability of the screening programme to ensure that they do more good than harm at a reasonable cost. Screening has important ethical differences from clinical practice as the health service is targeting apparently healthy people, offering to help individuals to make better informed choices about their health, so it is essential that individuals have realistic expectations of what a screening programme can deliver.

The UK National Screening Committee maintains an overview of existing and potential new programmes, regularly appraising and reviewing evidence and is an invaluable resource on the vast array of current and potential screening programmes. Second, public health practitioners are often involved in helping oversee the delivery and quality assurance of screening programmes. It is particularly important to ensure population coverage and high uptake of services for all groups, particularly those from vulnerable groups who may otherwise miss out. This may require engagement with professionals who are delivering the service, and for some front-line public health practitioners such as health visitors, discussion with individuals about whether they should use particular screening services. Ensuring that services are delivered in an appropriately culturally sensitive fashion may require grassroots work with local communities to ensure acceptability of services and information. A particular example is the introduction of screening for sickle-cell disease, an inherited blood condition that affects black and ethnic minority groups.

## Immunization

As with screening, immunization is primarily a population intervention. Public health practitioners will have a major role in appraising the evidence and supporting the case for the introduction of new programmes, for overseeing their delivery and ensuring effective population coverage. This will be particularly important for vulnerable groups such as those of no fixed abode, the homeless, travellers, and will depend on accurate population-based registers for identifying and recalling patients. Public health practitioners also have a key role in working closely with health professionals to promote an appropriate informed debate within the media and the public about immunization.

At local level, some public health practitioners will be in a position to encourage and support the uptake of immunization by individuals, particularly young children and the elderly, where advice from health professionals can be influential in encouraging the uptake of flu vaccination.

## Quality improvement

While it is important that appropriate levels of care are secured for population, the issue is not just about the provision of appropriate levels of health care but also about the quality and outcomes of care.

## Quality frameworks

A number of frameworks have been proposed to consider quality of health services. A commonly used one is that derived by Maxwell (1984) shown in Box 7.1. This provides a helpful framework for considering the contribution that public health practitioners can make to quality and each is considered further below.

---

**Box 7.1**   Dimensions of quality of health services

**Effectiveness**
**Acceptability**
**Efficiency**
**Access**
**Equity**
**Relevance**

(*Source*: Maxwell 1984)

---

## Effectiveness

The advent of the evidence-based medicine movement (Sackett *et al.* 1997) and the establishment of the international Cochrane Collaboration have led the way for a critical **systematic review** of the effectiveness of medical interventions. This has both stimulated large-scale randomized trials in key areas to determine the efficacy of interventions for common conditions, that have a large potential impact on population health, and paved the way for the emergence of national and international consensus statements and guidelines on effective practice.

Public health professionals in the UK have been prominent members of key initiatives that have developed systematic evidence-based approaches to the equitable delivery of high quality health care in the UK. These include the evidence-based medicine movement; the Cochrane Collaboration, the development of local and national guidelines for cancer care; the establishment of the National Institute for Clinical Excellence in England, and the establishment of National Service Frameworks. These are beginning to show an impact on population health with, for example, increases in cancer survival rates attributable to better treatment now occurring with dramatic decreases in breast cancer deaths due to wider more systematic use of effective treatment (Peto 1998). This focus on effectiveness has also lead to the recognition that some interventions are not effective and should be abandoned, thus releasing resources for cost-effective use elsewhere.

## Acceptability

Ensuring that services are delivered in a culturally competent fashion is paramount for effective uptake and utilization. This is particularly important in terms of key public health services such as family planning and sexual health services, but is relevant across the whole spectrum of health care.

Individuals wish to be treated in a holistic fashion recognizing that they have individual needs and circumstances. Services may need to be tailored to reflect both different socio-economic and ethnic backgrounds and different age ranges; the needs of adolescents are quite different to older people.

## Efficiency

The proper efficient use of resources is a legitimate concern of all public health professionals and ensuring that services are well organized and managed and provide value for money is an area of concern, particularly given the large expenditure in the field of health. This links with the amount of health gain per input spent for different interventions.

## Access and equity

Ensuring equitable access to services is a key public health challenge, even in countries such as the UK with a comprehensive health care system free at the point of delivery, where in theory, equitable access to health care should not be an issue.

However as identified by Julian Tudor Hart (1971) from his experience in South Wales, the availability of health care tends to vary inversely with the need for care, with sicker populations generally being less well served and having poorer access. He also stated that: 'This inverse care law operates more completely where medical care is most exposed to market forces, and less so where such exposure is reduced.' Indeed, there remain real issues of access to basic health care even in developed countries with market type insurance-based systems. For example, an estimated nine million children in the USA do not have health insurance (Campaign for Children's Healthcare 2006). However, even within countries that have comprehensive health care systems, access within populations can be problematic, particularly for certain groups such as the elderly and disabled, asylum seekers, the homeless, sex workers and those with learning difficulties. There is also evidence of systematic failings in health services to address the needs of indigenous populations within developed countries, and that the services provided are not always delivered in a culturally sensitive fashion (Ring and Brown 2003). There is also some evidence that those from disadvantaged socio-economic groups or from minority ethnic groups may fail to access care, and even if they do, may be less likely to receive active interventions such as cardiac revascularization (Ben-Shlomo and Chaturvedi 1995).

At a global level, access to basic health care services is highly variable and totally inadequate in many developing countries. In the World Health Report 'Make every mother and child count', WHO (2005a) estimates that out of a total of 136 million births a year worldwide, less than two-thirds of women in less developed countries and only one-third in the least developed countries have their babies delivered by a skilled attendant. Together with a lack of care for infants and young children, this is a major contributing factor to the 530,000 women a year who die in pregnancy or childbirth, the three million stillborn babies, and the 10.6 million children who die each year before their fifth birthday. Another study examining the availability and affordability of basic drugs required to treat common chronic health conditions such as hypertension and schizophrenia, has found that in many countries these are either not available, not affordable, or only at a price that impoverishes individuals and their families (Gelders et al. 2006).

Public health practitioners have a key role in both identifying, documenting and implementing action to address these inequities in access to effective services at local, national and international levels.

## Relevance

It is essential that relevant and appropriate services overall are delivered to populations. The balance of what is provided should be based on epidemiological needs assessments of the population, taking into account the different sub-groups within it.

### Methods of quality improvement

Alongside the recognition that there are different aspects to quality has come a more systematic approach to improving both the quality and the safety of health care. A wide variety of complementary and different approaches are used to improve different aspects of care. These include: clinical audit; the development of consensus and evidence-based guidelines; computer generated reminders; national standards; performance indicators; peer review and comparative feedback to name but a few.

In England, the concept of 'clinical governance' has been introduced, which for the first time has placed a statutory duty on all health organizations to seek quality improvement alongside the existing duties of financial control and service performance. It was specifically intended that this should be implemented through an organization-wide, developmental approach, which must encompass aspects of cultural change and integrate management and clinicians at every level (Scally and Donaldson 1998).

There is evidence that a concerted and integrated approach to quality improvement can have a substantial impact. In England and Wales a large national audit, the Myocardial Infarction National Audit Project (Royal College of Physicians 2006) has examined how well heart attacks have been managed by the health service over a five-year time period. It is known that early treatment with thrombolytic therapy, popularly known as 'clot busting' drugs given for a suspected heart attack is much more effective than that given at a later stage. The study has demonstrated a continuous improvement over each of the five years it has been running in the number of patients who were promptly treated, such that by 2006, almost 60 per cent of patients with suspected heart attacks in England received thrombolytic treatment within 60 minutes of calling for professional help, compared with only 22 per cent in early 2001.

## Quality and outcomes framework for general medical services

Other approaches to quality include the use of financial incentives for health care providers who meet various standards. An example is the use of a quality outcomes framework introduced as part of the contractual payment arrangements for general practitioners who deliver primary care services in England in 2004 (Department of Health 2004a). This provides financial rewards to general practices that can demonstrate the delivery of high quality systematic care to their practice population across a range of areas (Table 7.1). The framework includes evidence-based indicators in a number of clinical domains such as coronary heart disease, respiratory and other chronic diseases as well as organizational indicators such as cervical screening and maternity and child health surveillance and is subject to regular review. New areas such as chronic kidney disease, depression and obesity have been added for 2006 (NHS Employers 2006).

Work is ongoing to evaluate formally the impact of this system on the quality of general practice. However, significant improvements in the quality of care in general practice (as judged by three key conditions of coronary heart disease, asthma and diabetes) had already occurred in England prior to the introduction of the new contract (Campbell et al. 2005), probably as a result of the introduction of clinical audit, clinical governance and an increased emphasis on national standards and guidelines.

The content and delivery of the Quality and Outcome Framework and the contract provides a real opportunity for public health practitioners to work with primary care practitioners to ensure the delivery of high quality systematic care that addresses both key primary and secondary prevention for chronic diseases in primary care.

**Table 7.1** Quality and outcomes framework for UK general medical services 2006/07

| Domains | Areas covered |
| --- | --- |
| Clinical | Linked to care of patients with chronic diseases. |
| Organizational | Relating to records and information, communicating with patients, education and training, medicines management and clinical and practice management. |
| Additional services | Covering cervical screening, child health surveillance, maternity services and contraceptive services. |
| Patient experience | Based on patient surveys and length of consultations. |

The inclusion of targets in areas such as smoking and obesity provides a stimulus for general practitioners and others in primary care to consider these key public health issues. It also provides relevant and detailed data such as smoking rates and the prevalence of common chronic diseases in local populations not readily accessible elsewhere.

Developments are underway to try to identify and test a European-wide set of indicators that might be used in a similar fashion to examine and drive up the quality of primary care services across different health systems (Engels *et al.* 2005, 2006).

**Patient safety**

There is an increasing recognition that the delivery of health care itself has the potential to be associated with adverse events leading to harm or even death. While some adverse events may be due to unpredictable effects of interventions, others are due to systemic failures of health delivery systems. Estimates of the size of the problem are shown in Table 7.2. It is recognized that generally reporting and surveillance systems are inadequate to identify and manage these adverse events (Kohn *et al.* 1999).

Two key areas of concern are the use of medication and infection. The incorrect prescribing of drugs, or the inadvertent prescription of drugs that may interact together is a particular issue, drugs in an ageing population with multiple health problems is a common and serious problem. There is now increasing evidence that hospitals and other health care settings act as reservoirs of infection, leading to serious complications in individuals who acquire infection during a hospital stay – studies in a variety of different settings have found that between 3 and 20 per cent of patients admitted to hospital acquire an infection (Mayon-White *et al.* 1988).

These findings have led to many countries establishing more formal systems to try to both identify and manage adverse events and promote patient safety. To drive these developments, the World Health Organization (WHO) has supported the creation of a World Alliance for Patient Safety, launched in 2004. This has identified six action areas namely Patients for Patient Safety, Taxonomy, Research, Solutions for

Patient Safety, Reporting and Learning, and a biennial Global Patient Safety Challenge, the first of which, 'Clean Care is Safer Care' addresses health care-associated infection (Pittet and Donaldson 2006).

An example of an organizational approach to patient safety and quality improvement in hospitals in the USA is shown in Box 7.2.

**Table 7.2** United States and Australian research into adverse events in hospitals

|  | Havard Medical Practice Study 1991† | Quality in Australian Health Care Study 1995‡ |
|---|---|---|
| Proportion of inpatient episodes leading to harmful events | 3.7% | 16.6% (half preventable) |
| Proportion of inpatient episodes resulting in permanent disability or death in which harm was also caused* | 0.7% | 3% |
| Broad extrapolation of findings to the NHS based on 8.5 million inpatient episodes a year |  |  |
| Adverse events | 314,000 | 1,414,000 |
| Potential instances of permanent disability or death in cases where adverse events occurred* | 60,000 | 255,000 |

* Adverse events will not always be a causal or contributory factor in these cases.
† (Leape *et al.* 1991)
‡ (Wilson *et al.* 1995)
*Source*: adapted from Kohn *et al.* 1999

---

**Box 7.2**   The 100,000 lives campaign

A quality improvement initiative in the USA led by the Institute of Healthcare Improvement has enrolled over 3000 hospitals covering an estimated 75 per cent of all US hospital beds in a comprehensive programme to address unnecessary deaths through improving the quality of health care. The initial target of 100,000 reduced deaths was estimated to have been exceeded by 22,300 by June 2006 (IHI 2006). The campaign is based on a concerted organizational approach targeted on six key areas:

- preventing adverse drug events;
- deployment of rapid response teams;
- improving care for acute myocardial infarction (heart attacks)
- preventing surgical site infections;
- preventing central line infections; and
- preventing ventilator associated pneumonia.

Public health practitioners are engaged in many levels in these initiatives, from designing and implementing new surveillance and reporting systems, through to leading the organizational and cultural change required to promote patient safety, and through working in partnership with patients and patient groups to drive up quality.

### Adverse drug reactions

New drugs may come onto the market without serious side effects or adverse effects being identified. This is almost inevitable, given the limited number of patients included in clinical trials that some rare adverse events and side effects may emerge at a later stage after the drug has been in use for some time. National surveillance systems have been established in many countries to allow the reporting and identification of these as they emerge. In the UK, the 'Yellow Card' system allows health professionals and more recently, patients themselves, to report suspected adverse reactions to national regulatory body, the Medicines and Healthcare Products Regulatory Agency (MHRA) and the Commission on Human Medicines (CHM). The agency has the power to add product warnings, issues safety alerts and to recommend withdrawal of products and devices where appropriate.

Balancing the potential benefits from new drugs with the potential harm at a population level, particularly for those drugs that are prescribed commonly to large numbers of people is a complex task. Recent examples include the controversies over the appropriate use of certain antidepressant drugs that may induce suicidal thoughts in young people and adults with depression (CSM 2004), and withdrawal of some drugs commonly prescribed and used for arthritis after the finding that they may lead to an increased risk of heart attacks (CSM 2005).

Medicines regulators increasingly work as part of an international effort with the overarching European Medicines Agency (EMEA) and the Food and Drug Administration (FDA) in the USA as key players. Given the size of the pharmaceutical industry, there are potentially huge commercial gains and vested interests in this area. It is essential that there are robust independent regulatory measures in place based on sound surveillance systems that really do protect the public interest.

## Heath improvement

### Lifestyle advice

Health care professionals are well placed to provide individuals with tailored advice on how their lifestyle may impact on their health and what action they might take to change this. There is good evidence that patients may be receptive to information given in these settings. For example advice on smoking from a primary care doctor and nurses can be influential in helping individuals quit tobacco (Lancaster and Stead 2006; Rice and Stead 2006) and brief interventions from health care professionals about alcohol can be highly effective (Moyer et al. 2002). Advice might be in the context of primary or secondary prevention, where individuals have already experienced some adverse health effect, such as a heart attack, and may be keen to minimize the changes of further events occurring.

It is increasingly recognized that it is not just doctors but a wide range of health professionals that can have a role in health promotion and offering lifestyle advice to patients with whom they are in contact. Dentists are well placed to advise on smoking, as the impact of tobacco use on gum disease is highly significant, but are also in a position to be offering dietary advice to children who may be presenting both with dental caries and obesity related to similar underlying causes, such as a high consumption of sugary and carbonated drinks. Similarly, pharmacists are well placed to provide advice on a range of issues from contraception, smoking cessation, sun protection and raised blood pressure.

At another level, health care institutions can be organized actively to promote health. Recent moves to make the NHS smoke free in England have re-invigorated debates about the potential opportunity to provide pre-operative smoking cessation clinics so that those coming into hospital can cope with a smoke free environment, but also reduce the risks of their operation, and gain the long-term benefits of stopping smoking.

With an increase burden of long-term chronic disease in an ageing population, patients need to be supported to actively manage their illness, and to be empowered to take effective steps to ameliorate the impact of disease through steps such as exercise, diet and social support. Active rehabilitation after heart attacks and strokes has an appreciable impact on function, and can slow progression in chronic illnesses such as diabetes and arthritis.

If this potential is to be realized, health care professionals need to be supported routinely to provide non-directive accurate information in an appropriate fashion that does not lead to conflict with their primary duty to deal with illness. Public health practitioners will need to work carefully in partnership with health professionals in both primary and secondary care to ensure this happens. They will also wish to ensure that there is equitable access to active rehabilitation programmes for the population across a range of common chronic diseases.

## Building coalitions for change

Public health practitioners may also wish to engage doctors and other health care professionals as partners in terms of advocacy for key public health policies at national and local level. Doctors see at first hand adverse health effects from a variety of causes, and can make powerful allies in building a case for change and helping lobbying for appropriate regulatory or fiscal changes. The campaigning body Action on Smoking and Health (ASH) was in fact established by members of the UK Royal College of Physicians to campaign on tobacco control issues in direct response to the lack of action taken by the government of the day in response to their key report, *Smoking and Health* (RCP 1962). Doctors dealing with liver disease have been particularly concerned to find that in recent years they are starting to see, for the first time ever, young women with advanced liver disease. This has been a driving factor in the publication by the Academy of Medical Sciences of an authoritative report on alcohol (2004), which calls for action to be taken on the widespread promotion and availability of alcohol. A&E consultants and maxillofacial surgeons were concerned at the number of severe facial injuries after fights in pubs and bars at weekends and this paved the way for the use of shatterproof and toughened glasses (Shepherd 1994).

At local level health professionals may have a profound understanding of the impact of the socio-economic impact circumstances on health and be able to contribute to local public health practitioners attempts to ameliorate them.

Health care professionals also have an important role to play in multi-sectoral groups addressing public health issues such as injury prevention, domestic violence and child protection. Ensuring an appropriate response to such incidents by the health service is a key part of a co-ordinated multi-agency strategy to reduce the impact of injury and violence, and local health data may form a valuable part of the local evidence base for these groups.

## Organizational structures for delivery of the three domains of public health practice

Thus far this chapter has considered the evidence that health care interventions can have an impact on population health and has explored how public health practitioners might interface with health care systems to achieve this end, using the model of three domains of public health practice as outlined by Griffiths *et al.* (2005). Organizational structures for delivering health care and public health vary between different countries, and are increasingly divergent within the UK itself.

### Primary care trusts

In England, the establishment of primary care trusts (PCTs) in England as a result of the policy *Shifting the Balance of Power* (Department of Health 2001a) gave both the public health function and the majority of the NHS budget to PCTs. Each was required to appoint a director of public health (DPH), and for the first time this post was opened up to those from any background with the appropriate skills and experience in public health. This organizational structure provided a major opportunity for directors of public health to not only influence and lead work in the field of health improvement, working closely with local authorities, to link with colleagues in the Health Protection Agency to address health protection issues, and also to make inroads into health services improvement. To fulfil this potential, the DPH would need a strong support team with a range of complementary skills. The fact that PCTs were co-terminous with local authorities in most locations was a very helpful catalyst and support to working with local authorities to tackle both the wider determinants of health and health inequalities. In Wales the establishment of local health boards, co-terminous with local authorities, each with a director of public health led to similar opportunities.

There remain however, serious concerns about the capacity and resourcing of public health teams in PCTs in England at the present time as highlighted by both the UK Faculty of Public Health (Gray and Sandberg 2006) and the Chief Medical Officer (CMO) for England in his Annual Report *Raiding Public Health Budgets can Kill* (CMO for England 2006). This will seriously jeopardize the ability of PCTs to deliver on this ambitious public health agenda. Gray and Sandberg (2006) found that only 36 per cent of those working in PCTs perceived that their team was adequate to deliver the public health function. The CMO's report highlighted that senior staff levels in public health are almost static, in contrast with a striking and consistent expansion in all clinical specialities, and that spending on health improvement is failing to keep pace with the growth of NHS expenditure. Even more worryingly, the report identified 'a 20-fold variation in expenditure on health improvement by primary care trusts, much more than could be accounted for by differential need'. It highlighted significant concerns that the expressed commitments to public health by many health bodies are not matched by action, and in particular, that public health budgets are regularly 'raided' to reduce hospital deficits or to meet clinical productivity targets (Gray and Sandberg 2006).

It remains to be seen if the proposals to reduce the number of primary care trusts in England in 2006 through *Commissioning a Patient-Led NHS* (Department of Health 2005b) will provide an opportunity to address this. (See Chapter 5 for a detailed look at capacity and capability in public health.)

## Sustainability

Health services are large organizations with substantial resources and a significant number of employees; they consume large amounts of energy, produce waste, have massive purchasing power, and often have a significant impact on local travel congestion. There is potential to contribute to sustainability both by direct action and by acting as an exemplar organization that influences both other organizations and their own staff. The possible ways in which the NHS could make an impact are comprehensively reviewed by Coote (2002) and are summarized in Table 7.3.

**Table 7.3** Potential for NHS and other health care organizations to contribute to sustainability

| Area | Contribution |
| --- | --- |
| Employment | Recruit locally<br>Embed good practice with long-term view of training routes for local people<br>Collaborate and diversify |
| Purchasing policy | Support local economies<br>Promote 'whole life costing'<br>Fill knowledge and skills gap about sustainable purchasing |
| Procurement of food | Develop a long-term strategy |
| Procurement of child care policy | Follow a sustainable approach to provision of child care<br>Focus locally |
| Management of energy | Adopt a rounded approach<br>Prioritize energy efficiency<br>Promote health |
| Management of waste | Save costs<br>Recycle<br>Invigorate local communities |

*Continued*

**Table 7.3** Continued

| Area | Contribution |
| --- | --- |
| Travel | Work with local transport providers<br>Monitor costs<br>Use incentives and penalties<br>Reduce the burden of ill health |
| Commissioning new buildings | 'Design in' sustainable measures<br>Plan early |

*Source*: after Coote (2002)

## Conclusion

In conclusion, public health practitioners have much to gain from working in partnership with health care professionals. For some, this will mean active engagement in the process of commissioning and quality assuring health care to ensure that maximum gain is secured for a local population from a safe, comprehensive and equitable health care. For others it will mean working in partnership with health care professionals to advocate and lobby for changes to support the health of the public, or to support them to deliver appropriately tailored health promotion messages, and to ensure that these services are delivered in an appropriate, culturally sensitive and sustainable fashion.

---

**Suggested further reading**

Bunker, J.P. (2001) The role of medical care in contributing to health improvements within societies, *International Journal of Epidemiology*, 30: 1260–3.

Griffiths, S., Jewell T. and Donnelly, P. (2005) Public health in practice: the three domains of public health, *Public Health*, 119: 907–13.

Pencheon, D., Guest, C., Melzer, D. and Muir Gray, J. (eds) (2006) *Oxford Handbook of Public Health Practice*. Oxford: Oxford University Press.

Scally, G. (ed.) (1997) *Progress in Public Health*. London: Royal Society of Medicine Press.

# 8

## ALISON GILCHRIST
## Community development and networking for health

**Editors' introduction**

Evidence suggests that people's social environment and the quality and diversity of their informal networks are important for their health. This chapter describes the role of networks within the voluntary and community sectors. It particularly looks at the role of networks in building 'social capital' and community participation in order to strengthen the community sector's contribution to partnership working. It provides helpful insights into social networks which will be of value to all public health workers who work with and for communities.

The author describes the nature of networks within communities and identifies the role they play in helping people share information, make sense of their experiences and articulate their collective needs. Understanding and nurturing informal networks (weak ties) outside family and personal friendships (strong ties) is an essential prerequisite to community participation.

Networking is an integral part of many people's practice in paid and voluntary work, and is an essential feature of all aspects of partnership working. Community development practice and value base recognize the importance of networks within communities. Community development workers can connect 'weak tie' networks to foster greater cohesion and co-operation as well as countering the more negative aspects of elitism and exclusivity that can be characteristics of networks.

The author moves on to consider the way that social networks promote people's health by strengthening social relationships and combating social isolation, and how an understanding of networks can assist health promotion activity. She distinguishes between the activities that promote 'top–down' agendas and those that work with existing community generated concerns. Voluntary organizations, community groups and self-help activities are often connected through interpersonal networks, and these organizations are thus able to represent community and service user interests on partnerships. Opportunities for networking are stimulated by events and environments which encourage regular informal contact and interaction.

The author concludes by identifying the skills and activities necessary to promote and utilize networks. People with the responsibilities for fostering networks need to be able to work across organizational boundaries and have the skills and confidence to work in informal and unstructured ways, managing multiple accountabilities and issues of confidentiality.

## Introduction

Public health has been described as 'preventing disease, prolonging life and promoting health through the organised efforts of society' (Acheson 1988). It has both personal and collective dimensions, reflecting individual as well as social circumstances and choices. The concept of 'community', although problematic in sociological and policy terms (Hoggett 1997; Nash 2002), similarly encapsulates the idea that people's behaviour and well-being are influenced by interactions with others. Informal social networks contribute significantly to our quality of life, shaping our identities and sense of belonging, while enhancing many aspects of our health. Networks are evolving configurations in which some participants cluster together while others are only loosely connected. Those links that are characterized by close, overlapping or emotional relationships are known as '*strong ties*', while those between people who do not share a common allegiance have been termed '*weak ties*'. Granovetter (1973) first recognized the significance of 'weak ties' as forming 'bridges' between different sections of the community or between organizations, enabling the network to extend its reach and support a greater diversity of participants. It is these connections demonstrated in Figure 8.1 that provide the basis for collective action, alliances and partnership working, whether through formally constituted organizations or informal conversation and exchanges. Our experience of 'community' is derived from these informal social networks of neighbours, colleagues and fellow activists or associates (Wellman 1979), rather than more traditional (but often non-existent or overly intrusive) family relationships.

This rather compressed and simplified example illustrates how social networks are used to identify and articulate perceived needs and aspirations. People talk with one another, reflecting on their experience in order to share grievances, dreams and fears. They learn about different ways of seeing the world, new explanations for problems and, consequently, gain ideas for changing the status quo. This might involve challenging vested interests or conventional ways of working. Networks help to spread the risk and enable people to anticipate potential obstacles or consequences by drawing on a wider range of perspectives. Networks allow people to appreciate differences while also shaping their sense of collective identity, building common cause and mobilizing resources for joint action (Marwell and Oliver 1993; Klandermans 1997; Gilchrist 2004a).

But networks do not just happen. They are created, supported and shaped by people actively seeking out others and forging relationships that will help them in their own lives. Networking is an ancient, perhaps instinctive feature of human societies, but the term has been overused in recent years, acquiring pejorative connotations as

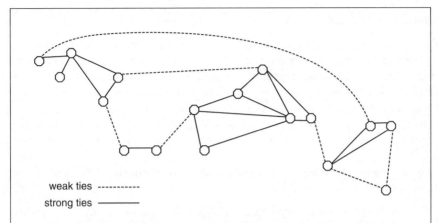

weak ties  -----------
strong ties  ─────

Simon, a community psychiatric nurse works in a team at the health centre. He has strong ties with his partner, Gavin, who is employed as a sports development officer. They play badminton together, and among the members of the badminton club, they have a couple of close friends, one of whom, Davina, is a local GP based in another area of the town. Through his acquaintance with Davina, Simon has got to know his equivalent, Jamal, who is concerned about the high levels of drug-related mental disorders within the Black communities. Simon raises this matter formally with members of his own team, who agree that a serious problem is brewing in the schools in the neighbourhood where the health centre is based. The social worker there has a brother who runs the youth club and agrees to find out what is already being done to work with young people to address this problem. They discover that the young people themselves are keen to organize activities to reduce boredom, and so a football league is set up with funding from Gavin's budget for community-based initiatives. The incidence of drug-use goes down and several of the young footballers find their way into permanent work through the contacts they have made on the pitch.

**Figure 8.1** Social networks

being manipulative and self-serving. I use the word more neutrally here to mean the practice of initiating, maintaining and using connections and relationships for individual and shared benefits.

This chapter considers how networks are useful for public health strategies, and argues that simply strengthening and diversifying social networks will improve health, as well as making health provision more effective. It explores the links between social capital, networks and community development, examining recent evidence connecting the quality of a person's relationships and social interaction with their levels of health. In doing so, the chapter uses the WHO definition of health as 'a state of complete physical, mental and social well-being, and not merely the absence of disease or infirmity' (WHO 1948). There is a particular focus on the role of networks in supporting community life and in co-ordinating the work of voluntary and community organizations. Networking is considered as an important strategy for encouraging community engagement and enhancing partnership working.

## Community development for health

Public health professionals have long recognized the value of a community-based approach and have looked to community development to provide them with tools and techniques for health education and health promotion projects (Labonte 1998). Community development is usually understood to mean a professional intervention that helps people to help themselves by encouraging them to set up or be involved in collective activities which address shared problems or achieve some common goal. The agreed occupational standards for community development work describe it as:

> An occupation dedicated to collectively bringing about social change and justice by working with communities to
>
> – identify their needs, opportunities, rights and responsibilities
> – plan, organise and take action
> – evaluate the effectiveness and impact of the action
>
> all in ways which challenge oppression and tackle inequalities.
>
> (Federation for Community Development Learning 2003)

The Department of Health guidance for community development workers in the Delivering Race Equality programme in mental health identifies four key roles: access facilitator, service developer, change agent and capacity builder (Department of Health 2005e). This highlights the way in which community development workers often play an inter-sectoral role, enhancing communication and co-operation between public authorities and communities. Community development is not, however, synonymous with community engagement although evidence shows that where there has been a tradition of community development in an area, community engagement strategies are more effective and sustainable because they are based on a foundation of strong and independent community activity. Nor is community development equivalent to health education although they may use many of the same techniques. The crucial distinction lies in community development's espoused value-base and orientation towards community perspectives and interests, even when employed by statutory health agencies. As Box 8.1 indicates, community development supports people to influence decisions and organize activities 'from the bottom–up'. In the context of public health, community development helps local people to establish and run groups and activities that specifically address health issues that community members have themselves identified.

## Promoting health 'in the community'

Health promotion often takes the form of services that reach out to or are located in communities in order to break down the formal boundaries between institutions and 'users'. Such schemes tend to work to an agenda set by health professionals or government priorities. In this respect, they differ from community development in being driven from the 'top–down'. Nevertheless, they may be designed and delivered according to the needs and wishes of the targeted populations.

---

**Box 8.1**   Social networks from the bottom–up

A campaign to raise awareness of heart disease among Asian people involved the social group for elders at the community centre as well as working through the local mosques, temples and gudwaras. The networks associated with these institutions were used to distribute leaflets about healthy eating, encourage people to join a walking group and attend for a cholesterol check at the clinic.

A group for teenage mothers undertook outreach work to schools and youth clubs, relating their own experiences and providing ideas and materials about contraception, relationships and safe sex. Because they were local and of similar ages to the young people, their advice seems to be more readily accepted than that of health professionals who are not so well-connected into the target groups.

Both of these are intended to increase people's knowledge of the risks involved in certain behaviours, with an expectation that habits will change as a result.

---

The government's latest strategy, *Choosing Health* (Department of Health 2004a), invites people to take more personal responsibility for improving their health by working with 'community health champions' to achieve individualized targets, such as weight loss or smoking reduction. Although in its early stages, this approach has immense potential to harness the power of peer pressure mediated through informal friendship and community networks.

Working with individuals to boost their self-esteem, to improve confidence in social settings and to coax them out of, sometimes self-imposed, isolation is especially important for people with mental health problems or who enjoy only intermittent good health. A community-based training project in the North-west of England deliberately included people who experienced mental ill health working alongside people from the same community who reported no such difficulties. This integrated approach was found to be especially important for developing the social networks of people who had previously felt isolated and stigmatized. The Developing Race Equality programme launched by the Department of Health across England in 2005 aims to reduce the fear of mental illness among Black and minority ethnic communities and improve their access to services. The programme builds on the learning from projects such as Sharing Voices in Bradford (Seebohm *et al.* 2005), which uses a community development approach to support mentally ill members of the community to take part in group activities. This is especially important for communities that experience high levels of poverty or oppression. Figure 8.2 exemplifies how different approaches to health promotion can be used to support the community development approach suggested.

Community development contributes to public health because it helps communities to tackle problems that threaten their well-being, such as a poor environment or high levels of crime (cf. Chu *et al.* 2004). Community development reinforces a holistic approach to service delivery by enabling communities to articulate and deliver their own solutions rather than relying on the medical expertise of others. It also encourages a more equal and positive interaction between community members and

| Decision making | Mode of intervention | Example |
|---|---|---|
| Top–down | Service delivery | User involvement on mainstream partnerships |
| | Outreach services | Community-based clinic, home visiting |
| | Health education | Talks and material given to community groups |
| | Community development | Action research, setting up community-led activities |
| Bottom–up | Collective action | Campaigns and user empowerment methods |

**Figure 8.2** Different approaches to health promotion

professionals who normally focus on their problems and deficiencies. Community-led initiatives (see Box 8.2) are more likely to be 'owned' (and therefore used) by local people and more likely to reach sections of the community that mainstream services neglect or inadvertently exclude. In addition to the development of specific projects or services, community development can also strengthen informal networks by helping people to work together and build trust within diverse communities, contributing to the long-term health of community members, and the sustainability of community-based health improvement programmes.

A networking approach to community development is based on practices and policies that strengthen and extend people's networks to promote better health

---

**Box 8.2**   Community-led Initiatives

A tenants' association was worried about the lack of play opportunities for children living in the high rise blocks. At the same time, the health visitors were concerned about levels of asthma among the younger residents. A joint group was set up and undertook a door-to-door survey to investigate the extent of the problem and to identify people who might be willing to help organize a campaign to improve things for the families. With the support of the tenants' association and involvement of the children themselves, a playground was designed and established on a disused site next to the local social club. With the help of a local community worker, they also made contact with similar groups around the country campaigning to improve the lives of children in tower blocks. Members of the group reported that they felt less isolated and visited the doctors less. One woman in particular was able to come off tranquillizers and used her newly discovered talents to successfully apply for a job at the primary school. Being involved in the group has restored her confidence and improved her mental health.

for individuals and benefit society as a whole (Campbell and Jovchelovitch 2000; Gilchrist 2004a). This applies to the fields of education, regeneration, employment and cultural activities as much as to health, and has important implications for professionals working for community benefit within and across all these policy areas (Banks *et al.* 2003). There is increasing recognition that health improvements can be gained through interdisciplinary, multi-agency partnerships that have strong levels of community involvement, hence the importance of promoting networks that work across organizational boundaries.

## The 'community' dimension to health and well-being

There is an accumulating body of evidence suggesting that people's social environment (the quality and diversity of their informal networks) is an important determinant of actual and perceived health (Pilisuk and Parks 1986; Campbell *et al.* 1999). In recent years this approach has focused on economic inequalities (Wilkinson 1996, 2005; Kawachi *et al.* 1997; Acheson 1998) and social capital (Gillies 1998c; Cooper *et al.* 1999; McKenzie and Harpham 2006)). As David Evans and Murray Stewart examine in their respective chapters on inequalities (Chapter 9), and regeneration and neighbourhood renewal strategies (Chapter 10), the government acknowledges that social exclusion, arising from poverty, discrimination and other life hazards is correlated with poor health. In this respect, health is an important dimension of social justice, especially as it applies to people's quality of life. Wilkinson's research powerfully demonstrates that this is in part linked to relative income levels within a given (national) population, and he suggests that it might be due to the associated stress and discontent experienced by poorer sections of society who witness the relative wealth of their counterparts, but feel they can do little to close the gap (Wilkinson 1996, 2000). Health and happiness are high when people are able to manage stress and develop a coherent view of their existence and status as meaningful and within their control (Antonovsky 1987). The empowerment aspects of community development would support this approach, particularly when linked to equalities-based practice (Gilchrist 2006 forthcoming).

Government policy has emphasized the importance of improving the quality of life for disadvantaged communities by reducing the gap between deprived areas and the average for the country as a whole (Social Exclusion Unit 2000). Local Government Acts (2000 in England; 2003 in Scotland) give local authorities the power to do virtually anything they choose to improve the 'well-being' of people in their area. Health is included as a dimension of Local Area Agreements that set out how the various partners will deliver the agreed aims. Similar policies and structures operate in Wales (Communities First), Northern Ireland (Targeting Social Need) and Scotland (Community Health Partnerships). This has resulted in some innovatory projects and health promotion programmes that attempt to boost both health and happiness by encouraging people to improve their social networks and to develop a more positive outlook on life. The initial results are promising, especially in relation to mental health. Box 8.3 gives an example of how involvement in self-help and mutual aid groups has also been shown to be beneficial to health, especially when these are peer-led.

---

**Box 8.3**   Self-help and mutual aid groups

---

- Members of Alcoholics Anonymous are more likely to stay sober if they increase their participation in the group over time, meet regularly with their sponsor and sponsor other AA members (Emrick *et al.* 1993).
- Similarly peer-led smoking cessation groups are more successful than the use of TV programmes and self-help manuals. Participants in the groups smoked significantly fewer cigarettes a day, and a follow-up three months later showed that a higher proportion were still not smoking compared to the people who had simply watched the TV programme and read the manual (Jason *et al.* 1987).
- The same findings appear in relation to participation in self-help tranquillizer groups (Tattersall and Hallstrom 1992).
- Groups providing support for the recently bereaved (Lieberman and Videka-Sherman 1986).
- Women attending a breast cancer support group that encouraged them to express their emotions and improve communication with family and friends (Spiegel *et al.* 1989).

The evidence suggests that these beneficial effects arise from the interactions and relationships that derive from membership of the group, including a sense of solidarity from knowing that there are people 'out there' with similar experiences who are available for mutual support. Informal networks often feed into and sustain self-help groups and they, in turn, generate new social networks that help people to manage their stress and increase their sense of security, leading to additional and sustainable health improvements (Holmes 2001).

## Informal networks and health

Empirical research indicates that relationships and regular interaction with others protects individuals against disease and mental distress. People with robust and diverse networks lead healthier and happier lives than those who are more isolated or whose networks are comparatively homogenous (Argyle 1989, 1996a; Yen and Syme 1999; Swann and Morgan 2002; Layard 2005). They have stronger immune systems, suffer less from heart disease, recover more quickly from emotional traumas such as bereavement, and seem to be more resistant to the debilitating effects of illness, possibly because of some kind of emotional buffer which gives them a more positive outlook on life generally (Pilisuk and Parks 1986; Blane *et al.* 1996; Kawachi 1997). While the physiological mechanisms for this resilience are unclear, it is probable that social networks provide a variety of forms of support and affirmation, including practical advice around health matters. It is known that people will seek information from non-professional sources about difficult or risky issues before they will approach the appropriate agencies (Gabarino 1983). Having knowledgeable people within one's social network is useful, assuming of course that any enquiries will be treated in confidence and not form the basis for gossip or disapproval. Similarly, role models and supporters can bolster self-esteem, enabling people to cope better during periods of distress and disaster. Neighbourhood networks provide practical assistance with a variety of tasks (Henning and Lieberg 1996; Williams and Windebank 2000) and family members can usually be relied on during a crisis and for long-term care (Bulmer 1987). Community groups and neighbourhood activities may also maintain individuals in a more active lifestyle by providing reasons for people to leave the house and meet other residents.

Relationships flourish when there is empathy and respect, a balance of giving and receiving (Duck 1992; Reilly 2001). People rarely like to feel that they are dependent on others and are more likely to accept help if they are able to reciprocate in some way. This aspect of networking deserves greater attention from health professionals. The 'gifted' time and skills of community members must be valued by recognizing that volunteers, activists and carers are not merely unpaid staff, but individuals with needs, talents and sometimes considerable expertise. The recognition that 'lay' people may be involved in the *co-production* of health reminds us that enabling patients and service users to give their time and effort to the shared experiences of caring and treatment, means that these relationships will be more balanced and more rewarding (see also Kretzmann 2000). In the past, however, work programmes and spending priorities were disproportionately dominated by the views of health professions, bolstered by their own close networks and organizational culture. Consequently many health initiatives were devised within a medical discourse, based on a deficit model which assumes that health problems occur because of some failing on the part of individuals or communities. There is now greater application of social models of health which acknowledge the impact that social and environmental factors have on actual and reported health. (See for example case studies published by the Community Health Exchange: www.chex.org.uk)

## The concept of social capital

There has been a growing interest in the concept of 'social capital', a term first coined by Harifan (1916), and elaborated since most notably by Jacobs (1961), Bourdieu (1993), Putnam (2000) and Halpern (2005). While there has been considerable discussion around the theoretical content of social capital and its application in practice (Field 2003), there is broad agreement that its core components consist of the 'shared understandings, levels of trust, associational memberships and informal networks of human relationships that facilitate social exchange, social order and underpin social institutions' (Richardson and Mumford 2002: 206). Woolcock (2001) builds on Granovetter's categories of 'strong' and 'weak' ties to suggest that social capital can be categorized as *bonding, bridging* and *linking*, referring respectively to:

- the ties that bind close friends, extended families and close-knit communities (bonding);
- the relationships between people who are in some ways different (bridging); and

- those connections that enable power, information and resources to flow between different levels of society (for example between the commissioners of strategic health authorities and community-led service providers) (linking).

Community development is mainly concerned with strengthening bridging and linking social capital and for the purposes of this chapter, social capital will be considered as a collective resource which is generated and maintained through networking interactions and voluntary associations, unmediated by formal contracts or financial exchange. The related concept of 'collective efficacy' has been developed by Sampson following research on community life in Chicago (2004). This refers to a *shared belief* by members of a community that by working together they can make a difference in their circumstances and life chances. The degree to which people are part of social networks operating in their locality seems to be an important aspect of this notion, and is probably related to their perceived willingness and capacity to organize collective action around common concerns, such as perceived threats to health, for example the siting of telephone masts.

## Networks and community participation

Networks provide both the motivation and the means for communities to undertake collective action to improve their lives. Personal contacts create a web of links and relationships, which support communication and co-operation between organizations and agencies, thereby creating routes for accessing health-related services or advices and encouraging community participation.

People are largely recruited to community activities and volunteering through word of mouth or knowing someone who is already involved. They may develop their social networks through such activities. Indeed, this is often given as a reason for volunteering or joining clubs especially when people's circumstances change or they move to a new area. The 'grapevine' is a wonderful source of information (and rumour) about what is going on and it allows 'private' issues to emerge into the public arena. Relationships among people active in the voluntary sector have been revealed as important channels for influencing policy and easing the sharing of facilities. Effective community leaders (see Box 8.4) are observed to have strong social networks, ensuring that they receive the support and feedback they need, and are held accountable by the people they claim to represent (Purdue *et al.* 2000).

However, networks can also perpetuate elite positions and exclude others from decision making (Skelcher *et al.* 1996). Networks inevitably reflect personal circumstances and preferences, often shaped by inequalities in society. These biases need to be countered through positive action measures or, at the very least, acknowledged in formal deliberations and through proper accountability mechanisms.

Community leaders sometimes find themselves resented by other residents or undermined by rivals (Richardson and Mumford 2002). Strong social capital can be divisive, maintaining the dominant status of an established community against incomers, for example when gypsies and travellers try to move onto a site. Such conflicts and tensions within communities are well documented, though not so commonly recognized within practice guidelines. These antagonisms frequently arise as a

---

**Box 8.4**   Effective community leaders

Maya was a middle-aged and newly divorced shop-owner who had recently moved into the area. Her children were grown up and she wanted to volunteer her services to the local community as a way of getting to know people. Maya's accountancy experience was particularly welcomed by the Community Association and she was elected treasurer at the next AGM. Her position in the community, as well as her links with the African-Caribbean communities from her earlier life, gave her a good sense of local needs and before long she found herself representing BME perspectives on the community health forum for that area. From here she stood as a local councillor and used her status to campaign to keep green spaces within inner-city neighbourhoods. She knew just how important these were for the peace of mind of local people, creating opportunities for residents to meet and greet each other and for children to play out.

---

result of different or competing lifestyles, and more powerful groups can unfairly occupy communal space and facilities. These forms of institutional discrimination are often unwitting: reflecting local norms and prevailing cultures rather than deliberate intentions to exclude. Such inequalities can be tackled by proactive networking to develop positive and more tolerant relationships (Gilchrist 2004b).

Communities are complex and dynamic systems, in a state of constant flux and with boundaries only 'fuzzily' defined. It is neither possible nor desirable to superimpose formal structures on this web of unchoreographed interaction and spontaneous self-organization. Network models of organization are well suited to such turbulent environments, since tightly managed programmes that are accountable through more formal hierarchies tend to stifle the essence of an effective community, namely its vibrancy and flexibility (Gilchrist 2001). Health promotion strategies should support and complement community-led initiatives, thereby invigorating community networks. This takes time and depends on long-term investment in generic community practitioners who can support a multiplicity of groups and activities, responsive to community-identified needs, rather than just focusing on short-term or externally designed projects.

## Building relationships, sharing power

Multi-agency or partnership working is considerably easier if trusting relationships exist between the people involved (Goss and Kent 1995; Means *et al.* 1997). By facilitating more effective partnership working, networking contributes to directly measurable outcomes because it reduces duplication and unhelpful antagonisms. Informal conversation enables partners and participants to anticipate where opinions are likely to diverge, and to pre-empt tensions by suggesting possible forms of negotiation or compromise. Box 8.5 gives an example to support these ideas. Dissenting views are accommodated by developing new forms of service delivery or finding ways around apparent obstacles to joint working. Research indicates that networking can be effective in developing user or community-orientated partnerships

---

**Box 8.5**  Building relationships and sharing power

---

Through the informal networks of a member of a neighbourhood watch group, attention was brought to the levels of isolation, depression and health problems experienced by older members of the Asian communities. After some preliminary research through home visits, the local community worker invited health visitors, community leaders and social workers to a meeting which agreed that some kind of social club should be established that catered for the cultural and religious needs of local Sikhs, Muslims and Hindus. The involvement of the (white) community worker was crucial in enabling this group to operate across the different community identities.

Visits were made to a day centre in Southall to see what could be done, and 'listening lunches' were held for local elders to sound out their views about what the social club should provide. As well as activities and refreshments, the group wanted access to chiropody services and psychiatric help, including counselling. Funding was obtained to run the group for one day a week with support from a part-time worker and over the years, the initiative has expanded to become a fully-fledged day centre with the full range of health-related support.

---

in service delivery (Beresford and Trevillion 1995; Taylor 1997; Mayo and Taylor 2001).

Learning about other people's cultures and histories is an important aspect of networking, enabling people to empathize with perspectives that are different from their own and to operate appropriately in different settings. Being aware of suspicions and assumptions that may exist across the community–institution boundary usually ensures that conflicts can be anticipated, clarified and resolved quickly. As well as more formal arrangements, co-operation between organizations relies on a regular and reciprocal exchange of information, favours and occasionally resources. This cannot be arrived at overnight or through paper memoranda. It involves a more organic process of developing linkages between individuals and addressing disagreements as and when they arise. In the context of public health, networks can be thought of as pathways across a complex organizational landscape connecting the various sectors, and providing routes into 'hard to reach' communities and signposts for navigating among sources of expertise and energy. Networks that support collaborative working are not necessarily formally constituted – they can be ad hoc arrangements that emerge around a specific need or goal and this is exemplified in Box 8.6.

Networking across boundaries should be recognized as difficult and sometimes risky work often requiring considerable ingenuity to find a connection or to step into unfamiliar cultural or organizational territory. Networking supports participation generally and can be used to reach and involve marginalized sections of the population. In particular, networking that is informed by an active commitment to inclusion, equality and anti-oppressive practices helps to tackle barriers to participation. Working to extend and maintain the 'weak ties' across community and agency boundaries will promote greater integration and ultimately improve service delivery. Working at the margins of organizations and across the edges of networks that are aligned but not

---

**Box 8.6** Collaborative working

---

Community workers based in a neighbourhood but employed by several different organizations jointly co-ordinated a Women's Health Day at the local clinic. Using their professional relationships and contacts in the community they were able to plan a programme of workshops and health promoting activities that drew together women from the statutory sector, higher education, the voluntary sector and, of course, women and girls from different ethnic communities in the area. The result was a successful event that strengthened local networks and further diversified access to health provision.

---

overlapping is important and can help communities to deal constructively with their own divisions by becoming more tolerant and cohesive, thus contributing to people's health and sense of well-being (Stafford *et al.* 2002). This can be a difficult role in which workers face dilemmas around multiple accountability and confidentiality.

Over the past decade or so government policy has promoted a much stronger role for community representatives and for people in the voluntary and community sectors whether on an unpaid basis or as professional workers. If these partnerships are to operate on a truly equal and participatory basis, they may require major shifts in attitude and practice from all concerned. Such arrangements can be fraught with difficulty, with a range of barriers identified that distort or undermine effective community engagement (Hastings *et al.* 1996; Popay *et al.* 2005). The existence of community forums or patient-led advocacy projects can make community participation more inclusive and democratic, as well as nurturing networks within communities and between sectors. Community development can help in the formation and maintenance of these, ensuring in particular that they are empowering for those whose voices are least heard.

General community activity is important in its own right but it is also the basis for community involvement in partnerships or consultation exercises. Just as people are persuaded to take part in communal activities and to serve on committees through their informal networks rather than through formal invitation, so networks are often used to recruit representatives on more formal decision-making arenas. Networks enable community members to succeed in these roles, to build links with people operating in other sectors and to develop the confidence and status to challenge some of the power inequalities that exist between communities and statutory institutions, or within communities themselves. Health practitioners need to understand and work with informal networks, encouraging them to 'build bridges' across community boundaries and to use informal networking to select and support representatives who can express community views (Mondros and Wilson 1994).

Partnership working demands clarity of purpose alongside a willingness to respond to divergent interests, not least within local communities. Some of the recurring problems in **cross-sectoral** partnerships arise because of differences in the ways that communities operate, and the mismatch between their more fluid structures and processes, and the rigid protocols of formal institutions. Numerous studies have shown that being connected to powerful individuals or agencies is itself a form of power (Laumann and Pappi 1976; Knoke 1990) and power relations are an important, although often neglected, aspect of social capital (Baum 2000). Consultation exercises can be enriched but also distorted by influential networks organizing to express particular views. Community representatives on partnership bodies benefit from being supported by formal democratic networks as well as through their informal connections in the community.

## Indirect outcomes of social networks

A 'solid foundation' of community activity and informal networks is a prerequisite for inclusive, democratic and sustainable community engagement (Chanan 2003). As well as the larger, well-established voluntary organizations (which are often managed and run by paid professionals), there exist myriad groups and local organizations that make a contribution to health within neighbourhoods and communities of interest. Some of these provide self-help activities with an explicit focus on a particular affliction (such as addiction to tranquillizers); many are patient or 'survivor' support groups to be found through the Internet. There are also thousands of organizations that actively promote healthy living, for example, through keep-fit classes and food co-operatives, as the example in Box 8.7 demonstrates.

---

**Box 8.7**   Action groups

The Hartcliffe Health and Environmental Action Group has been running activities for many years in an outer suburb of Bristol. The organization uses community development methods to work with local people, who are predominantly on low incomes, to encourage healthy eating and exercise. This addresses a range of issues around the affordability and accessibility of nutritious ingredients, while increasing people's confidence in food preparation. There is an emphasis on learning and sharing, with fun and networking being key ingredients.

---

Even when not directly related to improving diet or fitness, many community groups have a tangential impact on health through activities that indirectly maintain both physical and mental health. These include sports and cultural associations, encouraging people to come together to run, dance, play games, sing and so on. There are obvious physical advantages, but also psychological benefits through the enhanced interaction and improved social networks that are developed as a result (Argyle 1996b).

A new wave of Healthy Living Centres have resurrected the thinking behind the 'Peckham experiment' (Pearce and Crocker 1943) by providing or prescribing activities for their patients. However, the preventive function of community participation is still undervalued by the formal health sector. One reason for this resistance is the paucity of scientific evidence from action research or project evaluation. As a consequence there is plenty of anecdotal support for a positive link, but only limited and somewhat ambivalent hard evidence (Blaxter and Poland 2002). There is certainly more scope for communities to be involved in investigating the impact of social capital on health from their own perspectives, perhaps using methods of participatory appraisal and action research approaches as outlined in the LEAP framework described by Stuart Hashagen and Susan Paxton in Chapter 17.

## Networking in practice

Informal networks are part of the infrastructure and capacity of communities and can be developed (or eroded) through deliberate interventions and activities. In many areas, networks appear to evolve and function 'naturally' without any obvious forms of support or intervention. They contain individuals who are skilled organizers or intuitive networkers, who seem to know everyone and have the knack of putting the right people in touch with one another. They do not necessarily occupy visible 'leadership' roles, but operate behind the scenes, soothing ruffled feathers, resolving conflicts, referring others to the resources they need and generally acting as both 'connectors' and 'catalysts' to generate and maintain collective action (Gilchrist 1998; Gladwell 2002). Such people (among whom women seem disproportionately represented) are often unpaid and unproclaimed and yet their hidden networking is what weaves and mends the fabric of community life. This is especially so in areas experiencing high levels of deprivation and population mobility where there may be a high proportion of individuals experiencing isolation, low self-esteem and mental health difficulties due to social exclusion. These communities are more likely to benefit from professional help from community-based practitioners who can support their networking and help people to organize collective action. This is a role often played by community development workers.

Networking should be considered as a skilled and strategic aspect of community practice (Gilchrist 2005). It features strongly in the jobs or voluntary activity of many people working in communities using techniques that have been dubbed 'the 11 Ms of networking' (Gilchrist 1998) – see Figure 8.3.

Research into the practice of community development workers (Gilchrist 2001) found that good networkers are gregarious, compassionate, curious about cultures other than their own, generous with their time and attention, diplomatic and sensitive to the emotional and political dynamics of situations. Networkers are well organized, preparing themselves for different settings and following up conversations reliably so that trust and mutual respect develop. Networkers are able to assimilate information from a variety of sources and to communicate in a range of styles and modes. They are versatile and flexible in their approach, able to seize opportunities and use their imagination to conjure up exciting and innovative combinations, or simply to suggest interesting links between people from diverse backgrounds. Networkers demonstrate a confident awareness of self, and are able to convey their own identity and personal value system without being over-assertive or arrogant. They appear non-judgemental in their attitudes, open to criticism but also willing to challenge unfair or inefficient practices. They value their autonomy, welcome opportunities to use their own initiative and consequently are less tolerant of organizational constraints, such as those imposed by bureaucratic procedures.

Networking strategies include taking particular care during the early phase of any potential relationship, thinking about self-presentation, using non-verbal cues to

| | |
|---|---|
| Mapping | Finding out who else might have an interest in a particular issue: gathering information about them, including existing connections. |
| Making contacts | Introducing oneself and organization; making referrals. |
| Maintaining connections | Organizing meetings; sending out information bulletins; keeping up-to-date records of names and contact details for key individuals. |
| Managing the web | Servicing networks: making sure that power and inclusion issues are addressed. |
| Monitoring charges | Introducing and inducting new 'players': adjusting to shifts on the policy agenda or concerns arising in the community. |
| Mending | Identifying ruptures in the networks and addressing gaps that emerge through people leaving. |
| Merging | Helping separate groupings to recognize their common or overlapping interests: setting up joint organizational arrangements. |
| Mediating | Dealing with conflicts and misunderstandings: challenging prejudices and apprehensions. |
| Motivating | Persuading and encouraging people to link up with others: encouraging people to take on responsibilities and new roles. |
| Mobilizing | Using the network to form alliances and get involved in collective action. |
| Moving on | Making sure that network members have the confidence, information and support they need to sustain their own connections with one another. |

**Figure 8.3** Actions that facilitate and maintain networks

identify potential points of similarity and difference, and listening attentively to what the other person is saying. The initial contact often takes courage and networkers are assiduous in seeking out informal opportunities for conversation where the views divulged are more likely to express someone's real rather than official opinion. Making space for humour and serendipity on these occasions is useful for opening up dialogue and allows unexpected connections to be made. Networkers consciously monitor the holes and breaches in the web, moving to plug gaps and mend severed ties (see Box 8.8).

Within community development, networkers also need to think about the principles of equality and empowerment, ensuring that the contacts they make address power differentials and that their networks reflect the diversity of the population around them, rather than their own interests and preferences. Personal affinity will inevitably characterize one's networking practice, but these can be countered through a proactive and brave stance in building the more difficult or unfamiliar links.

Networking is facilitated by events that bring people together in semi-structured activity encouraging people who might not otherwise talk to one another to discover common interests and develop a sense of 'belonging'. Many of these interactions of everyday life take place in quasi-public spaces, such as outside schools, around the

---

**Box 8.8**   Networking

---

At a conference on HIV/AIDS, Mandeep, a PCT-based community development worker made sure that she looked through the participants list beforehand to identify the people she wanted to meet. She took with her leaflets about the projects she was currently supporting, and a supply of business cards. She arrived early enough to have a chat with colleagues she knew already, and during the lunch break made a point of making contact with people, who had asked interesting questions or whose name she had previously heard of. She was able to share information about her work plans and find others who were doing similar things to support HIV+ patients. Most excitingly, she found herself in conversation with a community development worker from Uganda who was working with HIV+ mothers to reduce the rates of transmission of the virus to their babies. Mandeep was fascinated to hear about the similarities in their approach to educating and empowering the women in relation to health issues generally. She returned to work the next day with renewed enthusiasm and several useful ideas about how to tackle some of the difficulties she had been encountering.

---

**Box 8.9**   Street parties

---

Street parties are organized on a street-by-street basis and are fun ways of reclaiming the communal space outside people's houses, creating opportunities for neighbours to meet and for children to play together outside. They usually involve clearing out the traffic, putting up some decorations, sharing food, some music and a few organized games that everyone can join in. The secret is to keep things low budget and simple. Street parties are a good way of distributing information about coming events and services that are available in the area, or they can provide a forum for consultation. They are also excellent for identifying residents who are willing to act as 'connectors'. The evaluation of street parties shows that many people meet or got to know their neighbours for the first time and this reduces fear of crime, as well as promoting social inclusion (www.streetsalive.net).

---

local shops and in pubs or parks. The quality of a built environment can have a huge impact on the nature of casual encounters, for example, whether places feel safe, accessible and welcoming to everyone who wishes to use them. They are often areas where people from different backgrounds mingle, but may also feel territorial as if available only to certain sections of the population. Wherever possible this should be challenged, perhaps through cultural activities such as street parties (see Box 8.9) or community art that incorporates local images and experiences.

## Conclusions

Community networks make an important contribution to the current social and health agenda. Networking is vital to the effective operation of multi-agency partnerships, especially those involving people from different disciplines and sectors. Extensive networks allow the identification and recruitment of useful allies and potential partners. Informal interaction associated with meetings, training and other joint events will encourage the development of mutual understanding and respect, making it easier to explore and resolve conflicts, to reach consensus or compromise where necessary, and to clarify aims and objectives as these inevitably change over time. Networking encourages community participation in formal consultation and programme delivery, as well as in activities that nurture mutuality and release social capital.

Although it is proving hard to trace a causal relationship between social networks and health, experience indicates that people who feel connected, rather than isolated or excluded, tend to engage more in communal activities and to report that they feel healthier as a result. The evidence reviewed above suggests that these subjective feelings can be translated into objective statistics in morbidity and mortality levels. Community development, especially in so far as it encourages informal networks and interagency working, has much to offer public health through building social capital and supporting community engagement.

## Acknowledgements

I would like to thank Amanda Inverarity, Janet Muir, Fiona Crawford, Paul Henderson, Jenny Fisher, Elspeth Gracey and Thara Raj for their encouragement and helpful comments on an earlier version of this chapter.

---

**Suggested further reading**

Bubb, S. (2005) *Only Connect: a Leader's Guide to Networking*. London: ACEVO.
Crawford, F. (2005) *Doing it Differently: An Asset-based Approach to Well-being*. Edinburgh: Scottish Council Foundation.
Halpern, D. (2005) *Social Capital*. Cambridge: Polity Press.
Gilchrist, A. (2004) *The Well-connected Community*. Bristol: The Policy Press.
McKenzie, K. and Harpham, T. (2006) *Social Capital and Mental Health*. Jessica Kingsley.
Taylor, M. (2003) *Community and Public Policy*. Basingstoke: Palgrave Macmillan.

# PART 3

# Major contemporary themes in public health

## Editors' overview

What are the key challenging issues in public health at the beginning of the 21st century?

Public health resource and action has always had to address some all-pervasive public health problems, such as the poor sanitation and lack of clean water tackled by the Victorians, and 'clean air' pollution control measures in the mid-20th century. Now, in the UK, public health faces new challenges. In this part of the book, we focus on five issues, selected because they are fundamental to today's task of improving public health: addressing inequalities in health; improving health and health inequality at a neighbourhood level; improving health in the cities of the world; looking at the wider picture of global influences on health and health inequalities; and protecting the health of the public.

These five issues have a central place in recent change in public health policy, participation and practice. They will continue to do so, and compel us to redefine public health for the 21st century and to explain why change has to happen.

In Chapter 9 David Evans considers new directions in tackling inequalities in health. He provides evidence of the socio-economic inequalities in the health of the UK population and assesses the UK policy response from successive governments. He notes recent government recognition of the link between poverty, inequalities and social exclusion and its translation into policy initiatives. Evans discusses whether current government policy towards reducing inequalities is working. In the final section of this chapter he gives practical options for public health workers about methods they might use in their work to reduce health inequalities.

In Chapter 10 Murray Stewart examines the re-emergence of 'neighbourhoods' as a concern of public health professionals and policy makers and their role in addressing health inequalities and improving health and well-being through 'neighbourhood renewal and regeneration'. Stewart outlines and assesses the success of national and local policy initiatives.

In Chapter 11 Colin Fudge takes an international perspective to discuss the implementation of sustainable futures in cities. He discusses the concept of 'sustainable development' and how urbanization and world population growth are threats to sustainable development and must be addressed in public health action. He provides case studies of his evaluative research in three Swedish cities. This gives useful pointers to public health workers and planners in growing urban city populations.

In Chapter 12 Stuart McClean examines the impact of globalization upon public health risks, global health inequalities and international trade policy. He summarizes conflicting views concerning the future impact of globalization on public health, arguing that events at some geographical distance from home will impact upon public health agendas and actions.

The traditional public health function of health protection, including disease surveillance and control, remain of central importance in contemporary public health. In Chapter 13 Melanie Grey, Mike Studden and Joyshri Sarangi examine new challenges, policy frameworks and organizational arrangements for health protection. They discuss underpinning guiding principles to inform judgements and decision taking, and engaging the public in understanding decisions about health risks. Grey, Studden and Sarangi also map the wide range of resources for protecting health, and analyse key issues for multidisciplinary working practice.

# 9

## DAVID EVANS
New directions in tackling inequalities in health

### Editors' introduction

When looking at the health of populations in the UK, a key issue is that health is not evenly spread: some groups of people are healthier than other groups. In particular, poorer people are, on average, less healthy than better-off people indicating an association between health and wealth. This uneven spread of health across populations is known as 'inequalities in health'. The existence of health inequalities challenges all public health workers to improve the health of less healthy groups of people so that it is as good as that of the healthiest; in other words to close the 'health gap' between rich and poor people.

Action to address health inequalities can take place at different levels of the population and the public health workforce. Policies can be implemented at different levels to tackle the root causes of ill health with, for example, actions to eliminate poverty, homelessness, lack of life chances and unemployment or by working directly to develop communities and individuals who have the worst health.

Reduction of health inequality should involve every public health worker, from those working for the government of the day in a health and public health capacity, the local authority, primary care trust members, social workers, community workers, nurses, environmental health practitioners, general practitioners, police and educators.

This chapter begins by looking at what we mean by 'inequalities' and whether they are always 'unfair'. It briefly examines the evidence for causes of health inequality between people in different socio-economic groups. Government policies over the past 25 years that aim to reduce health inequalities are assessed in terms of how successful they have been and what more could be done.

The author discusses five options for addressing health inequalities: lobbying, partnership working, community development, promoting healthy behaviours and improving access to health care. He concludes with practical pointers for the public health worker who wants to contribute to a reduction in health inequalities.

## Introduction

Health inequalities have been observed and reported in the UK since the ground-breaking work of William Farr on vital statistics, first published in 1837 (Davey Smith *et al.* 2001a). More recently the term has also been used to describe inequalities in the health experience of black and minority ethnic groups in Britain, although there are methodological difficulties in disentangling the effects of ethnicity and socio-economic status (Davey Smith *et al.* 2000a). There are, for example, significantly different standardized mortality ratios for men aged 20–64 resident in England and Wales but coming from different countries of origin, with most but not all non-British born groups experiencing higher standardized mortality ratios than the total population. Inequalities in health also exist between geographical areas and between women and men.

'Inequalities in health' have been defined as 'the virtually universal phenomenon of variation in health indicators (infant and maternal mortality rates, mortality and incidence rates of many diseases and so on) associated with socio-economic status and ethnicity' (Last 2001: 93). For almost every indicator, there is a clear positive correlation between health and wealth: on average, the wealthier people are, the better their health; the poorer, the worse their experience of health and disease, and the greater their risk of dying prematurely.

## Inequality and inequity

A key aspect of inequalities in health, not always explicit in the literature, is that inequalities are variations that are perceived to be unfair. On average, younger people experience better health than older people, but these differences are not usually regarded as unfair or defined as inequalities in health.

In practice when commentators discuss inequalities in health, they often mean inequities in health: that is, those inequalities which are perceived to be unfair. Concepts of equity and inequity are thus value based, and refer to 'what should be' (Baggott 2000). As Baggott points out, they are therefore contestable, and there is much controversy about whether certain inequalities are actually inequitable and what should be done about them. Are we concerned simply with inequality of outcome as measured by our various health indicators? Or are we also seeking to ensure equity of access to services (which may or may not lead to equitable outcomes) or equity of opportunity for people to attain their full health potential (World Health Organization 1981) which may require unequal input of resources towards poorer individuals and communities?

## Causes of inequality in health

As well as debates on the extent to which inequalities are inequitable, there is a considerable literature seeking to explain the causes of inequality in health. This is a complex field, beset with conceptual and methodological difficulties in measuring inequality and in demonstrating causal pathways. Following a discussion in the Black Report (DHSS 1980), four major potential causes of the observed inequalities generally have been considered: artefact, social selection, behavioural/cultural and material (Macintyre 1997). Although these debates are unresolved (and possibly irresolvable, as the different explanations are not necessarily mutually exclusive), the vast majority of researchers and policy analysts accept that artefact and social selection account for relatively little of the observed differences in health experience between rich and poor. There is more continuing debate on the relative importance of material and psychosocial factors.

What is most notable about this literature, however, is how much of it is concerned with documenting and explaining inequalities in health and how little focuses on describing and evaluating interventions to reduce such inequalities. It is relatively recently that significant attention has turned to synthesizing the evidence base on what works in reducing inequalities in health (Asthana and Halliday 2006). This chapter is intended to help redress the balance by primarily focusing on what the evidence base tells us works in reducing inequalities in health, particularly from the perspective of public health practitioners working at a community level. Before doing so, however, it is necessary briefly to summarize what we know about socio-economic inequalities in health, and how UK health policy has responded to this knowledge.

## The evidence for socio-economic inequalities in health

The last century has witnessed remarkable improvements in health both within Britain and in most other countries internationally. In developing countries, infant, child and maternal mortality have fallen dramatically. In the UK, Europe and the rest of the developed world mortality from the major killer diseases (chronic heart disease and cancer) has also been falling.

Despite these general improvements, however, socio-economic inequalities in health remain and are increasing between countries, regions, socio-economic groups and individuals. Inequalities in health are as obvious in Britain today as a hundred years ago, despite the creation of the welfare state and the virtual abolition of absolute poverty. The health of the poorest has improved over time, but not as fast as for the rest of the population; thus the health gap between rich and poor has widened. This gap in health is of course only one aspect of the widening socio-economic gap between rich and poor which can also be seen in income, housing, education and other aspects of social life.

Health inequalities are much greater in some countries than in others; for example, inequalities in health are markedly smaller in absolute terms in Sweden (which for many years has pursued equality orientated social and Labour market policies) than in the UK, thus suggesting that social policy can impact on health inequalities.

## The growing health gap in the UK

Health inequalities have been documented in the UK throughout the past 150 years. As well as the pioneering work of Farr, health inequalities were identified by Rowntree (1901), Booth (1902), Boyd Orr (1936), Titmuss (1943) and Tudor-Hart (1988) among many others (Davey Smith et al. 2001a). In 1977 the then Labour government commissioned Sir Douglas Black to lead a working group to review the evidence on inequalities in health and make policy recommendations (DHSS 1980). The conclusion of the Black Report was that:

> Most recent data show marked differences in mortality rates between the occupational classes, for both sexes and at all ages. At birth and in the first month of life, twice as many babies of 'unskilled manual' parents (class V) die as do babies of professional class parents (class I) and in the next eleven months nearly three times as many boys and more than three times as many girls . . . A class gradient can be observed for most causes of death, being particularly steep in the case of diseases of the respiratory system.
>
> (Townsend 1992: 198)

The rejection of the Black Report by the incoming Conservative government stimulated additional research into inequalities in health, the vast majority of which confirmed the fundamental link between growing inequalities in wealth and health. Nearly 20 years later the new Labour government, elected in 1997, commissioned Sir Donald Acheson to chair an independent inquiry into inequalities in health (Acheson 1998). The Acheson Report not only confirmed the existence of the inequalities identified in the Black Report, but concluded that in the intervening period the differences in the rates had widened:

> For example, in the early 1970s, the mortality rate among men of working age was almost twice as high for those in class V (unskilled) as for those in class I (professional). By the early 1990s, it was almost three times higher. This increasing differential is because, although rates fell overall, they fell more among the high social classes than the low social classes. Between the early 1970s and the early 1990s, rates fell by about 40 per cent for classes I and II, about 30 per cent for classes IIIN, IIIM and IV, but by only 10 per cent for class V. So not only did the differential between the top and bottom increase, the increase happened across the whole spectrum of social classes.
>
> (Acheson 1998: 11)

## Causal pathways

Some of the excess mortality and morbidity associated with poorer socio-economic position can be explained by recognized behavioural risk factors, in particular smoking, but also others including poor diet, high alcohol consumption and lack of physical exercise. Although such risk factors explain some of the inequality in health, particularly for cardiovascular disease where risk factors such as smoking, high serum cholesterol and high blood pressure play a part, they explain less than half of the socio-economic gradient in mortality (Mackenbach and Bakker 2002).

Some commentators have sought to explain this finding through the psychological effects of income inequality (Wilkinson 1996; Marmot and Wilkinson 2001) while others have stressed the cumulative impact of inequality over the life course (Kuh et al. 2003; Davey Smith et al. 2001c). The debates between these various schools of thought can be highly technical and difficult for non-specialists to assess. They are important because understanding the causal pathways leading to inequalities in health should help us plan interventions to reduce inequalities. The causal pathways are clearly complex and likely to be multifactoral. Recent research, for example, has demonstrated that there is significant variation in the association between socio-economic position and mortality for particular causes of ill health and death, with some risk factors having differing impacts at different stages of the life course (Davey Smith *et al.* 2001c). Although epidemiologists are increasingly accepting the life course perspective, as Asthana and Halliday (2006: 38) comment, it is probably premature to dismiss the psychosocial hypothesis.

## The UK policy response

### Conservative policy

Despite the publication of the Black Report and subsequent confirmatory research, for most of the 1980s and early 1990s the Conservative governments refused to accept the importance or even the existence of inequalities in health. From the mid-1990s the government grudgingly accepted what it termed 'variations in health' (Department of Health 1995) and began to discuss what it might do about them. Work at this time included the commissioning of a systematic review of research on the effectiveness of health service interventions to reduce variations in health (Arblaster *et al.* 1995).

### New Labour policy

However, it was not until the election of the new Labour government in 1997 that a comprehensive policy response to reduction of health inequalities was developed. Over its first term, the government launched a range of initiatives to tackle poverty, inequalities and social exclusion, including a specific focus on inequalities in health (Box 9.1). One of its first actions was to commission the *Independent Inquiry into Inequalities in Health* (Acheson 1998). The Acheson Report made a number of recommendations, but identified three key priorities:

- all policies likely to have an impact on health should be evaluated in terms of their impact on health inequalities;
- a high priority should be given to the health of families with children; and
- further steps should be taken to reduce income inequalities and improve the living standards of the poor.

The new government came to power with a commitment to tackle inequalities and a recognition that they needed to be tackled through 'joined-up' thinking across both central government and local partnerships. Thus the Prime Minister established a Social Exclusion Unit reporting directly to his office with a remit to work across departmental boundaries. Local authorities and other agencies were required to establish local strategic partnerships and multiagency community strategies, with a range

---

**Box 9.1**   Policies to tackle poverty, inequality and social exclusion

---

- Tackling low income through the national minimum wage, the Working Families Tax Credit, the Children's Tax Credit, income support for families and other changes to tax and benefit.
- Improving education by introducing policies to improve education standards, creating 500 Sure Start initiatives to improve early years' support to families and Education Action Zones.
- Improving employment opportunities through New Deal programmes, employment zones, action teams for jobs and the Connexions strategy for 13–19-year-olds.
- Rebuilding local communities through Local Strategic Partnerships, community strategies, the National Strategy for Neighbourhood Renewal, New Deal for Communities and Sure Start.
- Reducing crime through crime and disorder partnerships and the Street Crime Initiative.
- Addressing the housing needs of deprived areas through new standards of decency for social housing.
- Strategy to reduce the number of people sleeping rough.
- Drug and alcohol misuse prevention programmes, in particular through drug action teams.
- Helping vulnerable young people avoid conception and teenage pregnancy through the Teenage Pregnancy Strategy.
- Tackling health inequalities through Health Action Zones, Healthy Living Centres, healthy community collaboratives and new national targets for reducing health inequalities.

*Source*: Department of Health (2001c)

---

of national targets and performance indicators relating to inequalities. Following the priority given in both the Black Report and the Acheson Report, child and family poverty and child and family health are key policy priorities.

Within the health sector, the government has published new policy documents on health inequalities on an almost annual basis. In 1999 inequalities were addressed within the public health White Paper *Saving Lives: Our Healthier Nation* (Secretary of State for Health 1999) and an accompanying *Reducing Health Inequalities: An Action Report* (Department of Health 1999a) which laid out the range of government policies which addressed inequalities. *The NHS Plan* (Secretary of State for Health 2000) set out more concrete action and established two new national targets to reduce inequalities in life expectancy and infant mortality by 10 per cent by 2010. The HM Treasury and the Department of Health (2002) jointly published a *Cross Cutting Review on Tackling Health Inequalities* requiring joined-up working on inequalities across government, and included the restatement of the two national health inequalities targets as one PSA (Public Service Agreement) target. In 2003 the government launched *Tackling Health Inequalities: A Programme for Action* (Department of Health 2003) with confirmation of commitments across government. Figure 9.1 illustrates the key themes and principles of the *Programme for Action* which have continued to underpin government action.

2004 saw the publication of the Treasury commissioned second Wanless (2004) report and the subsequent White Paper *Choosing Health: Making Healthier Choices Easier* (Secretary of State for Health 2004), both addressing broader public health issues but also strongly focused on inequalities. In 2005 the Health Inequalities Unit (Department of Health 2005a) published *Tackling Health Inequalities: What Works* and the Department of Health (2005d) published a review led by Professor Sir Michael Marmot of progress towards the 2010 health inequalities target. (See also Chapters 1 and 2 for perspectives on government policy to tackle health inequalities.)

## UK policy effectiveness

### The evidence

What then is the evidence of the effectiveness of government policy in tackling inequalities in health? Given the complexity of the causal pathways and the long-term cumulative impact of health inequalities, it is unsurprising that definitive answers are not yet available. The review commissioned by the government (Department of Health 2005d) gave a mixed judgement on progress towards the national target and

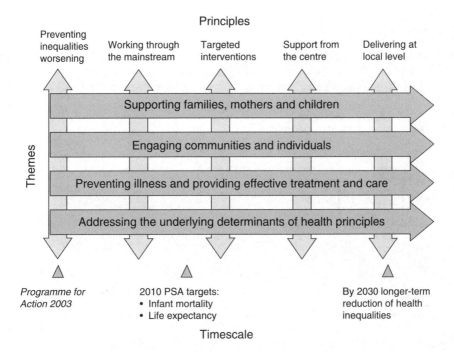

**Figure 9.1** Themes and principles of the *Programme for Action*

12 national headline indicators. In terms of the national target, the review concluded that there has been 'a continuing widening of inequalities as measured by infant mortality and life expectancy at birth in line with the previous trend' (p. 6). Figure 9.2 illustrates how life expectancy at birth has continued to widen for males although it has narrowed for females between the periods 1992–96 and 1997–2001. For the headline indicators, they found

> an inconclusive picture but with progress against two important headlines, child poverty and housing, and some signs of a narrowing of the gap in other areas, notably in circulatory (heart) disease mortality (in absolute terms) and, to a much lesser extent, cancer, as well as flu vaccinations and educational attainment. Other areas, like smoking, remain much less susceptible to change.
>
> (Department of Health 2005d: 6)

Shaw *et al.* (2005) independently assessed progress on health inequalities using somewhat different methods and came to a similar overall conclusion that inequalities in life expectancy between rich and poor areas of the UK continued to widen to 2003, the last year for which data were available. Moreover, they point out that inequalities in income and wealth also continue to widen, with wealth even more unequally distributed than income. From a life course perspective, wealth which reflects lifelong circumstances is an even more salient measure than income. They conclude that inequalities in health will not be reduced in the UK unless more redistributive economic policies are pursued.

## Problems of policy

A number of commentators have analysed policy on tackling health inequalities and concluded that it is beset with limitations and contradictions. The Acheson Report itself has been criticized for a lack of prioritization, a weak evidence base,

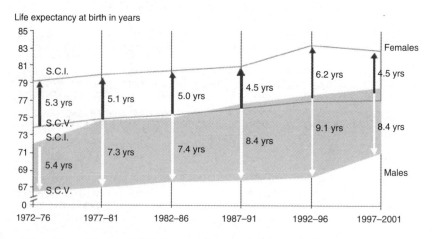

**Figure 9.2** Life expectancy at birth in years, by social class and gender
*Source:* ONS Longitudinal Survey

being inadequately concrete and uncosted (Davey Smith *et al.* 2001b; Exworthy *et al.* 2002).

The government's focus on area-based initiatives has been criticized because the majority of poor people live outside the specified areas of deprivation. For example, two-thirds of children living in poverty are outside Sure Start areas. Even within targeted areas, the resources allocated to tackling inequality are relatively small compared to mainstream spend in public services. Thus the government has emphasized the need for neighbourhood renewal and other regeneration funds to be used to 'bend mainstream services'. However, there is little evidence of effective practice in doing this. Different local agencies continue to receive differing 'must do's' from central government; for example, the drive for improved academic attainment in the education sector does not encourage schools to engage in local partnerships to tackle the broader determinants of inequality. Other aspects of government policy, particularly the short timescales within which regeneration funding has to be spent, often militate against coherent interagency planning for long-term service change.

Within the NHS, the major central policy drivers focus on improving access (for example, reducing hospital waiting times) and quality in secondary and primary care rather than on tackling the wider determinants of health inequalities. Despite the government's rhetorical commitment to tackling health inequalities, a number of commentators have suggested that there has been a '*de facto* relegation of health inequalities' in central priorities, resource allocation and performance management decisions (Exworthy *et al.* 2002). As Exworthy and colleagues conclude, tackling health inequalities is a policy priority for the government, but local 'implementation is hampered by deficiencies in performance management, insufficient integration between policy sectors and contradictions between health inequalities and other policy imperatives'. Many commentators have criticized the emphasis on 'choice' with *Choosing Health* (Department of Health 2004a) and other recent public health policy documents as returning to an excessively individualistic approach to tackling health inequalities (McKee 2005).

## Potential policies for reducing inequalities in health

### Upstream–downstream, universalist–selectivist policies

Interventions to reduce inequalities can be categorized as 'upstream' (tackling the fundamental causes of inequalities through national, social and economic policy) or 'downstream' (working directly with poor individuals and communities to tackle their immediate socio-economic and health problems). A second important distinction is between policies which are 'universalist' (ensuring everyone receives the same standard of service) and 'selectivist' (a means tested approach which targets benefits and services on those with greatest need). For some commentators the solution to health inequalities is clearly upstream and universalist:

> There is one central and fundamental policy that should be pursued: the reduction of income inequality and consequently the elimination of poverty. Ending poverty is the key to ending inequalities in health . . . Any child can tell you how

this can be achieved: the poor have too little money so the solution to ending their poverty is to give them more money. Poverty reduction really is something that can be achieved by 'throwing money at the problem'.

(Davey Smith *et al.* 1999: 163)

Other commentators have suggested that while there is good evidence for such downstream interventions as smoking cessation, there is a paucity of good quality studies of 'upstream' interventions (Macintyre *et al.* 2001), even though they largely support such policies. Davey Smith *et al.* (2001c), however, have countered that such analysis inappropriately focuses on individual level determinants of health while ignoring more important macro level determinants: 'The *Cochrane Library* is unlikely ever to contain systematic reviews or trials of the effects of redistributive national fiscal policies, or of economic investment leading to reductions in unemployment, on health' (Davey Smith *et al.* 2001b: 185).

A different type of evidence is needed to support macro-economic interventions to tackle poverty, an evidence-base that Davey Smith and colleagues have sought to provide in numerous publications (Davey Smith *et al.* 1999, 2001b; Shaw *et al.* 1999, 2005).

## Options for the public health practitioner

Such debates leave one with a conundrum: if the only fundamental way to tackle health inequalities is through national macro-economic policy, what can the public health practitioner working at the community level do? The choice is either to do nothing about inequalities which for most of us is ethically unacceptable – or to identify what can usefully be done at the local level. Fortunately, there is an increasing body of evidence to guide such decisions including reviews by Arblaster *et al.* (1995, 1996); Acheson (1998); Roberts' (2000) work on what works in reducing inequalities in child health; Mackenbach and Bakker's (2002) European survey; Asthana and Halliday (2006) and the ever growing literature available online via the National Electronic Library for Health (www.nelh.nhs.uk). Essentially, there are five options for the individual practitioner: lobbying, partnership working, community development, promoting healthy behaviours and improving access to health care.

## Lobbying

The practitioner can seek to influence how national policy addresses the upstream determinants of health inequalities by lobbying ministers, MPs, regulatory bodies and other national and local decision makers. Lobbying can be done on an individual basis (such as through letters to ministers and MPs) or through membership of national non-statutory organizations (for example, Child Poverty Action Group and the UK Public Health Association), professional organizations (such as the Community Practitioners and Health Visitors Association and the Faculty of Public Health), trade unions and/or political parties.

The media can be a very effective tool for public health lobbying (Chapman

2001). Lobbying national decision makers has the potential advantage of allowing the practitioner to address the upstream determinants of health and the decision makers who can shape policies to tackle these. At a local level the practitioner can act as an advocate for tackling inequalities within their own organization and across local partnerships.

It can be very difficult, however, to assess whether one is having an impact as a lobbyist or advocate. There has been little or no evaluative research on the impact or effectiveness of practitioners in lobbying for public health action to tackle health inequalities. However, an assessment of its value can be gleaned by examining the shifting national policy on health inequalities. Throughout the 1980s and early 1990s, the then government studiously ignored continued lobbying from the public health field on health inequalities. Most notably, the *Health of the Nation* White Paper (Secretary of State for Health 1992) did not address health inequalities despite this being the most common issue raised by those who responded to the preceding consultative Green Paper. However, a number of commentators are confident that the lobbying of the public health field was important in finally bringing the Conservative government to acknowledge and begin to address health 'variations', and for the new Labour government to have it as high upon its list of priorities as it did (Baggott 2000). Practical advice on how to lobby effectively for public health is given by Muir Gray (2001).

## Partnership working

Government policy on tackling inequality emphasizes the need for intersectoral and multidisciplinary partnership between local agencies and communities through the formation of local strategic partnerships. There is an increasing body of evidence that such partnership is an important prerequisite for effective local action on health inequalities. Arblaster et al. (1996) identify a multidisciplinary approach as an important characteristic of successful interventions to improve the health of disadvantaged groups in areas including injury prevention, reducing smoking and chronic heart disease risk, pregnancy prevention and sexual health. Gillies (1998a, b) has reviewed a range of studies of alliances and partnerships for health promotion and concluded there is strong evidence for their effectiveness.

The public health practitioner can contribute to partnership working on inequalities both by representing their agency on relevant partnership groups (such as Local Strategic Partnership/community strategy groups, equalities action groups, neighbourhood partnerships, Healthy Living Centres) and by facilitating partnership action on specific health-related issues (for example, promoting healthy eating, physical activity, tobacco control and so on).

Within such partnerships the practitioner can act as an advocate for local evidence-based, universalist and non-stigmatizing initiatives and services to tackle inequalities (such as universal preschool education, affordable high quality day care (Roberts 2000), vehicle speed reduction (Towner et al. 1993)) and targeted services where appropriate (for example, advice services to increase benefit uptake by disadvantaged groups (Greasley and Small 2002)).

Practitioners may also have skills in needs assessment, ensuring interventions are multifaceted and culturally sensitive, skills development, training and other factors identified by Arblaster *et al.* (1996) as important for successful interventions.

Important as partnership working undoubtedly is, however, there is also a large opportunity cost in the time necessary to make partnerships work. There has been little robust evaluation of the relative benefits and costs of different models of partnership working or comparisons of their impact on inequalities. Published evaluations often focus on process issues (for example, see Evans and Killoran 2000) and give practitioners only partial guidance on how to prioritize their time between the range of potential initiatives to tackle health inequalities.

(Part 2 of this book looks in depth at participation in public health work, including discussion of partnership working.)

## Community development

Community development has been defined as 'a process by which people are involved in collectively defining and taking action on issues that affect their lives' (Radford *et al.* 1997). For public health practitioners, it involves facilitating local communities to identify their own health needs and agenda, and to develop and implement their own solutions to improving health and reducing inequalities. (See Chapter 8 for discussion on community development approaches.)

Community development approaches have a long history in tackling inequalities and are often advocated (for example Benzeval *et al.* 1995). There is a substantial, diverse and mainly qualitative literature describing it (Stewart-Brown and Prothero 1988; Beattie 1991), which is methodologically very different from the experimental studies which form the basis for most of the reviews of interventions to tackle inequalities in health. Arblaster *et al.* (1996), for example, only included studies with an experimental design, and therefore unsurprisingly did not include any community development projects. The term 'community development' does not even feature in the indexes of two major recent collections on tackling inequalities in health (Leon and Walt 2000; Mackenbach and Bakker 2002). Health sector led community development projects have been reported to be critical catalysts for regeneration in a number of deprived communities (Hunt 1987; Smithies and Adams 1990; Roberts 1992; Whitehead 1995; Dalziel 2000; Roberts 2000).

## Promoting healthy behaviours

There is an expanding literature on the effectiveness of health promotion programmes (such as for smoking cessation, injury prevention, social support, breast-feeding) specifically targeted on individuals in lower socio-economic groups who are at higher risk of poorer health and/or health damaging behaviours. The majority of the studies in Arblaster *et al.* (1995), Roberts (2000) and Asthani and Halliday (2006) and other reviews are experimental evaluations of these types of intervention. For example:

- Connett and Stamler (1984) have shown that interventions can be successfully carried out to reduce the incidence of smoking in deprived groups (in this case middle-aged black and white Americans of varying socio-economic back-grounds). A recent NHS report from the North-west region (in the UK) (Lowey *et al.* 2002) provides additional evidence that smoking cessation services can effectively reach and help smokers from deprived communities.

- Colver *et al.* (1982) showed that pre-arranged home visits to identify specific targets for change in families living in a deprived area of Newcastle encouraged them to make changes in their homes that would be expected to reduce the risk of childhood accidents. More recent reviews (Lucas 2003) support the potential of home visiting to reduce accidental injuries in high risk groups.

- Oakley *et al.* (1990) demonstrated the effectiveness, appropriateness and safety of social support provided by midwives to women with high risk pregnancies. A review from the NHS Centre for Reviews and Dissemination (2000b) suggests that small group informal discussions appear to be the most effective way to encourage breastfeeding.

While many of these interventions have been shown to be effective, they are also largely focused downstream on individuals and their health problems associated with deprivation, rather than upstream on the determinants of health. Useful though this evidence base is, it does not offer practitioners guidance on how to balance their efforts between tackling inequalities through upstream determinants and downstream health problems.

## Improving access to health care

Access to NHS health care is mainly free at the point of service (except for dental, ophthalmic, prescription and some equipment charges) and, in principle, universally accessible to everyone in the population regardless of socio-economic position or ethnicity. In primary care, recent studies have found that lower income groups were more likely than higher income groups to use GP services, and that this higher usage broadly reflected need (Patterson and Judge 2002). There is also a strong positive relationship between levels of deprivation and hospital outpatient and admission rates. There is, however, convincing evidence of socio-economic differences in the likeli-hood of receiving some specialist services and in survival. Several studies have found that men living in more affluent areas were more likely to receive coronary revascu-larization surgery than men from poorer areas, despite having less need as measured by mortality rates (Ben-Shlomo and Chaturvedi 1995; Payne and Saul 1997).

More equitable access to health care can be pursued either through universal initiatives, including developing explicit referral guidelines and standards, such as maximum two week waits for cancer referrals. The alternative is selectivist approaches targeted on more deprived groups, such as targeted home visiting for families in areas of deprivation. Paterson and Judge (2002) identify thirty-six inter-ventions either aimed at lower income groups or which report separate results for them. Just over half (n = 19) report interventions aimed at lower income groups which were judged effective. These studies were mainly from the USA and included inter-ventions for cancer screening, treating health risks such as hypertension or substance misuse, improving maternal health and child health outcomes. The interventions were diverse and included hospital-based education programmes, community outreach activities and home visiting.

## Conclusion

The five options outlined above for practitioners to consider in tackling inequalities in health are not mutually exclusive and, indeed, many practitioners adopt several or all of these approaches in different contexts and/or at appropriate times. Unfortunately, there is no obvious evidence base on which to decide what level of effort it is sensible to put into each option or whether one should simply focus on universal health improvement and improved access, and not seek to specifically tackle inequalities at all. The evidence base for the last two options is the largest and easiest to interpret, simply because they are more amenable to the traditional randomized controlled trial method of evaluation.

There are a number of constructive responses to this uncertainty. First, the practitioner can seek to incorporate into their work Arblaster *et al.*'s (1996) characteristics of successful interventions to reduce inequalities in health:

- systematic and intensive approaches;
- improvements in access and prompts to encourage the use of services;
- multifaceted interventions;
- multidisciplinary approaches;
- ensuring interventions meet identified need of the target population; and
- involvement of peers in the delivery of interventions.

In addition, there are a small number of interventions which have a particularly strong evidence base for their effectiveness in tackling health inequalities including smoking cessation, breastfeeding support, early years day care, education and social support, and traffic speed reductions. Thus the practitioner can usefully begin by considering whether such interventions are in operation in their patch and, if not, work to put them in place.

The first steps in any initiative to tackle inequalities in health must be to identify the nature and extent of the inequality and then to search the literature to establish if any intervention has been shown to effectively reduce it. With the rapid expansion of Internet-based knowledge sources (in particular via the National Electronic Library for Health (www.nelh.nhs.uk), evidence of effective interventions will increasingly be most accessible online.

On a professional level, the public health practitioner can ensure they have the underpinning competencies and knowledge to effectively tackle inequalities. Necessary competencies include health needs assessment, equity audit, literature searching, critical appraisal, health promotion, community development, partnership working and evaluation including economic evaluation. (See also Chapter 5 on capacity and capability in public health.)

Tackling inequalities cannot be done as a distinct and separate programme of work. It requires integration across the range of professional activities including continuing professional development, clinical governance, teaching, research and development, and work programme planning.

What is most fundamentally required is a new perspective, a new set of reflexive questions. To effectively tackle inequalities in health, the practitioner must continually test out their activity and programmes against the question 'What is the evidence that this will contribute to reducing inequalities in health?'

---

**Suggested further reading**

Internet-based sources of relevant knowledge on tackling inequalities include:

- the Department of Health (www.dh.gov.uk);
- the Social Exclusion Unit (www.socialexclusionunit.gov.uk)
- the National Institute for Health and Clinical Excellence (NICE) (www.publichealth.nice.org.uk);
- on-line guide to what works in neighbourhood renewal (www.renewal.net);
- the Joseph Rowntree Foundation (www.jrf.org.uk)
- the Health Equity Network (www.ukhen.org.uk); and
- the *International Journal of Equity in Health* (www.equityhealthj.com).

# 10

## MURRAY STEWART
### Neighbourhood renewal and regeneration

**Editors' introduction**

The future of deprived neighbourhoods and their problems of poor health, crime, drugs, unemployment, community breakdown, poor housing and quality of life have recently become more visible to government, regions and 'neighbourhoods' themselves. Government 'modernization' policies and public health interventions that occur at neighbourhood level, including empowerment of people living in such neighbourhoods, can be viewed as the cornerstone for regeneration and renewal at the beginning of the 21st century.

Action to regenerate and renew neighbourhoods (for example, New Deal for Communities initiatives) takes place at different levels of the public health work. Policies can be implemented to tackle the root causes of neighbourhood deprivation including partnerships such as local strategic partnerships.

Renewal and regeneration is the remit of many multidisciplinary public health workers. Professionals and policy makers working for central government and regional government are crucial to regeneration and renewal in neighbourhoods in terms of tackling the policy elements governing economic and psychosocial determinants of health and well-being. Other people that are involved are local lay people, community leaders, local authority urban and transport planners, primary care trust health workers, social workers, community development workers, nurses, environmental health practitioners, general practitioners, police and educators.

In the first section of this chapter, the author traces the development of urban policy and neighbourhood renewal, highlighting the re-emergence of the neighbourhood and its rediscovery with the more holistic view of deprivation and disadvantage now evident in current urban policies. He then examines the link between neighbourhood policies and inequalities in health.

The last section explores the relationship between public health and the neighbourhood in depth, reflecting on the role of neighbourhood initiatives such as Health Action Zones, New Deal for Communities and the importance of 'social capital' and 'partnership working' in bringing about change in neighbourhoods.

## Urban policy and neighbourhood renewal: historical context

The history of cities has long been linked to concerns about public health. The record of town planning and housing is strewn with examples of the anti-urbanism which led so many to deplore the growth of cities and the conditions of life which they imposed on powerless populations. New Lanark, Saltaire, Bournville, Port Sunlight bear witness to the concerns of the 19th century community reformers whose benevolent, if paternalistic, initiatives sought to protect workers from the dangers of cramped and disease ridden city life. At the beginning of the 20th century Howard's garden cities aimed to expose residents to a healthy lifestyle and to housing characterized by lower densities and public open space. In the 1950s the New Towns movement was built around many of the principles of public health which half a century on we now seek to recreate.

It is against this anti-urbanism which runs so deep in the English psyche (Glass 1955) that we must understand the emergence of 'neighbourhood' as a foundation for regeneration and renewal at the beginning of the 21st century. We need to recognize the force both of the planning policies which supported urban expansion and of a half century of ad hoc area-based initiatives which have characterized urban policy (Stewart 2000). For many years after 1945 the physical and social reconstruction of cities was based on a belief that planning solutions – the New Towns and similar overspill initiatives – would lead to improvement in the conditions of life in the inner city. The planned, and much greater unplanned, movement of population and jobs away from cities led, however, to recognition of a geographical concentration of 'deprivation' in both inner city and peripheral estates. This in turn led to the establishment of successive central government programmes targeting 'deprived' areas.

The initiatives of the late 1960s and early 1970s were characterized both by a philosophy which suggested that communities should help themselves and, later, by a drive towards the improved management and co-ordination of public services. An increased interest in public participation (often area-based) accompanied these shifts in thinking. Thus the Educational Priority Areas, the Community Development Projects (CDPs), and the early Urban Programme, were accompanied by moves towards wider participation in planning (Skeffington 1969) and by further area-based initiatives – General Improvement Area and Housing Action Area legislation, Comprehensive Community Programmes (CCPs), the Inner Area Studies, and Area Management Trials.

Such initiatives were the antecedents of the rash of area-based initiatives – Health Action Zones included – of recent years. Educational Priority Areas were directed at similar issues as the recent Education Action Zones – raising educational standards and supporting disadvantaged schools. The CDPs were directed towards community empowerment; the Urban Programme funded projects many of which would sit comfortably in current programmes. The CDPs threw up numerous useful projects on the ground, but were above all characterized by their ability to raise the issue of whether/how far the structural, economic and social problems facing communities in local areas could be addressed by solutions based in those same areas. Evaluations of the CCP experiments in Gateshead and Bradford and the Area Management trials illustrated that area-based approaches attempt to deal with problems that are only partially spatially related, that political commitment to change is crucial and that traditional departmental structures are strongly resistant to change (Spencer 1982; Webster 1982).

In terms of formal policy, the CCP and Area Management experiments were overtaken by the inner city partnerships of the late 1970s within which vertical central–local partnership was pursued with ministers – chairing the partnerships – adopting a hands-on approach to fostering joint working. The 1980s saw area-based urban policy sustained both in response to the 'riots' of 1980–81 and later 1985, and to the government's wish to introduce new instruments of regeneration – urban development corporations, task forces, city action teams, housing action trusts. The urban programme was refocused on 57 targeted areas. Emphasis was laid on policies to draw in private sector investment, with incentives (urban development grants, then city grants) for property and development-led programmes.

In practice the 1980s represented a step backwards towards a reliance on single purpose agencies and the initiatives of that decade imposed fragmentation on urban policy. By 1991 relations between central and local government had improved and a new period of area-based working took off but this time characterized by the institutionalization of interurban competition. Two rounds of City Challenge, later superseded by the Challenge Fund element of Single Regeneration Budget (SRB) funding supported a wide range of area-based initiatives, a number in smaller towns and cities hitherto ineligible for, and inexperienced in, area-based working. By 2001, however, the circle had turned, with abolition of Single Regeneration Budget support for new schemes after six annual rounds, the transfer of regeneration responsibilities to Regional Development Agencies responsible to the Department of Trade and Industry and the emergence of the Neighbourhood Renewal Unit and a national strategy for neighbourhood renewal.

There were successes and failures over this period, but the evidence is that disparities between richer and poorer areas increased (Robson et al. 1994) and that those neighbourhoods identified as the most disadvantaged (for example, by census data) remained disadvantaged over long periods (Power and Tunstall 1995). Successive initiatives seemed to have only temporary impacts. There were few signs of the emergence of an evidence-based urban policy (Harrison 2000; Lawless et al. 2000). Regeneration had stumbled from one initiative to another, driven by shifting political ideologies, institutional proliferation and fragmentation, and re-organization of the mechanisms for delivery. But successive programmes revealed the intransigence of urban problems and the continuing plight of communities of place and interest.

## The development of the neighbourhood focus

### The re-emergence of the neighbourhood

It was against this background of concern about the effectiveness of urban initiatives to counter disadvantage that the Labour government of 1997 sought to re-examine the assumptions upon which area-based intervention was based, and indeed to develop a more formal statement of urban policy as a whole. A White Paper – the first ever to address urban policy as a whole (Department of Transport, Local Government and the Regions 2002) – and two Urban Summit conferences in 2003 and 2005 (Making Towns and Cities More Competitive, and Delivering Sustainable Communities) encouraged urban stakeholders to talk up the prospects of cities, to recognize their potential as well as their weaknesses and to concentrate on the exploitation of urban assets. It acknowledged the strengths of urban life – variety, community, diversity of faiths and cultures – and conveyed a new perception of cities from government, promising indeed 'a new focus for urban issues at the heart of government'. The White Paper did not introduce a new urban policy or programme per se. Rather, it represented a framework for policies across a wide range, reflecting several strands of thinking about regeneration and renewal which had emerged over the previous five years.

The Rogers Report (Department of the Environment, Transport and the Regions 2000b) had examined the ways in which there could be a renaissance in cities and an enhancement of the quality of urban life. Strongly influenced by considerations of urban design but also by the government's need to find space in cities for increased numbers of households, Rogers created a new climate for thinking about the future of cities, albeit a future smacking of architectural determinism.

A local government modernization programme (Department of the Environment, Transport and the Regions 2000c, 2001b) set out the principles which would support the enhancement of local democracy and the protection of standards of conduct in public life. It would assure the more effective delivery of services and demand a community leadership role from local authorities within a broader based local governance. Embedded in this modernization programme, through best value and local public service agreements, for example, was a commitment to a more responsive and community orientated approach to service planning and delivery in disadvantaged neighbourhoods. Equally central was the drive for more integrated working across sectoral boundaries in order to link local government with both central government agencies and other non-departmental public bodies in health, policing, training and employment, and housing. Better joined-up government within Whitehall was a further prerogative of reform (Cabinet Office 2000a). Indeed, from the work of the Central Policy Review Staff in the 1970s (Blackstone and Plowden 1988; Challis *et al.* 1988) to the analysis of cross-cutting failure in the 1990s (Richards *et al.* 1999; Stewart *et al.* 1999; Social Exclusion Unit 2000), there has been a saga of evidence about the fragmented nature of governmental activity at all levels, and about the tendency for departments and professions to operate within vertical silos with central and local levels combining to protect their particular domains and the budgets and responsibilities that go with them. (See also Chapter 2 on public health and the government modernization agenda.)

The emergence of a new regionalism together with the establishment of regional development agencies saw economic regeneration linked more closely to the competitiveness debate. Responsibility for the Single Regeneration Budget was passed to regional development agencies. At the same time the government was concerned about the role and function of government in the regions and in local areas and a further Cabinet Office report (2000b) heralded the arrival of the Regional Coordination Unit with a remit both to rationalize the web of area-based initiatives and to support the integration of government work at regional level.

The spatial dimension of social reform was reflected in the work of the Social Exclusion Unit. The Social Exclusion Unit has produced a series of reports, for example, on rough sleeping, truancy and school exclusions, teenage pregnancy and of most relevance on mental health (Social Exclusion Unit 2004), but its most influential work has been around the future of the deprived neighbourhood. In 1997 the Prime Minister gave the Social Exclusion Unit the remit to examine 'how to develop integrated and sustainable approaches to the problems of the worst housing estates including crime, drugs, unemployment, community breakdown and bad housing' (Social Exclusion Unit 2001b: 74).

*Bringing Britain Together* (Social Exclusion Unit 1998) provided a thorough and sophisticated analysis of the issues confronting deprived neighbourhoods reinforcing the observation that past policies had failed to arrest their relative decline. Over the next two years, 18 Policy Action Teams drew together a wide range of interests to develop further analyses and recommendations for action which were captured in a national framework for consultation (Social Exclusion Unit 2001a), which in turn, after consultation, was developed into the *National Strategy Action Plan* (Social Exclusion Unit 2001b).

As far as the resource argument was concerned, a cross-cutting Treasury-led review *Government Interventions in Deprived Areas* (HM Treasury 2000a), undertaken as background to the 2000 Comprehensive Spending Review, set out the spending and service delivery implications of the national neighbourhood renewal framework, establishing crucial principles for resource planning and programme delivery. The review concluded that main programmes should bear the primary responsibility for tackling deprivation. This would mean stipulating both national service standards and 'convergence' targets for tackling deprivation. Funding and process mechanisms might need to be changed. To combat the proliferation of partnerships and provide a single focus for setting local priorities, Local Strategic Partnerships should be established. Nevertheless, targeted initiatives including holistic regeneration programmes still had a role to play, but as part of a wider framework rather than as the main tool.

The *National Strategy Action Plan* for neighbourhoods embodied these principles. It rejected the proposition that deprivation can be combated solely through area-based initiatives. Instead (or, at least, as well) deprivation was to be tackled through the bending of main departmental programmes to focus more specifically on the most deprived areas. Neighbourhood renewal thus continues on two fronts.

On the one hand, there are moves towards the realignment of main programmes. This involves new 'floor targets' set for substandard social housing, for the reduction of burglary rates, for educational achievement, for longer life expectancy, for reduced teenage conception rates and for increased employment rates. Local Strategic Partnerships (LSPs) carry responsibility at the local level for neighbourhood renewal strategies, for meeting floor targets, for the rationalization of existing partnerships, and for new community strategies. In 2004 the announcement of Local Area Agreements heralded a further major initiative to encourage the joining up of programmes and the alignment of budgets (ODPM 2004; OPM *et al.* 2005; ODPM 2006a).

On the other hand, there continues a raft of specific initiatives. The Community Empowerment Fund has supported community and voluntary sector involvement in local strategic partnerships in the 88 areas eligible for a new Neighbourhood Renewal Fund. Neighbourhood Renewal Community Chests provided small grants to formal and informal community groups to support community activity and mutual self-help in the 88 Neighbourhood Renewal Fund areas. Until 2008 the Neighbourhood Renewal Fund itself provides extra resources for 88 of the most deprived local authority districts. The neighbourhood management programme helps deprived communities and local service providers work together at the neighbourhood level to improve and 'join up' local services, while New Deal for Communities partnerships were established in 39 neighbourhoods across England and over a 10-year period from 1998 will receive funding of £50 million per area – a total programme amounting to £1.9 billion. Neighbourhood wardens provide a uniformed, semi-official presence in residential areas with the aim of improving quality of life. Wardens may promote community safety, assist with environmental or housing improvements and they can assist with neighbourhood management as outlined above.

## Neighbourhoods and health

The key characteristic promised by the government in its rediscovery of the neighbourhood and its development of a new renewal/regeneration policy has been the departure from a predominantly physical and economic development focus to a more widely defined and holistic view of deprivation and disadvantage. The split of responsibilities between government offices in the regions and regional development agencies has led many observers to comment that there has been a separation rather than an integration between economic and social regeneration. It is clear at least in the social domain, however, that the neighbourhood agenda has stimulated a more holistic view of regeneration which both reflects the new thinking about public health (described in this book) and, at the same time, reinforces and helps to consolidate that thinking. In 1998 the Health Education Authority commissioned work which articulated clearly the links between health and regeneration (Russell and Killoran 1999). Drawing on the local government focused *New Commitment to Regeneration* on the one hand and the early years of Health Action Zones on the other, but at the same time firmly rooted in the health inequalities analysis (Department of Health 1998c), this work provided a stimulus to thinking about linkage and overlap between health and other policy areas. Evaluation of the *New Commitment to Regeneration* (Russell 2001) pointed out lessons for joined-up working – joint planning, pooled resources, integrated service delivery – and, reinforced by the findings of the Social Exclusion Unit's Policy Action Team 17, paved the way for the development of Local Strategic Partnerships.

The Health Act 1998 had already offered some scope for flexible working between health organizations and local government, but there is now a more explicit focus for developing joint action at neighbourhood level as a consequence of the Local Strategic Partnership responsibilities in relation to community planning (and the preparation of a community strategy) on the one hand, and the need to develop a neighbourhood renewal strategy to guide the allocation of the Neighbourhood Renewal Fund on the other. These requirements have stimulated much cross-sectoral activity (Hamer and Easton 2002; Hamer and Smithies 2002), activity further informed by the guidance issued by the Department of Health and the Neighbourhood Renewal Unit to stimulate good practice in the support of healthy neighbourhoods (Department of Health/Neighbourhood Renewal Unit 2002).

The guidance offers no new insights into the relationship between health and the neighbourhood. Indeed its main aims appear to be to inform non-health interests in neighbourhood partnerships – New Deal for Communities in particular but additionally neighbourhood management partnerships and local strategic partnerships – of the foundations upon which initiatives to counter health inequalities can be based.

## Neighbourhood policies and health inequalities

In terms of the five layers of influence often argued to determine health (Dahlgren and Whitehead 1992), the neighbourhood is a mediator in relation to social and community networks and living and working conditions, although it is also the setting within which individual behaviour and lifestyles are worked out. Poor housing, worklessness, crime and fear of crime, and low educational attainment are major features of disadvantaged neighbourhoods and, with poverty, are major determinants of health status. Improvements in these aspects of quality of life are thus a prerequisite of improved health outcomes. Neighbourhood renewal offers the potential for public health to work in conjunction with employment, education, housing and community safety policies to offer a holistic approach to reducing the gaps between the most disadvantaged neighbourhoods and other less deprived areas. (See also Chapter 9 for discussion of new directions for tackling health inequalities.)

### Neighbourhood initiatives to address health inequalities

It is impossible to do justice to the volume and variety of the new initiatives which these policies have spawned. Community safety partnerships support projects to reduce burglary, to support schemes for vulnerable groups, to introduce CCTV, to sustain higher levels of local policing, to combat vehicle crime, to introduce local neighbourhood wardens, to reveal and counter domestic violence and to stamp out racial harassment. In the field of employment there is major investment not simply to attempt to create more jobs and not least in the local social economy, but to ensure that as many of these jobs as possible go to local people. Intermediate labour market schemes, mentoring, work experience, support for employers and the whole employment New Deal programme aim to reduce worklessness and support the revival of an active local economy.

Transport provides an increasingly important example of the links between health and other sectors, although not one emphasized in the national neighbourhood strategy. A Social Exclusion Unit report on transport and exclusion (Social Exclusion Unit 2003) reinforces the messages from earlier research (Department of the Environment, Transport and the Regions 2000a; Hine and Mitchell 2001; Lucas *et al.* 2001), pointing to the fact that for those who rely on public transport, getting to hospitals is particularly difficult and can lead to missed health appointments. Thirty-one per cent of people without a car have difficulties travelling to their local hospital, compared to 17 per cent of people with a car. Seven per cent of people without a car say they have missed, turned down or chosen not to seek medical help over the past 12 months because of transport problems – double the rate in the general population. Thus the health and transport interface for those in disadvantaged neighbourhoods involves better advice on how to get to hospital through mainstream transport, greater publicity for the Hospital Travel Costs Scheme, and greater choice over the timing of hospital appointments to fit in with travel needs. Children from the lowest social class are five times more likely to die in road accidents than those from the highest social class (Social Exclusion Unit 2003).

Above all, however, the neighbourhood is characterized by its housing circumstances. Molyneux and Palmer (2000) pointed to the accumulation of housing issues with health implications – homelessness, poor housing, the quality of the environment – and to the links between housing costs, poverty and poor housing. The relationship between house condition – disrepair, damp and cold – has long been understood to have health impacts, while housing type and, in particular, living off the ground has been known to have consequences for mental and physical health. More recent longitudinal analysis (Marsh *et al.* 2000) reinforces these conclusions and in addition argues that the impact of poor housing on children may emerge as ill health only decades afterwards. There is growing recognition of, and research into, the important relationships between housing and health, as well as a more active debate about the precise nature of these relationships and about the causal linkages. One obvious consideration here is whether the causal relationships are unilateral or whether health affects housing as well as housing affecting health. If health status has traditionally been reflected in medical priority access to social housing, there is now more attention to the role of health condition in determining access to owner occupation and to the effect of health on long-term healthy living (Easterlow *et al.* 2000). At the same time, however, a major review of a range of housing interventions suggested that the health effects of housing improvement remain under-researched and consequently still poorly understood (Thomson *et al.* 2001).

A different dimension was examined by Allen (2000) who suggested that the housing renewal process itself may have health impacts and that the experience of renewal – uncertainty, upheaval, displacement cost, noise – can cause stress which induces health damage and mental illness. The possibility that regeneration may exacerbate health inequalities by imposing detrimental effects on already impoverished communities should not be ignored (Curtis *et al.* 2002). Crucial to this is the relationship between tenant and landlord with the distribution of control and power being dominant factors. It is interesting to juxtapose this point about the potential stress of regeneration/renewal with the now common observation of regeneration fatigue among community active members of area regeneration partnerships (Purdue *et al.* 2000), and to suggest that the pace and complexity of current renewal activity places unreasonable demands on communities. Seldom is the need for 'community capacity building' couched in health terms.

## Understanding inequalities in localities

What a neighbourhood approach demands is examination of the nature of the experience of residence within a particular locality – examination of the relationship with others in the home, with others in the building, with the immediate external environment and with neighbours and the neighbourhood. The residential experience may vary according to tenure, length of residence in the area, the condition of the building, neighbours and the connections from that residence to other activities – work, transport, shops and leisure. Experience of living will be dependent on sense of shelter, identity, status and security (Kearns *et al.* 2000).

Despite this and much more evidence about life and living within the neighbourhood, health inequalities cannot be addressed exclusively in the neighbourhood, and Acheson (1998), argues that many are the outcome of causal factors that run back into and from the basic structure of society. The parameters of such inequalities lie in poverty and income deprivation, in poorly maintained, cold and wet housing, in poor schooling and low educational attainment, in temporary and insecure employment, in vulnerability to crime and/or fear of it, in the absence of means of transport, and in the stress and mental ill health caused by one or more of the above. The work of the Social Exclusion Unit (1998) has illustrated graphically the relative deprivation experienced in the most deprived neighbourhoods and the *Indices of Deprivation* (Department of the Environment, Transport and the Regions 2000f) together with the availability of more disaggregated neighbourhood statistics highlight the disadvantaged position of certain neighbourhoods. Closing the gap between both disadvantaged localities and disadvantaged groups is a major objective of policy and there is extensive guidance about how best to approach the tasks of understanding inequalities in health, establishing a common language for expressing these inequalities and setting practical targets for meeting local needs (Bull and Hamer 2002).

It is also important to recognize, however, that while an emphasis on deprived neighbourhoods is the key feature of much government policy this excludes a significant number of people who do not live in those areas. The neighbourhood as a community of place must share attention with communities of interest – of ethnicity or disability – which may be widely spread across cities and regions rather than concentrated in particular localities. The Department of Health guidance on Health Action Zones (Department of Health 1999a) identified black and minority ethnic groups, people with disabilities, homeless people, travellers, single parents and their children, housebound older people, housebound disabled people, unemployed people, mentally ill people, former prisoners and vulnerable young people.

## The impact of neighbourhood initiatives

Assessing the impact either of health initiatives on neighbourhoods or of neighbourhood initatives on health invites a host of difficult questions about causality and attribution. Systematic review of a series of evaluations of urban regeneration over a 20-year period from 1980 offered mixed conclusions, reflecting a very weak evidence base in relation to health impact. Some impacts on the socio-economic determinants of health were noted, but in general positive impacts were small (and some negative), with improvements not greatly exceeding national trends (Thomson *et al.* 2006; Atkinson *et al.* 2006). The major observation from this work was that health represented only a small element (if any) within the regeneration evaluations included, that there was wide variation in the extent to which health impacts were measured, and that health impacts tended to be assessed in terms of activities such as raising health awareness or outputs such as facilities or services provided rather than outcomes. The consequence in the authors' views was a combination of myopia and amnesia in relation to the lessons learned for improved public health policy and practice.

**New Deal for Communities**

This somewhat negative view of the impact of regeneration on health outcomes pre-dated the most significant neighbourhood initiative – the 10-year New Deal for Communities (NDC), the evaluation of which espoused a more ambitious health domain incorporating a range of measures and indicators. The New Deal for Communities initiative operates in 39 localities with populations of around 8000–10,000 people and involves a 10-year programme which allocates around £50 million over the period to each New Deal for Communities initiative together with the support of all the relevant mainstream agencies. The areas experience disadvantage and inequal-ities as compared to the rest of their cities and the rest of the country, and all New Deal for Communities initiatives have some form of thematic health programme built into their delivery plans. New Deal for Communities partnerships were encouraged to undertake local surveys and to develop baseline indicators appropriate both to national targets and to local circumstances (standardized mortality ratios by disease category, teenage pregnancies, smoking, drug misuse, mental health and 'satisfaction with services').

Health work in New Deal neighbourhoods was informed by an early review of the emerging evidence-base on community health initiatives and of the lessons which the NDC initiative might learn – lessons which related both to evaluation methodology and regeneration practice (Bauld *et al.* 2001a). In terms of method the review stressed the need for a range of approaches, for cohort and panel studies, for intermediate outcome measures, and for selectivity in focus, while the lessons for NDC partner-ships themselves suggested the importance of comprehensive rather than particular interventions, the need for a robust evidence-based approach and the significance of links to the emerging national health agenda of health inequalities and service frame-works. Against these aspirations for a sound evaluation framework, however, a further review of the initial NDC delivery plans (Health Promotion Policy Unit 2002), showed that while New Deal for Communities initiatives had collected much informa-tion, there remained significant gaps not only in the basic data available but in their consistency and in terms of the indicators selected, interpretation, timescales and age groups. The review also argued that there were question marks over whether the outcomes set in the delivery plans were realistic, measurable and meaningful, whether planned activities were well specified, resourced and targeted, and whether the health plans of New Deal initiatives were embedded within the wider plans and structures of the New Deal for Communities partnerships. This confirms the conclusions from other studies which point to the fact that new neighbourhood partnerships – whether these be health partnerships or local strategic partnerships – need learning and devel-opment time to settle into new languages, new information sources and new planning mechanisms, before sensible, integrated plans and programmes can be developed (Department of Transport, Local Government and the Regions 2002; Hamer and Easton 2002; Hamer and Smithies 2002).

Four years on, however, the interim NDC evaluation report 2001–05 CRESR (2005) provides more evidence. By the end of the financial year 2003–04 NDC partnerships had implemented 720 health projects, costing on average £88,000 involving 72 new or improved facilities and with an aggregate 19,000 residents benefiting. NDC interventions were classified into four types – promoting healthy lifestyles (Ellis *et al.* 2005; Blank *et al.* 2005a), service provision to improve health (Peters *et al.* 2005a, b; Blank *et al.* 2005a, b), developing the workforce (Blank *et al.* 2005a; Peters *et al.* 2005a), and working with young people (Blank *et al.* 2005a, b; Goyder *et al.* 2005). By reference to both administrative data and to two major household surveys, the evaluation discusses lifestyle, self reported indicators of health, low birthweight, prescribing for mental illness, standardized health ratios, and access to health services. Against national equivalents and comparator areas, NDC localities demonstrated a range of modest improvements (although again a lack of improvement on some indicators). The NDC evaluation shows a stronger commitment from regeneration partnerships to engaging with the health agenda and a deeper level of analysis than any previous regeneration evaluation, and the links between health and other non-health issues (housing, employment, transport) are highlighted. Nevertheless even the four-year time-span of the first years of New Deal for Communities provide an insufficient basis for judging the long-term impacts of neighbourhood regeneration on health status and outcomes.

## Public health and the neighbourhood

What is the future direction of public health in the neighbourhood? What are the key issues which health professionals and communities need to address in conjunction with others? From the history of renewal and regeneration over many years and in the light of the policy context at the start of the 21st century a number of key issues emerge.

### The neighbourhood effect

Although renewal and regeneration are increasingly focused at the spatial level of the neighbourhood, there remains considerable uncertainty about the precise nature of the neighbourhood effect. Several of the determinants of health lie in the external environment and while problems of ill health (and of unemployment, crime and poverty) are to be found *in* the neighbourhood, they are not necessarily *of* the neighbourhood in the sense of being brought about by a 'neighbourhood effect'. There is much evidence, for example, that black and minority ethnic groups experience health inequalities, and also that in many cities they are concentrated into particular neighbourhoods. This does not mean, however, that the health problems particular to black and minority ethnic groups are caused by the 'neighbourhood'. Regeneration interventions may be appropriately focused at a neighbourhood level – on housing, on the environment or on traffic, for example – but may equally well be focused on solutions which must be generated externally in national policies – fiscal policies, benefits policies, industrial and economic policies. At the spatial scale of the neighbourhood there is likely to be a sharp illustration of the incidence of disadvantage, but it is at other scales – city, region and nation – that remedies are most likely to be found.

But while the neighbourhood may not be a determinant of health inequalities it remains an important focus for policy and practice and an arena for the expression of community of place, and it is in the links between neighbourhood communities and the wider networks of urban life that the most fruitful connections may emerge. Social networks have long been regarded as the foundation for strong community (see for example Dennis *et al.* 1957; Frankenberg 1957; Stacey 1960; Willmott and Young 1960), with strong ties to relatives, immediate friends and neighbours providing the basis for social interaction (Granovetter 1973). Extensive new evidence about the nature of local social networks has come from the Joseph Rowntree Foundation research on neighbourhood images (Andersen and Munck 1999; Cattell and Evans 1999; Silburn *et al.* 1999; Wood and Vamplew 1999). This complements other work on the strengths of, and pressures on, family life – the Bristol-based study by Gill *et al.* (2000), for example – and on the nature of social cohesion in disadvantaged neighbourhoods (Forrest and Kearns 1999; Page 2000). Much of the evidence focuses on the role of children as a pivotal element with networks mobilizing around issues of childcare and schooling. Women play a crucial role. It is important, however, to remember that some of the negative aspects of neighbourhood life stem from relations of trust and dependence built around drugs, crime, abuse and the function of illicit and often illegal power structures in maintaining oppressive systems of social relations (Hoggett 1997).

## Social capital

Much has been made in health literature of the role of social capital in fostering better health, and community-based preventive work has been a major strand of health initiatives such as Health Action Zones as well as of other area-based initiatives such as Sure Start and the New Deal for Communities. There is, however, a parallel strand of literature which points to the failure of initiatives predicated on community cohesion and community capacity building (Hastings 1996; Hastings *et al.* 1996), and to the difficulties inherent in generating genuine community engagement in the management of neighbourhoods and the provision of services. Why, after all, should communities be invited to take on responsibilities which professionals have been so lax in offering over decades? A key issue for public health in the 21st century therefore is to work through precisely which interventions to improve health may be best pursued through community-based initiatives and which through other routes.

This in turn relates to the function of 'weak ties' and of the social capital which provides access for disadvantaged communities to the mainstream of public service provision. Taylor recognizes the 'strong ties' interpretation of social capital but helpfully also points to the fact that what is needed for capacity building is exploration of the space between state and civil society, between levels of political power and decision making and the networks of everyday life (Taylor 2000).

## Main programmes

A significant route through which weak ties can be articulated lies in the reshaping of major mainline service provision to address the needs of local communities. Mainstreaming is seen as crucial to the sustainability of neighbourhood strategies in the long-term. The influence of Health Action Zones on policy and practice has been significant. They were able to undertake a range of innovative and often community-based initiatives on mental health, drug abuse, smoking and alcoholism, diet, health at work and so on. HAZs and sufficient resource and energy to lead interagency working on such issues were influential in transmitting some lessons to the mainstream. In some localities the HAZ programme acted as a catalyst for the integration of other programmes. In East London, for example, health gain work on the Ocean Estate led to the local primary care group being heavily involved in the Stepney New Deal for Communities after the realization that many local residents travelled long distances to access health services. In Plymouth the Programme Board for Children began to function as the single planning body for services to this group, integrating planning across providers. The Sandwell GrowWell and AgeWell programmes impacted on the main programmes of both health and other departments. Elsewhere the South Yorkshire Coalfields HAZ supported joint working with a Single Regeneration Budget scheme on a survey of social capital. HAZs were subject to national and local evaluations (Sullivan *et al.* 2004, 2006; Barnes *et al.* 2005; Bauld *et al.* 2005), the broad findings of which suggest that while there was some success in public involvement, in partnership building and in innovative service delivery, the impact of even this major area-based initiative on mainstream planning and practice was modest, fragile and short-lived.

This conclusion is borne out by evidence on mainstreaming from the NDC national evaluation (Stewart and Howard 2005). Partnership working between NDCs and health organizations had strengthened, and was felt to be producing demonstrable impacts both within the health organizations (restructuring, realignments) and on the ground. The evidence – from NDCs in Doncaster, Derby, Bristol, Kings Norton, Plymouth, Middlesbrough, Walsall – lay in increased PCT representation in NDC structures through secondees, staffing, and/or PCT management of a health theme group. Leadership was important. When an agency put senior representatives on the NDC board or manages a theme group, their mutual understanding, joint working, and interest in aligning work plans increased. In Plymouth, for example, the relationship with the PCT had improved considerably, largely as a result of the Chief Executive of the PCT sitting on the NDC Board and playing a very active and constructive role in both the Board and the relevant theme group. Increased joint working leads to shared information, improved networking, shared staff, all of which are conducive to consistent and efficient partnership working. Conversely, however, there was also evidence that where there is a lack of representation from the PCT in the NDC, this lack of involvement is 'stifling' strategic engagement.

There was widespread evidence of joint working (for example in Middlesbrough, Sandwell, Hartlepool), and also of PCTs taking up funding of NDC initiatives (Newham, Middlesbrough, Brent) (see Box 10.1). There was some evidence of the reconfiguring of mainstream services in order to work in closer partnership with NDC.

All this confirms that specific initiatives (such as Health Action Zones or New Deal for Communities) may provide some improvements, but that lasting change is dependent on the engagement of the much larger main programmes. Research on area-based initiatives (Department of Transport, Local Government and the Regions 2002: 31) argued that

> there was relatively little evidence of successful mainstreaming, in the sense of a mainstream agency adopting and reproducing examples of effective practice from initiative activity. When interviewees talked about mainstreaming, it was

---

**Box 10.1** Examples of partnership with NDC

---

*Example 1*

In Greets Green (Sandwell), the PCT was testing short-term mainstream pilots (for example smoking cessation sessions), and the Enhanced Nursing Service was a proto-type for a 'Managed Care' service in the Greets Green area before being rolled out in the wider area. A Neighbourhood Health team had been established and a jointly funded (NDC and PCT) Manager appointed. The PCT was working with the NDC to develop a Locality Health Plan next year, and the Manager was also the single point of contact for the Greets Green community and GP/Nursing community.

*Example 2*

In North Huyton (Knowsley) a web of structures integrated the NDC with the wider Knowsley health agenda. Although staff capacity was a continuing constraint, practitioner involvement in partnership working together with the consistent involvement of senior officers from key agencies – often acting as champions for pilot projects – drove mainstreaming forward. Portfolios of both quantitative and qualitative evidence demonstrating outputs and outcomes made the case for mainstreaming. Other illustrations of improved partnership working included improved access to health services (new health centres, healthy living centres, self care pharmacy, a men's health project).

---

often to explore the reasons why it was so slow. The mainstreaming that does happen tends to be piecemeal and opportunistic.

The Audit Commission (2002) identified similar constraints, many revolving around the inflexibility of organizational cultures to accommodate new ways of thinking and acting towards effective neighbourhood renewal. Mainstream change is a function of the interdependence of area-based, neighbourhood experience with the strategic capacity to alter the behaviour of the larger agencies. Partnership is now an over used, often abused, term for what occurs when two or more organizations sit down together. 'Talking shops' are perceived by many stakeholders to be wasteful – for the private sector because they divert from core business and for the voluntary and community sectors because they demand scarce time and energy, which again diverts from getting on with the 'real job'. Over the years there have been numerous studies looking at partnership working (Mackintosh 1993; Roberts *et al.* 1995; Hastings 1996; Hastings *et al.* 1996; Geddes 1997; Harding 1998; Lowndes and Skelcher 1998), and there is now an extensive literature on collaborative working across boundaries (Huxham 1996; Sullivan 2001). The impact of partnerships is a function of a number of features of joint working – membership, status, structures, leadership, agendas and organizational cultures. Health stakeholders are expected to participate in the new partnership structures and following Department of Health guidance the links with Local Strategic Partnerships have been reinforced (through the National Service Framework for Older People, the disability White Paper, arrangements for children's planning and so on). The lead role for Primary Care Trusts in Local

Strategic Partnerships has been messaged a number of times, for example, in the reform document *Shifting the Balance of Power* (Department of Health 2001a).

Participation in Local Strategic Partnerships is one matter, active engagement with a range of neighbourhood partnerships is another and health organizations, like others, need to think through their contribution to partnership working at regional, city and neighbourhood levels to ensure that role and function are understood. The evidence of the past is of complexity in the arrangements for joint working both vertically between centre and periphery, and horizontally between organizations at the same level.

If the health input to neighbourhood working is to be effective then a much clearer view about the protocols of working in partnership need to be developed. The neighbourhood can be a powerful arena for the development of cross-sectoral working between agencies and community, but it can also be a battlefield of competition and conflict. The key challenge for the new public health is to ensure that it is the former not the latter.

---

**Suggested further reading**

Barnes, M., Bauld, L., Benzeval, M., Judge, K., Mackenzie, M. and Sullivan, H. (2005) *Building Capacity for Health Equity*. London, Routledge.

**National evaluation of New Deal for Communities Reports**

Blank, L., Goyder, E., Ellis, E., Peters, J. and Johnson, M. (2005) *National Evaluation of New Deal for Communities: Improving Access to Health Care Services Introducing New Services for Residents*. Research Report 54. http:/ndcevaluation.adc.shu.ac.uk/ndcevaluation/reports.asp

Blank, L., Goyder, E., Peters, J. and Ellis, E. (2005) *National Evaluation of New Deal for Communities: Teenage Pregnancy and Sexual Health*. Research Report 53. http:/ndcevaluation.adc.shu.ac.uk/ndcevaluation/reports.asp

Ellis, E., Peters, J., Goyder, E. and Blank, L. (2005) *National Evaluation of New Deal for Communities: Healthy Lifestyle Interventions*. Research Report 57. http:/ndcevaluation.adc.shu.ac.uk/ndcevaluation/reports.asp

Peters, J., Ellis, E., Blank, L., Goyder, E. and Johnson, M. (2005) *National Evaluation of New Deal for Communities: Relocation or Extension of Health Care Services*. Research Report 55. http:/ndcevaluation.adc.shu.ac.uk/ndcevaluation/reports.asp

Peters, J., Ellis, E., Goyder, E. and Blank, L. (2005) *National Evaluation of New Deal for Communities: Healthy Eating Initiatives*. Research Report 56. http:/ndcevaluation.adc.shu.ac.uk/ndcevaluation/reports.asp

Social Exclusion Unit (2004) *Social Exclusion and Mental Health*. London: Cabinet Office.

Thomson, H., Atkinson, R., Pettigrew, M. and Kearns, A. (2006) Do urban regeneration programmes improve public health and reduce health inequalities? A synthesis of the evidence from UK policy and practice (1980–2004), *Journal of Epidemiological Community Health*, 60: 108–15.

# 11

## COLIN FUDGE
# Implementing sustainable futures in cities

**Editors' introduction**

'Sustainable development', put simply, means development which meets the needs of the present without damaging the health or environment of future generations. This is a huge challenge for cities.

The world contains hundreds of nations and thousands of cities at different stages of industrial development. Some of the features of increasing development are an ageing population in advanced industrialized countries, and a growing population with substantial movement of people into urban city living in less developed countries. What unites all cities and the citizens who inhabit them, whatever the level of their development, is whether the future can be guaranteed or is 'sustainable'. Public health workers can make an enormous contribution to creating sustainable futures in cities.

The tension between increased urbanization and a sustainable future for people living in cities reminds us of the origins of modern town planning and its close association with public health. In order for cities to be sustainable, town and transport planners and local authority employees, including health protection and environmental protection managers, must pay great attention to spatial planning, social housing and transport systems, and architects must consider the design of buildings. Central and local government politicians must tackle the problems of an ageing population and pension provision; the threat of terrorism in strategic buildings; quality of life; and that the governance of cities is appropriate for sustainability to be delivered.

This chapter begins by outlining some of the issues arising from increased urbanization, or movement of population into city living, against the backdrop of world and regional population change. It moves on to consider the policy approaches to creating sustainable futures in European cities. The author outlines some of his own evaluative research into sustainable futures in cities using some Swedish cities as examples. In the last part of the chapter he concludes with a number of strategic issues and propositions for the future sustainability of cities in the 21st century.

## Introduction

In this chapter sustainable development is identified as a much broader concept than environmental protection. This chapter argues that sustainable development has economic and social as well as cultural, health and environmental dimensions and embraces notions of equity between people in the present and between generations. This argument implies that further development should only take place within the carrying capacity of natural and social systems. In relation to work on the ecological footprint of cities, it could be suggested that a sustainable city is one that is attempting to reduce its ecological footprint (Douglas 1995, private communication; Rees 1992).

The first section of this chapter outlines some of the issues implicated in the current and future health of populations arising from urbanization and urban change and development against the backdrop of world and regional population change. This section also considers policy approaches adopted in Europe to take forward the sustainability agenda for cities. The second section describes some evaluative research that I carried out in Sweden, presenting findings from a case study in sustainable futures in cities. The final section of the chapter concludes with a number of strategic issues and propositions for the future sustainability of cities in the 21st century.

## Urbanization, urban change, development and policy

### The concept of sustainable development

Although the conceptual origins of sustainable development go back many years, for example, to the garden city movement in the UK and the Regional Planning Association of America, the more recent revival of the term comes from the 1980 World Conservation Strategy (International Union for the Conservation of Nature 1980), which suggested sustainable development as a means of integrating economic development with the essential conservation of the environment. The work of the World Commission on Environment and Development followed, leading to the publication of the Brundtland Report in 1987. In broad terms, the World Commission on Environment and Development rejected the (then dominant) argument that economic growth and maintenance of environmental quality were mutually exclusive. The report argued that development could and should be sustainable to meet the needs of the present, without compromising the ability of future generations to meet their own needs (Brundtland 1987).

Since the Brundtland Report there have been a number of significant policy debates and a range of reports addressing various aspects of sustainable development, as well as a growing body of practical experience in attempting to operationalize sustainability. The major stimulus has been the United Nation's Conference on Environment and Development (UNCED) in Rio in 1992, and the series of UN conferences that followed, culminating in the Habitat II conference in Istanbul in 1996. However, despite the widespread adoption internationally of the non-legally binding Agenda 21 action plan from Rio, many observers conclude that sustainable development is a challenge that remains to be confronted, and here the urban and regional level, as the interface between local and national, in an increasingly globalized environment of international interests and pressures, is of particular significance. The UN conference in South Africa in 2002 (Rio plus 10) emphasized the complexity of the task but called for an action oriented approach in the light of the impacts of global climate change.

## Population change and urbanization

This part of the chapter draws on statistical information from the UN Population Division, Department of Economic and Social Affairs and commentaries from the UN and academics specializing in the understanding of these statistics (United Nations 1996, 1998). The Population Division of the UN biennially prepares the official UN population estimates and projections for countries, urban and rural areas, and major cities. The summary information provides an overview for the reader illustrated by a number of graphs and tables.

## World population growth

The rapid growth of the world population is a recent phenomenon in the history of the world. World population was estimated at 791 million in 1750, with 64 per cent in Asia, 21 per cent in Europe, 13 per cent in Africa and 2 per cent in North and Latin America. By 1900, 150 years later, the world population had only slightly more than doubled, to 1650 million. The major growth had been in Europe, whose share of world population had increased to 25 per cent, and in North America and Latin America, whose share had increased to 5 per cent each. Meanwhile the share of Asia had decreased to 57 per cent and that of Africa to 8 per cent. The growth of the world population accelerated after 1900, with 2520 million in 1950, a 53 per cent increase in 50 years.

The rapid growth of the world population started in 1950, with a sharp reduction in mortality in the less developed regions, resulting in an estimated population of 6055 million in the year 2000, nearly two and a half times the population in 1950. With the declines in fertility in most of the world, the global annual growth rate of population has been decreasing since its peak of 2.0 per cent in 1965–70. In 1998, the world's population stood at 5.9 billion and was growing at 1.3 per cent per year, or an annual net addition of 78 million people.

By 2050 the world is expected to have 8909 million people, an increase of slightly less than half from the 2000 population. By then the share of Asia will have stabilized at 59 per cent, that of Africa will have more than doubled to 20 per cent, and that of North and Latin America nearly doubled to 9 per cent. Meanwhile, the share of Europe will decline to 7 per cent, less than one-third its peak level. While in 1900 the population of Europe was three times that of Africa, in 2050 the population of Africa will be nearly three times that of Europe. The world population will continue to grow after 2050. Long range population projections of the United Nations indicate population growth well into the 22nd century.

## United Nations' population revision

Some of the highlights of the UN's 1998 revision of the world population estimates and projections are summarized below:

- World population currently stands at 5.9 billion people and is growing at 1.33 per cent per year, or an annual net addition of 78 million people. World population in the mid-21st century is expected to be in the range of 7.3 to 10.7 billion people. The medium fertility projection, which is usually considered as 'most likely', indicates that world population will reach 8.9 billion in 2050.

- The global average fertility level now stands at 2.7 births per woman; in contrast to early 1950 when the average number was 5 births per woman. Fertility is now declining in all regions of the world. For example, during the last 25 years, the number of children per couple has fallen from 6.6 to 5.1 in Africa, from 5.1 to 2.6 in Asia and from 5.0 to 2.7 in Latin America and the Caribbean.

- The 1998 revision demonstrates a devastating mortality toll from HIV/AIDS. For instance, in the 29 hardest hit African countries, the average life expectancy at birth is currently seven years less than it would have been in the absence of AIDS.

- The results from the 1998 revision shed new light on the global population ageing process. In 1998, 66 million people in the world were aged 80 or over, that is about 1 in every 100 people (see Figure 11.1). This number is expected to

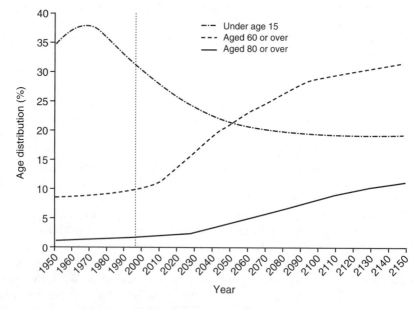

**Figure 11.1** Percentage of world population 1950–2150 in three age categories and medium fertility scenario
*Source*: Population Division of the Department of Economic and Social Affairs at the United Nations Secretariat, World Population Projections to 2150 (United Nations, New York, 1998)

increase almost sixfold by 2050 to reach 370 million people. The number of centenarians is projected to increase 16-fold by 2050 to reach 2.2 million people.

## World urban and rural populations

The percentage of population living in urban areas in 1996 and 2030 is given in Figure 11.2. Broadly this shows the urbanization trends in different regions of the world. The most noticeable changes are the very substantial increases in Africa and Asia.

### Large cities
In terms of the world's largest agglomerations (with populations of 10 million or more inhabitants) the UN Urban Agglomeration Statistics 1996 depicted in Figure 11.3 provide us with the evidence of the changes that have taken place from 1970 and the predictions for 2015.

Figure 11.4 is a graph demonstrating the growth in the number of urban agglomerations with 1 million or more inhabitants from 1950 to 2015. It shows dramatically the difference between the more developed and less developed regions.

The brief review of world population revised estimates and the urbanization trends from UN statistics demonstrate that there is a rapid shift for all regions of the world to becoming more and more urbanized. The growing urban agglomerations increasingly will be the focus for national economic performance and local and global environmental performance. The urban policies of governments and the planning, management and governance at the city level become critical in the realization of sustainable urban futures and increasingly national competitiveness in global markets.

In Europe, which has been urbanized for a long time, there have been a number of significant policy developments that provide frameworks for urban policy so more

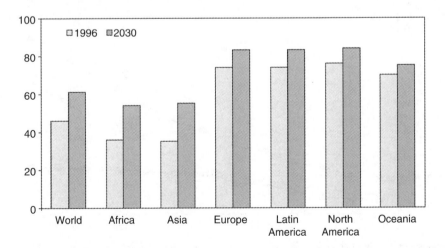

**Figure 11.2** Percentage of population living in urban areas in 1996 and 2030
*Source*: Population Division of the Department of Economic and Social Affairs at the United Nations Secretariat, World Population Projections to 2150 (United Nations, New York, 1998)

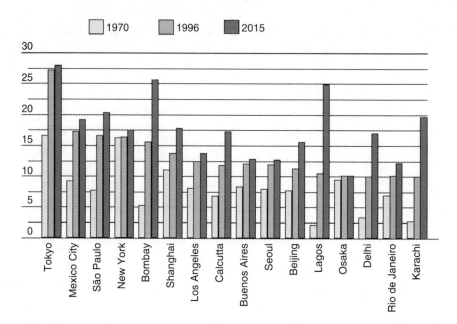

**Figure 11.3** World's urban agglomerations with populations of 10 million or more inhabitants in selected years
*Source*: UN Urban Agglomeration Statistics, Population Division, United Nations (1996)

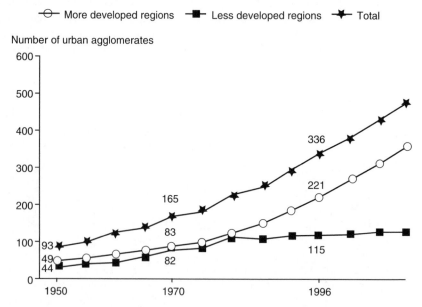

**Figure 11.4** Number of urban agglomerations from 1950 to 2015 with 1 million or more inhabitants
*Source*: UN Urban Agglomeration Statistics, Population Division, United Nations (1996)

sustainable futures can be developed in terms of energy use, transport, social exclusion, economic regeneration, cultural heritage and governance. These policies take on board the sustainable development agenda; provide for the sharing of local practice in towns and cities across Europe; and are supported by an increasing research interest in the 'city of tomorrow'.

## European urban focus

Over 80 per cent of the European population live in these towns and cities making them the cultural, economic and innovative centres of Europe. They function as the generators of local, regional and national economies, but together are the key localities in relation to European global competitiveness. They are also the centres of European social and cultural development and in recent times have undergone what is expressed as a 'renaissance' by some commentators. At the same time many of these localities are confronted with serious problems – high unemployment, social and spatial segregation, social exclusion; concerns over their future economy, crime and the general quality of life; negative impacts on health; and pressures on natural and historic assets. In addition they are handling wider global and societal changes due to the globalization of markets, shifts in demography and family structure and new technological innovations (see Chapter 12 for an in-depth discussion of globalization issues).

Along with cities worldwide, European cities are facing up to these challenges that are reshaping their futures. In work carried out for the European Commission and the World Health Organization over the last 15 years, a number of significant issues can be identified that are closely interrelated and that provide the agenda for policy development for both cities and member states, and for the European Union as a whole. These include increased competition among cities and regions both within the Union and between the Union and the rest of the world.

The accumulation of unemployment, poverty and social exclusion in larger cities are important issues for public health practitioners as urbanization is set to continue apace around the world. In-migration is an issue linked to these public health determinants. It is important that public health policy is directed towards sustainable urban development and reflects the influence of changes to public expenditure and social insurance on cities. Increasing concern over urban health; increasing inability to achieve access and mobility within and between cities; and concerns over the quality of local democracy appear to present many challenges for urban management, urban leadership and governance. Public health practitioners should be aware of such challenges in formulating their own actions and policy.

## European urban policies for sustainable futures

Since 1991 the European Community, now the European Union, has sought consolidation of its actions for environmental protection and re-orientation of environment policy to promote the objectives of sustainable development in relation to towns and cities. These policy shifts have key implications for the urban environment. The principal developments are described and elaborated in *European Sustainable Cities*

(Commission of the European Communities 1996). A selective policy history is provided in Table 11.1.

In the field of environmental policy, and by implication health, integration of the urban discussion has been extensively pursued. An integrated approach was first advocated in the Fourth Environmental Action Programme 1988–92; this led to the publication of the consultative *Green Paper on the Urban Environment* (Commission of the European Communities 1990) and in 1991 to the Council of Ministers establishing the Expert Group on the Urban Environment.

The rationale for detailed consideration of the urban environment is set out in the Green Paper, which was a response to pressures from three sources – the concern on the part of several European cities that a pre-occupation with rural development within the European Commission was overshadowing the interests of urban areas; the commitment of the then environment commissioner; and a resolution from the European Parliament urging for more studies on the urban environment. The Green Paper is a significant milestone in thinking about the urban environment in Europe, principally because it advocated a holistic view of urban problems and a policy integration approach to their solution.

**Table 11.1** Chronological policy history

| | |
|------|-----------------------------------------|
| 1972 | Stockholm Conference |
| 1980 | World Conservation Strategy |
| 1987 | Brundtland Report |
| 1987 | WHO Healthy Cities – Phase 1 |
| 1990 | Green Paper on the Urban Environment (EU) |
| 1991 | Expert Group on the Urban Environment (EU) |
| 1992 | Rio Conference (Agenda 21) |
| 1993 | Sustainable Cities Project (EU) |
| 1994 | Aalborg Conference – Charter and Campaign |
| 1996 | European Sustainable Cities Report |
| | Lisbon Action Plan |
| | Habitat II Conference, Istanbul |
| 1997 | Urban Communications (EU) |
| | Kyoto Conference |
| 1998 | Vth Framework for Research 'City of Tomorrow' |
| 2000 | Expert Group (new programme of studies) |
| | Hanover Conference |
| 2001 | Habitat plus 5 |
| 2002 | Rio plus 10 |
| 2005 | Urban Environment Strategy Statement (EU) |
| 2006 | Urban Forum, Vancouver |

The Green Paper sparked a number of debates. Perhaps the most heated debate concerned different views on urban form and the relationship between notions of 'compact cities' and sustainable futures. While the urban form and density of cities are clearly important, discussions since have widened the debate to consider ways in which 'cities and their hinterlands', regions and urban society are to be governed and managed to achieve sustainable futures. The Expert Group on the Urban Environment, established in 1991, developed the European Sustainable Cities Project in 1993 which led to a wider policy discussion in the European Commission with an urban focus. This work has been published in *European Sustainable Cities* (Commission of the European Communities 1994b, 1996). The European Sustainable Towns and Cities Campaign, launched in Aalborg in 1994, now includes over 2000 local authorities as well as the major European local authority networks, the International Council for Local Environmental Initiatives and WHO. The EU Urban Environment Expert Group has more recently advised the European Commission on the Sixth Environmental Action Programme. A series of studies and reports have been prepared for the Commission and have influenced the Urban Environment Strategy Statement (Commission for European Communities 2005) although the resulting policy is rather bland and inadequately deals with the urgency in relation to climate change and other issues put forward by the Expert Group studies.

## European sustainable cities

In 1997 the European Commission published its communication *Towards an Urban Agenda in the European Union* (Commission of the European Communities 1997). This communication established a process of consultation culminating in the November 1998 conference in Vienna where the urban action plan, *Sustainable Urban Development in the European Union: A Framework for Action* (Commission of the European Communities 1998), was discussed. This framework was organized under four substantive policy aims. These were:

- strengthening economic prosperity and employment in towns and cities;

- promoting equality, social inclusion and regeneration in urban areas;

- protecting and improving the urban environment towards local and global sustainability; and

- contributing to good urban governance and local empowerment.

Further the Fifth Framework for Research in the European Union, which commenced in 1999 and continued for four years, contained a strong focus on urban issues and included a research area called the 'City of Tomorrow'. Fudge and Rowe (1997) in a report on the development of socio-economic environmental research for the European Commission suggested some of the priorities for urban research to be included in the Fifth Framework programme should be:

- how to upgrade (towards sustainability goals) current urban stock – which will also comprise the fabric of the 'City of Tomorrow';

- developing models for the future of access and mobility which are affordable and sustainable;
- how to reduce inequality and counteract unemployment and social exclusion;
- investigating methods of implementing healthy public policy including community safety;
- investigating how to reduce energy consumption in all aspects of production and consumption in cities;
- attuning urban economies to sustainability goals, at the appropriate scale and without exporting problems, thus the research agenda must include city and hinterland;
- underpinning research into the changing nature of urban and social values; and
- examining approaches to urban management and governance that are required for sustainable futures for cities.

There has been a reduced focus on urban research in the Sixth Framework for research although in other policy arenas in the EU, urban and regional issues remain significant.

## Multidisciplinary policy issues in sustainable futures

The problems with both conceptualizing sustainable development and applying the principles derive from the requirement to bridge the very different paradigms of the so-called 'hard' disciplines associated with the environmental sciences, and those of management and social sciences. The extent to which different elements of the 'capital' of sustainability may be substitutable, for example whether an increase in human knowledge can compensate for resource losses, is also, by definition, unknown (see for example Pearce *et al.* 1990).

The concept of 'carrying capacity' seems to offer the possibility of setting objective limits upon the use of both natural and manmade resources. However, this concept too is interpreted differently by various users to reflect their own perceptions of value (see for example O'Neill 1996). Moreover, issues such as democratic probity have yet to be addressed at all (the majority may choose not to pay the price for sustainability policies and practice).

Tensions arise from the potential breadth and scope of sustainable development, both spatially (from global to local) and temporally (from 'as soon as possible' to the very long-term). Relevant policy areas include environment, transport, land use planning and practice, health, technology and business practice, as well as the frameworks for trade; the instruments which might be brought to bear thus range from legislation and market regulation to systems management and community action.

There are problems of definition, measurement, attribution of value and the use of indicators (see for example Local Government Management Board 1994b; Countryside Commission 1995). Work continues into green accounting (see for example Organization for Economic Cooperation and Development 1996; Green Alliance 1997) and, particularly through the Organization for Economic Cooperation and

Development (OECD), alternatives to gross national product as measures of national well-being.

However, it may be argued that the growth paradigm and the strength of business interests to a large extent still prevail. There is a dominant central commitment to international competitiveness which militates against business and capital engaging with more environmentally and socially beneficial forms of production and management (Welford 1995). Globalization, fostered by technological, informational and managerial change, proceeds apace; eco-efficiency may be superimposed but would require concerted international effort, of which there is little evidence (Fussler and James 1996). Localization, on the other hand, which underpins sustainability thinking in many countries emphasizes place, community and individual. The question which then arises is how urban and regional actors may most usefully resolve these dilemmas to make progress at the urban and regional level within an understanding and the real impacts of wider global imperatives and change.

## Ecological modernization

### Swedish cities case study

Given these generic approaches emerging from both European and international experience, the chapter now examines in more detail the experience of implementation of policies for sustainable futures from three cities in Sweden: Stockholm, Göteborg and Malmö.

Sweden has long been an acknowledged leader in Europe in terms of its commitment to environmental protection linked with ecologically based technological innovation, and to social democratization and high levels of welfare and health provision. Following the 1992 UN Conference on Environment and Development in Rio, Agenda 21 was received warmly in Sweden as codifying an existing determination to pursue development that may be sustainable.

However, over the last decade the economy has come under increasing pressure from globalization and social change. Although the environmental agenda remains strong, a schism seems to be developing with key socio-economic drivers. The Swedish government has responded with a policy framework of ecological modernization, through which it hopes to regain the high ground economically, environmentally and socially. This is reported elsewhere in the evaluative study of the implementation of the national framework for sustainable development and how it is being interpreted in cities and towns in Sweden (Fudge and Rowe 2000, 2001).

The three city mini case studies highlight different aspects of the utilization of sustainable development policies and initiatives and show the relative success of Swedish cities in facing the challenges identified earlier.

### Stockholm

The challenge for Stockholm (population 800,000) as capital lies in remaining a national leader in sustainable development in the face of rising consumer expectations in a globalizing society, ghettoization and developing 'edge crisis', and the ever-increasing costs of implementing sustainability principles as the public owner-ship of land, housing and other resources diminishes.

Many of the difficulties it faces were reflected in the increasing inner-city traffic congestion and air quality deterioration which characterize all of Sweden's major conurbations. A thematic 'flagship' project has been developed through the partly EU funded programmes, Zero Emissions in Urban Societies and Electric Vehicle City Distribution Systems. Standard traffic lights have been replaced with diode control systems, providing a significant energy saving. In the municipal fleet, 1500 petroleum and diesel vehicles have been replaced, or converted, to use methane from waste and sewage digestion, ethanol, rapeseed oil or electricity. Hybrid buses and heavy duty vehicles for waste management and food and goods distribution have also been introduced. Petroleum companies have co-operated in a new diverse fuelling infra-structure and, more recently, Stockholm has followed London with a congestion charging experiment.

Evaluation of performance, the effectiveness of incentives and transferability are built into the programmes and many achievements have been noted. One of these is the ongoing co-operation that has been achieved between public and private sectors. The project focus, led by deputy mayors, has also meant that various players within municipal governance across sectors and levels have worked together. However, this mutual working has yet to be translated into significant institutional change. The approach remains heavily 'expert' and the community at large has been little involved. Road traffic continues to increase and the costliness of the programmes limits their expansion and transferability. More ambitious development of new transport nodes and routes, including light rail, being pursued but is expensive and public ownership of land and resources continues to decline requiring new approaches to town planning and partnership working.

The project focus has also characterized neighbourhood regeneration projects in Stockholm. The adaptation of two 1960s suburbs to 'ecocycles principles' was the subject of an open ideas competition within the neighbourhoods themselves, among the professions and in senior school classes throughout Sweden, with the aims of inclusion and awareness raising. In what is intended to be an international proto-type for inner-city regeneration an 'ecological neighbourhood', Hammarby Sjöstad (undated), is being constructed on contaminated industrial land in south-central Stockholm. Aims include a halving of the usual environmental impacts of new-build housing. The neighbourhood will house 15,000 people in 8000 apartments within a mixed development of shops, offices, small businesses, schools and social and leisure facilities (Ministry of the Environment and Natural Resources 1992). Environmental and design objectives were agreed at the outset by a cross-sectoral partnership:

- to close resource loops at as local a level as possible;
- to minimize consumption of natural resources;
- to meet energy needs from renewable sources;
- to promote solutions that meet residents' and employers' needs; and
- to enhance social co-operation and ecological responsibility.

Technological solutions are already advanced. Thus, there will be district heating from heat recovery from local liquid biofuel boilers, supplemented by solar panels and heat pumps as necessary, and electricity supply in accordance with the Swedish Natural Environment Protection Agency's criteria for good environmental choice.

However, the commercial viability of the scheme has been questioned. Its social inclusiveness, its feasibility in relation to the right to personal choice of its inhabitants, and its transferability are also questioned. In this regard, an earlier experimental ecological neighbourhood, that of Ladugårdsängen in Örebro (Guinchard 1997), designed in 1989–90 for 3200 people and 500 businesses in public–private partnership, has to date largely survived commercial and ideological pressures. It continues to deliver successfully on waste and energy use minimization, and some transport parameters. Although almost complete and highly successful in terms of design and physical regeneration, the project still needs to demonstrate its social viability more fully and the realization of all of its original environmental goals. Nevertheless it is a case study worthy of a visit and would be welcomed in the UK as a great success.

## Göteborg

Göteborg (population 500,000) has an industrial past associated with the port and ferry industries and vehicle manufacturers (notably Volvo). Its re-invention of itself as a 'city of ideas' relies to a large extent on maintaining the close relationship between municipality, technological development and diversifying industry and academia. Its early lead in Sweden in comprehensive planning (Bergrund 1994) aimed to reconcile what are seen as the contradictory drivers of ecocycles-based sustainability – competitiveness and citizen empowerment.

The city council's green procurement policy is a key tool in the (pre-regionalization) context of 60,000 employees, having a procurement budget of SKr7 billion (about 3.5 billion euro), and in the potential to influence a wide constituency in the private and community sectors (European Commission 1996). The procurement department, a municipal company wholly financed through commissions on contracts which works closely with the environment department, develops and administers lists of environmental life cycle efficiency criteria and approved companies within 250 fields. Companies must commit to ongoing improvement through annual reporting, which tends to impact positively on all their business practice. Although initial investment by both the city and private business was high, contract suppliers (often small companies, where growth is needed) have won significant market advantage.

Systematic auditing shows unambiguous reductions in the city's environmental impacts, through lower resource use in products and packaging, delivery planning and high volume supplies. However, the procurement model depends on political commitment and leadership, widely accepted methodology, and a comprehensive strategy of ongoing cross-sectoral research, development and information dissemination, all of which are costly. In a changing political climate, and in the face of anti-competitiveness legislation from the EU and the dilution of local mutual responsibility (through regionalization as well as the globalization of markets), questions arise as to whether its devices and instruments will be strong enough to maintain it. Göteborg as 'second city' to the capital Stockholm is re-inventing itself with determination and on environmental, economic and social objectives. Unlike Stockholm it still has a large amount of brownfield land and the potential to become a more compact city.

## Malmö

Malmö (population 300,000) is at the forefront of the changes sweeping through Sweden. Its most pressing problem is unemployment, reaching more than 85 per cent in one inner-city neighbourhood among immigrant communities.

It is the national pathfinder in integrating cultural and socio-economic change with traditional values, and innovative thinking is reflected in the development of the new University College (Malmö Högskolen 1998). A key objective of the college is that it should make a significant contribution to the life of the city, and that its tuition and research should play a crucial part in the transition from a depleted industrial-based to a modern knowledge-based economy incorporating the highest environmental competencies. Development is publicly funded on publicly owned land on a complex disused shipyard/industrial site in the centre of Malmö, supported in part by parallel commercial development. Ecocycles thinking is being employed in both built form and curriculum development. The state programme for architecture and form underpins good functional and aesthetic design as well as sound, safe, manageable and ecologically durable technology at investment and operating costs appropriate to users' ability to pay. The college is expected to be self-sufficient in heating, with minimal electrical and cooling demands, and to incorporate systems to separate grey and foul water and waste close to source.

The curriculum is characterized by multidisciplinary and interdisciplinary activity. Departments and faculties are replaced by 'fields of training', all at basic, higher and research levels – for example, technology and economics, art and communication, health and community. Planning and implementation have been very rapid and thus strongly professional and 'top–down'.

The city's industrial, commercial and local communities generally have been little engaged. This is problematic both because the city is deeply divided socio-economically and politically, and because business remains strongly Conservative and tends to demand certain (sectoral) competencies in its potential employees. The extent to which the University College's ambitions can influence significantly the thinking and behaviour of the wider community remains in question although significant resources and positive policies have been put in place and much of this infrastructure is starting to demonstrate positive influences. Other projects such as the sustainable housing exhibition Malmö Bol and the so-called 'turning torso' building are changing internal and external perception of Malmö as a city with a sustainable future.

## Case study conclusion

The city case studies described above, implementing the national policy framework, provide compelling evidence of the progress Sweden has made towards sustainable development. In analytical work various needs were perceived in the municipality case studies (Fudge and Rowe 2001). These included:

- rebuilding power and trust in a new pluralist frame which can encompass the whole of the sustainable development agenda;

- strong and long-term leadership which may be able to survive the exigencies of party politics;

- clear methodologies, programmes and tools for vertical and horizontal integration in what remains a somewhat fragmented 'silo' culture; and

- a recognition of shifting public, private and community boundaries, so that expertise and experience at all levels in all sectors may be both governed and built upon.

## Strategic issues for the future of sustainability

Following the opening discussion of the definitions and meanings of sustainable development, this chapter has examined world population estimates and urbanization trends. These demonstrate that the 21st century will be an 'urban century' and that the growth rate of cities in all regions, but particularly in Asia and Africa, presents major problems in terms of spatial planning, infrastructure, housing, transport and quality of life. It also leaves governments with major policy questions around the future of growing urban and declining rural populations; significant demographic questions concerning the growing population of the elderly and children in different regions of the world; and for the UN and governments, major concerns about global climate change and poverty.

These changes have been explored in relation to the European Union where a considerable urban policy history exists. Urban policy, spatial planning and sustainable development are being pursued at European, national and city levels of government, within supportive networks with considerable sharing of practice and the sense of being involved in a meta-urban, sustainable development project. The chapter then has examined ecological modernization in Sweden as a selected case study focusing on three cities – Stockholm, Göteborg and Malmö. Sweden was chosen to demonstrate that even in some of the most advanced examples of urban sustainability in Europe, issues of history, culture, land, economics, demography and immigration, governance and political leadership all play significantly in the success of implementing sustainable development policy and practice.

This concluding discussion aims to expand on the emerging policy and management orthodoxy to achieve more sustainable futures for urban areas and proposes some steps for pursuing urban sustainability.

## Emerging policy on urban management

Despite considerable work by towns and cities and by national governments, urban settlements continue to face economic and social problems, environmental degradation and ill health. New ways of managing the urban environment need to be found so that cities can both solve local problems and contribute to regional and global sustainability. At the same time an urban renaissance in parts of the world and policies for regeneration and renewal can be used to advance the sustainability agenda.

This chapter highlights the notion that sustainable development must be planned for and that market forces alone cannot achieve the necessary integration of environmental, social, health and economic concerns. A form of urban management and urban governance is emerging which provides a framework within which innovative approaches to the planning of sustainability can be explored. In this respect, a set of ecological, social, economic, organizational and democratic principles and tools for urban management can be identified which may be applied in a variety of urban settings and which could be used selectively as cities move from different starting points and different circumstances towards contributing to local and global sustainability. The case study examples from practice across Europe clearly demonstrate that an institutional as well as a policy focus is required. The capacity of different levels of government, and particularly local government, to deliver sustainability is seen as crucial.

This may require fundamental reviews of the internal structure and working of local authorities and their relationship with their communities, as well as an examination of the relationship between central and local governments. A further dimension is that thinking about cities is undergoing a reappraisal with a return to a view of the city as a complex system requiring a set of tools that can be applied in a range of settings. Although the system is complex, it is appropriate to seek practical solutions, especially solutions which solve more than one problem at a time, or several solutions that can be used in combination. Illustrative examples of this are numerous – a Sheffield, UK, example in housing captures the essence of the new approach (Fudge 1995; Price and Tsouros 1996).

The challenge of urban sustainable development involves both the problems experienced within cities, the problems caused by cities and the potential solutions that cities themselves may provide. Managers of cities, if they are to meet more sustainable futures, must seek to resolve the social, economic, cultural and health needs of urban residents while respecting local, regional and global natural systems, broadly solving problems locally where possible, rather than shifting them to other spatial locations or passing them on to future generations. This prescriptive advice must, however, be interpreted within the complexity of regional and global economic and environmental relationships. This interpretation may raise broader issues about the 'production of space' and the 'production of nature' (Harvey 1996) and the wider economic and social forces that influence these decisions.

The preceding overview of the changes argued to be necessary to achieve a more sustainable future for cities is proactive, coherent and potentially radical. However, for it to be implemented a number of deeper questions and issues are raised that must also be addressed. First, considerable local changes that support sustainable futures (environmental strategies, recycling, environment centres, Agenda 21 co-ordinators, Agenda 21 plans, increases in cycling provision and so on) have occurred, but there seems to be limits to furthering this early progress. The spread of ideas and ownership of issues are limited within the population of cities. Mainstreaming of policy initiatives and demonstration projects seems difficult. Second, because the next developmental step cannot be accommodated alongside the existing economic functioning and economic relations within and between cities, it requires a more fundamental transformation of socio-ecological and political-economic processes and relations both within the locality and potentially at national and global levels. Third, as energy prices, water shortages and traffic congestion impact increasingly on government, business and the public in general, questions are raised about the choices we make in the management of our lives, the future of consumption and the inequalities locally and globally.

## Next steps

From policy development work, research and discussions with practitioners, general propositions implementing sustainable futures in cities include:

- Concerns of urban management and governance for sustainability are equally as important as the need for different substantive policies.
- Local authorities and their communities are crucial constituencies for sustainability, but regional and central government frameworks need to be supportive.
- Ecosystems thinking, particularly notions of resource flows, the recycling of land and buildings, the closing of resource loops, the principles of 'resource efficiency' and 'circularity' are the keys to adapting existing and designing new urban localities.
- Networks of actors engaging in this project are crucial to avoid duplication, share good practice and support problem solving (see network Winter Cities but also European Sustainable Cities and Towns Campaign network http://www.iclei.org/europe/la21/sustainable-cities.htm).
- Integration is needed between different sectors – economic, social, health, environmental and cultural; vertically between organizations and their communities; and horizontally within parts of organizations.
- Strategic planning and management, and infrastructure planning and provision at different spatial levels needs new approaches in terms of political leadership, technical competence, resource allocation and procurement.
- Conceptual and practical approaches need to be holistic at different spatial scales, not sectoral.
- Education and awareness need a strategic plan as well as 'bottom–up' initiatives and actions.
- Partnerships and collaboration between different sectors seem to provide more fruitful opportunities than relying on traditional categories of responsibilities.
- Demonstration projects are needed so that sustainable approaches can be experienced.
- Regular measurement of progress towards or away from sustainable futures related to baseline data is needed to understand progress and change.
- Democratic changes are implied through the involvement of communities (such as Agenda 21) and other factors.
- Action research is needed now to support and provide appropriate and timely feedback to practitioners.

- Longer-term developmental and evaluative programmes of research are needed to explore new ways of managing changing cities and evaluating existing policies and practices.

The focus on urbanization and the quality of life in cities in the 21st century raises issues of definition and scope for public health and public health interventions in society. It reminds us of the origins of modern town planning and its close association with public health and allows a closer relationship to be reconceptualized between health, town planning, global environmental change and the future of cities. In describing the urban context, the approaches to sustainable futures and the propositions for policy development and action, it is possible to see the implicit and explicit links to public health and indeed how mainline public health concerns may need to be reconceptualized to be able to take in the notion of sustainable development.

For the future the public health agenda, as well as concentrating on its core concerns, will probably have to engage with both the 'mitigation' and 'adaptation' responses to global climate change (Fudge and Antrobus 2002). In north-west European towns and cities, as in Japan and elsewhere, these 'new' concerns of the effects of global climate change will be coupled with the projected increase in the percentage of the population living until they are in their 80s or 90s, and the growing imbalance between those in work and providing services and a tax base, and those retired or in ill health. What then does the sustainable city look like and how will it be governed and managed? These questions give rise to further speculation on the nature of the public health agenda and the future public health discourse.

## Acknowledgements

I would like to acknowledge the assistance of my colleagues in the Faculty of the Built Environment at the University of the West of England, Bristol, particularly Dr Janet Rowe, and the work over the past 10–15 years in the European Union from the Expert Group on the Urban Environment, the European Sustainable Cities and Towns Campaign, and from colleagues in the research councils and in the universities in Sweden.

---

**Suggested further reading**

---

Barton, H. and Tsouros, C. (2000) *Healthy Urban Planning*, Spon. ISBN 0–415–24327–0.

Brown, V. A., Grootjans, J., Ritchie, J., Townsend, M. and Verrinder, G. (2005) *Sustainability and Health. Supporting Global Ecological Integrity in Public Health*. London: Earthscan.

CEC (2006) *European Sustainable Cities*. Report by the Expert Group on the Urban Environment, Brussels. ISBN 92–828–5176–1.

FORMAS (2005) *Sustainable Urban Development in Sweden*. Stockholm: FORMAS. ISBN 91–540–5948–8.

Fudge, C. and Rowe, J. (2000) *Implementing Sustainable Futures in Sweden*. Swedish Council for Building Research. ISBN 91–540–5862–7.

Takehito Takano (ed.) (2003) *Healthy Cities and Urban Policy Research*, Spon. ISBN 0–415–28844–4.

*Urban Design Quarterly* (2003) Topic: Healthy Cities. Summer 2003, Issue 87.

WHO (2003) *Healthy Cities in Europe: a Compilation of Papers on Progress and Achievements*, Agis D. Tsouros and Jill L. Farrington (eds). Copenhagen; WHO.

# 12

## STUART McCLEAN
Globalization and health

**Editors' introduction**

Globalization or 'growing interdependence' between different peoples, regions and countries in the world is the term used to describe social and economic relationships that stretch worldwide and will continue to do so.

All 21st century public health practitioners, as defined in the Introduction to this book, should be aware of the conjecture attached to the positive and negative impact of globalization on future public health by today's writers and thinkers.

Positive impacts are the spread of communication and media across the globe creating a 'global village'. This increases opportunities for public health practitioners to join forces in confronting issues such as the spread of infectious disease, the threat of terrorism, trafficking in illegal drugs, environmental health issues, climate change and matters concerning food, including GM foods and animal diseases. Globalization also has negative implications for public health practitioners: as national boundaries and controls are weakened, the historical concerns of public health workers over the past 200 years, including problems from the movement of goods and people, re-emerge into a 21st century context.

The uneven spread of new technology across the globe leaves two-thirds of the world disenfranchised technologically, with no obvious means to redress the situation. The pattern of technological exclusion does not conform to nation states, but in time will exacerbate health inequality in ways not conducive to lateral or unilateral governmental action. Global public health action is thus inextricably linked by geography and ecology to economic growth through technology and this has numerous implications for 21st century public health workers.

This chapter begins by exploring the contested definitions of globalization. The author goes on to discuss the positive and negative impacts of globalization on public health, examining the role of key international institutions such as the World Bank, World Trade Organization and World Health Organization. The impact of global trade policy on public health in the UK and global health inequalities and global divisions are assessed. Finally, globalization and emerging public health risks are discussed. The author concludes with a summary of the challenges for public health in the 21st century.

## Introduction

The aim of this chapter is to locate contemporary debates surrounding globalization and theories of global society within the domain of public health, and, in addition, to argue that these debates are central to the public health endeavour. A broad-based public health should take stock of significant economic, social and political changes that define and shape people's health. The following sections therefore map a range of debates that the public health discussion of globalization has raised.

There has been a considerable increase in interest into the issue of globalization within public health, but this emerging field is a contested one, insofar as public health writers are undecided, not only as to the impact of globalization on health, but also as to whether globalization has cemented its place in the public health lexicon. Nevertheless, I demonstrate how a key issue within public health is the need to understand the impact of macro processes of globalization on population health.

A theoretical approach to globalization is of key importance in helping us to understand the nature of contemporary economic, social and political changes, but at present globalization is generally undertheorized within the public health field. Therefore, by way of introduction, I shall briefly outline some of these issues as they are conceptualized within social science and consider how they illuminate wider debates within public health.

## The globalization debate

The term globalization has become increasingly central to academic discourse, particularly within the social and political sciences, but has only recently begun to play a part in discussions within public health (Lee 2003). Currently, it is argued that a key issue to emerge in 21st century public health is the challenge of globalization and how this affects individual and population level health (Zwi and Yach 2002: 1615). However, there has been a general shift in the awareness of globalization as a field of discussion, brought about partly by the public perception of events (such as war, conflict, famine and international level disputes) that occur at some distance from the recipient. As Hannerz states, 'Distances, and boundaries, are not what they used to be' (1996: 3). Globalization, then, undermines traditional perceptions and meanings of distance and national level boundaries.

Recent and high profile events such as the terrorist attacks that took place in New York and Washington on 11 September 2001, coupled with the global, cyclical risks posed by an avian influenza pandemic, have resulted in talk of globalization being no longer the sole preserve of lawyers, politicians, economists, sociologists and cultural theorists. These distant events, intensified and replayed through the role of the global media, have brought the 'new era' (United Nations Development

Programme 1999) of globalization to public consciousness, although it is generally argued that globalization is not a phenomenon of the modern age, but predates this era (Held and McGrew 2000: 6). Insofar as the presence of a global society has been brought to the attention of individuals and communities through the global media lens, these recent high profile events have meant that globalization, as both a word and a social condition, has become ubiquitous in Western society.

## Globalization – a contested term

Globalization is a greatly contested term in that it does not have a fixed meaning and therefore comes to mean different things to different people (Hannerz 1996; Held and McGrew 2000; Lee 2000b) (see Box 12.1). Indeed, discussions that explore the nature of globalization also engender fierce disagreement among those within the field of public health. A good example can be seen in both the number and range of electronic responses to Feachem's (2001) article in the *British Medical Journal.*

During the 1950s and 1960s the term modernization was used (predominantly within the social sciences) to describe the changes that underdeveloped nations would pass through on their route to full industrialization (Rostow 1966; Held and McGrew 2000). Westernization as a term has also featured heavily, particularly as the early stage/era of globalization; industrial and capitalist were other terms synonymous with Western societies (Hannerz 1996: 8).

Globalization should not be interpreted as the imposition of Western modernity across the globe (Giddens 1990; Beck 2000a). Globalization does not just refer to the 'Americanization' or 'McDonaldization' of the global order (Ritzer 1993), a process that has also been referred to as the 'convergence of global culture' thesis (Beck 2000a: 42), in which what we are witness to is a greater uniformity of lifestyles and modes of behaviour. As a counter-trend to this 'McDonaldization', globalization can also refer to 'reverse colonization', where non-Western or 'developing' countries have some bearing on events that take place in the West (Giddens 1999). For example, this can be seen in the 'latinizing' of Los Angeles and the emergence of a highly innovatory high-tech sector in regions of India (Giddens 1999).

Others argue that globalization as a concept is itself problematic and ill-defined, and that either 'internationalization' or 'transnational' are more apposite descriptions of these wider economic, social and political changes, particularly in relation to the erosion of state boundaries. Whereas internationalization refers to the continued primacy of the nation state in controlling territorial issues, transnational refers to the movement across bounded nation states that may not necessarily be global (Hannerz 1996), but trilateral (Giddens 1990). Furthermore, such transformations lend credence to the view that states are no longer the channels through which markets operate. As the German philosopher and sociologist Jurgen Habermas adroitly points out, 'Today it is more true to say that states are embedded within markets than that national economies are embedded within the boundaries of states' (Habermas 2006: 75). Globalization therefore radically alters the character of modern nations and their constitutive relations – between state, society and the economy.

Globalization is often seen to refer to 'interconnectedness' between individuals and communities across diverse and geopolitically separate nation states (McMichael and Beaglehole 2000; Stephens 2000). Moreover, globalization does not refer solely to processes which are remote from everyday personal lives (Giddens 1999). Individuals and communities can no longer consider themselves to be separate from wider global processes that have broader consequences for public health. We shall see how this issue of distant events shaped by and shaping local happenings is thereby central to public health debates surrounding the global society.

---

**Box 12.1**   What is globalization?

'[Globalization is] . . . the intensification of worldwide social relations which link distant localities in such a way that local happenings are shaped by events occurring many miles away and vice versa' (Giddens 1990: 64).

'Globalization as a concept refers both to the compression of the world and the intensification of consciousness of the world as a whole . . . both concrete global interdependence and consciousness of the global whole' (Robertson 1992: 8).

'[Globalization is] a process (or set of processes) which embodies a transformation in the spatial organization of social relations and transactions – assessed in terms of their extensity, intensity, velocity and impact – generating transcontinental or interregional flows and networks of activity, interaction, and the exercise of power' (Held et al. 1999: 16).

---

## Key features of globalization in relation to public health

Primarily, globalization has been brought about by, and is predominantly associated with, manifestly economic processes (Waters 1995; Price et al. 1999; O'Keefe 2000; Baum 2001; Woodward et al. 2001; Labonte and Torgerson 2005). Moreover, discussion surrounding the economic (as opposed to social, political or cultural) dimension of globalization has rather dominated the public health agenda. The argument here concerns the extent to which economic globalization has long been a feature of a world dominated by Western societies and ideology. Therefore, globalization in the economic context refers to a set of historical events which have their foundations in prior geopolitical events, such as the first period of European expansion from 1500 to 1800 (Feachem 2001: 506). As such, globalization is synonymous with the economic phenomenon of capitalism (Wallerstein 1979) and its neoliberal socio-economic agenda.

However, globalization does not refer merely to economic globalization: the economic integration of a global society has been overplayed (Turner 2001: 11). There are other spheres which we must take into account and are important in terms of public health. Globalization is engaged across a number of public and private spheres: the political, legal, military, socio-cultural and environmental as well as the economic (Held *et al.* 1999). These transformations within global society are central to contemporary social life and impact in both 'common sense' and unexpected ways on the health and well-being of individuals and communities.

There are clearly key links between the political economy of globalization (the manifest processes that drive globalization at an economic and structural level) and the various spheres that sustain health care and health care systems within capitalist Western societies. Woodward *et al.* (2001) in the *Bulletin of the World Health Organisation* have developed a useful conceptual framework with which to make sense of this emerging picture about how structural processes of globalization might impact on health (see Figure 12.1).

The model, albeit static, attempts to take into account the multiple 'routes' that globalization processes are implicit in, and how these might impact on health via a range of state, societal and supra-national level institutions.

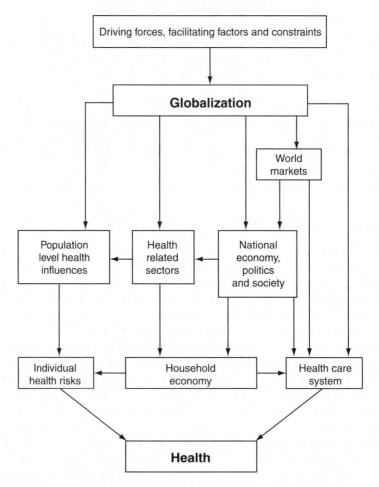

**Figure 12.1** Outline conceptual framework for globalization and health
*Source:* Woodward *et al.* (2001)

## The Janus faces: positive and negative impacts on public health

Central to this debate is the effect of these wider economic and socio-cultural changes (understood as globalization) on the health of individuals and populations. Public health writers have weighed up the effects of key global processes and have considered the extent to which they are either beneficial or harmful to population health. Hannerz argues that ambiguity and contestation over the meaning of the term is at the heart of the debate concerning its effects: 'One almost expects any mention of globalization to be accompanied by either booing or cheering' (1996: 5). However, globalization is not intrinsically either beneficial or harmful to people's health, although it appears that proponents of both sides of this debate have become entrenched in their attitudes towards it (Lee 2001; Labonte and Torgerson 2005).

We can observe and illustrate the positive and negative consequences of global processes (see Box 12.2). Globalization is widely perceived as 'Janus-faced' (Bettcher and Wipfli 2001: 617), as there are perceived to be two sides to the process, one promising, the other threatening (Yach and Bettcher 1998). Positive consequences stem from the idea that globalization increases the sharing of information, ideas and forms of knowledge, and this has important benefits for public health. Bettcher and Wipfli (2001) argue that these opportunities are often missed from the analysis of global processes. For example, the collaboration between states over shared global public health issues such as tuberculosis or tobacco control can be an important

---

**Box 12.2**

| Positive consequences | Negative consequences |
|---|---|
| The evidence that openness to trade and investment is good for economic growth is compelling and goes back several centuries . . . globalisation, economic growth, and improvements in health go hand in hand. Economic growth is good for the incomes of the poor is good for the health of the poor. Globalisation is a key component of economic growth. Openness to trade and the inflow of capital, technology, and ideas are essential for sustained economic growth.<br><br>(Feachem 2001: 504–5). | Globalisation is not just something 'out there', nor something out of control. It is the shirt you are wearing, that you now know better than ever was sewn in the sweatshops of India or China (whichever label) made from cotton (maybe) grown in export monocultures of a green 'revolution' that put immense power into the hands of transnational agrichemical industries . . . It is food – cheap, available and shiny – bought at the expense of contaminated land, air, and water and the working conditions of workers and their families internationally. It is the real cost of cheap petrol, cars, flights and holidays. It is water, air, food – and health.<br><br>(Stephens 2000) |

experience: 'the ease and rapidity of communications have facilitated the diffusion of ideas and policy concerns relating to health care and public health . . . to areas of the world previously beyond the reach of the public health community' (Bettcher and Wipfli 2001: 617). Globalization is also seen as having a positive effect in terms of promoting gender equality as well as human rights (Ganguly-Scrase 2003).

In addition, it is in the self-interest of high income countries to ensure that disenfranchised communities and nations do not become political vacuums of chaos in a globalizing world (Bettcher and Wipfli 2001: 617). In this respect political isolationism is seen as more of a threat to public health than openness to trade (Feachem 2001). The burgeoning of global travel, printed media and technologically enhanced media (such as the Internet) are viewed as positive aspects of global processes: 'Globalization of the world economy and the resulting increase in commerce, travel, and communication have benefited almost every country' (Howson *et al.* 1998: 586). Processes of technological innovation, for instance, have broader consequences for health. For example, the UK-based National Health Service has an Internet site called **NHS Direct**, and this is accessed by individuals and communities from all over the world as a resource for health.

For some writers within public health, globalization is something to be encouraged as it engenders 'openness' to ideas, people, trade and culture (Feachem 2001). This also seems to be the view of orthodox economists, in that globalization will lead to wealth accumulation. Such writers focus predominantly on the economic justification for globalization in terms of increased health equalling increased worker productivity: 'Healthy populations abroad represent growing markets for businesses of the industrial world. If developed countries invest in improving the health of other populations . . . their economic returns will be increased' (Howson *et al.* 1998: 589). Central to this argument is the view that globalization has helped to reduce inequities between and within countries (Frankel and Romer 1999). The World Trade Organization (WTO) and the World Bank (transnational and multinational level organizations) additionally support these views, and I explore these in more depth in the following section.

For others, however, globalization is creating rising social and health inequalities. Negative consequences are again viewed in terms of economic shifts; the market liberalization that global trade fosters: 'At the start of the 21st century one of the major threats to global health comes from the transnational financial interests who speculate against the world currencies' (Baum 2001: 613). Globalization is perceived as generating negative effects on national level health care systems, through the restrictive 'market promoting' policies of the WTO (Price *et al.* 1999), and that these policies have led to a disproportionate effect on the health of the vulnerable groups in the global society (Pollock and Price 2000: 13).

In addition, the public health concern has focused on equating globalization with direct health impacts, such as shifting disease patterns, climate change, poorer working conditions in the developing nation states and effects on food security. I will return to these issues in the final section examining contemporary public health risks.

## The promoters of economic globalization and other key players

Global interconnectedness has been achieved largely on an economic scale, although we can also see that there has been significant erosion of boundaries in other spheres such as the cultural and political. Yet, economic globalization is not the serendipitous result of contemporary economic policy. This manifestation of globalization has long been a feature of Western states, and now the neoliberal socio-economic agenda of the Organization for Economic Cooperation and Development countries receives extra backing through the work and policy directives of the WTO, the World Bank and the International Monetary Fund. These organizations are widely regarded as the promoters of economic globalization (McMichael and Beaglehole 2000: 496).

However, we should recognize that the global health arena is a plural setting. For example, globally the health sector additionally consists of multinational companies, the independent sector, non-governmental organizations, WHO and the bilateral sector (Howson *et al.* 1998: 588). Also, the private and not-for-profit sector has become an important force in promoting global health as new organizations such as the Global Fund for Aids, Tuberculosis and Malaria (www.theglobalfund.org), and the Bill and Melinda Gates Foundation (www.gatesfoundation.org) raise the profile of global infectious disease. Yet the WTO, the World Bank, the International Monetary Fund and WHO take centre stage in discussions surrounding globalization and public health, so I will turn to these briefly.

### The World Trade Organization

A replacement for the General Agreement on Tariffs and Trade is the WTO, an international body based in Geneva which was created in 1995 to 'lower import taxes, remove barriers to free trade and resolve trade disputes' (Pollock and Price 2000: 12). The aim of the General Agreement on Tariffs and Trade was to reduce tariffs and thereby liberalize trade. It has also been perceived as an opportunity for the United States to create a trading system that best suited its interests during the post-war period (Waters 1995: 68).

A broader objective of the WTO has been to expand private markets by removing political/trade barriers to the global movement of goods, services and capital. A key component of these talks was that of public services. For example, a major aim of the WTO talks scheduled in Seattle in November 1999 was the restructuring of public services. Here, the focus was on prising open public funding streams that pay for public services. Therefore, the WTO is devising the international laws and regulatory frameworks that will allow it to open up public services to market forces: 'WTO plans are about dismantling public services in the interests of private sector corporations' (Pollock and Price 2000: 13).

Engagement with the promotion of economic globalization has been implemented through a number of strategies and trade laws, such as the promotion of free trade and the enforcement of structural adjustment policies (McMichael and Beaglehole 2000). Other strategies include the additional incentives that are offered to developing nations through a relaxation of wage controls and workplace standards (Daykin and

Doyal 1999; McMichael and Beaglehole 2000). The specific role of the WTO is spelt out more clearly by O'Keefe (2000). O'Keefe argues that the WTO:

> sets the regulatory framework for the multi-lateral trading system including contractual obligations, which are legally binding on member states . . . It sets the rules applying to intellectual property rights, trade in goods and services, settles disputes and co-operates with other international agencies in developing global economic policy.
>
> (O'Keefe 2000: 174)

Some writers within public health interpret these trading obligations as a beneficial process. For example, Feachem argues that a key economic benefit of globalization is that countries that have gone through a process of trade liberalization will have an increase in GNP, and this has an equal effect on the health status of populations (Feacham 2001: 504). The notion of trade liberalization is crucial to the argument, and most commentators equate globalization with trade liberalization and the freeing of trade.

Trade liberalization refers to the relaxing of controls on the movement of capital, goods and services. The WTO website states it thus: 'one of the principles of the WTO system is for countries to lower their trade barriers and to allow trade to flow more freely. After all, countries benefit from the increased trade that results from lower trade barriers' (www.wto.org). However, the main questions that are posed in relation to trade liberalization are whether it promotes economic growth for poorer nations and whether it is equally practised (Labonte 2001: 620). It is perhaps no surprise therefore that the WTO has frequently become a major target for anti-globalization protests.

A good example of trade liberalization is the General Agreement on Trade in Services – one of the trade agreements devised by the WTO to encourage 'progressive liberalization' (Labonte 2002). Progressive liberalization essentially means that countries can only increase their commitments to free trade (Labonte 2002: 65). The WTO talks in Seattle were to focus on the revision of the General Agreement on Trade in Services: 'a system of international law intended to expand private-enterprise involvement in the increasingly important service sector' (Price *et al.* 1999: 1889).

Therefore, the General Agreement on Trade in Services opens up public service provision to foreign competition and ownership. This includes, for example, many service sectors such as health, education and housing (Price *et al.* 1999). The General Agreement on Trade in Services permits member countries to force the removal of barriers to foreign participation in the health services of other WTO members.

## The World Bank and the International Monetary Fund

Other organizations worth mentioning briefly are the World Bank and the International Monetary Fund. Based in Washington DC and currently headed by Paul Wolfowitz (a controversial figure who helped to implement the foreign policy of the present Bush administration in the USA), the World Bank is a source of financial assistance primarily for developing countries, and is seen as one of the largest multilateral funders of health care projects (O'Keefe 2000). The International Monetary Fund, based in Washington, also provides temporary economic assistance, but exists primarily to eliminate restrictions that hamper the promotion of free trade. The International Monetary Fund has been criticized particularly for its imposing of the structural adjustment programmes for developing countries that are in debt. The structural adjustment programmes exist in order to promote the private sector, and it is argued that this can lead to impaired population health (McMichael and Beaglehole 2000: 496). This is due to their part in driving for-profit insurance medical care, as opposed to encouraging developing nations to expand their public services (Navarro 1998). As a consequence, the combined result of debt repayment and structural adjustment programmes has resulted in developing nations dramatically cutting their social spending (Braveman and Tarimo 2002: 1627).

## The World Health Organization

The WHO additionally plays a crucial role in defining the field in terms of global institutions that have a stake in health. Generally, the WHO is viewed in positive terms in that its focus has been on reducing inequalities and identifying the inseparable nature of global-based inequalities in health. As O'Keefe explains: 'The World Health Organization (WHO) has repeatedly insisted that policy at national and international levels should be linked and that we should be attempting to reduce inequalities between and within countries at the same time. A commitment to equity should guide health sector reform' (2000: 168).

Furthermore, the WHO has been influential in a number of forms of collaboration around health problems, such as tobacco consumption. As the WHO explains, tobacco consumption is a challenge to population health that 'cuts across national boundaries, cultures, societies and socio-economic strata' (www.who.int/en/). However, the WHO has not been exempt from criticism. Indeed, some have questioned its ability to address issues of global inequity when it has seen to become increasingly 'impotent' as a global player (Baum 2001: 615), while others have questioned its future global strategy and mandate (Ruger and Yach 2005).

So far I have outlined the debates surrounding the role and influence of the international and transnational organizations, and have considered the extent to which economic/trade liberalization is exacerbating the gap between the rich and poor in the developing regions.

I now turn to examining the knock-on effect this will have on the vulnerable groups in the UK (the poor, the elderly, disabled and unemployed), due to privatization of public services, which is a product of key economic and political global trends.

## Global trade policy and the UK health care context

National health systems are increasingly influenced by global factors that transcend state borders (Yach and Bettcher 1998). In addition, domestic policies have effects beyond the nation state: 'the domestic and international spheres of public health policy are becoming more intertwined and inseparable' (Yach and Bettcher 1998: 735).

A key issue here concerns the changing role of the state and the widening influence of the private sector. In this context, the UK is seen as an important domestic setting with which to discuss the changing relationship between global trade policies and public services (Price *et al.* 1999).

It is generally argued that the foundations of the NHS were based on a traditional nation state model of society. In addition, the NHS has been a public institution, but increasingly writers have argued that it is under threat partly due to the movement towards private enterprise, but also because of the power of markets to undermine broader social goals. A key question, then, is whether this form of global competition spells the end for the welfare state (Held and McGrew 2000: 19). Habermas' following statement spells out the wider implications of these concerns: 'Restrictions on the room to manoeuvre of national governments simultaneously endanger the welfare state, and thereby the sole example of the successful offsetting of the socially undesirable effects of capitalism' (Habermas 2006: 76).

The UK is leading the way in restructuring and modernizing its public sector services, and this can be seen as a threat to the viability of the state and the future of public health. This restructuring is linked in the West to an increased use of experimentation with health care markets via deregulation and privatization methods such as private finance initiatives (PFI) (see Pollock 2004 for a recent critique of PFI). Markets and quasi-markets for health care have been seen as a solution to rising health care expectations in the West, and as Braveman and Tarimo explain: 'Globally, there has been a downsizing of government and a marked trend towards privatization of many functions formally within the public health domain. To varying degrees, many countries have experienced a shift from centrally planned and regulated to market-dominated economies' (2002: 1627).

Pollock and Price (2000) explore some of the wider implications in addressing the reforming of public sector services, and these are also taken up in an article in the *Lancet* (Price *et al.* 1999). The example they give is that of the funding arrangements for public services. The NHS, they explain, has been funded on the basis of geographical area needs. Since 1991 and the creation of the internal market, funding is allocated as a payment per patient which follows them to the point of delivery. Pollock and Price argue that pro-liberalization organizations like the World Bank favour this 'capitation' payment as it allows the substitution of public for private sources of funding, such as private insurance and an incentive to withhold care (Price *et al.* 1999).

These authors argue that these wider structural changes in the delivery and funding of health care services hold key implications for public health. One of the most important of these is that of the effect on income and health inequalities in the UK, which are continuing to widen (Acheson 1998). It is argued that the WTO, through the General Agreement on Trade in Services, places restrictions on national sovereignty, although the wide ranging effects of these policies are yet to be explored in relation to inequalities in health.

## Global inequalities in health: the local impact of global divisions

Some writers exploring the international health scene have argued that events like that of 11 September in New York symbolize the failure to address global inequities (Zwi and Yach 2002: 1618). Globalization is seen, on one hand, as exacerbating inequalities of resources. On the other hand, the World Bank and WTO have argued that economic globalization and trade liberalization (free trade) would bring benefits for all, and would act as a trigger for economic development within low income countries.

### The impact of trade liberalization on health inequalities

The evidence largely points to the fact that trade liberalization has increased inequalities both between and within countries (see Navarro 1998; Walt 1998; Hurrell and Woods 1999; Lee 2000a; Rowson 2000). As Hurrell and Woods explain, 'Economic liberalization is exacerbating the gap between rich and poor within virtually all developing countries' (1999: 1). Moreover, these changes have effects wider than the developing nations. For example, Navarro argues that inequalities have increased substantially in both Western and non-Western societies. As he explains:

> These inequalities are growing at an unprecedented rate, not only among countries but also within most of the developed and developing countries . . . the globalization they extoll has meant an unprecedented growth in wealth and income, for others the process has meant an unprecedented deterioration in their standard of living, health, and well being.
>
> (Navarro 1998: 742)

### Inequalities between and within countries

The United Nations Development Programme report 2001 produces some key data on inequalities between and within countries. On balance, global level inequality is very high. For example, in 1993 the poorest 10 per cent of the world's population had only 1.6 per cent of the income of the richest 10 per cent. Conversely, the richest 10 per cent of the US population had a combined income greater than that of the poorest 43 per cent (United Nations Development Programme 2001: 19). However, as the report details, income deprivations are not limited to developing countries or regions. For example, within OECD countries more than 130 million are calculated as income poor and 34 million are unemployed (United Nations Development Programme 2001: 10), which raises some important questions regarding the relationship between global employment status and health (Daykin and Doyal 1999).

In addition, countries in eastern Europe and countries of the former Soviet Union have experienced some of the largest growths in income inequality and this has had a major impact on the recent resurgence of tuberculosis. Furthermore, since the political transition of the former Soviet Union and eastern European states, there has been a large and significant impact on life expectancy and personal security (United

Nations Development Programme 2001: 13). For example, the report states, 'Global-ization has created many opportunities for cross-border crime and the rise of multi-national crime syndicates and networks' (United Nations Development Programme 2001: 13). This also has implications for the displacement of refugee populations across Europe.

More importantly, the report also notes that countries do not have to wait for economic prosperity to make progress in human development such as public health. This echoes some of the ideas of Wilkinson (1996) who argues that more egalitarian societies are healthier and more socially cohesive. Examples given such as South Korea and Costa Rica suggest that domestic social policies also contribute to and promote aspects of human development such as population health; this is not just the by-product of economic growth (United Nations Development Programme 2001: 13).

This also raises the issue of social capital, viewed by Putnam (1993) as stretching across four characteristics: existence of community networks, participation in net-works (civil engagement), sense of local identity and solidarity, and norms of trust and reciprocity. The United Nations Development Programme report states that income inequality diminishes social capital (2001: 17). This also has major implica-tions for public health: 'A deficiency of social capital (social networks and civic institutions) adversely affects the prospects of health by predisposing to widened rich–poor gaps, inner urban decay, increased drug trade, and weakened public-health systems' (McMichael and Beaglehole 2000: 497).

(Health inequalities in the UK are discussed in depth in Chapter 9.)

## Technological inequalities

Another major factor raised by the United Nations Development Programme report (2001) is that of technological advance and its association with progress in human development. This is a moot point as inequalities of resources can draw attention to the technological capabilities of nation states. Sachs (2000), for example, argues that the world is split into regions that score highly on technological innovation and those that have limited technological expertise, although, interestingly, these regions that lack technological innovation do not necessarily conform to national borders (Sachs 2000). Sachs' argument is that technological inequality is synony-mous with other risks, such as those connected with public health. However, unlike many economic-based arguments, Sachs explains that it is not the free market which can help provide technological innovations within these excluded regions, but partnerships and interaction between governments and scientific institutions (Sachs 2000).

The scope of contemporary public health is the reduction of social and health inequalities, and the striving for health sustaining environments (McMichael and Beaglehole 2000). In this way, we can see that exploring the effects of globalization on health inequalities is crucial. Additionally, it means that those professionals working within the broad gamut of public health may have to be more creative in exposing the multiple factors that contribute to continuing health inequalities.

## Globalization and emerging public health risks

This section examines the wider impact of globalization on public health, particularly as it pertains to current key concerns within public health in the UK. It is argued by those in the public health field that people in the Western world are experiencing a major transition in the main causes of disease and must now address the challenges that these new public health risks bring to population health (McMichael and Beaglehole 2000: 495). (See also Chapter 13 for discussion on new threats to health and health protection issues in the UK.)

### Non-communicable diseases

The 'epidemiological transition' brings new public health risks within the UK and the Western world in general (Gwatkin *et al.* 1999). For example, we see this with the rise of non-communicable diseases, such as coronary heart disease, cancers and forms of substance abuse such as alcoholism. A primary concern in terms of public health and in terms of the WHO agenda is that of tobacco-related diseases (Lee 2000b). Although it could be argued that tobacco-related markets are shrinking in Western Europe and North America, the impact of market/trade liberalization has meant that new markets have been fostered in Asia, Africa, South America, Eastern and Central Europe (Lee 2000b: 256). Other related public health issues such as substance abuse are also linked to emerging global trends, such as changing work patterns and lifestyles which are a result of the global economy (Lee 2000b: 257).

The greatest public health changes have been created through the global liberal-ization of trade (Walt 1998). As such, tobacco-related morbidity and disease has been placed high on the WHO agenda. For example, WHO member states are involved in the negotiation of a law/treaty to assist in the regulation of tobacco companies – the Framework Convention on Tobacco Control (Bettcher and Wipfli 2001: 617) (see Box 12.3).

Although the extent to which the WHO can set global policy on tobacco control has been perceived as heavily limited (*Lancet* 2002: 267), engagement with global and regional level public health policy has led to further debate and sharing of ideas. This highlights a point made earlier – that globalization encapsulates positive and negative expressions. For example, the negativity of the increase in tobacco-related trade in Eastern and Central Europe contrasts with the increased co-operation among organizations on global public health issues. Globalization is both dynamic and contradictory (O'Keefe 2000: 172).

### Communicable diseases

Non-communicable diseases aside, it is also true that globalization is changing the nature of infectious/communicable diseases (Lee 2000a: 14), highlighted most recently in the case of SARS (see Box 12.4). Infectious diseases such as tuberculosis, malaria, the plague and cholera, are interpreted as 're-emerging'. For example, the WHO (1997) explains that the re-emergence of malaria is seen in areas where it had been thought it was eradicated, such as Azerbaijan, Iraq and Turkey.

---

**Box 12.3**   Case study: framework convention on tobacco control

---

In 1999 the WHO began work on the framework convention on tobacco control; the first time the WHO had used legal frameworks to help population health. The framework is a binding international legal instrument which embraces a general commitment and system of governance, and was developed in response to the globalization of the tobacco epidemic. The Convention was endorsed by member states on 21 May 2003 and entered into force on 27 February 2005.

The Convention consisted both of a number of price and tax-related measures to reduce the demand for tobacco, as well as a range of non-price-related measures. Among its range of measures, the treaty requires countries to impose restrictions on tobacco advertising, the sponsorship and promotion of tobacco, establishing new packaging and labelling of tobacco products, as well as providing protection from exposure to tobacco smoke and strengthening legislation to reduce tobacco smuggling.

*Source*: Shibuya *et al.* 2003; WHO 2005b

---

**Box 12.4**   Case study: SARS

---

Risk has increasingly become part of our vocabulary for making sense of new health scares, from NV-CJD to MMR and mobile phones, so it is no surprise that other more sinister health threats have arisen. The more recent outbreak of the Severe Acute Respiratory Syndrome (SARS) for example, demonstrates the potential of newly emerging infectious diseases to spread rapidly in a globalized world, increasing the risk of a global pandemic. But, it also demonstrates the dangers of raising the spectre of risk without due consideration to its proper place within the panoply of possible environmental and public health risks. Like other newly emerging global public health risks, SARS was inextricably linked to the dark side of modernity – spread along the global air travel routes, with their links between a 'global cities network' (Ali and Keil 2006). The outbreak occurred between November 2002 and July 2003, spread between more than two dozen countries (and global cities such as Beijing, Hong Kong, Singapore and Toronto), and resulted in over 8000 cases and 774 deaths. While the death toll was relatively low, its effect on local economies, trade and travel were more widespread. The danger of SARS was limited, in the end, by mass quarantine measures. The WHO highlighted, among others, the role of a 'responsible' global media and improved global electronic communications as key factors in the successful public health response. The WHO has recently declared that the SARS virus has been effectively eradicated.

*Source*: WHO 2003c; Ali and Keil 2006

Also, there are other newly emerging diseases like HIV, Ebola and NV-CJD (WHO 1997). Indeed, the WHO claims that over the last 20 years 30 new infectious diseases have emerged (WHO 1997: 148). This is particularly the case among the low income countries, and regions which have experienced significant economic crises: 'Overall, communicable diseases were much more important for the poor than was suggested by global averages' (Gwatkin *et al.* 1999: 588). Such findings are supported by the work of the US physician and anthropologist Paul Farmer, who has consistently argued for increased understanding of the links between infectious diseases and structurally embedded social inequalities (Farmer 1999).

It has also been argued that widening inequality within and between countries (identified by the United Nations Development Programme report 2001) is contributing to poorer people's vulnerability to infectious diseases, illustrated by the multi-drug resistant strains of tuberculosis and HIV (Farmer 1997, 1999; Howson *et al.* 1998; Lee 2000a). This is particularly interesting in the case of tuberculosis, where there has been a reversal of the trends in the West, with an increase of cases in particular with Multi-drug Resistant (MDR) TB (Farmer 1997). Furthermore, this has taken place in areas populated by the poor and most vulnerable groups in society: 'Significant outbreaks of MDR TB have been reported in homeless shelters, prisons and medical facilities from Washington DC to Boston to San Francisco' (Farmer 1997: 348). Tuberculosis increases in Russia and Eastern Europe during the 1990s have also been noted and this is seen as illustrative of the breakdown of the social order and social cohesion since the political fragmentation of the former Russian states.

Infectious diseases, therefore, have increased partly because of increased poverty and also because they are the product of widening inequalities. Infectious diseases are therefore treated as 'sociomedical phenomena' (Farmer 1997: 348). However, with the increase in global travel, tourism (to places like Africa, the Indian subcontinent and South America), population migration and displacement, other diseases like malaria and cholera are proving to be a public health threat once again (Lee 2000b: 256).

## Food-borne disease

The increase and intensification of worldwide mobility in both people and trade also has key public health risks and implications for the transportation of food and the increased incidence of transborder food-borne disease (Lee 2000b: 258). This has led to certain authors claiming that we should source food from local farms – the 'proximity principle' (El Din 2000: 16). Other commentators such as Shiva (2000) argue that trade agreements like the Trade Related Intellectual Property Rights Agreement of the WTO have increased the patents on indigenous food varieties, which Shiva argues destroys the diversity of local food cultures and their rich biological heritage (Rowson and Koivusalo 2000; Shiva 2000).

## Environmental change

Another key public health issue, in terms of risk, is that of global environmental change (see Box 12.5 for details of Kyoto Protocol). It has long been argued that key

---

**Box 12.5** Case study: Kyoto Protocol on climate change

The Kyoto Protocol is an international agreement drawn up in 1997 in Kyoto, Japan, under the United Nations Framework Convention on Climate Change, to set targets for industrialized nations to cut their greenhouse gas emissions (such as carbon dioxide and methane), which is seen as partly responsible for global warming. The protocol has its roots in the United Nations conference in Rio in 1992, known since as the 'Earth Summit'. To date 141 countries have signed up to the treaty, with the USA a notable exception, and each country was set its own target, depending largely on its stage of industrial development. Russia's signature in 2004 was widely perceived as a significant moment in helping the treaty to come into force. The Kyoto Protocol became a legally binding treaty on 16 February 2005, once particular conditions were met. Differences in opinion continue to exist between the USA and European nations, as well as 'developing' nations, over both the scientific 'value' of reducing gas emissions, as well as the 'fairness' in differences in emissions targets. Such debates also highlight the increasing importance attached to global social responsibility, both at a governmental and corporate level.

*Source:* Stevrer 2003

---

global environmental changes, brought about by the intensity of modern consumer driven economics, hold risks for public health: 'These changes to the earth's basic life-supporting processes pose long-term risks to the health of populations' (McMichael and Beaglehole 2000: 497). McMichael and Beaglehole explore the potential risks of global climate change to health, for example, in the geographical range of vector-borne infectious diseases such as malaria. Strains of malaria have now been discovered in parts of south-east England, and this has been put down to global climate change (Brown 2001). Climate change can therefore bring about a greater spread in infectious diseases: 'many of the biological organisms and problems linked to the spread of infectious diseases are especially influenced by fluctuations in climate variables, notably temperature, precipitation and humidity' (WHO 1997: 124).

## Health care organizations

I argued previously that the boundaries of the nation state are in the process of being eroded and challenged by the counter movement of globalization. One area in which there has been a key impact is that of health care organizations. We have witnessed one aspect of this in terms of the privatization of services and market orientated policies, such as the private finance initiative (Pollock and Price 2000: 12; Pollock 2004).

But there are other key issues regarding health care systems that pose potential risks as well as opportunities. Lee notes a particular movement in the UK, 'towards an increasingly transborder provision of health care through the physical migration of health professionals and the development of telemedicine and teleconsulting across national boundaries' (2000b: 259). For instance, the number of overseas trained nurses and midwives relocating to the UK has risen to record levels. The biggest overseas 'suppliers' of nursing staff are the Philippines, New Zealand, the West Indies, Zimbabwe and now Spain. It is argued that this is causing a 'brain drain' in these countries as the most skilled staff will often be recruited. In addition, instances of 'medical tourism' may increase as patients in the UK seek speedier or less expensive health care elsewhere (Walt 1998: 436).

## Conclusion: the challenges for public health in a global era

We are witness to an emerging picture of public health risks and this picture is changing fast, a situation acutely exemplified by Giddens' metaphor of the 'juggernaut' of modernity (Giddens 1990). Can public health keep up with the pace of change brought about by globalization? A more pertinent question for those working in public health fields is what role they might play in utilizing the positive forces of globalization and/or alleviating its more negative effects. More simply, it can just mean public health practitioners identifying the newly emerging issues that are impinging on their practices that can be directly or indirectly related to globalization. For some, globalization retains the mystique of being something that happens elsewhere, and that people are powerless to have any impact on the risks recounted above. Others may feel that there are now opportunities to harness the effects of globalization for the good, and to become informed about the impact of globalization.

The 'new era' of globalization brings welcome opportunities as well as risks; it enables new technological solutions aimed at growing inequalities, as well as helping to create some of its own. For public health specialists (utilizing the Chief Medical Officer's distinction) such identifiable risks may be the continued sponsorship of sporting events by global food corporations, such as Coca-Cola. In contrast, the new global partners for health and the potential for sharing practice may be widely perceived by specialists as a welcome opportunity. So, it is this paradoxical situation that leads the commentators on globalization to reach an impasse over whether its benefits outweigh the disadvantages. One thing is certain: major economic and socio-cultural processes of globalization cannot be reversed, at least not without increasing certain risks and inequalities that have already been identified.

In exploring the relationship between globalization and public health, two key issues can be identified. The first concerns that of the threats that global society and a global level trade system poses to public health. This issue throws up key questions surrounding inequalities, global climate change, global working conditions, regulations and so on. The second issue raises slightly different questions as it concerns the continued relevance of the nation state in relation to regional and global public health issues, particularly in the light of increased involvement of transnational and multinational level organizations in the global health arena. I have expounded on the notion that globalization poses particular challenges (and opportunities) to public health workers. For example, writers such as Feachem (2001) remain largely positive about the long-term effects of globalization on population health, whereas others like Pollock and Price (2000) imply that globalization is an inherently unfair process and that markets are not the solution to rising health care needs. They suggest that the trade policies and ideology of the WTO and the World Bank are loaded in favour of private initiatives, and that these are having a detrimental impact on domestic health policy in the UK.

Further, their argument extends to the notion that this affects and restricts national sovereignty. However, discussions surrounding the decline of the welfare state and indeed the nation state may be premature (Turner 2001: 12); great importance continues to be attached to the notion of sovereignty and state legitimacy:

> While some feared that the intensification of globalisation would lead to greater diminution of state roles, others have argued that it is precisely because of global-isation that key state roles such as the promotion of equity, the development of a policy framework within which services can be provided, and the regulation of service and provider quality, need to be reinforced.
>
> (Zwi and Yach 2002)

Perhaps globalization is a trend we do not want to reverse, but merely to bring into play greater equity and adapt the rules and policies of the WTO, in short, to further democratize the transnational trade organizations. This proposal is supported by Labonte (2001: 621), who argues that the WTO should be reformed and not abolished. Others, such as Zwi and Yach (2002) argue that we should further support and extend the role of the WHO and the UN, as these are perceived as providing the widest fora for debate. This brings to light a question that should be raised in address-ing the promotion of globalization – globalization for the benefit of whom? Therefore, we need to explore increasing the public health benefits of globalization for the dis-enfranchised and the poor, and not just the higher income nations and social groups.

Furthermore, globalization (as a movement that cuts across various spheres) should be linked to the notion of sustainability, and in particular sustainable develop-ment. This term had particular resonance within the 2002 Earth Summit debate in Johannesburg, and sustainability is certainly something desirable to those in the West. In this context, sustainable development can be seen as addressing the essential health needs of people in the present without threatening the health needs of those in the future. (See Chapter 11 for discussion on sustainability in urban environments.)

Nevertheless, for all the talk of globalization which has been addressed in this chapter, the key issue is how public health professionals in the UK will respond to these ever changing geopolitical events at the local level. Admittedly, local/regional issues are the most important and relevant to public health workers, although I have shown in this chapter how key events at some geographical distance from home will increasingly impact on the agenda of public health professionals in the UK.

---

**Suggested further reading**

Farmer, P. (1999) *Infections and Inequalities: the Modern Plagues.* Berkeley, CA: University of California Press.

Giddens, A. (1990) *The Consequences of Modernity.* Cambridge: Polity Press.

Held, D. and McGrew, A. (eds) (2000) *The Global Transformations Reader: An Introduc-tion to the Globalization Debate.* Cambridge: Polity Press.

Lee, K. (2003) *Globalization and Health: An Introduction.* London: Palgrave Macmillan.

# 13

## MELANIE GREY, MIKE STUDDEN AND JOYSHRI SARANGI
Protecting the public's health

### Editors' introduction

Threats to public health are not new; for as long as human kind has existed there has been a constant interface with the dangers of the surrounding environment. Since the 1800s, protection from threats to health in people's environment – such as air pollution, lack of adequate sanitation, poor housing, contaminated food, disease transmitted by people or animals – have been an essential and fundamental part of public health action.

But what is new about health protection in the 21st century? Who plays a part? What partnerships and agencies are involved? These questions are addressed in this chapter. It will be of interest to any public health worker who wants a contemporary overview of public health action to protect the population's health.

This chapter is concerned with threats to health from the physical and biological environment, which are moderated by global, national and local, socio-economic and political circumstances. It takes a wide view of protecting the public health, beyond that of protection for basic human needs, to providing human environments which make a positive contribution to health and addressing inequalities in exposure to environmental hazards.

The authors start with an overview of current threats to health, the disease burden and emerging health protection policy. Global, technological, population and societal changes are resulting in new threats, such as climate change and terrorism, as well as the re-emergence of existing threats, such as infectious diseases common in the 19th century. They discuss underpinning guiding principles to inform judgements and decision taking, including the precautionary principle, principles around uncertainty of hazard and risk assessment, and engagement of society in understanding risk decisions.

The chapter maps the wide range of resources for protecting health in different sectors and organizations, and analyses key issues for multidisciplinary working practice. The authors conclude that protecting the public's health in the 21st century requires collaborative partnerships at local and regional level, supported and informed by an integrated national and regional expertise, and an explicit, well driven policy framework.

## Health threats and emerging health protection policy

### The scope of health protection

Health protection has its origins and organizational arrangements based on the prevention and control of communicable disease, non-infectious environmental hazards and health-related emergency planning (Regan 1999). Incident response, as well as proactive intervention, is required to deal with the diverse nature of risks to a particular population. The Department of Health and the Welsh Office consultation document on health protection (Department of Health/Welsh Office 2002) distinguishes hazards to health as *involuntary* hazards. Although very different in nature they have the following characteristics in common (Department of Health/Welsh Office 2002):

- they can affect large groups of the population in a relatively short space of time, for example, epidemics;
- when a problem arises it may not be clear initially which hazard has caused it – infectious agent, chemical or radiological hazard;
- speedy and co-ordinated action to trace the source and deal with it is of the essence to ensure infection and contamination do not spread;
- management of these hazards requires collaboration between the NHS and other agencies such as emergency services and local authorities.

To this we must add protection from hazards which have longer-term affects related to life time exposure or where there is a long latency period before onset of the health affects, together with the synergistic (combined) affects of hazards such as a cocktail of air pollutants.

The emergence and re-emergence of significant public health threats, assessment of risk, development of policies and organizational systems and aspects related to practice for the preventive and emergency health response provide the focus for protecting the public's health.

### Contemporary health threats

The scale and nature of health threats from infectious diseases or environmental hazards are very wide ranging, including:

- an acute major incident; such as a radioactive leak from a nuclear installation site;
- a major food poisoning outbreak or food contamination;
- a public accident; such as a major rail crash;
- longer-term and chronic health threats: such as exposure to hazardous materials from a landfill site or the effects of air pollution;
- the uncertain hazards of new technologies; such as genetic modification of foods; telecommunication technology and nanotechnology;

- newly emerging infectious diseases including zoonotic infections (of animal origin).

A health impact can be small and limited to the local population, or widespread extending to whole populations. An effect on the public's health can be acute and immediate and/or chronic and delayed over a period of many years.

The risks to health increasingly include those of global origin and have international and national as well as local implications. Global and local environmental changes resulting from the impact of resource over-utilization and ecosystem degradation are now presenting themselves and are being linked to newly emerging diseases (Lee 2000a) and to global environmental hazards including stratospheric ozone depletion, loss of biodiversity, and stresses on food-producing systems (WHO 2005c). The scale is illustrated by the emergence of at least 30 previously unknown infectious diseases since the 1970s (Department of Health 2002d). As well as the direct health impacts, these health threats have also resulted in indirect effects such as the impact on national economies and the destabilizing effect on populations and communities. Over the past three decades threats to health have included:

- extreme climate affects such as, flooding in the UK in 2000 and abnormally high temperatures in Europe in the summer of 2003 (Department of Health 2001a; McMichael *et al.* 2003);

- bioterrorism risks (anthrax, smallpox) post-11 September 2001 (House of Commons Defence Committee 2001/02);

- infectious diseases such as tuberculosis, malaria, that are interpreted as 're-emerging' (Morens *et al.* 2004; Department of Health 2002c);

- food implicated health threats such as new variant Creutzfeldt-Jacob Disease (nvCJD) from bovine spongiform encephalopathy (BSE) in cattle (Patterson and Painter 1999; Phillips Report 2000);

- newly emergent communicable diseases such as HIV/AIDS in the 1980s (Department of Health 2002c: 39);

- newly emergent diseases of animal origin, such as in the 1990s Severe Acute Respiratory Syndrome (SARS), thought to be caused by a coronavirus of animal origin, which originated in China in November 2002 (WHO 2003a) and the potential risk of a human influenza pandemic (worldwide epidemics) from Avian Influenza H5N1 strain (Capua and Marangon 2006).

## The burden of disease

*Health Protection in the 21st Century, Understanding the Burden of Disease; Preparing for the Future* (Health Protection Agency 2005) is the first step in assessing and quantifying the disease burden of infectious and environmental hazards in the UK, to assist in strengthening the evidence base for health protection (see Table 13.1).

**Table 13.1** Infectious and environmental hazards – the disease burden in the UK

| | |
|---|---|
| Infectious disease | Approximately 10% of all deaths. Respiratory infections; infectious intestinal disease; health care associated infections and HIV/AIDS. |
| Radiation | Naturally occurring Radon and UV radiation: estimated 100,000 or more new skin cancers every year; uncertainty of electromagnetic risks. |
| Environmental pollution | Up to 57 children per 1000 in England and Wales may have long-term lung function affected by air pollution. |
| Chemicals | Estimated 50,000 people over a five-year period were exposed to chemicals as a result of reported incidents. |
| Poisons | In 2002, around 6600 deaths were attributable to poisonings or exposures to noxious chemicals (11 per 100,000 population). |
| Injury | Falls and road traffic accidents are the main causes of injury. 3% of all deaths in the UK. |
| Environmental inequalities | Environmental quality varies between different regions and communities and there is an inequitable distribution of environmental hazards among children of different social groups and different regions of England and Wales. |
| Health inequalities | Gastrointestinal infection leading to hospital admission was 2.4 times higher in the poorest fifth of the population than in the most affluent quintile. The most deprived children are more likely to be injured or killed in pedestrian incidents than the most affluent. |
| Children's health | Asthma: an estimated 30% of childhood asthma is related to air pollution. Injuries: estimated 2 million children are taken to hospital after accidents every year. |

*Source*: adapted from Health Protection Agency (2005)

For environmental hazards it is difficult to evaluate the burden of disease as often many factors are involved and health impacts can be long-term with current estimates generally based on very uncertain data and on limited datasets. Thus for example asthma has been linked to infections, allergies, both indoor and outdoor pollution and household moulds and it is difficult to look at quantifying the impact that each of these factors has on the burden of disease without taking all factors into consideration (Health Protection Agency 2005). In addition the disease burden of lower income groups are only beginning to be identified as population socio-economic datasets and environmental datasets are integrated within spatial (geographic) and temporal (time) domains. In this context children's health and inequalities in health are identified as key cross-cutting health protection themes which contribute to the government's public health programmes on health inequalities and children's health (Department of Health 2002a).

## Emerging health protection policy and organization

The policy and public communication disasters of the BSE crisis and the lessons to be learnt from this (O'Brien 2000), undoubtedly have informed a number of changes in European and British policies for protecting health. Openness and transparency in relation to health hazards and risk uncertainty are key changes, as well as development of precautionary and preventive policies which are integrated into all policies (European Community 1999). Political and economic constraints including the influences of the World Trade Organization and free trade agreements, coupled with challenges to the strength of the scientific evidence and risk, make implementing these policies a slow process. (Globalization and health is discussed in depth in Chapter 12.)

The UK Food Standards Agency (FSA) was created in 1998 in response to the number of food safety issues including the BSE crisis (MAFF 1998). The setting up of the FSA went some way to addressing the criticism of government departments regarding the interests of commercial producers, agri-business and the food industry over that of consumer and public health. Public concern and heightened risk perception regarding food safety issues in the UK continues to have a significant influence, for example, on policies in relation to genetically modified food controversies.

European Union policy, and implicitly that of the member states, requires a high level of health protection to be adopted through Article 152 of the Amsterdam treaty of the EU (European Community 1999) and since 1996 public health has become a European policy objective. The European Public Health Action programme 2003–08 sets out the need for and the direction of improvements in health information and rapid response to health threats (European Community 2001). This required comparability and co-ordination Europe-wide, as well as greater co-operation with international organizations such as the World Health Organization (WHO), Organization for Economic Cooperation and Development (OECD), Food and Agriculture Organization and the World Trade Organization (WTO). (See Table 13.2 for a list of organizations and their functions in health protection.) The communicable disease network of the EC set up in 1999 (Giesecke and Weinberg 1998; European Community 1999) was enhanced to provide a telematic early warning response system (EWRS) in 2000 and since 2002 this also provides for a co-ordinated response to biological, chemical and nuclear threats.

In the UK the policy roots for environment and health protection exist within the public health regulations of the 19th century. The piecemeal and separate development of policies that followed resulted in lack of integration of both policies and administrative arrangements to implement them. It was not until the mid-1990s that moves to integrate policies to protect the environment and health began to develop (Department of the Environment/Welsh Office 1993) with the creation of the Environment Agency. Policy mechanisms such as, for example, Integrated Pollution Prevention and Control have enabled the integrated assessment of the environment and health impacts of industrial processes (CHMRC 2002). Protection from workplace hazards have also developed through a complex set of regulatory requirements that were integrated, after 1974, under the national Health and Safety Commission

**Table 13.2** Organizations and their functions in protecting health

| Organization/Abbreviation | Function |
| --- | --- |
| Cabinet Office (CO) | Government office – co-ordinating/cross-cutting: includes the UK Resilience Unit and Civil Contingencies Secretariat. |
| Department for Communities and Local Government | Government office – for regional and local government. Regional Co-ordination Unit. |
| Department of Environment, Food and Rural Affairs (DEFRA) | Government department for environment, food and rural affairs. (Sponsoring department for Environment Agency.) |
| Department for Transport (DfT) | Government department for transport. |
| Environment Agency (EA) | National agency for environmental protection. |
| Emergency Preparedness Division | Department of Health unit for health services emergency planning co-ordination. |
| European Environment Agency | European agency for environmental protection. |
| Expert Panel on Air Quality Standards (EPAQ) | Government standing expert panel. |
| Food and Agricultural Organization (FAO) | United Nations international body for food policy, food security and agricultural development and standards. |
| Food Standards Agency (FSA) | National body monitoring food safety and health. |
| Health and Safety Executive (HSE) | Executive arm of the HSC for implementation of health and safety of the workplace. |
| Health and Safety Commission (HSC) | National commission for health and safety. |
| Health Protection Agency (HPA) | National co-ordinating body for health protection. (Under the Department of Health.) |
| – Local and Regional Services (LRS) | Division of the HPA supports local and regional health protection services. |
| – Centre for Infections (CfI) | Specialist centre of the HPA which support national and regional health protection. |
| – Centre for Emergency Preparedness and Response (CEPR) | Specialist centre of the HPA which support national and regional health protection. |
| – Centre for Radiation Chemical and Environmental Hazards (CRCEH) | Specialist centre of the HPA which support national and regional health protection. |
| – Chemical Hazards and Poisons Division (CHaPD) | Specialist division of the HPA which support national and regional health protection. |
| – Regional Microbiology Network (RMN) | Specialist network of the HPA. |
| Local Authorities Coordination of Regulatory Services (LACORS) | Co-ordinates local government regulatory services such as food and consumer safety. |

| Organization for Economic Cooperation and Development (OECD) | International organization on social and economic development. |
| --- | --- |
| Public Health Observatories (PHO) | Regional NHS organizations for non-communicable health and disease monitoring and co-ordinating information and health trends. |
| World Health Organization (WHO) | International United Nations sponsored organization for health. |

and its executive arm, the Health and Safety Executive. A more proactive approach to implementing workplace health protection has been strengthened through policies such as *Revitalising Health and Safety* (HSC/DETR 1999) and the European *Community Strategy on Health and Safety* (European Commission 2002).

Protection from outbreaks of communicable diseases in the UK was weakened by lack of direction and expertise in the period following changes to the NHS and local authority services in 1974. The loss of the expertise of the Medical Officer of Health from local authorities was cited as a key factor in the failures of public health services during the infectious disease outbreaks in the 1980s (Acheson 1988). From 2003 onwards the HPA Regional Microbiology Network and Centre for Infection provides this co-ordination and expertise, working with local health protection units and local authority services.

It can be seen that policy development and implementation is directed towards preventive approaches and preparedness, based on co-ordinated surveillance and assessment of risks, integration of environment and health impacts, and development of resilience for emergencies that occur, together with an overarching theme of transparency and a wider communication and engagement of people in the processes involved.

### Towards prevention

European Community policy on the environment makes it explicit that a precautionary principle based on preventive action is to be taken having regard to the size of the risk (proportionality), analysis of costs and benefits and consistency of application. Conditions under which the precautionary principle would apply were defined in the *Rio Declaration on Environment and Development* (UNCED 1992b) as they relate to development. These are:

- when there are threats of serious or irreversible damage;
- when there is lack of scientific certainty; and
- when cost-effective measures are possible to prevent environmental degradation.

'When in doubt about the impact of a development it will be managed according to the worst case scenario of its impact on the environment and human health' (UNCED 1992b). The implementation of the precautionary principle has been considered and developed by the European Environmental Agency (EEA) and by the World Health Organization (Europe region) and is being used more as 'a framework of thinking and action that governs the use of foresight in situations characterized by uncertainty and ignorance and where there are potentially large advantages and disadvantages of both regulatory action and inaction' (Martuzzi and Bertollini 2004).

Early preventive environmental policy mechanisms such as 'polluter pays' principle involving punitive fines and environmental remediation have moved towards the inclusion of other policy mechanisms such as fiscal measures, for example, a carbon tax as an energy and greenhouse gas reduction measure and a landfill tax as a waste reduction measure. This is shifting environmental policy away from control and clean-up, towards prevention of activities involving adverse environmental and health impacts. The European Union Sixth Environment Action Programme commenced in 2001 to further action on environment and human health threats as well as on quality of life issues through integrated approaches (European Community 2002). Similarly the *European Environment and Health Strategy* (European Commission 2003) and *Environment and Health Action Plan* (European Commission 2004) aim is to integrate the information on the state of the environment, the ecosystem and human health and reduce the burden of disease caused by environmental pollution.

Food quality and safety aspects in reducing the disease burden are now considered within food and farming policies for example the 'farm to fork' whole life cycle approach, integrating environmental and health impact, such as minimizing 'food miles' travelled (Cabinet Office 2002b).

This raises inequality issues about pricing of goods and services, for example, food and energy costs related to fiscal environmental measures and the differential impact on low income households. Such developments in policy aimed at reducing global environmental effects and achieving a more sustainable approach to resource utilization and minimizing overall population health impacts, need to be considered in terms of sustainable communities and the specific health impacts on population groups at community level, such as those living in fuel or food poverty. (Sustainability and health is discussed in depth in Chapter 11.)

### Responding to new threats

The spectre of deliberate releases of biological and chemical agents and terrorist activities heightened global and national awareness of the potential impacts on health and on economic and social stability. This highlighted the need for better surveillance and integration and co-ordination of policy and organizational systems for the identification and management of newly emerging health threats and for improved horizon scanning and preparedness. The WHO's global alert and response systems supported by global and national networks, such as the *Global Outbreak Alert and Response Network* (GOARN), are major pillars of health security aimed at the detection, verification and containment of epidemics. At national level the Chief Medical Officer's report *Getting Ahead of the Curve* (Department of Health 2002c) sets out the strategies for England and Wales (with parallel arrangements in Scotland and Northern Ireland) to integrate policies and programmes under the umbrella of health protection which has been established throughout the UK. The broad strategy aims cover:

- scoping of health threats;
- establishing priorities; and
- integrating infectious disease challenges within wider health protection needs.

At the same time contingency planning for emergencies moved to an integrated 'resilience' approach at national level supporting and co-ordinating regional and local level services.

## The organizational framework for protecting health

### At national level

The increasing range and complexity of health threats focused attention on the need for national expert advice and information to support improved co-ordination at all levels of surveillance and response. Planning for or dealing with any health threat event, where causation may very well be unknown in the early stages, requires broadly similar emergency response and investigation, whether the threat is chemical, biological or radiological (Department of Health/Welsh Office 2002).

The Health Protection Agency (HPA) for England and Wales is a non-departmental public body charged with co-ordinating health protection across the UK and providing the portal for the European Union early warnings and alerts and for assistance calls. The Local and Regional Division (LRS) of the HPA works through nine regional offices in England that correspond to the government offices of the regions. The services provided to local authorities and public health authorities are for routine and incident-based environmental and infectious disease monitoring with a laboratories maintained in the regions. These facilities are augmented by partnerships with NHS trusts who support the work of the HPA through collaborating laboratories. A co-ordinating health protection function exists within Scottish and Northern Ireland administrations.

Interface working between the Health Protection Agency and other national organizations such as the Environment Agency, the Health and Safety Executive, the Food Standards Agency is facilitated by national high level memoranda of understanding and at local level through working agreements. UK-wide co-ordination on major national emergencies requires government cross-cutting approaches, provided for by the Civil Contingencies Secretariat and the UK Resilience Unit of the Cabinet Office, as well as the regional co-ordination function of the Department for Communities and Local Government Resilience Teams (www.ukresilience.info/home/htm). Figure 13.1 provides an overview of the organizations contributing to protection of the public's health.

### At regional and local level

The enhanced regional focus for health protection through the HPA and the Regional Resilience Forum enables co-ordination between regional government, local authorities, regional agencies, health services and other essential services. Regional teams support the Regional Director of Public Health in managing the response to major

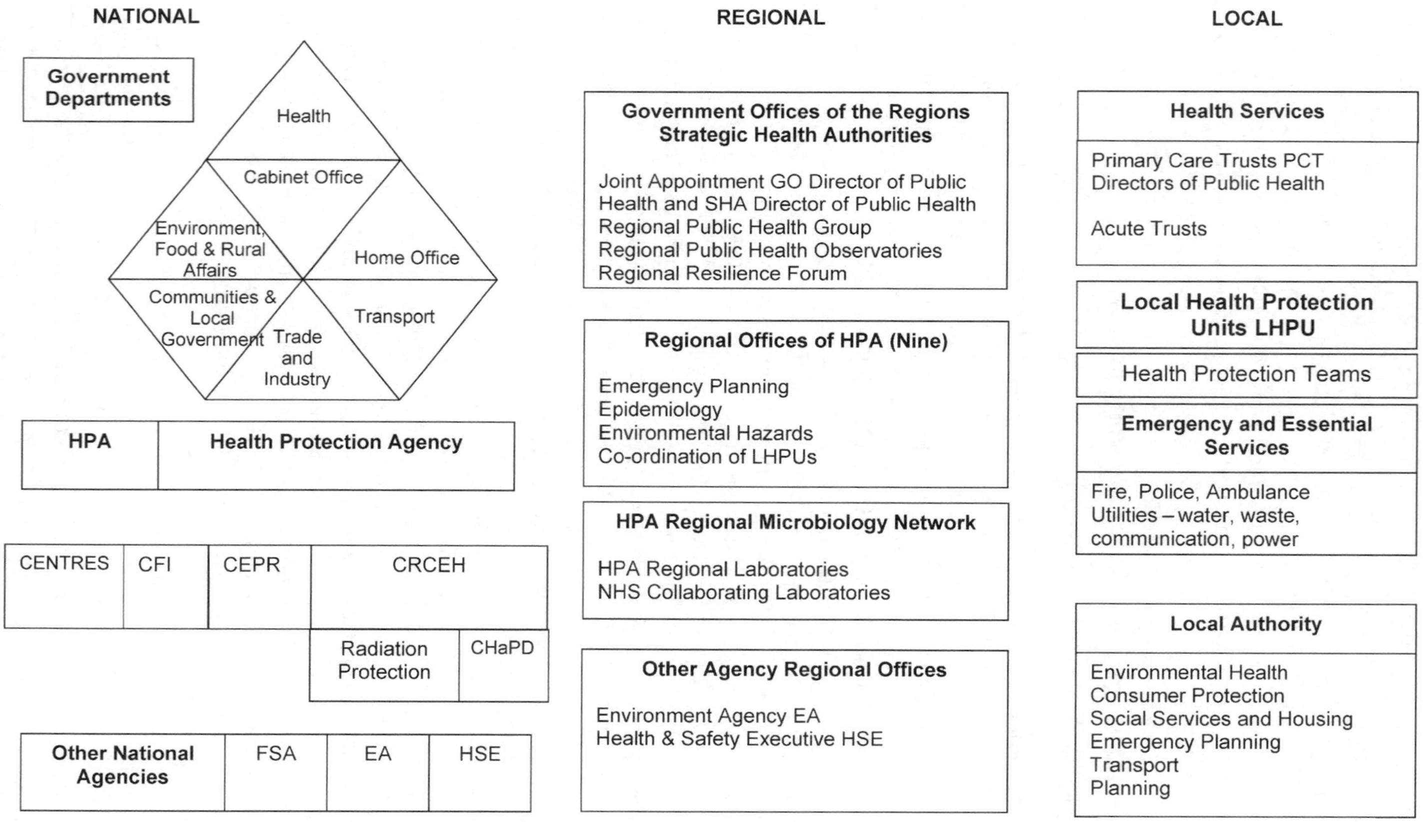

**NATIONAL**

**Government Departments**

Health
Cabinet Office
Home Office
Transport
Trade and Industry
Communities & Local Government
Environment, Food & Rural Affairs

**Health Protection Agency**

| HPA | | | | |
|---|---|---|---|---|
| CENTRES | CFI | CEPR | CRCEH | |
| | | | Radiation Protection | CHaPD |

**Other National Agencies**

| FSA | EA | HSE |
|---|---|---|

**REGIONAL**

**Government Offices of the Regions Strategic Health Authorities**

Joint Appointment GO Director of Public Health and SHA Director of Public Health
Regional Public Health Group
Regional Public Health Observatories
Regional Resilience Forum

**Regional Offices of HPA (Nine)**

Emergency Planning
Epidemiology
Environmental Hazards
Co-ordination of LHPUs

**HPA Regional Microbiology Network**

HPA Regional Laboratories
NHS Collaborating Laboratories

**Other Agency Regional Offices**

Environment Agency EA
Health & Safety Executive HSE

**LOCAL**

**Health Services**

Primary Care Trusts PCT
Directors of Public Health

Acute Trusts

**Local Health Protection Units LHPU**

Health Protection Teams

**Emergency and Essential Services**

Fire, Police, Ambulance
Utilities – water, waste, communication, power

**Local Authority**

Environmental Health
Consumer Protection
Social Services and Housing
Emergency Planning
Transport
Planning

**Figure 13.1** Overview of organizations contributing to the protection of the public's health (England)

incidents, and co-ordinate the activities of several local Health Protection Units (HPU). The structures and functions of regional and local teams vary to take into account the local populations and the risks to their health such as nuclear plants, major chemical industries, or significant infectious disease problems, or low rates of childhood immunization. The establishment of a regional focus has shown that multi-agency working can impact on the effectiveness of response, such as to a major Legionnaires disease outbreak in 2002, whereby a significant reduction in the fatality rate for this disease was achieved (Spear 2003).

Public health expertise is required at regional and local level in environment and health impact assessment (HIA), for example making local decisions about the disposal of carcasses following the foot and mouth outbreaks (Department of Health 2002d: 125) and there is a statutory public health consultee role under the Integrated Pollution Prevention and Control regulatory regime to prevent pollution from specific industrial processes (Kibble and Saunders 2001; CHMRC 2002).

## The health services role

In England at local level, responsibility for the health of the population rests with the NHS Primary Care Trusts, working with other services and in relation to health protection the PCT is supported by the local health protection units (HPU) of the HPA ensuring local delivery and monitoring of national action plans with broadly equivalent arrangements in Scotland, Wales and Northern Ireland devolved administrations.

Local NHS bodies have been responsible for many years for ensuring that they have plans for responding to major incidents and mass casualties, together with local stakeholders – the emergency services and local authority emergency planning teams. A review of emergency planning services to deal with identified deficiencies followed the NHS structural changes in April 2002 and new guidance was adopted in 2005 within the context of the Civil Contingencies Act 2004 (Department of Health 2005b).

## Local authority role – environmental health and civil contingencies

Since the establishment of the 19th century local boards of health local authorities have had responsibility at local level for environmental health and public protection, dealing with risk factors in the environment such as environmental conditions (sanitation, air, water and waste pollution), infectious disease control, food hazards, housing and working condition and emergencies and civil contingencies. In the national devolved administration areas of Scotland, Wales and Northern Ireland and for some English local authority areas, local government is organized as a single tier (unitary authorities) which in most cases have common boundaries with local health service provision. The so-called 'regulatory services' of local authorities are supported by a co-ordinating body at national level LACORs which contributes to the development of best practice and comparability of regulation across local authorities.

Local authorities are part of the multi-agency resilience arrangements at local level as Category 1 responders under the Civil Contingencies Act 2004 and the

Regional Resilience Forum facilitates co-ordinated planning and implementation. Local authorities have a leading role in the aftermath of emergencies, as in the major flooding at Boscastle, north Cornwall in 2004 (South West Regional Resilience Forum 2006).

Environmental health practitioners working in local government to protect health, have wide ranging statutory powers and responsibilities to prevent the impact of environmental and communicable disease hazards and in addition contribute to promoting the well-being of communities working under the broad 'well-being' power of local authorities as discussed in Chapter 1.

## Health protection: principles and practice

### Hazards, risk and health impact assessment

The first principle in establishing an effective system for protecting health is the identification of hazards and their potential to cause harm – the risk. While hazard is the intrinsic ability of an agent to cause a specific adverse consequence in terms of population health and/or environmental impact, the risk can be described as the potential of a hazard to cause harm depending on specific circumstances. This can be considered in terms of:

- the host (human exposure, susceptibility, response);
- the harmful agent (infectious, chemical, physical, biological);
- the external influences (socio-economic, environmental, cultural), the pathway or mechanism for the agent to cause harm.

Risk assessment is the process of estimating the potential impact of a chemical, physical, microbiological or psychosocial hazard on a specified human population or ecological system under a specific set of conditions for exposure and for a certain time frame (Pencheon et al. 2001: 208). For certain hazardous agents dose response relationships and toxicological and epidemiological data exist and risk assessment can be quantified in terms of a specified human population exposure under a specific set of conditions and over a specific time frame.

However, in many situations, especially for complex and long-term patterns of exposure, the assessment of the acceptable risk level is uncertain, due to weaknesses in the evidence arising from:

- incomplete data (lack of exposure data, unreliable health data or low statistical power);
- variability inherent in the data (difficulties in measuring human exposure and dose response studies, which are often retrospective or opportunistic, and of extrapolating high dose acute exposure studies to low dose exposure);
- confounding factors (other factors which affect health status which cannot be removed).

(Developed from SWPHO 2002: 25)

**Table 13.3** Risk and uncertainty – levels of proof, descriptors and examples in regulation and control mechanisms

| **Quantitative** descriptor (probability bands IPCC 2001) | **Qualitative** descriptor | Examples of where used |
|---|---|---|
| Very likely 90–99% | Statistical significance Beyond all reasonable doubt | To show scientific causation. Used in criminal law. |
| Likely 66–90% | Reasonable certainty Sufficient scientific evidence | Food quality protection law. World Trade Organization (WTO) trade description – Sanitary and Phyto sanitary (SPS) Agreement Article 2.2 1995. |
| Medium likelihood 33–66% | Balance of evidence | Intergovernmental Panel on Climate Change (IPCC) 1995 and 2001. |
| | Balance of probabilities | Much civil and administrative law (e.g. negligence action for damages under civil law). |
| Low likelihood 10–33% | Scientific suspicion of risk | Sufficient for precautionary action on potential harm from substances. The burden of proof is on the regulator to demonstrate (the Precautionary Principle). |
| | Available as pertinent information to consider | To justify a provisional trade restriction under WTO (SPS) agreement Article 5.7 where scientific information is insufficient. |
| Very unlikely 1–10% | Low risk | Basis for household fire insurance. |

Source: adapted from Intergovernmental Panel on Climate Change (IPPC 2001), and European Environment Agency (EEA 2003). http://org.eea.europa.eu/documents/budapest2004/Compilation_of_EEA_background_papers.pdf

## Making decisions about hazards and risks

Decision-making models which take account of uncertainty and lack of knowledge about risks are required in order that appropriate interventions can be undertaken. Table 13.3 illustrates the levels of proof (degrees of uncertainty) in decision making, with some examples of their use in regulation. For example a 'scientifically based suspicion of risk' may be sufficient for action by the *regulator* (for example to restrict a chemical substance) and this then may only be overturned by a higher burden of proof 'beyond reasonable doubt' from the *producer* that the substance is 'safe' (European Environment Agency 2003).

Where evidence exists and is strong, exposure indices can be developed and applied in order to reduce exposure and prevent harm. Developed exposure indices for hazards include:

- ambient (background) environmental exposure for all individuals;
- individualized exposure (for example, for occupational exposure or high risk groups);
- exposure through combined exposure pathways (for example, through inhalation, ingestion and contact).

An example of ambient exposure indices is air quality standards for individual pollutants such as ozone and particulate matter, set by the government's Expert Panel on Air Quality Standards on advice from the Department of Health Committee on Medical Effects of Air Pollution (Department of Health COMEAP 1995, 1997). In Europe it is claimed that poor air quality, through causing premature death, claims as many lives as AIDS (European Commission 2002). In 1997 in England and Wales, the national air quality management strategy was adopted to secure improvements in local air quality, applying standards at local level for eight key air pollutants (Department of the Environment, Transport and the Regions 1997).

In relation to the public health implications of diverse and complex environmental hazards, the epidemiological and toxicological evidence is more often than not insufficient or inconclusive. A study evaluating the state of the evidence into waste management activities and health (SWPHO 2002) concluded that 'the nature of existing epidemiological research in this area is such that most studies are useful for generating hypotheses, but are unable to test the hypotheses or provide convincing evidence of association between exposure and health impacts' (SWPHO 2002: 40). Miller (1996) came to a similar conclusion for studies on the health impacts of hazardous waste. It is also needs to be recognized that the evidence available about health impacts may ignore the wider qualitative health impacts, for example the effects of psycho-social effects of environmental hazards such as noise, disturbance, isolation, anxiety, or loss of amenity.

### Assessing risks to children from environmental hazards

The science of linking environmental factors to the health of children is, with a few well studied exceptions such as lead in petrol, some air pollutants, and some radiations, in its early stages of development (Briggs 1999, 2003). Children are at most risk from environmental hazards due to a number of factors including genetics, host state, such as immune system immaturity and exposure pathways. The World Health Organization (WHO 2002a, b) considers the use of a Multiple Exposures Multiple Effects (MEME) model. This is an example of a conceptual and theoretical model which attempts to take account of the fact that individual exposures can lead to many different health outcomes. It is also however, important to highlight that both exposures and health outcomes and the associations between them are affected by contextual conditions, such as social, economic or demographic factors (WHO 2002b; Briggs 2003). This approach supports precautionary based decisions about risk to children from environmental hazards.

## Health and Environmental Impact Assessment

Health and Environmental Impact Assessment is a decision-making approach evolved from Environmental Impact Assessment (EIA) introduced as regulatory mechanism by the European Community to require the assessment of the impacts of major development projects. Fehr (1999) describes the use of integrated environmental and health impact assessment for the planned extension of a non-toxic waste disposal facility where both environmental and health impacts of the development are assessed. Fehr argues that such an assessment should be used more often as a tool in health protection, but that consensus is needed on the concept and further development needed of the tool. The National Assembly for Wales in its guidelines on the use of health impact assessment (HIA) stresses that it must do more than just indicate that a development may create pollution or a health hazard; it must assess options in relation to health outcomes (National Assembly for Wales 1999: 19). HIA is discussed further in Chapter 17.

## Risk perception and communication

In situations of uncertainty and where there is lack of knowledge, risk-based decisions about hazards to health are variable. When there is little knowledge and much uncertainty about risks, experts are prone to use the same mental strategies, known as heuristics, as the non-scientifically trained public (SWPHO 2002: 35). Thus scientists tend to underestimate the risk of technologies they are familiar with based on scientific probability, while the public tend to overestimate the risk, based more on intuition, as they unfamiliar with the technology (see Figure 13.2).

Other aspects influence perception and outcomes, such as outrage factors, which cover qualitative aspects of a judgement, including lack of choice, global catastrophic potential and affecting people personally (SWPHO 2002: 36). For example, involuntary man-made hazards such as pollution, especially if poorly understood by science, are perceived to be a higher risk than voluntary ones, such as dangerous sports or smoking. These perceptions of risks are not of necessity unpredictable and are not unreasonable. The BSE crisis in the UK is an example of a vacuum in risk communication – 'mad cows or crazy communication' (Powell and Leiss 1997: 4–25) and there is now recognition that communication strategies which inform, engage and empower

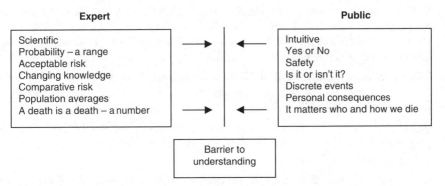

**Figure 13.2** The barriers to understanding of risk between the expert and the public
*Source*: adapted from Powell and Leiss (1997: 27)

the public, should be employed within decision-making processes in preparing for responses to health threats.

## Surveillance, prevention and control

The UK government's strategy document, *Getting Ahead of the Curve*, established measures to deal with emerging and re-emerging infections including a surveillance system with comprehensive coverage to detect unusual disease presentations and changes in occurrence or profile of micro-organisms, and the use of data to predict outbreaks or epidemics and prevent them (Department of Health 2002c: 56). The Health Protection Agency Centre for Infection states that communicable disease surveillance is:

> the continuous monitoring of the frequency and the distribution of disease, and death, due to infections that can be transmitted from human to human or from animals, food, water or the environment to humans, and the monitoring of risk factors for those infections.
>
> HPA 2006

In England the Health Protection Agency is responsible for most of the surveillance programmes for health protection, including those for infectious diseases. At a global level, the World Health Organization (WHO), as the United Nation's specialist agency for health, working through networks, is responsible for surveillance of infection. The European Centre for Disease Prevention and Control (ECDC) co-ordinates European strategy and European surveillance networks such as Enter-*net*, a surveillance network for salmonella and Verotoxin-producing *E. coli* O157 which is supported by the UK HPA.

The global surveillance systems cover the following areas:–

- **Epidemic intelligence-systematic event detection**. Formal and informal reporting of suspected disease outbreaks and related conditions such as food and water safety and chemical events.

- **Event verification**. Raw intelligence from all sources must be converted into meaningful intelligence in order to avoid false alerts causing unnecessary public anxiety and inappropriate response and disruption to travel, trade and economic loss (Grein *et al.* 2000).

- **Information management and dissemination**. WHO *Outbreak Verification List* (OVL) and the *Weekly Epidemiological Record for Disease* for public health professionals, WHO *Disease Outbreak News* for public information.

- **Real time alert**. A network of electronically interconnected WHO member countries (192), disease experts, institutions, agencies and laboratories which share information globally.

- **Co-ordinated rapid outbreak response**. A pooled resource for alert and response operations in countries drawing on technical resources from within the global networks.

- **Outbreak response logistics**. Standardized procedures for the alert and verification process, communications, co-ordination of the response, specialist equipment, medical supplies, emergency evacuation, research, evaluation, and relations with media.

### Surveillance data sources

Use of routine sources of information is described as 'passive' surveillance, while 'active or enhanced' surveillance requires special effort to collect the data and confirm the diagnosis.

There are many surveillance data sources for infectious diseases, some of which are given in Table 13.4. In the UK most infectious disease surveillance data comes from two sources: laboratory reports and statutory notifications. With the exception of some infections which are part of the Department of Health's mandatory

**Table 13.4** Examples of surveillance systems in the UK

| Name and type | Source information | Purpose and description |
|---|---|---|
| **RCGP Weekly Returns Service (WRS)** Royal College of General Practice | Enhanced surveillance GP practices covering 600,000 population | Infectious diseases: notably the incidence of influenza-like illness and other common respiratory conditions. Weekly incidence rates calculated per 100,000 population. |
| **NHS Direct/HPA Syndromic Surveillance** | NHS Direct calls: cough, cold/flu, fever, diarrhoea, vomiting, eye problems, double vision, difficulty breathing, rash and lumps | Significant statistical excesses ('exceedances'); abnormal clusters, age-group specific trends and HPA region specific trends. Identify early stages of illness caused by the deliberate or accidental release of a biological or chemical agent, or more common infections. http://www.hpa.org.uk/infections/topics_az/primary_care_surveillance/NHSD.htm |
| **QRESEARCH** | GP practice data base Health needs, risks, care and outcome for a population of over 4 million currently registered patients from a national database | A national, primary care surveillance system analysed to Strategic Health Authority level. Links morbidity data to prescribing and vaccination data. Extracts various risk factors such as socio-demographic indicators, ethnicity and rurality. http://www.nottingham.ac.uk/~mczqres/whatis.html http://www.qresearch.org/. |
| **Tuberculosis Surveillance** | Newly diagnosed TB cases | Enhanced tuberculosis surveillance including outcome data organized by the HPA. |

*Continued overleaf*

**Table 13.4** Continued

| Name and type | Source information | Purpose and description |
|---|---|---|
| **Healthcare Associated Infection (HAI)** | Example MRSA bacteraemics | Mandatory Department of Health Surveillance. Used to track progress towards targets. www.hpa.org.uk/cdr/pages/news.htm |
| **Regional Public Health Observatories** | Various sources | Monitors patterns of non-communicable disease, identifying gaps in information, studying patterns, cancer incidence or guidance on improving children's health. www.apho.org.uk |
| **SWESS Pilot South West Environmental Surveillance System** | Pilot Scheme HPA Quarterly reports South West Multiagency participation | Monitors incidents leading to acute or chronic exposures to chemical substances and other environmental stressors. www.hpa.org.uk/southwest/env_surv_news/SWESS_Quarterly_Report_Oct_Dec_2005.pdf |

surveillance programme of health care-associated infections, laboratory reporting in the UK is voluntary. The system, which is managed by the Health Protection Agency, takes data from hospital microbiology laboratory information systems.

The second system, which runs in parallel to the microbiology system, is based on notification of clinical diagnoses. There is a legal requirement to notify specified diseases such as, food poisoning, tuberculosis, malaria, mumps and rubella. The fact that these notifications are often based only on clinical suspicion means that accuracy is compromised; however they can be a useful source of information about trends in incidence of some viral infections, in particular, which do not lend themselves to laboratory diagnosis.

For some infections there is no single source of information available and multiple datasets have to be used to get a composite surveillance picture of the disease. Such an example is influenza where routine data is very incomplete because few samples are submitted to the laboratory and, influenza is not a notifiable disease and only a small proportion of people present to their GP. The most useful data in determining the prevalence of influenza is GP and NHS Direct data.

In the UK enhanced surveillance programmes have been established for some infections, this includes for tuberculosis and for invasive meningococcal disease. Enhanced meningococcal surveillance helped establish the need to introduce meningococcal C vaccine and to evaluate the national programme after its introduction.

### Primary and secondary prevention

Surveillance information is necessary to determine the need to undertake health interventions. Prevention can be divided into two main categories, primary and secondary. Primary prevention of infectious diseases is used to prevent the onset of a targeted infection at a time prior to any exposure to that infection. The national childhood immunization programme is an example of primary prevention against a range of childhood infections and is one of the best examples of preventive action to safeguard public health. Health promotion activities, aimed at reducing the incidence of certain infections, such as sexually transmitted infections, are also examples of primary prevention.

Secondary prevention is used to identify and treat asymptomatic persons who have already developed risk factors or pre-clinical disease, but in whom the condition is not clinically apparent. Good examples in the area of infectious diseases are chemoprophylaxis for family contacts of cases of invasive meningococcal disease, post-exposure immunization against hepatitis B following a needle-stick injury and ante-natal screening of mothers for various infections that can affect the foetus or newborn.

### Monitoring risk factors for disease

Surveillance and monitoring of risk factors in the environment – air, water, food, soil and vegetation and animal health surveillance – provide points at which early intervention can prevent disease. This is the responsibility of several government departments and national and regional agencies (see Table 13.2) and at local level, the local authority environmental health and consumer protection services.

Animal health surveillance and control of diseases contributes to prevention of human diseases that are transmitted by animals – zoonotic diseases. This is important for emerging transboundary diseases where organisms causing animal disease may cross the species barrier and become pathenogenic for humans. In 1994, the agreements that led to the creation of the World Trade Organization (WTO) included specific measures on the management of sanitary and phytosanitary problems (SPS Agreements) relating to the risks posed by trade in animals and animal products.

A specific animal health surveillance network is that for Avian Influenza established in 2006 to monitor and control this disease in poultry and other bird species (Edwards 2006). See Box 13.1 for an example of the UK response to an incident of Avian Influenza virus in birds.

### Monitoring of food hazards and chemical hazards in the environment

Food hazard product alert and information systems controlled under the auspices of the Food Standards Agency through local authority services and the food industry, enables rapid response and recall of contaminated food at the earliest point in the supply chain, for example, at the port of entry or recall from food suppliers or consumers. Special monitoring and control measures are in place for imported food due to the higher associated risks both of animal and human disease through, for example, illegal imports such as bush meat (DEFRA 2004).

The Chemical Releases Inventory was first introduced in 1991 in England and

---

**Box 13.1**  Case study of Avian Influenza, surveillance and intervention measures

*The incident*: In April 2006, H7N3 Low Pathogenic Avian Influenza was confirmed on a poultry farm in Dereham, Norfolk. Subsequent tests provided positive results for avian influenza in chickens on two further poultry farms near Dereham but it was later confirmed that the virus was also H7N3 Low Pathogenic Avian Influenza. A poultry worker on one of the poultry farms was later diagnosed as suffering from conjunctivitis caused by H7 avian influenza.

*Response*: All strains of H5 and H7 avian influenza viruses, plus any other H subtypes that show pathogenic traits in poultry, are formally notifiable.

Although H7 does not transmit easily from human to human and only has extremely limited implications for human health; the poultry worker was given the antiviral drug oseltamivir as a precautionary measure and offered seasonal influenza vaccine to prevent the H7 virus from mixing with any human flu viruses that may be circulating. Household contacts were identified and followed up with guidance, advice and preventive medication as appropriate.

*Health impact*: Although only minor health effects resulted from exposure in this particular case, early human health interventions helped to allay public concerns and reduce anxiety in the wider community and to reduce the risk of avian influenza strains mixing with human influenza strains with the potential for changes to pathenogenicity in humans.

*Lessons for planning*: Vigilance is essential to ensure that mutation of viruses is identified at an early stage in any reported cases. Co-ordination of animal and human health responses is vital in preventing emerging zoonotic infections.

*Source*: press release HPA East of England: Conjunctivitis caused by H7 avian influenza in poultry worker 28 April 2006
http://www.hpa.org.uk/eastofengland/press/060428_avian_flu_h7.htm

---

Wales by the Environment Agency to provide data on an annual basis of emissions from industrial processes under the regulatory Integrated Prevention and Pollution Control regime. Despite the apparent transparency of this information, there are limitations through inconsistencies, lack of reporting and many industrial activities are excluded and are separately regulated, such as landfill waste, mining and sewage treatment. Of over 100,000 chemicals catalogued as being in commercial use, many had not been fully assessed for toxicity, persistence and bioaccumulation at the start of the 21st century (Murkerjee 1995; Santillo *et al.* 1999). Gaps in knowledge or lack of systematic methodologies to monitor the occurrence of chemicals mean delays in establishing routine monitoring and protection policies as in the case of chemicals which mimic human reproductive hormones (endocrine disrupting chemicals). These are suspected of decreasing sperm counts and increasing the incidence of cancers (IEH 1995; Colborn *et al.* 1997).

Where monitoring outputs are available, the analysis of population health impacts can be facilitated by datasets on health and environmental quality being co-ordinated on common geographical boundaries, so that links between health events, ambient environmental quality changes or pollution release incidents can be ascertained. Geographic Information Systems (GIS) enable geomapping of population and boundaries with other datasets and tools for analysis of the information and is relevant to:

- mapping infectious disease outbreak and related environmental data;
- emergency incident planning and response;
- population data such as standardized deprivation indexes and environmental exposure;
- mapping ambient air quality monitoring data;
- mapping chemical release inventories, waste sites facilities or *Control of Major Accident Hazard Regulations 1999* (COMAH 1999) sites.

Modelling of routine, accidental or deliberate releases, together with GIS is developing as a powerful tool in mapping long-term trends of health impact and in predicting patterns of exposure for acute hazard incidents of use to health protection organizations in developing systems for integration of health informatics with environmental data.

## Health emergency planning and response

Tertiary prevention consists of measures to reduce or eliminate the adverse health effects of particular incidents or outbreaks. In relation to the acute response the nature, degree and timing of specific health protection responses will vary depending on the circumstances and potential population health implications.

A major incident may be defined as:

Any occurrence which presents a serious threat to the health of the community, disruption to the service or causes (or is likely to cause) such numbers or types of casualties as to require special arrangements to be implemented by hospitals, ambulance services or health communities.

(NHS Executive 1998b: glossary)

Thus an acute response is required for a major incident such as a fire in a chemical plant, as well as ongoing longer-term measures consisting of health impact assessment and health surveillance. In order to achieve a combined and co-ordinated response to a major incident, the capabilities of the emergency services must be closely linked with those of local authorities and other agencies. The management of the response can be divided into three levels: operational, tactical and strategic (NHS Executive 1998b).

- Operational (bronze): this is the front-line control at the scene of any incident.

- Tactical (silver): the tactical level of command is used to determine priority in allocating resources, to plan and co-ordinate tasks, and to obtain other resources as required.

- Strategic (gold): this senior tier of management would only be used in a large incident to make strategic decisions about deployment of resources, managing populations, providing information and restoring normality.

The requirement to implement one or more of these management levels will depend upon the nature of the incident.

### Emergency planning

Following the fuel crisis and severe flooding in 2000, the Cabinet Office undertook an extensive emergency planning review and set up the UK Resilience Unit and the Civil Contingencies Secretariat to support national and regional resilience to emergencies which in turn support local services (Cabinet Office 2001c).

Individual emergency plans need to reflect the concept of integrated emergency management, where the aim is to achieve maximum effectiveness by integrating the contribution made by a number of different agencies and authorities, with the emphasis on planning the response to an incident regardless of cause. While the lead agency is usually the police in the acute phase of a response and the local authority in terms of dealing with the aftermath, there are situations where the lead co-ordinating role is undertaken by another agency at a local or national level. For example, during the foot and mouth crisis the Cabinet Office provided the necessary lead for co-ordinated national action (Cabinet Office 2002a). The Civil Contingencies Act 2004 introduced a new statutory framework for civil protection at the local level, setting out clear roles and responsibilities for front-line organizations in preparing for emergencies. Ongoing preparation and training for emergencies is required at all levels. This is enhanced through table top as well as practised exercises. For example '*Exercise Arctic Sea*', based on a 'rising tide' situation (Cabinet Office Resilience Unit 2005).

### Dealing with major incidents

The United States terrorist incident on 11 September 2001 indicated that extensive emergency planning arrangements would need to be consolidated in the UK in order to deal with the implications of a terrorist incident resulting in mass casualties.

In practice a major health incident may start in a number of ways (NHS Executive 1998b: 6).

- Big bang: a health service major incident is classically triggered by a sudden major transport or industrial accident such as a chemical explosion (see Case Study – Box 13.2).

- Rising tide: the problem creeps up gradually such as occurs in a developing infectious disease epidemic or a winter bed availability crisis.

- Cloud on the horizon: an incident in one place may affect others following the incident.

---

**Box 13.2**   Case study: a major incident – the Buncefield oil depot fire

---

*The incident*: In December 2005, the Buncefield oil depot in Hemel Hempstead exploded into flames starting the largest fire in Europe since the Second World War. It took four days to bring the fire under control, by which time 22 tanks of diesel, kerosene and aviation fuel had been destroyed. Fumes from the fire caused a black plume of smoke so dense that it could be seen on satellite images.

*Emergency response*: The immediate concern was to assess the risk to health and provide advice on how to reduce any threat to people in the vicinity or those fighting the fire. The air quality was monitored during the incident and this indicated that the plume was not significantly adding to existing levels of air pollution, with particulate levels no worse than that found near a busy main road.

The public was informed that the risk to health was low and should not be associated with increased illness. However, caution was still recommended and residents in the area where they directly experienced smoke were advised to shelter.

*Health impacts*: It was considered that the plume of smoke posed a minimal risk to health. In the very high temperatures of the fire, it was predicted that all organic chemicals in the fuel would be completely destroyed, leaving few pollutants.

*Lessons for planning*: The incident demonstrated the value of an integrated health protection service, able to work across different sectors and provide comprehensive advice and support.

*Reference*: The Public Health Impact of the Buncefield Oil Depot Fire, Health Protection Agency, 2006. ISBN: 0 901144 82 7

*Source*: http://www.hpa.org.uk/publications/2006/buncefield/buncefield

---

- Headline news: a wave of public or media alarm over a health issue as a reaction to a perceived threat may create a major incident for the health services even if fears are unfounded.
- Internal incidents: the service itself may be affected by its own internal major incident or by an external incident that impairs its ability to work normally.
- Deliberate release: a deliberate release of chemical, biological, radiological or nuclear materials requires specific action to be taken in terms of public health intervention.

## The range of responses to incidents

Environmental incidents with less extensive population health implications also require co-ordinated action to be taken by relevant local agencies. A low scale incident at local level may escalate into a situation which requires particular action to be taken by statutory agencies with health protection responsibilities, for example, the Health and Safety Executive regarding a Legionnaire's Disease outbreak which is usually associated with workplaces. While a limited health protection response is required in terms of contact tracing in relation to a case of, for example, non-infectious tuberculosis, a far more extensive response may be required for a case of infectious tuberculosis on a hospital ward catering for cancer patients whose immune system is already weakened.

A case study of a multiple incident is summarized in Box 13.3.

---

**Box 13.3**   Case study: a recurring incident – multiple accidental release of refrigerant gas

*The incident*: Over a three-month period, four separate incidents were recorded involving the accidental release of refrigerant gas in supermarkets undergoing refurbishment. Twelve customers and members of staff required hospital treatment in one of the incidents and the premises were evacuated in all cases.

*Health response*: Enforcement of health and safety provisions is a local council function in retail premises and three of the incidents occurred in different local authority areas. Common threads were picked up in the HPA environmental surveillance system that identified the same supermarket chain operating the stores. As a result links were made with the local environmental health departments and the authority in whose area the supermarket head office was located allowing information sharing and investigation across all of the incidents. The company were able to review safety procedures with their contractors to prevent further accidental releases.

*Health impacts*: Acute incidents with no ongoing health effect are normally recorded but rarely investigated and rely on trend spotting to entrain preventive action. Accidental exposures tend to go unchecked with a resulting ongoing burden across NHS acute care services.

*Lessons for planning*: Active cross boundary surveillance of acute exposures to chemical substances can identify potential preventive measures to reduce risk of recurring incidents.

*Source*: HPA South West Environmental Surveillance System Newsletter Issue 8 January/ February 2006
http://www.hpa.org.uk/southwest/env_surv_news/Jan_06.pdf

---

## Overview: the challenges

The diverse health threats of the past few decades have undoubtedly moved health protection needs, particularly health and hazard surveillance and emergency response, up the political agenda, not least because of the economic and destabilizing effects of such threats nationally and globally.

Health protection policy and strategy is implicitly about prevention and improvement of health influenced by intervention and control models of health. While key successes have been made, for example, in global and national surveillance networks for communicable disease and in rapid hazard alert systems, there is a continuing need to review and evaluate the criteria for and implementation of systems for prevention and response to health threats and emergencies.

Policies and interventions must be related to the assessment of the risk and health outcomes, but while there is complexity and uncertainty in risk assessment this must not hinder the implementation of preventive and precautionary approaches. While integrated health and environmental information, modelling and health impact assessment tools together with geographic information systems are being refined, there needs to be consensus in policy and strategic development about their use in determining national regional and local priorities for protecting the public's health.

Transparency, information and communication about health risks in decision making are key requirements, whether concerning acute incident response or in relation to planned hazard prevention. There is an important role for public health practitioners working with communities in a range of contexts – in neighbourhoods or working with the business community – to inform and engage them in the process of understanding risks and the requirements that need to be taken to prevent and reduce them, and to enable an appropriate response to emergencies when they occur.

'Think globally and act locally' is perhaps an overused phrase, but has some resonance here, not only in relation to the broad concept of sustainable development and natural resource utilization to which it usually refers, but also in relation to health risks and specific national and local responses. Collaborative partnerships focused on communities, local agencies and services are as relevant to health protection as they are in the broader context of health improvement. Protecting public health within the wider public health context is not only about targeting whole population risks, it is also concerned with local population needs and health threats and addressing health inequalities that exist. This includes attention to the environmental justice agenda – the excess burden of environmental hazards borne by socially deprived communities.

This requires explicit policy and regulatory drivers for health protection and adapting within organizational structures to enable integration of health protection provision through effective partnership arrangements, having regard to the disciplines and expertise available and the effective co-ordination of expertise and support at the national and regional level.

**Suggested further reading**

Bennett, P. and Calman, K. (eds) (1999) *Risk Communication and Public Health*. Oxford: Oxford University Press.

British Medical Association (1998) *Health and Environmental Impact Assessment: An Integrated Approach*. London: Earthscan.

Department of Health (2002) *Getting Ahead of the Curve – A Strategy for Infectious Diseases (Including Other Aspects of Health Protection)*, Chief Medical Officer's Report. London: The Stationery Office.

Health Protection Agency (2005) *Health Protection in the 21st Century – Understanding the Burden of Disease; Preparing for the Future: October 2005*. Health Protection Agency.

Hunter, P. and Syed, Q. (2006) *Public Health Protection Handbook*. London: Taylor & Francis.

Pencheon, D., Gust, C., Melzer, D. and Muir Gray, J. (eds) (2001) *Oxford Handbook of Public Health Practice*. Oxford: Oxford University Press.

# PART 4

## Evaluation evidence and guidance in 21st century public health

### Editors' overview

What actions should be taken in public health policy, participation and practice in the 21st century in order to improve health and well-being? How can we demonstrate whether and why these actions are successful?

Some of the responses to these questions are tackled, by no means exhaustively, in Part 4 of this book. It explores new thinking about what should constitute the evidence base for contemporary multidisciplinary public health practice. It outlines three separate disciplinary approaches to evaluation from: epidemiology, economics and community health and well-being. These disciplines were selected because of their traditional and emerging contributions to the questions that concern a multi-professional workforce.

There is a growing requirement for robust, theory-based evaluation frameworks, appropriate for complex, context specific public health programmes. These requirements depart somewhat from the traditional, medically dominated evaluation questions in public health practice and have created a movement towards evidence informed public health or 'How and why programmes work?' as opposed to evidenced-based public health or 'What interventions work?' These chapters will be useful to all public health practitioners who face the growing need to evaluate their work.

In Chapter 14 Tony Harrison explores the challenging question of developing an evidence-based multidisciplinary public health. He reviews the recent sources of evidence and the proliferation of internet-based resources. He concludes with suggestions concerning the ways in which the professions and disciplines that constitute 21st century public health can work together and move forward to implement the evidence.

In Chapter 15 Jon Pollock discusses the use of epidemiological evidence in public health. He reviews the role of classical epidemiology in public health before going on to examine the ways in which the discipline is responding to new challenges in public health. In particular he concentrates on methodological developments which attempt to disentangle the effect of different influences (such as environmental as opposed to genetic) on ill health and well-being.

In Chapter 16 Jane Powell explains the key concepts, thinking and techniques of health economics for public health work. The two Wanless reviews are held up as setting the economic background for the future of public health and the move from a sickness to health service. She reviews recent NICE guidance for incorporating economics into the evaluation of public health programmes in order to allocate resources across all services in like terms and the ethical basis of economics as a discipline is laid bare. Steps in a framework to support the economic evaluation of a complex, context specific public health Family Alcohol Service are exemplified for readers.

In Chapter 17 Stuart Hashagen and Susan Paxton define community health and well-being work as a core area of 21st century public health, with a range of public health professionals acting in partnership, and communities themselves as one of the driving forces of change. They discuss the tensions between non-traditional evaluations in the community health and well-being field and more traditional evaluation frameworks, arguing that the established 'hierarchy of evidence' that dominates evidence-based public health practice is inappropriate for community health and well-being work. They present useful new frameworks for evaluating community health and well-being and examples of the ways these have been applied in Scotland in practice.

# 14

## TONY HARRISON
Evidence-based multidisciplinary public health

**Editors' introduction**

What does 'evidence-based public health' mean? At its simplest, it is about ensuring that any intervention (such as a patient's treatment or a public health programme) can be backed up with evidence to show that the intervention is likely to be effective and successful. This is in contrast, for example, to giving treatments or running programmes just because they follow a historical pattern, or are based solely on beliefs or opinion. This evidence-based approach is widely accepted and adopted in the health field.

Creating an evidence-based multidisciplinary public health is difficult because the disciplines and practices that contribute to public health have different approaches to gathering and analysing evidence; also, many policies and practices are aimed at long-term improvements in health and it is difficult in the short-term to demonstrate whether or not they are effective.

The movement towards an evidence-based approach to practice and policy has been dominated by a quantitative and statistical approach to demonstrating the effectiveness (or otherwise) of specific interventions. This has been particularly successful in medicine and health care. But in public health this quantitative and statistical approach could result in marginalizing some important areas of practice. This is true especially of interventions that address social and economic conditions. Here the context within which they are implemented may be particularly important and it is more difficult to describe this using quantitative and statistical data.

This chapter distinguishes between evidence-based public health (which specifically tries to measure the effectiveness of interventions), evidence-informed public health (where evidence of a wider type informs judgements) and the evidence base for public health (which includes all evidence, however it is used).

The author looks at the development of evidence-based public health in the UK. He suggests that problems of incorporating different types of evidence into public health could be reduced by recognizing the essential tension between quantitative and qualitative approaches, and between those that aim to demonstrate the effectiveness of interventions regardless of context and those that emphasize the importance of context. The importance of theory, or identifying the mechanisms linking interventions to outcomes, in evidence-based public health is briefly reviewed.

## Introduction

This chapter looks at the problems of developing an evidence-based *multidisciplinary* public health. This is defined as an evidence-based approach which all disciplines that contribute to public health can share. It is not, therefore, about a more restricted evidence-based public health medicine, neither is it a review of the movement towards evidence-based policy and practice in all those separate professional areas that arguably contribute to public health. It is about the problems of creating an approach to public health, which, while being evidence-based, does not place a boundary around the concept of evidence that results in the effective exclusion of some disciplines from public health. Its particular focus is the problem of extending the evidence-based approach to complex community-based interventions which aim to impact on health in the longer run through improvements in the social and economic determinants of health.

The chapter is primarily based on UK material. Specific evidence databases are referred to in this chapter, but as this is about the problems of an evidence-based multidisciplinary public health they are discussed only in terms of what they say about criteria for inclusion in evidence bases. They are not reviewed for their detailed content. Website addresses were correct at the time of writing.

While there is considerable material on developments in evidence-based public health in general (for example Heller and Page 2002; Rychetnik *et al.* 2002), that which specifically addresses the issue of multidisciplinarity is more sparse. There is, though, a growing literature on evidence-based policy and practice across different sectors (Nutley *et al.* 2002) and on the general debate about the use of evidence in public policy and in health (McQueen 2002; Solesbury 2002; Young *et al.* 2002). The most interesting formal development towards creating a synthesis of evidence for an evidence base for multidisciplinary public health in the UK was associated with the establishment of the Health Development Agency in England under the Director of Evidence and Guidance Professor Mike Kelly. This is heavily drawn on to illustrate the issues that need addressing in an evidence-based multidisciplinary public health. The Health Development Agency is now part of the Centre for Public Health Excellence with the National Institute for Health and Clinical Excellence (NICE) and the evidence base for multidisciplinary public health is still under Professor Kelly's leadership.

The argument in this chapter is essentially twofold. First, unless multidisciplinary public health is evidence-based, then it is open to the charge that while its intentions are well meaning, its prescriptions require better demonstration of their effectiveness. Second, because the disciplines that contribute to multidisciplinary public health have such different research traditions and even conceptions of what is meant by evidence, the main prerequisite for multidisciplinary work is a common understanding of where each comes from and of the strength and limitations of each other's evidence. This, it is argued, is essential if collaborations (a key vehicle through which new public health is to be delivered) are to work in the manner hoped and expected of them. If the evidence on which policy and practice is based in different sectors remains part of a specialist preserve, then the understanding by different disciplines of what each has to offer by way of improving public health will elude policy makers and practitioners alike.

## The structure of this chapter

This chapter is structured in the following way:

- First, because the term evidence-based public health is open to some ambiguity it is defined and contrasted with the broader ideas of evidence-informed public health decisions, and the evidence base for public health.

- Second, because the chapter is specifically about multidisciplinary public health, the development of the wider evidence-based policy and practice movement in the UK is reviewed. This section looks at some of the major developments in the creation of an infrastructure to support evidence-based policy and practice. It also looks at how far this has gone in multidisciplinary public health. It concludes by setting out a simple model of evidence-based policy and practice.

- Third, the central part of the chapter considers the problems of producing evidence for a multidisciplinary public health and getting it accepted as useful and valid. It reviews the methodological problems involved, shows how these are reflected in the debates about the criteria for inclusion in evidence databases. It examines controversies around the concept of a hierarchy of evidence, which is widely accepted in evidence-based medicine but questioned elsewhere. This section proposes a framework for resolving disputes around the idea of a hierarchy and for clarifying the contributions that different disciplines can make to public health.

- Fourth, the next section briefly reviews some of the arguments about the role of theory in evidence-based policy and practice, and relates these to public health.

- Finally, the chapter concludes by arguing that if multidisciplinary public health is ever to become truly evidence-based, a number of difficult conditions need to be satisfied. But it also argues that evidence-based public health can only be a part of a wider public health.

## Defining evidence-based multidisciplinary public health

Evidence-based policy and practice in general has come to take on a particular meaning. This is that interventions (acts designed to bring about an outcome that would not have happened in their absence) should be based on clear and rigorous evidence about their efficacy (in other words, on whether or not they work). Interventions may be at the level of the individual (for example, the use of a drug or therapy), a group (a school class being taught skills associated with literacy or numeracy) or of a community. Examples of the latter would be local policies designed to reduce crime or regenerate neighbourhoods, or to reduce the incidence of disease through behavioural changes induced by a health promotion campaign.

The evidence base for interventions may come from prospective trials conducted under rigorous conditions that leave little room for doubt that it was the intervention and not something else that brought about any improvement in outcomes. In medicine, greatest emphasis is placed on randomized controlled trials, and on systematic reviews that amalgamate the results of different randomized controlled trials. Where prospective trials are not possible then the evidence may be based on retrospective evaluations of interventions and observational studies. Often sophisticated statistical methods are employed in an attempt to measure the extent to which improved outcomes may be due to chance as opposed to being a direct result of the intervention.

Whatever methodologies are used, evidence-based policy and practice as characterized here rely on the ability to set up 'counterfactuals' (or clear predictions of what would have happened in the absence of the intervention). It depends, obviously, on the ability to measure outcomes (an issue of potential controversy, especially in public health where some would dispute that the traditional epidemiological outcome measures of mortality and morbidity should enjoy the dominance that they do). It also relies on the ability to isolate interventions (and in some conceptions of evidence-based policy to reduce these to single, simple actions) as part of this process of eliminating other possible causes of any change in outcomes.

Evidence-based policy and practice as outlined above also has another very important characteristic. That is the generalizability of the evidence (or the ability to replicate the effect of the intervention in different places at different times). In other words, one criterion for evidence-based policy and practice, as seen by some, is that the effect of an intervention should be independent of context. This is a major issue for an evidence-based multidisciplinary public health where many interventions at the community level (for example, those designed to promote community safety and reduce crime, or to provide social and economic regeneration in neighbourhoods) are so clearly highly context dependent.

## A spectrum of use of evidence

The concept of evidence-based policy and practice implies a somewhat mechanistic process leading from the identification of a problem, to the selection of a preferred intervention, to implementation. Of course things are never this simple. Choice and judgement is involved at all stages. However, for the purposes of this chapter a distinction is made between the use of evidence in decision making at different points along a spectrum where the differences involve the level of judgement and an associated risk that the intervention may not work. In this chapter:

- Evidence-*based* policy and practice refer to a situation where least judgement and risk is involved in the decision to use a specific intervention. The decision is based on clear evidence as to what the effectiveness of the intervention is likely to be; the evidence is most likely to be of an experimental nature. This is most likely to be relevant to practice decisions, or to policy decisions which are specific to a defined group or locality.

- Evidence-*informed* policy and practice refer to a situation where evidence has been used as a basis for a more complex judgement. The evidence may be of a wider nature, including, for example, evidence of social and economic conditions, and of the links between these and health (the social and economic determinants of health). (See Chapter 9 for discussion about socio-economic determinants of health and health inequalities.)

- The evidence base for public health is the broadest term, including all the evidence that may be used in one way or another for public health decisions. It includes evidence of conditions (including, for example, health inequalities) as well as of the effectiveness of interventions. It carries no particular implications as to *how* it may be used – it could be as part of health impact assessments (for example Jaffe and Mindell 2002), or even to inform legislative change in a very broad way.

## The development of evidence-based public policy and public health

The development of evidence-based policy and practice has been an important feature of public sector policy in the United Kingdom over the last decade. The significance and breadth of this development is illustrated in important publications (see for example Davies *et al.* 2000), the establishment of collaborations for systematic reviews of studies of the effectiveness of interventions (for example, the Cochrane and Campbell collaborations), and a network for the development of evidence-based policy and practice by the Economic and Social Research Council. Few policy sectors have been left untouched by the evidence-based idea. It is best developed (both in terms of methodologies for providing and validating the evidence, and of the associated infrastructure for disseminating it to the policy community and practitioners) in medicine and health care. It has also influenced policy and practice in areas as diverse as crime prevention and community safety, education, social work, transport and many others (for example, Macdonald *et al.* 1992; Terry 1999; Coe *et al.* 2000; Davies *et al.* 2000: part 2; Sherman *et al.* 2002; Tilley and Laycock 2002), and generated debate about the extent to which existing housing policy is evidence-based (for example Maclennan and More 1999).

### The Cochrane and Campbell collaborations

The best known development in evidence-based policy and practice is the Cochrane Collaboration (http://www.cochrane.org/). This international collaboration concentrates on the preparation, maintenance and dissemination of systematic reviews of the effects of health care interventions. In many respects it sets a 'gold standard' for evidence-based policy and practice. The collaboration is international and its coverage correspondingly wide, it specifies rigorous criteria for reviewing and synthesizing studies as part of systematic reviews, and has developed an accessible infrastructure (including the use of web technology) for the dissemination of its work. It includes centres in countries in all continents.

It is structured around review groups which cover different areas of health care. Currently there are over 30 of these – examples are the Heart Group, Oral Health Group and Schizophrenia Group. Methods groups deal with methodological aspects of systematic reviews (including, for example, health economics, health-related quality of life and statistical methods) and fields/networks are organized around areas of interest which extend across different health problems. Examples are child health, health promotion and public health, and primary health care.

The more recent Campbell Collaboration (C2 Steering Group and Secretariat 2001) has developed from the Cochrane initiative and concentrates on systematic reviews of studies of the effectiveness of social and behavioural interventions, including education (http:www.campbellcollaboration.org). This was inaugurated in 2000 and consequently is at a relatively early stage of development, but its structure suggests its usefulness to public health. Sub-groups include those concerned with methods (including statistics, quasi-experiments and process and implementation), crime and justice, social welfare, and education.

An early paper produced by the Campbell Collaboration (C2 Steering Group and Secretariat 2001) is instructive in identifying both the ambitions of the evidence-based movement and some of the associated problems. C2's aim is 'to produce reviews that are useful to policymakers, practitioners and the public'. In doing this it seeks to challenge a situation in which 'scepticism if not outright cynicism' exists about the use of evidence in some policy sectors. It sees this scepticism as resulting from advocacy groups using evidence which they claim supports their positions, even though their positions are in conflict, and by a number of characteristics of social research that appear to diminish its value as evidence for public policy. These include the fact that policy and practice are implemented in a real world in which context and circumstance matter, whereas experiments often take place in an altogether different context under artificial and controlled conditions. Also, it is argued, the inevitable flaws in social research mean that there is invariably more than one explanation for the outcome of policy.

C2 seeks to guarantee the quality of its output by, among other things, ensuring the integrity of the methods it employs by the adoption of transparent and uniform standards of evidence and the use of rigorous procedures to avoid bias in the screening of studies and in producing reviews. Coverage is international and access to its findings is facilitated by the combination of new technologies with conventional methods and the development of end user networks.

## UK Economic and Social Research Council evidence network

The further extension of the evidence-based movement is well illustrated by the establishment by the UK Economic and Social Research Council of an 'evidence network' in 1999. The remit and approach of this reflects some of the tensions in the social sciences about the concept of evidence-based policy and practice – particularly in relation to the question of whether any particular research methodology deserves a privileged position. Thus it states that research should 'play to its strengths as one kind of evidence among others'. But it also recognizes the advantages of 'greater rigour, replicability and independence' (http://www.evidencenetwork.org/history.asp)

and the need for agreed standards for policy research. The interests of the node organizations that make up the network illustrate the scope of this. These include 'What Works for Children', a centre for neighbourhood research, a centre for evidence-based public health policy, a centre for evidence in ethnicity, health and diversity, systematic reviews in social policy and social care, and a research unit for research utilization (http://www.evidencenetwork.org.org/nodes.asp). The spread of this initiative illustrates its potential for multidisciplinary public health.

## UK developments in public health

If we look more specifically at evidence-based public health in the UK, two developments are interesting. First, the House of Commons Health Select Committee's work and report on public health in 2001 (House of Commons Health Select Committee 2001a, b) included both evidence from expert witnesses and a comment in its report on evidence-based public health. This arose from the earlier White Paper, *Saving Lives: Our Healthier Nation* (Secretary of State for Health 1999) in which public health and the reduction in health inequalities were seen as central to health policy. Given the range of factors implicated in these, the intention here would seem to be that public health should be a multidisciplinary activity. The Committee's terms of reference included specific mention of initiatives that cut across departmental and disciplinary lines such as Health Action Zones, Employment Action Zones, Education Action Zones and Community Plans. (See Chapters 2 and 3 for detailed discussions of public health policy.)

In a written memorandum, Professor Sally Macintyre illustrated some of the problems of an evidence-based public health which covers such complex interventions (Macintyre 2001). She argued that in spite of the richness of research analysing health inequalities in Britain, there was a dearth of research into the effectiveness of interventions designed to reduce these, and that 'one reason for this is the perceived difficulty in applying experimental methods to the evaluation of social or public health interventions'. She went on to suggest that it should be possible to use such methods and find out something about their effectiveness if area-based interventions (initiatives based on defined geographical areas, such as inner-city areas or housing estates, with specific characteristics) were set up specifically to test these. This, she suggested, may involve identifying twice as many areas as money was available for, randomly allocating these to 'trial' and 'control' (no intervention) categories, and then rigorously evaluating outcomes in the two.

In other words, she was suggesting the possibility of a kind of randomized controlled trial to provide good evidence on whether this sort of area-based initiative works in reducing health inequalities. In its report the Committee cast doubt on the practicality of this idea, but acknowledged that there was a void in relation to evidence of the effectiveness of public health interventions which it hoped could be filled. This has happened as a result of the work of the Centre for Public Health Excellence (NICE).

## NICE public health guidance and evidence database

The second development in evidence-based public health in the UK is the development of the NICE database. This is in effect multidisciplinary, as part of NICE's remit is to identify 'evidence of what works to improve people's health and reduce health inequalities'. It advises and supports policy makers and practitioners, helping them to get evidence into practice (www.nice.org.uk). While this may sound clear cut it quickly becomes evident that the ambition of this project in addressing long standing health inequalities and the complex of causes that lie behind these, gives rise to fundamental problems of what is meant by evidence. Thus, the website introduction to NICE public health guidance says:

*About public health guidance*
NICE produces two types of guidance on public health:

**Public health intervention guidance** makes recommendations on clear activities (interventions) to promote a healthy lifestyle or reduce the risk of developing a disease or condition. For example, giving advice in GP's offices to encourage exercise.

**Public health programme guidance** deals with broader activities for promoting good health and preventing ill health. This guidance may focus on a topic (such as smoking) particular population (such as young people) or a particular setting (such as the workplace). For example: strategies to improve the diet and nutrition of mothers and infants.

*Aim of public health guidance*
NICE public health guidance aims to help public health professionals and practitioners in local government and NHS organizations achieve the targets set out in the 2004 White Paper *Choosing Health: making healthy choices easier.*

- The NICE public health guidance (http://www.nice.org.uk/page.aspx?o=295876) has two versions. The full guidance is written for health professionals, NHS bodies, local government and wider public health audiences using language suitable for people without specialist medical knowledge. The quick reference guide presents recommendations in a suitable format for those responsible for implementing the guidance in the wider public health arena and the general public. Other types of information: a database containing examples of systematic and other reviews of effectiveness, and evidence-based briefing documents is also accessible. The old database adopted an 'inclusive' approach that initially did not attempt to develop a consensus among professionals as to what constitutes 'best evidence' (Swann *et al.* 2002).

## A model of evidence-based policy and practice

Figure 14.1 attempts to show in diagrammatic form different stages in the development and use of infrastructure to support evidence-based policy and practice. As it is

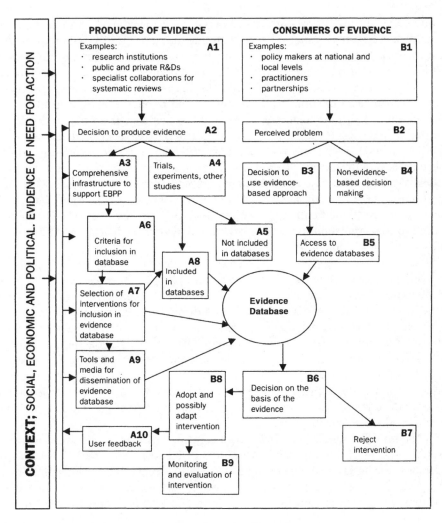

**Figure 14.1** Simplified model of evidence-based policy and practice
(EBPP = evidence-based policy and practice; R&Ds = researchers and developers)

specifically concerned with evidence of the effectiveness of interventions, and not evidence in the broader sense, it separates the external context which influences the development of evidence-based systems from the systems themselves and their use (vertical box to the left of the diagram). This includes not only political pressures, such as those currently evident in the UK, but evidence of need for policy or practice change.

Two aspects of evidence-based public health are shown inside the main box. One (boxes labelled A) outlines key stages in the decision to produce evidence in support of policy and practice, and the other (the Bs) stages in the decision to use it. The 'production' side of the diagram gives examples of the types of bodies that may produce evidence in support of evidence-based public health (A1), and distinguishes comprehensive systems (such as the Cochrane and Campbell collaborations, A3), from individual trials and studies (A4). At a later stage these may or may not become part of comprehensive databases (A5 or A8) depending on how these are set up and on the criteria for inclusion (A6, A7 and A9). These boxes show three key stages in setting up databases in support of evidence-based public health and in identifying their contents. A6 shows the criteria for including evidence from trial and studies – and this includes both search strategies and criteria based on methodologies (for example, whether to restrict the database to systematic reviews of randomized controlled trials, and these trials themselves). These criteria may be used at two levels. At the highest level, what kind of studies are accepted and, at a lower level, what kinds may be used in systematic reviews of studies. A7 shows that decisions have to be made about which interventions to include, and A9 about the type of media that will be used for dissemination to users. A10 shows how user feedback may influence the infrastructure and content of databases.

The user side of the diagram attempts to show key stages in the decision to use evidence-based public health. B1 gives examples of different kinds of users and B2 shows that decisions are made only in response to a perceived problem (influenced by the context of decision making). B3 and B4 distinguish between an evidence-based approach to decisions and other approaches, and B5 that if an evidence-based approach is adopted it requires access to some form of evidence database. B7 and B8 show different outcomes of the decision process, and B9 that a decision to use an evidence-based approach may feed back into an evidence database through monitoring and evaluation of the implementation of an intervention. Further user feedback may influence the form, structure and content of evidence-based systems; this is shown on the left-hand side of the diagram.

This simplified model helps make clear some of the central difficulties involved in the development of a multidisciplinary evidence-based public health. These are the issues of the criteria for the inclusion of evidence, the selection of interventions for which evidence of their effectiveness is provided, the mechanisms by which evidence is disseminated to users, and who the users are. These are considered in the next section.

## Main problems of evidence-based systems for multidisciplinary public health

The first and central problem revolves around the debate about criteria for inclusion of evidence in databases and about the relative merits of data based on different methodologies.

### A hierarchy of evidence

Evidence-based medicine and health care emphasize the concept of a hierarchy of evidence in which evidence from some methodologies is given higher status than that from others. The idea of a hierarchy of evidence has come to be widely accepted internationally in the health field.

Top of the hierarchy (type 1 evidence) is evidence from at least one good systematic review, including at least one randomized controlled trial. A systematic review, as the term implies, reviews and aggregates evidence from as many individual trials and experiments as are accepted by the criteria for inclusion in the review. The use of these criteria lies behind the adjective 'systematic', and distinguishes this type of review from other literature reviews where both the search criteria and the criteria for inclusion are less rigorously specified. One particular type of systematic review is a meta-analysis. This is a quantitative analysis, which aggregates the results of as many different studies as are found and accepted by the criteria, and then analyses these statistically. It thus increases the sample on which statistical statements of the strength of a relationship between an intervention and an outcome are made and in principle reduces the confidence intervals. It is thus designed to increase confidence in the efficacy of a specific intervention.

Mulrow (1995) explains the rationale behind systematic reviews and this provides the logic for their position at the top of the hierarchy. They reduce large quantities of information to useable dimensions and are an efficient scientific technique which may be both less time consuming and more reliable than instigating a new study. As a result of the diversity of circumstances in which individual studies are carried out they are generalizable across different contexts and have increased power when compared with individual studies as a result of the aggregation of data.

At the second level of the hierarchy comes type II evidence, the criteria for which is at least one good randomized controlled trial. Type III includes at least one well designed intervention study (that is a study that attempts to estimate the effect of an intervention compared with 'do nothing'), but without randomization. This would include, for example, retrospective studies that attempt to measure the impact of an intervention (such as improved domestic heating) on the health of a group subject to this intervention, compared with a control group with the same basic characteristics but which had not been subject to the intervention. Type IV evidence includes at least one well designed observational study. Bottom of the hierarchy comes expert opinion, including the opinions of service users and carers.

## Applying the hierarchy to public health

The logic of this hierarchy is clear in relation to evidence-based medicine and health care. At the top of the hierarchy comes evidence that is objective and strives to eliminate bias. This has the greatest explanatory power in terms of its ability to measure the effectiveness of an intervention (and, conversely, the risk that it will not work) and thus gives decision makers the greatest confidence. At the bottom comes evidence that may be biased by the interests of those expressing opinions. This ordering within the hierarchy is not surprising given that one of the objectives of evidence-based practice is to not take the opinions of experts and others at face value, but to subject their practices to rigorous and independent testing.

However, the question is raised as to whether this hierarchy is appropriate for *all* aspects of evidence-based public health, particularly where we are talking not just about public health medicine but about a range of interventions that come from different professional practices and disciplines. The strength of the hierarchy lies in the ability to isolate discrete interventions, to identify measurable outcomes and assess the impact of interventions independent of context, and to measure the strength of a 'dose–response' relationship. As such it is based on a reductionist approach. But many interventions where there are grounds for believing there would be beneficial public health impacts do not fit this model. This would seem to apply particularly to the complex community-based initiatives associated with regeneration and neighbourhood renewal. There are three main reasons for this:

- First, the precise circumstances or context in which initiatives are being implemented is likely to have a significant effect on outcomes. Charismatic and energetic leadership, strong community bonds and the physical characteristics of an area, including its connectivity with other areas are likely to influence the success of such interventions.

- Second, the very principle of partnership is supposed to ensure that the details of projects are finely tuned to the local context, making generalization across different areas difficult.

- Third, initiatives commonly have long-term and complex aims. It may be optimistic to hope for measurable outcomes in relatively short periods of time.

The logic of these complex community-based interventions is based on well grounded research linking social and economic conditions (or the determinants of health) to health and the reduction in health inequalities (Acheson 1998; Wilkinson and Marmott 1998). This research is different in nature from evaluations of specific interventions. It is more complex, dealing with a multitude of factors that have a bearing on health. It is often based in the social sciences and on a range of methodologies. Its findings tend to be more provisional and context dependent, particularly where the work is case study based. This is particularly so with research into regeneration, housing and neighbourhood renewal where there are 'few high quality intervention studies which address the impact of housing and health' (Thompson et al. 2002).

The tensions involved in attempting to absorb this disparate work into the evidence base for public health is well illustrated in a discussion paper on this topic for the King's Fund by Gowman and Coote (2000). This argues that 'in the first instance, it is essential that any new evidence base relates to the full range of public health objectives and activities', as set out in Saving Lives: Our Healthier Nation. These include specific disease-based targets for health improvement, as well as the broader goals to improve health and reduce health inequalities. The paper goes on to say:

As visions of health have become increasingly broad, the range of activities encompassed by the public health umbrella has widened correspondingly. Initiatives and interventions across a range of sectors have a part to play in improving health, and a growing number are expected to link with the Government's public health strategy . . . Too narrow a definition of public health, or of what constitutes evidence, will work against joined-up thinking, and work against mainstreaming of health improvement . . . A medically oriented evidence base will mean that evidence about health improvement remains the preserve of mainstream public health practitioners, excluding many others within local government or the voluntary and business sectors who have a significant part to play. A new framework for evidence needs to be based on a clear understanding of these different players and functions.

(Gowman and Coote 2000: 14)

Gowman and Coote's paper argues forcefully for an evidence base that is not restricted to medically orientated conceptions of a hierarchy of evidence. This, they say, would exclude much potentially valuable research and evidence from a new public health evidence base. They stress that a new framework has to recognize that 'in place of a hierarchy of evidence, it should be possible to accommodate different kinds of evidence, acknowledging their respective strengths in appropriate settings' (Gowman and Coote 2000).

## Locating different research traditions in public health

One way out of what appears to be an impasse is to start by identifying the essential tensions between evidence that comes from different research traditions. Two such tensions are suggested:

- The first tension is between the quantitative and a qualitative tradition. The former seeks to establish measured relationships between variables, uses statistical analysis to estimate the likelihood that these relationships are due to chance, and uses a scientific and reductionist approach to isolate the influence of different variables. The latter's strengths lie more in its ability to convey meaning and the interpretation of complex situations including those involving attitudes and perceptions.

- The second tension is between approaches that seek to establish relationships that are independent of context and provide robust information about interventions which is replicable in different circumstances, and those which place much greater emphasis on the circumstances in which things happen.

These tensions are represented in Figure 14.2. In this the horizontal axis XY represents the spectrum from a wholly quantitative to qualitative approach, and the vertical axis AB, from one which attempts to generalize about cause and effect independently of context, to one which focuses on the effect of context on how things work.

It is possible to locate in this diagram different research methodologies. Thus, meta-analyses which attempt to establish measures of the effectiveness of interventions independent of context, would come towards the bottom left-hand corner of the south-east quadrant, and individual randomized controlled trials, further to the north. Observational studies, particularly those which are retrospective, come still further to the north. Case studies, with their emphasis on a variety of data, on the importance of context and on a process of triangulation to validate findings would come towards the top of the north-west quadrant.

The heavy arrow in this diagram tentatively sets out the main line of tension in the current debate about evidence in public health. The validity of the concept of a

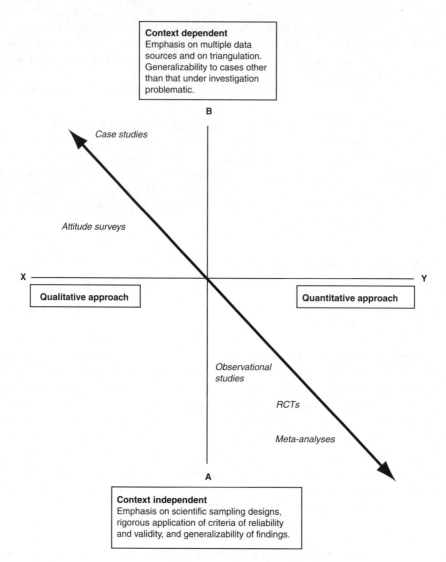

**Figure 14.2** Locating different research traditions in public health

hierarchy of evidence applies largely to the south-east quadrant. As one shifts to the north-west the idea of a hierarchy becomes more questionable for three reasons. First, there is greater reliance on different types of data based on different notions of evidence, for example, interviews, attitude surveys, demographic data, documentary historical data and narratives. This especially applies to case studies. Second, conclusions from research are based more on interpretation and judgement than on conventional scientific ideas of 'proof'. The whole notion of proof is a much more problematic concept in relation to this part of the diagram; evidence tends to be from the social sciences where there is much greater debate and controversy about methodology (Flyvbjerg 2001). Third, it is also notable that the critical appraisal skills

(Critical Appraisal Skills Programme) that are increasingly now part of the training in evidence-based health are more easily applied to the lower right-hand part of the diagram than elsewhere.

In the diagram the south-west and north-east quadrants are shown as being empty. This is not to deny that there are qualitative research methodologies that come closer to quantitative, context independent studies in their approach. Indeed Silverman (1998) argues the case for greater emphasis on this type of qualitative work in health research and less on interviews.

The diagram is also suggestive of the ways in which evidence may be used to inform public health decisions – particularly along the north-south axis. At the lower end, where evidence is less context dependent, interventions for which evidence is available are likely to be discrete, controlled and at the individual level. It is also more likely to be outcome-based – and consequently particularly useful for practitioners. At the top end, interventions are more likely to be complex, often at the community level and often concerned with processes rather than with final outcomes (for example, with public participation, capacity building and with developing social capital). Interventions in this area are more likely to deal with the environmental (in the wide sense) determinants of health, and evidence here is likely to be more provisional and so more likely to be used at the level of political interventions involving higher levels of uncertainty and greater judgement.

This diagram potentially offers a way forward in terms of identifying a common framework for the public health evidence base. The lower half of the diagram, with its emphasis on context independence and replicability is that to which the term 'evidence-based' public health in the conventional sense is best applied. The upper half of the diagram maps a different part of the evidence base for public health – particularly that concerned with evidence of the social, economic and environmental determinants of health. Interventions in this area are often long-term in their intention, consequently it would be inappropriate to look for the sort of summative outcomes (such as changes in mortality and morbidity) in evaluation as are used towards the bottom of the diagram.

However, there is a potential link with the lower part through interventions that are designed to change behaviour (like journeys to work or school, exercise, diet and smoking) where there is plausible evidence that such behavioural change will in the longer term lead to health improvements. Here the behavioural change represents an intermediate outcome and one that is amenable to relatively short-term measurement. This suggests that the link between evidence-based public health and evidence of the determinants of health comes in the identification of short-term outcome indicators where there is an accepted theoretical link between these and a longer-term health gain. An example (see Box 14.1) from a complex multifaceted intervention like neighbourhood renewal may make this clear. (See Chapter 10 for more about neighbourhood renewal and regeneration.)

---

**Box 14.1**   Case study: neighbourhood renewal

---

Neighbourhood renewal strategies involve a range of objectives that depend heavily on the nature of the locality involved, on the outcome of processes of community participation and on processes of partnership working. The ultimate goal is improvement in the conditions in which people live their lives and may involve housing improvement, jobs and employment, skills enhancement, environmental improvement, community safety and crime reduction initiatives, and attempts to reduce feelings of social exclusion. The approach is holistic and involves cross-cutting/joined-up initiatives in which the contributions of different agencies and organizations to the fundamental goals of improvement are integrated through partnership working. This type of intervention does not readily lend itself to the reductionist, context independent, measurement-based approach of evidence-based policy and practice. However, it should be possible to identify process and intermediate outcomes from the improvement strategy which can be tested against evidence, where a link with health can be established.

A number of examples of intermediate and process outcomes, for which evidence of the link between neighbourhood improvement interventions and health may exist, can be given. Examples are housing improvements as measured by improvements in the internal environment (damp and temperature), young people brought into long-term employment through training and skills development, improvements in perceived safety from crime, and reductions in traffic noise. And the links between these and health is established by more fundamental research on the determinants of health (Acheson 1998).

It should be noted that there are two stages in connecting the evidence base from the top half of the diagram with evidence-based policy and practice in the lower half. One involves the identification of outcomes that can be measured and subject to the rigorous analytical treatment of evidence-based work, and the other involves the establishment of a sound theoretical link between these outcomes and longer-term health gains. This raises the issue of the role of theory in an evidence-based public health to which we now turn.

---

## The role of theory in evidence-based public health

In an obvious sense all evidence-based policy and practice is theory driven. Even the most pragmatic trial that seeks to evaluate whether a specific intervention 'works' is based on a theory that links an action (the intervention) with an outcome (for example, reduced vulnerability to heart disease) through some intervening mechanism (a behavioural change, for example). In this sense it may seem surprising that a lively debate has arisen around the issue of theory in evaluations for evidence-based policy and practice (for example Pawson and Tilley 1997; Davies *et al.* 2000: 265–70).

The essence of this debate revolves around two linked issues. The first is the role of randomization in trials and its objective of isolating one factor (the intervention) from the circumstances or context in which it operates. A pragmatic view would be that what is important is the demonstration of effectiveness – not the underlying reason for it. Second, set against this, is a theoretically informed view that the real world is one of context and circumstances; these cannot be assumed away, and neither can it simply be assumed that the intervention will work everywhere. Therefore, what is important is to find out *why* an intervention works or does not work, what the mechanisms linking the intervention and the outcome are, and the ways in which context influences success or failure.

The importance of context and the dangers of pure empiricism are nicely characterized in Lytton Strachey's study of Florence Nightingale in his *Eminent Victorians* (1918). He says,

---

**Vignette: Florence Nightingale**

> she was simply an empiricist. She believed in what she saw and acted accordingly; beyond that she would not go . . . She had found that fresh air and light played an effective part in the prevention of the maladies with which she had to deal: and that was enough for her. What were the general principles underlying the fact – or even whether there were any she refused to consider . . . she had seen the good effects of fresh air, therefore there could be no doubt about them . . . the bedrooms of patients should be well ventilated. Such was her doctrine . . . But it was a purely empirical doctrine, and thus led to some unfortunate results.
>
> (Strachey 1918: 155–6)

Strachey goes on to relate how Nightingale tried to insist that the fresh air remedy, which proved to be successful in the Crimea, should be adopted in India. Those who understood Indian conditions knew this would be disastrous. In the end their wisdom prevailed, but the point of this is that the intelligent application of successful innovations requires understanding of *why* they work and the circumstances in which they both do and do not work. However, Florence Nightingale was not actually a pure empiricist. She was a miasmatist whose underlying theory was that illness came from bad air, rather than from 'germs'. Consequently this example demonstrates the dangers of elevating pure empiricism over theory. It may obscure an entirely false theory on which it is based.

---

Developments of the underlying theories associated with policy and practice evaluation can be found in Weiss (1995), Pawson and Tilley (1997), Connell and Kubisch (1998) under the title 'theories of change', and Pawson (2002a, b, c) under the heading 'realist evaluation'. These approaches are particularly appropriate to complex community-based interventions, and seek to uncover the actual mechanisms that link an intervention with what actually happens. Their relevance to this chapter lies in their application to complex community-based interventions, such as neighbourhood renewal strategies and Health Action Zones. In these the notion of replicability is problematic; conditions matter and the process of implementation is likely to influence outcomes. These theoretical developments provide a useful way forward in incorporating social scientific thinking into evidence-based policy and practice, while avoiding the dangers of pure empiricism so feared in the social sciences.

## Conclusion

The challenge of developing an evidence-based multidisciplinary public health is considerable. It involves, among other things, complex theoretical and methodological debates across disciplines, realignments of power and influence within the public health community, an open-mindedness combined with rigour about evidence among those training for public health practice, and the development of accessible mechanisms for the dissemination of evidence. The magnitude of this task should not be underestimated.

It could be argued that the complexity of the task raises questions about whether evidence-based multidisciplinary public health is actually necessary at all. Given that all the disciplines that arguably contribute in some way to the health of the public are, in themselves, being influenced by the evidence-based movement in its broadest sense, there may be an argument for leaving specialists in different fields to do their own thing and to capitalize on the division of Labour that this could bring. But the argument for evidence-based multidisciplinary public health is not an argument against specialisms and acknowledging the benefits this brings. It is an argument for recognizing the contributions of different disciplines to public health and for incorporating these into a framework that does not exclude. This should allow partnerships and other multidisciplinary teams to appraise and use evidence on the basis of its fitness for purpose rather than for its adherence to specific methodological traditions.

This is not to say that an evidence-based approach should dominate all aspects of public health. Public health is a complex activity, involving long-term goals and fundamental shifts in both policy and practice. This means that it is 'both an art and a science, but it shouldn't be an act of faith' (Gowman and Coote 2000). The role of evidence will in some cases be scientific, but in others it will be to inform complex decision making. Multidisciplinary evidence-based public health should help inform that decision making. It should make risks of failure clearer, encourage monitoring of outcomes so that corrective action can be taken when things turn out not to be as predicted and add to the constant improvement of the evidence base on which future informed decisions can be made.

---

**Suggested further reading and useful website references**

Rychetnik, L., Frommer, M., Hawe, P. and Shiell, A. (2002) Criteria for evaluating evidence on public health interventions, *Journal of Epidemiology and Community Health*, 56: 119–27.

Smith, S., Sinclair, D., Raine, R. and Reeves, B. (2005) *Health Care Evaluation*. Berkshire: Open University Press.

The evidence base for public health policy and practice – see evidence briefings http://www.publichealth.nice.org.uk/page.aspx?o=500082

The Cochrane Collaboration: http://www.cochrane.org

The Campbell Collaboration: http://campbellcollaboration.org

The Evidence Network: http://www.evidencenetwork.org

The Joseph Rowntree Foundation: http://www.jrf.org.uk/knowledge/findings

# 15

## JON POLLOCK
## Epidemiology for 21st century public health

**Editors' introduction**

The purpose of this chapter is to draw attention to the changing requirements of data acquisition and analysis, and the broader methodology skill base required by epidemiologists working in the developing, wider arena of 21st century public health.

Epidemiology is the main discipline in public health. Epidemiology is used to analyse the relationship between disease and ill health on the one hand, and causative factors, like exposure to infected water, polluted air or contact with other individuals carrying infections, on the other. It has resulted in major breakthroughs in public health, such as identifying the link between smoking and lung cancer. Epidemiology analyses patterns of disease in populations and attempts to identify causes by relating these patterns to known measurable risk factors. But as we become better informed and more sophisticated in our understanding of ill health and well-being, so we need more sophisticated and complex epidemiological methods to tell us something about the contribution that *different* factors (be they environmental, genetic, behavioural or life history) make to health and well-being.

This chapter reviews approaches and developments in epidemiology and looks at the contribution these make to 21st century public health. First, the author reviews classical epidemiological approaches and their contribution to understanding the causes of ill health and the risks associated with exposure to different agents, and the effectiveness of therapies. Second, the chapter examines emerging demands that contemporary public health is placing on epidemiology as a tool. The third section reviews the ways in which epidemiology is responding to these new demands by way of methodological developments and use of the Internet for global data acquisition. In the fourth section the author examines meta-analysis, Bayesian statistics, life course approaches and multi-level approaches and their role in the public health epidemiology of the future.

The author concludes that epidemiology is the main component in the public health practitioner's tool box and should remain as the main form of methodological guidance for understanding the causes of poor population health and to evaluate preventive and therapeutic measures into the future.

## Defining the scope

The use of epidemiology in public health has evolved in numerous ways since its original formulation as the science investigating patterns of disease within and between populations. In its classical form epidemiology developed as a method for exploiting the information content of natural variation in the prevalence of disease in order to generate testable hypotheses of aetiology and hence afford opportunities for prevention. The successful prosecution of an epidemiological investigation initially involved the systematic collection of numerical data on disease distribution and the identification of associative relationships with 'risk factors'. This was followed by postulating causative relationships between risk factors and disease in the form of hypotheses and proposing interventions which could break the relationships. Finally, the implementation of these interventions and the evaluation of their effects in reducing disease incidence would complete the task.

As such, the classical epidemiological approaches involved the following skills and processes:

- definition, diagnosis, characterization and classification of disease states;
- insight and experience in identifying and defining potential risk factors;
- rigour and accuracy in recording disease risk factor distributions;
- quantitative skills in demonstrating relationships between disease states and risk factors;
- applying deductive processes in the formulation of testable hypotheses of aetiology;
- proposing measurable interventions and applying quantitative skills in their linkage with disease incidence; and
- formulation of mechanistic explanations and further hypotheses to account for patterns of diseases.

The classical epidemiological approach, therefore, primarily involves the application of precision in measurement and the identification of putative causal factors through the quantitative demonstration of associations that are unlikely to occur by chance or be accounted for by confounders. As such it involves clinical, scientific and statistical approaches that have been the dominating themes, to date, in training public health specialists. Both hypothetico-deductive (hypothesis testing using traditional frequentist statistics) and inductive (identification of possible risk factors) mental processes are involved.

The identification, isolation and control of communicable diseases, while the traditional bread-and-butter work of the public health practitioner, is only part of the heritage of epidemiological work. (See Chapter 13 for more about health protection.) First, epidemiological risk factor analysis and, specifically, modelling risk, enables aetiological risk factor reduction programmes in public health to be proposed. This can range from the identification of a single key risk factor and the measurement of the risk attributable to it (for example, smoking as a risk factor for lung cancer), to the statistical creation, using multivariate statistical techniques, of scoring systems that enable a variety of modifiable risk factors to be addressed together as in, for example, cardiovascular event scoring systems (Shaper *et al.* 1987).

Second, the inclusion in 'epidemiology' of the evaluation of therapeutic interventions other than those relating to the control and prevention of disease outbreaks, has widely expanded its relevance into areas such as health service research, community-based programme evaluations, consumer satisfaction, social care and other areas. Traditionally, epidemiologists are involved in the quantification of effects attributable to clinical interventions of all kinds, ranging across the spectrum of surgical and medical practice. The classical clinical trial of a new drug or the comparison of radiotherapy and chemotherapy in the post-operative care of cancer patients are good examples. Skills required include an awareness and experience of the advantages and disadvantages of different designs in research methodology, and the knowledge of the increasingly complex medical statistical requirements of evaluative work. The distinction between the epidemiologist and the medical statistician has become increasingly blurred. These skills now need to be used in the more complex scenarios of the community setting, multi-factor intervention in health and social care, and diverse outcomes that include concepts such as 'quality of life'.

Where then do classical epidemiology and public health epidemiology begin and end? Disease control in the community clearly remains a public health function. While the evaluation of new surgical techniques on its own might not constitute 'public health', the extension of epidemiological principles to the evaluation of virtually any health- or social care-related intervention (drugs, therapy, advice, education programme, community regeneration) in primary care or in the community can be considered as part of 'public health epidemiology' (Table 15.1 illustrates the subject matter of classical and public epidemiology.)

### Identifying appropriate epidemiological approaches for contemporary public health

What then are the challenges for epidemiology in 21st century public health? As a tool there are three answers to this question.

- To guide and promote ways of using research and analytical methods for the investigation of broader sets of problems in the public health arena (McKee 2001).

- To evolve and disseminate new methodologies to cope with the particular demands of epidemiological investigation in the widening public health agenda.

- To inculcate good practice in the distribution of skills of evaluation and appraisal throughout the community of public health professionals in order to progress evidence-based health and, hopefully, social care (MacDonald 1998).

**Table 15.1** Activity areas in classical and public health epidemiology

| Classical epidemiology | 21st century public health epidemiology |
| --- | --- |
| • Communicable disease outbreak control and surveillance | • Communicable disease outbreak control and surveillance |
| • Monitoring prevalence, incidence, trends in the social, demographic and geographic distribution of diseases and conditions | • Modelling disease risk and developmental outcome |
| • Identifying and quantifying disease risk factors | • Evaluating health and social care interventions and programmes within and across the community |
| • Evaluating surgical and medical treatments | • Health service system evaluations |
| | • Health needs assessments |
| | • Injury and accident prevention |
| | • Disseminating critical appraisal skills |

Epidemiology depends on accurate, complete data; data limitations having a profound effect on the value and potential for epidemiological analysis in public health. Classical epidemiology has used disease recording systems to promote the surveillance (and hence control) of disease and the identification of risk factors (especially modifiable risk factors) that introduce the possibility of making effective interventions. It should be pointed out, however, that much of the informational requirements of public health epidemiology derives, with the exception of death certification, from information rooted in secondary and tertiary health care systems, rather than in the community or from social care sources.

While the NHS could provide the medium for structuring an integrated health and social care data collection system (and much important work has been successfully undertaken on registries and record linkage systems, and more recently the Electronic Patient Record) a strong case remains for the collection of standardized data on disease presentation and management in primary care to facilitate epidemiological studies in public health. With General Practitioners' self-employed status this is restricted to voluntary schemes such as the Royal College of General Practitioners' 'spotter' practice scheme (www.rcgp-bru.demon.co.uk/) and the RCGP General Practitioner National Morbidity Surveys (McCormick *et al.* 1995) that are used to monitor outbreaks and longer-term disease trends respectively. In addition data are collected on prescribing practice by the Prescription Pricing Authority, on specific diseases from research networks such as the Medical Research Council's General Practice Research Framework, and the national notifiable disease system. The newly developed GP activity database initiated commercially by VAMP and now MIQUEST (through the Collection of Health Data from General Practice project; http://www.connectingforhealth.nhs.uk/miquest), may in time fulfil part of this primary public health monitoring role for providing data for epidemiological analysis. Of critical importance will be the success in developing a culture of research-valuable data collection processes in the social care arena and the mechanisms for accurately linking health and social data together.

While classical epidemiological approaches to risk, disease surveillance and control, and clinical intervention evaluations remain important core components, the new public health demands assistance from methodologists in:

- specifying individual risk more accurately;
- understanding interactions between risk factors more deeply;
- investigating the **proximal mechanisms** for and wider ramifications of poor health on individuals, groups and societies; and particularly
- evaluating the impact of complex social/behavioural and/or community-based interventions in the wider public health.

Simple dose-responsive aetiological explanations of disease (smoking and lung cancer, cholesterol and heart disease) are becoming less common as more clear-cut relationships become understood. Attention is therefore naturally turning to complex influences and interactions in which single agent models are insufficient to account for much of the individual variation in disease susceptibility. A prime example of this are the factors involved in the risk of stomach cancer. Here the proximal agent involved in most cases is a bacterium (*Helicobacter pylori*) but individual risk of cancer is affected by both genetic variation between individuals (El-Omar *et al.* 2000) and dietary intake (Ekstrøm *et al.* 2000).

When the number of independent contributory factors is large the size of epidemiological investigation required to assess each factor's independent and combined effects needs to increase. Larger studies with large numbers of independent factors increases the complexity of analysis. Epidemiology in the wider public health is likely not only to have to address a very much broader array of topics and settings than previously, but also to manage mixed health and social care settings and interventions with small effect sizes over long time periods involving complex interactions. As more independent explanatory variables are considered in studies measurement moves towards nominal, or at best, ordinal scales of measurement rather than number or scale measures. Increasingly the central measurements in 21st century public health as it widens towards more sociological and psychological horizons encompass subjective factors such as quality of life, satisfaction, feelings, moods and attitudes as outcomes. The use of scales formed to quantify these subjective components of public health require detailed assessments and evidence of the validity and reliability of scales to measure nebulous concepts such as well-being and quality of life (see Box 15.1).

## Epidemiology: changes to support 21st century public health

### Ecological epidemiology for patterns of killer diseases

The epidemiological method can be traced, as an evolutionary course, back to investigations of the distribution patterns of disease such as cholera and the method of ecological epidemiology which depended heavily on accurate case definitions and reporting systems, the fabric of epidemiological study. Later studies involved

---

**Box 15.1** Case study: treatment of offenders – a 21st century public health problem

Consider a modern public health issue: the treatment of offenders to achieve a reduction in the physical abuse of others. A traditional approach would use mostly process evaluation methodologies to undertake an audit of management, mark instances of 'good practice' based on assumptions of efficacy or from expert opinion, or both, and identify markers of offender behavioural change based on interviews with offenders themselves, corrective institution workers, and other stakeholders. Long-term follow-up would be unlikely (although the number of recidivists might be recorded). It is unlikely that information on the social and educational background of the offenders would be systematically collected and most of the evaluation would be undertaken at the level of the institution rather than the individual.

How could the further application of epidemiological methods be of benefit and what would be the consequences for costs and timings? First, detailed qualitative research would be required to identify examples of 'good practice' based on explicit criteria that, for firm theoretical reasons, were grounded in evidence and involved agreed and validated outcome measures. Subsequent audit would categorize institutional activity as a function of such criteria so as to locate and identify those more likely to succeed. Longitudinal studies of a substantial number of individual offenders would be instigated, stratified across institutions, covering the range of practice variations and using prospective (as well as retrospective) data collection starting on entry to the institution. Details would be obtained of offenders' social, economic and educational backgrounds, behavioural history and measures of psychological health. Sampling of offenders within and between institutions would involve multi-level approaches (see section below on multi-level approaches) and outcomes would be universally recorded by record linkage with police and other databases. Risk of discovered recidivism would be statistically related both to personal and institutional factors through multivariate analysis providing information on how different types of offenders respond to different forms of corrective care over the longer term.

Clearly the main disadvantage of this approach lies in the resources required for data collection over the long term, for the large sample size required and for the need to plan for early base-line measures, expert statistical and analytical support. These considerations, however, need to be balanced against the adverse long-term fiscal and social costs of under-funded, poorly designed research which has to be repeated (Freiman *et al.* 1992).

---

monitoring cohorts prospectively, employing retrospective case-control methodology as used in the seminal papers linking smoking with lung cancer, through to experimental trials of intervention to attribute causation in therapy.

These developments in method accompanied a conceptual shift in scientists' perceptions of the causes of ill health. The revolutionary changes in methods of hygiene, the disposal of sanitary waste, and the prevention of contamination of drinking water that occurred from the middle of the 19th century were motivated initially by the avoidance of the putrefying and obnoxious smells of the 'miasma' that characterized diseased environments. (See Chapter 1 Introduction for more about the history of public health.) As two eminent epidemiologists have pointed out in a seminal account of the history of epidemiology in public health (Susser and Susser 1996a), the transition from miasma to the bacteriological era led to the notion of disease specificity and the 'one agent (germ): one disease paradigm' that proved so successful in understanding infectious diseases, the development of methods of immunization through exposure and vaccination and, ultimately, antibiotic agents. It is noteworthy, however, that it was the *non-specificity* of the poisoning effected by the miasma that led to a multiplicity of major changes in public health as policies enabled improvements to be made in the collection and disposal of dangerous materials, the provision of clean drinking water, in housing and in personal hygiene, with many health benefits.

On the other hand it was the very *specificity* of the germ theory that encouraged disease susceptibility to be seen as more of an individual risk rather than as a measure to promote public health. The germ theory dominated medical thinking in public health from around the 1870s to the 1950s and, indeed, the practice of clinical epidemiology became very much the investigation of the health of the individual rather than the population – despite the clear benefits of mass vaccination and the evidence of declining mortality from infectious disease prior to the introduction of mass vaccination campaigns, presumably as a result of improved nutrition, social conditions and medical care (McKeown 1976).

### The black box approaches for chronic ill-health and disease

The rise of mortality attributable to cancer and chronic diseases that has afflicted populations in developed countries since the Second World War led to epidemiologists using case-control and cohort studies effectively to characterize individual risk without a deep understanding of the aetiological mechanisms involved. This 'black box' approach was accompanied by the notion of the 'web of causation' (MacMahon *et al.* 1960), the multi-causal nature of public health problems and the establishment of statistical measures of risk and odds to characterize disease susceptibility. Further developments in quantitative methodologies have characterized the 'black box' era to substantiate the paradigm.

### Eco-epidemiology and population-level approaches for individuals within communities and 21st century society

To this analysis has been recently added a new paradigm that returns epidemiology firmly in the direction of population health. The Sussers have termed this 'eco-epidemiology' (Susser and Susser 1996b) and have emphasized the need for modern epidemiology to embrace causal mechanisms and pathways at the societal level as well as at the molecular level, citing the HIV epidemic as an example. Here while molecular level investigations are needed to understand the precise mechanisms and characteristics of infection and viral replication, details of the specific personal and sexual behaviour of individuals, and population mixing, is needed at other levels. The public health implications of HIV require understanding at all levels, demanding skills in biology, ecology, psychology, anthropology, population genetics and medical statistics, at the very least.

Consider sick person A in Group GA, part of population PA. Traditional epidemiological approaches might assess risk to A by measuring disease susceptibility in PA and approach prevention by identifying preventable risk factors in PA and applying them to A. The eco-epidemiological approach would prioritize the social and economic factors that predict risk, identify the personal factors that exacerbate risk within the social context, and, with the knowledge of the biological mechanisms of disease contraction established, evaluate the efficacy of preventive measures targeted at the group and individuals within the group.

A number of epidemiologists have followed this approach (Pearce 1996). The ecologic model for epidemiology has been supported by McMichael (1999), for example, who calls for replacing the preoccupation with individual level risk factors and cross-sectional measures of exposure with the development of 'dynamic, interactive, life-course models of disease risk acquisition . . .' in a wider socio-ecologic perspective.

One driving force for this redirection is dissatisfaction with the measured proportion of variation in disease explained by conventional, individual-based predictive risk factors such as those measured on the British civil servants in the Whitehall study on heart disease (Marmot *et al.* 1984). Illustrating the poor predictability of health outcomes, Marmot *et al.* (2001) states that while 95 per cent of lung cancer deaths in the first Whitehall study occurred in smokers, the factors of age, smoking and employment *together* accounted for no more than 7 per cent of the individual variation in lung cancer mortality because most smokers do *not* die of it. A population-based public health epidemiology has probably been delayed not only by the understandable focus on individually targeted disease risk assessments but also by the fall from grace of ecological studies following the wide dissemination of 'ecological fallacy' arguments (see below). Concepts and measures of population health have been relegated in priority although the purpose of the Public Health Observatory system (www.pho. org.uk) might be seen to now include this brief.

Large randomized controlled trials (RCTs) and their meta-analysis form part of the evidence-based medicine move towards drawing generalizable, group-level conclusions of efficacy of treatment. But while specific individual interventions can have large effects on individual health, it is also the case that small effect sizes in large populations can have substantial public health consequences. Modest population-level reductions in blood pressure or blood cholesterol concentrations, or increases in exercise, can have substantive population-level health effects and confer benefits on community health and reduce demands on health services (Morris 1975).

However, care is needed in integrating the results of individual-level and population-level studies. The 'ecological fallacy' emphasizes the differences in the determinants of disease between and within populations and cautions against interpreting the first as a mirror of the second (Rose 1985; Greenland and Robins 1994). Heavy smoking populations, for example, are likely to have lung cancer risk factors that differ from abstinent populations although the difference in risk of lung cancer between these populations will be largely attributed to smoking behaviour (Davey Smith and Ebrahim 2001). Population-specific risk factors analysis has been recognized in less developed countries as an important epidemiological approach. Accordingly, optimal prevention measures are likely to vary between populations. The experience of individually targeted health promotion and health education programmes in failing to reduce chronic disease indices is an example (Ebrahim and Davey Smith 1997). Furthermore ecological studies are being revisited as important sources of information on population-level risk factors and on interactions between these and those operating solely at the individual level (Schwartz 1994; Mackenbach 1995). The other prime tool in population-level epidemiological studies, the community trial, is discussed in more detail later in the chapter.

## Genetic epidemiology

Other factors, to be discussed in more detail below, include the need for understanding more about the distribution of risk factors and combinations of risk factors within populations, the measurement of low or intermittent exposure rates over long periods of time, and the interactions between genetic, environmental and societal factors in the generation of disease (McKee 2001).

Genetic epidemiology, through the potential of the Human Genome Project, provides an additional new major opportunity for public health progress. Some of the hype surrounding the public health impact of this initiative seems excessive as even modest risk levels for disease attributable to specific genes or gene combinations generate great excitement in comparison to more conventional physical or behavioural characteristics (Davey Smith and Ebrahim 2001). Here the challenge lies in the analysis of interactions between genes and the environment and finding its significance in the context of the realities of public health such as the massive and increasing burden of ill health related to the rapid rise in obesity and diabetes.

As in the case of the 'ecological fallacy' an equivalent 'genetic fallacy' exists. This can demonstrate an individual risk *within populations* that varies substantially with individuals' genetic constitutions while these factors are not strongly correlated with variation *between populations* (Maes et al. 1997; Mokdad et al. 2000). It remains probable, therefore, that the ethical conundrum of providing a chemical solution to a lifestyle caused health problem, notwithstanding the exciting developments in the availability of genetic information, are probably unlikely to impact in a revolutionary way on public health in its wider context.

## Other developments

### Use of the Internet for global data acquisition

Having considered the need for epidemiology to adopt a more ecological stance to service public health in the future, there are a number of other areas where technical and methodological development is occurring.

These other areas of development include the use of the Internet in data acquisition for a global approach to public health (LaPorte et al. 1994). It was envisaged in this initiative that international registries, surveys and disease monitoring programmes could be undertaken throughout the world using Internet-based technology. Disease distribution patterns, especially in more remote parts of the world can exploit the technical advances in spatial statistics based on geographical information systems (GIS) (Robinson 2000; LaPorte *et al.* 1996). While e-mail and web pages, user lists and the like undoubtedly foster communication patterns among epidemiologists, as they do for everyone, this approach is more immediately finding a particular niche in education and training. The SuperCourse in Epidemiology (www.pitt.edu/~super1/index.htm) is a new resource for those presenting public health oriented epidemiology courses around the world using well referenced materials including visual aids. Particularly suited to developing countries, the SuperCourse may prove to be a significant force for training the wider cadres of public health practitioners envisaged in coming decades.

### Health statistics

Another area in which technical improvement is occurring is in the definition and classification of diseases, and conditions of ill health and the design and availability of health statistics. An example of excellence is the raw data on levels of pollutants in the air, as assessed by over 100 automated monitoring sites managed by the Department for the Environment and Rural Affairs, which are updated hourly and published freely on the internet (www.airquality.co.uk). This provides a new level of accurate data on a few environmental exposures which are often so difficult to obtain.

### Classification of diseases and health-related problems

In the area of health measurement major advances have been made with international agreements on definition such as the International Statistical Classification of Diseases and Related Health Problems whose tenth edition (ICD10) is now established within clinical epidemiology (www.who.int/whosis/icd10). But major faults remain in both voluntary and obligatory disease registration systems in the UK that confound their wider use for research purposes. These exist because of their development as structures of management (for example Hospital Episode Statistics) rather than specifically for disease monitoring or research. Limitations in primary care data sources have already been referred to. Much has been written about the strengths and weaknesses of these systems (Kerrison and MacFarlane 2000; Leadbetter 2000), but in general they cannot be used for dedicated 'casewise' epidemiological studies in public health. The light might be appearing at the end of the tunnel, however, as the new electronic health record and electronic patient record which, in theory, will provide both the source data for aggregate statistics on health service provision and (suitably anonymized) case-wise, record-linked epidemiological data for research.

## Future developments in public health epidemiology: concepts and methods

For reasons already discussed it is probable that public health epidemiology will come to develop particular approaches and methods to satisfy demand for a better understanding of population-based measures of risk, integrating information from diverse sources, evaluation of complex interventions, and the challenges of life-course exposure measurement and outcome assessments. In this section I shall visit four topics which, it is envisaged, will emerge as more prominent areas in future public health epidemiology. Two of these: meta-analysis and Bayesian methods, concern primarily statistical or mathematical progress more than, or at least as much as, conceptual and theoretical development. Life course approaches and community evaluations are areas demanding wider acceptance and understanding of the methods of design and analysis (and funding) required for their scientific development.

## Meta-analysis

The statistical summation of different epidemiological studies on the same subject is becoming an essential tool in understanding the variation and complexities of research results. This is not only because of contradictory results of different studies of the same topic (Mayes *et al.* 1989) but because of variation or 'heterogeneity' of results due to chance effects or effects related to characteristics of the studies themselves. For example, separate meta-analyses of the effects of dietary beta-carotene intake on cardiovascular mortality conducted on cohorts and in trials indicate worrying discrepancies which are probably the result of inherent differences in study design (especially risk of selection bias in observational studies) as similar discrepancies have also been found in studies of cancer and in studies of other anti-oxidants (Egger *et al.* 2001; Davey Smith and Egger 1999).

In the wider public health, where observational studies are the norm and trials of intervention unusual, steps need to be taken to enable conclusions to be drawn from the widely ranging results of public health interventions. This area is controversial with opinions ranging from finding such meta-analytical systematic reviews of observational studies unacceptable (Shapiro 1994) to cautious conditional approval (Egger *et al.* 2001). The arguments governing this process include, first, the importance of avoiding selection and recall bias and confounding, particularly in observational studies, and second, concentration on investigating the sources of heterogeneity between observational studies rather than blindly presenting a single 'conclusive' meta-analytical result. The alternative, a cumbersome assessment of a set of narrative views, may be less useful. Ensuring that observational studies are undertaken with a rigorously scientific approach is likely to be helpful. One recommendation, that *individual* patient or client data (Altmann 2001) are utilized in a meta-analysis, while desirable is unlikely to be achievable in the near future within the remit of the wider public health because of inherent non-conformity in the settings, researchers and interventions being employed.

Another developing role for meta-analysis in public health, where it has emerged from a careful process and where heterogeneity is limited, lies in identifying the realities of health behaviour impact as outcome, in contrast to interventionist studies of limited usefulness for broad health promotion or health education campaigns. For example, strong evidence that dietary changes effected in the animal or human laboratory setting have a marked effect on blood cholesterol concentration, may not be reflected in community-based populations with wide-ranging prior risk profiles, baseline health behaviour activity and attitudes (Davey Smith and Ebrahim 1998).

The 'context-specific' differences in subject characteristics, compliance and overall diets may be of paramount importance, leading to disappointing results for the population as a whole (Brunner *et al.* 1997; Ebrahim and Davey Smith 1997). However, this finding is of great significance as broad-spectrum health promotion campaigns might not be as effective as specific measures targeted at high risk individuals (Davey Smith and Ebrahim 1998).

## Bayesian approaches

One of the more challenging developments for epidemiologists to incorporate in their approach to the statistical treatment of public health data is Bayesian analysis (Bland and Altmann 1998). Traditional 'frequentist' statistics is used to ascribe probabilities to obtaining the sample data observed assuming that *no* association, difference or effect actually exists (the so-called Null hypothesis) in the underlying population. This is worthwhile doing because simply by chance unusual results can be obtained on a sample, just as we might – although it is unlikely – obtain 40 heads and 10 tails in a normal coin tossed 50 times.

If, for example, we are measuring the impact of an intervention such as nicotine replacement therapy (NRT) our Null hypothesis would be that those receiving NRT are equally likely to continue smoking as those not receiving it. If our *observed* data then seem to show that smoking rates are lower in the NRT group we can use frequentist statistics to quantify the probability that such a result could occur by chance if, in fact, the underlying smoking rates in the population were equal. We then, to follow the frequentist paradigm, continue by judging whether this probability is acceptable or not. It is a convention, although in fact entirely arbitrary, to regard the probability (that the research *sample* data could have come from a *population* with equal smoking rates in the NRT and no-NRT groups) as 'unreasonably low' if it is less than about 1 in 20 (or 0.05 or 5 per cent). If the probability is below this criterion a decision is taken to reject the Null hypothesis as 'reasonably unlikely' and the result is taken to indicate a 'statistically significant difference'. It is an assumption of the frequentist method that, according to the Null hypothesis, the *expected* smoking rates in the NRT group is fixed at the rate equivalent to those not receiving NRT. In other words the data are being used to estimate the probability that a specific, and perhaps unreasonable hypothesis, is *unlikely to be the case.*

For decision making in health, however, we really want to follow a converse reasoning, that is, estimate the probability or risk that a (positive or negative) outcome *will occur* given the data we observe in the research study. In order to do this we may need to use all the information we have about the probable outcome rather than assume that a positive one is as likely as a negative one.

It is a central principle of the Bayesian approach in clinical medicine that the starting point for assessing therapeutic efficacy of some intervention is some probability that a specific outcome will be obtained (from all previous knowledge of the subject). Of course it *may* be that no such knowledge exists, but in many cases it does. This probability is called the 'prior probability' (or 'prior') and how the results of a new study might change this probability is the essence of Bayesian calculations. A major strength of the Bayesian approach is, as we shall see, that it naturally takes into consideration the incremental process of research evidence as more information, data and analysis emerge: these knowledges change the 'prior' as research into a subject evolves and grows.

It is because the prior can vary according to information from previous studies that Bayesian statisticians regard the method as more realistic. To take the coin tossing example, most coins will have some (probably very small but nevertheless existent) bias (based on its uniformity of weight distribution and shape irregularities) and this should be taken into account. Furthermore, as many public health interventions or public policy changes are one-off events, the probability of obtaining an advantageous outcome by chance is of limited meaningfulness using frequentist statistics that are based on the theory of multiple events or samples.

In public health the need to incorporate information from *observational* studies, including specifically qualitative research, is of particular relevance in assessing the outcome of interventionist studies. In these cases the prior probability of an outcome is 'informed' by these sources of intelligence and the effects of the intervention judged against it in the 'posterior probability' (that is the probability of the event given the data observed and the assumed prior), using Bayesian techniques. For example to assess the impact of a home-based rehabilitation programme for the elderly returning from hospital on independent functioning, pilot interviews and discussions could be used before the programme started to enable a set of possible priors to be estimated. It could be argued that such an approach provides a more reasonable baseline against which to assess intervention impact.

However, the difficulty lies in the validity of the estimate of the prior and this is one main thrust of the anti-Bayesian critics. Sensitivity analysis (incorporating a range of priors to cover a variety of contingencies) often accompany Bayesian estimates of probability. This makes results messier, conditional and continuous (rather than the apparently clear cut notion of statistical significance), albeit based on more realistic assumptions and theory (Spiegelhalter *et al.* 1999). Some modern statistical packages now include Bayesian programmes as use of the method had previously been compromised by the tedious nature of the calculations.

Another potentially important use of Bayes theorem in public health lies in the methods of meta-analysis. Here, it provides a conceptual and mathematical foundation for synthesizing research evidence and, especially, in moderating the quantitative influence of a large trial with unusual or unexpected results. As the results are presented in the form of probability distributions it naturally fits into the meta-analytical technique of 'random-effects modelling', often used when research evidence on the same topic is internally discordant and heterogeneous.

Because Bayesian methods involve the interpretation of data in the light of existing evidence, it is particularly suited to policy makers (Lilford and Braunholtz 1996; Ashby and Smith 2000). It provides a method of analysis that allows the policy maker to formulate the questions they wish to ask: 'how does the new evidence of a recent study affect our current view that service X is most unlikely to have adverse effect Y?' or 'if we are dealing with the particular scenario S, what is the risk of Y being reduced by 25 per cent?' This is also equivalent to the doctor's assessment of the probability of a patient having a disease given the presence of certain symptoms. These computations are possible because the outcome is calculated as a *probability distribution* (with 'credible' rather than 'confidence' intervals) not as the 'p-value' for a fixed risk (Lilford and Braunholtz 2000).

For public health epidemiology where properly conducted community trials are required but prove to be resource-sapping, expensive and lengthy, it is important to use the maximum amount of information available in designing and interpreting the study. In particular there is a need for decision making based on information which derives from some combination of routine data, observational studies and controlled trials (Ashby and Smith 2000). Inevitably this will necessitate the incorporation of lower hierarchy evidence into estimation of the design parameters such as overall sample size, acceptable statistical error rates, cluster size, cluster numbers, in addition to data interpretation. Here the value of the prior can be adjusted accordingly. Adjusting the prior enables valuable information to be gained about sub-groups on the basis of assumptions that can be informed from qualitative or observational evidence. As Freedman explains, in a well written introduction (Freedman 1996), while Bayesian approaches might seem to be most useful in meta-analysis and assisting individual patient decision-making processes, its impact on public health may also lie in areas such as population screening (Eddy et al. 1990), assessing the cost-effectiveness of trials (Detsky 1985), and sub-group analyses (Dixon and Simon 1992).

## Life course approaches

Two relatively recent methodological approaches typify developments of major interest in public health epidemiology. The first, which can be packaged under the generic term of 'life course epidemiology' encompasses long-term exposures, weak associations (Florey 1988), epidemiology of chronic conditions expressing themselves in older age, and foetal programming. The common denominators here are, on the one hand, the determination of weak, longer-term adverse exposures affecting health, their interactions both with other environmental exposures and genetic factors, and on the other, early exposures during critical periods of development having major long-term effects.

The notion of single, acute exposures resulting in specific measurable outcomes after brief intervals may be paradise for the epidemiologist, but is now an unrealistic model for elucidating the causes of major public health concerns such as the common chronic diseases of diabetes, asthma and other respiratory diseases, rheumatoid arthritis (and health risk 'conditions' such as essential hypertension). The reality, in complex, adaptive and responsive biological systems, is that temporal ordering, dose, exposure intervals, interactions between exposures, exposure duration, the presence of critical periods, and interactions with genetic and social factors are all likely to alter the course of outcome expression. While the simultaneous modelling of all the influences is both conceptually and mathematically challenging, life course approaches to aetiological understanding can be initiated more simply.

By way of example Ben-Schlomo and Kuh (2002) diagrammatically illustrate the biological and psychosocial exposures acting over a lifetime that may influence lung function/respiratory disease. These include, in chronological order, factors varying from genetic predisposition to poor uterine growth to passive smoking, air pollution, to occupational hazards, with socio-economic status, housing conditions, and poor educational attainment also being contributory.

Such a life course model can incorporate 'critical periods', usually early developmental 'windows' which can irreversibly channel the structure and function of biological systems so that they are much more sensitive to risk factors in later life. Evidence that poor foetal growth, for example, can lead to non-insulin dependent diabetes, obesity, hypertension and cardiovascular disease as a result of 'biological programming' of metabolic physiology at early developmental stages of life form part of the so-called 'foetal origins of adult disease' hypothesis (Barker 1998; Book and Whelan 1991). This in turn owes part of its conception to seminal studies of the long-term effects on the infant and child of undernutrition at different stages of the mother's pregnancy (Stein *et al.* 1975). There remain, however, many careful clarifications to be made in elucidating the mechanisms involved in foetal programming (Gillman 2002). The picture is made yet more complex by the existence of trans-generational effects on outcomes such as cardiovascular mortality, emphasizing that public health measures may require even longer acting programmes of research and prevention (Davey Smith *et al.* 2000b).

In contrast to the longer-term impact of acute events in critical periods are the weak exposures that accumulate over lengthy periods. The adverse effects of exposure to ionizing radiation are now known to be additive and not threshold specific, although their *impact* (for example, diagnosis of effects on function) may become evident rather suddenly. In the social context, epidemiological approaches can be used to characterize risk of, for example, depression following the accumulative impact over time of 'life events' such as mental breakdown, bereavement, unemployment and divorce (Brown and Harris 1978).

As populations age and knowledge of long-term risk factors and their interactions matures, public health professionals will increasingly require epidemiologists to steer them, using new methodologies, including sophisticated statistical techniques (such as meta-analysis and Bayesian approaches), in directions where meaningful policies can be successfully implemented. Life span perspectives will probably depend on the establishment, maintenance and full exploitation of large life-course cohorts prospectively enrolled in previous generations (Golding *et al.* 2001). It is as apposite now, as it always has been, since the days of John Graunt's Bills of Mortality, to note that the foetal programming hypothesis which places new longer-term perspectives on public health and its causes, depends on accurate record keeping of birth weights, placental weights and maternal characteristics at a time when their ultimate usefulness could not have been foreseen. Investment in longitudinal data collection is likely to reap important public health benefits from the epidemiological analysis of cohorts in future years (Gillman 2002). The multiplicity of aetiological and contributory factors and the likely absence of strong associations require such cohorts to be sizeable and, consequently, expensive to manage and maintain.

## Multi-level approaches

The second methodological approach of increasing potential in public health lies in multi-level modelling and, specifically, the epidemiological analysis of community intervention trials. Much of conventional medical statistics is based on the integrity of the individual as a unit of response to interventions to improve health. While this may be true in the individualistic treatment scenarios of the consultant's examination room, it is much less so in the field of public health. Here, individuals are physically arranged and characterized by clusters of spatial, social and genetic relationships. This non-random distribution also imparts non-independence of responsiveness to exposures and to public health measures. For example, individuals living in the same inner city housing estate are more likely to be similarly affected by pollution from a nearby factory than those living in another, more distant, housing estate; or patients on the same GP list might be more likely to be given similar advice on smoking, exercise and weight control and, possibly pursue a healthier lifestyle with health benefits, than those on another's list. Health measures in such common instances require evaluation to take into account the different levels of operation and this constitutes the principle of the process of multi-level approaches to the design and analysis of epidemiological studies.

The non-independence of individuals in many fields of public health measurement emphasizes the need for multi-level analysis. An eminent statistician recently drew attention to the general unawareness (including experienced researchers) of the need to take the clustering of individuals in society into account in public health studies (Bland 2001). The problem concerns any situation where a health intervention, be it a preventive measure or a positive intervention – including health education, vaccination, provision of a clean water supply and so on – is applied at the level of a group or community but where outcomes are assessed individually. The effect of the correlation of outcomes within groups containing individuals similar in some way is to reduce the effective sample size of independent units and, hence, diminish the power of the study. If ignored this, in effect, underestimates the statistical error and exaggerates the statistical significance of differences between groups or relationships between variables, leading to 'false positive' results.

What are the consequences of this apparent statistical nicety for epidemiology in 21st century public health? Unfortunately, the answer is that they are quite profound. This is because much public health work involves a few units of large size, such as the patients in two or three surgeries or a few large schools or housing estates. The practical implications of this have been simply and well presented by Ukoumunne and colleagues (Ukoumunne *et al.* 1999). They identified key considerations including the careful selection (and, generally also the maximization) of numbers of clusters, cluster randomization, and allowing for clustering effects at the time of analysis. It is in any case very common for the size of trials of intervention to be woefully underestimated in public health interventions as well as in clinical medicine. This problem is exacerbated by the effects of clustering where, to maintain power, studies have to be increased in size by the 'design effect' (Donner and Klar 1994) – a quantity that takes into account the 'intra-class correlation coefficient', a measure of the non-independence of individuals within clusters. Properly including the design effect in power calculations can increase the required size of research studies twofold or more. Probably of greater difficulty, however, will be the resource implications for increasing the number of clusters with some authors recommending an absolute minimum of six with strong indications for substantially increasing this number

(Grossdkurth *et al.* 1995), especially where, as is the case for many modern public health interventions, the effect size is modest or small. A recent example of a large scale public health intervention that has properly addressed this issue in both design and analysis is the evaluation of the Sure Start programme for young children and their families (Carpenter *et al.* 2005).

Multi-level regression analysis may also be required and, fortunately, software is now more widely available to assist in this endeavour. A more detailed discussion on the theory and practice of multi-level and cluster designed studies can be found in Von Korff *et al.* (1992) and Donner and Klar (2000).

## Conclusion

Epidemiology is the main component in the public health practitioner's tool box and should remain as the primary form of methodological guidance for understanding the causes of poor health and to evaluate preventive and therapeutic measures. It can also be concerned with the elucidation of the mechanisms – from molecular to societal – of perturbation of health.

If a modern definition of public health such as the collective efforts by society to prevent premature death, illness, injury and disability and to promote population health (Beaglehole and Bonita 1997) is adopted, then epidemiology must prepare for the task of developing methodologies to use in a much broader array of concerns such as poverty, war and global warming (*Lancet* 1997). There is little doubt that advantages would accrue were the development of a *population-oriented* evidence-based public health to follow from the successes of the evolution of evidence-based medicine from clinical epidemiology (Heller and Page 2002). Indeed this is already happening specifically with the widening agenda of the Cochrane and Campbell collaborations into social care, educational methodologies and corrective behaviour, and an increasing focus on appropriate population-based measures of health (Aspinall 1999) such as those within the remit of the Public Health Observatories (Ashton 2000). (See Chapter 14 on evidence-based public health for further discussion of these issues.)

The *methodological* changes that are foreseen to implement this re-orientation include the introduction of population services audit, dissemination of critical appraisal skills to managers and policy makers and improved population-based health data collection and dissemination (Davey Smith and Ebrahim 2001). Analytical innovation is also required, including further developing group and population-oriented study designs and data analysis for health assessment and intervention evaluations.

Epidemiology is simply a tool to be used for public health as its practitioners demand. New focuses on evidence summations, ecological contexts, life course effects, health and social inequalities, and community health interventions must ener-gize epidemiologists to develop the methodological and analytical skills to support these demands. Additionally, however, epidemiologists have the right to expect public health workers to listen to the advice they offer in appraising the evidence correctly and in designing research studies appropriately. This is of particular importance as the wider public health often requires more complex, more expensive and more resource-hungry study designs than hitherto. These messages have passed from clinical medicine to traditional public health and now need to continue the journey towards the broader reaches of public health and social care.

---

**Suggested further reading**

---

Beaglehole, R., Bonita, R. and Kjellstrom, T. (1993) *Basic Epidemiology*. Geneva: World Health Organization.

Bhopal, R. (2002) *Concepts of Epidemiology*. Oxford: Oxford University Press.

Black, N., Brazier, J., Fitzpatrick, R. and Reeves, B. (1998) *Health Services Research Methods: A Guide to Best Practice*. London: BMJ Books.

Vetter, N. and Matthews, I. (1999) *Epidemiology and Public Health Medicine*. Churchill Livingstone.

# 16

## JANE POWELL
## Health economics and public health

**Editors' introduction**

Health economics is a way of thinking and a set of tools and techniques associated with this way of thinking. It is concerned with resources and how they are allocated and distributed in society.

This chapter presents a case study that will aid public health practitioners in 'how to do' an economic evaluation. The role of needs assessment and health impact assessment in relation to economic analysis is also considered.

Most public health professionals will benefit from knowledge of the key concepts, thinking and techniques of health economics in their day-to-day work. A balance sheet framework for economic evaluation of all types of public health programmes and interventions is an especially helpful tool for evaluating all kinds of public health programmes and interventions. We need to identify good public health programmes which incorporate a service user perspective and are effective and cost-effective, in that beneficial outcomes should outweigh costs for society as a whole.

In the first section of this chapter, the author focuses briefly on economics as a discipline through introduction of a case study in economic evaluation. She outlines key concepts from the perspective of public health professionals, and tools and techniques that are closely associated with the work of health economists. The author concludes that the time is right to further develop the framework for economic evaluation in public health research and practice around the balance sheet approach.

## Key concepts in health economics for public health professionals

Orthodox economic theory is founded upon numerous principles and is full of jargon. Fortunately, for those in public health who have not had a thorough grounding in economic theory, explanation of a few key concepts will cover a substantial amount of what is needed to use an economic evaluation approach. Resources are scarce or finite. Public health professionals cannot do everything for groups and populations that they would wish as demands are infinite and resources do not allow it. Therefore, they have to make choices about how to allocate the scarce resources at their disposal.

## Efficiency and equity

Efficiency is a criterion for sharing out or allocating resources among all competing uses in public health. According to an economist's perspective, resources should be allocated in order to obtain the maximum 'health improvement' from the finite amount of resource. However, most public health professionals would be concerned to allocate resources equitably as well. Unfortunately, there is almost always a trade-off between efficiency and equity in allocating resources, so it is unlikely that in public health care, an efficient allocation of resources will also be equitable (Dolan 1998).

## Quality adjusted life years (QALYs)

Despite their numerous difficulties, development of QALYs, as a tool for measuring outcome or the benefit of interventions, can be viewed in retrospect as one of the most well known, tangible contributions that health economists have made to the development of evaluation in health care.

A QALY is a number indicating the size of health gain from an intervention. It is created by combining quantitative information of length of survival with scores related to patient perceptions of quality of life (Bush *et al.* 1972; Weinstein and Stason 1977; Williams 1985) so that:

a QALY = estimate of length of life × estimate of quality of life.

## Opportunity cost

Resources are limited and if they are used in one way they are then not available to be used in another way. Very few activities are costless and costs can be incurred without money necessarily changing hands. For example, if a public health professional fore-goes the opportunity to visit an elderly house accident victim in order to attend to an emergency road accident victim then there is a cost involved to the elderly patient, which is the benefit foregone in not having immediate emergency care. The value of the best opportunity foregone as a result of undertaking an activity or the sacrifice involved is the opportunity cost.

Usually money is used as a means of measuring opportunity cost. Definitions of cost in economics and accounting are different. The economist's notion of cost extends beyond the cost falling on the public health service. All sacrifices involved in pursuing a particular public health policy should be incorporated within any measure of opportunity cost, including those on other agencies in society, individuals and their families.

## Incorporating health economics in public health guidance

Economic analysis and economic evaluation has become an essential part of the public health guidance development process (NICE 2006). This has arisen as a consequence of the two Wanless reports (Wanless 2002, 2004). The first Wanless report argued that government needed to refocus on health improvement by becoming a health service rather than a sickness service (Wanless 2002). Wanless went on to investigate the cost-effectiveness of improving the health of the whole population and reducing health inequalities by supporting people to become fully engaged in their own good health (Wanless 2004). Wanless recommended that a common framework should be used to evaluate the cost-effectiveness of interventions and programmes across health care and public health.

This framework should allow a comparison of the cost effectiveness of public health interventions:

- within and between risk factors and disease areas;
- involving screening and treatment within and across disease areas;
- directed towards tackling the wider determinants of health.

(NICE 2006: 41)

Economic analysis relating to public health guidance should adopt the public sector, NHS and personal social services perspectives and other perspectives when appropriate. Where a range of perspectives is used within one economic evaluation study this is known as a balance sheet approach to economic evaluation.

## Economic evaluation methods

Cost–effectiveness analysis incorporating QALYs as the health-related outcome measure is the main method recommended by NICE for economic evaluation in public health, so that all uses of resources can be compared in like terms. In addition, a cost–consequences analysis can also be applied to evaluate public health interventions with more than one multidimensional outcome. Cost–consequences analysis does not attempt to combine measures of benefit into a single measure of effectiveness, so it cannot be used to rank interventions in terms of their effectiveness and efficiency. Nevertheless, it is a systematic technique that allows decision makers to weight and prioritize the outcomes of an evaluation and is relevant to the complexity and multi-dimensional character of public health interventions and programmes (Kelly *et al.* 2005; NICE 2006).

## A case study example: the economic evaluation of family and child alcohol services

### The stages

### 1. The problem

Alcohol problems affect families negatively and in many diverse ways. These effects in the problem drinker include deteriorations in physical and psychological health, employment, education, ability to parent, relationships, family finances, and a range of family dynamics and functioning. Certain families may be at even higher risk: those living in poverty for example, or dealing with unemployment or lacking in social support. Children and family members in these families can have a particularly hard time, often suffering from a wide range of behavioural difficulties, problems with the school environment, emotional and psychological difficulties, and (in younger children) development delay. Yet despite this huge range of problems, most services are focused on problem drinkers, not on their family members, so there is a huge gap in service provision for the family members of problem drinkers (Velleman et al. 2003).

Where specific services have been established, they tend to be in their infancy and are few and far between (Templeton et al. 2005). There are also cases where generic services (an umbrella term that includes, for example, children and family services, children and adolescent mental health services, alcohol and drug agencies, adult mental health services, social services, probation teams, youth offending teams and so on) may have a dedicated post to work with this client group; but workers undertaking these roles can be particularly isolated (sometimes the only person within their organization with this focus) and often constrained by the same resource and other issues that are faced by their organization. An online toolkit for setting up and sustaining a Family Alcohol Service (FAS) on the AERC website http://www.aerc.org.uk (Templeton et al. 2006).

The stress-strain-coping-support model suggests that the stress of living with a problem drinker can lead to strain, often shown via high levels of physical and psychological symptoms (Velleman et al. 2003). The amount of strain is influenced by two key factors: coping and social support. This means the strain arising from living with a problem drinker can be reduced by altering or improving coping and support. The model suggests that changes in symptom levels would occur only once changes in coping and support have taken effect and that an effective family alcohol service will provide substantial non-health benefits in terms of 'coping' and 'social support' outcomes. Therefore in any economic evaluation it would be sensible to attempt to capture family assessments of change on this front that arise from the FAS intervention as well as the more obvious health benefits or outcomes.

Service provision for the family members of alcohol misusers is very limited. Many commentators have called for a more integrated approach, a more family focused approach to working both with affected children and parents and with problem drinkers, which concentrates on parenting and family functioning, instead of purely on simple child protection or drinking outcomes. There has also been a considerable national policy drive towards such a family-focused approach, and this impetus has continued with the publication of the NHS *National Service Framework for Children* (Department of Health 2004d). Unfortunately though, despite a clear focus on the family in its interim report, the final Alcohol Harm Reduction Strategy for England failed to deliver supportive recommendations about service provision for 'vulnerable' and 'at risk' children in families with a problem drinker (Cabinet Office, Prime Minister's Strategy Unit 2004).

## The knowledge base for economic evaluation of alternative services

It is important to examine the evidence base for effectiveness of family alcohol services before proceeding to examine cost-effectiveness. Economic evaluation is meaningless if this service or any other for that matter does not work in the first place. The technical merits of any programme intervention or service must be established before an evaluator moves on to determine cost-effectiveness.

It is necessary therefore to review the evidence for effectiveness in a systematic way or to search for systematic reviews of effectiveness on the many databases currently available for that purpose. The best source of evidence for the effectiveness of medical community and psycho-social public health interventions are available on the National Institute for Health and Clinical Excellence (NICE) website in the Centre for Public Health Excellence. Readers are referred to this excellent resource for evidence briefings. Public health interventions are complex and there are various issues and considerations to their conduct compared with those undertaken for medical interventions (Kelly *et al.* 2005).

Recent evidence from the USA represents a preliminary effort to study patients' and family members' experiences and levels of satisfaction for structured family group sessions for a problematic drinker in an outpatient setting (Marshall *et al.* 2005). This study reported positive outcomes from counsellors working with multi-family groups. These arose from sharing family time rather than the specific topics that were covered. UK-based work that reports upon Social Behaviour and Network Therapy for families with a substance misuser, also reports positive preliminary outcomes and a recommendation for further evaluation (Copello *et al.* 2006). A Cochrane review of family therapy for anorexia nervosa has yet to report (Kolliakou *et al.* 2006). However the protocol for this systematic review suggests that its future findings would be of considerable interest to the evaluation of family alcohol services, as there is considerable cross-over between anorexia nervosa and alcohol problems in terms of the nature of the syndrome and the impact on families. Family interventions have been previously demonstrated to be effective in the long-term treatment and rehabilitation process of anorexia nervosa (Dare *et al.* 1995).

## Describing the different Family Alcohol Services to be compared precisely

The lack of national alcohol policy for families, it is doubly important to evaluate services in economic terms to ensure that evidence is collected that will support continued and increased resource allocation.

One type of Family Alcohol Service is described fully below to illustrate the descriptive information that is likely to be relevant. Other services may take different forms from this, but each should be described precisely. The process of economic evaluation is the same for each alternative form of Family Alcohol Service. Each alternative form of service delivery should be comparatively evaluated in the same way.

### The Family Alcohol Service, North London

The Family Alcohol Service, launched in north London in 2002, has established both a new service and new practice in an area of social care that has been almost completely neglected. The therapeutic model which it has developed offers a solution-focused therapeutic service to all family members that want to engage, and to significant others who have an influence over the welfare of the child/children. The focus is on the child and working with family members to minimize the effect of parental drinking upon them. At its core is a model of an integrated service:

- As a fully multi-disciplinary service, utilizing a range of professions and integrating both alcohol-focused and child and family focused professionals and ways of working. The team establishment consists of a manager, a specialist adviser, two alcohol workers, two half-time family support workers, a social worker and an administrator.
- By aiming to work with the whole family: the non-problem drinking parent, the children, other family members, and the drinker himself or herself.

FAS intervention has two stages. A first stage intervention with each family normally consists of five sessions, usually with two workers co-working and seeing some family members individually. In these sessions information is gathered from the whole family about all aspects of their lives, with the emphasis on what the family feel that they do well, rather than focusing on the presenting problem. This positive reframing helps families become motivated to change by focusing first on their values, looking at what is important to them as a family, and then focusing on their strengths, looking at what they are already doing well (Templeton *et al.* 2006).

### What is being evaluated?

This economic evaluation aims to assess the extent to which the comparative costs of Family Alcohol Services result in children and family members with a problem drinker in the family improve in terms of change in outcomes over time. It also aims to assess whether different types of Family Alcohol Service result in resource savings to family members, other statutory and voluntary agencies (for example crime and criminal justice system and society) as a whole.

### The perspective

In this example the costs and outcomes relevant to the funders of FAS will mainly concern us in terms of detail. When a societal perspective is taken, all costs, resource savings and outcomes that arise from each type of Family Alcohol Service, to the organization, service users, other agencies and society should be identified. Even though it may not be possible to measure and value all costs, all relevant costs and savings associated with FAS must be identified so that the decision maker is fully aware of all the consequences of FAS as a programme or intervention. A 'balance sheet' approach to economic evaluation might be taken that shows the ratio of costs to outcomes for all services from a range of perspectives, that is the organization or society as a whole.

The opportunity cost of running an FAS or any service or programme for that matter, should always be borne in mind. In many cases the price a person pays or could pay (if free at the point of use or a non-money valued resource) could be used to value resources like time when money does not necessarily change hands.

Use of time is not free, even if a person is not paid for this time and is a volunteer. Market prices can be used to make a monetary value of resources like time where money does not change hands but valuable resources are used up.

Estimates of resources saved in £s from running an intervention, programme or service are important as they are subtracted from the total cost of a programme before this is compared with benefit later on.

## The costs of FAS

*Costs*: There are four broad categories of cost for each alternative to be evaluated, that should be considered in economic evaluation:

- Programme costs arise from the direct cost of providing a public health intervention.
- Direct costs include all of the individual elements of an intervention, such as staff, volunteer time, buildings, equipment, transport, support services and so on (Building Cost Information Service 2004; Curtis and Netten 2005).
- Non-programme intangible costs (or savings) arise from the resultant programme effects, such as the savings that may result due to a reduction in the need for alternative programmes.
- **Indirect costs**, such as child, family and wider agency costs (or savings), for example, the salary of carers should also be included in economic evaluation.

Establishment of FAS:
- refurbishment of premises;
- publicity materials;
- equipment;
- discussions with funders;
- appointment of staff; and
- furniture.

Running costs:
- salary/ies of all FAS staff (and on-costs National Insurance and pension);
- maintenance of premises;

- heating and lighting;
- rent and rates; and
- telephone.

Problem drinker's costs and families' costs:
- time for attendance at the FAS;
- travel to FAS;
- expenses (for example food);
- lost earnings; and
- loss of well-being costs.

Resource cost savings:
- decreased burden on crime and criminal justice systems, housing sector, education sector, health and social care services and other statutory and voluntary agencies;
- improved well-being; and
- behaviour change.

The next stage is to measure the costs incurred to the FAS and its service users and the resource savings in terms of pounds sterling (£). The cost for the entire caseload of service users (including their families) needs to be estimated by the evaluator/s in each of the identified categories. Much of this data, especially time for attendance and costs of travel, needs to be recorded on a computer or records system. Cost data can be obtained from whoever does accounts or from published sources available online at the Personal Social Services Research Unit, University of Kent and the Building Cost Information Service. These online sources are an excellent way to work with, building up a picture of the costs of a service. It may be necessary to up-rate for inflation or make some assumptions in order to arrive at a £ cost you can use, but this top–down approach is entirely acceptable within the framework of an economic evaluation.

Strenuous efforts should be made within public health economic evaluations to ensure appropriate costing methodology is applied by considering resources used and their unit cost separately, following Beecham (2000).

## Outcomes or consequences of Family Alcohol Services

An FAS in common with many public health interventions is likely to lead to multiple outcomes. The trick is to think creatively in how to measure and reflect these numerous outcomes.

*Benefits*: economic evaluation should be comprehensive and have a societal perspective. It should therefore consider outcomes that may not be referred to in the objectives including the impact upon parties other than the main target group.

*Outcome measures*: outcome evaluation will also recognize that programmes impact at different levels. It will be important to evaluate the impact of these programmes on the community and organization in which the programme is set as well as on individuals, in order to capture the full impact of a programme.

There are two types of outcomes to be evaluated:

- final outcomes arise from the populations impacted by a public health programme; and
- process outcomes arise from achievement of potential, actual joint working processes and partnership arrangements that arise from a public health programme.

Process outcomes relating to the manner in which an organization and its workers implement a programme are not part of traditional economic evaluation that focuses upon inputs and outputs. But it is difficult to ignore process outcomes within public health programme evaluation as it is essential to uncover the reasons why a public health programme succeeds or fails and add this knowledge to the analysis and findings (Sefton *et al.* 2002).

## Final outcomes

1   Improved quality of life.
2   Change in Quality Adjusted Life Years.

The EQ-D5 health-related quality of life measure could be used to measure 1 and 2. Available at: http://www.euroqol.org/web/

3   Improved behaviour.
4   Improved feelings of coping and social support.

The Strengths and Difficulties Questionnaire for measuring emotional and behavioural problems in children and adolescents could be used to measure 4. Available at: http://www.sdqinfo.com/b2.html

5   Improved educational opportunities, re-training or employment opportunities.
6   Increased school attendance reduction in truanting.

## Activity outcomes

1   Number of people referred to FAS.
2   Number of people who attended after receiving an initial appointment.
3   Number of people who attended after receipt of a second appointment who did not attend first appointment.
4   Number of people provided with a personal action plan.
5   Number of people who attended for follow-up interviews or sessions.

The problems and issues with use of activity measures rather than final outcome measures is that the former can be affected by non-attendees and non-adherents. The fact that people are not attending a service or programme or not adhering to treatment is important and needs to be reflected in the economic evaluation somehow.

The final outcomes or consequences need to be measured where they can be. All activity outcomes need to be recorded as this is valuable information to evaluate a service. If possible the measured final consequences or outcomes need to be con- verted into pounds sterling (£) so they can be compared with the costs. Activity outcomes do not need to be converted into pounds sterling as their relative number can be divided into the cost to get a cost per case figure. This is useful information in its own right.

## Discounting costs and benefits

If your evaluation extends beyond a 12-month period it is conventional to employ the discounting technique. The different levels of costs and outcomes and these impacts over time must be reflected in economic evaluation. Time differences in the occur- rence of costs and outcomes can be reflected with discounting by the public sector discount rate (Drummond and McGuire 2001).

## Sensitivity analysis

Sensitivity analysis can be applied to test the robustness of any data to assumptions that might underlie the production of cost and outcome information. This is import- ant in economic evaluation because assumptions will most probably have to be made. The estimation of risk and uncertainty in economic evaluation has become an indus- try in itself particularly when cost-effectiveness ratios are estimated from the results of randomized controlled trials. Bootstrap methods are used to estimate confidence intervals around the ratios. Interested readers are referred to the chapter by Briggs (2001) cited in Drummond and McGuire (2001).

## Calculation of cost-effectiveness ratios

The formula for this is the same whether you are dividing the final outcome by cost or the activity outcome by cost. You will need to subtract the costs savings you have identified to other statutory and voluntary agencies and society as a whole, from the cost side of the ratio.

$$\text{Cost per QALY} = \frac{(\text{Cost} - \text{the resource savings})}{(\text{number of QALYs})}$$

or

$$\text{Cost per service user} = \frac{(\text{Cost} - \text{the resource savings})}{(\text{number of service users})}$$

The conversion of final outcomes into a monetary value allows the economic benefits of FAS to health and social care organizations and society as a whole to be estimated.

## Equity or utilization and/or equal access

An FAS might be in an area with an above average number of families with problem drinkers. In turn there may be equality and diversity issues to take into consideration. There may be equal access factors in relation to those who choose to attend the service, where the issue is equity in relation to use rates rather than equal access.

It might be the case that costs and outcomes and the interaction effects between organizations, individuals, communities and society may not be apparent at first or may quickly fall off. It is important that economic evaluators embrace the users of services and become involved with the data generated, as it is then much more meaningful and provides richness to the process of interpreting the data generated.

Economic evaluation is focused upon efficiency or cost-effectiveness. Health Needs Assessment and Health Impact Assessment are two evaluative techniques that should be considered alongside economic evaluation, as they are more conducive to evaluations in which equity or health inequalities are an issue.

### Health needs assessment

This is a systematic method for reviewing the health issues facing a population leading to agreed priorities and resource allocation that will improve health and reduce inequalities (Cavanagh and Chadwick 2005).

### Health impact assessment

Health impact assessment is a relatively new approach which accepts that social, economic and environmental factors, as well as genetic make up and health care, make a difference to people's health. It is a systematic way of assessing what difference a policy, programme or project (often about social, economic or environment factors) makes to people's health. For example, it has been used when public sector organizations and partnerships have wanted to understand the effect on people's health of policies on transport, air quality, economic development, regeneration or housing.

The assessment can be carried out before, during or after a policy is implemented, but ideally it is done before so that the findings can inform decisions about whether and how to implement the policy. Key steps are to:

- select and analyse policies, programmes or projects for assessment;
- profile the affected population – who is likely to be affected and their characteristics;
- identify the potential health impacts by getting information from the range of people who have an interest in the policy or who are likely to be affected by it;
- evaluate the importance, scale and likelihood of the potential impacts; and
- report on the impacts and make recommendations for managing the impacts.

Health impact assessment is a tool for bringing public health issues into the foreground when organizations and partnerships are making policies and decisions. Public health workers may find it useful if they are considering new policies on, for example, transport or regenerating areas of social deprivation (Ewles and Simnett 2003: 141).

## The economic worth of each Family Alcohol Service

Cost per service user or change in cost per service user and cost per QALY or change in cost per QALY are resource allocation terms that will stand you in very good stead when funding opportunities arise because they are comparative and can be compared with the output of other treatments and services that compete for scarce resources in funding exercises. In public health interventions the usefulness of qualitative data should not be overlooked. It is usually a good source for trying to tease out what people actually mean by what they are saying and for gauging how and why public health programmes work as opposed to what works in evidenced-based public health. (See Chapter 14 for a discussion of evidence-based public health.)

### Strengths of economic evaluation

The great strength of economic evaluation as a technique is that it follows a systematic, rational and logical approach that leads beguilingly to an answer or, in public health, to a range of answers that can be applied with other types of analysis and information in decision-making processes. It is, when conducted as it should be, much more transparent than deployment of 'expert judgement' as a basis for making decisions about public health resource allocation. Decision-making processes in public health may still be very cloudy, but the evidence from economic evaluation should at least act to create some discussion about values, viewpoints and judgements before decisions are made.

The thinking time or problem definition time of an economic evaluation is also extremely worthwhile. If deficiencies in services and need have not been identified correctly or at all, then it becomes a rubber stamping exercise to support vested interest, which it is not meant to be.

### The ethical stance of public health professionals

According to Mooney (1992) there are three principal ethical theories: virtue, duty and the common good. Virtue and duty are essentially individual ethical theories and the common good a societal ethical theory. Jonsen and Hellegers suggest that: 'traditionally medical ethics has dealt mostly within . . . the theories of virtue and of duty . . . the nature of contemporary medicine [new public health] demands that they be complemented by the third essential theory – the common good' (Jonsen and Hellegers 1987: 4).

It can be argued that there is much more that can be identified as the doctrine of the common good in the contemporary ethics of 'new public health care' than the individual ethic that predominates in medical health care.

## The ethical stance of economists

Utilitarianism forms the ethical basis of economics as a discipline. Utilitarian ideas, theories and techniques are concerned with 'the common good or the greatest happiness of the greatest number' and this philosophy is closely associated with the writings of Jeremy Bentham (1834). Vilfredo Pareto also brought concepts of social welfare into economics with his notion that improvement in the allocation of resources takes place if at least one person is made better off and nobody else worse off (Pareto 1935). The translation of utilitarian, social welfare concepts into economics revolves around the issue of distributive justice which is the ethical concept most relevant to choosing priorities.

There are question marks over a number of issues, for example, whether it is possible to measure utility, health, ill health or social welfare. Another issue is whether the economic deprivation suffered by one group of individuals can be offset by the freedom from economic deprivation of another group of individuals. According to most economists, it is possible to measure these things and to make trade-offs between population groups. Economics is a mostly 'positivist' discipline that takes an aggregate, societal view of resource allocation. From this perspective it concurs reasonably well with traditional population-based, health promotion approaches that form part of contemporary public health (Lupton 1995).

## Efficiency and equity – the trade-off and ethical dilemma

There are competing theories of social justice. Rawles (1972) had a concern with both liberty and the social good, which he argued should be distributed to the advantage of those at the 'bottom of the pile'. The worst that could happen to people in a society run according to Rawlsian social justice would be better than the worst that could happen under a utilitarian regime. Economic evaluation techniques highlight the importance of using scarce resources in the most efficient way possible to maximize overall health gain. Ideas of prioritization and rationing of health care are closely linked to concerns that health demand is infinite and yet resources are finite. The argument that a public, taxation-funded NHS and primary care led public health system will never be able to meet all the demands of an expectant public, new expensive technologies, new drugs and an ageing population concur with the view expressed in both Wanless reports (Wanless 2002, 2004). (See Chapter 2 for a perspective on government policy for public health.)

Few people would argue against spending public health resources in the best way possible. The argument about what is the 'best way' is a normative question that can be viewed from the perspective of maximizing health gain or addressing health inequalities. Current government policy gives a strong direction to the latter. But there are many more attendant difficulties attached to the notion of reducing health inequalities than there are to achieving efficiency or maximizing health gain. Reduction of health inequality requires that equity be defined for these purposes, but as Pereira (1993) notes, there are at least six main definitions of equity which makes its pursuit problematic. (See Chapter 9 on approaches to tackling inequalities in health.)

Using QALYs as the measure of maximizing health gain has been criticized on numerous fronts. Unfortunately, economic evaluation as a technique does not seem to have evolved in order to encompass renewed emphasis upon equity in public health policy and requirements to consider user perspectives in evaluating services. It can be argued, therefore, that economic evaluation focusing as it does upon individual value does not adequately reflect social values (Dolan 1998) and is not the best guide to the distributional effects of a given course of public health action in many cases.

Economic evaluation is ethical from the standpoint of the utilitarian. In the utilitarian welfare function (Bergson 1938) that applies to health, 'happiness' is replaced by 'health gain' and the philosophy of spending resources to maximize health gain is applied.

## Conclusion

The application of economic evaluation within the arena of public health research and practice has become a given. Cost-effectiveness analysis using QALYs and a balance sheet approach to a range of perspectives in economic evaluation is the way forward. However, the involvement of service users, their families and carers should be sought at both the problem definition and equity assessment stages of evaluation. (See Chapters 6 and 8 for more about involvement of the public in health care decisions.) The use of systematic review of the current economic knowledge of a problem is an essential step in the development of public health guidance as an end in itself and a check and balance.

Public health interventions have numerous outcomes, many levels and objectives that are not always clear. In view of these features, and cost-consequences are recommended by NICE for further development and application at a local level.

More effort should be made to ensure greater scientific validity of evaluations in public health research. However, the complexity of many public health interventions may require non-standard modifications to study designs or a greater role for qualitative methods in the practice of economic evaluation.

**Suggested further reading**

I make a strong recommendation to readers to look up the following evidence briefing on the issues and considerations involved in the 'economic appraisal of public health' programmes and interventions.

Kelly, M., McDaid, D., Ludbrook, A. and Powell, J.E. (2005) *Economic Appraisal of Public Health Interventions: Evidence Briefing*. London: National Institute for Health and Clinical Excellence. http://www.publichealth.nice.org.uk/page.aspx?o=513209

Two books from the Understanding Public Health Open University Press are accessible and well worth dipping into for more about evaluation in health care and economic evaluation. These are:

Fox-Rusby, J. and Cairns, J. (2005) *Economic Evaluation*. Berkshire: Open University Press.

Smith, S., Sinclair, D., Raine, R. and Reeves, B. (2005) *Health Care Evaluation*. Berkshire: Open University Press.

A good guide to health needs assessment is:

Cavanagh, S. and Chadwick, K. (2005) *Summary Health Needs Assessment at a Glance*. London: Health Development Agency.

Finally an oldie but a goodie on economic evaluation in social welfare, excellent summary of the relevant considerations in measuring costs and outcomes and some suggestions of ways to capture 'hard' and 'soft' information to incorporate within an appraisal is:

Sefton, T., Byford, S., McDaid, D., Hills, J. and Knapp, M. (2002) *Making the Most of it: Economic Evaluation in the Social Welfare Field*. York: York Publishing Services for the Joseph Rowntree Foundation.

# 17

# STUART HASHAGEN AND SUSAN PAXTON
## Frameworks for evaluation of community health and well-being work

**Editors' introduction**

Community health and well-being work is a core area of 21st century public health. Complex programmes are implemented by a range of professionals working in partnership for health and well-being, linking with communities themselves who are one of the driving forces.

A feature of the public health guidance from NICE is a renewed focus on the *outcomes* of public health interventions that seek to improve health and well-being in communities. But evaluation of complex, context-specific health and well-being programmes is difficult; as outcomes do not readily lend themselves to the established 'hierarchy of evidence' that has dominated traditional evidence-based public health practice.

In this chapter, all public health workers involved in community health and well-being programmes will find something useful in the mix of theory and practical advice for 'measuring' outcomes in terms of community health and well-being.

The authors from the Scottish Community Development Centre start by discussing what is meant by community health and well-being and the core values that inform policy and practice. A model of health and well-being developed by Labonte is used to inform a model for planning and evaluation called the Learning Evaluation and Planning model (LEAP). It focuses on the three core elements of healthy people; strong communities, sustainability and good quality of life.

The authors conclude that the current emphasis on evidence-based practice challenges public health workers to establish approaches to planning and evaluation that are informed by social principles, shifting the culture towards a more participative and empowering ethos.

## Introduction

This chapter is concerned with approaches to planning and evaluation for practice in the new public health. Its focus is mainly on tools for planning and evaluating community development work developed by the Scottish Community Development Centre. These tools are discussed with reference to policy in Scotland and more widespread issues in the evaluation and validation of what we shall call 'community health and well-being action'. This area of practice combines community development with action on health inequalities, and informs partnership work. Community health and well-being action is characterized by:

- a concern with health inequalities: a recognition that unacceptable inequalities in health persist, that they affect the whole of society, and that they can be identified at all stages of the life course from birth to old age;

- a focus on community development: working to support communities to take action on needs and issues that they identify as critical;

- linking a social model of health to the medical approach: recognizing that good health is a product of social, economic and psychological factors, and not simply a medical or physiological matter;

- recognition of policy and organizational change: the health and quality of life in communities is affected as much by the policies and practices of the NHS and other organizations, as by the nature of the communities themselves;

- an emphasis on partnerships: acknowledging that effective strategies for change often require a partnership approach – drawing on the knowledge, skills and resources of the community and service agencies, working to a shared vision for change; and

- clear and explicit value systems: these help to shape and frame planning, action and evaluation of practice; these values are, of course, subject to review and debate.

A good conceptual basis for the approach is provided by Labonte (1998), who encourages us to take a fresh look at health and well-being and to consider how those interested in promoting good health might understand their task.

Labonte's model encourages those involved in community health and well-being action to consider what actions can facilitate outcomes for health and well-being for people and communities. Labonte goes on to describe the risk factors that prevent people from enjoying health and well-being and these risk factors are identified in Figure 17.1.

The application of the model in Figure 17.1 helps to understand the connection between risk factors and well-being. By focusing on the way people relate to communities and services, well-being action is particularly concerned with psychosocial factors and the risk conditions described therein. Where community empowerment leads to people in communities having more skills and confidence, better networks, more control and influence over their lives, the psychosocial risk factors are addressed. Similarly, engagement in well-being activity to improve the quality of community life will have an impact on risk conditions such as poverty, pollution and low socio-economic status.

From a community well-being practice perspective it is helpful to understand

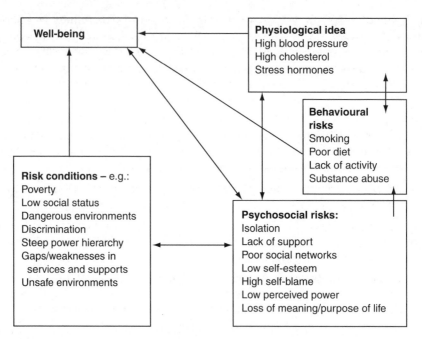

**Figure 17.1** Risk factors in Labonte's model

behavioural factors as largely consequent on psychosocial factors and risk conditions. Thus, if people feel better about themselves and if they are less exposed to external risk conditions, they are more likely to pay attention to their behaviour patterns and be more prepared to take action. If we can accept this approach a chain of actions and impacts can be established and built into our evaluation frameworks.

The above discussion locates 'community health and well-being action' in Scotland firmly within 21st century public health as defined in the Introduction to this book.

## Powers of well-being in Scotland

The term 'well-being' is used for two reasons in the definition of community health and well-being action. First, the outcome of new public health interventions is to improve the health and well-being of a community. This distinguishes new public health interventions from 'health' interventions by the medical emphasis that links them to the outcome of control or absence of illness (Jones 1999). Second, in the Scottish legislation for local government, the power to promote 'well-being' has been introduced and each local authority now leads a Community Planning Partnership, involving health services, police and fire, economic development and other partners, alongside the community and voluntary sector, to realize this goal. A linked development is the establishment of Community Health Partnerships (NHS Scotland 2003) which have responsibility for developing and managing primary care and community health services, again on a partnership basis involving community representation. Each CHP is linked to a Patient Partnership Forum through which the participation of patients and the community is routed. The Scottish Health Council (SHC), which replaced the former local health councils, has a role to monitor and report on the performance of NHS Boards in the areas of community engagement and public involvement. To inform its work, the SHC has adopted the National Standards for Community Engagement (Communities Scotland 2005). One may thus conclude, that at a policy and structural level, there is a significant recognition of the importance of at least involving the public in decisions about priorities and plans, and that the importance of multi-agency actions to address health and well-being matters is recognized.

In 2003, the Minister for Health in the Scottish Executive issued a 'challenge' to the community development and health sector to demonstrate and evidence the impact that the approach has, and could potentially have in informing and influencing policy. A multi-agency 'task group' was established to work on the three elements of the challenge: to develop an approach, strategy and action plan for the community-led pillar of the Health Improvement Challenge; to engage in a capacity building process to enable local, regional and national stakeholders to be involved in the process of informing a strategy; and to work closely with the Scottish Executive and other partners to support effective action on key elements of the approach within the overall Health Improvement Challenge. Four themes emerged during the development of recommendations: these were the importance of securing sustainability (including funding) of community health initiatives, the need to improve the quality of planning and partnership work, the need to build the capacity of all partners in taking forward the agenda, and the need for a greatly improved evidence base on the impact and value of community-led approaches.

## Learning organizations

Learning organizations have to be able to evaluate their actions in order to learn from experience. The link between learning and evaluation is reinforced in community health and well-being action because of the difficulty of establishing direct connections between causes and effects in this field. Learning organizations need to be able to monitor the environment in order to be able to identify critical change rapidly and accurately and be able to base their future action on such evidence.

## Participative evaluation

If the aim of community health and well-being action is to increase participation and ownership, it follows that the planning and evaluation process should be consistent with this. Thus, the community must be included as partners in the process. Community development action seeks to develop agendas for change from within communities and to draw on the resources of the community to lead them towards change. It follows that community development cannot be evaluated appropriately using externally imposed, cost-based or output quantifying models or measures. Having clear goals and considering the costs involved are important, but these should be established collaboratively by the community and other partners in consultation with funders or policy makers (Hancock *et al.* 1999).

## Challenges in evaluating community well-being

Community development work has outcomes that can be isolated and measured. Community development has to communicate how the things it does (actions) have effects (outcomes) which may be described as 'empowering communities'. But there are ways in which 'empowering communities' can be defined and measured, provided that those involved in community health and well-being action take the trouble to specify both outcomes and outputs and how they are linked (Hashagen 1998).

In Box 17.1 we show with an example how community development needs

---

**Box 17.1**   Food co-operatives for community health and well-being

A food co-operative might provide a wider range of foodstuff at a lower price than retail shops. It may provide recipes and cookery classes, and it may involve a number of community members as volunteers and helpers. All these things are outputs and all can be measured as such. But their presence may also contribute to wider outcomes of benefit to the well-being of families and the wider community.
  These wider benefits are:

• the provision of food at low cost allows residents to save the time and money other-wise used to travel to distant supermarkets with gains to family (and community) income;

• a cooking class or group might support families to ensure that children eat more healthily, as well as increasing skills;

• the voluntary activity around the co-op may bring gains in social contact and social support, both of which contribute to well-being; and

• the co-op may be able to source local products, and supply local schools, care homes or community centres, thus contributing to the local economy.

  These outputs all contribute to community health and well-being but are difficult to capture with data, but each of these outcomes can be measured using quantitative or qualitative information.
  To evaluate a community initiative such as a food co-op the traditional approach has been to look directly at the outputs and ask:

• How many people are members?

• How well run is the co-op?

• What is the turnover of the co-op?

• What foods are actually available?

Many approaches to evaluation ask for little more than numbers, but what we should really be interested in capturing is the wider impact of the co-op on the well-being of the community. It may be harder to assess this, but ways can be found. In the example above, additional income to families can be calculated, and any changes in skills and diets can be assessed through feedback. The gains from voluntary activity and local sourcing or supply can be observed or self-reported. It is important to define possible outcomes in order to know where to look for the evidence of change. While many other factors may impinge on such factors, it is nevertheless important to recognize that the co-op should be able to assess its own value.

indicative rather than prescriptive approaches to evaluation. The stakeholders in any community development initiative must develop and agree the measures and indicators of change that they intend to use, and these will be unique to the particular situation and context of the work. While the indicators chosen may reflect national targets or may use examples set elsewhere, the actual choice should be made by the stakeholders in the initiative so that the things that are assessed are those that are of key significance to that initiative and owned by all the participants (Dixon 1995).

## The Scottish Community Development Centre: Learning Evaluation and Planning framework

The LEAP (Learning Evaluation and Planning) framework, developed at the Scottish Community Development Centre (SCDC) offers an approach to planning and evaluation that has been widely adopted in Scotland, in community health, community learning, volunteering and environmental programmes (Chanan 2002; NHS Health Scotland 2003).

The Scottish Community Development Centre (www.scdc.org.uk) was established in 1994, and is a partnership between the Community Development Foundation and the University of Glasgow. SCDC aims to encourage the adoption of community development approaches in public policy and to support and promote best practice in the field by developing practice frameworks and supporting their use, and encouraging networking and learning. LEAP was originally written to support the work of community learning and development partnerships in Scotland, having been commissioned by the Scottish Executive. The model was found to be helpful by practitioners in a range of disciplines, and SCDC has subsequently been commissioned to write versions tailored to the role of several stakeholder groups in community development (see Box 17.2).

The *LEAP for Health* framework suggests that there are three broad areas in which outcomes can be sought and that each of these can be divided into several major 'dimensions' on which plans and evaluation can be framed. These dimensions are expressed in Figure 17.2.

---

**Box 17.2**   The principles of *LEAP for Health*

---

- Needs, problems and issues: the first principle is that community health and well-being work must start with a clear understanding of the needs, problems and issues experienced by the people, groups or communities in question. This is in contrast to the idea of resource-led planning, in which agencies start with a known level of resources, equipment and budgets, and decide how those resources will be applied. Such an approach is unlikely to be accepted by the recipients. A need-led approach implies that time and energy can be wisely invested in reaching a clear understanding of issues that can be owned and shared by the community.

- Clarity about outcomes and outputs: the need to specify the outcomes that are expected from a piece of work, and how they will impact on health, how they will be measured, and how action can be directed towards achieving the outcomes.

- Participative learning: community health and well-being learning requires a different sort of culture to the 'experts on top' model. It thrives within an 'experts on tap' environment. To do this, and to establish ways of working that are based on empowerment, we need to move towards a culture where people, whether patients, local groups or community organizations, are engaged in defining needs and developing solutions, drawing on the expertise of others where appropriate. This means moving to a culture based on dialogue, equality and involvement. The effectiveness of moving towards this can itself be planned for and evaluated.

- Partnership-based: the earlier discussion about the complexity of health and well-being, and the importance of physical, mental, community and policy factors in experiencing well-being, leads to the inevitable conclusion that no single agency or interest can promote well-being alone. Partnerships are needed both to bring a range of perspectives to bear on a problem or issue and to work to find solutions that are likely to work. Partnerships are also vehicles for securing participative practice and a needs-led approach.

---

## Well-being practice: healthy people

*LEAP for Health* proposes four main areas within which the idea of 'healthy people' can be defined and organized into an analytical framework. These are:

- Awareness and knowledge: the extent to which people have the knowledge they need to be able to exercise informed choices about the way they live. This is an important factor in mental well-being and a prerequisite for the other factors.

- Confidence, choice and control: the extent to which people are able to make informed decisions in their own interests and are able to assert themselves in social situations and in their dealings with public agencies.

- Self-reliance and independence: which suggests that 'community health' is where people are able to lead and control their own lives relatively autonomously,

Community networks: linking people and communities

Healthy people: capable, confident and connected

Community environment: promoting well-being

Strong community: skilled, organized and involved

Quality of life: economic skill, environmental, cultural, political

Healthy community
• Equitable
• Sustainable
• Liveable

Community participation: engaging in change

**Figure 17.2** A model of community well-being

drawing on services and supports where necessary, but not being over-dependent on them.

• Connection to community: responding to the idea that well-being is a social idea; the way in which people contribute to and draw from their relationship to others is crucial.

If it can be agreed that these things are indeed core aspects of 'well-being', the activities of partners can be directed towards achieving them, and that they can in some way be measured. For some agencies in the NHS it can be a considerable culture shift to accept that such outcomes should be recognized and measured, and that it is an important part of well-being practice to encourage such a shift. To reach a clear understanding of what outcomes can be expected and how these might be measured is a central part of this debate. The LEAP model is intended to facilitate this process.

## Well-being practice: strong communities

The second main area of well-being practice is in the area of communities. The culture and structure of communities is a significant part of the context in which people, especially excluded people, live their lives. Community well-being practitioners should therefore be interested in the way communities work and organize themselves, how they contribute to well-being, and how they interact with the wider political and economic environment. Box 17.3 indicates the features of strong communities.

Participation is a crucial component of well-being as Box 17.3 demonstrates. Consequently those involved in community health and well-being practice should attend to the ways in which communities are encouraged to participate. This will include consideration of practical and financial barriers, the response of public

---

**Box 17.3**   The dimensions of strong communities

---

- *Community skills*: the knowledge, skills and confidence of people in the community have a direct relationship to the 'connection to community' dimension discussed above. Communities do need community skills to be successful and the idea of a 'learning community' encapsulates this idea.

- *Equalities*: given that inequality and exclusion are key factors in poor health, work in communities should reflect an explicit equalities and justice agenda. This principle is core to community development work and must consequently be built into its evaluation. It is possible to define equalities and develop indicators or measures to assess progress and change.

- *Community organization*: in simple tasks such as sharing childcare or helping a housebound neighbour, or major initiatives like a healthy living centre, people in communities can organize to meet needs, solve problems or make good use of common assets. Communities can also develop strong networks of care and support, and can also establish networks between communities, or between groups of people confronting similar issues (see Chapter 8 for a detailed look at networking for health).

- *Community involvement*: the fourth area is the nature of the interaction between a community and the social, economic and political forces that shape its experience. The term 'community' refers not only to communities of place (villages, streets and housing estates) but also to communities of common interest. It is important to note that community as a term extends to people with diabetes, parents with pre-school children, or senior citizens, members of the same church or social club.

---

agencies or the availability of information, advice and support. As noted earlier, indicators for all these areas of community strength can be developed. The *Achieving Better Community Development (ABCD)* handbook (Barr and Hashagen 2000) does so, and a more recent publication by Skinner and Wilson (2001) gives useful guidance on how these factors may be assessed and evaluated. (See also Chapters 4, 6 and 8 for more about participation.)

## Well-being practice: quality of community life

The third broad area of interest for community health and well-being is the quality of the environment in which people and communities live and work. Again it is possible to recognize that some environments will tend to promote well-being, while others will have an opposite effect. Individuals and communities are of course interested in quality of life; partnerships have a central role in helping identify visions for change and strategies for shared action. Outcomes in this area are very much specific to a given context, but are likely to be concerned with one or more of the issues in Table 17.1.

**Table 17.1** Quality of life

| Dimension | Health-related outcomes |
|---|---|
| Community economy | Increased community income<br>Reduced community expenditure<br>Enhanced community assets<br>Elimination of waste and wasteful practices<br>Beneficial external investment decisions |
| Community service | Good networks of care and support<br>Accessible services<br>Responsive services<br>Community involved in service decisions and priorities |
| Community health and safety | Safe routes and spaces<br>Environmental pollution control<br>Energy efficient housing and community buildings<br>Knowledge and awareness of healthy behaviours and choices |
| Community culture | A sense of identity and culture<br>Celebration of difference<br>Opportunities for recreation, physical activity, self-expression<br>Freedom of religious expressions |
| Local democracy | Elected representatives and policy makers engage with the community<br>Organizations adopt democratic and participative practices<br>Community institutions are open, accountable and democratic |

## Action planning

The discussion above should have helped to establish that health and well-being are broad concepts that must be tackled robustly and in partnerships involving communities as well as agencies. In addition, health and well-being is crucially about the outcomes from practice, not simply the outputs. It may be difficult, but it is possible to find and agree ways to measure well-being and the process of change in community development. Figure 17.3 summarizes the integrated action planning and evaluation framework at the heart of the LEAP approach.

Good planning and evaluation helps to focus on change and to improve practice. It provides evidence that action is making the best use of limited resources and thus provides partners and communities with confidence that they are benefiting from the action. Put simply, good practice requires that all participants in action for community development have:

- a clear view of what they are trying to achieve (*vision*);
- agreement on how they intend to get there (*planning*);

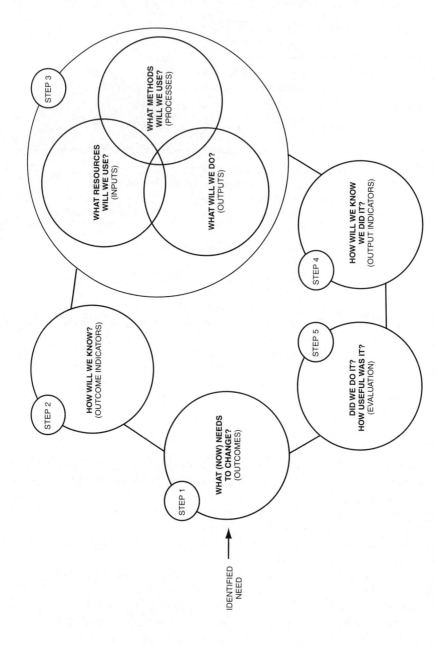

**Figure 17.3** LEAP action planning and evaluation framework

The figure contains the following labelled elements:

- IDENTIFIED NEED
- STEP 1 — WHAT (NOW) NEEDS TO CHANGE? (OUTCOMES)
- STEP 2 — HOW WILL WE KNOW? (OUTCOME INDICATORS)
- STEP 3 — WHAT RESOURCES WILL WE USE? (INPUTS); WHAT METHODS WILL WE USE? (PROCESSES); WHAT WILL WE DO? (OUTPUTS)
- STEP 4 — HOW WILL WE KNOW WE DID IT? (OUTPUT INDICATORS)
- STEP 5 — DID WE DO IT? HOW USEFUL WAS IT? (EVALUATION)

- evidence to show whether they have done what they said they would do (*monitoring*); and
- evidence to tell them whether they achieved what was intended, whether anything else happened and whether these things were helpful or not (*evaluation*).

*LEAP* materials go into detail about the way in which this model may be applied in practice. The key points are that:

- At step 1, a future vision should be established, again through dialogue and debate. This vision should be described as a set of desired outcomes or future conditions to be achieved.
- Step 2 requires indicators or measures for these outcomes to be agreed, so that all participants will have a common understanding of how success will be recognized, or evidence that the action had not succeeded in achieving the intended outcomes. It is important to note that these discussions can apply at a high level over the long-term (for example in planning a local authority-wide five-year health improvement conference) as well as a short-term, local level event such as a health fair. It is also important that local indicators are set to reflect community priorities, and these may reflect or interpret higher level policy indicator. It is also important to value anecdotal and qualitative evidence, for example, the isolated elderly man who was prescribed an exercise class following a heart attack, but who derived the greatest benefit from building a new network of friends in the coffee bar afterwards.
- Step 3 asks those involved in partnerships to consider and specify the resources they have; the methods they intend to use; and what actions they will implement to lead towards the outcomes desired.
- Step 4 asks partners to monitor whether what they intended actually took place. This is a key aspect of their accountability to each other. The collection of evidence for monitoring and evaluation is critical: in this way we can begin to understand and analyse change and its impact.
- Step 5 the relationship between the outputs (what was actually done) and the outcomes (the effect of what was done) is examined in order to learn and shape future action. Again this is a critical opportunity to take stock, to review progress, to learn lessons about practice, and to feed back.
- The cycle iterates and Step 1 then asks, 'What now needs to change?'

The LEAP model outlined in Box 17.4 thus provides a framework within which both the quantity and the quality of the inputs, processes and outputs can be measured, as well as the impact. In assessing impact, considerations of effectiveness, equity and efficiency can be included. The approach integrates planning and evaluation, emphasizing process and qualitative factors, and attempts to specify the types of outcomes that can emerge from community development-based work.

---

**Box 17.4**   A checklist for community development programme evaluation

- Are we gaining a new understanding of community needs and issues?
- Are we being effective in tackling them?
- Are we being inclusive?
- Are the participants achieving their personal goals?
- Are we building community assets and resources?
- Is our work empowering people?
- Are we building a culture of collaboration, participation and sustainable change?
- Are we learning from our experience?
- Are we contributing to health and well-being?
- Are we making the best possible use of the resources we have?
- Do we have the evidence we need to influence future decisions?

*Source:* Barr 2002

---

## Tensions between LEAP-like and traditional frameworks for evaluation

Traditionally the field of health has invested heavily in evaluation, with medical practitioners needing to know as much as possible concerning the impact and possible side effects of a particular course of action. This has led to an emphasis on calls for epidemiological and quantitative evidence and, in the field of community well-being, evidence that community activities are having a demonstrable impact on rates of illness or on behaviours such as people's diets, their exercise or smoking habits. Needless to say, such connections are almost impossible to substantiate and alternative approaches to evaluation are needed if, in the longer term, the health impacts of well-being work are to be acknowledged. (This reflects the tensions inherent in an evidence-based approach to health care and public health discussed in Chapter 14.)

The tradition of evaluation in community participation is rather different. It has often emphasized process over outcome, looking at the quality of people's experience rather than the impact of the work (East End Health Action 2000; Partners in Change 2001). Until recently, community development has not been good at establishing or 'owning' the criteria on which it can be evaluated. In these circumstances, participants and practitioners in community health and well-being have criticized funders for:

- imposing agendas that may have little to do with local views of needs and issues;
- emphasizing value for money above all else;
- giving more weight to the quantity of the outputs than the quality of the outcomes; and
- giving too little attention to understanding the processes of achieving change.

## LEAP and Healthy Living Centres in Scotland

A Leap Support Unit (LSU), funded by NHS Health Scotland and the Big Lottery Fund is based at the Scottish Community Development Centre and among other activities provides support based on the LEAP model to all the Healthy Living Centres in Scotland. An example of the way one of these has drawn on this support is discussed below. Box 17.5 provides background information about the project.

---

**Box 17.5**   Healthy Living Centre Dumfries and Galloway

Building Healthy Communities (BHC) was initiated in January 2001 through the Lottery funded Healthy Living Centre National Programme to tackle health inequalities in the four most deprived areas of Dumfries and Galloway. This is a large rural area with distinct communities and poor access to health services. Neighbourhoods here have a combination of social, economic, and built environment-related problems that contribute towards poor health and well-being. Dumfries and Galloway (D&G) Partnership for Health concluded that action should be taken 'at strategy and policy level as well as within communities themselves to reduce inequalities' and 'to enable communities to work alongside policy and decision makers'. In 2004, BHC reached the end of its Big Lottery funding but successfully negotiated continuation of its work with local service providers. As a result of sustainable change, local staff are now employed within D&G NHS as part of the Health Improvement Team and their budget is augmented by four other local funding streams, including Community Regeneration Funding.

BHC comprises a regional consortium and four local partnerships based in targeted areas of Dumfries and Galloway – Upper Nithsdale, Stranraer and West Wigtownshire, Wigtown and the Machars, and North West Dumfries. This structure is designed 'to strengthen the infrastructure for health both regionally and locally by building healthy communities from the bottom up' (BHC Strategic Plan). 'There is a particular focus on tackling the root causes of ill health through increasing activity in social support and community development targeted at the most vulnerable' (BHC Bid Paper 2001). BHC does this by: providing access to volunteering opportunities thus building local people's skills, confidence and knowledge; developing a range of health initiatives such as self-help groups, befriending, counselling, healthy eating and exercise activities. It thus contributes towards health improvement and supporting local groups and representatives to participate in decision-making structures. The impact on health inequalities is achieved by focusing on those areas designated as those most experiencing poor health.

---

## Case study – Building Healthy Communities in Dumfries and Galloway

### Building Healthy Communities in Dumfries and Galloway – the vision of change

BHC seeks to influence cultural change within the NHS by promoting a community development approach to tackling health inequalities in a wider policy and operational context. The emergence of Community Planning Partnerships and Community Health Partnership structures, which are based on national policy objectives, provides new avenues for BHC to widen its influence and scope for delivery. BHC participation within these partnership structures provides them with opportunities to evidence their impact on community health and well-being to a range of statutory and voluntary service providers, and in turn promotes the success of this approach.

BHC actively embraced the purpose of LEAP in its ability to inform and create learning opportunities for participants. The organization was not afraid to highlight where initiatives were not achieving an impact on health outcomes and relished the opportunity to tackle new needs as expressed by the communities in which they operated.

The setting up of the HLC Support Programme as part of the LEAP Support Unit provided BHC with the opportunity to take up a variety of supports that were previously missing or too costly. Following a process of negotiation with all the stakeholders, the regional partnership agreed on the following common vision:

> Building Healthy Communities is a strong dynamic partnership which reduces health inequalities using a community development approach to promote the health and well-being of the most disadvantaged individuals, families, communities and organisations in Dumfries & Galloway.

The Partnership felt that this encapsulated their overall purpose and identity, based on the needs they felt were important.

### Building Healthy Communities in Dumfries and Galloway – the process of change

The process used involved setting aside a number of planning development days involving both the Regional Partnership and the four local partnerships. As part of the LEAP process, the Regional Partnership was encouraged to think about the lessons they had learned from previous work, and the needs they hoped to commonly address. Following negotiation and as part of the overall strategic process, the Partnership agreed that the need to reflect their values and principles (community development, empowerment, participation) and approaches (capacity building, evaluation, training) should be detailed as such in the strategic plan. It was clear that these issues required attention to make the partnership effective in achieving their impact on reducing health inequalities, promoting health and well-being, and influencing policy and sustainability.

## Building Healthy Communities in Dumfries and Galloway – the outcomes of change

The outcomes sought were that:

- BHC Regional Partnership is a strategic, inclusive and effective partnership.
- BHC contributes towards reducing health inequalities and promotes a sense of well-being throughout Dumfries & Galloway in supporting the area partnerships to impact at local level.
- BHC influences local and national policies, decision makers and service providers.
- BHC is sustainable and financially viable at all levels within its structure.
- BHC supports the use of innovative practices with communities, statutory and voluntary agencies at local, regional and national levels.
- BHC takes a common approach in supporting the area partnerships in their development and capacity to tackle health inequalities at a local level.

The area partnerships identified needs to be addressed around the following categories:

- Partnership – improved communication, trust, knowledge and practice exchange, joint working, confidence, profile, practice, capacity.
- Health – raise awareness of and promote use of supports and services available, challenge stigmas, promote healthy lifestyles.
- Community – identify needs, support groups, build skills, knowledge and confidence, ensure participation, support networks.

In expressing these needs, they recognized that the need to strengthen their partnership had a direct influence on their ability to impact on health outcomes and the relation associated with achieving these through a capacity building approach. This is also evident with the Regional Partnership in that their first outcome is being a strategic, inclusive and effective partnership. As such the local partnerships identified the following outcomes:

1 To be dynamic effective organizations which promote joint working and stakeholder involvement.
2 To provide leadership in the local community by raising awareness, promotion and use of support, challenging stigma, barriers to health and promoting healthy lifestyles.
3 To assist communities to be fully engaged in identifying community needs and are empowered to be involved in decision making which affects them within their areas.
4 To empower individuals, families and communities by building on their existing skills, confidence and knowledge.

## Outcome indicators

Having agreed the outcomes sought, attention was paid to negotiating and establishing a series of outcome measures and indicators which would allow them to gather useful evidence and assess successful achievement of outcomes. Participants were encouraged to think about what would tell them their outcomes would be achieved, and if both the qualitative and quantitative information required was readily available to those tasked with gathering it. The need to gather baseline data was emphasized and indicators were revised if this was not available.

These indicators were identified by the Regional Partnership in relation to the outcome: 'BHC contributes towards the reduction of health inequalities and promotes a sense of well being in Dumfries & Galloway'.

- Increased referrals and self-referrals to BHC and associated health care providers (statistics of referrals against existing baseline information).
- Increase in BHC users' personal satisfaction on individual and community well-being (user feedback – a well-being tool or Richter scale used at regular intervals with individuals and groups).
- Requests for BHC to expand to other areas (number and nature of requests recorded).
- Number of SIMD (Scottish Index of Multiple Deprivation) areas targeted within area partnerships (existing number of areas and number of SIMD areas increased).
- Number of direct beneficiaries – those who are in receipt of services across the local partnerships.
- Number of volunteers (local partnership records).
- Quality of volunteer support (feedback forms, Individual Learning Plans demonstrating progress).
- Number of local initiatives (Local Partnership Plans and recordings).
- Quality of local initiatives (initiative evaluations identifying participant levels and quality of involvement, staff and volunteer recorded observations).

These indicators were developed at regional level, although it is clear that they rely heavily on the local partnerships recording and gathering information on their outcomes and outputs. This demonstrates the clarity of purpose required in terms of setting inter-related outcomes at different levels of an organization, and in this instance the regional partnership's ability to impact on this outcome was largely through their ability to co-ordinate and support work at local partnership level.

## Action planning

The Regional Partnership identified a number of inputs, processes and outputs to achieve their outcomes which were negotiated and agreed on by all participants. The Partnership found it relatively easy to identify what resources were required as this reflected their existing budgets, staffing and volunteering levels and organizational capacity which in turn reflects the reality of funding restrictions, or arguably the realistic focusing on what they knew to be achievable while still aspiring to their agreed outcomes.

The processes identified were a combination of participants evaluating what had been successful in their past experience and identifying any other approaches which were required to best achieve the desired results. Again, the processes reflected the purpose of the organization, so at regional level this focused on their ability to co-ordinate an impact on health outcomes at a local level and the promotion of this impact with a number of strategic partners and agencies. Their processes therefore identified strategic promotion, co-ordination, and support and recording mechanisms.

The outputs of the Regional Partnership were specific to their role with the local partnerships and their strategic purpose. These included a regional strategy, marketing strategy, volunteering strategy, accumulation of all area health impact outcomes data, staff supervision, six monthly review sessions, and participation in a number of strategic forums and partnerships.

## Monitoring

The partnership was encouraged to think about what arrangements they would need to put in place to effectively monitor their activities and impact as initiatives were progressed. These were identified as:

- Regular local partnership reports – quarterly.
- Evaluations from local initiatives detailing quantitative and qualitative data – participants identify achievement of outcomes and quality of involvement.
- Staff supervision mechanisms – observations through experience/analysis/learning.
- Budget reports.

## Evaluation

The partnership agreed on the following arrangements based on their monitoring arrangements and evidence criteria as specified in their outcome indicators.

A six month review process – to review progression towards outcomes by identifying barriers/difficulties to achievement, produce and review evidence accumulation in relation to indicators, and record lessons learned with all stakeholders through allocated development days.

Annual evaluations – to co-ordinate formal recordings and assessment of staff, volunteers and participants judgement of achievement towards outcomes.

Development days will be set aside to allow participants to assess the impact against outcomes and the value of outputs/methods in achieving them. Used in conjunction with the monitoring data, these evaluations will directly affect the future direction of outputs and methods in the longer-term outcomes of BHC. It has also been agreed that external evaluations will be commissioned as and when appropriate by BHC.

## Lessons learned

### Level of stakeholder involvement

This is arguably *the* most significant factor in the LEAP process adopted by BHC. The impact of area staff and representatives involvement in each other's development was recognized as invaluable to progressing not only the process, but the appropriateness of setting outcomes, indicators and the realistic identification of action plans. This resulted in levels of peer support never before experienced by participants, and the exchange of learning and experience facilitated the way in which participants enjoyed, valued and responded to the task at hand. Significantly, these levels of stakeholder involvement are actively highlighted and promoted with other Healthy Living Centres in their ability to achieve sustainability and success.

### Commitment and investment in learning

The levels of participation in evaluating previous work and the focus of those involved to honestly judge the effectiveness of these initiatives indicated an overall commitment to learning what was successful and unsuccessful. This resulted in a number of initiatives being passed to other agencies where appropriate, or 'dropped' as a result of being unrealistic or unachievable. While it could be argued that this would have happened without the use of LEAP, the implementation of the process through support of the LSU, helped partners to think about their activities, and provided them with an opportunity to review these activities in relation to their purpose.

By identifying and revising a series of outcome indicators, BHC hopes to actively contribute towards the emerging evidence base within the field of community health and well-being. These indicators should provide BHC with a set of evidence criteria which can be used to indicate progression towards/achievement of their outcomes. The fact that the indicators have been revised as part of the planning process in terms of learning and continuous improvement will further enhance their ability to assess the achievement of outcomes. Further revisions through the evaluation process are inevitable and this is arguably the most valuable part of the LEAP process in terms of improved learning and efficiency using a participatory planning and evaluation approach with all stakeholders.

## Conclusion

The new approach to 21st century public health is in its infancy (although many have been arguing its value for some time). The encouragement in policy to adopt innovative approaches, to engage communities and to work in partnership provides new challenges and opportunities. Equally, the emphasis on evidence-based practice challenges those of us committed to a social model of practice to propose and establish approaches to planning and evaluation that are informed by social principles.

Working to give such approaches a weight equal to traditional methods is an effective strategy in shifting the culture towards a more participative and empowering ethos. Frameworks such as LEAP offer a set of critical questions that all participants can use, and which encourage public health programmes to work effectively in partnership, and to work collaboratively with communities.

Building Healthy Communities in Dumfries and Galloway has invested heavily in integrating LEAP, a planning and evaluation tool which allows them to focus on their purpose and practice. It also allows stakeholders to judge their effectiveness in tackling health inequalities in line with national and local priorities. Ultimately the evaluation process will determine the achievement of outcomes, and this will inform the continuous and integrated planning and evaluation process required of evolving, learning organizations within this field. This will hopefully inform those organizations involved in the work of community health and well-being, and provide practical lessons in the effort, evidence and ability to impact on health inequalities using a community development approach.

---

**Suggested further reading**

Barrett, G., Sellman, D. and Thomas, J. (2005) *Interprofessional Working in Health and Social Care. Professional Perspectives*. Basingstoke: Palgrave Macmillan.

Smith, S., Sinclair, D., Raine, R. and Reeves, B. (2005) *Health Care Evaluation*. Basingstoke: Open University Press.

# 18

## GABRIEL SCALLY
# Sustainable development and public health: arm in arm

**Editors' introduction**

In this chapter, the author highlights the importance of the relationship between sustainability and public health. The chapter helps public health workers to think about the future by focusing on several core themes. These include learning from historical public health, the need to function in a shared power world, the impact of excessive consumption on the health profile of populations and the impact on the well-being of the planet. Focus moves to the global issues of AIDS, transportation, obesity and tobacco as complex public health issues which impact considerably on sustainable development.

The impact of transportation on global warming is discussed as a global problem. The author moves to focus on the UK and demonstrates that the dilemma appears to be the chasm between a high level of public recognition of the existence of climate change and the causative link to transportation and subsequent personal choice.

The author discusses the obesity time bomb and provides the links for the reader between the macro and micro level considerations in this complex area and advocates that public health programmes on food and health need to have sustainable agriculture at their core.

The final section of the chapter considers the environmental impact of tobacco recognizing that the struggle to win people away from tobacco is usually waged on the ground of personal health. The author argues that there is a low awareness of the very strong evidence of the disastrous effects that tobacco cultivation, manufacture and usage have on environments worldwide.

The author concludes by reiterating that the connections between sustainability and public health are very clear and that public health professionals must ensure they enhance their natural role in sustainable development.

## Introduction

Convinced as we all are of the high ideal and real value of the health of all, we must stop being indifferent toward questions of hygiene and public health, and each one of us must make it his duty, so far as in him it lies, to promote this object in the future.

(Max Von Pettenkofer 1873)

Attempts to write about the future of public health are blessed with certain advantages as well as disadvantages. Among the advantages are both the indisputable importance of the public health function and the certainty that a collective response to ill health will be a core requirement of whatever civil and political structures are in place in the future. The nature of threats to health and well-being may alter, sometimes decisively, over time but nonetheless the principles of public health responses will undoubtedly remain reasonably consistent. The response needs to be timely, effective and acceptable. What has developed, and will develop further, is the importance of working across organizational boundaries whether at local, national or international level. The climate within which public health practice is conducted is changing and the centrality of health concerns is emerging in many areas of civil society. Nowhere is this more apparent than in sustainable development where the crisis of global warming has catapulted concerns about the physical and human environment to the fore.

## A shared power world

One of the immense advantages possessed by our predecessors in public health was the simplicity of the organizational structures with which they had to deal. The sanitary revolution in the United Kingdom in the 19th century was closely linked to the full flowering of municipal power. The role of central government was much more limited than today and the range of powers and responsibilities exercised by the corporations and councils that ran civil society at the local level was truly enormous. Their responsibilities literally ranged from the cradle to the grave and their full control of housing and utilities meant that their influence over the conditions under which people lived was all pervasive. When harnessed for the improvement of health this range of powers placed local authorities in a position of enormous strength. They were of course also responsible for the employment of the public health workforce including medical officers of health and sanitary inspectors. The role of the public health officials was largely to convince their employers, and important colleagues such as the borough engineer, that action to improve health needed to be taken.

The successes of the sanitary revolution in developed countries created a change situation. The decline in infectious diseases, largely due to improvements in the living and working conditions of the population, left a gap in expectation in relation to the public health function. The steady growth in organized health services during the 20th century created the opportunity for the development of a new skill set based on the organization and administration of medical services. Endeavour in relation to the organization of health services is an important part of public health practice. In particular the issue of quality of health services is a central issue and one where public health skills are important. This has been particularly so in the area of screening where the development of screening services and their quality assurance is highly dependent on the application of specialist public health skills. The retreat into matters of personal health service provision represented a trend in many developed countries and by the end of the 20th century public health had moved far from its nineteenth century routes.

## Recapturing the common ground

The successful worldwide eradication of smallpox and the control of many of the common infectious diseases seemed, in the second half of the twentieth century, to have reduced the need for traditional public health approaches. The emergence of AIDS, multiple drug resistance and other novel threats have altered this view and led to a resurgence of traditional public health approaches. The effect of AIDS in many lesser-developed countries has been to set back the economic and social prospects of entire continents. This has happened before in history. In medieval times bubonic plague devastated the population of Europe and caused the most profound of social upheavals. Bubonic plague however soon ran its course and the process of economic development regained momentum. AIDS, however, after almost two decades shows little sign of abating in developing countries and its social and economic effects are devastating.

In the countries of Western Europe in contrast, the effects of AIDS have been moderated by a combination of behavioural change and the availability of expensive pharmaceutical therapies. The plagues that continue to affect developed countries are, in contrast, the diseases of over-consumption. Consumption not only in the tradition-ally understood way of oral indulgence but also associated with the unsustainable consumption of the earth's resources. Although the effects of tobacco consumption and excessive dietary animal fats have been known for decades to be linked to the epidemic of coronary heart disease, the lessons of the necessity of health supporting lifestyles have been focused on the reduction of known individual risk factors, rather than an approach which takes a global and holistic approach to human health and also locates in the context of place and community. Thus while the war against tobacco consumption may slowly be being won in the developed countries the profit hungry tobacco industry develops new markets in the developing world. And while effort was expended in tackling tobacco the patterns of dietary consumption, in league with the decline in physical activity has led to the epidemic of obesity that now threatens to overwhelm developed societies. When hospitals and crematoria are forced to invest in new operating tables and furnaces because of the huge increase in the weight of the people with which they deal, then the time for a new approach has surely come.

The response of health professionals and the pharmaceutical industry to the epidemic of obesity has predominately been to develop new ways of helping indi-viduals cope with or control already gained weight. This has, in some cases, taken the form of substances to inhibit absorption of some nutrients or the development of exercise prescription schemes. The health sector has not yet fully appreciated the connection between the pattern of diseases of consumption and the structure and organization of our collective functioning as communities. The decline in physical activity as part of the routine of daily life requires a response from the health community which sees the reversal of that decline as just as important as the development of therapies for the diseases that result. Thus the design of hospitals and health centres which must, of course make access a priority, must make it easy for those using or working in the facilities to journey to and from in ways which incorporate exercise, whether it be walking or cycling.

> Healthy diets and physical activity, together with tobacco control, constitute an effective strategy to contain the mounting threat of noncommunicable diseases.
> (World Health Organization 2004)

## Global warming and human decline

Just as the impact of excessive consumption has had a major and potentially devastating effect on the health profile of humankind so has it had an equally, if not potentially more, serious impact on the well-being of the planet. The intellectual struggle to achieve consensus on the existence of global warming has been successful and 'denyers' are retreating in the face of overwhelming evidence of global climate change.

The potential effects on the health of populations are enormous. The change in growing conditions in general and rainfall in particular, will mean that agricultural activity will alter or cease altogether in many parts of the world. Change in climate will also change the pattern of distribution of vector borne disease and render existing control mechanisms inadequate. The very things that are responsible for the destruction of human health are also responsible for the destruction of the global ecosystem and the creation of global warming. However the connections have yet to be made in a way that commands the attention of the public health community and provokes concerted action on behalf of those whose main concern is the health of the population rather than the planet.

## Transportation and global warming

It is estimated that in developed countries the transport sector is responsible for approximately 25 per cent of the production of the gases contributing to global warming but only about half this amount in the cities of developing countries. However the net effects of global warming are likely to have a much more serious impact on the livelihoods and well-being of people in developing countries, with a rise in sea level threatening the continued existence of a small number of them. Despite the clear connection there is yet to be a commensurate response in terms of action to achieve modal shift in transport methods. Indeed the trends seem to be going the other way (World Bank 2002).

The substitution of car-based transport for walking and cycling is an international phenomenon seen as far apart as China and the UK. In China the number of cars has exploded from around 1 million in 1994 to 5 million in 2001, and to 16 million in 2004 (World Bank 2006). Attempts to create space for all these cars has resulted in the reduction of long-standing pedestrian and cycling rights of way and even the removal of urban greenery. Despite these efforts the growth in car ownership has resulted in a steady decline in travel speeds in Beijing. The enormous amount of urbanization that has taken place in China has increased home to work travel distances but public transport infrastructure has failed to keep pace.

In the UK the number of trips undertaken per person by foot or on bicycle declined by 15 per cent between 1996 and 2005 (Department for Transport 2006). In 2005 only 19 per cent of adults lived in households without access to a car. In 2005 car travel accounted for four-fifths of the total distance travelled and this has remained stable in the last 10 years. The potential for modal shift in transport is indicated by the fact that in 2005 nearly a quarter of all car trips were less than two miles in length. The amount of scope for shift is indicated by the fact that more trips of between one and two miles were made as a car or van driver than by walking and cycling combined.

Research in the UK has demonstrated that while public recognition of the existence of climate change has reached the maximum feasible level there is a much lower appreciation of the causative link to transportation and to personal choice in this area (Anable *et al.* 2006). The achievement of substantial modal shift would seem to require a major increase of understanding and the translation of that understanding into intention to make changes. A key influence will be the available infrastructure for walking and cycling. It will be a major task to achieve the necessary investment in new facilities. The evidence in favour of such investment is convincing. Analysis of the costs and benefits of a number of cycling and walking schemes in the UK has suggested that there is a benefit to cost ratio of 20 : 1 (Sustrans 2006).

## Obesity time bomb

The World Health Organization estimates that more than 1 billion people worldwide are overweight and that 300 million of them are clinically obese. They believe that this constitutes an epidemic and is a time bomb in terms of non-communicable diseases. The distribution of obesity worldwide varies and often exists alongside gross undernutrition. Current levels of obesity levels range from less than 5 per cent in China, Japan and some parts of Africa, to over 75 per cent in urban Samoa. But within-country variation is common so even in relatively low prevalence countries such as China, rates are almost 20 per cent in some urban areas (World Health Organization 2006).

In the UK it is estimated that in 2003 22 per cent of males over the age of 16 years were obese and a further 43 per cent were overweight. With respect to women the relative figures were 23 per cent and 33 per cent. In respect of children aged 2 to 15 years 17 per cent of boys were obese and a further 15 per cent overweight. For girls the relative figures were 16 per cent and 15 per cent. Predictions for 2010 have been made on the basis of current trends and they indicate the proportion of men that are obese will have risen from 22 per cent to 33 per cent and for women the proportion that are obese will have risen from 23 per cent to 28 per cent. Among children the estimates are that the proportion of boys that are obese will have gone from 17 per cent to 19 per cent and for girls obesity will have gone up from 16 per cent to 22 per cent.

The precise causation of the increase in obesity is not completely understood. In the UK food consumed outside the home is excluded from the National Food Survey (NSF) and this calls into question whether the fall in calorie intake that the NFS demonstrates is an accurate reflection of overall dietary intake. It is however certain that obesity is a function of the combination of calorie intake and physical activity. Thus the effort required to reverse the global trend must be active in both the areas of diet and physical activity. In respect of food there is a recognized need to increase understanding of food and nutrition and to engage people of all ages in developing an appreciation of where their food comes from and how it is produced.

The UK government's approach in its key policy report *The Strategy for Sustainable Farming and Food* linked food, health and sustainable development together for the first time in an official document (Department for Environment, Food and Rural Affairs 2002). It was brought about by the enormous consequences of both the foot and mouth outbreak in 2001 and the emergence of Bovine Spongiform Encephalitis. The strategy quotes estimates that it takes 10 tons of raw food materials to make one ton of processed food. The remaining 90 per cent is discarded as waste, along with packaging waste including 12 billion plastic carrier bags and 29 billion food and drink cans every year in the UK (Department for Environment, Food and Rural Affairs 2002).

The distance our food travels is one area where the environmental costs can potentially be enormous and where public health programmes aimed at increasing consumption of fruit and vegetables must be linked to sustainability. The amount of kilometres of air freight of food for the UK has increased by 140 per cent between 1992 and 2002. Although air freight represents only 0.1 per cent of food-related vehicle kilometres it creates a grossly disproportionate 11 per cent of food transport $CO_2$ emissions (Smith *et al.* 2005). The inclusion of crunchy vegetables in the government's School Fruit Scheme has enabled a higher level of domestic sourcing to be achieved. There is however much further effort needed by all those working in public health to ensure that programmes on food and health have sustainable agriculture at their core.

## Tackling tobacco via environmental activism

According to the World Health Organization, tobacco accounts for about 5 million deaths every year. It seems sure to be central to public health concerns for decades to come. The battle against tobacco is fought with vigour by public health practitioners across the world. There has been substantial progress in a growing number of developed countries in protecting people in the workplace from the effects of environmental tobacco smoke. The example of Ireland in particular, which became smoke free in 2004, has had a substantial influence in this regard. Little attention is however paid to the wider environmental costs of tobacco. In the Framework Convention on Tobacco Control there is one short paragraph (Article 18) that hints at the environmental aspects of tobacco production.

> In carrying out their obligations under this Convention, the Parties agree to have
> due regard to the protection of the environment and the health of persons in

relation to the environment in respect of tobacco cultivation and manufacture within their respective territories.

(World Health Organization 2003c)

Tobacco is produced in more than 100 countries and its cultivation occupied more than 4.1 million hectares of land in 2000 with 32 per cent of that total being in China and a further 11 per cent in India. The world trade in tobacco increased from 1.3 million tonnes in 1971 to 2.0 million tonnes in 1997 (Food and Agriculture Organization 2003). The major environmental degradation caused by this cultivation is explained by the nature of the plant, its cultivation and the process of curing. It has been estimated that worldwide 200,000 hectares of deforestation occurred annually between 1990 and 1995 due to tobacco cultivation and curing. This constituted almost 5 per cent of the deforestation occurring in tobacco growing countries (Geist 1999). In some countries it has a disproportionate effect, with tobacco causing 26 per cent of deforestation in Malawi, 31 per cent of Bangladesh, 41 per cent in Uruguay and 45 per cent in the Republic of Korea (World Health Organization 2002c). In addition to deforestation, the delicate nature of the tobacco plant and its susceptibility to disease means that huge amounts of fertilizers, pesticides and herbicides are used in its production. Up to 16 applications of potentially toxic chemicals may be made during the growing cycle (Action on Smoking and Health 2004).

The process of turning tobacco into consumer products generates enormous amounts of waste. The global tobacco industry produced in 1995 an estimated 2,262 million kilos of manufacturing waste and 209 million kilos of chemical waste. The production of tobacco is only the beginning of the effect of tobacco on the environment however. In 1995 it is estimated that globally 5.535 trillion cigarettes were sold by the tobacco industry and of these an estimated 83 per cent had filters. The waste generated by tobacco is visible each time you walk on a city street or visit a beach used for recreation.

The struggle to win people away from tobacco is usually waged on the grounds of personal health. The very strong evidence of the disastrous effects that tobacco cultivation, manufacture and usage have on environments worldwide has not reached the consciousness of the public. At a time when environmental awareness is at an all-time high this provides an outstanding opportunity for public health advocates to open up another front in the war against tobacco. The environmental argument might well have an effect on many whom while willing to run a risk with their own health will not wish to be associated with damage to the global environment.

## Conclusion

It should be especially clear in medicine that we cannot have well humans on a sick planet. Medicine must first turn its attention to protecting the health and well-being of the Earth before there can be any effective human health.

Thomas Berry (1991)

As long ago as 1991, in his Schumacher Lecture, Thomas Berry, a Catholic priest and cultural historian in the United States, issued a clarion call for health professionals to address the issues of the global environment. The public health fraternity could have been expected to be in the forefront of that effort, but have on the contrary been virtually absent from the development of sustainable development in the public policy arena. The connections between sustainability and public health are blindingly obvious, except perhaps to those who are content being blind. If public health professionals do not assume their rightful place in the vanguard of sustainable development then they will in due course be judged to have failed their professional duties and their fellow citizens.

---

**Suggested further reading**

---

Anable, J., Lane, B. and Kelay, T. (2006) *An Evidence Base Review of Public Attitudes to Climate Change and Transport Behaviour.* London: Department for Transport.

Brown, V.A., Grootjans, J., Ritchie, J., Townsend, M. and Verrinder, G. (2005) *Sustainability and Health. Supporting Global Ecological Integrity in Public Health.* London: Earthscan.

HM Government (2005) *Securing the Future: Delivering UK Sustainable Development Strategy.* CM 6467. London: The Stationery Office.

HM Treasury (2006) *Stern Review: Economics of Climate Change.* London: The Stationery Office.

Secretary of State for Environment, Food and Rural Affairs (2005) *The UK Government Sustainable Development Strategy.* London: The Stationery Office.

# Glossary

Website glossaries and other sources used:

http://www.thecareforum.org.uk

http://www.neighbourhood.gov.uk/glossary.asp?pageid=10#n

Ewles, L. and Simnett, I. (2003) *Promoting Health: a Practical Guide*, 5th edn. Edinburgh: Baillière Tindall.

The Glossary contains explanations of jargon and abbreviations used in this book and in public health generally.

**Advocacy**  Representing the interests of people who cannot speak up for themselves because of illness, disability or other disadvantage.

**Aetiological explanations**  Explanations of causation, often to be carefully distinguished from associations by epidemiological elimination of bias, chance and confounding.

**Agenda 21**  A worldwide movement to address environmental concerns for the 21st century, focusing on *sustainable development*. All local authorities are required to develop a Local Agenda 21 Strategy.

**Anti-urbanism**  A movement that fulfils a desire for people to move from city and town dwelling.

**Average/unit cost**  The total cost of a treatment or programme divided by the total units.

**Bayesian statistics**  The main distinguishing feature of the Bayesian approach is that it makes use of more information than a frequentist approach. Whereas the latter is based on analysis of what we could call 'hard data', that is data which are generally well-structured and derived from a well-defined observation process, Bayesian statistics also accommodate 'prior information' which is usually less well specified and may even be subjective.

**Best value**  It replaced compulsory competitive tendering. It requires all local authority service providers, both internal and external, to justify the efficiency and effectiveness of their services. It aims to ensure that local councils get the best service provider to deliver each local service whether this is the council, voluntary or private sector. It emphasizes quality and service user involvement as well as cost. Councils must carry out best value reviews on all their services.

**Boards** Governing bodies of many organizations including the NHS hospital trusts and *primary care trusts*. A board decides on the overall strategic direction of the organization and ensures that it meets its statutory financial and legal obligations. Boards are usually made up of executive and non-executive directors. The board is answerable for the actions of the organization.

**Care Standards Act 2001** Established for the first time a national regulatory body for both the independent and statutory sector. From April 2002 the National Care Standards Commission (NCSC) will take over all the present functions of local authorities and health authorities on the registration and regulation of children's homes, independent hospitals, independent clinics, care homes, residential family centres, independent medical agencies, domiciliary care agencies, fostering agencies, childminding, nurses agencies and voluntary adoption agencies. The Act also set up a General Social Care Council to register social care workers, set standards in social care work and regulate the education and training of social care workers.

**Care Trust** NHS organization which provides *health and social care* services, formed by the merger of local authority social care services with NHS primary and *community health services*. Care trusts started to be set up in 2002.

**Case controlled study** A research study that compares the characteristics of a group with a specific characteristic such as a disease ('cases') with a comparable group without that characteristic ('controls').

**Centre for Public Health Excellence** Develops public health guidance on the promotion of good health and the prevention of ill health.

**Chemoprophylaxis** The administration of a chemical, including antibiotics, to prevent the development of an infection or the progression of an infection to actively manifest disease, or to eliminate the carriage of a specific infectious agent to prevent transmission and disease in others.

**Chronic disease** Refers to disease which is recurrent or long lasting.

**City Challenge** A five-year government initiative, now completed, aimed at transforming specific rundown inner city areas and significantly improving the quality of life for local residents within its policy area.

**Clinical governance** A system for ensuring high quality NHS treatment and care services. It is the framework by which NHS organizations are accountable for continuously improving the quality of their services through a systematic process that is underpinned by a commitment to lifelong learning.

**Clinical networks** Networks of health professionals for treating patients by sharing information and resources.

**Clinical surveillance** Refers to the systematic collection, analysis and interpretation of health data and other hazards which can impact on public health.

**Cohort study** A research study that examines a whole group over time.

**Collaboration** A generic term referring to all processes where people work together as individuals, collectives or societies.

**Commission for Health Improvement (CHI)** A national body responsible for ensuring good quality services in the NHS.

**Commissioning** In the context of commissioning health services, this means deciding what health services and programmes are needed to improve the health status of the local population and ensuring that they are provided.

**Communicable disease** Diseases which can be transmitted from one person to another; often called infectious or contagious diseases.

**Community action** Activity carried out by people under their own control in order to improve their collective conditions. It may involve campaigning, negotiating with or challenging authorities and those with power.

**Community development** Working with people to identify their concerns, and support them in collective action for the good of the community as a whole.

**Community Health Council (CHC)** An independent body which advised the local NHS until it was replaced in 2002 by *Patient Advice and Liaison Services (PALS)*. Was sometimes known as 'the patients' watchdog'.

**Community health project** A programme of work organized by an agency or a local organization with the aim of improving health by some combination of community activity, self-help, *community action* and/or *community development*.

**Community health services/community services** Health services provided in people's homes or from premises in the community such as GP surgeries, health centres, clinics and small community hospitals (as distinct from services provided in major hospitals).

**Community health champions** Refers to local people or workers who are seen to have a particular role or commitment to health issues in a community and will be referred to by local people for advice. The role of health trainers is modelled on this.

**Community health work** This is *community work* with a focus on health concerns, but generally health is defined broadly to include social and economic aspects, so that community health work may encompass almost as broad a range of activities as community work which does not have a specific health remit.

**Community Planning** Refers to an approach to planning which is based in local communities and begins with the views and opinions of local residents.

**Community safety partnerships** Multi-agency partnerships which work to create safer places for people to live and work in. They tackle problems such as anti-social behaviour, domestic violence and crime. They aim to reduce accidents and injuries.

**Community strategy** The Local Government Act 2000 requires local authorities to prepare a community strategy to promote the social, economic and environmental well-being of their communities. A community strategy should offer a 10-year perspective. *Local strategic partnerships* will co-ordinate the community strategy.

**Community work** Working with community groups and organizations to overcome the community's problems and improve people's conditions of life. Community work aims to enhance the sense of solidarity and competence in the community.

**Confidence interval** The range of values above and below a statistic, such as an average or a percentage, within which the real value probably lies. Values outside these limits could have happened by chance. A reduced confidence interval means that we can be more certain that the result did not happen by chance.

**Confounders** Variables that affect the apparent strength of relationship between a risk factor and a health outcome due to their own relationship with both; for example, smoking confounds the strength of the relationship between exercise and heart disease because it is itself related to both exercise and heart disease. Only by controlling for the effects of confounders can the true relationship be determined.

**Consequence** Any change in the natural history of an illness or disease brought about by the intervention.

**Cost-effectiveness analysis** A type of economic evaluation study design in which the consequences of different interventions are measured in terms of a uni-dimensional outcome measure, for example, life years or blood pressure.

**Cost-utility analysis** A type of economic evaluation study that compared competing interventions in terms of cost per utility. Utility is an outcome measure comprising quantity and quality of life following an intervention and is usually expressed in quality-adjusted-life-years (QALYs).

**Cost/QALY gained** The ratio used in cost-utility analyses to make comparisons between competing interventions programmes. The ratio for each intervention is expressed in terms of monetary cost per QALY gained.

**Critical Appraisal** The process of assessing and interpreting evidence, by systematically considering its validity, results and relevance to your own work.

**Cross-sectoral** Working across the boundaries of different *sectors*, e.g. health services working together with businesses and voluntary organizations. Sometimes also called intersectoral or multi-sectoral.

**Decile** In describing distribution of a variable (such as income), a decile describes one-tenth of the total population.

**Demography** The study of the statistics about a population such as birth, death and age profile.

**Department for Transport, Local Government and the Regions (DTLR)** Government department also responsible for housing, regeneration and elections.

**Devolution** The responsibility for the overall management of relations between the UK government and the devolved administrations in Scotland, Wales and Northern Ireland has moved from the then Office of the Deputy Prime Minister (ODPM) to the Department for Constitutional Affairs (DCA). The Department for Communities and Local Government (replaced ODPM in May 2006) is now responsible for the English region.

**Director of Public Health** Currently describes the role of an individual who has responsibility for the health of the local population covered by the primary care trust he/she is appointed to. Each year the Director of Public Health is legally required to produce an annual report addressing local population health concerns.

**Do nothing** Used in research as a comparator. A scenario in which the present system of intervention or delivery of health care is described as it currently is with no changes.

**Double devolution** 'Double devolution' refers to the government's commitment that they will devolve to local government, and councils will seek to devolve to, and engage with neighbourhoods and communities.

**Downstream policy** Tackling health problems that have not been prevented.

**Ecological fallacy** The error in assuming that factors influencing the different incidences of disease *between* large populations (such as whole nations) are necessarily the same as those influencing individual variation in disease susceptibility *within* populations.

**Economic evaluation** A comparative analysis of two or more alternatives in terms of their costs and consequences.

**Effectiveness** The extent to which a programme, activity, service or treatment achieves the result it aimed for, e.g. the effectiveness of a public health programme would mean the extent to which it had achieved objectives such a specified positive change in the population's health.

**Efficiency** A term applied to a programme or activity to denote how good the *process* (as distinct from the *outcome*) is in terms of, for example, value for money or use of time; it is about how results are achieved compared with other ways of achieving them.

**Epidemiology** The study of the distribution, determinants and control of disease in populations.

**Evaluation** The process of assessing what has been achieved (the *outcome*) and how it has been achieved (the *process*).

**Evidence-based** Based on reliable evidence that something works. For example, 'evidence-based health promotion' means health promotion projects or programmes based on sound research which shows that they are likely to be successful in achieving their aims.

**Evidence-informed** Wider evidence than evidence-based. Evidence-informed comes from a range of quantitative and qualitative methods that informs decision making.

**Expert Patient programme** A government programme set up in 2002 as a self-management course giving people confidence, skills and knowledge to manage long-term health conditions.

**Fiscal policy** An economic term describing the actions of government in setting the level of public expenditure and funding it.

**Geographic Information Systems (GIS)** For example enables mapping of population data on geographic boundaries together with other data sets.

**Gini coefficient** An indicator of income inequality in a population. If income is distributed equally, the coefficient is equal to 0 and if a few people hold most of the wealth, the coefficient is closer to 1.

**Global Outbreak Alert and Response Network (GOARN)** Supported by the World Health Organization as socio-economic and environmental and tools for analysis of the information.

**Grassroots workers** Refers to people working in communities and providing face-to-face services to local people.

**Green Paper** A government policy document issued for consultation. Becomes a *White Paper* when it is finalized and formally agreed as government policy.

**Hard to reach groups** Refers to those groups in the population who do not easily engage with formal activities or use services for a variety of reasons. These groups often suffer high levels of disadvantage.

**Health 21** A policy framework published by the World Health Organization in 1999, which set out 21 targets for the European region in the 21st century.

**Health Act 1999** It gave powers to health and local authorities, Primary Care Trusts (PCT) and NHS Trusts to make arrangements to pool funds, have a lead organization commission services and/or provide integrated services. The Act also allows health authorities and PCTs to transfer money to local authorities or the voluntary sector for any health-related local authority function. Local authorities can transfer funds to health authorities and PCTs to improve the health of people in their areas.

**Health Action Zones (HAZs)** Established to provide a framework for the NHS, local authorities and other partners to work together in reducing local health inequalities. HAZs vary in size and type of area they cover. They are areas of high health need selected by government for special funding and health programmes.

**Health alliance** Partnership of two or more organizations working together to promote health. Often also called health 'partnership'.

**Health and social care services** A wide range of services to meet people's health and social needs. Health care tends to mean services provided by the NHS, and social care usually refers to services provided by local authorities, especially social services departments. In many instances, services are provided by both. They may also be provided by the *voluntary sector*.

**Health authority** The statutory NHS organization responsible for health services for a defined population until abolished in 2002, when its responsibilities were largely taken on (in England) by *primary care trusts* and *care trusts*.

**Health Development Agency (HDA)** National public body established in 2000 which is a resource for public health work in England. Its remit includes maintaining a database of research evidence about what works to improve health and providing information about the effectiveness of health improvement programmes. There are comparable bodies in Scotland (the Health Education Board for Scotland), Wales (the Health Promotion Division of the National Assembly for Wales) and Northern Ireland (the Health Promotion Agency for Northern Ireland).

**Health education** Planned opportunities for people to learn about health, and to undertake voluntary changes in their behaviour.

**Health For All** A movement started in the 1980s by the World Health Organization. It included *health targets* for year 2000 and stressed basic principles of promoting positive health through health promotion and disease prevention; reducing *inequalities in health*; community participation; co-operation between health authorities, local authorities and others with an impact on health; and a focus on *primary care* as the main basis of the health care system.

**Health gain** A measurable improvement in health status, in an individual or population, attributable to earlier intervention.

**Health gap** The difference between the overall health of the better off and more deprived communities in a population.

**Health impact assessment (HIA)** Systematic process to estimate the effects of a specified action – a programme, policy or project – on the health of a defined population, e.g. what difference a new transport policy would have on the health of the population affected by it.

**Health Improvement and Modernisation Plan (HIMP)** A three-year local rolling plan of action to improve health and services for health and social care, led by local NHS organizations such as *primary care trusts*. (Formerly known as Health Improvement Programme.)

**Health inequalities** The gap between the health of different population groups. People who are better off have better health and are less likely to die under the age of 75 from all the main diseases that kill. Improving the health and life expectancy of the less well-off to reduce this gap is a priority of the NHS Plan.

**Health needs assessment** A systematic method for reviewing the health issues facing a population group leading to agreed priorities and resource allocation that will improve health and reduce health inequalities.

**Health promotion** The process of enabling people to increase control over, and to improve, their health.

**Health target** A quantified, measurable improvement in health status, by a given date, which achieves a health objective. It provides a yardstick against which progress can be monitored.

**Health trainers** These are new public health roles intended to work in local communities with local people providing information to help them develop and implement personal health plans.

**Health-related behaviour** What people habitually do in their daily life which affects their health. Usually refers to issues such as whether they smoke, whether they take exercise, what they eat, their sexual behaviour, how much alcohol they drink, and drug use. Sometimes simply called 'health behaviour'.

**Healthy Cities** A WHO initiative started in 1987 to improve health in urban areas. Involves collaborative work between local government, health services, local businesses, community organizations and citizens. The Health for All (UK) Network is the co-ordinating body for action on Healthy Cities within the UK.

**Healthy Living Centres** Centres or networks of activity which aim to promote good health, developed by partnerships with local participation. Funded from the National Lottery. HLCs are more people-centred than resource-centred and are based on programmes of activities, which can be held in existing premises. Examples are health and fitness screening in pubs and betting shops, health promotion in schools, linking arts and health, fitness for people with chronic conditions.

**Healthy Universities** WHO initiative to promote health in university settings.

**High risk approach** Public health approach which prioritizes people particularly at risk of ill health. (Compare with *whole population approach*.)

**Holistic** In the health context (as in 'holistic approach to health'), this means taking into account all aspects of a person – physical, mental, emotional, social – as well as their social, economic and physical environment. (As distinct from an approach which only focuses on, for example, the physical functioning of the body.)

**Hypertension** High blood pressure.

**Impact** A term sometimes used to describe short-term *outcomes*, e.g. the impact of a programme to encourage women to attend for a breast cancer screening test (mammogram) might be assessed in terms of how many women attended; the long-term outcome could be a change in the rate of women who died of breast cancer.

**Immunization** The use of vaccines to prevent individuals contracting serious and contagious diseases and so containing the spread of disease.

**Incidence** The number of new episodes of illness arising in a population over a specified period of time.

**Index of Deprivation (IOD)** It ranks districts to show relative deprivation. It uses 12 indicators of deprivation, covering such things as income, housing, education, environment, crime and health, and measures how much a district is above or below the national average. The individual scores are then added together to produce an overall 'deprivation' score for each district.

**Indirect costs** Productivity losses (decreases in the output of the economy) that occur as a result of health care interventions, for example, a person will need to take time from work to attend hospital for an operation.

**Infrastructure** All the things and systems that are not directly involved in providing a service, but which have to be there for services to operate efficiently or consistently, like management and administration, or communications and distribution networks. In the voluntary sector, the word is often used to describe organizations like local development agencies and umbrella groups which help other voluntary organizations work better by providing them with things like information, advice, training, co-ordination, representation.

**Input** The resources that go into a programme or activity, including money, time, staff and materials.

**Lay Members** Members of the public who sit on the boards of public bodies such as the health authority, the primary care groups and *primary care trusts*. They are sometimes called Non-Executive Directors. They are involved with the overall strategic direction of an organization rather than the day-to-day administration, which is done by paid staff. They are usually part-time. NHS lay members are usually recommended by the NHS locally from a regional register of potential members. The Secretary of State makes the final decision. Confusingly some primary care trusts and primary care groups also have lay representatives who can also be called lay members. The job of these lay representatives is to ensure the views of local people are taken into account and to help develop public participation.

**Lifecourse Approaches** Using a multidisciplinary framework to understand the importance of time and timing in association between exposures and outcomes at the individual and population levels.

**Life expectancy** The average number of years a given group of people can expect to live based on known statistics.

**Local Area Agreements (LAAs)** Government scheme giving local authorities more control over their finances and more freedom to work in innovative ways to benefit their communities.

**Local and Regional Services (LRS)** Division of the HPA, which supports local and regional services.

**Local Government Act 1999** It introduced *Best Value* and placed a duty on councils to continuously improve their services and replaced the previous Conservative government's compulsory competitive tendering (CCT) regime.

**Local Government Act 2000** It required all local authorities to introduce new ways of making decisions. All local authorities are required to choose between three different decision-making models all of which involve separating powers between an executive and assembly. The three models are: directly elected mayor with cabinet, cabinet with leader, directly elected mayor with a council manager.

**Local Involvement Networks (LINks)** In the Department of Health document 'A Stronger Local Voice' proposals for new Local Involvement Networks or 'LINks' are highlighted. These will gather and analyse information from patients and make recommendations to commissioners, providers and Overview and Scrutiny Committees.

**Local Public Service Agreement** Agreements between individual local authorities and the Government setting out the authority's commitment to deliver specific improvements in performance, and the Government's commitment to reward these improvements. The agreement also records what the Government will do to help the authority achieve the improved performance. http://www.local-regions.odpm.gov.uk/lpsa/index.htm

**Local Strategic Partnership (LSP)** Local NHS, local authority and other agencies working together to develop and implement local strategy for *neighbourhood renewal*.

**Meta-analysis** An overview of all the valid research evidence. If feasible, the quantitative results of different studies may be combined to obtain an overall result, referred to as a 'statistical meta-analysis'.

**Methicillin-resistant *Staphylococcus Aureus* (MRSA)** A Hospital Acquired Infection (HAI).

**Modernization Agency** Set up in the *NHS Plan* to support local NHS clinicians and managers redesign services to make them more patient-friendly, quicker and efficient, and to secure continuous service improvements across the NHS. It is responsible for the NHS leadership centre, and the NHS beacon services programme.

**Morbidity/morbidity rate** Illness/incidence of illness in a population in a given period.

**Mortality/mortality rate** Death/incidence of death in a population in a given period.

**Multi-disciplinary** Involving people from different professions (disciplines) and backgrounds.

**Multilevel approach** Can consider measures of health variation (for example, neighbourhood variance, intra-class correlation) to understand the distribution of health in the general population rather than only applying measures of association (for example, regression co-efficients, odds ratios) to understand contextual determinants of individual health.

**Multivariate techniques** Analytical and statistical methods that examine simultaneously the influence of many variables together on an outcome.

**Mutual Aid** Voluntary reciprocal exchange of resources and services for mutual benefit.

**National Health Service (NHS) & Community Care Act 1990** It gave local authorities the lead responsibility for the social care of older people and disabled people (including people with learning difficulties and mental health problems). It also acknowledged the role of carers.

**National Health Service (NHS) & Social Care Act 2001** It enables new integrated care trusts to be created, with health and social services working under one roof. It also made the NHS responsible for paying for nursing care in nursing homes but not personal care. It included proposals for major investment in GP surgeries; incentives to improve NHS perform-ance; a new contract for GPs and extending the scope of the direct payments scheme for disabled people. It also said that Patients' forums and Patient Advocacy Liaison Services would be set up in every NHS Trust. It established local authority overview and scrutiny committees to monitor the NHS locally.

**National Institute for Health and Clinical Excellence (NICE)** National body which provides patients, health professionals and the public with authoritative, robust and reliable guidance on 'best practice' in relation to drugs, treatments and services across the NHS.

**National Service Framework (NSF)** National document which sets out the pattern and level of service (standards) which should be provided for a major care area or disease group such as mental health or heart disease.

**National strategies for health** Government strategies to improve the health of national populations. Strategies current in 2006:

Northern Ireland: '*Investing for Health*' '*Health and Wellbeing: into the Millennium*'
England: '*Choosing Health: Making healthy choices easier*'
Scotland: '*Our National Health: A Plan for Action*'
Wales: '*Well-being in Wales*'.

**Neighbourhood Renewal Strategy** Strategy developed by local agencies with a co-ordinated approach to tackle the social and economic conditions in the most deprived local authority areas.

**Neighbourhood Management Programme** A way of encouraging stakeholders to work with service providers to help improve the quality of services delivered in deprived neighbour-hoods. http://www.neighbourhood.gov.uk/nmanagement.asp

**Neighbourhood Renewal Community Chests** A total of £50 million central govern-ment money in England over three years 2001–04 for small grants to community groups. http://www.neighbourhood.gov.uk/commchest.asp

**Neighbourhood Renewal Fund** Provides public services and communities in the 88 poorest local authority districts with extra funds to tackle deprivation. The original £900 million pot has been extended for a further three years and has been increased by a further £975 million. http://www.neighbourhood.gov.uk/nrfund.asp

**Neighbourhood Support Fund** Government grants of £10,000 upwards to community groups to enable them to re-engage disaffected young people. http://www.dfes.gov.uk/nsf/

**Network** A group of people who exchange information, contacts and experience for mutual benefit.

**New Deal for Communities** Government funding for deprived communities to support plans that bring together local people, community and voluntary organizations, public agencies and local business in an attempt to make improvements in health, employment, education and the physical environment.

**New public health** An approach to public health which emerged in the 1980s. It shifted emphasis from a *lifestyle* approach focused on people's individual health behaviour to a new focus on political and social action to address underlying issues which affect health such as poverty, employment, discrimination and the environment people live in.

**New Deal for Regeneration** It provides money through the *Regional Development Agencies* to 'regenerate' urban areas in England. Bids should be from partnerships of local authorities, LSCs, other public bodies, the private sector, the voluntary sector and local communities. Another strand of this is the *New Deal for Communities* which operates in areas with the highest levels of disadvantage and aims to tackle social exclusion.

**New NHS Modern Dependable** Government's White Paper published in December 1997 which outlined the government's plans for modernizing the NHS. It introduced *Primary Care Groups* and Health Improvement Programmes and announced the end of fund-holding.

**NHS Direct** A national NHS telephone help line (0845 4647) staffed by specially trained nurses.

**NHS Reform and Health Care Professions** Bill was published in November 2001. It means that most of the functions and commissioning budgets of health authorities will be transferred to *primary care trusts*. It will also establish the Commission for Patient and Public Involvement in Health which will encourage the public to get more involved with their local health trusts.

**NHS National Plan** It was published in July 2000, and is the Government's strategy for reforming and modernizing the NHS over 10 years. The plan says that the NHS has to be redesigned around the needs of the patient with fast, convenient care delivered to a consistently high standard. It acknowledges that the NHS cannot tackle health inequalities alone and calls for a new partnership between health and local government. Local government will be given power to scrutinize the NHS locally and Best Value will be extended to health.

**NHS Trust** An independent body within the NHS which provides health services in hospitals. Some NHS trusts provide specialized services such as ambulance services or mental health services.

**Noblesse Oblige** This is an expression used to infer that those with wealth, power or privileges have social obligations to those without such resources. Sometimes it is used negatively to imply that this can be done hypocritically or in a patronizing fashion.

**Nominal variable** A variable composed of categories with qualitatively different values, e.g. occupation or gender.

**Non-Governmental Organization (NGO)** Organization which is independent of government control.

**Non Statutory Sector** Anybody who is not part of the statutory sector. This includes voluntary and community organizations, private sector organizations, service users and carers.

**Null Hypothesis** The hypothesis that no association exists between two variables or no difference exists between two groups. Frequentist statistics only test the probability that the observed data are consistent with the Null Hypothesis.

**Obesity** A high level of body fat which is believed to carry a high risk of health problems.

**Opportunity costs** Potential benefits which will not be realized if one thing is done instead of another. For example, if there is only enough time and money for one health programme (A or B), and it is spent on A, the opportunity costs are the potential benefits of spending on B which will be foregone or sacrificed.

**Ordinal** A variable composed of categories with quantitatively ordered values, e.g. council tax bands.

**The OECD Organization for Economic Co-operation and Development (OECD)** This numbers 30 member nations, including Australia, Canada, Germany, Japan, Spain, UK and the USA.

**Ottawa Charter** A document launched in 1986 at an international World Health Organization conference in Ottawa, Canada, which identified key themes for health promotion practice.

**Our Healthier Nation** A government *Green Paper* published in 1998. It was the first government health strategy document in recent years to acknowledge the link between poverty and ill health and the need to do something about the social causes of ill health. Key aims were to improve the health of the population as a whole, to improve the health of the worst off and to narrow the health gap. It introduced Health Improvement (now Health Improvement and Modernization) Programmes and the idea of local authorities having a new duty to promote economic social and environmental well-being in their areas.

**Outcome** The end-product of a health programme or activity, expressed in whatever terms are appropriate, e.g. changes in people's attitudes or knowledge, changes in health policy, changes in the uptake of services or changes in the rate of illness.

**Overview and Scrutiny Committees (OSCs)** Set up in January 2003 in local authorities with social services responsibilities these committees have the power to scrutinize a range of local decisions and issues including those involved in health services. This contributes to local authorities wider role in health improvement and reducing health inequalities for their area and its inhabitants.

**Partnership** Different organizations such as Social Services, Health and the voluntary sector working together to achieve a common aim. The Partnership ideal is one of independent and equal partners who work closely within a common framework. Partnership is a key word for new Labour. All their policies stress the importance of departments and sectors working together to provide better and more seamless services.

**Partnership boards/forums** There is a partnership board/forum in each of the local authority areas. Partnership boards replaced the Joint Consultative Committees. They have wide representation with representatives from the health authority, local authority (a range of departments) primary care organizations and NHS Trusts as well as the voluntary sector, service users and carers. Partnership Boards aim to work together to develop a joint understanding of the need for health and social services within each area and to plan services from different agencies.

**Pathogenic** Causing disease.

**Patient Advice and Liaison Services (PALS)** Established from April 2002 within NHS trusts to help patients, families and carers to resolve problems or air concerns. Replaced *Community Health Councils*.

**Patient forums** Independent statutory bodies established within every NHS Trust to provide direct input from patients into how local NHS services are run. They will be expected to find out what patients and their carers think about the services they use. They will also monitor the quality of local services from the patient perspective and to work with the local NHS Trust to bring about improvements. See the Commission for Patient and Public Involvement in Health. Legislation is awaited to establish patient forums so there could still be changes.

**Performance management** Systematic management practices and monitoring systems which support people so that they can achieve their work objectives.

**Policy** A broad statement of the principles of how to proceed in relation to a specific issue, such as a national policy on transport, a local authority policy on housing, or a policy on how to deal with alcohol issues in a workplace.

**Pooled Budgets** The Health Act 1999 enabled Health Authorities, Primary Care Trusts, and local authorities to pool budgets. This means that they can each agree to put in funding to be used to meet the needs of a specific group of people, e.g. people with learning difficulties. Once the money is pooled it loses its identity as health or Social Services so that the expenditure will be based on the needs of the people who use the services and not on the level of contribution of each partner. Each partner still has statutory responsibility for functions carried out using the pooled fund.

**Portfolio approach** An approach to qualification through gathering pieces of evidence to meet a range of competencies.

**Powers of well-being** Under section 2 of the Local Government Act 2000 councils have the power to do anything which they consider is likely to promote the economic, social and environmental well-being of their areas, in order to respond to the needs of their local communities.

**Practice Based Commissioning (PBC)** PBC is about engaging practices and other primary care professionals in the commissioning of services. Through PBC, front-line clinicians are being provided with the resources and support to become more involved in commissioning decisions.

**Primary Care Organization (PCO)** A term used to describe *care trusts, primary care groups* and *primary care trusts.* Since 1997 there have been different initiatives in England, Northern Ireland, Scotland and Wales. In England the development of primary care has been focused on **primary care groups** and **trusts** (PCGs/PCTs) who have gradually taken on the majority of health care services and public health functions. In Northern Ireland health boards currently retain most commissioning and public health functions although there are proposals to develop English-type PCTs. In Scotland non-commissioning PCTs have been developed with Health Boards retaining commissioning and strategic public health roles. In Wales there are local health groups that have a wider **voluntary sector** and local authority representation than in England with the Welsh Assembly playing a strong strategic public health role.

**Prevalence** Measure of how much illness there is in a population at a particular point in time or over a specified period of time.

**Preventive** Used to describe something or some action which prevents something happening when it is undesirable.

**Primary care** Services which are people's first point of contact with the NHS, e.g. services provided by GPs, practice nurses, district nurses and health visitors. (As distinct from *secondary care* provided in hospitals.)

**Primary Care Groups (PCG)** NHS bodies which were first set up around 1999, formed from groups of GP practices in a locality. In the early 2000s PCGs became *primary care trusts* and were given more responsibilities.

**Primary Care Trust (PCT)** An NHS body whose main tasks are to assess local health needs, develop and implement *Health Improvement and Modernisation Plans*, provide *primary care* services and commission *secondary care* services from hospitals and specialized services run by

*NHS trusts*. PCTs have a board with a majority of non-executives and a separate professional executive committee whose members include GPs, nurses and representatives from local authority social services. In 2006 a reorganization of primary care will reduce the numbers of PCTs in England.

**Primary health care team** Health workers usually based at a GP surgery or health centre who provide *community health services*. They include GPs, district nurses, practice nurses and health visitors.

**Primary prevention** Stopping ill health arising in the first place. For example, eating a healthy diet, not smoking and taking enough exercise are factors in the primary prevention of heart disease.

**Process** All the implementation stages of a health programme or activity which happen between *input* and *outcome*.

**Proximal mechanisms** Pathways of influence that most immediately lead to the outcome. Poor diet may be the proximal effect on the health of low income families.

**Public health** Preventing disease, prolonging life and promoting health through work focused on the population as a whole.

**Public health network** An initiative linking people involved in public health work together to develop skills, share good practice, develop joint practice and tackle local public health issues.

**Public health teaching networks** Links public health departments and educational institutions to maximize opportunities to teach public health and ensure all relevant groups in the workforce are exposed to PH learning.

**Public sector** A collective term for organizations which are controlled by the state and publicly funded, such as the NHS, local authorities, and the police, fire, probation and prison services. Often also called statutory sector/services because they are governed by laws (statutes). (See also *sector*.)

**Public Service Agreements** Agreements that set out what government departments should achieve in return for the money allocated to them.

**Qualitative** Concerned with quality – how good or bad something is according to specified criteria, usually expressed as a description in words rather than numbers. For example qualitative data about the outcome of a breast screening programme could include users' descriptions of how they felt about it: whether they found it painful, embarrassing, well-organized etc. (Compare with *quantitative*.)

**Quality** How 'good' something (such as health service) is when judged against a number of criteria.

**Quality Protects** Services for children in need, including vulnerable children in local authority care.

**Quality standard** An agreed level of performance negotiated within available resources.

**Quantitative** Concerned with measurable quantity, usually expressed in numbers. For example quantitative data about the outcome of a breast screening programme could include the percentage of the women invited who actually attended, the percentage called back for further assessment, and (ultimately) the decrease in rates of illness and death from breast cancer. (Compare with *qualitative*.)

**Randomized controlled trial (RCT)** An experimental method whereby subjects are allocated randomly between an experimental group which receives an intervention and a control group which does not, so that the two groups can be compared to see the effect of the intervention.

**Recall bias** A bias affected by differences in obtaining accurate information on historical events or exposures between groups of subjects with different characteristics, irrespective of their true exposures. For example, women experiencing a miscarriage are more likely to remember and report specific events early in their pregnancy than those who had uneventful pregnancies.

**Regeneration** The revitalization and renewal of deprived areas, often inner city urban areas. It involves reviving local economies and communities and improving services. It is about improving the quality of life and promoting equality of opportunity for all communities. It involves tackling social exclusion, unemployment and training.

**Regional Assemblies** Voluntary, multi-party and inclusive regional assemblies have been established in each of the eight English regions outside London, building on the partnership working arrangements that already existed in some regions between local authorities and regional partners. Assemblies operate within the same boundaries of the government offices in the regions and the RDAs. Their constitutions vary from region to region.

**Regional Development Agencies (RDAs)** The government has established RDAs to promote sustainable economic development and social and physical regeneration, and to co-ordinate the work of regional and local partners in areas such as training, investment, regeneration and business support. RDAs are quangos. They each have a board which is mainly made up of business people and four local authority members. A high priority for RDAs will be the development of regional strategies, to improve economic performance and enhance their region's competitiveness and to provide a framework for regional economic decision taking.

*Saving Lives: Our Healthier Nation* *A national strategy for health* in England, published in 1999, which sets out priority areas (cancer; heart disease and stroke; accidents; and mental health) and sets national targets.

**Screening** The application of a special test for everyone at risk of a particular disease to detect whether the disease is present at an early stage. It is used for diseases where early detection makes treatment more successful.

**Secondary care** Specialized health care services provided by hospital inpatient and outpatient services.

**Secondary prevention** Intervention during the early stages of a disease so that further damage can be prevented.

**Selection bias** A bias effected in a sample by systematically choosing certain subject types in preference to others; for example, selecting a sample of persons from a football crowd is unlikely to give you a study group representative of the whole population.

**Self-help** Refers to an individual or a group attempts self improvement – economically, emotionally or intellectually.

**Service user** An individual who uses health or local authority services. They may also be referred to as a client, patient or consumer.

**Single Regeneration Budget (SRB)** A major source of government funding since 1994. The funding concentrates on specific local areas, usually with high levels of deprivation. It aims to help them improve by developing more economic and social activities. It is linked to job creation, training opportunities and partnerships between the statutory, private and voluntary sectors. It brought *City Challenge* and a number of other urban funding programmes into a single budget. It is distributed annually by the Department of the Environment who choose the most successful bids across a large region.

**Social capital** Investment in the social fabric of society, so that communities have characteristics such as high levels of trust, and supportive networks for the exchange of information, ideas and practical help.

**Social inclusion/exclusion** A sense of belonging to/feeling alienated from the community in which a person lives.

**Stages of Change** A cycle of stages a person usually goes through when they change a health-related behaviour, such as stopping smoking. Stages are: (1) not yet thinking about it, (2) thinking about changing, (3) being ready to change, (4) action – making changes, (5) maintaining change; then either maintaining the changed behaviour permanently or (6) relapsing – often then repeating the cycle by thinking about changing again (2).

**Standardized Mortality Ratio (SMR)** A way of comparing death rates in which allowances have been made for the different age structures of populations. This means that fair comparisons can be made between populations with, for example, different proportions of children or older people.

**Statutory organizations/agencies** *Public sector* organizations or agencies such as local authorities and NHS organizations.

**Statutory sector** Another term for the *public sector.*

**Strategy** A broad plan of action that specifies what is to be achieved, how and by when; it provides a framework for more detailed planning.

**Strategic Health Authority (SHA)** From 2002, 30 new strategic health authorities replaced the 95 health authorities. They are a bridge between the Department of Health and local NHS services and to provide strategic leadership to ensure the delivery of improvements in health, well-being and health services locally.

**Stratospheric ozone** Ozone in the upper layers (stratosphere) of the atmosphere (as opposed to ozone at ground level). Depletion in this layer contributes to global warming effects. At ground level ozone is a respiratory irritant.

**Sure Start** Part of the government's drive to eradicate child poverty in 20 years and to halve it by 2010. It aims to improve the health and well-being of families and children from birth so they can flourish when they go to school. Government schemes are targeted in areas of high health need and aim to support parents and children under 4. This initiative is aimed at improving services for expectant parents and for children aged 0–3 in deprived areas. It is a partnership of local parents and statutory and voluntary organizations. It aims to promote the physical, intellectual and social development of babies and young children breaking the cycle of disadvantage.

**Sustainable development** Development which meets the needs of the present without damaging the health or environment of future generations.

**Synergistic effect** As applied to chemicals in the environment which act together to give a combined effect on humans.

**Systematic review** A review of the literature that uses an explicit approach to searching, selecting and combining the various studies.

**Target group** The people who are intended to benefit from a public health or health promotion activity.

**Targets** Quantified and measurable achievements to aim for, by specified dates, which provide yardsticks against which progress can be monitored. (See also *health target.*)

**Teaching Public Health Networks** Supports the Choosing Health requirements of educating the whole workforce about the determinants of health.

**Tertiary Care Services** Very specialized NHS services which cannot be provided within every health authority area, for example a unit for treating eating disorders or specialist cancer clinic. Access is through GPs or local hospital consultants.

**Third Sector** Voluntary organizations, community groups and other non-profit organizations are sometimes called the third sector because they are not part of the public or private sector. The phrase is sometimes used instead of the voluntary sector because people think 'voluntary sector' is misleading as it implies that the sector is only about volunteers.

**Trilateralism** The interconnections between Europe, North America and East Asia which accounts for 85 per cent of world trade. Connected terms: regionalization and triadization.

**Upstream Policy** Tackling the fundamental causes of ill-health through national, social and economic policy thus preventing many problems.

**Urbanization** Movement of people to live in cities and towns.

**User Involvement** People who use services are involved in making decisions about, and planning those services. *Service users* could be asked for their views on a particular subject or may join a working group which decides how a service will develop.

**User-led initiatives** Refers to initiatives that have been devised, planned and managed by people who use services.

**Voluntary organizations** Not-for-profit organizations, ranging from large national ones to small groups of local people, run by volunteers but possibly employing paid staff. Small local voluntary organizations are often called community groups.

**Voluntary sector** A collective term for *voluntary organizations*, community groups and charities. (See also *sector.*)

**White Paper** Government policy, often accompanied by legislation. Usually follows a *Green Paper.*

**Whole population approach** Public health approach which focuses on a whole community rather than individuals who are identified as being in particular need. (Compare with *high risk approach.*)

**Wicked issues** Have incomplete, contradictory and changing requirements. Solutions to such issues are difficult to define because of complex interdependencies. The solution of one 'wicked issue' may reveal or create an even more complex problem.

**World Health Organization (WHO)** An inter-governmental organization within the United Nations system whose purpose is to help all people attain the highest possible level of health through public health programmes. Its headquarters are in Geneva, Switzerland.

**World Trade Organization Sanitary and Phyto sanitary agreements (WTO SPS)** Relate to world animal and plant trade including health and disease.

**Zeitgeist** A German word meaning 'spirit of the time'. It describes the intellectual and cultural climate of an era.

**Zoonotic infections** Infections of animals which are communicable to humans; animals are the main reservoir of the infection.

# Bibliography

Abbott, S., Florin, D., Fulop, N. and Gillam, S. (2001) *Primary Care Groups and Trusts: Improving Health*. London: King's Fund.

Abbott, S., Petchey, R., Kessel, A. and Killoran, A. (2006) What sort of networks are public health networks? *Public Health*, 120(6): 551–6.

Academy of Medical Sciences (2004) *Calling Time. The Nation's Drinking as a Major Health Issue*. London: Academy of Medical Sciences.

Acheson, D. (1988) *Public Health in England. Report of the Committee of Inquiry into the Future of the Public Health Function*, Cm289. London: HMSO.

Acheson, D. (1998) *Independent Inquiry into Inequalities in Health*. London: The Stationery Office.

Action on Smoking and Health (2004) *Factsheet no. 22: Tobacco and the Environment*. http://www.ash.org.uk/ (accessed 17 September 2006).

Active Community Unit (ACU) (2001) *Funding Community Groups – A Consultation Document Issued by ACU on Behalf of the Inter-Departmental Working Group on Resourcing Community Capacity Building*. London: ACU, Home Office.

Ahmad, Y. and Broussine, M. (2003) The UK public sector modernisation agenda – reconciliation or renewal? *Public Management Review*, 5(1): 45–62.

Ali, S.H. and Keil, R. (2006) Global cities and the spread of infectious disease: the case of severe acute respiratory syndrome (SARS) in Toronto, Canada, *Urban Studies*, 43(3): 491–509.

Allen, P. (2001) Health promotion, environmental health and local authorities, in A. Scriven and J. Orme (eds) *Health Promotion: Professional Perspectives*. Basingstoke: Palgrave.

Allen, T. (2000) Housing renewal – doesn't it make you sick? *Housing Studies*, 15(3): 443–63.

Altmann, D.G. (2001) Systematic reviews of evaluations of prognostic variables, in M. Egger, G. Davey Smith and D.G. Altmann (eds) *Systematic Reviews in Health Care: Meta-analysis in Context*. London: BMJ Books.

Anable, J., Lane, B. and Kelay, T. (2006) *An Evidence Base Review of Public Attitudes to Climate Change and Transport Behaviour*. London: Department for Transport.

Andersen, H. and Munck, R. (1999) *Neighbourhood Images in Liverpool*. JRF Area Regeneration Series. York: York Publishing Services.

Anie, A., Daniel, N., Tah, C. and Petruckevitch, A. (2005) *An Exploration of Factors Affecting the Successful Dispersal of Asylum Seekers*. London: Home Office. www.homeoffice.gov.uk/rds/pdfs05/rdsolr5005.pdf (accessed 28 July 2006).

Annandale, E. (1998) *The Sociology of Health and Medicine: A Critical Introduction*. Cambridge: Polity Press.

Antonovsky, A. (1987) *Unravelling the Mystery of Health: How People Manage Stress and Stay Well*. San Francisco: Jossey-Bass.

Arblaster, L., Entwistle, V., Lambert, M. *et al.* (1995) *Review of the Research on the Effectiveness of Health Service Interventions to Reduce Variations in Health*, CRD Report 3. York: NHS Centre for Reviews and Dissemination, The University of York.

Arblaster, L., Lambert, M., Entwistle, V. *et al.* (1996) A systematic review of the effectiveness of health service interventions aimed at reducing inequalities in health, *Journal of Health Services Research and Policy*, 1(2): 93–103.

Argyle, M. (1989) *The Psychology of Happiness*. London: Routledge.

Argyle, M. (1996a) The effects of relationships on well-being, in N. Baker (ed.) *Building a Relational Society: New Priorities for Public Policy*. Aldershot: Arena.

Argyle, M. (1996b) *The Social Psychology of Leisure*. Harmondsworth: Penguin.

Ashby, D. and Smith, A.F. (2000) Evidence-based medicine in Bayesian decision-making, *Statistics in Medicine*, 19: 3291–305.

Ashton, J. (1992) The origin of healthy cities, in J. Ashton (ed.) *Healthy Cities*. Milton Keynes: Open University Press.

Ashton, J.R. (2000) Public health observatories – the key to timely public health intelligence in the new century, *Journal of Epidemiology and Community Health*, 54: 724–5.

Ashton, J. and Seymour, H. (1988) *The New Public Health*. Buckingham: Open University Press.

Aspinall, J. (1999) Ethnic groups and our healthier nation: whither the information base? *Journal of Public Health Medicine*, 21: 125–32.

Asthana, S. and Halliday, J. (2006) *What Works in Tackling Health Inequalities?: Pathways, Policies and Practice Through the Lifecourse*. Bristol: The Policy Press.

Atherton, G. and Hashagen, S. with Chanan, G., Garratt, C. and West, A. (2003) *Including Local People in Community Planning in Scotland*. London: Community Development Foundation.

Atkinson, R. (1999) Discourses of partnership and empowerment in contemporary British urban policy, *Urban Studies*, 36(1): 59–77.

Atkinson, R., Thomson, H., Kearns, A. and Pettigrew, M. (2006) Giving urban policy its medical: assessing the place of health in area-based regeneration, *Policy and Politics*, 34(1): 5–26.

Audit Commission (1998) *A Fruitful Partnership: Effective Partnership Working*. London: Audit Commission.

Audit Commission (2002) *Neighbourhood Renewal: Policy Focus*. London: Audit Commission.

Baggot, R. (2000) *Public Health: Policy and Politics*. Basingstoke: Macmillan Press.

Ball, R., Heafey, M. and King, D. (2001) Private finance initiative – a good deal for the public or a drain on future generations? *Policy and Politics*, 29(1): 95–108.

Banks, S., Butcher, H., Henderson, P. and Robertson, J. (2003) *Managing Community Practice: Principles, Policies and Programmes*. Bristol: The Policy Press.

Barker, D.P. (1998) *Mothers, Babies and Health in Late Life*. Edinburgh: Churchill Livingstone.

Barnes, M. (1997) *Care Communities and Citizens*. London: Longman.

Barnes, M. (1999) Users as citizens: collective action and the local governance of welfare, *Social Policy and Administration*, March, 33(1): 73–90.

Barnes, M. and Sullivan, H. (2002) Building capacity for collaboration in English health action zones, in C. Glendinning, M. Powell and K. Rummery (eds) *Partnerships, New Labour and the Governance of Welfare*. Bristol: The Policy Press.

Barnes, M., Harrison, S., Mort, M. and Shardlow, P. (1999) *Unequal Partners: User Groups and Community Care*. Bristol: The Policy Press.

Barnes, M., Matka, E. and Sullivan, H. (2003) Evidence, understanding and complexity: evaluation in non-linear systems, *Evaluation*, 9(3): 263–82.

Barnes, M., Bauld, L., Benzeval, M., Judge, K., Mackenzie, M. and Sullivan, H. (2005) *Building Capacity for Health Equity*. London: Routledge.

Barr, A. (2002) *Learning Evaluation and Planning*. London: Community Development Foundation.

Barr, A. and Hashagen, S. (2000) *Achieving Better Community Development*. London: Community Development Foundation.

Barr, A., Hamilton, R. and Purcell, R. (1996) *Learning for Change*. London: Community Development Foundation.

Bartley, M., Blane, D. and Montgomery, S. (1997) Health and the lifecourse: why safety nets matter, *British Medical Journal*, 314: 1194–6.

Barton, H. and Grant, M. (2006). The determinants of health and well being in our neighbourhoods, *Journal for The Royal Society for the Promotion of Health*, 126(6): 252–3.

Baud, L., Clarke, K. and Maltby, T. (eds) (2006) *On Behalf of the Social Policy Association, Social Policy Review 18: Analysis and Debate in Social Policy, 2006*. Bristol: The Policy Press.

Bauld, L. and Judge, K. (2002) *Learning from Health Action Zones*. London: Aeneas Press.

Bauld, L., Mackinnon, J. and Judge, K. (2000) *Community Health Initiatives: Recent Policy Developments and the Emerging Evidence Base*. www.renewal.net

Bauld, L., Mackinnon, J. and Judge, K. (2001a) *Community Health Initiatives: Recent Policy Developments and the Emerging Evidence Base*. Glasgow: University of Glasgow.

Bauld, L., Judge, K., Lawson, L. *et al.* (2001b) *Health Action Zones in Transition: Progress in 2000*. Glasgow: University of Glasgow.

Bauld, L., Judge, K., Barnes, M., Benzeval, M., MacKenzie, M. and Sullivan, H. (2005) Promoting social change: the experience of health action zones in England, *Journal of Social Policy*, 34(3): 427–45.

Baum, F. (2000) Social capital, economic capital and power: further issues for a public health agenda, *Journal of Epidemiology and Community Health*, 53: 195–6.

Baum, F. (2001) Health, equity, justice and globalisation: some lessons from the People's Health Assembly, *Journal of Epidemiology and Community Health*, 55: 613–16.

Beaglehole, R. and Bonita, R. (1997) *Public Health at the Crossroads*. Cambridge: Cambridge University Press.

Beattie, A. (1991) *Success and Failure in Community Development Initiatives in National Health Service Settings: Eight Case Studies*. Milton Keynes: Open University Press.

Beck, U. (1992) *Risk Society: Towards a New Modernity*. London: Sage.

Beck, U. (1999) *World Risk Society*. Boston, MA: Blackwell.

Beck, U. (2000a) *What is Globalisation?* Cambridge: Polity Press.

Beck, U. (2000b) *The Brave New World of Work*. Cambridge: Polity Press.

Beecham, J. (2000) *Unit Costs not Exactly Child's Play: A Guide to Estimating Unit Costs for Children's Social Care*. London: Department of Health.

Bennett, P. and Calman, K. (eds) (1999) *Risk Communication and Public Health*. Oxford: Oxford University Press.

Bennis, W. (1988) *On Becoming a Leader*. New York: Addison-Wesley.

Ben-Shlomo, Y. and Chaturvedi, N. (1995) Assessing equity in access to health care provision in the UK: does where you live affect your chances of getting a coronary artery bypass graft? *Journal of Epidemiology and Community Health*, 49: 200–4.

Ben-Schlomo, Y. and Kuh, D. (2002) A life course approach to chronic disease epidemiology:

conceptual models, empirical challenges and interdisciplinary perspectives, *International Journal of Epidemiology*, 31: 285–93.

Ben-Shlomo, Y., White, I.R. and Marmot, M. (1996) Does the variation in the socio-economic characteristics of an area affect mortality? *British Medical Journal*, 312: 1013–14.

Bentham, J. (1834) *Deontology: Or, the Science of Morality*, J. Bowring (ed.), 2 volumes. London: Longman.

Benzeval, M., Judge, K. and Whitehead, M. (eds) (1995) *Tackling Inequalities in Health: An Agenda for Action*. London: King's Fund.

Benzeval, M., Taylor, J. and Judge, K. (2000) Evidence on the relationship between low income and poor health: is the government doing enough? *Fiscal Studies*, 21(3): 375–99.

Beresford, P. (2001) Service users, social policy and the future of welfare, *Critical Social Policy*, 21(4): 494–512.

Beresford, P. and Croft, S. (1993) *Citizen Involvement*. Basingstoke: Macmillan.

Beresford, P. and Trevillion, S. (1995) *Developing Skills for Community Care: A Collaborative Approach*. Aldershot: Arena.

Bergrund, L. (1994) Eco-balancing: a Göteborg example, in UNCED, *Agenda 21, Report to the Manchester Conference*, 199–59.

Bergson, A. (1938) A reformulation of certain aspects of welfare economics, *Quarterly Journal of Economics*, 98: 371–400.

Berridge, V. (1999) *Health and Society in Britain Since 1939*. Cambridge: Cambridge University Press.

Berry, T. (1991) *The ecozoic era*. Eleventh annual E. F. Schumacher lecture, Great Barrington, MA: The E. F. Schumacher Society.

Bettcher, D.W. and Wipfli, H. (2001) Towards a more sustainable globalisation: the role of the public health community, *Journal of Epidemiology and Community Health*, 55: 617–18.

Beveridge, W. (1942) *The Beveridge Report*, Cmnd 6404. London: HMSO.

Biles, A., Mornement, A. and Palmer, H. (2001) From the ballot box to the real world, *Regeneration and Renewal*, 8 June, 14–15.

Blackman, T., Elliott, E., Greene, A. *et al.* (2006) Performance assessment and wicked problems: the case of health inequalities, *Public Money & Management*, 26 (in press).

Blackstone, T. and Plowden, W. (1988) *Inside the Think Tank*. London: Heinemann.

Blair, T. (1996) *New Britain: My Vision of a Young Country*. London: Fourth Estate.

Blair, T. (1998a) *Leading the Way: A New Vision for Local Government*. London: Institute for Public Policy Research.

Blair, T. (1998b) *Compact on Relations between Government and the Voluntary and Community Sector in England*, Cm 4100. London: HMSO.

Blair, T. (2002) *The Courage of our Convictions: Why Reform of the Public Services is the Route to Social Justice*. London: Fabian Society.

Blair, T. (2006) *Speech on Healthy Living*, 26 July, Nottingham. www.number10.gov.uk/output/Page9921.asp

Blamey, A., Hanlon, P., Judge, K. and Murie, J. (eds) (2002) *Health Inequalities in the New Scotland*. Glasgow: Public Health Institute Scotland.

Bland, M. (2001) Cluster Designs: A Personal View. Talk given at The Contributions of Statistics to Public Health meeting at the Public Health Laboratory Service Communicable Disease Centre, Colindale, London, 11 October. www.sghms.ac.uk/depts/phs/sta./jmb/clustalk.htm (accessed 1 January 2003).

Bland, J.M. and Altmann, D.G. (1998) Bayesians and frequentists, *British Medical Journal*, 317: 1151.

Blane, D., Brunner, E. and Wilkinson, R. (eds) (1996) *Health and Social Organization: Towards a Health Policy for the 21st Century*. London: Routledge.

Blank, L., Goyder, E., Ellis, E., Peters, J. and Johnson, M. (2005a) *National Evaluation of New Deal for Communities: Improving Access to Health Care Services Introducing New Services for Residents*, Research Report 54. http:/ndcevaluation.adc.shu.ac.uk/ndcevaluation/reports.asp

Blank, L., Goyder, E., Peters, J. and Ellis, E. (2005b) *National Evaluation of New Deal for Communities: Teenage Pregnancy and Sexual Health*, Research Report 53. http:/ndcevaluation.adc.shu.ac.uk/ndcevaluation/reports.asp

Blaxter, M. (1990) *Health and Lifestyles*. London: Routledge.

Blaxter, M. (1995) *Consumers and Research in the NHS: Consumer Issues within the NHS*. London: Department of Health.

Blaxter, M. and Poland, F. (2002) Moving beyond the survey in exploring social capital, in C. Swann and A. Morgan (eds) *Social Capital for Health: Insights from Qualitative Research*. London: Health Development Agency.

Blythman, J. (2004) *Shopped: The Shocking Power of British Supermarkets*. London: Fourth Estate.

Bogdanor, V. (ed.) (2005) *Joined-Up Government*. Oxford: Oxford University Press/The British Academy.

Book, G.R. and Whelan, J. (eds) (1991) *The Childhood Environment and Adult Disease*, CIBA Foundation Symposium 156. Chichester: John Wiley.

Booth, C. (1902) *Life and Labour of the People in London*. London: Macmillan.

Bourdieu, P. (1993) *Sociology in Question*. London: Sage.

Bovaird, T. and Halachmi, A. (2001) Learning from international approaches to best value, *Policy and Politics*, 29(4): 451–63.

Boyle, D., Clark, S. and Burns, S. (2005) *Hidden Work: Co-production by People Outside Paid Employment*. York: Joseph Rowntree Foundation.

Boyd Orr, J. (1936) *Food, Health and Income*. London: Macmillan.

Boyne, G. and Law, J. (2005) Setting public service outcome targets: lessons from local public service agreements, *Public Money and Management*, 25(4): 254–60.

Braveman, P. and Tarimo, E. (2002) Social inequalities in health within countries: not only an issue for affluent nations, *Social Science and Medicine*, 54: 1621–35.

Brenton, M. (1985) *The Voluntary Sector in British Social Services*. London: Longman.

Briggs, A. (2001) Handling uncertainty in economic evaluation and presenting the results, in M. Drummond and A. McGuire (eds) *Economic Evaluation in Health Care Merging Theory with Practice*. Oxford: Oxford University Press.

Briggs, D. (1999) *Environmental Health: Framework and Methodologies*. Geneva: World Health Organization.

Briggs, D. (2003) Environmental pollution and the global burden of disease, in D.J. Briggs, P. Elliott and M. Joffe (eds) Impact of environmental pollution on health: balancing risk, *British Medical Bulletin*, 68: 1–24.

British Thoracic Society (2000) The Joint Committee of the British Thoracic Society: control and prevention of tuberculosis in the UK, code of practice, *Thorax*, 55: 887–901.

Brown, G. and Harris, T. (1978) *Social Origins of Depression*. London: Routledge.

Brown, P. (2001) Return of malaria feared as climate warms, *Guardian*, 10 February.

Brown, V.A., Grootjans, J., Ritchie, J., Townsend, M. and Verrinder, G. (2005) *Sustainability and Health. Supporting Global Ecological Integrity in Public Health*. London: Earthscan.

Brundtland, G. (ed.) (1987) *Our Common Future: World Commission on Environment and Development*. Oxford: Oxford University Press.

Brunner, E., White, I., Thorogood, M. *et al.* (1997) Can dietary interventions change diet and cardiovascular risk factors? A meta-analysis of randomized controlled trials, *American Journal of Public Health*, 87(9): 1415–22.

Bryson, J.M. and Crosby, B.C. (1992) *Leadership for the Common Good*. San Francisco: Jossey-Bass.

Buchan, J. (2002) Rallying the troops, *Health Service Journal*, 30 May, 24–6.

Buckland, S., Lupton, C. and Moon, G. (1994) *An Evaluation of the Role and Impact of Community Health Councils*. Portsmouth: Social Services Research and Information Unit, Portsmouth University.

Building Cost Information Service (2004) *Surveys of Tender Prices, March BICS*. London: Royal Institution of Chartered Surveyors.

Building Healthy Communities Bid Paper (2001) unpublished.

Building Healthy Communities Strategic Plan (2002) unpublished.

Bull, J. and Hamer, L. (2002) *Closing the Gap: Setting Local Targets to Reduce Health Inequalities*. London: Health Development Agency.

Bulmer, M. (1987) *The Social Basis of Community Care*. London: Unwin Hyman.

Bunker, J.P. (1995) Medicine matters after all, *Journal of the Royal College of Physicians*, 29: 105–12.

Bunker, J.P. (2001) The role of medical care in contributing to health improvements within societies, *International Journal of Epidemiology*, 30: 1260–3.

Bunton, R. and Macdonald, G. (eds) (1992) *Health Promotion: Disciplines and Diversity*. London: Routledge.

Bush, J., Fanshel, S. and Chen, M. (1972) Analysis of a tuberculin-testing program using a health status index, *Socio-Economic Planning in Science*, 6: 49–68.

BVSC The Centre for Voluntary Action (2006) Accessed at www.bvsc.org/files/images/layout/laa.gif

C2 Steering Group and Secretariat (2001) *The Campbell Collaboration: Concept, Status and Plans* (revision date 6/01/01). http://econ.dur.ac.uk/eb2003/proceedings.htm (paper under Boruch, Robert F. *et al.*).

Cabinet Office (1999) *Modernising Government*, Cm 4310. London: HMSO.

Cabinet Office (2000a) *Wiring It Up*. London: Performance and Innovation Unit, The Stationery Office.

Cabinet Office (2000b) *Reaching Out: The Role of Central Government at Regional and Local Level*. London: Performance and Innovation Unit, The Stationery Office.

Cabinet Office (2001a) *Better Policy Delivery and Design*, discussion paper. London: Performance and Innovation Unit, The Stationery Office.

Cabinet Office (2001b) *Strengthening Leadership in the Public Sector*, a research study by the Performance and Innovation Unit. London: Performance and Innovation Unit, The Stationery Office.

Cabinet Office (2001c) *The Future of Emergency Planning in England and Wales: Results of the Consultation*. London: UK Resilience Unit, The Stationery Office. www.ukresilience.info.epr/eprconsltres.pdf (accessed 23 January 2003).

Cabinet Office (2002a) *Roles of Lead Government Departments on Planning and Managing Crises*. London: UK Resilience Unit, The Stationery Office.

Cabinet Office (2002b) *Farming and Food, a Sustainable Future*, report of the Policy Commission on the Future of Farming and Food Cabinet Office. www.cabinetoffice.gov.uk/farming (accessed on 9 August 2006).

Cabinet Office, Prime Minister's Strategy Unit (2004) *Alcohol Harm Reduction Strategy for England*. London: Cabinet Office.

Cabinet Office, Resilience Unit (2005) *Exercise Arctic Sea*, a regional table top exercise June 2005, Cabinet Office. http://www.ukresilience.info/preparedness/exercises/regional casestudies/arcticsea.shtm (accessed on 28 July 2006).

Cameron, E., Mathers, J. and Parry, J. (2006) Being well and well being: The value of community and professional concepts in understanding positive health, in L. Baud, K. Clarke and T. Maltby (eds) on behalf of the Social Policy Association, *Social Policy Review 18: Analysis and Debate in Social Policy, 2006*. Bristol: The Policy Press.

Campaign Against Racism and Facism (2000) *Dispersal and the New Racism*. www.carf. demon.co.uk/feat35.html (accessed 2 August 2002).

Campaign for Children's Healthcare (2006) http://www.familiesusa.org/ (accessed 15 July 2006).

Campbell, C. and Jovchelovitch, S. (2000) Health and community development: towards a social psychology of participation, *Journal of Applied and Community Social Psychology*, 10: 255–70.

Campbell, C., Wood, R. and Kelly, M. (1999) *Social Capital and Health*. London: Health Education Authority.

Campbell, S., Roland, M.O., Middleton, E. and Reeves, D. (2005) Improvements in quality of clinical care in English general practice 1998–2003: longitudinal observational study, *British Medical Journal*, 331: 1121–8.

Capua, I. and Marangon, S. (2006) Control of avian influenza in poultry, *Emerging Infectious Disease* (serial on the Internet). http://www.cdc.gov/ncidod/EID/vol12no09/06-0430.htm (accessed on 2 August 2006).

Carpenter, J., Griffin, M. and Brown, S. (2005) *The Impact of Surestart on Social Services*. Research Report SSU/2005?FR/015. Durham: University of Durham.

Cartwright, A. (1979) *The Dignity of Labour?* London: Tavistock.

Cattell, V. and Evans, M. (1999) *Neighbourhood Images in East London*, Joseph Rowntree Foundation Area Regeneration Series. York: York Publishing Services.

Cattell, V. and Herring, R. (2002) Social capital, generations and health in East London, in C. Swann and A. Morgan (eds) *Social Capital for Health: Insights from Qualitative Research*. London: Health Development Agency.

Cavanagh, S. and Chadwick, K. (2005) *Summary Health Needs Assessment at a Glance*. London: Health Development Agency.

Centre for the Advancement of Interprofessional Education (CAIPE) (1997) *Interprofessional Education – A Definition*, Bulletin 13. London: CAIPE.

Centre for Regional Economic and Social Research (2005) *New Deal for Communities 2001–2005 Interim Evaluation*, Neighbourhood Renewal Unit Research Report 17. London: Office of the Deputy Prime Minister.

Challis, L., Fuller, M., Henwood, M. *et al.* (1988) *Joint Approaches to Social Policy: Rationality and Practice*. Cambridge: Cambridge University Press.

Chanan, G. (2002) *Measures of Community*. London: Community Development Foundation.

Chanan, G. (2003) *Searching for Solid Foundations*. London: ODPM research report.

Chapman, S. (2001) Using media advocacy to shape policy, in D. Pencheon, C. Gust, D. Melzer and J. Muir Gray (eds) *Oxford Handbook of Public Health Practice*. Oxford: Oxford University Press.

Chapman, J. (2004) *System Failure: Why Governments Must Learn to Think Differently*, 2nd edn. London: DEMOS.

Charlton, J.R.H., Hartley, R.M., Silver, R. and Holland, W.W. (1983) Geographical variation in mortality from conditions amenable to medical intervention in England and Wales, *Lancet*, i: 691–6.

Chief Medical Officer (CMO) (1997) *Avian (H5N1) Influenza in Hong Kong*, PL/CMO/97/3, Department of Health. London: The Stationery Office.

Chief Medical Officer for England (2006) *Annual Report: Raiding Public Health Budgets Can Kill*. London: Department for Health.

CHMRC (Chemical and Hazard Management Research Centre) (2002) *IPPC: A Practical*

*Guide for Health Authorities*. Birmingham: University of Birmingham. (www.doh.gov.uk/pdfs/ippchag.pdf).

Chu, A., Thorne, A. and Guite, H. (2004) The impact on mental well-being of the urban and physical environment: an assessment of the evidence, *Journal of Mental Health Promotion*, 3(2): 17–31.

Clarence, E. and Painter, C. (1998) Public services under new Labour: collaborative discourses and local networking, *Public Policy and Administration*, 13(3): 8–22.

Clarke, M. and Newman, J. (1997) *The Managerial State*. London: Sage.

Coe, R., Fitz-Gibbon, C. and Tymms, P. (2000) *Promoting Evidence-based Education: The Role of Practitioners*. Durham: Durham University Curriculum, Evaluation and Management Centre, Mountjoy Research Center.

Coker, N. (2001) Asylum seekers' and refugees' health experience, *Health Care UK*, autumn, 34–40.

Colborn, T., Myers, J.P. and Dumanoski, D. (1997) *Our Stolen Future – Are We Threatening Fertility, Intelligence and Survival – A Scientific Detective Story*. London: Abacus.

Coleman, A. and Harrison, S. (2006) *The Implementation of Local Authority Scrutiny of Primary Health Care 2002–2005*. Manchester: National Primary Care Research and Development Centre.

Colver, A., Hutchinson, P. and Judson, E. (1982) Promoting children's home safety, *British Medical Journal*, 285: 1177–80.

COMAH (Control of Major Accident Hazard Regulations) (1999) *Control of Major Accident Hazard Regulations 1999*. London: The Stationery Office.

Commission of the European Communities (1990) *Green Paper on the Urban Environment*, COM(90) 218. Luxembourg: OOPEC.

Commission of the European Communities (1994a) *Community Initiative Concerning Urban Areas*, (URBAN) COM(94) 61 Final, 2 March. Brussels: Commission of European Communities.

Commission of the European Communities (1994b) *European Sustainable Cities*, Part One. Luxembourg: OOPEC.

Commission of the European Communities (1994c) *State of Europe's Environment*. Brussels: Commission of European Communities.

Commission of the European Communities (1996) *European Sustainable Cities*. Luxembourg: OOPEC.

Commission of the European Communities (1997) *Towards an Urban Agenda in the European Union*, COM (97) 197 Final. Luxembourg: OOPEC.

Commission of the European Communities (1998) *Sustainable Urban Development in the European Union: A Framework for Action*, COM (98) 605 Final. Luxembourg: OOPEC.

Commission of the European Communities (2001) *Amended Proposal for a Decision of the European Parliament and of the Council Adopting a Programme of Community Action in the Field of Public Health (2001–2006)*, COM(2001)302. Brussels: Commission of the European Communities.

Commission of the European Communities (2005) *Sixth Environment Action Programme – Urban Environment Strategy Statement*, COM(05) Final. Brussels: Commission of the European Communities.

Commission for Health Improvement (2002) *Nothing About Us Without Us*. London: The Stationery Office.

Committee on Safety of Medicines (CSM) (2004) *Report of the CSM Expert Working Group on the Safety of Selective Serotonin Reuptake Inhibitor Antidepressants (2004)*. London: Committee on Safety of Medicines.

Committee of Safety of Medicines (2005) Updated advice on the safety of Cox2 inhibitors

17 February 2005. http://www.mhra.gov.uk/home/idcplg?IdcService=SS_GET_ PAGE&ssDoc Name=CON1004250&ssSourceNodeId=227&ssTargetNodeId=221

Communities Scotland (2005) *National Standards for Community Engagement*. Edinburgh: Scottish Executive.

Connell, J.P. and Kubisch, A.C. (1998) Applying a theory of change approach to the evaluation of comprehensive community initiatives: progress, prospects and problems, in K. Fulbright-Anderson (ed.) *New Approaches to Evaluating Community Initiatives. Volume 2. Theory, Measurement and Analysis*. Washington, DC: Aspen Institute.

Connett, J. and Stamler, J. (1984) Responses of black and white males to the special intervention programme of the Multiple Risk Factor Intervention Trial, *American Heart Journal*, 108: 839–49.

Cooke, S. and Yarrow, D. (1993) Culture and organisational learning, *Journal of Management Inquiry*, 2(4): 373–90.

Cooper, H., Arber, S., Fee, L. and Ginn, J. (1999) *The Influence of Social Support and Social Capital on Health*. London: Health Education Authority.

Coote, A. (ed.) (2002) *Claiming the Health Dividend: Unlocking the Benefits of NHS Spending*. London: The King's Fund.

Copello, A., Williamson, E., Orford, J. and Day, E. (2006) Implementing and evaluating social behaviour and network therapy in drug treatment practice in the UK: a feasibility study, *Addictive Behaviours*, 31(5): 802–10.

Cornwall, J. (1984) *Hard Earned Lives: Accounts of Health and Illness from East London*. London: Tavistock.

Corrigan, P. and Joyce, P. (1997) Reconstructing public management, *International Journal of Public Sector Management*, 10: 417–32.

Countryside Commission (1995) *State of the Countryside – Environmental Indicators*. Cheltenham: Countryside Commission.

Cowe, R. (2000) Swap shop, *Guardian*, 30 August.

Craig, P. and Lindsay, G. (2000) *Nursing for Public Health: Population Based Care*. London: Churchill Livingstone.

CRESR (2005) New Deal for Communities 2001–2005: An Interim Evaluation, CRESR, Sheffield Hallam University *et al.* including EIUA, NRU Research Report 17.

Curtis, L. and Netten, A. (2005) *Unit Costs of Health and Social Care 2004*. Kent: Personal Social Services Research Unit, University of Kent.

Curtis, S., Cave, B. and Coutts, A. (2002) Is urban regeneration good for health? Perceptions and theories of the health impacts of urban change, *Environment and Planning Government and Policy*, 20(4): 517–34.

Cutler, T. and Waine, B. (2000) Managerialism reformed? New Labour and public sector management, *Social Policy and Administration*, September 34(3): 318–32.

Dahlgren, G. and Whitehead, M. (1992) Policies and strategies to promote equity in health. Unpublished. Geneva: World Health Organization.

Dalziel, Y. (2000) Community development as a strategy for public health, in P. Craig and G.M. Lindsay (eds) *Nursing for Public Health. Population-based Care*. London: Churchill Livingstone.

Dare, C., Eisler, I., Colahan, M., Crowther, C., Senior, R. and Asen, E. (1995) The listening heart and the chi-square: clinical and empirical perceptions in the family therapy of anorexia nervosa, *Journal of Family Therapy*, 171: 31–57.

Davey Smith, G. and Ebrahim, S. (1998) Commentary: dietary change, cholesterol reduction, and the public health: what does meta-analysis add? *British Medical Journal*, 316: 1120.

Davey Smith, G. and Ebrahim, S. (2001) Epidemiology – is it time to call it a day? *International Journal of Epidemiology*, 30: 1–11.

Davey Smith, G. and Egger, M. (1999) Meta-analysis of observational data should be done with due care, *British Medical Journal*, 318: 56.

Davey Smith, G., Dorling, D., Gordon, D. and Shaw, M. (1999) The widening health gap: what are the solutions? *Critical Public Health*, 9(2): 151–70.

Davey Smith, G., Chaturvedi, N., Harding, S., Nazroo, J. and Williams, R. (2000a) Ethnic inequalities in health: a review of UK epidemiological evidence, *Critical Public Health*, 10(4): 375–408.

Davey Smith, G., Harding, S. and Rosato, M. (2000b) Relation between infants' birthweight and mothers' mortality: prospective observational study, *British Medical Journal*, 320: 839–40.

Davey Smith, G., Dorling, D. and Shaw, M. (2001a) *Poverty, Inequality and Health in Britain: A Reader*. Bristol: The Policy Press.

Davey Smith, G., Ebrahim, S. and Frankel, S. (2001b) How policy informs the evidence: 'Evidence based' thinking can lead to debased policy making, *British Medical Journal*, 322: 184–5.

Davey Smith, G., Gunnell, D. and Ben-Shlomo, Y. (2001c) Life-course approaches to socio-economic differentials in cause-specific adult mortality, in D. Leon and G. Walt (eds) *Poverty, Inequality and Health*. Oxford: Oxford University Press.

Davey Smith, G., Dorling, D., Mitchell, R. and Shaw, M. (2002) Health inequalities in Britain: continuing increases up to the end of the 20th century, *Journal of Epidemiology and Community Health*, 56: 434–5.

Davies, A. (1993) Who needs user research? Service users as subjects or participants, in M. Barnes and G. Wistow (eds) *Researching User Involvement*. Leeds: Nuffield Institute for Health Service Studies.

Davies, J.K. and Kelly, M.P. (1992) *Healthy Cities: Research and Practice*. London: Routledge.

Davies, H.T.O., Nutley, S.M. and Smith, P.C. (eds) (2000) *What Works? Evidence-based Policy and Practice in the Public Services*. Bristol: The Policy Press.

Day, P. and Klein, R. (1987) *Accountabilities: Five Public Services*. London: Tavistock.

Daykin, N. and Doyal, L. (eds) (1999) *Work and Health*. London: Palgrave.

D'Cruze, S. (2000) Don't reject asylum seekers, *Nursing Standard*, 15(7): 28.

Deacon, A. (2000) Learning from the US? The influence of American ideas upon 'new Labour' thinking on welfare reform, *Policy and Politics*, 28(1): 5–18.

DEFRA (2004) *Delivering the Animal Health and Welfare Strategy in England Implementation Plan 2004*. London: Department for Environment, Food and Rural Affairs.

Dennis, N., Henriques, F.M. and Slaughter, C. (1957) *Coal is Our Life*. London: Eyre and Spottiswoode.

Department for Communities and Local Government (DCLG) (2006) *Partnerships and Local Area Agreements*. www.communities.gov.uk (accessed 27 July 2006).

Department for Education and Skills (2003) *Every Child Matters*. London, Department for Education and Skills.

Department for Education and Skills (2004) *Implementing Sure Start – An In Depth Study Report Part 1*. London: Department of Education and Skills.

Department of Environment, Food and Rural Affairs (DEFRA) (2002) *Farming and Food. A Sustainable Future*, policy commission report. London: The Stationery Office.

Department for Environment, Food and Rural Affairs (DEFRA) (2002) *The Strategy for Sustainable Farming and Food*. London: DEFRA.

Department of the Environment, Transport and the Regions (DETR) (1997) *The UK National Air Quality Strategy*. London: The Stationery Office.

Department of the Environment, Transport and the Regions (DETR) (1998) *Modern Local Government – In Touch with the People*, Cm 4014. London: DETR.

Department of the Environment, Transport and the Regions (DETR) (2000a) *Preparing Community Strategies: Guidance to Local Authorities*. London: DETR.

Department of the Environment, Transport and the Regions (DETR) (2000b) *Our Towns and Cities: the Future: Delivering an Urban Renaissance*. London: DETR.

Department of the Environment, Transport and the Regions (DETR) (2000c) *Modernising Local Government*. London: DETR.

Department of the Environment, Transport and the Regions (DETR) (2000d) *Joining It Up Locally*. Report of policy Action Team 17. London: DETR.

Department of the Environment, Transport and the Regions (DETR) (2000e) *Social Exclusion and the Provision and Availability of Public Transport*. TraC at the University of North London for DETR. London: DETR.

Department of the Environment, Transport and the Regions (DETR) (2000f) *Indices of Deprivation 2000*. London: DETR.

Department of the Environment, Transport and the Regions (DETR) (2001a) *Strong Local Leadership – Quality Public Services*. London: DETR.

Department of the Environment, Transport and the Regions (DETR) (2001b) *Local Strategic Partnerships – Government Guidance*. London: DETR.

Department of the Environment/Welsh Office (1993) *Integrated Pollution Control, A Practical Guide*. London: The Stationery Office.

Department of Health (1995) *The Health of the Nation: Variations in Health. What Can the Department of Health and the NHS Do?* London: HMSO.

Department of Health (1997a) *The New NHS: Modern, Dependable*, Cm 3807. London: The Stationery Office.

Department of Health (1997b) *Communications about Risk to the Public Health – Pointers to Good Practice*. London: The Stationery Office.

Department of Health (1998a) *Screening of Pregnant Women for Hepatitis B and Immunisation of Babies at Risk*, HSC (98) 127. London: The Stationery Office.

Department of Health (1998b) *A First Class Service: Quality in the New NHS*, a consultation paper. London: The Stationery Office.

Department of Health (1998c) *The Health of the Nation – A Policy Assessed*. London: The Stationery Office.

Department of Health (1999a) *Reducing Health Inequalities: An Action Report*. London: The Stationery Office.

Department of Health (1999b) *Health Impact Assessment: Report of a Methodological Seminar*. London: The Stationery Office.

Department of Health (1999c) *Reducing Mother to Baby Transmission of HIV*, HSC, 1999/183. London: The Stationery Office.

Department of Health (2000a) *The Expert Patient: A New Approach to Chronic Disease Management for the 21st Century*. London: Department of Health.

Department of Health (2000b) *Asylum Seekers – Access to National Health Service Treatment*. www.doh.gov.uk/hsd/asylumseekers.htm (accessed 21 June 2002).

Department of Health (2000c) *NHS Plan Technical Supplement on Target Setting for Health Improvement*. London: Department of Health.

Department of Health (2001a) *Shifting the Balance of Power: Securing Delivery*. London: The Stationery Office.

Department of Health (2001b) *The Report of the Chief Medical Officer's Project to Strengthen the Public Health Function*. London: The Stationery Office.

Department of Health (2001c) *Tackling Health Inequalities: Consultation on a Plan for Delivery*. London: The Stationery Office.

Department of Health (2001d) *Vision to Reality*. London: The Stationery Office.

Department of Health (2001e) *Involving Patients and the Public in Healthcare*. London: The Stationery Office.

Department of Health (2001f) *A Research and Development Strategy for Public Health*. www.doh.gov.uk

Department of Health (2001g) *Health Effects of Climate Change: An Expert Review*. London: The Stationery Office.

Department of Health (2002a) *Tackling Health Inequalities*, the results of the consultation exercise. London: The Stationery Office.

Department of Health (2002b) *Shifting the Balance of Power: Next Steps*. London: The Stationery Office.

Department of Health (2002c) *Getting Ahead of the Curve – A Strategy for Infectious Diseases (Including Other Aspects of Health Protection)*, Chief Medical Officer's report. London: The Stationery Office.

Department of Health (2002d) *Building Healthy Cities – What works in regeneration*. London: Department of Health.

Department of Health (2003) *Tackling Health Inequalities: A Programme for Action*. London: Department of Health.

Department of Health (2004a) *Choosing Health: Making Healthy Choices Easier*, CM6374. London: The Stationery Office.

Department of Health (2004b) *General Medical Services Contract*. Department of Health, London.

Department of Health (2004c) *Community Development Workers for Black and Minority Ethnic Communities: Interim Guidance*. London: Department of Health.

Department of Health (2004d) *National Service Framework for Children, Young People and Maternity Services*. London: Department of Health.

Department of Health (2005a) *Tackling Health Inequalities: Status Report on the Programme for Action*. London: Department of Health.

Department of Health (2005b) *Commissioning a Patient-led NHS: Delivering the NHS Improvement Plan*. London: Department of Health.

Department of Health (2005c) *Emergency Planning Guidance*. London: Department of Health.

Department of Health (2005d) *Self Care – A Real Choice*. London: Department of Health.

Department of Health (2005e) *Delivering race equality in mental health care, an action plan for reform inside and outside services and the Government's response to the independent inquiry into the death of David Bennett*. London: Department of Health.

Department of Health (2006a) *On the State of the Public Health: Annual Report of the Chief Medical Officer 2005*. London: Department of Health.

Department of Health (2006b) *Health Reform in England: Update and Commissioning Framework*. London: Department of Health.

Department of Health (2006c) *A Stronger Local Voice: A Framework for Creating a Stronger Local Voice in the Development of Health and Social Care Services*. London: Department of Health.

Department of Health (2006d) *Our Health, Our Care, Our Say: A New Direction for Community Services*. London: Department of Health.

Department of Health (2006e) *Practice Based Commissioning: Achieving Universal Coverage*. London: Department of Health.

Department of Health COMEAP (Committee on the Medical Effects of Air Pollutants) (1995) *Non Biological Particles and Health*. London: The Stationery Office.

Department of Health COMEAP (Committee on the Medical Effects of Air Pollutants) (1997) *Handbook on Air Pollution and Health*. London: The Stationery Office.

Department of Health EPCU (Emergency Planning Coordination Unit) (2002a) *Emergency*

*Planning and Response to Major Incidents: Summary of Roles and Responsibilities.* London: The Stationery Office. www.doh.gov.uk/epcu (accessed 24 January 2003).

Department of Health EPCU (Emergency Planning Coordination Unit) (2002b) *Planning for Major Incidents: Updated NHS Guidance.* London: The Stationery Office. www.doh.gov.uk/epcu (accessed 24 January 2003).

Department of Health/Neighbourhood Renewal Unit (DoH/NRU) (2002) *Health and Neighbourhood Renewal: Guidance from the Department of Health and the Neighbourhoood Renewal Unit.* London: DoH/NRU.

Department of Health/Welsh Office (2002) *Health Protection: A Consultation Document on Creating a Health Protection Agency.* London: The Stationery Office.

Department of Social Security (1998) *New Ambitions for Our Country: A New Contract for Welfare,* Cm 3805. London: The Stationery Office.

Department of Transport, Local Government and the Regions (DTLR) (2001) *Strong Local Leadership: Quality Public Services.* London: DTLR.

Department of Transport, Local Government and the Regions (DTLR) (2002) *Collaboration and Co-ordination in Area based Initiatives.* London: NRU/RCU.

Department for Transport (2006) *National Travel Survey 2005.* London: Department for Transport.

Detsky, A.S. (1985) Using economic analysis to determine the resource consequences of choices made in planning clinical trials, *Journal of Chronic Diseases,* 38: 753–65.

DHSS (1980) *Inequalities in Health: Report of a Research Working Party.* London: DHSS.

DHSS (1986) *Primary Health Care: An Agenda for Discussion,* Cmnd. 9771. London: HMSO.

DHSS (1987) *Promoting Better Health: The Government's Programme for Improving Primary Health Care,* Cmnd. 249. London: HMSO.

Dickson, D. (1997) UK policy learns about risk the hard way, *Nature,* 385: 8–9.

Dixon, J. (1995) Community stories and indicators for evaluating community development, *Community Development Journal,* 30: 327–36.

Dixon, D.O. and Simon, R. (1992) Bayesian subset analysis in a colorectal cancer trial, *Statistics in Medicine,* 11: 13–22.

Dixon, J., Kouzmin, A. and Korac-Kokabadse, N. (1998) Managerialism – something old, something borrowed, little new, *International Journal of Public Sector Management,* 11(2/3): 164–87.

Dolan, P. (1998) The measurement of individual utility and social welfare, *Journal of Health Economics,* 17: 39–52.

Donaldson, L. (1999) Strengthening public health. Speech at the Public Health Grand Rounds, London School of Hygiene and Tropical Medicine, 4 October.

Donaldson, L. (2000), *Association of Surgeons of Great Britain and Ireland, Yearbook 2000,* London: The Rowan Group.

Donner, A. and Klar, N. (1994) Cluster randomization trials in epidemiology: theory and application, *Journal of Statistical Planning and Inference,* 42: 37–56.

Donner, A. and Klar, N. (2000) *Design and Analysis of Cluster Randomization Trials in Health Research.* London: Arnold.

Dooris, M. (2006) Healthy settings: challenges to generating evidence of effectiveness, *Health Promotion International,* 21: 55–65.

Dowling, B., Powell, M. and Glendinning, C. (2004) Conceptualising successful partnerships, *Health and Social Care in the Community,* 12(4): 309–17.

Douglas, I. (1995) Private communication.

Driver, S. and Martell, L. (1998) *New Labour: Politics after Thatcherism.* Cambridge: Polity Press.

Drummond, M. and McGuire, A. (2001) *Economic Evaluation in Health Care: Merging Theory with Practice*. Oxford: Oxford University Press.

Drummond, M.F., Sculpher, M.J., Torrance, G.W., O'Brien, B.J. and Stoddart, G.L. (2005) *Methods for the Economic Evaluation of Health Care Programmes*. Oxford: Oxford University Press.

Duck, S. (1992) *Human Relationships*. London: Sage.

Duggan, M. (2001) *Healthy Living: The Role of Modern Local Authorities in Creating Healthy Communities*. Birmingham: Society of Local Authority Chief Executives.

Duggan, M. (2002) Social exclusion, discrimination and the promotion of health, in L. Adams, M. Amos and J. Munro (eds) *Promoting Health: Politics and Practice*. London: Sage.

Dunkley, R. and Rao, M. (2006) *Developing the Public Health Workforce*. ph.com. newsletter of the Faculty of Public Health. London: Faculty of Public Health www.fph.org.uk

Earl, P. (1995) *Microeconomics for Business and Marketing*. Hampshire: Edward Elgar.

East End Health Action (2000) *Report of Participatory Appraisal Workshops*. Glasgow: East End Health Action.

Easterby-Smith, M. (1997) Disciplines of organisational learning: contributions and critiques, *Human Relations*, 50(9): 1085–113.

Easterlow, D., Smith, S.J. and Mallinson, S. (2000) Housing for health: the role of owner occupation, *Housing Studies*, 15(3): 443–63.

Ebrahim, S. and Davey Smith, G. (1997) Systematic review of randomised controlled trials of multiple risk factor interventions for preventing coronary heart disease, *British Medical Journal*, 314: 1666–74.

Eddy, D.M., Hasselblad, V. and Shachter, R. (1990) A Bayesian method for synthesising evidence: the confidence profile method, *International Journal for Technological Assessment in Health Care*, 6: 31–55.

Edwards, R.T. (2001) Paradigms and research programmes: is it time to move from health care economics to health economics? *Health Economics*, 10: 635–49.

Edwards, S. (2006) The OFFLU Network on avian influenza, *Emerging Infectious Diseases* (serial on the Internet), 12(8). http://www.cdc.gov/ncidod/EID/vol12no08/06-0380.htm (accessed on 1 August 2006).

Egger, M., Davey Smith, G. and Schneider, M. (2001) Systematic reviews of observational studies, in M. Egger, G. Davey Smith and D.G. Altmann (eds) *Systematic Reviews in Health Care: Metanalysis in Context*. London: BMJ Books.

Ekström, A.M., Serafini, M., Nyren, O. *et al.* (2000) Dietary antioxidant intake and the risk of cardia cancer and non-cardia cancer of the intestinal and diffuse types: a population-based case control study in Sweden, *International Journal of Cancer*, 87: 133–40.

El Ansari, W., Phillips, C.J. and Hammick, M. (2001) Collaboration and partnerships: developing the evidence base, *Health and Social Care in the Community*, 9(4): 215–27.

El Din, E.Z. (2000) Buy organic – local or global? *Health Matters*, 41: 16.

El-Omar, E.M., Carrington, M., Chow, W.H. *et al.* (2000) Interleukin-1 polymorphisms associated with increased risk of gastric cancer, *Nature*, 404: 398–402.

Elixhauser, A., Halpern, M., Schmier, J. and Luce, B. (1998) Health care CBA and CEA from 1991 to 1996: an updated bibliography, *Medical Care*, 31: 7 (suppl).

Elliot, E., Landes, R., Popay, J. *et al.* (2001) *Regeneration and Health: A Selected Review of the Literature*. London: King's Fund.

Ellis, E., Peters, J., Goyder, E. and Blank, L. (2005) *National Evaluation of New Deal for Communities: Healthy Lifestyle Interventions*, Research Report 57. http:/ndcevaluation.adc.shu.ac.uk/ndcevaluation/reports.asp

Elson, T. (2004) Why public health must become a core part of council agendas, in K. Skinner (ed.) *Community Leadership and Public Health: the Role of Local Authorities*. London: The Smith Institute.

Emrick, C., Tonigan, J. *et al.* (1993) Alcoholics anonymous: what is currently known? in B. McCrady and W. Miller (eds) *Research on Alcoholics Anonymous*. New Brunswick: Rutjers Centre of Alcohol Studies.

Engels, Y., Campbell, S., Dautzenberg, M. *et al.*; EPA Working Party (2005) Developing a framework of, and quality indicators for, general practice management in Europe, *Family Practice*, 22: 215–22.

Engels, Y., Dautzenberg, M., Campbell, S., *et al.* (2006) Testing a European set of indicators for the evaluation of the management of primary care practices, *Family Practice*, 23: 137–47.

Environment Agency (2000) *Environmental Impact of the Foot and Mouth Outbreak – an Interim Assessment*. www.environment-agency.gov.uk (accessed 14 January 2003).

European Commission (1996) *European Sustainable Cities Report*. Brussels: Expert Group on the Urban Environment. http://europa.eu.int

European Commission (1998) Setting up a network for epidemiological surveillance and control of communicable diseases in the Community, *Official Journal of the European Community*, OJL 268, 3 October, 1.

European Commission (2002) *European Community Strategy on Health and Safety at Work 2002–2006*, COM (2002) 118. European Commission.

European Commission (2003) Science, Children, Awareness, Legal instruments and Evaluation (SCALE), *European Environment and Health Strategy*, COM (2003) 338. European Commission.

European Commission (2004) *The European Environment and Health Action Plan 2004–2010*, COM (2004) 416 final. European Commission.

European Commission Air Pollution and Health European Environmental Information System (APHEIS) (2002) *Report of the Investigation of Premature Deaths from Exposure to PM10 Particulates*. Brussels: EC APHEIS.

European Community (1999) *Fourth Report on the Integration of Health Protection Requirements in Community Policies*, V/99/408-EN. Brussels: European Community.

European Community (2001) *A Programme of Action in the Field of Public Health 2001–2006*, COM 302. Brussels: European Community.

European Community (2002) Environment 2010: our future, our choice. The sixth environment action programme of the European Community, *Official Journal of the European Community*, OJL 242, 10 September.

European Environment Agency (EEA) (2003) *A Framework for Evaluating Complex Scientific Evidence on Environmental Factors in Disease Causation*, Background paper No. 3, the European Environment Agency, October 2003 (Rev. June 2004). http://org.eea.europa.eu/documents/budapest2004/Compilation_of_EEA_background_papers.pdf (accessed on 4 August 2006).

European Sustainable Cities and Towns Campaign (1996) The Lisbon Action Plan, *Brussels Eurosurveillance Weekly*, European communicable disease surveillance network and reports. www.eurosurveillance.org

Evans, D. and Killoran, A. (2000) Tackling health inequalities through partnership working: learning from a realistic evaluation, *Critical Public Health*, 10(2): 125–40.

Ewles, L. and Simnett, I. (2003) *Promoting Health: A Practical Guide*, 5th edn. Edinburgh: Baillière Tindall.

Exworthy, M. and Powell, M. (2000) Variations on a theme: new Labour, health inequalities and policy failure, in A. Hann (ed.) *Analysing Health Policy*. Aldershot: Ashgate.

Exworthy, M., Berney, L. and Powell, M. (2002) How great expectations in Westminster may be dashed locally: the local implementation of national policy on health inequalities, *Policy and Politics*, 30(1): 79–96.

Faculty of Public Health Medicine (2002) *Statement on Managed Public Health Networks*. www.fphm.org.uk/Policy/Policy_frame.htm

Faculty of Public Health Medicine and Health Development Agency (2001) *Statement on Managed Public Health Networks*. London: Faculty of Public Health Medicine.

Fahey, D.K., Carson, E.R., Cramp, D.G. and Muir Gray, J.A. (2003) User requirements and understanding public health networks in England, *Journal of Epidemiology and Community Health*, 57: 938–44.

Farmer, P. (1997) Social scientists and the new tuberculosis, *Social Science and Medicine*, 44(3): 347–58.

Farmer, P. (1999) *Infections and Inequalities: the modern plagues*. Berkeley, CA: University of California Press.

Fassil, Y. (2000) Looking after the health of refugees, *British Medical Journal*, 321: 59.

Feachem, R.G.A. (2001) Globalisation is good for your health, mostly, *British Medical Journal*, September, 323: 504–6.

Federation for Community Development Learning (2003) *National Occupational Standards in Community Development Work*. Sheffield: FCDL. www.fcdl.org.uk

Fehr, R. (1999) Environmental impact assessment: evaluation of ten-step model, *Epidemiology*, 10(5): 618–25.

Fernie, K. and McCarthy, J. (2001) Partnership and community involvement: institutional morphing in Dundee, *Local Economy*, 16(4): 299–311.

Field, J. (2003) *Social Capital*. London: Routledge.

Finch, J. and Groves, D. (1983) *A Labour of Love: Women, Work and Caring*. London: Routledge and Kegan Paul.

Fine, B. (1999) The developmental state is dead – long live social capital? *Development and Change*, 30: 1–19.

Fitzpatrick, M. (2001) *The Tyranny of Health. Doctors and the Regulation of Lifestyle*. London: Routledge.

Florey, C. du V. (1988) Weak associations in epidemiological research: some examples and their interpretation, *International Journal of Epidemiology*, 17(4): 950–4.

Flyvbjerg, B. (2001) *Making Social Science Matter. Why Social Inquiry Fails and How it Can Succeed Again*. Cambridge: Cambridge University Press.

Food and Agriculture Organization (2003) *Projections of Tobacco Production Consumption and Trade to the Year 2010*. Rome: Food and Agriculture Organization.

Forbes, J. and Sashidharan, S. (1997) User involvement in services – incorporation or challenge? *British Journal of Social Work*, 27(4): 481–98.

Forrest, R. and Kearns, A. (1999) *Joined Up Places? Social Cohesion and Neighbourhood Regeneration*. York: York Publishing Services.

Fox-Rusby, J. and Cairns, J. (2005) *Economic Evaluation*. Berkshire: Open University Press.

Foucault, M. (1979) Governmentality, *Ideology and Consciousness*, 6: 5–22.

Frankel, J.A. and Romer, D. (1999) Does trade cause growth? *American Economic Review*, 89: 379–99.

Frankel, S., Davidson, C. and Davey Smith, G. (1991) Lay epidemiology and the rationality of responses to health education, *British Journal of General Practice*, 41: 428–30.

Frankenberg, R. (1957) *Village on the Border*. London: Cohen and West.

Freedman, L. (1996) Bayesian statistical methods: a natural way to assess clinical evidence, *British Medical Journal*, 313(7057): 569–70.

Free, E. (2003) *Young Refugees: Providing Emotional Support to Young Separated Refugees in the*

*UK*. London: Save the Children. www.savethechildren.org.uk/scuk_cache/scuk/cache/cmsattach/48_youngref4.pdf (accessed 28 July 2006).

Free, E. (2005) *Young Refugees: A Guide to the Rights and Entitlements of Separated Refugee Children*. London: Save the Children. www.savethechildren.org.uk/scuk_cache/scuk/cache/cmsattach/3173_rightsandentitlements.pdf (accessed 28 July 2006).

Freidson, E. (1986) *Professional Power: A Study of the Institutionalisation of Formal Knowledge*. Chicago: University of Chicago Press.

Freiman, J.A., Chalmers, T.C., Smith, H. and Kuebler, R.R. (1992) The importance of beta, the type II error, and sample size in the design and interpretation of the randomized controlled trial: survey of two sets of 'negative' trials, in J.C. Bailar and F. Mosteller (eds) *Medical Uses of Statistics*, 2nd edn. Boston, MA: NEJM Books.

Frenk, J. (1992) The new public health, in Pan American Health Organization, *The Crisis of Public Health: Reflections for Debate*. Washington: PAHO/WHO.

Fry, J. and Hodder, J.P. (1994) *Primary Health Care in an International Context*. London: Nuffield Provincial Hospitals Trust.

Fudge, C. (1995) *International Healthy and Ecological Cities Congress: Our City, Our Future*, Rapporteur's Report. Copenhagen: WHO.

Fudge, C. and Antrobus, J. (2002) *Climate Change Research: Scoping Exercise*, MISTRA Research Programme, June. Bristol: University of the West of England.

Fudge, C. and Rowe, J. (1997) *Urban Environment and Sustainability: Developing the Agenda for Socio-Economic Environmental Research*, research report for DG XII. Bristol: University of the West of England.

Fudge, C. and Rowe, J. (2000) *Implementing Sustainable Futures in Sweden*. Stockholm: BFR.

Fudge, C. and Rowe, J. (2001) Ecological modernisation as a framework for sustainable development: a case study in Sweden, *Environment and Planning A*, 33: 527–1546.

Fulop, N. and Hunter, D.J. (1999) Saving lives or sustaining the public's health? *British Medical Journal*, 319: 139–40.

Fussler, C. and James, P. (1996) *Driving Eco-Innovation: A Breakthrough Discipline for Innovation and Sustainability*. London: Pitman Publishing.

Gabarino, J. (1983) Social support networks for the helping professions, in J. Whittaker and J. Gabarino (eds) *Social Support Networks: Informal Helping in the Human Services*. Hawthorne, NY: Aldine DeGruyter.

Ganguly-Scrase, R. (2003) Paradoxes of globalization, liberalization and gender equality: the world of the lower middle classes in West Bengal, India, *Gender and Society*, 17(4): 544–66.

Gaster, L. and Deakin, N. (1998) Quality and citizens, in A. Coulson (ed.) *Trust and Contracts: Relationships in Local Government, Health and Public Services*. Bristol: The Policy Press.

Geddes, M. (1997) *Partnership Against Poverty and Exclusion: Local Regeneration Strategies and Excluded Communities in the UK*. Bristol: The Policy Press.

Geist, H.J. (1999) Global assessment of deforestation related to tobacco farming, *Tobacco Control*, 8: 18–28.

Gelders, S., Ewen, M., Noguchi, N. and Laing, R. (2006) *Price, Availability and Affordability: An International Comparison of Chronic Disease Medicines*. World Health Organization and Health Action International.

Giddens, A. (1990) *The Consequences of Modernity*. Cambridge: Polity Press.

Giddens, A. (1994) *Beyond Left and Right: The Future of Radical Politics*. Cambridge: Polity Press.

Giddens, A. (1999) *Reith Lecture on 'Globalisation'*. London: BBC. http://news.bbc.co.uk/hi/english/static/events/reith_99/week1/week1.htm

Giesecke, J. and Weinberg, J. (1998) A European centre for infectious disease? *Lancet*, 352: 1308.

Gilchrist, A. (1998) Connectors and catalysts, *SCCD News*, 18: 18–20.

Gilchrist, A. (2001) Strength through diversity: networking for community development. Unpublished PhD thesis. Bristol: University of Bristol.

Gilchrist, A. (2003) Partnerships and networks, in S. Banks, H. Butcher, P. Henderson and J. Robertson (eds) *Managing Community Practice*. Bristol: The Policy Press.

Gilchrist, A. (2004a) *The Well-connected Community*. Bristol: The Policy Press.

Gilchrist, A. (2004b) *Community Development and Community Cohesion: Bridges or Barricades?* London: Community Development Foundation.

Gilchrist, A. (2005) *Community Development and Networking*, 2nd edn. London: Community Development Foundation.

Gilchrist, A. (2006 – forthcoming) *Challenge, Choice and Change – Equalities-Based Community Development*. London: Community Development Foundation.

Gill, O., Tanner, C. and Bland, L. (2000) *Family Support; Strengths and Pressures in a 'High Risk' Neighbourhood*. Ilford: Barnardo's.

Gillam, S. and Smith, K. (2002) in Wilkin *et al*. (eds) *The National Tracker Survey of Primary Care Groups and Trusts 2001/2002: Taking Responsibility?* Manchester: National Primary Care Research and Development Centre, University of Manchester.

Gillam, S., Abbott, S. and Banks-Smith, J. (2001) Can primary care groups and trusts improve health? *British Medical Journal*, 323: 89–92.

Gilliatt, S., Fenwick, J. and Alford, D. (2000) Public services and the consumer: empowerment or control? *Social Policy and Administration*, 34(3) September, 333–49.

Gillies, P. (1998a) Effectiveness of alliances and partnerships for health promotion, *Health Promotion International*, 13(2): 1–21.

Gillies, P. (1998b) Effectiveness of alliances and partnerships for health promotion, *Health Promotion International*, 13: 99–120.

Gillies, P. (1998c) Social capital and its contribution to public health, *Forum*, 8.2(5): 47–51.

Gillman, M.W. (2002) Epidemiological challenges in studying the fetal origins of adult chronic disease, *International Journal of Epidemiology*, 31: 294–9.

Ginnety, P. (2001) *Tools of the Trade – A Toolkit for Those Using Community Development Approaches to Health and Social Wellbeing*. Newry: Community Development and Health Network, Northern Ireland.

Gladstone, F. (1979) *Voluntary Action in a Changing World*. London: The Bedford Square Press.

Gladwell, M. (2002) *The Tipping Point: How Little Things can Make a Big Difference*. London: Abacus.

Glass, R. (1955) Urban sociology in Great Britain, *Current Sociology*, 4: 5–19.

Glendinning, C. (2002) Partnerships between health and social services: developing a framework for evaluation, *Policy and Politics*, 30(1): 115–27.

Glendinning, C., Powell, M. and Rummery, K. (eds) (2002) *Partnerships, New Labour and the Governance of Welfare*. Bristol: The Policy Press.

Golding, J., Pembrey, M. and Jones, R. (2001) ALSPAC – the Avon longitudinal study of parents and children. I. Study Methodology, *Paediatric and Perinatal Epidemiology*, 15: 74–87.

Goss, S. and Kent, C. (1995) *Health and Housing: Working Together? A Review of the Extent of Inter-agency Working*. Bristol: The Policy Press.

Gowman, N. and Coote, A. (2000) *Evidence and Public Health. Towards a Common Framework*. London: King's Fund.

Goyder, E.C., Blank, L., Ellis, E., Furber, A., Peters, J., Sartain, K. and Massey, C. (2005)

Reducing inequalities in access to health care: developing a toolkit through action research, *Quality and Safety in Health Care*, 14: 336–9.

Graham, H. (1993) *When Life's a Drag: Women, Smoking and Disadvantage*. London: HMSO.

Granovetter, M. (1973) The strength of weak ties, *American Journal of Sociology*, 78: 1360–80.

Grant, M., Orme, J., Powell, J.E. and Grey, M. (2006 unpublished) Healthy Communities and the professions which support them. Conference poster at the Convergence of Public Health and Sustainability Agendas Conference, Bristol, 24 April.

Gray, S. and Sandberg, E. (2006). *The Specialist Public Health Workforce in the UK: 2005 Survey*. London: Faculty of Public Health.

Greasley, P. and Small, N. (2002) Welfare advice in primary care. Nuffield portfolio programme report no 17. http://www.leeds.ac.uk/hsphr/nuffield_publications/documents/welfare.pdf (accessed 17 July 2006).

Green Alliance (1997) *Making Environmental Decisions: Cost Benefit Analysis, Contingent Valuation and Alternatives*, proceedings of a conference, Green Alliance/Centre for the Study of Environmental Change, January. London: Green Alliance.

Green, G. and Grimsley, M. (2002) *4 Capitals for Neighbourhood Sustainability*. Paper presented to the Health Development Agency conference Social Action for Health and Wellbeing: Experiences from Policy, Research and Practice, 20–1 June. London: Health Development Agency.

Greenland, S. and Robins, J. (1994) Ecologic studies; biases, misconceptions and counter-examples, *American Journal of Epidemiology*, 139: 747–71.

Greer, S. (2001) *Divergence and Devolution*. London: Nuffield Trust.

Greer, S. (2004) *Four Way Bet: How Devolution Has Led to Four Different Models For the NHS*. London: University College London.

Greer, S. (2006) The politics of health policy divergence, in J. Adams and K. Schmueker (eds) *Devolution in Practice 2006: Public Policy Differences Within the UK*. Newcastle upon Tyne: IPPR North.

Grein, T.W., Thomas, W., Kamara Kande-Bure, O. *et al.* (2000) Rumors of disease in the global village: outbreak verification, *Emerging Infectious Diseases (serial on the Internet)*, 6(2). http://www.cdc.gov/ncidod/EID/vol6no2/contents.htm (accessed 11 August 2006).

Griffiths, S., Jewell, T. and Adshead, F. (2003) Stand and deliver, *Health Service Journal*, 113(6 November), 18–19.

Griffiths, S., Jewell, T. and Donnelly, P. (2005) Public health in practice: the three domains of public health, *Public Health*, 119: 907–13.

Grossdkurth, H., Mosha, F. and Todd, J. (1995) Improved treatment of sexually transmitted diseases on HIV infection in rural Tanzania: randomised controlled trial, *Lancet*, 346: 530–6.

Guinchard, C-G. (1997) Swedish planning: towards sustainable development, special edition of PLAN, *Swedish Journal of Planning*, Stockholm.

Gwatkin, D.R., Guillot, M. and Heuveline, P. (1999) The burden of disease among the global poor, *Lancet*, 354: 586–9.

Habermas, J. (2006) *Time of Transitions*. Cambridge: Polity Press.

Halpern, D. (2005) *Social Capital*. Cambridge: Polity Press.

Hamer, L. and Easton, N. (2002) *Community Strategies and Health Improvement: A Review of Policy and Practice*. London: I&DeA/DTLR/HDA.

Hamer, L. and Smithies, J. (2002) *Planning Across the Local Strategic Partnership: Case Studies of Integrating Community Strategies and Health Improvement*. London: HDA/LGA/DTLR.

Hammarby Sjöstad (undated) Stockholm City Council, Stockholm, Sweden.

Hampshire, M. (2001) Out of reach, *Nursing Standard*, 15(51): 16–17.

Hancock, T., Labonte, R. and Edwards, R. (1999) Indicators that count! Measuring population health at the community level, *Canadian Journal of Public Health*, 90: 522–6.

Hannerz, U. (1996) *Transnational Connections: Culture, People, Places*. London: Routledge.

Harding, A. (1998) Public–private partnerships in the UK, in J. Pierre (ed.) *Partnerships in Urban Governance*. Basingstoke: Macmillan.

Harifan, L.J. (1916) The rural school community centre, *Annals of the American Academy of Political and Social Science*, 67: 130–8.

Harris, A. (1995) Fresh fields: the relationship between public health medicine and general medical practice, *Primary Care Management*, 5(7): 3–9.

Harrison, A. (2000) Urban policy: addressing wicked issues, in H. Davies, S. Nutley and P. Smith (eds) *Evidence Based Policy and Practice in Public Services*. Bristol: The Policy Press.

Harrison, S. and Mort, M. (1998) Which champions, which people? Public and user involvement in health care as a technology of legitimation, *Social Policy and Administration*, 32(1): 60–70.

Harvey, D. (1996) *Justice, Nature and the Geography of Difference*. Oxford: Blackwell.

Hashagen, S. (1998) *Strengthening Communities*. Edinburgh: Health Education Board for Scotland.

Hastings, A. (1996) Unravelling the process of partnership in urban regeneration policy, *Urban Studies*, 33: 2.

Hastings, A., McArthur, A. and McGregor, A. (1996) *Less than Equal: Community Organizations and Estate Regeneration Partnerships*. Bristol: The Policy Press.

Hawe, P. and Shiell, A. (2000) Social capital and health promotion: a review, *Social Science and Medicine*, 51: 871–85.

Health Education Unit and Open University (1991) *Roots and Branches: Papers from the Open University / Health Education Authority 1990 Winter School on Community Development and Health*. Milton Keynes: Open University.

Health Promotion Policy Unit (2002) *An Analysis of the Health Domain of the Delivery Plans*. London: New Deal for Communities National Evaluation.

Health Protection Agency (2005) *Health Protection in the 21st Century – Understanding the Burden of Disease; preparing for the future*. Health Protection Agency. http://www.hpa.org.uk/publications/2005/burden_disease/full_doc.pdf (accessed 18 July 2006).

Health and Safety Commission and Department of Environment, Transport and the Regions (HSC/DETR) (1999) *Revitalising Health and Safety*. London: The Stationery Office.

Healthwork UK (2001) *National Standards for Specialist Practice in Public Health*. Dorset: Healthwork UK.

Held, D. and McGrew, A. (eds) (2000) *The Global Transformations Reader: An Introduction to the Globalization Debate*. Cambridge: Polity Press.

Held, D., McGrew, A.G., Goldblatt, D. and Perraton, J. (eds) (1999) *Global Transformations: Politics, Economics and Culture*. Cambridge: Polity Press.

Heller, D. (2002) *How Can Primary Care Trusts Develop and Implement their Public Health Roles to Help Reduce Health Inequalities?* Paper to the HDA seminar on tackling health inequalities, June. London: Health Development Agency.

Heller, R.F. and Page, J. (2002) A population perspective to evidence-based medicine: evidence for population health, *Journal of Epidemiology and Community Health*, 56: 45–7.

Henning, C. and Leiberg, M. (1996) Strong ties or weak ties? Neighbourhood networks in a new perspective, *Scandinavian Housing and Planning Research*, 13: 3–26.

Hine, J. and Mitchell, F. (2001) Better for everyone? Travel experiences and transport exclusion, *Urban Studies*, 38(2): 319–32.

HM Government (2005) *Securing the Future: Delivering UK Sustainable Development Strategy* Cm 6467. London: HMSO.

HM Treasury (2000a) *Government Interventions in Deprived Areas*. London: The Stationery Office.

HM Treasury (2000b) *Public Private Partnerships: The Government's Approach*. London: The Stationery Office.

HM Treasury (2006) *Stern Review: Economics of Climate Change*. London: The Stationery Office.

HM Treasury and Department of Health (2002) *Tackling Health Inequalities: Summary of the 2002 Cross-Cutting Review*. London: HM Treasury and Department of Health.

Hogg, C. (1999) *Patients, Power and Politics: From Patients to Citizens*. London: Sage.

Hoggett, P. (ed.) (1997) *Contested Communities: Experiences, Struggles, Policies*. Bristol: The Policy Press.

Holmes, J. (2001) *The Search for the Secure Base: Attachment Theory and Psychotherapy*. Hove: Brunner-Routledge.

Home Office (1998) *Compact: Getting it Right Together – Compact on Relations Between Government and the Voluntary and Community Sector in England*, Cm 4100. London: The Stationery Office.

Home Office (1999) *Standards for Civil Protection in England and Wales*. London: The Stationery Office.

Home Office (2001) *Secure Borders, Safe Haven: Integration with Diversity in Modern Britain February 2002*. London: The Stationery Office.

Home Office (2005) *The National Community Safety Plan 2006–09*. London: Home Office.

Hood, C., James, O. and Scott, C. (2000) Regulation of government: Has it increased, is it increasing, should it be diminished? *Public Administration*, 78(2): 283–304.

Hornby, S. (1993) *Collaborative Care*. Oxford: Blackwell.

Horton, S. and Farnham, D. (2000) New Labour and the management of public services: legacies, impact and prospects, in S. Horton and D. Farnham (eds) *Public Management in Britain*. Basingstoke: Macmillan.

House of Commons Defence Committee (2001/02) *Report of the Proceedings of the House of Commons Defence Committee, Defence and Security in the UK*. Sixth report, session 2001–02, Vol. 1. London: The Stationery Office.

House of Commons Health Select Committee (2001a) *Public Health*. Second report, Vol. I report and proceedings of the committee, session 2000–01, HC30-I. London: The Stationery Office.

House of Commons Health Select Committee (2001b) *Public Health*. Second report, Vol. II minutes of evidence and appendices, session 2000–01, HC30-II. London: The Stationery Office.

House of Commons Health Select Committee (2001c) *Second Report for the Session 2000–2001*. www.parliament.the-stationery-o.ce.co.uk/pa/cm200001/cmselect/cmhealth/30/3002.htm (accessed 2 December 2002).

House of Lords (1995) *Report from the Select Committee on Sustainable Development*, session 1994–95, June. London: HMSO.

Howson, C.P., Fineberg, H.V. and Bloom, B.R. (1998) The pursuit of global health: the relevance of engagement for developed countries, *Lancet*, 351: 586–90.

Hudson, B. (1987) Collaboration in social welfare: a framework for analysis, *Policy and Politics*, 15(3): 175–82.

Hudson, B. (1999) Dismantling the Berlin Wall: developments at the health–social care interface, in H. Dean and R. Woods (eds) *Social Policy Review 11*. Luton: SPA.

Hudson, B. and Hardy, B. (2001) Localization and partnership in the New National Health Service: England and Scotland compared, *Public Administration*, 79(2): 315–25.

Hudson, B., Hardy, B., Henwood, M. and Wistow, G. (1997) *Inter-agency Collaboration: Primary Health Care Sub-study*, final report. University of Leeds: Nuffield Institute for Health.

Hudson, B., Callaghan, G., Exworthy, M. and Peckham, S. (1999) *Locality Partnerships: The Early PCG Experience*, report to Northern and Yorkshire NHS Executive Research and Development. Luton: Social Policy Association.

Hunt, S. (1987) Evaluating a community development project, *British Journal of Social Work*, 17: 661–7.

Hunter, D. (1997) Managing the public health, in G. Scally (ed.) *Progress in Public Health*. London: RSM Press.

Hunter, D. (1998) *The Health of the Nation – A Policy Assessed*. Leeds: University of Leeds, University of Glamorgan and London School of Hygiene and Tropical Medicine.

Hunter, D.J. (2003) *Public Health Policy*. Oxford: Polity Press.

Hunter, D.J. (2005) Choosing or losing health? *Journal of Epidemiology & Community Health*, 59: 1010–12.

Hunter, D.J. (ed.) (2007) *Managing for Health*. London: Routledge.

Hunter, D.J. and Marks, L. (2005) *Managing for Health: What Incentives Exist for NHS Managers to Focus on Wider Health Issues?* London: King's Fund.

Hunter, D.J., Wilkinson, J. and Coyle, E. (2005) Would regional government have been good for your health? *British Medical Journal*, 330: 159–60.

Hurrell, A. and Woods, N. (eds) (1999) *Inequality, Globalization, and World Politics*. Oxford: Oxford University Press.

Huxham, C. (ed.) (1996) *Creating Collaborative Advantage*. London: Sage.

Huxham, C. and Macdonald, D. ([1882] 1999) Introducing Collaborative Advantage, in H. Ibsen (ed.) *An Enemy of the People*. Oxford: Oxford Paperbacks.

Illich, I. (1976) *Limits to Medicine*. London: Marion Boyars.

Institute for Environment and Health (IEH) (1995) *Environmental Oestrogens – Consequences for Human Health and Wildlife*. Leicester: University of Leicester.

Institute of Healthcare Improvement (IHI) (2006) Press Release. IHI announces that hospitals participating in 100,000 lives campaign have saved an estimated 122,300 lives. http://ihi.org/NR/rdonlyres/1C51BADE-0F7B-4932-A8C3-0FEFB654D747/0/UPDATED100kLivesCampaignJune14milestonepressrelease.pdf (accessed 16 July 2006).

Institute of Medicine (1988) *The Future of Public Health*. Washington: National Academy Press.

Institute of Medicine (2000) *The Future of the Public's Health in the 21st Century*. Washington: The National Academies Press.

Institute of Medicine (2003) *Who Will Keep the Public Healthy? Educating Public Health Professionals for the 21st Century*. Washington: Committee on Educating Public Health Professionals for the 21st Century.

Intergovernmental Panel on Climate Change (IPCC) (1995) *Second Assessment Climate Change 1995*. A report of the intergovernmental panel on climate change.

Intergovernmental Panel on Climate Change (IPCC) (2001) *Third Assessment Report from the Intergovernmental Panel on Climate Change, Summary for Policymakers* final. Intergovernmental Panel on Climate Change, United Nations Environment Programme. United Nations.

International Union for the Conservation of Nature (IUCN) (1980) *World Conservation Strategy: Resource Conservation for Sustainable Development*. Geneva: IUCN.

Isaacs, W. (1993) Taking flight: dialogue, collective thinking, and organisational learning, *Organisational Dynamics*, 22(2): autumn, 24–39.

Jacobs, J. (1961) *The Death and Life of Great American Cities*. New York: Random House.

Jaffe, M. and Mindell, J. (2002) A framework for the evidence base to support health impact assessment, *Journal of Epidemiology and Community Health*, 56: 132–8.

Jason, L., Gruder, C. *et al.* (1987) Work site meetings and the effectiveness of a televised smoking cessation intervention, *American Journal of Community Psychology*, 15: 57–77.

Jones, J. (1999) *Private Troubles and Public Issues: A Community Development Approach to Health*. Edinburgh: Community Learning Scotland.

Jones, D. and Gill, P.S. (1998) Refugees and primary care: tackling the inequalities, *British Medical Journal*, 317(7170): 1444–6.

Jonsen, A.R. and Hellegers, A.E. (1987) Conceptual foundations for an ethics of medical care, in L.R. Tancredi (ed.) *Ethics of Health Care*. Washington, DC: National Academy of Sciences.

Kavanagh, D. and Richards, D. (2001) Departmentalism and joined-up government: back to the future, *Parliamentary Affairs*, 54: 1–18.

Kawachi, I. (1997) A prospective study of social networks in relation to total mortality and cardiovascular disease in the USA, *Journal of Epidemiology and Community Health*, 50: 245–91.

Kawachi, I., Kennedy, B.P., Lochner, K. and Prothrow-Stith, D. (1997). Social capital, income and inequality, *American Journal of Public Health*, 89(9): 1491–8.

Kearns, A., Hiscock, R., Ellaway, A. and Macintyre, S. (2000) Beyond four walls: the psycho-social benefits of home: evidence from west-central Scotland, *Housing Studies*, 15(3): 443–63.

Kelly, M. and Capewell, S. (2004). Briefing paper. Relative contributions of changes in risk factors and treatment to the reduction in coronary disease mortality. London: Health Development Agency.

Kelly, M., McDaid, D., Ludbrook, A. and Powell, J.E. (2005) *Economic Appraisal of Public Health Interventions: Evidence Briefing*. London: National Institute for Health and Clinical Excellence. http://www.publichealth.nice.org.uk/page.aspx?o=513209

Kelly, R. (2006) Speech to Local Government Conference, 5 July. www.communities.gov.uk (accessed 27 July 2006).

Kerrison, S. and MacFarlane, A. (eds) (2000) *Official Health Statistics: An Unofficial Guide*. London: Arnold.

Kibble, A.J. and Saunders, P. (eds) (2001) *Integrated Pollution Prevention and Control – A Practical Guide for Health Authorities, Version 1*. Birmingham: University of Birmingham.

Klandermans, B. (1997) *The Social Psychology of Protest*. Oxford: Blackwell.

Klein, R. (1998) *The New Politics of the NHS*, 4th edn. London: Longman.

Knoke, D. (1990) *Political Networks: The Structural Perspective*. Cambridge: Cambridge University Press.

Kohn, L.T., Corrigan, J.M. and Donaldson, M.S. (eds) (1999). *An Organisation With a Memory*. Report of an expert group on learning from adverse events in the NHS chaired by the Chief Medical Officer. Department of Health. London: HMSO.

Kolliakou, A., Holliday, J. and Murphy, R. (2006) *Family Therapy for Anorexia Nervosa (Protocol)*, The Cochrane Collaboration. London: John Wiley.

Kretzmann, J. (2000) Building capacity from the bottom-up in P. Ashton and A. Hobbs (eds) *Community Development for Health*. London: Health For All Network.

Kuh, D., Ben-Shlomo, Y., Lynch, J., Hallqvist, J. and Power, C. (2003) Life course epidemiology, *Journal of Epidemiology and Community Health*, 57: 778–83.

Labonte, R. (1998) *A Community Development Approach to Health Promotion*. Edinburgh: Health Education Board for Scotland and RUHBC, University of Edinburgh.

Labonte, R. (2001) Liberalisation, health and the World Trade Organisation, *Journal of Epidemiology and Community Health*, 55: 620–1.

Labonte, R. (2002) International governance and World Trade Organisation (WTO) reform, *Critical Public Health*, 12(1): 65–86.

Labonte, R. and Torgerson, R. (2005) Interrogating globalization, health and development: Towards a comprehensive framework for research, policy and political action, *Critical Public Health*, 15(2): 157–79.

Lancaster, T. and Stead, L. (2006) Physician advice for smoking cessation, *The Cochrane Database of Systematic Reviews*, Issue 2.

*Lancet* (1997) Putting public health back into epidemiology, *Lancet*, 350(907): 229.

*Lancet* (2002) Who has the power over tobacco control? *Lancet*, 360: 267.

LaPorte, R.E., Akazawa, S., Hellmonds, P. *et al.* (1994) Global public health and the information superhighway, *British Medical Journal*, 308: 1651–2.

LaPorte, R.E., Bavinas, E., Chang, Y.-F. and Libman, I. (1996) Global epidemiology and public health in the 21st century: applications of new technologies, *Annals of Epidemiology*, 6: 162–7.

Lang, T. (2000) Cheap food, poor policy, *Times Higher*, 10 November.

Larson, M. (1977) *The Rise of Professionalism: A Sociological Analysis*. Berkeley: University of California Press.

Last, J. (2001) *A Dictionary of Epidemiology*, 4th edn. Oxford: Oxford University Press.

Laumann, E. and Pappi, F. (1976) *Networks of Collective Action: A Perspective on Community Influence Systems*. New York: Academic Press.

Lawless, P., Dabinett, G., Rhodes, J. and Tyler, P. (2000) *The Evidence Base for Regeneration Policy and Practice*, DETR Regeneration Research 39. London: DETR.

Layard, R. (2005) *Happiness: Lessons From a New Science*. London: Penguin.

Leadbetter, D. (ed.) (2000) *Harnessing Official Statistics*, Harnessing Health Information Series No. 3. Oxford: Radcliffe Medical Press.

Leape, L.L., Brennan, T.A., Laird, N.M. *et al.* (1991) Incidence of adverse events and negligence in hospitalized patients: results of the Harvard Medical Practice Study II, *New England Journal of Medicine*, 324: 377–84.

Lee, K. (2000a) Global sneezes spread diseases, *Health Matters*, 41: 14–15.

Lee, K. (2000b) The impact of globalisation on public health: implications for the Faculty of Public Health Medicine, *Journal of Public Health Medicine*, 22(3): 253–62.

Lee, K. (2001) A dialogue of the deaf: the health impacts of globalisation, *Journal of Epidemiology and Community Health*, 55: 619.

Lee, K. (2003) *Globalization and Health: An Introduction*. London: Palgrave Macmillan.

Le Grand, J., Mays, N. and Mulligan, J.A. (eds) (1998) *Learning from the NHS Internal Market: A Review of Evidence*. London: King's Fund.

Leifler, D. (1999) Giving refuge to those in need, *Nursing Standard*, 13(43): 16–17.

Leon, D. and Walt, G. (eds) (2000) *Poverty, Inequality and Health*. Oxford: Oxford University Press.

Levitas, R. (1998) *The Inclusive Society?* Basingstoke: Macmillan.

Levitt, I. (1988) *Poverty and Welfare in Scotland*. Edinburgh: Edinburgh University Press.

Lewis, J. (1991) The public's health: philosophy and practice in Britain in the twentieth century, in E. Fee and R. Acheson (eds) *A History of Education in Public Health*. Oxford: Oxford University Press.

Lewis, M. and Hartley, J. (2001) Evolving forms of quality management in local government: lessons from the best value pilot programme, *Policy and Politics*, 29(4): 477–96.

Lieberman, M. and Videka-Sherman, L. (1986) The impact of self-help groups on the mental health of widows and widowers, *American Journal of Orthopsychiatry*, 56(3): 435–49.

Lilford, R.J. and Braunholtz, D. (1996) The statistical basis of public policy: a paradigm shift is overdue, *British Medical Journal*, 313: 603–7.

Lilford, R.J. and Braunholtz, D. (2000) Who's afraid of Thomas Bayes? *Journal of Epidemiology and Community Health*, 54: 731–9.

Lindow, V. (1993) *User Participation in Community Care*. London: Department of Health, Community Care Support Unit.

Ling, T. (2000) Unpacking partnership: the case of health care, in J. Clarke, S. Gerwitz and E. McLuaghlin (eds) *New Managerialism, New Welfare?* London: Sage.

Lister, R. (2001) New Labour: a study in ambiguity from a position of ambivalence, *Critical Social Policy*, 21(4): 425–47.

Local Government Act 2000. Available via the ODPM website at the Local Regions area of the site. The Act is also available from The Stationery Office.

Local Government Association and UK Public Health Association (2000) *Joint Response to the Public Health White Paper: Saving Lives: Our Healthier Nation*. London: Local Government Association.

Local Government Management Board (LGMB) (1994a) *Local Agenda 21: Principles and Process. A Step-by-Step Guide*. London: LGMB.

Local Government Management Board (LGMB) (1994b) *Sustainability Indicators Research Project: Report of Phase One*. London: LGMB.

Longford, E. (2001) *Wellington*. London: Abacus.

Lovelock, J. (2006) *The Revenge of Gaia*. London: Allen Lane Penguin Books.

Low, J. (ed.) (2001) *Regeneration in the 21st century*. London: Policy Press.

Lowey, H., Fullard, B., Tocque, K. and Bellis, M. (2002) *Are Smoking Cessation Services Reducing Inequalities in Health?* Liverpool: North West Public Health Observatory.

Lowndes, V. and Skelcher, C. (1998) The dynamics of multi-organisational partnership: an analysis of changing modes of governance, *Public Administration*, 76(2): 313–33.

Lucas, K., Grosvenor, T. and Simpson, R. (2001) *Transport, the Environment and Social Exclusion*. York: York Publishing Services.

Lucas, P. (2003) Home visiting can substantially reduce childhood injury. What Works for Children Group. www.whatworksforchildren.org.uk (accessed 17 July 2006).

Lupton, D. (1995) *The Imperative of Health: Public Health and the Regulated Body*. London: Sage.

Lupton, C. and Taylor, P. (1994) *Consumer Involvement in Healthcare Commissioning*. Portsmouth: Social Services Research and Information Unit, University of Portsmouth.

Lupton, R. and Power, A. (2002) Social exclusion and neighbourhoods, in J. Hills and J. Le Grand (eds) *Understanding Social Exclusion*. Oxford: Oxford University Press.

Lupton, C., Peckham, S. and Taylor, P. (1998) *Managing Public Involvement in Healthcare Purchasing*. Buckingham: Open University Press.

Lynch, M.A. and Cuninghame, C. (2000) Understanding the needs of young asylum seekers, *Archives of Disease in Childhood*, 38(5): 384–7.

MacDonald, G. (1998) Promoting evidence-based practice in child protection, *Clinical Child Psychology and Psychiatry*, 3(1): 71–85.

Macdonald, J. (1992) *Primary Health Care: Medicine in its Place*. London: Earthscan.

Macdonald, G.M., Sheldon, B. and Gillespie, J. (1992) Contemporary studies of the effectiveness of social work, *British Journal of Social Work*, 22(6): 5–43.

Macintyre, S. (1997) The Black report and beyond: what are the issues? *Social Science and Medicine*, 44(6): 723–45.

Macintyre, S. (2001) Memorandum, in House of Commons Health Select Committee, *Second Report for the Session 2000–2001*. London: The Stationery Office.

Macintyre, S., Maciver, S. and Soomans, A. (1998) Area, class and health: should we be focussing on places or people? *Journal of Social Policy*, 22(2): 213–34.

Macintyre, S., Chalmers, I., Horton, R. and Smith, R. (2001) Using evidence to inform health policy: case study, *British Medical Journal*, 322: 222–5.

Mackenbach, J.P. (1995) Public health epidemiology, *Journal of Epidemiology and Community Health*, 49: 333–4.

Mackenbach, J.P. (1996). The contribution of medical care to mortality decline: McKeown revisited, *Journal of Clinical Epidemiology*, 49: 1207–13.

Mackenbach, J. and Bakker, M. (eds) (2002) *Reducing Inequalities in Health: A European Perspective*. London: Routledge.

Mackenbach, J.P., Looman, C.W.N., Kunst, A.E., Habbema, D.F. and van der Maas, P.J. (1988) Post-1950 mortality trends and medical care: gains in life expectancy due to declines in mortality from conditions amenable to medical intervention in The Netherlands. *Social Science and Medicine*, 27: 889–94.

Mackintosh, M. (1993) Partnership: issues of policy and negotiation, *Local Economy*, 7(3).

Maclennan, D. and More, A. (1999) Evidence, what evidence? The foundations for housing policy, *Public Policy and Management*, January–March.

MacMahon, B., Pugh, T.F. and Ipsen, J. (1960) *Epidemiological Methods*. Boston: Little, Brown and Co.

Macpherson, W. (1998) *Report of the Inquiry into the Death of Stephen Lawrence*. London: Home Office.

Maddock, S. and Morgan, G. (1997) Barriers to Professional Collaboration and Inter-agency Working Within Health and Social Care. Paper presented at the Public Services Research Unit Conference, May.

Maes, H.M., Neale, M.C. and Eaves, L.J. (1997) Genetic and environmental factors in relative body weight and human adiposity, *Behavior Genetics*, 27: 325–51.

MAFF (1998) *The Food Standards Agency; A Force for Change*. London: The Stationery Office.

Malmö Högskolen (1998) Utbildningskatalog 1998/99, Malmö, Sweden, *Management Decision*, 30(3): 50–6.

Marks, N. (2005) *The Power and Potential of Well-being Indicators: Measuring Young People's Well-being in Nottingham*. London: The New Economics Foundation.

Marks, L. and Hunter, D.J. (2005) Moving upstream or muddying the waters? Incentives for managing for health, *Public Health*, 119: 974–80.

Marmot, M. and Wilkinson, R.G. (2001) Psychosocial and material pathways in the relation between income and health: a response to Lynch *et al.*, *British Medical Journal*, 322: 1233–6.

Marmot, M.G., Shipley, M.J. and Rose, G. (1984) Inequalities in death: specific explanations of a general pattern, *Lancet*, 1: 1003–6.

Marmot, M., Shipley, M., Brunner, E. and Hemingway, H. (2001) Relative contribution of early life and adult socioeconomic factors to adult morbidity in the Whitehall II study, *Journal of Epidemiology and Community Health*, 55(5): 301–7.

Marsden, R., Aldegheri, E., Khan, A. *et al.* (2005) 'What's going on?' A Study of Destitution and Poverty Faced by Asylum Seekers and Refugees in Scotland. Edinburgh: The Refugee Survival Trust. http://oxfamgb.org/ukpp/resources/downloads/Whats_going_on.pdf (accessed 6 July 2006). www.rst.org.uk (accessed 6 July 2006) – executive summary.

Marsh, A., Gordon, D., Heslop, P. and Pantazis, C. (2000) Housing deprivation and health: a longitudinal analysis, *Housing Studies*, 15(3): 411–29.

Marshall, J.P., Kimball, T.G., Shumway, S.T., Miller, M.M., Jeffries, V. and Arredondo, R. (2005) Outcomes of a structured family group in an outpatient alcohol/other drug treatment setting, *Alcoholism Treatment Quarterly*, 23(4): 39–53.

Martell, R. and Murray, K. (2001) Carers who cross a chasm, *Nursing Standard*, 16(4): 12.

Martuzzi, M. and Bertollini, R. (2004) The precautionary principle, science and human health protection, *International Journal of Occupational Medicine and Environmental Health*, 17(1): 43–6.

Martuzzi, M. and Tickner, J. (2003) *Evaluating and Choosing Policy Options in Environmental and Health, Role of the Precautionary Principle*. World Health Organization. http://ec. europa.eu/health/ph_determinants/environment/EMF/Conf24_26feb2003/martuzzis.pdf (accessed on 2 August 2006).

Marwell, G. and Oliver, P. (1993) *The Critical Mass in Collective Action: A Micro-social Theory*. Cambridge: Cambridge University Press.

Matka, E., Barnes, M. and Sullivan, H. (2002) Health action zones: creating alliances to achieve change, *Policy Studies*, 23(2): 97–106.

Maxwell, R. (1984) Quality assessment in health, *British Medical Journal*, 288: 1470–2.

Mayes, L.C., Horwitz, R.I. and Feinstein, A.R. (1989) A collection of 56 topics with contradictory results in case-control research, *International Journal of Epidemiology*, 3: 725–7.

Mayo, M. (1997) Partnerships for regeneration and community development, *Critical Social Policy*, 52, 17(3), August.

Mayo, M. and Taylor, M. (2001) Partnerships and power in community regeneration, in S. Balloch and M. Taylor (eds) *Partnership Working: Policy and Practice*. Bristol: The Policy Press.

Mayon-White, R.T., Ducel, G., Kereselidze, T. and Tikomirov, E. (1988) An international survey of the prevalence of hospital-acquired infection, *Journal of Hospital Infection*, 11 (Suppl A): 43–8.

McArthur, A. (1996) The active involvement of local residents in strategic community partnerships, *Policy and Politics*, 23(1): 61–71.

McCormick, A., Fleming, D. and Charlton, J. (1995) *Morbidity Statistics from General Practice: Fourth National Study 1991–92*, Series MB5, No. 3. London: HMSO.

McDonald, R. (2006) Creating a patient-led NHS: empowering 'consumers' or shrinking the state? in L. Baud, K. Clarke and T. Maltby (eds) *On behalf of the Social Policy Association, Social Policy Review 18: Analysis and Debate in Social Policy, 2006*. Bristol: The Policy Press.

McEwen, J. (2006) Routes to registration: the UK Voluntary Register for Public Health Specialists. *Ph.com Newsletter of Faculty of Public Health*. June. London: Faculty of Public Health.

McIver, S. (1991) *Obtaining Views of Users of the Health Services*. London: King's Fund.

McKee, M. (2001) Epidemiology in the 21st century: the challenges ahead, *European Journal of Public Health*, 11: 241–2.

McKee, M. (2005) Choosing health? First choose your philosophy, *Lancet*, 365: 369–71.

McKee, M., Stott, R. and Garner, P. (2001) *International Co-operation and Health*. Oxford: Oxford University Press.

McKenzie, K. and Harpham, T. (2006) *Social capital and mental health*. London: Jessica Kingsley.

McKeown, T. (1976) *The Modern Rise of Population*. London: Edward Arnold.

McMichael, A.J. and Beaglehole, R. (2000) The changing global context of public health, *Lancet*, 356: 495–9.

McMicheal, A.J., Campbell-Lendrum, D.H., Corvalán, C.F. *et al.* (2003) *Climate Change and Human Health, Risks and Responses*. Geneva: World Health Organization.

McMichael, M. (1999) Prisoners of the proximate: loosening the constraints on epidemiology in an age of change, *American Journal of Epidemiology*, 149: 887–97.

McPherson, K. and Fox, J. (1997) Public health: an organized multidisciplinary effort, in G. Scally (ed.) *Progress in Public Health*. London: Royal Society of Medicine Press.

McQueen, D.V. (2002) The evidence debate, *Journal of Epidemiology and Community Health*, 56: 83–4.

Meads, G., Killoran, A., Ashcroft, J. and Cornish, Y. (1999) *Mixing Oil and Water: How can Primary Care Organizations Improve Health as Well as Deliver Effective Health Care?* London: Health Education Authority.

Means, R., Brenton, M., Harrison, L. and Heywood, F. (1997) *Making Partnerships Work in Community Care: A Guide for Practitioners in Housing, Health and Social Services*. Bristol: The Policy Press.

Medical Research Council (2000) *A Framework for Development and Evaluation of RCTs for Complex Interventions to Improve Health*. London: Medical Research Council.

Merkel, B. and Hubel, M. (1999) Public health policy in the European Community, in W. Holland and E. Mossialos (eds) *Public Health Policies in the European Union*. Aldershot: Ashgate.

Middleton, J. (2002) Doctors in public health. Who needs them? in A. Watterson (ed.) *Public Health in Practice*. Basingstoke: Palgrave.

Milburn, A. (2000) A Healthier Nation and a Healthier Economy: The Contribution of a Modern NHS. LSE Health Annual Lecture, London, 8 March.

Milburn, A. (2002) *Tackling Health Inequalities, Improving Public Health*. Speech to the Faculty of Public Health Medicine, 20 November, London.

Milewa, T., Harrison, S., Ahmad, W. and Tovey, P. (2002) Citizens' participation in primary healthcare planning: innovative citizenship practice in empirical perspective, *Critical Public Health*, 12(1): 39–53.

Miller, A.B. (1996) Review of extant community based epidemiological studies on health effects of hazardous wastes, *Toxicology and Industrial Health*, 12(2): 225–33.

Miller, C. (2003) Public health meets modernisation, in J. Orme, J. Powell, P. Taylor, T. Harrison and M. Grey. *Public Health for the 21st Century. New Perspectives on Policy, Participation and Practice*. Maidenhead: Open University Press/McGraw-Hill.

Miller, C., Hoggett, P. and Mayo M. (2007). The obsessions with outputs: Over regulation and the impact on the emotional identities of public service professionals, *Journal of Work, Organisation and Emotions*.

Ministry of the Environment and Natural Resources (1992) *Eco Cycles: The Basis of Sustainable Urban Development*, SOU, 43. Stockholm: Ministry of the Environment and Natural Resources.

Mokdad, A.H., Serdula, M.N., Dietz, W.H. *et al.* (2000) The continuing epidemic of obesity in the United States, *Journal of the American Medical Association*, 284: 1650–1.

Molyneux, P. and Palmer, J. (2000) *A Partnership Approach to Health and Housing. A Good Practice Briefing for Primary Care Practitioners*. London: Health and Housing Network and UKPHA.

Mondros, A. and Wilson, S. (1994) *Organizing for Power and Empowerment*. New York: Columbia University Press.

Moon, G., Myles, G. and colleagues (2000) *Epidemiology: An Introduction*. Buckingham: Open University Press.

Mooney, G. (1992) *Economics Medicine and Healthcare*. Brighton: Wheatsheaf.

Morens, D.M. *et al.* (2004) The challenge of emerging and re-emerging infectious diseases, *Nature*, 430: 242–9.

Morrell, G. and Wainwright, S. (2006) *Destitution Amongst Refugees and Asylum Seekers in the UK*. London: Information Centre for Asylum Seekers and Refugees (ICAR). www.icar.org.uk/?=6572 (accessed 28 July 2006).

Morris, J. (1991) *Pride Against Prejudice: Transforming Attitudes to Disability*. London: The Women's Press.

Morris, J.N. (1975) *Uses of Epidemiology*. Edinburgh: Churchill Livingstone.

Morrow, V. (2002) Children's experiences of 'community': implications of social capital discourses, *Social Capital: Insights From Research*. London: Health Development Agency.

Mossialos, E. and McKee, M. (2002) Health care and the European Union, *British Medical Journal*, 324: 991–2.

Moyer, A., Finney, J.W., Swearingen, C.E. and Vergun, P. (2002). Brief interventions for alcohol problems: a meta-analytic review of controlled investigations in treatment-seeking and non-treatment-seeking populations. *Addiction*, 97: 279.

Muir Gray, J. (2001) The public health professional as political activist, in D. Pencheon, C. Gust, D. Melzer and J. Muir Gray (eds) *Oxford Handbook of Public Health Practice*. Oxford: Oxford University Press.

Mulrow, C.D. (1995) Rationale for systematic reviews, in I. Chalmers and D.G. Altman (eds) *Systematic Reviews*. London: BMJ Publishing Group.

Murkerjee, M. (1995) Toxins abounding – despite the lessons of Bhopal chemical accidents are on the rise, *Scientific American*, June, 15–16.

Mykhalovskiy, E. and McCoy, L. (2002) Troubling ruling discourses of health: using institutional ethnography in community-based research, *Critical Public Health*, 12(1): 17–37.

Naidoo, J. and Wills, J. (1998) *Practising Health Promotion: Dilemmas and Challenges*. London: Baillière Tindall.

Nash, V. (2002) *Reclaiming Community*. London: Institute for Public Policy Research.

National Assembly for Wales (NAW) (1999) *Developing a Health Impact Assessment Toolkit in Wales*. Cardiff: NAW.

National Association of County and City Health Officials (2002) *National Public Health Performance Standards Program*. www.naccho.org/project48.cfm (accessed 2 December 2002).

National Audit Office (2002) *Facing the Challenge: NHS Emergency Planning in England*. Report by the Comptroller and Auditor General, HC 36 Session 2002–03, 15 November. www.nao.gov.uk/publications/nao_reports/02–03/020336es.pdf (accessed 24 January 2003).

National Health Services Management Executive (NHSME) (1992) *Local Voices: The Views of Local People in Purchasing for Health*. London: NHSME.

National Institute for Health and Clinical Excellence (2005) *Putting NICE Guidance into Practice: How NICE is Supporting the Implementation of its Guidance*. London: NICE.

National Institute for Health and Clinical Excellence (2006) *Methods for Development of NICE Public Health Guidance*. London: NICE.

National Social Marketing Centre (2006) *It's Our Health! Realising the Potential of Effective Social Marketing*. London: National Consumer Council.

Navarro, V. (1998) Comment: Whose Globalization? *American Journal of Public Health*, 88(5): 742.

Nazroo, J. (1997) *The Health of Britain's Ethnic Minorities*. London: Policy Studies Institute.

Neighbourhood Renewal Unit (2001) *Accreditation Guidance for Local Strategic Partnerships*. London: Department of Transport, Local Government and the Regions.

Neighbourhood Renewal Unit (2002) *The Learning Curve: Developing Skills and Knowledge for Neighbourhood Renewal*. London: Neighbourhood Renewal Unit, Office of the Deputy Prime Minister.

Nettleton, S. (1998) Women and the new paradigm of medicine, *Critical Social Policy*, 18(2).

New Economics Foundation (2006) http://www.neweconomics.org/gen/well-being_power. aspx (accessed on 14 August 2006).

Newman, J. (2001) *Modernising Governance*. London: Sage.

Newman, J. and Vidler, E. (2006) More than a matter of choice? Consumerism and the modernisation of health care, in L. Bauld, K. Clarke and T. Maltby (eds) *On Behalf of the Social Policy Association, Social Policy Review 18: Analysis and Debate in Social Policy, 2006*. Bristol: The Policy Press.

Newman, J., Barnes, M., Sullivan, H. and Knops, A. (2004) Public participation and collaborative governance, *Journal of Social Policy*, 33(2): 203–23.

NHS Centre for Reviews and Dissemination (1995) *Review of the Research on the Effectiveness of Health Service Interventions to Reduce Variations in Health*. York: University of York.

NHS Centre for Reviews and Dissemination (2000a) *Evidence from Systematic Reviews of Research Relevant to Implementing the Wider Public Health Agenda*. York: University of York.

NHS Centre for Reviews and Dissemination (2000b) Promoting the initiation of breastfeeding, *Effective Healthcare Bulletin*, 6(2). York: NHS Centre for Reviews and Dissemination, University of York.

NHS Employers (2006) *Delivering Investment in General Practice. Revisions to the GMS Contract, 2006/7*. London: NHS Employers.

NHS Executive (1998a) *Establishing Primary Care Groups*, HSC 1998/065. Leeds: NHS Executive.

NHS Executive (1998b) Department of Health NHS executive guidance, *Planning for a Major Incident*. London: The Stationery Office.

NHS Executive (1999) *Quality and Performance in the NHS: High Level Performance Indicators*. Leeds: NHS Executive.

NHS Health Scotland (2003) *Leap for Health*. Edinburgh: NHS Health Scotland.

NHS Scotland (2003) *Partnerships for Care, Scotland's Health White Paper*. Edinburgh: NHS.

Nolte, E. (2004) New citizens, in J. Healy and M. McKee (eds) *Accessing Health Care*. Oxford: Medical Publications.

Nolte, E. and McKee, M. (2004) *Does Health Care Save Lives? Avoidable Mortality Revisited*. London: The Nuffield Trust.

Nolte, E., Scholz, R., Shkolnikov, V. and McKee, M. (2002) The contribution of medical care to changing life expectancy in Germany and Poland, *Social Science and Medicine*, 55: 1905–21.

Nord, E. (1999) *Cost-value Analysis in Health Care*. http://assets.cambridge.org/0521643082/sample/0521643082WSN01.pdf (accessed 30 August 2002).

North, N. (1991) Neighbourhoods: the local population as health care consumers, citizens or providers? *Critical Public Health*, 4: 8–15.

Northern Ireland Department of Health and Social Services (1995) *Regional Strategy for Health and Social Well-being 1997–2002*. Belfast: Northern Ireland Department of Health and Social Services.

Northern Ireland Department of Health and Social Services Voluntary Activity Unit (1996) *Monitoring and Evaluating Community Development in Northern Ireland*. Belfast: Northern Ireland Department of Health and Social Services.

Northern Ireland Executive (2002) *Investing for Health*. Belfast: Department of Health Social Services and Public Safety.

Novotny, T. and Zhao, Z. (1999) Consumption and production waste: another externality of tobacco use, *Tobacco Control*, 8: 75–80.

Nutbeam, D. (2002) Unpublished address to UK Public Health Alliance Conference, March, Glasgow.

Nutbeam, B. and Wise, M. (2002) Structures and strategies for public health intervention, in R. Detels, J. McEwen, R. Beaglehole and H. Tanaka (eds) *Oxford Textbook of Public Health Volume 3. The Practice of Public Health*, 4th edn. Oxford: Oxford University Press.

Nutley, S., Davies, H. and Walter, I. (2002) *Evidence Based Policy and Practice: Cross Sector Lessons from the UK*. Working paper 9. London: ESRC Centre for Evidence Based Policy and Practice, University of London.

Office of the Deputy Prime Minister (ODPM) (2003) *Egan Review: Skills for Sustainable Communities Sustainable Communities*. Norwich: HMSO.

Office of the Deputy Prime Minister (ODPM) (2004) *Local Area Agreements: A Prospectus*. London: Office of the Deputy Prime Minister.

Office of the Deputy Prime Minister (ODPM) (2006a) *Local Area Agreements: Guidance for Round 3 and Refresh on Rounds 2 and 3*. London: Office of the Deputy Prime Minister.

Office of the Deputy Prime Minister (ODPM) (2006b) Empowerment and the Deal for Devolution: Speech by Rt Hon David Miliband MP Minister of Communities and Local Government. London: Office of the Deputy Prime Minister. February.

Office of the Deputy Prime Minister (ODPM) (2006c) *The Challenges of Local Governance in 2015*. The Tavistock Institute, SOLON Consultants and the Local Government Information Unit, local: vision. London: The Stationery Office. April.

Office for National Statistics (2006) *Cancer Survival: England and Wales 1991–2001*. London: Office for National Statistics.

Office of Public Management, University of the West of England, Warwick University (2005) *A Process Evaluation of the Negotiation of Local Area Agreements*, for the Local Government Research Unit, ODPM. London: Office of the Deputy Prime Minister.

O'Brien, M. (2000) Have lessons been learned from the UK bovine spongiform encephalopathy (BSE) epidemic? *International Journal of Epidemiology*, 29: 730–3.

O'Keefe, E. (2000) Equity, democracy and globalisation, *Critical Public Health*, 10(2): 167–77.

O'Neill, J. (1996) Cost benefit analysis: rationality and the plurality of values, *The Ecologist*, 16(3): 98–103.

Oakley, A., Rajan, L. and Grant, A. (1990) Social support and pregnancy outcome, *British Journal of Obstetrics and Gynaecology*, 97: 155–62.

Oliver, M. (1996) *Understanding Disability: From Theory to Practice*. London: Macmillan.

Oliver, M. and Barnes, C. (1998) *Disabled People and Social Policy: From Exclusion to Inclusion*. London: Longman.

Organization for Economic Cooperation and Development (OECD) (1996) *Integrating Environment and Economy: Progress in the 1990s*. Paris: OECD.

Organization for Economic Cooperation and Development (OECD) (2001) *Public Sector Leadership for the 21st Century*. Paris: OECD.

Orme, J., Powell, J., Taylor, P., Harrison, T. and Grey, M. (eds) (2003) *Public Health for the 21st Century: New Perspectives on Policy, Participation and Practice*. Maidenhead: McGraw-Hill/Open University Press.

Ormerod, P. (1994) *The Death of Economics*. London: Faber & Faber.

Ottewill, R. and Wall, A. (1990) *The Growth and Development of Community Health Services*. Sunderland: Business Education Publishers.

Owen, D. (1965) *English Philanthropy 1660–1960*. Cambridge, MA: Harvard University Press.

Page, D. (2000) *Communities in the Balance: The Reality of Social Exclusion on Housing Estates*. York: York Publishing Services.

Palmer, S. (2006) *Sustainable communities – the right paradigm for health protection*, in A. Furber (ed.) *Ph.com The Newsletter of the Faculty of Public Health*. London: Faculty of Public Health.

Pan American Health Organization (2000) *Essential Public Health Functions*. www.paho.org/english/gov/cd/cd42_15-e.pdf (accessed 2 December 2002).

Pareto, V. (1935) *Mind and Society*. New York: Harcourt Brace Javanovich.

Partners in Change (2001) *Communities and Health – Report from Outcomes Workshop*. Edinburgh: Partners in Change.

Patterson, I. and Judge, K. (2002) Equality of access to healthcare, in J. Mackenbach and M. Bakker (eds) *Reducing Inequalities in Health: A European Perspective*. London: Routledge.

Patterson, W.J. and Painter, M.J. (1999) Bovine spongiform encephalopathy and new variant Creutzfeldt-Jakob disease: an overview, *Communicable Disease and Public Health*, 2: 5–13.

Pawson, R. (2002a) Evidence-based policy: in search of a method, *Evaluation*, April, 8(2): 157–81.

Pawson, R. (2002b) *Evidence Based Policy: II. The Promise of 'Realist Synthesis'*. Working paper 4. London: ESRC Centre for Evidence Based Policy and Practice, University of London.

Pawson, R. (2002c) *Does Megan's Law work? A Theory-driven Systematic Review*. Working paper 8. London: ESRC Centre for Evidence Based Policy and Practice, University of London.

Pawson, R. and Tilley, N. (1997) *Realistic Evaluation*. London: Sage.

Payne, N. and Saul, C. (1997) Variations in use of cardiology services in a health authority: comparison of coronary artery revascularisation rates with prevalence of angina and coronary mortality, *British Medical Journal*, 314: 257–61.

Pearce, D., Barbier, E. and Markayanda, A. (1990) *Sustainable Development*. London: Earthscan.

Pearce, I.H. and Crocker, L.H. (1943) *The Peckham Experiment: A Study of the Living Structure of Society*. London: Allen & Unwin.

Pearce, N. (1996) Traditional epidemiology, modern epidemiology and public health, *American Journal of Public Health*, 86(5): 678–83.

Peckham, S. (2004) Reconciling individual and community needs: community orientated approaches to health, in J. Kai and C. Drinkwater (eds) *Primary Care in Urban Disadvantaged Communities*. Oxford: Radcliffe Medical Press.

Peckham, S. and Exworthy, M. (2003) *Primary Care in the UK: Policy, Organization and Management*. Basingstoke: Macmillan/Palgrave.

Pencheon, D., Gust, C., Melzer, D. and Muir Gray, J. (eds) (2001) *Oxford Handbook of Public Health Practice*. Oxford: Oxford University Press.

Pereira, J. (1993) What does equity in health mean? *Journal of Social Policy*, 22(1): 19–48.

Peters, J., Ellis, E., Blank L., Goyder, E. and Johnson, M. (2005a) *National Evaluation of New Deal for Communities: Relocation or Extension of Health Care Services*, Research Report 55: http:/ndcevaluation.adc.shu.ac.uk/ndcevaluation/reports.asp.

Peters, J., Ellis, E., Goyder, E. and Blank, L. (2005b) *National Evaluation of New Deal for Communities: Healthy Eating Initiatives*. Research Report 56. http:/ndcevaluation.adc.shu.ac.uk/ndcevaluation/reports.asp

Petersen, A. and Lupton, D. (1996) *The New Public Health*. London: Sage.

Peto, R. (1998) Mortality from breast cancer in UK has decreased suddenly, *British Medical Journal*, 317: 476.

Pfeffer, J. (1992) *Managing with Power: Politics and Influence in Organizations*. Boston: Harvard Business School Press.

Philip, W., James, T., Nelson, M., Ralph, A. and Leather, S. (1997) Socio-economic determinants of health: The contribution of nutrition to inequalities in health. *British Medical Journal*, 314: 1545. May.

Phillips Report (2000) *BSE Enquiry Report*. London: HMSO.

Pickard, S. (1998) Citizenship and consumerism in healthcare: a critique of citizens' juries, *Social Policy and Administration*, 32: 226–44.

Pilisuk, M. and Parks, S.H. (1986) *The Healing Web: Social Networks and Human Survival.* Hanover, NE: University Press of New England.

Pill, R. and Stott, N.C.H. (1982) Concept of illness causation and responsibility, *Social Science and Medicine,* 16: 43–52.

Pittet, D. and Donaldson, L. (2006) Challenging the world: patient safety and health care-associated infection, *International Journal for Quality in Health Care,* 18(1): 4–8.

Plsek, P.E. and Greenhalgh, T. (2001) The challenge of complexity in health care, *British Medical Journal,* 323: 625–8.

Policy Action Team 17 (2000) *Joining it up Locally, National Strategy for Neighbourhood Renewal.* London: Department of the Environment, Transport and the Regions.

Pollitt, C. (1993) *Managerialism and the Public Services,* 2nd edn. Oxford: Blackwell.

Pollock, A. (2004) *NHS Plc: The Privatisation of Our Health Care.* London: Verso Books.

Pollock, A. and Price, D. (2000) Globalisation? Privatisation! *Health Matters,* 41: 12–13.

Pollock, A., Shaoul, J., Rowland, D. and Player, S. (2001) *Public Services and the Private Sector: A Response to the IPPR.* A catalyst working paper. London: Catalyst.

Popay, J. (ed.) (2001) *Regeneration and Health: A Selected Review of Research.* London: King's Fund.

Popay, J., Williams, G., Thomas, C. and Gatrell, T. (1998) Theorising inequalities in health: the place of lay knowledge, *Sociology of Health and Illness,* 20(5): 619–44.

Popay, J. *et al.* (2005) *Taking Strategic Action For Engaging Communities (SAFEC).* Lancaster: University of Lancaster.

Porter, M. and MacIntyre, S. (1984) What is, must be best: a research note on Conservative or deferential responses to antenatal care provision, *Social Science and Medicine,* 19: 1197–200.

Portes, A. (1998) Social capital – its origin and applications in modern society, *Annual Review of Sociology,* 24: 1–24.

Powell, D. and Leiss, W. (1997) *Mad Cows and Mothers Milk, the Perils of Poor Risk Communication.* Quebec, Canada: McGill Queens University Press.

Powell, M. (1998) *New Labour, New Welfare State? The 'Third Way' in British Social Policy.* Bristol: The Policy Press.

Powell, M. (2000) New Labour and the third way in the British welfare state: a new and distinctive approach? *Critical Social Policy,* February, 20(1): 39–59.

Powell, M. and Exworthy, M. (2001) Joined-up solutions to address health inequalities analysing policy, process and resource streams, *Public Money and Management,* January–March, 21–6.

Powell, M. and Exworthy, M. (2002) Partnerships, quasi-networks and social policy, in C. Glendinning, M. Powell and K. Rummery (eds) *Partnerships, New Labour and the Governance of Welfare.* Bristol: The Policy Press.

Powell, M. and Glendinning, C. (2002) Introduction, in C. Glendinning, M. Powell and K. Rummery (eds) *Partnerships, New Labour and the Governance of Welfare.* Bristol: The Policy Press.

Power, A. and Tunstall, R. (1995) *Swimming Against the Tide: Polarisation or Progress on 20 Unpopular Council Estates.* York: Joseph Rowntree Foundation.

Pratt, J. (1995) *Practitioner and Practices: A Conflict of Values.* Oxford: Radcliffe Medical Press.

Pratt, J., Plamping, D. and Gordon, P. (1998) *Partnership Fit for Purpose?* London: King's Fund.

Price, C. and Tsouros, A. (eds) (1996) *Our Cities, Our Future.* Copenhagen: WHO.

Price, D., Pollock, A.M. and Shaoul, J. (1999) How the World Trade Organisation is shaping domestic policies in health care, *Lancet,* 354: 1889–91.

Pugh, G. (ed.) (1997) *Partnerships in Action.* London: NCB.

Purdue, D., Razzaque, K., Hambleton, R. and Stewart, M. (2000) *Community Leadership in Urban Regeneration.* Bristol: The Policy Press.

Putnam, R. (1993) *Making Democracy Work: Civic Traditions in Modern Italy.* Princeton, NJ: Princeton University Press.

Putnam, R. (2000) *Bowling Alone – The Collapse and Revival of American Community.* London: Simon and Shuster.

Radford, G., Lapthorne, D., Boot, N. and Maconachie, M. (1997) Community development and social deprivation, in G. Scally (ed.) *Progress in Public Health.* London: FT Healthcare.

Ramadan, N. (2006) *Seeking Asylum: A Report on the Living Conditions of Asylum Seekers in London.* London: Refugee Media Action Group. www.migrantsresourcecentre.org.uk (accessed 28 July 2006).

Ranade, W. (1998) *A Future for the NHS? Health Care for the Millennium.* Harlow: Longman.

Randall, E. (2001) *The European Union and Health Policy.* Basingstoke: Palgrave.

Rao, M. (2006) *Editorial. ph.com. newsletter of the Faculty of Public Health.* June. London: Faculty of Public Health.

Raphael, D. and Bryant, T. (2002) The limitations of population health as a model for a new public health, *Health Promotion International,* 17(2): 189–99.

Rawles, J. (1972) *A Theory of Justice.* Oxford: Oxford University Press.

Rawnsley, A. (2001) *Servants of the People: The Inside Story of New Labour.* London: Penguin.

Rees, W. (1992) Ecological footprints and appropriated carrying capacity: what urban economics leaves out, *Environment and Urbanisation,* 4(2): 121–30.

Rees, W.E. (1998), Is 'sustainable city' an oxymoron? *Local Environment,* October, 2(3): 303–10.

Refugee Council (2002) *Government Announcement and Proposal Since its White Paper on Asylum: A Summary.* London: Refugee Council.

Refugee Council (2006a) *Asylum and Immigration Status and Educational Entitlement.* London: Refugee Council. www.refugeecouncil.org.uk/downloads/entitlements_table.pdf (accessed 26 June 2006).

Refugee Council (2006b) *The National Asylum Support Service.* London: Refugee Council. www.refugeecouncil.org.uk/infocentre/entit/sentit001.htm (accessed 26 June 2006).

Refugee Council (2006c) *Entitlement to Education.* London: Refugee Council. www.refugee council.org.uk/infocentre/entit/sentit005.htm (accessed on 26 June 2006).

Regan, M. (1999) Health protection in the next millennium: from tactics to strategy, *Journal of Epidemiology and Community Health,* 53: 517–18.

Reilly, D. (2001) Enhancing human healing, *British Medical Journal,* 322: 120–1.

Rice, V.H. and Stead, L.F. (2006) Nursing interventions for smoking cessation, *The Cochrane Database of Systematic Reviews,* Issue 2.

Richards, S., Barnes, M., Coulson, A. *et al.* (1999) *Cross-cutting Issues in Public Policy and Public Services.* London: DETR.

Richardson, A. and Goodman, M. (1983) *Self Help and Mutual Care: Mutual Aid Organisations in Practice.* London: Policy Studies Institute.

Richardson, L. and Mumford, C. (2002) Community, neighbourhood and social infrastructure, in J. Hills and J. Le Grand (eds) *Understanding Social Exclusion.* Oxford: Oxford University Press.

Ring, I. and Brown, N. (2003) The health status of indigenous peoples and others, *British Medical Journal,* 327: 404–5.

Ritzer, G. (1993) *The McDonaldization of Society.* London: Sage.

Roberts, E. (1992) *Healthy Participation: An Evaluative Study of the Hartcliffe Health and Environment Action Group – A Community Development Project in South Bristol.* London: South Bank Polytechnic.

Roberts, H. (2000) *What Works in Reducing Inequalities in Child Health*. Barkingside: Barnardo's.

Roberts, K. and Harris, J. (2002) *Disabled People in Refugee and Asylum Seeking Communities*. Bristol: The Policy Press.

Roberts, V., Russell, H., Harding, A. and Parkinson, M. (1995) *Public/Private Voluntary Partnerships in Local Government*. Luton: Local Government Management Board.

Robertson, R. (1992) *Globalization*. London: Sage.

Robinson, T.P. (2000) Spatial statistics and geographical information systems in epidemiology and public health, *Advances in Parasitology*, 47: 81–128.

Robson, B., Brodford, M. and Deas, I. (1994) *Assessing the Impact of Urban Policy*. London: HMSO.

Rose, G. (1985) Sick individuals and sick populations, *International Journal of Epidemiology*, 14: 32–8.

Rostow, W.W. (1966) *The Stages of Economic Growth: A Non-communist Manifesto*. Cambridge: Cambridge University Press.

Rowntree, S. (1901) *Poverty: A Study of Town Life*. London: Macmillan.

Rowson, M. (2000) Blueprint for an unequal world, *Health Matters*, 41: 10–11.

Rowson, M. and Koivusalo, M. (2000) Who will inherit the earth? *Health Matters*, 41: 16–17.

Royal College of Physicians (RCP) (1962) *Smoking and Health*. London: Royal College of Physicians.

Royal College of Physicians (RCP) (2006) *Myocardial Infarction National Audit Project. Fifth Public Report. How the NHS manages heart attacks*. London: Royal College of Physicians.

Royal Society (1992) *Risk: Analysis, Perception and Management*. London: The Royal Society.

Ruger, J.P. and Yach, D. (2005) Global functions at the World Health Organization. *British Medical Journal*, 330: 1099–100.

Rummery, K. and Glendinning, C. (1997) *Working Together: Primary Care Involvement in Commissioning Social Care Services. Debates in Primary Care No 2*. Manchester: NPCRDC, University of Manchester.

Russell, H. (2001) *Local Strategic Partnerships: Lessons from New Commitment to Regeneration*. Bristol: The Policy Press.

Russell, H. and Killoran, A. (1999) *Public Health and Regeneration: Making the Links*. London: Health Education Authority.

Rutstein, D.D., Berenberg, W., Chalmers, T.C. *et al.* (1976) Measuring the quality of medical care: a clinical method, *New England Journal of Medicine*, 294: 582–9.

Rutstein, D.D., Berenberg, W., Chalmers, T.C. *et al.* (1980) Measuring the quality of medical care: second revision of tables of indexes. *New England Journal of Medicine*, 302: 1146.

Rychetnik, L., Frommer, M., Hawe, P. and Shiell, A. (2002) Criteria for evaluating evidence on public health interventions, *Journal of Epidemiology and Community Health*, 56: 119–27.

Sachs, J. (2000) A new map of the world, *Economist*, 355(8176): 81–3.

Sackett, D.L., Richardson, W.S., Rosenberg, W. and Haynes, R.B. (1997) *Evidence Based Medicine: How to Practice and Teach EBM*. London: Churchill Livingstone.

Sackett, D.L., Straus, S.E., Richardson, W.S., Rosenberg, W. and Haynes, R.B. (2000) *Evidence-based Medicine*. London: Churchill Livingstone.

Saffron, L. (1993) The consumers perception of risk, *Consumer Policy Review*, 3(4): 213–21.

Sampson, R. (2004) Networks and neighbourhood in H. McCarthy *et al.* (eds) *Network Logic*. London: DEMOS Collection 20.

Sandford, I. (2001) *Mainstreaming of HAZ Projects in LSL*. Lambeth, Southwark and Lewisham: HAZ.

Santillo, D., Johnstone, P. and Singhofen, A. (1999) *The Way Forward – Out of the Chemical Crisis*. Stockholm: Greenpeace International.

Scally, G. (ed.) (1997) *Progress in Public Health*. London: Financial Times Healthcare.

Scally, G. and Donaldson, L.J. (1998) Looking forward: Clinical governance and the drive for quality improvement in the new NHS in England, *British Medical Journal*, 317: 61–5.

Scally, G. and Womack, J. (2004) The importance of the past in public health, *Journal of Epidemiology and Community Health*, 58: 751–5.

SCDC (Scottish Community Development Centre) (2001) *Achieving Better Community Development*. http://www.scdc.org.uk/abcd_summary.htm (accessed 20 July 2002).

Schein, E. (1993) On dialogue, culture, and organisational learning, *Organisational Dynamics*, autumn, 22(3): 40–51.

Schuller, T., Baron, S. and Field, J. (2000) Social capital: a review and critique, *Social Capital: Critical Perspectives*. Oxford: Oxford University Press.

Schwartz, S. (1994) The fallacy of the ecological fallacy: the potential misuse of a concept and the consequences, *American Journal of Public Health*, 84(5): 819–24.

Scott, T. (2002) *Report of the First Meeting of the Joint NHS Leadership Centre and Faculty of Public Health Medicine, Public Health Leadership Thinking and Planning Group*, 16/17 May. Oxford: NHS Leadership Centre.

Scottish Executive (1998) *Working Together for a Healthier Scotland*, Cm 3854. Edinburgh: The Stationery Office.

Scottish Executive Health Department (2001) *Our National Health: A Plan for Action, a Plan for Change*. Edinburgh: Scottish Executive Health Department.

Scottish Office Department of Health (1999) *Towards a Healthier Scotland*. Edinburgh: The Stationery Office.

Scriven, A. and Orme, J. (2001) *Health Promotion: Professional Perspectives*, 2nd edn. Basingstoke: Palgrave/Open University.

Secretary of State for Health (1992) *The Health of the Nation. A Strategy for Health in England*, Cm 1986. London: HMSO.

Secretary of State for Health (1998) *Our Healthier Nation: A Contract for Health, A Consultation Paper*, Cm 3852. London: HMSO.

Secretary of State for Health (1999) *Saving Lives: Our Healthier Nation*, Cm 4386. London: The Stationery Office.

Secretary of State for Health (2000) *The NHS Plan: A Plan for Investment, a Plan for Reform*, Cm 4818. London: The Stationery Office.

Secretary of State for Health (2004) *Choosing Health: Making healthier choices easier*, Cm 6374. London: The Stationery Office.

Secretary of State for Health (2006) *Our Health, Our Care, Our Say: A New Direction for Community Services*, Cm 6737. London: The Stationery Office.

Secretary of State for Northern Ireland (1998) *Fit for the Future: A Consultation Document on the Government's Proposals for the Future of Health and Personal Social Services in Northern Ireland*. Belfast: The Stationery Office.

Secretary of State for Wales (1998) *NHS Wales: Putting Patients First*, CMB 3841. Cardiff: The Stationery Office.

Seebohm, P., Henderson, P. *et al.* (2005) *Together we will Change: Community Development, Mental Health and Diversity*. London: The Sainsbury Centre for Mental Health.

Sefton, T., Byford, S., McDaid, D., Hills, J. and Knapp, M. (2002) *Making the Most of It: Economic Evaluation in the Social Welfare Field*. York: York Publishing Service.

Senge, P. (1999) *The Dance of Change: The Challenge of Sustaining Momentum in Learning Organisations*. London: Nicholas Brealey.

Sennett, R. (2006) *The Culture of the New Capitalism*. New Haven and London: Yale University Press.

Service Users Advisory Group (2001) *Nothing About Us Without Us*. London: Department of Health.

Shaper, A.G., Pocock, S.J., Phillips, A.W. and Walker, M. (1987) A scoring system to identify men at high risk of heart attack, *Health Trends*, 19: 37–9.

Shapiro, S. (1994) Meta-analysis/schmeta-analysis, *American Journal of Epidemiology*, 140: 771–8.

Shaw, S. and Abbott, S. (2002) Too much to handle? *Health Service Journal*, 27 June, 28–9.

Shaw, M., Dorling, D., Gordon, D. and Davey Smith, G. (1999) *The Widening Gap: Health Inequalities and Policy in Britain*. Bristol: The Policy Press.

Shaw, M., Davey Smith, G. and Dorling, D. (2005) Health inequalities and New Labour: how the promises compare with real progress, *British Medical Journal*, 330: 1016–21.

Shepherd, J. (1994). Preventing injuries from bar glasses. *British Medical Journal*, 308: 932–3.

Sherman, L.W., Farrington, D.P., Welsh, B.C. and Mackenzie, D.L. (eds) (2002) *Evidence-based Crime Prevention*. London: Routledge.

Shibuya, K., Ciecierski, C., Guindon, E., Bettcher, D.W., Evans, D.B. and Murray, C.J.L. (2003) WHO Framework Convention on Tobacco Control: development of an evidence based global public health treaty, *British Medical Journal*, 327: 154–7.

Shiva, V. (2000) *Respect for the Earth: Globalisation*. http://news.bbc.co.uk/hi/english/static/events/reith_2000/lecture5.stm

Silburn, R., Lucas, D., Page, R. and Hanna, L. (1999) *Neighbourhood Images in Nottingham*, JRF Area Regeneration Series. York: York Publishing Services.

Silverman, D. (1998) The quality of qualitative health research: the open-ended interview and its alternatives, *Social Sciences in Health*, 4(2): 104–17.

Singleton, C. and Aird, B. (2002) As good as new: will the primary care infrastructure deliver the public health agenda? *Health Service Journal*, 27 June, 28–9.

Skeffington, A. (1969) *People and Planning*. London: HMSO.

Skelcher, C., McCabe, A. and Lowndes, V. with Nanton, P. (1996) *Community Networks in Urban Regeneration*. Bristol: The Policy Press.

Skills for Health (2002a) *National Occupational Standards/Competencies for Public Health Practice*. Bristol: Skills for Health.

Skills for Health (2002b) *Functional Map of Public Health Practice*. Bristol: Skills for Health.

Skinner, S. and Wilson, M. (2001) *Assessing Community Strengths*. London: Community Development Foundation.

Smaje, C. (1996) The ethnic patterning of health: new directions for theory and research, *Sociology of Illness and Health*, 18(2): 139–71.

Smith, A., Watkiss, P., Tweddle, G. *et al.* (2005) *The Validity of Food Miles as an Indicator of Sustainable Development: Final Report*. London: DEFRA.

Smith, S.J., Alexander, A. and Easterlow, D. (1997) Rehousing as health intervention; miracle or mirage, *Health Place*, 3: 203–16.

Smithies, J. and Adams, L. (1990) *Community Participation in Health Promotion*. London: Health Education Authority.

Smithies, J. and Webster, G. (1998) *Community Involvement in Health: From Passive Recipients to Active Participants*. Aldershot: Ashgate.

Social Exclusion Unit (1998) *Bringing Britain Together: A National Strategy for Neighbourhood Renewal*, Cm 4045. London: HMSO.

Social Exclusion Unit (2000) *National Strategy for Neighbourhood Renewal*. London: HMSO.

Social Exclusion Unit (2001a) *A New Commitment to Neighbourhood Renewal: National Strategy Action Plan*. London: Cabinet Office.

Social Exclusion Unit (2001b) *National Strategy for Neighbourhood Renewal: A Framework for Consultation*. London: Cabinet Office.

Social Exclusion Unit (2002) *Transport and Social Exclusion*. London: Cabinet Office.

Social Exclusion Unit (2003) *Making the Connections: Final Report on Transport and Social Exclusion*. Summary. February. London: Social Exclusion Unit.

Social Exclusion Unit (2004) *Social Exclusion and Mental Health*. London: Cabinet Office.

Solesbury, W. (2002) The ascendancy of evidence, *Planning Theory and Practice*, 3(1): 90–6.

South West Regional Resilience Forum (2006), *Major Flooding at Boscastle and Surrounding Areas of North Cornwall 16th August 2004, a Summary of Lessons Learned*. Multi-agency report of the South West Regional Resilience Forum (SWRRF) At: www.devon-cornwall.police.uk/v3/showpdf.cfm?pdfname=boscastledebrief.pdf (accessed 14 August 2006).

Spear, S. (2003) Terrorism contingency planning saved lives during last legionnaires outbreak, *Environmental Health News*, 16 January.

Spencer, K. (1982) Comprehensive Community Programmes, in S. Leach and J. Stewart (eds) *Approaches to Public Policy*. London: Allen & Unwin.

Spiegel, D., Bloom, R. *et al.* (1989) Effect of psychosocial treatment on survival of patients with metastatic breast cancer. *The Lancet*, October 14: 888–91.

Spiegelhalter, D.J., Myles, J.P., Jones, D.R. and Abrams, K.R. (1999) An introduction to Bayesian methods in health technology assessment, *British Medical Journal*, 319: 508–12.

Stacey M, (1960) *Tradition and Change: A Study of Banbury*. Oxford: Oxford University Press.

Stacey, M. (1969) The myth of community studies, *British Journal of Sociology*, 20(2): 134–47.

Stacey, M. (1976) The health service consumer: a sociological misconception, in M. Stacey (ed.) *Sociology of the NHS*, Sociological Monograph no. 22. Keele: University of Keele.

Stafford, M., Bartley, M., Wilkinson, R. *et al.* (2002) Healthy neighbourhoods: investigating the role of social cohesion. Paper presented to the Health Development Agency conference Social Action for Health and Wellbeing: Experiences from Policy, Research and Practice, London, 20–1 June.

Standing Conference for Community Development (SCCD) (2001) *Strategic Framework for Community Development*. Sheffield: SCCD.

Starfield, B. (1998) *Primary Care: Balancing Health Needs, Services and Technology*. New York: Oxford University Press.

Starkey, F., Taylor, P. and Means, R. (2001) Coming to terms with primary care trusts: the views of PCG board members, *Managing Community Care*, 9(2): 22–9.

Stein, Z., Susser, M., Saenger, G. and Marolla, F. (1975) *Famine and Human Development: the Dutch Hunger Winter of 1944–45*. New York: Oxford University Press.

Stephens, C. (2000) La globalisacion nos matan – globalisation is killing us, *Health Matters*, 41: 6–8.

Stevrer, R. (2003) The US's retreat from the Kyoto Protocol: An account of a policy change and its implications for future climate policy, *European Environment*, 13: 344–60.

Stewart, M. (2000) Local action to counter exclusion: a research review, *Joining It Up Locally – The Evidence Base*, report of Policy Action Team 17, Vol. 2. London: DETR.

Stewart, M. (2002) Systems governance: towards effective partnership working. Paper to the HAD Seminar Series on Tackling Health Inequalities, September, London.

Stewart, M. and Howard, J. (2005) *Mainstreaming: Evidence from the National Evaluation*, Research Report 66. http:/ndcevaluation.adc.shu.ac.uk/ndcevaluation/reports.asp

Stewart, M., Goss, S., Clarke, R. *et al.* (1999) *Cross-cutting Issues Affecting Local Government*. London: DETR.

Stewart-Brown, L. and Prothero, L. (1988) Evaluation in community development, *Health Education Journal*, 4447(4): 156–61.

Stewart-Brown, S., Shaw, R. and Morgan, L. (2002) *Social capital in the home and health in later life*. Paper presented to the Health Development Agency conference Social Action for Health and Wellbeing: Experiences from Policy, Research and Practice, London, 20–1 June.

Stevens, A. and Raftery, J. (eds) (1997) *Health Care Needs Assessment*, 2nd edn. Oxford: Radcliffe Medical Press.

Strachey, L. ([1918] 1948) *Eminent Victorians*. London: Penguin.

Sullivan, H. (2001) Maximising the contributions of neighbourhoods – the role of community governance, *Public Policy and Administration*, 16(2): 29–48.

Sullivan, H. and Skelcher, C. (2002) *Working Across Boundaries. Collaboration in Public Services*. Basingstoke: Palgrave.

Sullivan, H., Root, A., Moran, D. and Smith, M. (2001) *Area Committees and Neighbourhood Management*. London: Local Government Information Unit.

Sullivan, H., Judge, K. and Sewell, K. (2004) 'In the eye of the beholder': perceptions of local impact in English Health Action Zones, *Social Science and Medicine*, 59: 1603–12.

Sullivan, H., Barnes, M. and Matka, E. (2006) Collaborative capacity and strategies in area based initiatives, *Public Administration*, 84(2): 289–310.

Summerton, N. (1999) Accrediting research practices, *British Journal of General Practice*, 49(438): 63–4.

Susser, M. and Susser, E. (1996a) Choosing a future for epidemiology: I. Eras and paradigms, *American Journal of Public Health*, 86(5): 668–73.

Susser, M. and Susser, E. (1996b) Choosing a future for epidemiology: II. From black box to Chinese boxes and eco-epidemiology, *American Journal of Public Health*, 86(5): 674–7.

Sustrans (2006) *Economic Appraisal of Local Walking and Cycling Routes*. Bristol: Sustrans.

Swann, C. and Morgan, A. (2002) *Social Capital: Insights From Research*. London: Health Development Agency.

Swann, C., Falce, C., Morgan, A. and Kelly, M. (2002) *HDA Evidence Base. Work in Progress. Process and Quality Standards Manual for Evidence Briefings*. Health Development Agency. http://194.83.94.80/hda/docs/evidence/eb2000/corehtml/ebmanual.pdf

SWPHO (South West Public Health Observatory) (2002) *Waste Management and Public Health: The State of the Evidence. A Review of the Epidemiological Research on the Impact of Waste Management Activities on Health*. London: SWPHO.

Szreter S. (1988) The importance of social intervention in Britain's mortality decline c.1850–1914: a reinterpretation of the role of public health, *Journal of the Society of Social History and Medicine*, 1: 1–37.

Tarrow, S. (1994) *Power in Movement: Social Movements, Collective Action and Politics*. Cambridge: Cambridge University Press.

Tattersall, M. and Hallstrom, C. (1992) Self-help and benzodiazepine withdrawal, *Journal of Affective Disorders*, 24(3): 193–8.

Taylor, L. and Blair-Stevens, C. (eds) (2002) *Introducing Health Impact Assessment (HIA): Informing the Decision-making Process*. London: Health Development Agency.

Taylor, M. (1995) *Unleashing the Potential: Bringing Residents to the Centre of Regeneration*. York: Joseph Rowntree Foundation.

Taylor, M. (1997) *The Best of Both Worlds: The Voluntary Sector and Local Government*. York: Joseph Rowntree Foundation.

Taylor, M. (2000) Communities in the lead: organisational capacity and social capital, *Urban Studies*, 37(5–6): 1019–35.

Taylor, M. and Hoggett, P. (1994) Trusting in networks? The third sector and welfare change, in P. Vidal and I. Vidal (eds) *Delivering Welfare: Repositioning Non-profit and Co-operative Action in Western European Welfare States*. Barcelona: Centro de Iniciativas de la Economia Social.

Taylor, P. (2002) *Understanding the Policy Maze*. Glasgow: Community Health Exchange, Glasgow Healthy City Partnership and Health Education Board for Scotland.

Taylor, P., Peckham, S. and Turton, P. (1998) *A Public Health Model of Primary Care – From Concept to Reality*. Birmingham: UK Public Health Association.

Taylor, P., Vegoda, M. and Leech, S. (2001) Exploring the experience of a group of lay members on primary care groups, *Local Governance*, 27(4): 231–8.

Taylor, R. and Guest, C. (2001) Protecting health, sustaining the environment, in D. Pencheon, C. Guest, D. Melzer and J.A. Muir Gray (eds) *Oxford Handbook of Public Health Practice*. Oxford: Oxford University Press.

Templeton, L., Zohhadi, S. and Velleman, R. (2005) *Working with Family Members in Specialist Drug and Alcohol Services: Findings from a Feasibility Study, Research Briefing*. Bath: Mental Health R & D Unit, The University of Bath.

Templeton, L., Zohhadi, S., Velleman, R. and Powell, J.E. (2006) [online] *Working with the Children and Families of Problem Alcohol Users: a Toolkit*. http://www.aerc.org.uk/documents/pdf/finalReports/toolkit/toolkit.pdf (accessed 30 June 2006).

Terry, F. (1999) The impact of evidence on transport policy-making: the case of road construction, *Public Policy and Management*, January–March.

The Stationery Office (2000) *Local Government Act 2000*. London: The Stationery Office.

Thomson, H., Pettigrew, M. and Morrison, D. (2001) Health effects of housing improvement: systematic review of intervention studies, *British Medical Journal*, 323: 187–90.

Thompson, H., Pettrigrew, M. and Morrison, D. (2002) *Housing Improvement and Health Gain: A Systematic Review*. Occasional paper no. 5. Glasgow: MRC Social and Public Health Sciences Unit, Glasgow.

Thomson, H., Atkinson, R., Pettigrew, M. and Kearns, A. (2006) Do urban regeneration programmes improve public health and reduce health inequalities? A synthesis of the evidence from UK policy and practice (1980–2004), *Journal of Epidemiological Community Health*, 60: 108–15.

Tilley, N. and Laycock, G. (2002) *Working Out What to Do; Evidence-based Crime Reduction*. Crime reduction research paper 11. London: Home Office Policing and Reducing Crime Unit.

Titmuss, R.M. (1943) *Birth, Poverty and Wealth*. Philadelphia, PA: University of Pennsylvania Press.

Tones, K. (2001) Health promotion: the empowerment imperative, in A. Scriven and J. Orme (eds) *Health Promotion: Professional Perspectives*. Basingstoke: Palgrave.

Towner, E., Dowswell, T. and Jarvis, S. (1993) *The Effectiveness of Health Promotion Interventions in the Prevention of Unintentional Childhood Injury: A Review of the Literature*. London: Health Education Authority.

Townsend, P. (ed.) (1988) *Inequalities in Health*. London: Penguin.

Townsend, P. (1992) *Inequalities in health. The Black report*. London: Penguin.

Townsend, P., Davidson, N. and Whitehead, M. (eds) (1992) *Inequalities in Health*. London: Penguin.

Treurniet, H.F., Boshuizen, H.C. and Harteloh, P.P. (2004) Avoidable mortality in Europe (1980–1997): a comparison of trends, *Journal of Epidemiology and Community Health*, 58: 290–5.

Treurniet, H.F., Boshuizen, H.C. and Harteloh, P.P.M. (2005) Avoidable mortality in Europe (1980–1997): a comparison of trends, *American Journal of Public Health*, 95: 103–8.

Tudor Hart, J. (1971). The inverse care law, *Lancet*, 1(7696): 405–12.

Tudor-Hart, J. (1988) *A New Kind of Doctor*. London: Merlin Press.

Turner, B. (1985) *Health and Illness*. London: Allen & Unwin.

Turner, B.S. (2001) Risks, rights and regulation: an overview, *Health, Risk and Society*, 3(1): 9–17.

Ukoumunne, O.C., Gulliford, M.C., Chinn, S. *et al.* (1999) Evaluation of health interventions at area and organisation level, *British Medical Journal*, 319: 376–9.

UKPHA (UK Public Health Association) (2006) *Learning from Differences Between the Four Countries of the United Kingdom and Ireland*. The first Report of the UKPHA Devolution Special Interest Group. London: UKPHA.

UNCED (United Nations Conference on Environment and Development) (1992a) *Agenda 21*. Rio de Janeiro: UNCED.

UNCED (United Nations Conference on Environment and Development) (1992b) *The Rio Declaration on Environment and Development*. Rio de Janeiro: UNCED.

Ünal, B., Critchley, J.A., Fidan, D. and Capewell, S. (2004) Life-years gained from modern cardiological treatments and population risk factor changes in England and Wales, 1981–2000, *Journal of Epidemiology and Community Health*, 8: 290–5.

United Nations (UN) (1992) *Earth Summit. Agenda 21: The United Nations Programme of Action from Rio*. New York: UN Department of Information.

United Nations (UN) (1996) *World Urbanization Prospects Database – 1996 Revision*. New York: UN Department of Economic and Social Affairs, Population Division.

United Nations (UN) (1998) *World Population Estimates and Projections – 1998 Revision*. New York: UN Department of Economic and Social Affairs, Population Division.

United Nations Development Programme (1999) *Human Development Report 1999: Globalisation With a Human Face*. Oxford: Oxford University Press.

United Nations Development Programme (2001) *Human Development Report 2001*. http://www.undp.org/hdr2001/

Vaill, P. (1999) *Spirited Leading and Learning: Process Wisdom for a New Age*. Englewood Cliffs: Prentice-Hall.

Velleman, R., Templeton, L., Taylor, A. and Toner, P. (2003) *The Family Alcohol Service: Evaluation of a Pilot*, Research Briefing. Bath: Mental Health R & D Unit, The University of Bath.

Vernon, G. and Feldman, R. (2006) *Refugees in Primary Care: from Looking After to Working Together*, a paper reviewing the provision of primary care for refugees and asylum seekers. www.networks.nhs.uk/networks.php?pid+256 (accessed 29 June 2006).

Von Korff, M., Koepsell, T., Curry, S. and Diehr, P. (1992) Multi-level analysis in epidemiologic research on health behaviors and outcomes, *American Journal of Epidemiology*, 135(10): 1077–82.

Von Pettenkofer, M. ([1873] 1941) *The Value of Health to a City*, two lectures delivered in 1873. Baltimore: The Johns Hopkins Press.

Walker, P., Lewis, J., Lingayah, S. and Sommer, F. (2000) *Prove it! Measuring the Effect of Neighbourhood Renewal on Local People*. London: New Economics Foundation.

Wallerstein, I. (1979) *The Capitalist World Economy*. Cambridge: Cambridge University Press.

Wallerstein, N. (1993) Empowerment and health: theory and practice of community change, *Community Development Journal*, 28: 218–27.

Walsh, J.A. and Warren, K.S. (1979) Selective primary care: an interim strategy for disease control in developing countries, *New England Journal of Medicine*, 301: 967–74.

Walt, G. (1998) Globalisation of international health, *Lancet*, 351: 429–33.

Wanless, D. (2002) *Securing our Future Health: Taking a Long-Term View. Final Report*. London: HM Treasury.

Wanless Report (2002) *NHS Funding and Reform: The Wanless Report*. Research paper 02/30. http://www.parliament.uk/commons/lib/research/rp2002/rp02–030.pdf (accessed 17 July 2002).

Wanless, D. (2004) *Securing Good Health for the Whole Population*. Final report. London: HM Treasury.

Warren, R., Rose, S. and Bergunder, A. (1974) *The Structure of Urban Reform*. Lexington, MA: Lexington Books.

Warren, M.D. (2000) *The Origins of the Faculty of Public Health Medicine*. Faculty of Public Health.

Waters, M. (1995) *Globalisation*. London: Routledge.

Webster, B. (1982) Area management and responsive policy-making, in S. Leach and J. Stewart (eds) *Approaches to Public Policy*. London: Allen & Unwin.

Weinstein, M. and Stason, W. (1977) Foundations of cost-effectiveness analysis for health and medical practices, *New England Journal of Medicine*, 296(13): 716–21.

Weiss, C.H. (1995) Nothing as practical as good theory: exploring theory-based evaluation for comprehensive community initiatives for children and families, in J. Connell *et al.* (eds) *New Approaches to Evaluating Community Based Initiatives: Concepts, Methods and Contexts*. Washington, DC: Aspen Institute.

Welford, R. (1995) *Environmental Strategy and Sustainable Development: The Corporate Challenge for the Twenty-First Century*. London: Routledge.

Wellard, S. (2003) *The hostility begins to melt*, Community Care, 16–22 October.

Wellman, B. (1979) The community question: the intimate networks of East Yorkers, *American Journal of Sociology*, 84: 1201–31.

Welsh Assembly Government (2002) *Well-being in Wales: Consultation Document*. Cardiff: Public Health Strategy Group, Office of Chief Medical Officer, Welsh Assembly Government.

White, A.K. and Johnson, M. (2000) Men making sense of chest pain – niggles, doubts and denials, *Journal of Clinical Nursing*, 9: 534–41.

Whitehead, M. (1995) Tackling inequalities: a review of policy initiatives, in M. Benzeval, K. Judge and M. Whitehead (eds) *Tackling Inequalities in Health: An Agenda for Action*. London: King's Fund.

Widgery, D. (1991) *Some Lives! A GP's East End*. London: Sinclair-Stevenson.

Wilkin, D., Gillam, S. and Coleman, A. (eds) (2001) *The National Tracker Survey of Primary Care Groups and Trusts 2000/2001: Modernising the NHS?* Manchester: National Primary Care Research and Development Centre, University of Manchester.

Wilkin, D., Coleman, A., Dowling, B. and Smith, K. (2002) *The National Tracker Survey of Primary Care Groups and Trusts 2001/2002: Taking Responsibility?* Manchester: National Primary Care Research and Development Centre, University of Manchester.

Wilkinson, R. (1996) *Unhealthy Societies: The Affliction of Inequality*. London: Routledge.

Wilkinson, R.G. (1997) Health inequalities: relative or absolute material standards? *British Medical Journal*, 314: 591–5.

Wilkinson, R. (2000) *Mind the Gap: Hierarchies, Health and Human Evolution*. London: Weidenfield.

Wilkinson, R.G. (2005) *The Impact of Inequality: How to Make Sick Societies Healthier*. London: Routledge.

Wilkinson, R. and Marmot, M. (eds) (1998) *The Solid Facts: Social Determinants of Health*. Copenhagen: Regional Office for Europe, WHO.

Williams, A. (1985) The economics of coronary artery bypass grafting, *British Medical Journal*, 291: 326–9.

Williams, C. and Windebank, J. (2000) Helping each other out? Community exchange in deprived neighbourhoods, *Community Development Journal*, 35(2): 146–56.

Williams, G. and Popay, J. (2002) Lay knowledge and the privilege of experience, in J. Gabe, D. Kelleher and G. Williams (eds) *Challenging Medicine*. London: Routledge.

Williamson, C. (1992) *Whose Standards? Consumer and Professional Standards in Health Care.* Oxford: Oxford University Press.

Williamson, O. (1975) *Markets and Hierarchies: Analysis and Antitrust Implications.* London: The Free Press.

Willmott, P. and Young, M. (1960) *Family and Class in a London Suburb.* London: Routledge and Kegan Paul.

Wilson, G. (1998) Staff and users in the postmodern organisation: Modernity, postmodernity and user marginalisation, in M. Barry and C. Hallett (eds). *Social Exclusion and Social Work: Issues of Theory, Policy and Practice.* Lyme Regis: Russell House.

Wilson, R.M., Runciman, W.B., Gibberd, R.W. *et al.* (1995) The quality in Australian health care study, *Medical Journal of Australia* 163(4): 58–471.

Winkler, F. (1987) Consumerism in health care: beyond the supermarket model, *Policy and Politics,* 15: 1–8.

Wistow, G. and Barnes, M. (1993) User involvement in community care: origins, purposes and applications, *Public Administration,* 71: 279–99.

Wong, K. and Butler, G. (2000) *Taking Asylum: A Guide to Community Safety Partnerships on Responding to the Immigration and Asylum Act 1999.* London: National Association for the Care and Rehabilitation of Offenders.

Wood, M. and Vamplew, C. (1999) *Neighbourhood Images of Teesside JRF Area,* Regeneration Series. York: York Publishing Services.

Woodhead, D., Jochelson, K. and Tennant, R. (2002) *Public Health in the Balance: Getting it Right for London.* London: King's Fund.

Woodward, D., Drager, N., Beaglehole, R. *et al.* (2001) Globalization and health: a framework for analysis and action, *Bulletin of the World Health Organisation,* 79(9): 875–81.

Woolcock, M. (2001) The place of social capital in understanding social and economic outcomes, *Isuma – Canadian Journal of Policy Research,* 2(1): 11–17.

World Bank (2002) *Cities on the Move: A World Bank Urban Transport Strategy Review.* Washington D.C.: The World Bank.

World Bank (2006) *China: Building Institutions for Sustainable Urban Transport.* EASTR Working Paper no. 4. Washington D.C.: The World Bank.

World Commission on Environment and Development (1987) *Our Common Future (The Brundtland Report).* Oxford: Oxford University Press.

WHO (World Health Organization) (1948) *Constitution.* Geneva: WHO.

WHO (World Health Organization) (1978) *Report on the International Conference on Primary Care, Alma Ata, 6–12 September.* Geneva: WHO.

WHO (World Health Organization) (1981) *Global Strategy for Health for All by the Year 2000.* Geneva: WHO.

WHO (World Health Organization) (1985) *Health For All in Europe by the Year 2000, Regional Targets.* Copenhagen: WHO.

WHO (World Health Organization) (1986) *Ottawa Charter for Health Promotion: An International Conference on Health Promotion, November 17–21.* Copenhagen: WHO.

WHO (World Health Organization) (1991) *Health For All Targets: The Health Policy for Europe.* Copenhagen: WHO.

WHO (World Health Organization) (1997) *Health and Environment in Sustainable Development: Five Years after the Earth Summit.* Geneva: WHO.

WHO (World Health Organization) (2002a) *Children and Environmental Health Risks.* Geneva: WHO. http://www/who.int/ceh/risk/en (accessed on 5 August 2006).

WHO (World Health Organization) (2002b) *Children's Environmental Health Indicators.* Geneva: World Health Organization. http://www.who.int/ceh/indicators/en/ (accessed 5 August 2006).

WHO (World Health Organization) (2002c) *The Tobacco Atlas*. Geneva: WHO.

WHO (World Health Organization) (2003a) *SARS Affected Areas*. http://www.who.int/csr/sar-sareas/en/ (accessed 20 May 2003).

WHO (World Health Organization) (2003b) *Severe Acute Respiratory Syndrome (SARS): Status of the Outbreak and Lessons for the Immediate Future*. Geneva: WHO.

WHO (World Health Organization) (2003c) *WHO Framework Convention on Tobacco Control*. Geneva: WHO.

WHO (World Health Organization) (2004) *Global Strategy on Diet, Physical Activity and Health*. Geneva: WHO.

WHO (World Health Organization) (2005a) *The World Health Report 2005 – Make Every Mother and Child Count*. Geneva: WHO.

WHO (World Health Organization) (2005b) *WHO Framework Convention on Tobacco Control*. Geneva: WHO.

WHO (World Health Organization) (2005c) *Ecosystems and Human Well-being: Health Synthesis: a Report of the Millennium Ecosystem Assessment*. Geneva: WHO. http://www.who.int/globalchange/ecosystems/ecosystems05/en/index.html (accessed 15 July 2006).

WHO (World Health Organization) (2006) *Chronic Disease Information Sheets: Obesity and Overweight*. http://www.who.int/dietphysicalactivity/publications/facts/obesity/en/index.html (accessed 17 September 2006).

Yach, D. and Bettcher, D. (1998) The globalization of public health, I: threats and opportunities, *American Journal of Public Health*, 88(5): 735–8.

Yen, I. and Syme, S. (1999) The social environment and health: a discussion of the epidemiological literature, *Annual Review of Public Health*, 20: 287–308.

Yorkshire Forward (2001) *Active Partners*. York: Yorkshire Forward.

Young, K., Ashby, D., Boaz, A. and Grayson, L. (2002) Social science and the evidence based policy movement, *Social Policy and Society*, 1(3): 215–24.

Zakus, J.D.L. and Lysack, C.L. (1998) Revisiting community participation, *Health Policy and Planning*, 13(1): 1–12.

Zaninotto, P., Wardle, H., Stamatakis, E., Mindell, J. and Head, J. (2006) *Forecasting Obesity to 2010*, a report prepared for the Department of Health. London: Joint Health Surveys Unit.

Zwi, A.B. and Yach, D. (2002) International health in the 21st century: trends and challenges, *Social Science and Medicine*, 54: 1615–20.

# Index

ABCD (Achieving Better Community Development), 310
Acheson, Sir Donald
report on health inequalities (1998), 13, 26, 141, 158–159, 164, 214, 262, 266
report on public health in England (1988), 12, 13, 136, 229
action planning, 311–312, 318
ageing population, 9, 119, 131, 185, 299
Agenda, 21, 12, 49, 186, 192, 195, 200–201, 329
air pollution, 223–224, 226, 236, 245, 282
animal disease, 241
Arblaster, L., 159, 164–165, 168
Arts for Health Movement, 80
asylum seekers, 83, 89, 92–97, 126, 329
Audit Commission, 64, 68, 80, 96, 183

Bayesian approaches to epidemiology, 269, 279–283
Bentham, Jeremy, 299
biomedical model, *see* medical model
bioterrorism, 225
Black Report on health inequalities, 12, 156, 158–160
Blair, Tony, 32, 45
*Bringing Britain Together* (Social Exclusion Unit), 174
British Medical Association, 248
*British Medical Journal*, 206
Brundtland Report (1987), 85, 186, 192
BSE (bovine spongiform encephalitis), 77, 225, 227, 237

Buncefield oil depot fire, 245
built environment, 16, 151, 202, 315
Butler, Josephine, 104

Cabinet Office, 36, 43, 52, 76, 173, 184, 228, 230–231, 244, 291
Campbell collaboration, 256, 268
cancer, 269, 271–276, 279
capacity and capability in public health, 61, 83–84, 87–88, 91, 133, 168
asylum seekers case study, 92–97
and the public health professional project, 88
and the public health workforce, 155, 323, 2, 14–15, 34, 40, 83–84, 87
skills and competencies, 83–84, 86, 87, 89, 91
and training needs, 83, 87, 90–91, 94
capitalism, and globalization, 41, 207, 214
carers, 100, 108, 143, 261, 293, 300
carrying capacity, and sustainable futures in cities, 186, 194
central–local partnerships, 74
Chadwick, Edwin, 10, 104
change management, and future public health policy, 36, 40
Chapman, J., 40
Chemical Releases Inventory, 241
Chief Medical Officer, 1, 13–14, 26, 32, 41, 84, 87, 132, 221, 230, 248
children
asylum seeking, 94, 96
and children's services, 51

and community health and well being, 54,
    79, 92, 93, 106–108, 114, 115, 126,
    140, 145, 151, 159–163, 177–178
and economic evaluation, 290–295
and environment, 226, 236, 240
and Every Child Matters, 77
and National Service Framework, 69, 183
and overweight and obesity, 30, 68, 81,
    123, 130, 326
cholera, 11, 217, 219, 273
*Choosing Health: Making Healthy Choices
    Easier*, 21, 27, 30, 31, 32, 44, 56, 69,
    85, 86, 139, 161, 163, 258
cities, *see* sustainable futures in cities
City Challenge, 172
Civil Contingencies Act (2004), 233, 244
CJD (new variant Creutzfeldt-Jacob
    Disease), 218–219, 225
climate change, 19, 187, 193, 199, 202, 204,
    210, 220–223, 235, 322, 325, 326, 329
clinical audit, 126, 128
Cochrane collaboration, 124–125, 255, 268
collaborative partnerships, 223, 247
collaborative working, 15, 18, 52, 61, 74,
    82–86, 91, 96, 146–147, 183
Commission for Patient and Public
    Involvement in Health, 38, 52, 103
common good, 298–299
communicable diseases,
    and European Union health strategy, 39
    and health protection, 225, 229, 270
    and globalization, 217, 219
Community Chests, 52, 174
community development
    and action, 305
    and approaches, 166, 307
    and empowerment, 316
    needs, 306
    practice, 135
    programme evaluation, 314
    projects, 105, 166, 171
    work/worker/working, 90–91, 135, 138,
        149, 151, 170, 303, 306, 310
Community Empowerment Fund, 52, 174
community focus, and leadership, 6, 42
community health councils, 101
community health and well being,
    action, 303–306
    and evaluation of, 302–303, 305, 307–321
    fields of, 320

LEAP (Learning Evaluation and Planning)
    model of, 307–321
community nurses, 84, 90–91, 101
community partnerships, 49, 75, 79, 175, 179
conservative governments, 65, 158–159, 165
Consumers,
    expectations, 195, 271
    feedback, 102
    of healthcare, 101
    as patients, 101
    of policy, 27, 241
    interests, 77
    and public health, 227
    and safety, 228
context dependence/independence, and
    evidence-based public health, 254,
    262, 265
cost–consequences analysis, 289
cost–effectiveness analysis, 289, 300
counterfactuals, and evidence-based public
    health, 254
Critical Appraisal Skills Programme, 265
Cyclebag, 22

Davey Smith, G., 156–159, 163–164,
    276–279
*Delivering Choosing Health*, 27, 31
deprived neighbourhoods, 18, 80, 170, 174,
    178
devolution, 19, 25, 30, 33–37, 43, 48, 55–57,
    77
directors of public health, 12, 37, 52, 73, 84,
    87, 101, 122, 132, 231
disabled people, 178

Earth Summit debate (Johannesburg, 2002),
    222
Eastern Europe, globalization and health
    inequalities in, 215, 219
eco-epidemiology and population level
    approaches, 275–276
ecological fallacy arguments, and
    epidemiology, 276–277
economic evaluation, 168, 250, 287–301
    *see also* health economics
Economic and Social Research Council,
    255–256
educational priority areas, 171
efficiency and equity, in health economics,
    288, 299

emergency planning and response, 18, 243
empiricism, and theory in evidence-based
    public health, 267
employers, 196, 198, 266, 272, 323
employment, neighbourhood policies on,
    176, 178, 180, 193, 257, 266, 315, 323
employment, global, 215
Environment Agency, 21, 227, 228, 231, 235,
    242
environmental hazards, and health protection,
    223–228, 236, 247
environmental health officers, 12, 15, 75, 84,
    86, 89–91, 101, 155, 170
epidemiology, 270–281
    Bayesian approaches to, 280–282
    classical and public health, 272–273
    ecological epidemiology and population
        level approaches, 273–275
    eco-epidemiology and population level
        approaches, 275–276
    future developments in, 278–279
    genetic, 277
    history of, 275–276
    importance of, 2, 3, 15, 16, 249, 254, 269
    life course approaches to, 282–283
    medical versus lay, 109–110
    and meta-analysis, 276, 278–281
    multilevel approaches to, 283–285
    needs assessment, 122, 126
    scope of, 270–272
equity
    and access, 125, 156, 297
    audit, 168
    efficiency and, 156, 288, 299–300, 313
    and opportunity, 156
    partnership for, 75
    social, 86, 186, 213, 222
ethics, and health economics, 21, 87, 90, 97,
    123, 164, 250, 277, 298
European cities, 185, 191–192
*European Sustainable Cities*, 191–193,
    201–202
European Union (EU)
    future public health policy, 191, 193, 199
    and health protection, 227, 231
    and international partnerships, 76
    Sixth Environmental Action Programme,
        230
    and social policy, 39
    and smoking bans, 21

and urban growth, 191
evidence and guidance, 249, 252
evidence-based public health, 9, 11, 27
    multidisciplinary, 88, 260, 268
    defining, 251–253, 259–260
    development of, 255–257
    and different research traditions,
        263–265
    problems of, 260–263
    role of theory in, 265–267
evidence-informed policy and practice, 255
Exercise Arctic Sea, 244

family,
    alcohol service, 250, 290–294, 298
    focused, 290
    members, 92–93, 143, 290–292
    working with families, 104, 292
Farr, William, 156
fertility levels, global, 188
Fifth Framework for Research in the
    European Union, 193
food implicated health threats, 227–228
Food Standards Agency (FSA), 77, 81,
    227–228, 231, 241
food-borne disease, 219
Frenk, Julio, 35
future of public health policy, 25–30, 33–41,
    46, 63–65, 153
    health inequalities, 163, 288
    health protection, 217
    and neighbourhoods, 178, 191, 214
    and public health history, 5, 61
    and public health services, 81–82

garden cities, 171, 186
General Agreement on Trade in Services,
    212, 214
genetic epidemiology, 277
Geographic Information Systems (GIS), 243,
    278
*Getting Ahead of the Curve*, 230, 238
global,
    climate change, 187, 199, 202, 220, 221,
        325
    and environmental, 187, 189, 202,
        219–220, 225, 230, 328–329
    health inequalities, 154, 204
    and influences, 2, 153
    and population, 188

responses, 76
travel, 76, 210, 219
warming, 9, 220, 285, 322, 323, 325
globalization, 2, 154, 204–222
  and emerging public health risks, 154, 205,
    217, 225–231
  global trade policy, and the UK health care
    context, 204, 210, 213, 214
  and the 'global village', 204
  the globalization debate, 205–207
  and health, 7, 81, 204, 208, 222, 227,
  and health care organizations, 213,
    220–221
  and health inequalities, 215–216
  positive and negative impacts on public
    health, 35, 128, 209–210
  promoters of economic globalization,
    211–213
  and sustainability, 3, 187, 189, 193–194,
    199, 200, 202
  and sustainable futures in cities, 193–195,
    199–200, 202
Global Outbreak Alert and Response
  Network (GOARN), 230
Göteborg, sustainable development in, 195,
  197, 199
governing partnerships, 73
Government Interventions in Deprived Areas
  (HM Treasury), 174
GPs (general practitioners), 90, 93–94, 110,
  115, 127–128, 155, 170, 272
Green Paper on the Urban Environment
  (Commission of the European
  Communities), 192
Guidance,
  and economics, 289, 300
  and health inequalities, 178
  and health protection, 240, 242
  and neighbourhoods, 175
  NICE, 10, 90, 250, 252, 258, 302
  NSFs, 183

HAZs, see Health Action Zones (HAZs)
health action zones (HAZs), 26, 28, 66, 69,
  78, 160, 171, 175
Health for All movement, 12
health authorities, 68–69, 101–102, 112, 144,
  231
Health Development Agency (HDA), 26–28,
  72, 252, 301

health economics, 1, 250, 256, 287–301
  see also economic evaluation
Health Education Authority, 28, 175
health impact, 80, 178, 230, 242–243, 245,
  277
  assessment, 233–234, 237, 243, 247, 255,
    287, 297, 298
health inequalities,
  Acheson Report on, 12, 77, 158–160, 162
  addressing, 5, 153, 155, 247, 299
  causes of, 76
  and equity, 297
  and impact on, 315, 321
  and tackling, 315, 317, 321
  and reductions in, 49, 160, 257, 289, 299,
    316–318
The Health of the Nation (Department of
  Health), 26, 28, 65, 165
health professionals, 43, 53, 58, 131
  adverse drug reactions, 130
  challenging the dominance of, 5, 35
  and collaboration, 19, 59, 131
  and community focus, 7, 138–139, 143
  and globalization, 222
  and health promotion, 130
  and lay involvement in public health,
    102–3, 105, 107–111, 113
  and leadership, 72, 220
  and neighbourhoods, 153, 180
  and networks, 116
  and silos, 61
  and sustainability, 322, 329
health promotion, 12, 18, 168, 277
  and collaboration, 165
  and community health and well being, 135
  'in the community', 35, 80, 138–141, 145
  and ethics, 299
  and the evidence base, 125, 258, 271, 283,
    287–288, 298
  knowledge and skills, 15, 29
  and immunization, 124
  and lifestyle, 130
  and messages, 118, 125, 254, 279, 280
  promoting healthy behaviours, 14, 72, 166
  and public health policy,
  workforce, 84, 90
health protection, 2, 8, 9, 121
  and contemporary health threats, 9, 217,
    224, 230
  domains of, 12

emergency planning and response, 18, 22
emerging policy and organization, 227,
      229, 243–245
   global, 247
   hazards and risk assessment, 234, 237
   and health inequalities, 226
   and local authorities, 122
   organizations and structures for, 231–233
   PCTs, 233
   surveillance and prevention, 238–243, 246
   sustainability, 185
Health Protection Agency (HPA), 21, 132,
      225–228, 231, 238, 240, 245, 248
Health and Safety Executive (HSE),
      228–229, 231
Health trainers, 17, 31, 44, 53, 59, 86
health visitors, 12, 15, 17, 89, 101, 115, 123,
      140, 146, 164
Healthy Cities movement, 12, 105
healthy living centres (HLCs), 26, 28, 66, 69,
      73–75, 78, 148, 160, 165, 183, 315,
      320
hierarchy of evidence, and multidisciplinary
      public health, 250–264, 302
history of public health, 10–11, 23, 103, 275
HIV/AIDS, 76, 151, 188, 225–226
HLCs, see Healthy Living Centres (HLCs)
hospitals, 27, 30, 118, 128–129, 176, 243,
      324–325
HPA, see Health Protection Agency (HPA),
      21, 132, 225–226, 228, 231, 238, 240,
      245
HSE, see Health and Safety Executive (HSE),
      228–229, 231
Human Genome Project, 277
Huxham, C., 67

IMF (International Monetary Fund),
      211–213
immunisation, 11, 12, 14, 96, 104, 119,
      123–124, 233, 241, 275
individualism, pitfalls of, 67
inequalities, see health inequalities
infectious diseases, 12, 119, 217–220,
      223–225, 238–241, 275, 323–324
influenza virus, 241–242
   'Avian Flu', 242
Integrated Prevention and Pollution Control
      regime, 242
interest groups, 9, 105, 112, 113

international partnerships, 63, 76
International Statistical Classification of
      Diseases and Related Health Problems,
      278
Internet, 148, 168–169, 210, 249, 269,
      277–278

'joined up government', 38, 65, 69, 76, 78,
      173
'joined up policy', 18, 36, 76, 77

Kavanagh, D., 76
Kelly, R., 46, 56–57
Kelly, M., 252

Labonte, R., model of community health and
      well being, 302–304
Labour movement, 103–5
Larson, M., 88
lay contribution to public health, 98–100, 112
leadership,
   adequate, 75
   and advocacy, 19
   community development, 36, 54, 56, 262,
      317
   health, 1
   horizontal, 36
   and partnership, 89
   party, 45
   political, 43–44, 57–58, 199, 201
   and roles, 149, 173
   strategic, 15, 86, 97
   strong, 25, 40, 54
LEAP (Learning Evaluation and Planning),
      model of community health and well
      being, 149, 302, 307–309, 311–316,
      320–321
Legionnaires Disease, 233
lobbying, 96, 131, 155, 164–165
local authorities/government and future
      public health policy, 2, 11, 38, 47, 48
   and communities, 49, 67
   and Double Devolution, 56–57
   and health protection, 224, 228–229, 231,
      233–234, 243
   and lay action, 105
   and Local Area Agreements (LAAs), 38,
      49, 53–55
   and Local Strategic Partnerships (LSPs),
      51–53

and loss of power, 44
and neighbourhoods, 173
and the NHS, 73, 101–102, 122
Overview and Scrutiny Committees
    (OSCs), 49
and partnerships,
and Powers of Well being, 21, 43, 50, 141,
    323
and Primary Care Trusts (PCTs), 132
and public health concerns, 58
Public Service Agreements, 55–56
regional context of, 21
and sustainable futures in cities, 193,
    200–201
and Sustrans, 22
Local Area Agreements (LAAs), 38, 51, 53,
    55, 66, 69, 141, 174
Local Exchange Schemes, 80
Local Involvement Networks (LINks), 38,
    53, 103
local partnerships, 51, 65, 74, 78–80, 159,
    163, 165, 315–319
local politics, 59
Local Strategic Partnerships (LSPs), 38, 42,
    48, 51, 53, 55, 66, 69, 74, 75, 78, 79,
    82, 159–160, 165
  and neighbourhood renewal and
    regeneration, 170, 174–176, 179,
    183–184
Local Voices (National Health Services
    Management Executive), 102
localization, and sustainable futures in cities,
    195
London, Greater London Authority, 48

Macdonald, D., 67
Macintyre, Professor Sally, 257
malaria, 211, 217, 219, 220, 225, 240
Malmö, sustainable development in, 195–199
management
  of neighbourhoods
  performance
  quality
  risk
  systems
  urban
  see also leadership
media, 97, 107, 124, 164, 204–206, 210, 218,
    239, 245, 260
medical model, 28, 32, 48, 98, 105, 109–110

medical officers of health, 101, 323
meta-analysis, 261, 269, 276, 279, 281–283
miasma theory of disease, 1, 267, 274–275
Milburn, Alan, 79, 99
minority ethnic groups, 126, 156, 178,
    180
MMR (Measles, Mumps and Rubella),
    218
Mooney, G., 298
mortality rates, 95, 118, 120, 156, 158, 167
multidisciplinary public health, 2, 5, 7, 61, 63,
    68, 83, 92, 98–99, 124
  development of, 25
  evidence-based, 249, 251–254, 257,
    260
  and neighbourhoods, 170
  and partnerships, 75
  and the professional project, 85, 87
  and public health policy, 24
  and the public health workforce, 86
multi-drug resistant tuberculosis
    (MDR-TB), 219
multilevel approaches to epidemiology, 269,
    274, 283–285

National Commission for Patient and Public
    Involvement, 103
National Cycle Network, 22
National Institute for Health and Clinical
    Excellence (NICE), 27, 90, 169, 252,
    291
National Strategy Action Plan, 174
Navarro, V., 215
neighbourhood effect, 180
Neighbourhood Renewal Community
    Chests, 174
Neighbourhood Renewal Fund, 51, 53,
    174–175
Neighbourhood Renewal programme, 80
neighbourhood renewal and regeneration, 18,
    153, 170, 265
  historical context, 171–172
  main programmes, 181–184
  neighbourhood policies and health,
    175–176
  inequalities, 176–180
  re-emergence of the neighbourhood,
    172–175
Neighbourhood Renewal Unit, 51–52, 76,
    172, 175,

neighbourhood wardens, 175, 176
networks
    Economic and Social Research Council
        evidence network, 256
    clinical, 34
    closed, 143–144
    and community, 102, 135, 137, 139,
        144–145, 151, 176, 216, 310–311, 317
    friendship, 107
    globalization and health, 72, 82, 89–90,
        146
    informal, 98, 113, 116, 135, 140–143,
        146–149, 152
    involvement, 38, 49, 53, 103
    local, 147
    national, 230
    personal, 62, 99, 109, 135, 141
    professional, 75
    social, 108, 135–137, 139, 141–142, 144,
        148, 152, 181, 216
    surveillance, 238, 247
    and sustainable futures, 134
    teaching public health, 18, 85, 89–90
New Commitment to Regeneration, 175
New Deal for Communities, 28, 80, 160, 170,
    175–176, 179–184
New Labour government, 13, 25–26, 45, 65,
    158–159, 165
New variant CJD, 219
public health policy, 24–25, 30, 65
    and devolution, 33–34
    and Europe, 39, 191
    the future of, 2, 25
    and joined up government, 38, 65, 69, 76,
        78, 173
    and joined up policy, 46
    and neighbourhoods, 178
    and opportunity cost, 288
    and partnerships, 65, 81–82
    and QALYs, 300
    see also health inequalities
'new' public health, 12, 13, 17, 30, 39, 86,
    184, 217, 253, 263, 273, 298, 302, 304
new social movements, 105
new technology, 204
new towns movement, 171
NHS (National Health Service)
    and clinical practice, 90
    and community health, 105
    and community partnerships, 99
    constraints on implementation, 34–35
    and devolution, 33
    and emergency planning and response, 224
    and epidemiology, 272
    and government modernization agenda,
        29, 38
    and health inequalities, 26
    and health trainers, 17, 31, 44, 53, 59, 86
    and improving health, 31–32
    and involvement, 100–101
    and national partnerships, 76
    and the National Service Frameworks, 291
    and the NHS Centre for Reviews and
        Dissemination (NHSCRD), 167
    and Overview and Scrutiny Committees
        (OSCs), 38
    partnerships with local authorities, 27, 48,
        80, 90
    and primary care, 103, 233
    and public health history, 11, 12, 101, 102
    and public health policy, 14, 27, 163
    and regionalism, 37, 76
    and social marketing, 31
    and the welfare state, 14, 27, 29–30, 104,
        214
    workforce skills and competencies, 81
NHS Direct, 210, 239–240
NHS Plan, 26, 28, 33, 37, 69, 160
National Sickness Service, 1, 15
    see also Wanless Report and Wanless, D.,
nicotine replacement therapy, 280
Nightingale, Florence, 267
Northern Ireland, 5, 21, 25, 33, 48, 66, 77,
    141, 230–231, 233
nuclear threats, 227
Null hypothesis, 280
Nurses, 15–17, 75, 84, 86, 89–90, 101, 121,
    130, 155, 220

OECD (Organization for Economic
Cooperation and Development), 195, 215,
    227–229
offenders, epidemiology and the treatment of,
    274
O'Keefe, E., 212–213
opportunity cost, 166, 288, 293
Oversee and Scrutiny Committees (OSCs),
    38, 49, 58

Pareto, Vilfredo, 299

participation,
  and community, 52, 135, 144, 147–148,
    152, 266, 314
  and lay contribution to public health, 112,
    115
  multi-agency, 240
  and public, 43, 52, 171, 265
  widening, 16
partnerships,
  and agency, 40, 141, 151
  area, 317–318
  building, 67
  collaboration and, 63, 223, 247
  community partnerships, 75
  creating, 69
  developing, 65, 66
  formal, formalised, 74, 75–82
  health, 53, 64–65, 82, 108, 110, 141, 179,
    304
  international, 376
  local authority, 58, 73
  local, 51, 65, 74, 78–80, 159, 163, 165,
    315–319
  national, 76
  neighbourhood, 165, 176, 179, 184
  sectoral, 78, 147
  specialized, 51
  strategic, 74
  successful, 75
  sustainable, 56
  thematic, 51
  vertical, 65
  working with the public and communities,
    44
  see also collaborative partnerships; Local
  Strategic Partnerships (LSPs)
Patient Advice and Liaison Services (PALS),
  102
patient and public involvement, 101, 110
PCTs (primary care trusts), 14, 17, 33,
    43–44, 54–59, 72–77, 82–91, 102,
    132–133, 233, 182
Pettenkofer, Max Von, 323
police officers, and the public health
  workforce, 84
pollution
  air pollution, 77, 153, 223–226, 236, 245,
    282
  and health protection, 9, 22, 226, 230, 233,
    237, 243, 284, 311

  and community health and well being, 303
  Integrated Pollution Prevention and
    Control, 227, 233, 242
  and local authorities, 233
population change, 185–187
poverty
  asylum seekers, 93, 96
  child, 28, 160, 162–164, 290
  Child Poverty Action Group, 164
  Food, 230
  health, 76
  health inequalities, 13, 105, 153–157,
    163–164, 219, 303
  ill-health, 96
  Joseph Rowntree surveys on, 104
  neighbourhoods, 176–178, 180
  and oppression, 139
  social exclusion, 9, 69, 141, 159–160, 191
  sustainability, 199
  and war, 285
  welfare state, 104, 164
Pratt, J., 67
Practice based commissioning, 14, 122
pregnancy
  childbirth, 126
  nutrition and, 283
  teenage, 14, 17, 58, 78, 160, 165, 174
  Teenage Pregnancy Strategy, 160
  Teenage Pregnancy Unit, 76
primary care, 14, 67, 94, 102, 127–128, 130,
    163, 167, 271–272, 299, 304
  data services, 278
  organizations, 33, 66
  professionals, 69, 122, 128
  surveillance, 239
  see also PCTs (primary care trusts)
primary care organizations, 33, 66
professional closure, 85
professional project, 83–84, 88
public health action
  and advocacy, 165
  and communities, 72
  and geography, 204
  and health protection, 22, 223
  and international context of, 19, 21, 227
  and lay involvement, 100
  and occupational health, 18
  and organizational structures, 18, 22
  and settings for, 19
  and scope of, 3, 7–10, 61, 98, 100, 103, 111

and Sustrans, 22
and Wanless Report, 26
Public Health Observatories, 229, 240, 285
public health professionals, *see* health
    professionals
public health resources, 2, 8, 100, 299
public involvement 69, 98–100, 102–103,
    107, 112–114, 116, 182, 305)
public services, 30, 35, 43, 49, 51, 57, 82, 99,
    101, 105, 107, 163, 171
    and globalization and the reform of,
        211–214
purchaser-provider, 34, 73

quality adjusted life years (QALYs), 288,
    295–296, 300
quality of life,
    and ecological model, 8
    and economics, 288
    and epidemiology, 256, 271, 273
    good, 191, 302
    improved, 185, 230, 295
    measures of, 295
    and neighbourhoods, 18, 141, 170,
        175–176, 303
    people and, 9, 136, 141, 310–311
    sustainability, 199, 202
quantitative/qualitative research, and
    evidence-based public health, 265,
    274, 281

randomized controlled trials, 254, 263, 276,
    296
Rathbone, Eleanor, 104
*Reducing Health Inequalities: An Action Report,*
    160
Regional Coordination Unit, 173, 228
regional health protection services, 228
regionalism, 3, 37, 38, 49, 173
*Research and Development Strategy for Public
    Health,* 88
reverse colonization, 206
*Revitalising Health and Safety,* 229
*Rio Declaration on Environment and
    Development,* 229
risk assessment, 86, 223, 234, 247
risk factor analysis, and epidemiology, 271
Rogers Report on urban life (2000), 173
rough sleepers initiative, 76
Rushey Green Time Bank, 80

SARS (Severe Acute Respiratory
    Syndrome), 217, 218, 225
*Saving Lives: Our Healthier Nation,* 13, 26, 28,
    33, 69, 160, 257, 262
Scotland
    community development, 303, 307
    Community Health Partnerships
    community planning, 67
    and devolution, 19, 25, 48, 77
    and Healthy Living Centres, 304, 315
    local authorities in, 141
    and powers of well-being, 304
    public health strategy, 21, 66
    and smoking ban, 31–32
Scottish Community Development Centre,
    302, 303, 307, 315
self-help groups, 59, 102, 105, 112, 113, 135,
    141, 142, 148, 315
    and voluntary and community
        organizations, 116
    and neighbourhood renewal, 175
service users,
    and Family Alcohol Service, 293–294, 296,
        300
    opinions of, 102, 261
    process of engagement of, 48
    and regeneration, 80
*Shifting the Balance of Power: Next Steps*
    (Department of Health), 26, 52, 97,
    184
    and primary care, 14, 132
Single Regeneration Budget, 172, 173, 182
Snow, John, 10–11
social capital, 113, 141, 143–144, 152, 216
    and community participation, 135
    and neighbourhoods, 181
    and networking, 152
    and partnership working, 170
    and power relations, 148
    for public health, 85
social class, and health inequalities, 158, 162
social exclusion,
    and community engagement, 22
    in European cities, 191
    and networks, 149
    and the *NHS Plan,* 69
    policies to tackle, 43, 68, 159–160
    and poor health, 141
    and poverty, 9, 69
Social Exclusion Unit, 69, 76, 159, 173–175

social model of health, 67, 71, 303
social workers, 15, 27, 84, 91, 101, 110, 146, 155, 170, 215
Soviet Union (former), globalization and health inequalities in, 215
Standard Regeneration Budget, 80
Stockholm, sustainable development in, 195–197, 198–199, 202
Strachey, Lytton, *Eminent Victorians*, 267
strategic leadership, 97
    for health and well-being, 15, 86
structural adjustment policies, 211
Sure Start, 25, 28, 74–76, 79
    evaluation of, 285
    and health improvement, 79
    projects, 78, 160
    programmes, 14
    and inequality,
    Rose Hill, 79
Sustainable development, 12, 185, 186
    agenda, 191
    and Brundtland Report, 85
    and food, 327
    and globalization, 222, 247, 323
    and healthy communities, 8
    and health, 13
    in Sweden, 195, 198–199
    and public health, 322
    scope of, 194
    strategy, 49
    threats to, 154
    and urban policy, 191, 200
    World Summit on, 86
*Sustainable Development, Securing the Future,* 8
sustainability and health, 88
sustainable futures in cities, 153, 185, 186, 194–195, 199, 201
    local changes that support, 200
    measurement of progress towards, 201
    multidisciplinary policy issues in, 194
    policy for, 191, 202
    Swedish cities case study, 195
*Sustainable Urban Development in the European Union* (Commission of the European Communities), 193
Sustrans, 22, 23, 326
systematic reviews, and evidence-based public health, 257

*Tackling Health Inequalities* reports, 14, 26, 27, 160–161, 163
targets
    Choosing Health Delivery Plan, 27
    for climate change, 220
    for health gain and partnership, 14
    health inequalities, 13, 26, 38, 160
    for Health for Europe, 12
    for joint health and social care, 76
    and primary care trusts, 43, 58
    as Public Service Agreement (PSA), 27, 161
    for smoking and obesity, 128, 139
teachers, and the public health workforce, 15, 16, 84, 86, 89, 110
teamwork, and the professional project,
terrorism threats, 185, 204, 223, 225
Time Banks, 80
tobacco related diseases, and globalization, 217
tourism, and infectious diseases, 219, 221
*Towards an Urban Agenda in the European Union* (Commission of the European Communities), 193
trade liberalization
    and globalization, 212, 215, 217
    and health inequalities, 213, 215
trade union movement, 104
training in public health, 89
    integrating and financing, 83
transport
    effect on global warming, 322, 325–326
    of food, 327
    neighbourhood policies on, 176–178
    policy, 77
    in Stockholm, 196
    sustainable systems of, 22, 185
tuberculosis (TB), 119, 209, 211, 215, 217, 219, 225, 239, 240, 246

unemployment, in European cities, 191, 194, 198
United Nations, 187–188
    Conference on Environment and Development (Rio, 1992), 220
    Development Programme report (2001), 215–216, 219
United States
    access to health care in, 167
    community programmes in, 79

Framework Convention on Climate
    Change, 220
life expectancy in, 119
quality improvement initiative in, 129
terrorist incident in, 244
and World Trade Organization, 211
upstream policies, for tackling health
    inequalities, 24, 25, 28, 29, 40,
    163–165, 167
Urban Summit Conferences, 173
urbanization and urban development, 186
    emerging policy on urban management,
    186
    European cities, 191
    and quality of life in cities, 202
    and sustainable development, 154, 185
    and world population change, 187, 189,
    199
utilitarianism, and health economics, 299

Vision to Reality (2001), 26
voluntary sector,
    and community-based activities, 144
    and local strategic partnerships, 174
    as part of public health workforce, 84
    and powers of well-being, 304
    role in highlighting problems, 105

Wales
    case study of working class women,
    107
    and Health Impact Assessment, 237
    and inverse care law, 125
    local health boards, 132
Wanless Report (2002), 26, 43, 289, 299

Wanless Report (2004), 27, 30, 43, 46, 289,
    299
wardens, neighbourhood, 175, 176
waste management activities, 236
welfare state, 104
    and the NHS, 157, 214, 222
WHO (World Health Organization),
    and collaboration, 66
    and European cities, 191
    and global policy on tobacco control,
    327–328
    and health protection, 238
    and international partnerships, 75, 227
    and obesity, 81, 326
    role in globalization, 204, 208
workforce, see capacity and capability in
    public health
workplace hazards, 227
World Bank, 85, 186, 210–212, 214–215, 221
World Commission on Environment and
    Development, 85, 186
world population growth, 154, 187
WTO (World Trade Organization), 204, 210,
    227, 241
    and health protection, 235
    Trade Related Intellectual Property Rights
    Agreement, 219

young people,
    and well-being, 50
    policy for, 54
    health of, 68
    sexual health of, 72, 160
    and social networks, 139
    and neighbourhood renewal, 266

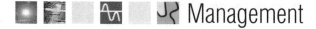